Annual Register
of Book Values

THE ARTS & ARCHITECTURE

1994

Annual Register of Book Values

THE ARTS & ARCHITECTURE

Series Editor: Michael Cole

1994

The Clique

7 Pulleyn Drive, York YO2 2DY, England

Annual Register of Book Values - The Arts & Architecture

ISBN 1 870773 42 X
ISSN 0968-7505

Typesetting by Maxiprint, York, England
Printed and bound by Redwood Books, Trowbridge , England

Contents

Introduction and Notes

The annual *ARBV* series, now in its eighth year, provides annual records of the pricing levels of out-of-print, rare or antiquarian books within a number of speciality subject areas and gives likely sources and suppliers for such books in Britain and the United States of America. It is intended to be used by both the experienced bookman and the newcomer to book-collecting.

Sources of information:

The books recorded each year in the various subject volumes of *ARBV* have been selected from catalogues of books for sale issued during the previous year by numerous bookselling firms in Britain and the United States. These firms, listed at the end of this volume, range in nature from the highly specialized, handling books solely within closely defined subject areas, through to large concerns with expertise across a broad spectrum of interests.

Extent of coverage:

ARBV concentrates exclusively on books published in the English language and, throughout the series as a whole, encompasses books published between the 16th century and the 1980s.

The 30,000 or so separate titles recorded in the annual volumes of *ARBV* vary greatly from year to year although naturally there is a degree of overlap, particularly of the more frequently found titles. Consecutive annual volumes do not, therefore, merely update pricings from earlier years; they give substantially different listings of books on each occasion. The value of the *ARBV* volumes lies in providing records of an ever-increasing range of individual titles which have appeared for sale on the antiquarian or rare book market.

Emphasis is placed throughout on books falling within the lower to middle range of the pricing scale (£10 - £250; $20 - $500) rather than restricting selection to the unusually fine or expensive. In so doing, *ARBV* provides a realistic overview of the norm, rather than the exception, within the booktrade.

Authorship and cross-references:

Authors are listed alphabetically by surname.

Whenever possible, the works of each author are grouped together under a single form of name irrespective of the various combinations of initials, forenames and surnames by which the author is known.

Works published anonymously, or where the name of the author is not recorded on the title-page, are suitably cross-referenced by providing the main entry under the name of the author (when mentioned by the bookseller) with a corresponding entry under the first appropriate word of the title. In cases of unknown, or unmentioned, authorship, entry is made solely under the title.

Full-titles:

Editorial policy is to eschew, whenever possible, short-title records in favour of full-, or at least more complete and explanatory, titles. Short-title listings do little to convey the flavour, or even the content, of many books - particularly those published prior to the nineteenth century.

Descriptions:

Books are listed alphabetically, using the first word of the title ignoring, for alphabetical purposes, the definite and indefinite articles *the, a* and *an.* Within this alphabetical grouping of titles, variant editions are not necessarily arranged in chronological order, i.e., a 2nd, 3rd or 4th edition might well be listed prior to an earlier edition.

Subject to restrictions of space and to the provisos set out below, the substance of each catalogue entry giving details of the particular copy offered for sale has been recorded in full.

The listings have been made so as to conform to a uniform order of presentation, viz: Title; place of publication; publisher or printer; date; edition; size; collation; elements of content worthy of note; description of contents including faults, if any; description and condition of binding; bookseller; price; approximate price conversion from dollars to sterling or vice versa.

Abbreviations of description customary within the booktrade have generally been used. A list of these abbreviations will be found on page *x*.

Collations:

Collations, when provided by the bookseller, are repeated in toto although it should be borne in mind that booksellers employ differing practices in this respect; some by providing complete collations and others by indicating merely the number of pages in the main body of the work concerned. The same edition of the same title catalogued by two booksellers could therefore have two apparently different collations and care should be taken not to regard any collation recorded in *ARBV* as being a definitive or absolute record of total content.

Currency conversion:

ARBV lists books offered for sale priced in either pounds sterling (£) or United States dollars ($). For the benefit of readers unaccustomed to one or other of these currencies, an approximate conversion figure in the alternative currency has been provided in parentheses after each entry, as, for example, **"£100 [≈ $150]"**, or, **"$60 [≈ £40]"**. The conversion is based upon an exchange rate of £1 sterling ≈ US $1.50 (US $1 ≈ £0.667 sterling), the approximate rate applicable at the date of going to press.

It must be stressed that the conversion figures in parentheses are provided merely as an indication of the approximate pricing level in the currency with which the reader may be most familiar and that fluctuations in exchange rates will make these approximations inaccurate to a greater or lesser degree.

Acknowledgements:

We are indebted to those booksellers who have provided their catalogues during 1993 for the purposes of *ARBV*. A list of the contributing booksellers forms an appendix at the rear of this volume.

This appendix forms a handy reference of contacts in Britain and the United States with proven experience of handling books within the individual specialist fields encompassed by the series. The booksellers listed therein are able, between them, to offer advice on any aspect of the rare and antiquarian booktrade.

Many of the listed books will still, at the time of publication, be available for purchase. Readers with a possible interest in acquiring any of the items may well find it worth their while communicating with the booksellers concerned to obtain further and complete details.

Caveat:

Whilst the greatest care has been taken in transcribing entries from catalogues, it should be understood that it is inevitable that an occasional error will have passed unnoticed. Obvious mistakes, usually typographical in nature, observed in catalogues have been corrected. We have not questioned the accuracy in bibliographical matters of the catalogues concerned.

The Clique

Abbreviations

advt(s)	advertisement(s)
addtn(s)	addition(s)
a.e.g.	all edges gilt
ALS	autograph letter signed
altrtns	alterations
Amer	American
bibliog(s)	bibliography(ies)
b/w	black & white
bndg	binding
bd(s)	board(s)
b'plate	bookplate
ctlg(s)	catalogue(s)
chromolitho(s)	chromo-lithograph(s)
ca	circa
cold	coloured
coil	collected
contemp	contemporary
crnr(s)	corner(s)
crrctd	corrected
cvr(s)	cover(s)
dec	decorated
detchd	detached
diag(s)	diagram(s)
dw(s)	dust wrapper(s)
edn(s)	edition(s)
elab	elaborate
engv(s)	engraving(s)
engvd	engraved
enlgd	enlarged
esp	especially
ex lib	ex library
f (ff)	leaf(ves)
f.e.p.	free end paper
facs	facsimile
fig(s)	figure(s)
fldg	folding
ft	foot
frontis	frontispiece
hand-cold	hand-coloured
hd	head
ill(s)	illustration(s)
illust	illustrated
imp	impression
imprvd	improved
inc	including
inscrbd	inscribed
inscrptn	inscription
intl	initial
iss	issue
jnt(s)	joint(s)
lge	large
lea	leather
lib	library
ltd	limited
litho(s)	lithograph(s)
marg(s)	margin(s)
ms(s)	manuscript(s)
mrbld	marbled
mod	modern
mor	morocco
mtd	mounted
n.d.	no date
n.p.	no place
num	numerous
obl	oblong
occas	occasional(ly)
orig	original
p (pp)	page(s)
perf	perforated
pict	pictorial
port(s)	portrait(s)
pres	presentation
ptd	printed
qtr	quarter
rebnd	rebind/rebound
rec	recent
repr(d)	repair(ed)
rvsd	revised
roy	royal
sep	separate
sev	several
sgnd	signed
sgntr	signature
sl	slight/slightly
sm	small
t.e.g.	top edge gilt
TLS	typed letter signed
unif	uniform
v	very
vell	vellum
vol(s)	volume(s)
w'engvd	wood-engraved
w'cut(s)	woodcut(s)
wrap(s)	wrapper(s)

The Arts & Architecture 1993 Catalogue Prices

Abbey, J.R.

- Life in England in Aquatint and Lithography 1770-1860 ... Folkestone & London: 1972. 4to. 32 plates, 50 text ills. Orig cloth. Dw. *(Traylen)* **£320 [≈$480]**
- Scenery of Great Britain and Ireland in Aquatint and Lithography 1770-1860 ... London: 1972. 4to. 34 plates, 54 text ills. Orig cloth. Dw. *(Traylen)* **£320 [≈$480]**

Abercrombie, D. (editor)

- The Book of the Modern House. A Panoramic Survey ... London: Waverley, 1939. 1st edn. 4to. xl,378 pp. Errata slip. 6 cold plates, 244 b/w plates. Orig dec cloth. *(Clevedon Books)* **£50 [≈$75]**

Acharya, Prasanna Kumar

- Architecture of Manasara. London: OUP, (1933). 1st edn. 2 vols. 4to. 157 plates. Orig cloth, rubbed, inner hinges strengthened, spine sunned. *(Bookpress)* **$285 [≈£190]**

Achdjian, A.

- A Fundamental Art of the Rug. Paris: Editions Self, 1949. 4to. 287 ,[11] pp. Mtd cold plates, b/w ills. Orig cloth. *(Spelman)* **£80 [≈$120]**

Achilles Tatius

- The Loves of Clitophon and Leucippe ... Stratford-upon-Avon: Shakespeare Head Press, 1923. One of 498 (of 503). Sm folio. Sl tape staining free endpapers. Orig qtr canvas, minor worming front hinge. *(Blackwell's)* **£50 [≈$75]**

Ackermann, James S.

- The Architecture of Michelangelo. Studies in Architecture. Volumes IV and V. London: Zwemmer, 1964. 2nd edn, rvsd. 2 vols. 4to. 83 plates. Orig cloth. Price-clipped dws. *(Sotheran's)* **£120 [≈$180]**

Adams, Eric

- Chelsea Porcelain. London: Barrie & Jenkins, 1987. 224 pp. 172 plates. Orig cloth. Dw. *(Castle Bookshop)* **£20 [≈$30]**
- Francis Danby: Varieties of Poetic Landscape. Yale: UP, 1973. 1st edn. xviii, 207 pp. 6 cold plates, 160 b/w ills. Dw (sl soiled). *(Spelman)* **£60 [≈$90]**
- Francis Danby: Varieties of Poetic Landscape. New Haven: Yale UP, 1973. xviii, 208 pp. 166 ills. Orig cloth. Dw. *(Leicester Art Books)* **£60 [≈$90]**

Adams, Philip R.

- Mary Callery: Sculpture. New York: Wittenborn, 1961. Sq 4to. 151 pp. Num ills. Orig cloth. *(Ars Libri)* **$75 [≈£50]**

Adams, William Howard

- The French Garden, 1500-1800. New York: Braziller, (1979). 1st edn. 4to. Ills. Ex-lib. Orig cloth. Dw. *(Bookpress)* **$50 [≈£33]**

Adamson, Jeremy

- Lawren S. Harris. Urban Scenes and Wilderness Landscapes, 1906-1930. Toronto: Art Gallery of Ontario, 1978. Sq 4to. 231 pp. 175 ills, 34 figs. Orig cloth. Dw. *(Ars Libri)* **$65 [≈£43]**

Addison, J. de S.

- Arts and Crafts of the Middle Ages. A Description of Mediaeval Workmanship ... London: Bell, 1908. 8vo. xix,378 pp. Cold & b/w plates, ills. Orig dec cloth, t.e.g. *(Clevedon Books)* **£28 [≈$42]**

Addison, William

- English Fairs and Markets. London: Batsford, 1953. 1st edn. 199 pp. Cold frontis, ills by Barbara Jones. Orig cloth gilt. Price-clipped dw. *(Hollett)* **£35 [≈$53]**

Ades, Dawn

- Dada and Surrealism Reviewed. London:

Arts Council of Great Britain, 1978. 4to. xi,475 pp. 32 cold plates. Orig wraps.
(Mendelsohn) **$110 [≈£73]**

Adhemar, Jean

- Toulouse-Lautrec: His Complete Lithographs and Drypoints. New York: Abrams, n.d. Folio. 370 pp. 368 ills (54 cold). Orig cloth. Dw (few short tears).
(Abacus) **$100 [≈£67]**

Adhemar, Jean & Cachin, Francoise

- Degas. The Complete Etchings, Lithographs and Monotypes. London: 1974. 4to. 288 pp. 18 cold plates, 293 ills. Lib stamp on title. Dw (spine sl faded).
(Francis Edwards) **£40 [≈$60]**
- Degas: The Complete Etchings, Lithographs and Monotypes. New York: Viking, (1975). 1st edn. Folio. 288 pp. 201 ills. Orig cloth. Dw. *(Abacus)* **$100 [≈£67]**

Aeschylus

- The Oresteia. Translated from the Greek by E.D.A. Morshead. Illustrated by Michael Ayrton. New York: Limited Editions Club, 1961. One of 1500 sgnd by Ayrton. 4to. Orig qtr leather. Slipcase (faded).
(Oak Knoll) **$75 [≈£50]**

Aesop

- The Fables of Aesop, and Others. With Designs on Wood by Thomas Bewick. Newcastle: E. Walker for T. Bewick & Son, 1823. 2nd edn. Ltd edn. xxiv,376 pp. 188 w'engvs by Thomas Bewick, other ills. New three qtr leather. With thumb print receipt bound in as issued. *(Argonaut)* **$500 [≈£333]**
- Fables. A New Translation by V.S. Vernon Jones. Introduction by G.K. Chesterton. Illustrated by Arthur Rackham. London: 1911. 8vo. 13 cold plates, text ills. Contemp prize calf. *(Robertshaw)* **£55 [≈$83]**
- The Fables of Aesop. Translation of Roger L'Estrange. Golden Cockerel Press: 1926. One of 350. Thin 4to. 108 pp. 11 w'engvs by Celia M. Fiennes. B'plate. Orig qtr buckram.
(Waddington) **£55 [≈$83]**

Agius, Pauline

- Ackermann's Regency Furniture & Interiors. London: Crowood Press, 1984. 200 pp. 200 plates. Dw. *(Fine Art)* **£35 [≈$53]**

Aglionby, William

- Choice Observations upon the Art of Painting. Together with Vasari's Lives ... London: for R. King, 1719. 2nd edn. Cr 4to. [xxx],1-(128), 125-132, 129-(376) pp. Sl dusty & browned, some tears, some leaves cropped. Mod half calf. Anon.
(Ash) **£125 [≈$188]**

Ahlberg, Hakon

- Swedish Architecture of the Twentieth Century. New York: Scribner, 1925. 1st edn. Folio. xvi,41,[5] pp. 152 plates. Orig cloth, sl rubbed, number on spine.
(Bookpress) **$375 [≈£250]**

Ainslie, George Robert

- Illustrations of the Anglo-French Coinage ... London & Edinburgh: 1830. Only edn. 4to. x,[ii],(168) pp. Errata slip. 7 plates. Orig qtr mor, sl rubbed, cloth sl marked. Author's presentation copy. Anon.
(Clark) **£75 [≈$113]**

Ainsworth, Ed

- The Cowboy in Art. New York: World, (1968). 1st edn. 4to. xiv,242 pp. Cold & b/w ills. Orig cloth gilt. Dw.
(Karmiole) **$100 [≈£67]**

Akiyama, Terukazu & Matsubara, Saburo

- Arts of China. Buddhist Cave Temples. New Researches. Tokyo: Kodansha, (1969). 1st edn. Folio. 248 pp. 218 ills. Orig cloth. Dw. Slipcase. *(Bookpress)* **$150 [≈£100]**

Akurgai, Ekrem

- The Art of the Hittites. Translated by Constance McNab. New York: Abrams, [ca 1962]. 1st US edn. 4to. 315 pp. 174 plates, text ills. Orig cloth, sl rubbed, hd of spine sl torn. *(Worldwide)* **$95 [≈£63]**

Alain-Fournier

- The Wanderer (Le Grand Meaulnes). Translated from the French by Francoise Delisle ... Illustrations by Dignimont. New York: Limited Editions Club, 1958. One of 1500 sgnd by Dignimont. Tall 8vo. Orig cloth (spine age-yellowed). Slipcase.
(Oak Knoll) **$45 [≈£30]**

Alarcon, Pedro Antonio de

- The Three-Cornered Hat ... Translated by Martin Armstrong. Illustrated by Roger Duvoisin. [New York]: The Limited Editions Club, 1959. One of 1500 sgnd by Duvoisin. Sm 4to. Orig cloth-backed bds. Slipcase.
(Oak Knoll) **$45 [≈£30]**

Aldin, Cecil

- An Artist's Models. London: (1930). One of 310 signed by the author. Sm folio. 20 tinted plates. Orig vellum, t.e.g. *(Traylen)* **£400 [≈$600]**

- Cathedrals and Abbey Churches of England. London: Eyre & Spottiswoode, 1929. 1st cheap edn. Sm 4to. vii,111 pp. 16 cold plates, 15 text ills. half-titlespotted. Orig cloth gilt, trifle used. *(Hollett)* **£60 [≈$90]**
- Cathedrals of England. London: Eyre & Spottiswoode, n.d. 1st edn. Sm 4to. vii,111 pp. 16 cold plates, 15 text ills, dec endpapers. A few spots to prelims. Orig cloth gilt, faded. *(Hollett)* **£85 [≈$128]**
- Old Inns. London: Heinemann, 1921. One of 380 signed by the author. 4to. viii,149 pp. 16 mtd cold plates, 45 plates. Orig qtr vellum & pict bds gilt, edges sl rubbed. *(Gough)* **£325 [≈$488]**
- Old Inns. London: Heinemann, 1925. Lge 8vo. viii,149 pp. 16 cold plates, num text ills. Photos & ills pasted to endpapers, b'plate. Orig cloth gilt, spine faded. *(Hollett)* **£60 [≈$90]**
- Old Manor Houses. London: Heinemann, 1923. 1st edn. Sm 4to. 109 pp. 12 cold plates, num ills. Orig cloth gilt, extrs sl worn, a few marks. *(Hollett)* **£95 [≈$143]**

Aldridge, James

- Living Egypt. Photographs by Paul Strand. London: (1969). 1st edn. Over 100 photo ills. Dw (tip of spine chipped). *(Rob Warren)* **$175 [≈£117]**

Alexander, Christopher

- The Linz Cafe. New York: OUP, 1981. 1st edn. 8vo. 92,[4] pp. Name. Orig cloth. *(Bookpress)* **$45 [≈£30]**

Alexander, Russell George

- The Engraved Work of F.L. Griggs, A.R.A., R.E. Etchings and Drypoints 1912-1928. Shakespeare Head Press: 1928. One of 325. xviii, 93 pp. Orig cloth. *(Fine Art)* **£85 [≈$128]**

Allen, Charles Dexter

- American Book-Plates. A Guide to their Study with Examples. With a Bibliography by Eben Newell Hewins ... New York: Macmillan, 1905. 8vo. xvi,438 pp. 22 plates, num ills. Orig cloth gilt. *(Karmiole)* **$35 [≈£23]**

Allen, Frank J.

- The Great Church Towers of England, chiefly of the Perpendicular Period. Cambridge: UP, 1932. 4to. xiii,206 pp. Frontis, 52 plates, 59 text ills. Orig cloth. Dw (reprd). *(Quest Books)* **£75 [≈$113]**
- The Great Church Towers of England chiefly of the Perpendicular Period ... Cambridge: UP, 1932. 1st edn. 4to. xiii,206 pp. 53 plates, 59 text ills. Endpapers sl spotted. Orig cloth gilt. *(Hollett)* **£85 [≈$128]**

Allen, Hervey

- Christmas Epithalamium. New York: William Edwin Rudge, 1925. 1st edn thus. One of 325. 8 ff. Orig bds. Tissue dw, fine. Typography by Bruce Rogers. *(Hermitage)* **$75 [≈£50]**

Allingham, Helen

- Happy England. With Memoir and Descriptions by Marcus B. Huish. London: A. & C. Black, 1903. One of 750 signed by Allingham. Thick 4to. Cold port, 80 cold plates. Orig dec buckram, fine. *(Traylen)* **£460 [≈$690]**

Alloway, Lawrence

- American Pop Art. New York: Collier, 1974. 4to. xii,[2],144,[2] pp. 105 plates. Orig wraps. *(Ars Libri)* **$40 [≈£27]**
- Network: Art and the Complex Present. Ann Arbor: UMI Research Press, 1984. 4to. 302 pp. Orig cloth. Dw. *(Ars Libri)* **$85 [≈£57]**

Alpatov, M.W.

- Art Treasures of Russia. London: Thames & Hudson, n.d. Lge 4to. 178 pp. 104 mtd cold plates. Orig cloth gilt. Price-clipped dw. *(Hollett)* **£30 [≈$45]**

Alsop, Joseph

- The Rare Art Traditions. The History of Art Collecting and its Linked Phenomena wherever these have appeared. Princeton: UP, Bollingen Series, 1982. Roy 8vo. 96 ills, frontis sl creased. Dw. *(David Slade)* **£25 [≈$38]**
- The Rare Art Traditions: The History of Art Collecting and its Linked Phenomena. Princeton: UP, 1982. xxiii,691 pp. 95 ills. Orig cloth. Dw. *(Fine Art)* **£35 [≈$53]**

Alston, J.W.

- Hints to Young Practitioners in the Study of Landscape Painting ... Third Edition. London: Longman, [ca 1805]. 8vo. [6],67 pp. Etched title, 5 plates. Some foxing & old waterstaining to text. Orig linen backed bds, spine & crnrs worn. *(Spelman)* **£50 [≈$75]**

Amaya, Mario

- Pop Art ... And After. New York: Viking,

1966. 4to. 148 pp. 48 plates. Orig cloth. Dw. *(Ars Libri)* **$60 [≈£40]**

Ames, Joseph

- Typographical Antiquities ... Origin and Progress of Printing in Great Britain and Ireland ... London: for the editor ..., 1785-90. 3 vols. 4to. Plate of marks as vol 2 title, text ills. Subscribers. Mod buckram, partly unopened. *(Lamb)* **£400 [≈$600]**

Amiranashvili, Shalva

- Mediaeval Georgia Enamels of Russia. New York: [ca 1960]. 4to. 64 mtd cold plates. orig bndg. *(Hollett)* **£40 [≈$60]**

Anacreon

- Anacreon: Done Into English out of the Original Greek by Abraham Cowley. Soho: The Nonesuch Press, 1923. One of 725. Engvs by Stephen Gooden. Orig vellum backed bds, gilt spine. Dw (sl chipped). *(Hermitage)* **$125 [≈£83]**

Ancient Reliques ...

- Ancient Reliques; or Delineations of Monastic, Castellated, & Domestic Architecture and other Interesting Subjects ... (engraved and published by J. Greig ... A. Storer). London: the proprietors ..., 1812-13. 2 vols. 100 plates, inc tail-pieces. Sl marg worm. Contemp calf. *(Waterfield's)* **£180 [≈$270]**

Andersen, Hans Christian

- Fairy Tales. Illustrated by E.A. Lemann. London: Arnold, 1893. 1st edn thus. 8vo. xii, 219,[8 advt] pp. Ills. Prize b'plate. Endpapers browned. Orig pict buckram. *(Sotheran's)* **£45 [≈$68]**
- Hans Andersen's Fairy Tales. Illustrated by A. Duncan Carse. London: Adam & Charles Black, [1912]. One of 250 signed by the publishers. Sm 4to. xvi,373,[ii] pp. 12 mtd cold plates, ills. Crnr of 1 plate creased. Orig pict white cloth gilt, t.e.g. *(Sotheran's)* **£298 [≈$447]**
- Hans Andersen's Fairy Tales. Edited by Capt. Edric Vredenburg. Illustrated by Mabel Lucie Attwell. Phila: David McKay, n.d. 1st Amer edn. 4to. 12 cold plates, ills. Orig gilt dec cloth, v sl worn. *(Jo Ann Reisler)* **$300 [≈£200]**
- Fairy Tales. Illustrated by W. Heath Robinson. London: Boots the Chemists, (1913). 8vo. 320 pp. 16 mtd cold plates. Orig cloth gilt. *(Davidson)* **$295 [≈£197]**
- Fairy Tales. Illustrated by Harry Clarke. London: Harrap, 1916. 1st Clarke edn. 4to. 319 pp. 16 mtd cold plates, b/w ills. Orig illust cloth, t.e.g., spine sl faded. *(Davidson)* **$1,400 [≈£933]**
- Fairy Tales. Illustrated by Kay Nielsen. London: Hodder & Stoughton, 1924. 1st English edn. 4to. 197 pp. 12 mtd cold plates, b/w ills, dec endpapers. Stain on free endpaper. Orig cloth gilt, spine ends worn, sm hole in spine. *(Davidson)* **$650 [≈£433]**
- Fairy Tales. Illustrated by Kay Nielsen. London: Hodder & Stoughton, [1924]. One of 500 signed by Nielsen. 4to. 12 mtd cold plates, num plates & ills. Orig elab gilt vellum, t.e.g., spine sl soiled, one tiny chip edge of lower bd. *(Sotheran's)* **£1,700 [≈$2,550]**
- Fairy Tales. Illustrated by Kay Nielsen. New York: Doran, 1924. 1st Amer edn. 4to. 280 pp. 12 mtd cold plates, b/w ills, dec endpapers. Orig dec cloth, sl soiled, spine sl faded. *(Davidson)* **$650 [≈£433]**
- Fairy Tales. Illustrated by Harry Clarke. London: Harrap, 1931. 4to. 319 pp. 16 mtd cold plates, 12 b/w ills. Inscrptn. Orig dec cloth. *(Davidson)* **$185 [≈£123]**

Andersen, Wayne

- Cezanne's Portrait Drawings. Cambridge: The MIT Press, (1970). 1st edn. sq 4to. xii, 248 pp. Ills. Name. Orig cloth. Dw. *(Karmiole)* **$40 [≈£27]**

Anderson, C.

- Ancient Models or Hints on Church Building. London: Burns, 1841. 2nd edn. 12mo. 211 pp. Ills. Sl dusty. Binder's cloth. *(Monmouth)* **£20 [≈$30]**

Anderson, John, Jr.

- The Unknown Turner: Revelations concerning the Life and Art of J.M.W. Turner. New York: privately printed for the author, 1926. One of 1000. Folio. 154 pp. Cold frontis, num b/w ills. Orig cloth. *(Abacus)* **$125 [≈£83]**

Anderson, Joseph

- Ancient Scottish Weapons ... see Drummond, James

Anderson, Sherwood

- Winesburg, Ohio. Illustrations by Ben F. Stahl. New York: The Limited Editions Club, 1978. One of 1600 sgnd by Stahl. 4to. Orig qtr leather. Slipcase (faded in spots). *(Oak Knoll)* **$75 [≈£50]**

Anderson, W.

- Japanese Wood Engravings. Their History, Technique and Characteristics. London: Portfolio, 1895. Lge 8vo. 80 pp. 6 cold plates, text ills. Sm lib stamp on title verso. Later lib cloth. *(Bow Windows)* **£45 [≈$68]**

Anderson, William J. & Stratton, Arthur

- The Architecture of the Renaissance in Italy ... London: Batsford, 1927. 5th edn. 8vo. 316 pp. 90 plates, 150 text ills. Orig cloth gilt. *(Hollett)* **£20 [≈$30]**

Andre, G.G.

- The Draughtsman's Handbook of Plan and Map Drawing ... London: Spon, 1874. 4to. 150 pp. 31 plates. Cloth backed bds, orig title panel laid on. *(Monmouth)* **£50 [≈$75]**

Andrews, Edward D.

- The Community Industries of the Shakers. New York: State Museum Handbook, 1933. 322 pp. 65 plates. Inscrptn. Orig wraps. *(Hollett)* **£30 [≈$45]**

Andrews, Keith

- Adam Elsheimer. Paintings, Drawings, Prints. Oxford: Phaidon, 1977. 178 pp. 142 ills. Orig cloth. *(Leicester Art Books)* **£60 [≈$90]**

Andrews, William

- Old-Time Punishments. Hull: 1890. One of 100. 4to. x,251 pp. Frontis, num text ills. Orig cloth gilt, t.e.g., sl rubbed, spine dull. *(Taylor & Son)* **£46 [≈$69]**

Andreyev, Leonid

- Abyss. Golden Cockerel Press: 1929. One of 500. 31 pp. W'engvs by Ivan Lebedeff. Endpapers browned. Orig qtr buckram, t.e.g. *(Waddington)* **£36 [≈$54]**

Angel, Marie

- Beasts in Heraldry. Vermont: The Stephen Greene Press, 1974. 1st edn. 12mo. Name. Orig box, sl soiled, one corner split. *(Davidson)* **$85 [≈£57]**

Anker, Peter & Andersson, Aron

- The Art of Scandinavia. London: Paul Hamlyn, (1970). 2 vols. 452; 392 pp. Plates. Orig cloth. Dws. *(Abacus)* **$75 [≈£50]**

Anscombe, Isabelle

- Omega and After. Bloomsbury and the Decorative Arts. London: Thames & Hudson, 1981. 1st edn. 4to. Num ills. Name. Dw. *(Virgo)* **£35 [≈$53]**

Antal, Frederick

- Fuseli Studies. London: Routledge, 1956. xii, 176 pp. 64 plates. Orig buckram. *(Leicester Art Books)* **£36 [≈$54]**
- Hogarth and His Place in European Art. London: Routledge, 1962. 1st edn. Lge 8vo. 152 plates. Some soiling. Dw (worn). *(Spelman)* **£40 [≈$60]**
- Hogarth and His Place in European Art. London: Routledge, 1962. xxi,270 pp. 152 plates. Orig cloth. Dw. *(Leicester Art Books)* **£65 [≈$98]**

Antiquarian ...

- Antiquarian Book Monthly Review. Volume 1, Issue No. 1, February 1974 to Vol XIII Number 12, Issue 152, December 1986. Olney & Oxford: 1974-86. 13 vols. Ills. Binder's cloth. *(Cooper Hay)* **£130 [≈$195]**
- The Antiquarian Itinerary, comprising Specimens of Architecture, Monastic, Castellated and Domestic ... Accompanied with Descriptions. London: for the proprietors by Wm. Clarke ..., 1815-18. 7 vols. 8vo. Num plates. Occas foxing & offsetting. Orig bds, sl worn. *(Taylor & Son)* **£110 [≈$165]**

Anton, Ferdinand

- Art of the Maya. New York: 1970. 1st US edn. Thick folio. 365 ills. Dw. Slipcase. *(Rob Warren)* **$150 [≈£100]**
- Art of the Maya. London: Thames & Hudson, 1978. 1st English edn. 4to. 299 plates. Orig cloth. Slipcase. *(Baker)* **£34.50 [≈$53]**

Antrim, Benajah J.

- Pantography, or Universal Drawings. Phila: the author, 1843. 1st edn. 12mo. 161,[1] pp. 11 plates. Foxed. Orig cloth, rebacked, ink stain lower bd. *(Bookpress)* **$250 [≈£167]**

Apollinaire, Guillaume

- The Cubist Painters. Aesthetic Meditations 1913. Translated from the French by Lionel Abel. New York: Wittenborn, 1944. 4to. Ills. Orig wraps, worn. *(Ars Libri)* **$60 [≈£40]**
- The Cubist Painters. Aesthetic Meditations 1913. Second Revised Edition. New York: Wittenborn, Schulz, 1949. 4to. Ills. Orig wraps. *(Ars Libri)* **$50 [≈£33]**
- The Poet Assassinated. Translated from the French with a Biographical Notice and Notes by Matthew Josephson. New York: The Broom Publishing Co., 1923. One of 1250. Sm 4to. 158 pp. Port frontis, 4 w'cut ills.

Orig wraps. *(Ars Libri)* **$100 [≈£67]**

Apollonius of Tyre

- Apollonius of Tyre. Translated and Introduced by Paul Turner. Golden Cockerel Press: 1956. One of 300. 76 pp. Engvs by Mark Severin. Orig qtr mor, t.e.g., fine. *(Bookworks)* **£115 [≈$173]**

Apuleius

- Cupid and Psyche, translated by William Aldington. Golden Cockerel Press: 1934. One of 150. W'engvs by Lettice Sandford. Endpapers v sl browned. Crnrs v sl worn. *(Waddington)* **£68 [≈$102]**

Apuleius, Lucius

- The Golden Asse ... Translated out of Latin by William Adlington ... and Illustrated ... by Jean de Bosschere. London: John Lane, 1923. One of 3000. 8vo. 16 plates. Orig cloth gilt, t.e.g. *(Claude Cox)* **£25 [≈$38]**

Aquinas, Saint Thomas

- Selections from his Works made by George N. Shuster. Wood Engravings by Reynolds Stone. New York: Limited Editions Club, 1979. One of 1500 sgnd by Stone. Sm 4to. Orig cloth. Slipcase. *(Oak Knoll)* **$100 [≈£67]**

Arabian Nights

- The Arabian Nights. Illustrated by E.J. Detmold. London: Hodder & Stoughton, [1924]. 1st edn. Lge 4to. 12 mtd cold plates. V sl foxing. Orig gilt dec white cloth. *(Jo Ann Reisler)* **$985 [≈£657]**

Aragon, Louis

- Henri Matisse. A Novel. Translated by Jean Stewart. London: Collins, 1972. 2 vols. 234 + 307 ills. Orig cloth. Dws. Slipcase. *(Leicester Art Books)* **£160 [≈$240]**

Archer, W.G.

- Indian Paintings from the Punjab Hills. London: Sotheby Parke Bernet, 1973. 1st edn. 2 vols. Sm folio. Num ills. Orig cloth. Dws (sl chipped & soiled). *(Bookpress)* **$225 [≈£150]**

Archipenko, Alexander

- The Archipenko Exhibition. Introduction and Catalogue by Christian Brinton. New York: Kingore Gallery, 1924. Sm 4to. [6] pp. 7 plates. Orig dec wraps. *(Ars Libri)* **$300 [≈£200]**
- Archipenko. Fifty Creative Years, 1908-1958. New York: Tekhne, 1960. Lge 4to. [2], 109 pp. 292 ills. Orig buckram. Dw. *(Ars Libri)* **$400 [≈£267]**

Architectural Notices ...

- Architectural Notices of the Churches of the Archdeaconry of Northampton. Deaneries of Higham Ferrers and Haddon. London: John Henry Parker, 1849. Lge 8vo. xii,283,[5] pp. Errata slip. 41 (of 42) plates. Contemp half calf, rubbed. *(Spelman)* **£30 [≈$45]**

Arciniegas, German

- Fernando Botero. New York: Abrams, 1977. 56, (168) pp. 179 ills. Orig cloth. Dw. *(Leicester Art Books)* **£95 [≈$143]**

Ardizzone, Edward

- Indian Diary 1952-1953. Introduction by Malcolm Muggeridge. London: 1984. 1st edn. Num ills. Orig cloth. Dw (sm tear to rear). *(Margaret Nangle)* **£20 [≈$30]**
- Paul. The Hero of the Fire. London: 1948. 1st edn. Cold ills by the author. Free endpapers v sl browned. Orig pict bds, ft of spine bumped, hd of spine splitting. Dw (sl used). *(Ulysses Bookshop)* **£55 [≈$83]**

Argan, Giulio Carlo

- Henry Moore. New York: Abrams, [ca 1972]. Sq 4to. Orig cloth. Dw. *(First Folio)* **$75 [≈£50]**

Aries, R.S.

- Mane-Katz 1894-1962. The Complete Works. London: Jacques O'Hana, 1970-72. One of 1000 & 500. 2 vols. Num ills. Orig cloth. *(Leicester Art Books)* **£180 [≈$270]**

Aristophanes

- The Birds. Illustrations by Marian Parry. New York: Limited Editions Club, 1959. One of 1500 sgnd by Parry. 4to. Orig qtr leather. Outer wraparound cover. Slipcase. *(Oak Knoll)* **$75 [≈£50]**
- The Birds. An English Version by Dudley Fitts. Illustrated by Quentin Blake. London: Lion & Unicorn Press, 1971. One of 400. 4to. Num ills. Orig pict wraps. *(Barbara Stone)* **£55 [≈$83]**
- The Eleven Comedies. Illustrated by Jean de Bosschere. New York: Liveright, 1928. One of 2050. 2 vols. 16 cold & 16 b/w plates. Orig gilt dec cloth, tiny snag hd of 1 spine. *(Hermitage)* **$200 [≈£133]**
- The Frogs. Wood-Engravings by John Austen. New York: Limited Editions Club, 1937. One of 1500 sgnd by Austen. 4to. Orig cloth. Board wraparound protective wrapper

(sm damaged spot). Slipcase. *(Oak Knoll)* **$95 [≈£63]**

Aristotle

- Politics & Poetics. Portraits by Leonard Baskin. New York: Limited Editions Club, 1964. One of 1500 sgnd by Baskin. Sm 4to. Orig cloth (spine darkened). Slipcase. *(Oak Knoll)* **$100 [≈£67]**

Ark ...

- Ark. The Journal of the Royal College of Art. London: 1950-56. Nos 1-17. Oblong 4to. Orig wraps. *(Ars Libri)* **$450 [≈£300]**

Arlott, John

- Clausentum, Sonnets. London: Cape, 1946. 1st edn. Cr 8vo. 7 ills by Michael Ayrton. Orig cloth. *(Blackwell's)* **£85 [≈$128]**
- Clausentum. London: Cape, 1946. 1st edn. Ills by Michael Ayrton. Dw. *(Any Amount)* **£36 [≈$54]**

Arman, Mark

- Fleurons: their Place in History and in Print. Dunmow, Essex: Workshop Press, 1988. One of 170 signed by the author. Roy 8vo. Orig qtr cloth. *(Blackwell's)* **£40 [≈$60]**
- Seventeen 18th and 19th Century Boxwood Blocks. Thaxted: The Workshop Press, 1982. One of 80 signed by the author. Lge 8vo. [vi], 30 pp. 12 plates. Orig cloth backed bds. Sep portfolio of prints. Slipcase. *(Bookpress)* **$85 [≈£57]**

Armfield, Maxwell

- An Artist in Italy. London: Methuen, 1926. 1st edn. 16 cold plates by the author. Orig buckram backed bds, sl rubbed & marked. *(Bookworks)* **£18 [≈$27]**

Armi, C.E.

- Masons and Sculptors in Romanesque Burgundy: The New Aesthetic of Cluny III. Penn State UP: 1983. 2 vols (text & plates). 4to. 238 plates. Dws. *(Monmouth)* **£50 [≈$75]**

Armitage, Ella S.

- The Early Norman Castles of the British Isles. London: Murray, 1912. 8vo. 46 plates & plans. Orig cloth, spine gilt dull. *(David Slade)* **£35 [≈$53]**

Armitage, Merle

- The Lithographs of Richard Day. With a Foreword by Carl Zigrosser. New York: E. Weyhe, 1932. One of 500. 4to. x,[2] pp. Orig litho frontis signed by the artist, port, 12 plates. Orig bds. *(Ars Libri)* **$175 [≈£117]**

Arms, Dorothy Noyes

- Churches of France. New York: Macmillan, 1929. 1st edn. 4to. xv,[i],179 pp. 50 plates. Orig cloth, sl worn. *(Bookpress)* **$65 [≈£43]**

Arms, Dorothy Noyes & Taylor, John

- Churches of France. New York: Macmillan, 1929. 1st edn. 4to. 179 pp. 51 ills. Orig cloth. *(Rona Schneider)* **$85 [≈£57]**
- Hill Towns and Cities of Northern Italy. New York: Macmillan, 1932. 1st edn. 4to. 217 pp. 56 ills. Orig cloth. *(Rona Schneider)* **$105 [≈£70]**

Armstrong, A.

- Axel Herman Haig and His Work. Illustrated from his Etchings, Pencil Drawings and Watercolours, with a Biography and a Descriptive Catalogue of his Etched Work. London: The Fine Art Society, 1905. x,176 pp. 46 ills. Binder's cloth, t.e.g. *(Leicester Art Books)* **£45 [≈$68]**
- Axel Herman Haig and his Work ... With a Biography and a Descriptive Catalogue of his Etched Works. London: Fine Art Society, 1905. Ltd edn. 4to. Orig signed etching frontis, 45 plates (4 cold). Orig half mor, t.e.g., cloth sl marked. *(Monmouth)* **£50 [≈$75]**

Armstrong, Lilian

- Renaissance Miniature Painters and Classical Imagery. The Master of the Putti & His Workshop. London: Harvey Miller, (1981). 1st edn. Sm 4to. viii,223 pp. Frontis, 152 ills. Orig cloth. Dw. *(Bookpress)* **$75 [≈£50]**

Armstrong, Tom, & others

- 200 Years of American Sculpture. New York: Whitney Museum of American Art, 1976. 4to. 336 pp. Num ills. Orig cloth. *(Rona Schneider)* **$50 [≈£33]**

Arnason, H.H.

- Robert Motherwell. New York: Abrams, (1977). 1st edn. Oblong 4to. 251 pp. 325 ills. Orig dec cloth. Plastic wraparound band. *(Abacus)* **$300 [≈£200]**
- The Sculptures of Houdon. London: Phaidon, 1975. 294 pp. 393 ills. Orig cloth. Dw. *(Leicester Art Books)* **£40 [≈$60]**

Arnold, Sir Edwin

- Japonica. New York: Scribner, 1891. 1st edn. 8vo. xv,[i],128 pp. Frontis, ills by Robert

Blum. Orig cloth gilt, t.e.g. *(Bookpress)* **$325 [≈£217]**

- The Light of Asia. Illustrations by Ayres Houghtelling. Avon, CT: Limited Editions Club, 1976. One of 2000 sgnd by Houghtelling. 4to. Orig pict cloth. Slipcase. *(Oak Knoll)* **$45 [≈£30]**

Arnold, Hugh

- Stained Glass of the Middle Ages in England and France. London: A. & C. Black, Twenty Shilling Series, 1913. 1st edn. 50 cold plates by L.P. Saint. Orig cloth, fine. *(Old Cathay)* **£59 [≈$89]**
- Stained Glass of the Middle Ages in England and France. London: Adam & Charles Black, 1913. 4to. 1st edn. xiv,269 pp. 50 plates. Orig pict cloth gilt. *(Taylor & Son)* **£45 [≈$68]**
- Stained Glass of the Middle Ages in England and France. With Fifty Plates in Colour by Lawrence B. Saint. London: Adam & Charles Black, (1955). 8vo. [xiv],269,[3 blank] pp. 50 cold plates. Orig cloth. Dw (spine ends chipped). *(Bow Windows)* **£30 [≈$45]**

Arnold, Matthew

- The Scholar Gipsy and Thyrsis. Illustrated by W. Russell Flint. London: Philip Lee Warner, 1919. Reprint of 1911 edn. 4to. [12], 68 pp. 10 mtd cold plates, endpaper maps. Orig cloth gilt. *(Karmiole)* **$75 [≈£50]**

Arnold, Sir Thomas W.

- Painting in Islam ... Oxford: Clarendon Press 1928. 1st edn. 4to. xviii,159,[1] pp. Frontis, 64 plates. Orig cloth, sl rubbed, tips sl worn, number on spine. *(Bookpress)* **$250 [≈£167]**

Arp, Jean

- On My Way. Poetry and Essays 1912-1947. The Documents of Modern Art. New York: Wittenborn, Schulz, 1948. 148 pp. 2 orig w'cuts by Arp, 48 ills. Orig wraps. *(Leicester Art Books)* **£35 [≈$53]**

Arrowsmith, H.W. & A.

- The House Decorator and Painter's Guide; containing a Series of Designs for Decorating Apartments, suited to the Various Styles of Architecture. London: Thomas Kelly, 1840. 1st edn. 4to. 61 plates (26 hand cold). Few plates foxed. Lacks intl advt leaf. Later half calf. *(Traylen)* **£800 [≈$1,200]**

Ars Typographica

- Ars Typographica. Edited by Frederic W. Goudy [then by Douglas McMurtrie]. New York: The Marchbanks Press, 1918-34. 9 issues (vols 1:1-4, 2:1-4, 3:1), complete. 4to. Orig stiff paper wraps. *(Oak Knoll)* **$250 [≈£167]**

Art ...

- The Art Journal Illustrated Catalogue. The Industry of all Nations, 1851. London: Virtue, [1851]. Folio. Num w'engvd ills. Orig pict gilt cloth, extrs sl worn. *(Barbara Stone)* **£125 [≈$188]**
- The Art Journal Illustrated Catalogue. The Industry of all Nations, 1851. London: George Virtue, [1851]. 1st edn. Lge 4to. Advt leaf at end. W'engvd ills. Few margs sl frayed. Inner hinges cracked. Orig cloth gilt, sl soiled & marked. *(Claude Cox)* **£45 [≈$68]**
- The Art of Painting in Miniature. Teaching the Speedy and Perfect Acquisition of that Art without a Master. London: for J. Hodges, 1752. 6th edn. 12mo. [x],1-132, 135-150,[6] pp. Frontis. Sheep, worn. Anon. *(Bookpress)* **$285 [≈£190]**
- The Art of Tanning and Currying Leather ... see Vallancey, Charles

Arthaud, Claude

- Enchanted Visions: Fantastic Houses and their Treasures. New York: Putnam, (1972). 1st Amer edn. Folio. 355,[4] pp. Ills. Orig cloth. Dw (torn). *(Bookpress)* **$75 [≈£50]**

Art-Union

- Art-Union. Monthly Journal of the Fine Arts. London: 1847-48. 2 vols. Lge 4to. Plates. Occas v sl foxing. Qtr calf, rubbed. *(Monmouth)* **£60 [≈$90]**

Ash, Douglas

- How to Identify English Drinking Glasses & Decanters 1680-1830. London: Bell, 1962. Cr 8vo. 200 pp. B/w ills. Dw. Inscribed by the author. *(Paul Brown)* **£22 [≈$33]**

Ashbee, C.R.

- Conradin, a Philosophical Ballad. Broad Campden: Essex House Press, 1908. One of 250. [viii],26,[viii] pp. 6 ills by P.A. Mairet. Orig qtr linen, edges sl rubbed. *(Michael Taylor)* **£55 [≈$83]**

Ashdown, Charles H.

- British Castles. London: Adam & Charles Black, 1911. 1st edn. Lge 8vo. xx,208 pp. 37 cold plates. Foredge sl spotted. New endpapers. Orig dec cloth gilt, t.e.g. *(Hollett)* **£48 [≈$72]**

Ashdown, Mrs Charles H.

- British Costume during XIX Centuries (Civil and Ecclesiastical). London: Nelson, [1910]. Sm 4to. xiii,376 pp. 8 cold plates, num ills. Orig cloth gilt. Dw (sl worn). *(Hollett)* **£30 [≈$45]**

Ashford, Faith

- A Soul Cake. Ditchling: St. Dominic's Press, 1919. [One of 240]. Cr 8vo. [vi],53 pp. Orig ptd wraps, unopened. *(Blackwell's)* **£90 [≈$135]**

Ashley, Alfred

- The Art of Etching on Copper. London: John & Daniel A. Darling, [1849]. Oblong 4to. 14 plates inc title vignette. Sl spotted. Orig cloth. *(Waterfield's)* **£85 [≈$128]**

Ashley, C.W.

- The Ashley Book of Knots. London: (1948). 1st London edn. Lge 8vo. [x],620 pp. Num ills. Orig cloth. *(Bow Windows)* **£65 [≈$98]**

Ashton, Dore

- Richard Lindner. New York: Abrams, 1969. 217 pp. 187 ills. Orig cloth. Dw. *(Leicester Art Books)* **£70 [≈$105]**
- Richard Lindner. New York: Abrams, [1969]. Sm oblong folio. 217 pp. 187 ills. Orig cloth. Dw. *(Ars Libri)* **$225 [≈£150]**

Ashton, John

- Chap-Books of the Eighteenth Century ... London: Chatto & Windus, 1882. 1st edn. 8vo. xvi,(488),[32 ctlg] pp. Ills. Orig cloth, sl rubbed. *(Clark)* **£60 [≈$90]**
- English Caricature & Satire on Napoleon I ... London: Chatto & Windus, 1884. 1st edn. 2 vols. 8vo. 115 ills. Orig cloth gilt, dusty, extrs sl worn. *(Claude Cox)* **£40 [≈$60]**

Ashton, Julian & Lindsay, Norman

- The Art of Elioth Gruner. Sydney: Art in Australia, 1923. One of 600 signed by the artist. 16 pp. 42 plates. Orig cloth & bds. *(Leicester Art Books)* **£90 [≈$135]**

Ashton, Leigh

- An Introduction to the Study of Chinese Sculpture. London: 1924. 4to. 63 plates. Orig buckram. *(Traylen)* **£48 [≈$72]**

Asmi, Iftikhar

- The Garden of the Night. Twenty-Six Sufi Poems. Translated by Iftikhar Asmi. Andoversford: The Whittington Press, 1979. One of 240 signed by translator and artist, Richard Kennedy. [72] pp. Ills. Orig qtr buckram, t.e.g. Slipcase. prospectus. Advt card. *(Bookworks)* **£65 [≈$98]**

Atkins, Guy

- Asger Jorn: The Final Years, 1965-1973. A Study ... and a Catalogue ... London: Lund Humphries, 1980. Lge 4to. 241,[1] pp. 676 ills. Orig cloth. Dw. *(Ars Libri)* **$600 [≈£400]**

Atkinson, Thomas Dinham

- Local Style in English Architecture ... London: Batsford, 1947. 1st edn. 8vo. viii, 183 pp. 126 ills. Orig cloth. Dw (extrs trifle rubbed). *(Hollett)* **£25 [≈$38]**

Audsley, William & Audsley, George

- Cottage, Lodge, and Villa Architecture. London: William Mackenzie, [ca 1870]. Folio. 32 pp. Litho title, 91 litho plates on 85 ff. Occas spotting, few sl marks. Mod half mor gilt. *(Hollett)* **£160 [≈$240]**
- Polychromatic Decoration as applied to Buildings in the Mediaeval Styles. London: Sotheran, 1882. 1st edn. Folio. [viii],32 pp. Red & black title & half-title, 36 chromolitho plates. Lib stamp on endpaper. Occas sl spotting. Orig cloth, spine reprd. *(Robert Frew)* **£200 [≈$300]**

Auerbach, Erna

- Nicholas Hilliard. Boston: Routledge, 1961. xxiv,352 pp. 269 ills. Orig buckram. Dw. *(Leicester Art Books)* **£65 [≈$98]**
- Nicholas Hilliard. London: 1961. xxiv,352 pp. 7 cold plates, 245 ills. Orig cloth. Dw. *(Fine Art)* **£85 [≈$128]**

Augustine, Saint

- The Confessions. Illustrated with Paintings by Edy Legrand. New York: The Limited Editions Club, 1962. One of 1500 signed by Legrand. 4to. Orig qtr leather. Slipcase. *(Oak Knoll)* **$55 [≈£37]**

Auslander, Joseph

- Letters to Women. London: [1929]. 1st edn. W'cuts by Clare Leighton. Orig cloth, pict onlay. Dw (worn). *(Margaret Nangle)* **£35 [≈$53]**

Ausonius, Decimus Magnus

- Patchwork Quilt. Done into English by Jack Lindsay, with Decorations by Edward Bawden. London: Fanfrolico Press, (1930). One of 400. Orig cloth bds. *(Michael Taylor)* **£80 [≈$120]**

- Patchwork Quilt. Done into English by Jack Lindsay, with Decorations by Edward Bawden. London: Fanfrolico Press, (1930). Unnumbered. Orig cloth bds, sl rubbed, spine faded. *(Michael Taylor)* **£42 [≈$63]**

Austen, Jane

- Northanger Abbey. Illustrations by Clarke Hutton. N.p.: Limited Editions Club by The Garamond Press, 1971. One of 1500 sgnd by Hutton. Tall 8vo. Orig cloth (some fading of spine). Slipcase. *(Oak Knoll)* **$55 [≈£37]**
- Persuasion. Illustrations by Tony Buonpastore. Westport: Limited Editions Club, 1977. One of 1600 sgnd by Buonpastore. Tall 8vo. Orig cloth. Slipcase. *(Oak Knoll)* **$55 [≈£37]**
- Pride and Prejudice. Illustrated by Hugh Thomson. London: 1894. 1st edn thus. 8vo. Inscrptn. Orig elab gilt cloth, a.e.g., front hinge just starting, spine just a little dull. *(Adam Blakeney)* **£45 [≈$68]**
- Sense and Sensibility. Introduction by Austin Dobson. Illustrated by Hugh Thomson. London: Macmillan, 1896. Ills. Inscrptn. Orig bndg, a.e.g. *(Limestone Hills)* **$75 [≈£50]**

Austin, Alfred

- The Garden That I Love. London: A. & C. Black, 1905. One of 250 signed by the author. 16 cold plates by George Samuel Elgood. Orig cloth. *(Old Cathay)* **£75 [≈$113]**
- Lamia's Winter Quarters. London: A. & C. Black, 1907. One of 250 signed by the author. 16 cold plates by George Samuel Elgood. Orig cloth, fine. *(Old Cathay)* **£110 [≈$165]**

Austin, Stephen

- Sakoontala. Hertford: Stephen Austin, 1855. Sm 4to. Frontis, title & num dec borders printed in colours and gold. Orig cream leather gilt, spine ends reprd, extrs sl rubbed. *(Barbara Stone)* **£150 [≈$225]**

Austin, William

- Poems. Edited with an Introduction by Anne Ridler. Oxford: Perpetua Press, 1983. One of 150 signed by Ridler and the printer. Imperial 8vo. Orig qtr buckram. Slipcase. *(Blackwell's)* **£45 [≈$68]**

Avery, Charles (introduces)

- Fingerprints of the Artist. European Terracotta Sculpture from the Arthur M. Sackler Collection. Washington: 1980. Folio. 298 pp. Ca 300 ills, 32 cold plates. Orig cloth. Dw. *(Washton)* **$150 [≈£100]**

Axsom, Richard H.

- The Prints of Frank Stella, 1967-1982. A Catalogue Raisonee ... New York: Hudson Hills Press, 1982. Lge sq 4to. 192 pp. Num ills. Orig wraps. *(Ars Libri)* **$200 [≈£133]**

Ayrton, Elizabeth

- The Cook's Tale. Illustrated by Michael Ayrton. London: 1957. 1st edn. Ills. Orig bndg. Dw. *(Words Etcetera)* **£24 [≈$36]**

Ayrton, Michael

- Golden Sections. With an Introduction by Wyndham Lewis. London: 1957. One of 1500. Sl offsetting to endleaves. Dw (sl sunned & marked). *(Blakeney)* **£55 [≈$83]**
- William Hogarth. Drawings. Edited and Introduced by Michael Ayrton. Notes on the Plates by Bernard Denvir. London: Avalon Press, 1948. 1st edn. 4to. 88 pp. 78 ills. Orig cloth, sl faded. *(Spelman)* **£20 [≈$30]**

Ayrton, Michael & Silcock, Arnold

- Wrought Iron and its Decorative Use. London: Country Life, [1929]. 4to. [vi],196 pp. Num b/w ills. Orig qtr cloth gilt, backstrip sl marked. *(Cooper Hay)* **£55 [≈$83]**

Babcock, Alfred

- Old Stuff, Selected by Alfred Babcock, Printed by Alfred Babcock, and Bound by Albert Babcock. [Cranford, NJ]: Alfred Babcock, 1964. One of 75. Sm 8vo. [iv],201 pp. Orig cloth, paper labels. *(Oak Knoll)* **$45 [≈£30]**

Bacon, Francis

- The Essays. New York: Limited Editions Club, 1944. One of 1100 signed by the designer, Bruce Rogers. Sm folio. Orig cloth backed bds, t.e.g. Cloth case. *(The Veatchs)* **$150 [≈£100]**

Bacou, Roseline

- Millet. One Hundred Drawings. New York: Harper & Row, (1975). 1st US edn. Folio. 216 pp. 100 plates. Orig cloth gilt. Dw. Cardboard slipcase. *(Karmiole)* **$75 [≈£50]**
- Millet. One Hundred Drawings. Translated by James Emmons. London: Phaidon, 1975. 216 pp. 102 ills. Orig cloth. Dw. *(Leicester Art Books)* **£45 [≈$68]**
- Piranesi. Etchings and Drawings. Boston: New York Graphic Society, 1975. 200 pp. 178 ills. Orig cloth. Dw. *(Leicester Art Books)* **£50 [≈$75]**

Bahr, A.W.

- Old Chinese Porcelain and Works of Art in China. London: 1911. Roy 8vo. 120 plates (12 cold). Sl foxing. Orig cloth gilt. Author's presentation copy. *(Traylen)* **£55 [≈$83]**

Baigell, Matthew

- Charles Burchfield. New York: Watson-Guptil, 1976. 208 pp. 149 ills. Orig cloth. Dw. *(Leicester Art Books)* **£80 [≈$120]**
- Thomas Hart Benton. New York: Abrams, [1974]. 282 pp. 229 ills. Orig cloth. Dw. *(Leicester Art Books)* **£70 [≈$105]**
- Thomas Hart Benton. New York: Abrams, [1974]. Oblong folio. 278,[4] pp. 229 plates. Orig cloth. Dw. *(Ars Libri)* **$125 [≈£83]**

Bail, Murray

- Ian Fairweather. Sydney: Bay Books, 1981. 264 pp. 212 ills. Orig cloth. Dw. *(Leicester Art Books)* **£60 [≈$90]**

Bailey, Arthur L.

- Library Bookbinding. White Plains: H.W. Wilson Co., 1916. 1st edn. 8vo. Orig cloth. Dw (v worn). Author's pres inscrptn. *(Oak Knoll)* **$65 [≈£43]**

Bain, Iain

- The Watercolours and Drawings of Thomas Bewick and His Workshop Apprentices ... London: Gordon Fraser, [1981]. 2 vols. 4to. 233; 230 pp. Num ills. Orig buckram. *(Sotheran's)* **£58 [≈$87]**

Bain, James

- A Bookseller Looks Back. The Story of Bains. London: Macmillan, 1940. 8vo. xv,304 pp. Frontis, 7 plates. Orig cloth gilt. *(Cooper Hay)* **£18 [≈$27]**

Baines, Anthony

- European and American Musical Instruments. New York: The Viking Press, (1966). 1st edn. 4to. x,174 pp. Frontis, ills. Orig cloth. Dw. *(Bookpress)* **$75 [≈£50]**

Bairnsfather, [Charles] Bruce

- Bullets & Billets. London: Grant Richards, [1917]. 1st edn. 8vo. 304,[2] pp. 20 plates inc frontis & title. Orig pict cloth, lower cvr sl marked. *(Claude Cox)* **£25 [≈$38]**

Baker, C.H. Collins

- Crome. Introduction by C.J. Holmes. London: Methuen, 1921. Lge 4to. Port, 52 plates. Orig buckram, sl rubbed. *(Traylen)* **£90 [≈$135]**
- Lely & the Stuart Portrait Painters: A Study of English Portraiture before and after Van Dyck. London: Philip Lee Warner, 1912. One of 375. 2 vols. x,218; x,280 pp. 240 plates. Orig vellum backed bds, hd of one spine worn with sm split. *(Fine Art)* **£550 [≈$825]**
- Lely and the Stuart Portrait Painters. A Study of English Portraiture before and after Van Dyck. London: Philip Lee Warner, 1912. One of 375. 2 vols. 165 plates. Orig buckram, t.e.g. *(Leicester Art Books)* **£375 [≈$563]**

Baker, Charles (editor)

- Bibliography of British Book Illustrators 1860-1900 ... Birmingham: 1978. One of 1000. Sm 4to. xii,186 pp. 2 mtd cold ills, num ills. Dw (chipped, sl worn). *(Francis Edwards)* **£25 [≈$38]**

Baldass, Ludwig

- Giorgione. London: Thames & Hudson, 1965. 188 pp. 82 plates. Orig cloth. *(Leicester Art Books)* **£60 [≈$90]**
- Hieronymus Bosch. London: Thames & Hudson, 1960. 242 pp. 161 ills. Orig cloth. Dw. *(Leicester Art Books)* **£48 [≈$72]**

Baldry, Alfred Lys

- Albert Moore. His Life and Work. London: George Bell, 1893. 109 pp. 63 plates. Orig dec cloth gilt, t.e.g. *(Leicester Art Books)* **£110 [≈$165]**
- Sir John Everett Millais. His Art and Influence. London: George Bell & Sons, 1899. xv,123 pp. 61 ills. A few marks. Orig cloth gilt, t.e.g., sl rubbed. *(Hollett)* **£65 [≈$98]**

Ball, Katherine M.

- Decorative Motives of Oriental Art. London: John Lane; The Bodley Head, (1927). 1st edn. Sm folio. xxvi,[ii],286,[2] pp. Lib marks. Cloth, sl worn. *(Bookpress)* **$150 [≈£100]**

The Ballads of Robin Hood ...

- The Ballads of Robin Hood. Illustrated by David Gentleman. N.p.: The Limited Editions Club, 1977. One of 1600 sgnd by Gentleman. Tall 8vo. Orig cloth-backed bds. Slipcase (faded). *(Oak Knoll)* **$55 [≈£37]**

Balston, Thomas

- John Martin 1789-1854: His Life and Works. London: 1947. 309 pp. Cold frontis, 26 plates. Orig cloth. *(Fine Art)* **£28 [≈$42]**
- John Martin. His Life and Works. London:

Duckworth, 1947. 309 pp. 27 plates. Orig cloth. *(Leicester Art Books)* **£40 [≈$60]**

Balzac, Honore de

- Droll Stories. Translated into Modern English by Alec Brown, with Drawings by Mervyn Peake. London: Folio Society, 1961. Slipcase. *(Mermaid Books)* **£15 [≈$23]**
- Eugenie Grandet. Introduction by Richard Aldington. Illustrations by Rene Ben Sussan. New York: Limited Editions Club, 1960. One of 1500 sgnd by Ben Sussan. Tall 8vo. Orig cloth. 2 leather wraparound labels. Slipcase. *(Oak Knoll)* **$55 [≈£37]**
- Old Goriot. Introduction by Francois Mauriac. Illustrations by Rene Ben Sussan. New York: Limited Editions Club, 1948. One of 1500 sgnd by Ben Sussan. Tall 8vo. Orig qtr leather. Slipcase. *(Oak Knoll)* **$55 [≈£37]**
- Ten Droll Stories ... Illustrations by Jean de Bosschere. London: John Lane, 1926. One of 3000. 8vo. 25 plates. Orig cloth gilt, backstrip sl faded. *(Claude Cox)* **£30 [≈$45]**

Bampfylde, John

- Poems. Edited and Introduced by Roger Lonsdale. Oxford: Perpetua Press, 1988. One of 300 signed by Lonsdale. 8vo. 80 pp. Port frontis. Orig cloth gilt. *(Blackwell's)* **£30 [≈$45]**

Bandinelli, Ranuccio Bianchi

- Rome: the Late Empire. Roman Art A.D. 200-400. Translated by Peter Green. New York: Braziller, (1971). 4to. 430 ills. Orig cloth. Dw. *(Karmiole)* **$75 [≈£50]**

Banister, Judith

- Old English Silver. London: Evans Bros., 1965. Tall 8vo. 287 pp. Ills. Orig cloth gilt. Dw (sl worn & chipped). *(Hollett)* **£25 [≈$38]**

Bankart, C.P.

- The Art of the Plasterer. London: Batsford, [ca 1910]. 4to. 350 pp. Num ills. Stamp on front free endpaper. Orig bndg, marked & soiled. *(Monmouth)* **£60 [≈$90]**

Barbier, Carl Paul

- William Gilpin. His Drawings, Teaching and Theory of the Picturesque. Oxford: Clarendon Press 1963. xiv,196 pp. 17 plates. Orig cloth. *(Leicester Art Books)* **£62 [≈$93]**

Barclay, John

- Euphormio's Satyricon. Translated and Introduced by Paul Turner. Golden Cockerel Press: 1954. One of 150 (of 260). Tall 4to. 162 pp. W'engvs by Derrick Harris. B'plate. Orig qtr canvas, crnrs & hd of spine bumped. *(Waddington)* **£95 [≈$143]**

Barham, R.H.

- The Ingoldsby Legends. Illustrated by Arthur Rackham. London: Dent, 1898. 1st edn thus. Cold plates, ills. Some foxing to text. Rec half calf, gilt dec spine. *(Old Cathay)* **£59 [≈$89]**
- The Ingoldsby Legends. Illustrated by Arthur Rackham. London: 1898. 1st edn thus. Cold plates, ills. Sl soiling. Prelims foxed. Orig cloth, t.e.g., sl marked, rubbed & worn. *(Susan Wood)* **£65 [≈$98]**
- The Ingoldsby Legends. By Thomas Ingoldsby. Illustrated by Arthur Rackham. London: Dent, 1907. 1st edn thus. 4to. 24 mtd cold plates. Pict endpapers. Orig buckram gilt, t.e.g., fine. * Rackham first illustrated this title in 1898 (12 cold plates, smaller format). *(Sotheran's)* **£148 [≈$222]**

Barker, Nicolas

- Bibliotheca Lindesiana. London: Quaritch for the Roxburghe Club, 1978. Crrctd reprint. 4to. xviii,415 pp. 24 plates. Orig cloth. *(Bookpress)* **$135 [≈£90]**

Barman, Christian

- The Bridge. Illustrated by Frank Brangwyn. London: John Lane; The Bodley Head, 1926. 1st edn. 24 cold plates. Orig cloth gilt, sl worn. *(First Folio)* **$40 [≈£27]**
- Sir John Vanbrugh. London: Benn, Masters of Architecture Series, 1924. Lge 8vo. 28 pp. 34 plates. Few marg lib stamps. Orig cloth backed bds. *(Hollett)* **£25 [≈$38]**

Barnard, George

- Drawing from Nature: a Series of Progressive Instructions in Sketching ... New Edition. London: Routledge, 1877. Roy 8vo. 18 cold ills (sl foxed), 107 text w'cuts. Orig cloth gilt. *(Traylen)* **£55 [≈$83]**
- The Theory & Practice of Landscape Painting in Water-Colours. London: Wm. S. Orr, 1855. 1st edn. 176 pp. 26 cold plates, num text engvs. Orig gilt dec cloth, sl worn. *(Willow House)* **£65 [≈$98]**
- The Theory and Practice of Landscape Painting in Water-Colours. London: W.S. Orr, 1855. 1st edn. [6],176 pp. Advt slip on front endpaper. 26 cold or tinted plates, w'cuts in text. Final index leaf holed with loss. Orig cloth, sometime rebacked. *(Spelman)* **£50 [≈$75]**

Barnard, J.

- Victorian Ceramic Tiles. L: Studio Vista, 1972. Sm 4to. 184 plates. Edges sl browned. Dw (sl chipped & worn). *(Monmouth)* **£20 [≈$30]**

Barnard, Julian

- The Decorative Tradition. Princeton: The Pyne Press, (1973). 1st edn. 4to. 150 photo ills. Name. Orig bds. Dw (sl used). *(Bookpress)* **$30 [≈£20]**

Barnes, Albert C. & Mazia, Violette de

- The Art of Cezanne. London: 1939. 1st edn. 171 b/w ills. Orig cloth, edges sl spotted, hd of spine & one crnr v sl bumped. Dw (dusty, rubbed, sl nicked & creased). *(Ulysses Bookshop)* **£55 [≈$83]**

Barnicoat, John

- A Concise History of Posters. London: Thames & Hudson, 1972. Sm 4to. 288 pp. 273 ills. Orig cloth. Dw. *(Ars Libri)* **$50 [≈£33]**

Barr, Alfred H.

- Matisse, his Art and his Public. Reprint Edition. New York: MoMA, 1966. Lge 8vo. 591 pp. Ills. Orig cloth. *(Spelman)* **£20 [≈$30]**

Barret, George

- The Theory and Practice of Water Colour Painting. Elucidated in a Series of Letters. London: Ackermann, 1840. 1st edn. 8vo. viii, 123, [1],[11 advt] pp. Half-title. Orig cloth, recased. *(Spelman)* **£120 [≈$180]**

Barrett, Franklin A.

- Caughley and Coalport Porcelain. With a Foreword by W.B. Honey. Leigh-on-Sea: F. Lewis, 1951. One of 500. Sm 4to. 108 pp. 162 ills. Orig buckram gilt, sm lib numbers ft of spine. *(Hollett)* **£75 [≈$113]**
- Worcester Porcelain. London: Faber, 1953. 1st edn. Tall 8vo. xiv,53 pp. 4 cold & 96 other plates. Orig cloth gilt. Dw. *(Hollett)* **£35 [≈$53]**

Barrett, Franklin A. & Thorpe, Arthur L.

- Derby Porcelain 1750-1848. London: Collectors' Book Club, 1973. xv,206 pp. 8 cold plates, 177 ills. Orig cloth gilt. Price-clipped dw. *(Hollett)* **£45 [≈$68]**

Barrett, Timothy

- Japanese Papermaking, Traditions, Tools, and Techniques. New York: Weatherhill, (1983). 1st edn. Sm 4to. x,317,[1] pp. 3 mtd specimens, 37 ills. Orig cloth. Dw. *(Oak Knoll)* **$65 [≈£43]**

Barrie, J.M.

- George Meredith. New York: William Edwin Rudge, 1924. One of 500. 13 pp. Orig bds. Tissue dw, fine. Typography by Bruce Rogers. *(Hermitage)* **$75 [≈£50]**

Barrington, Archibald

- Manual for Students of British Architecture ... London: George Bell, 1843. 8vo. 36 pp. Orig wraps. With 20-section linen-backed "Tabular Display of British Architecture". *(Hollett)* **£55 [≈$83]**

Barrow, John

- Dictionarium Polygraphicum: Or, The Whole Body of Arts Regularly Digested ... The Second Edition, Corrected and Improved. London: Hitch & Hawes, 1758. 2 vols. 8vo. [viii], 432; [iv],398 pp, extra title vol 2. Frontis vol 1, 54 plates, correct. Rec qtr calf. *(Rankin)* **£300 [≈$450]**

Bartlett, William Henry

- Forest, Rock, and Stream: A Series of 20 Steel Line Engravings. Boston: Estes & Lauriat, 1886. 4to. 84 pp. 19 ills. Sev pp loose. Orig dec bndg. *(Rona Schneider)* **$160 [≈£107]**

Barwick, G.F.

- A Book Bound for Mary Queen of Scots. being a Description of the Binding of a Copy of the Geographia of Ptolemy at Rome, 1490 ... London: Chiswick Press for the Bibliographical Society, 1901. 4to. 2 cold plates. Orig canvas backed bds. *(Traylen)* **£38 [≈$57]**

Basile, Giambattista

- Stories from the Pentamerone. Illustrated by Warwick Goble. London: Macmillan, 1911. 1st edn thus. 4to. 32 cold plates. Orig pict cloth gilt. *(Barbara Stone)* **£125 [≈$188]**

Baskerville, John

- A Preface being that written by John Baskerville for his 1758 edition of Milton's Paradise Lost. Chalvey Park, Slough: Rampant Lions Press, 1934. One of 50. 14 pp. Orig wraps. *(Michael Taylor)* **£85 [≈$128]**

Baskin, Esther

- Creatures of Darkness. Drawings by Leonard Baskin. Boston: Little, Brown, (1962). 1st edn. Edges of bds sl faded. Price-clipped dw. *(Hermitage)* **$40 [≈£27]**

Baskin, Leonard

- Ars Anatomica: A Medical Fantasia. New York: (1972). One of 300 Roman-numbered copies with an extra suit of plates signed by Baskin. Lge folio. 13 lithos. Loose sheets as issued in qtr leather portfolio. Cardboard slipcase (sm split one edge). *(Black Sun)* **$325 [≈£217]**
- A Book of Etchings. Irises. Northampton: The Eremite Press, 1988. One of 35. Folio. 17 etchings. Orig leather. Fldg case. *(Bookpress)* **$8,500 [≈£5,667]**
- Demons, Imps & Fiends. Drawings by Leonard Baskin. Northampton: The Gehenna Press, 1976. One of 450 signed by Baskin. Tall 4to. (42) pp. 18 plates. Orig mrbld bds, leather label. *(Karmiole)* **$250 [≈£167]**
- Jonathan Swift: A Modest Proposal. Written and Illustrated by Leonard Baskin. New York: Grossman, 1969. Folio. [38] pp. Ills. Orig cloth. *(Ars Libri)* **$50 [≈£33]**

Basler, Adolphe

- Despiau. New York: E. Weyhe, [1927]. Lge 4to. [6] pp. 24 plates, 2 text ills. Orig qtr cloth, soiled. *(Ars Libri)* **$45 [≈£30]**

Bastien, Alfred & Freshwater, G.J.

- Printing Types of the World. A Comprehensive Manual ... London: Pitman, 1931. 1st edn. Sm 4to. x,212 pp, advt leaf. Orig cloth, sl soiled & rubbed. *(Claude Cox)* **£18 [≈$27]**

Bate, Percy

- English Table Glass. London: Batsford, 1913. Reprint. 8vo. xiii,130 pp. 67 plates. Name. Orig bds, faded. *(Paul Brown)* **£25 [≈$38]**

Bates, H.E.

- Achilles and Diana. Illustrated by Carol Barker. London: 1963. 1st edn. Cold ills. Free endpapers sl spotted. Foredge sl thumbed. Orig pict bds, spine ends & crnrs bumped. Price-clipped dw (dusty, spotted, torn, chipped and creased). *(Ulysses Bookshop)* **£80 [≈$120]**
- My Uncle Silas. Illustrated by Edward Ardizzone. London: 1939. 1st edn. 4to. Ills. Orig bndg, fine. Dw (nicked, v sl creased, marked & dusty). *(Ulysses Bookshop)* **£250 [≈$375]**
- Through the Woods. Illustrated by Agnes Miller Parker. London: 1936. 1st edn. Cr 4to. 142 pp. 73 w'engvs. Orig cloth gilt, hd of spine sl worn, ft of spine sl marked, few tiny marks front cvr. *(Stella Books)* **£18 [≈$27]**
- Through the Woods. London: Gollancz, 1936. 1st edn. Sm 4to. 142 pp. 73 w'engvs by Agnes Miller Parker. Orig cloth gilt. Dw (few short tears & creases). *(Hollett)* **£35 [≈$53]**

Battiscombe, C.F. (editor)

- The Relics of Saint Cuthbert. OUP: for Durham Cathedral, 1956. One of 750. Stout 4to. 3 cold & 55 other plates. Dw (sl frayed). *(David Slade)* **£100 [≈$150]**

Baudoin, Frans

- Rubens. New York: 1977. Lge 4to. 406 pp. 278 ills (96 cold). Orig cloth. Dw. *(Washton)* **$75 [≈£50]**

Baur, John I.H.

- The Inlander. Life and Work of Charles Burchfield (1893-1967). Newark & New York: Delaware UP, 1984. Lge 4to. 288 pp. 259 ills. Orig wraps. *(Ars Libri)* **$45 [≈£30]**
- Philip Evergood. New York: Abrams, (1975). Oblong 4to. 215 pp. 151 ills. Orig cloth. Dw. *(Abacus)* **$100 [≈£67]**

Bawden, Edward

- A Book of Cuts. London: 1979. 1st edn. Folio. Num b/w ills. Orig card cvrs (handled). *(Margaret Nangle)* **£22 [≈$33]**
- Portfolio of Prints. London: Royal College of Art Printmaking Department, Lion and Unicorn Press, 1984. One of 200. Sm 4to. Linocut & 10 prints. Loose as issued in buff paper folder. *(Barbara Stone)* **£95 [≈$143]**

Bayes, Walter

- The Art of Decorative Painting. London: Chapman & Hall, 1927. 1st edn. 268 pp. Frontis, 79 plates, text figs. Orig cloth, uncut. *(Willow House)* **£18 [≈$27]**

Bayley,Nicola

- Nicola Bayley's Book of Nursery Rhymes. London: Cape, 1975. 1st edn. Num cold ills. Orig laminated illust bds, fine. *(Words Etcetera)* **£75 [≈$113]**

Bean, Jacob

- 100 European Drawings in the Metropolitan Museum of Art. Greenwich: [1964?]. One of 500. 223 pp. Cold frontis, 100 b/w plates. Orig qtr vellum, t.e.g. Slipcase (sl worn). *(Clarice Davis)* **$125 [≈£83]**

Bean, Percy & McCleary, William

- The Chemistry and Practice of Finishing. Manchester: Hutton, Hartley, 1926. 3rd edn.

2 vols. Sm 4to. Num plates, 96 cloth samples. Orig cloth. *(Bookpress)* **$175 [≈£117]**

Beard, Charles R.

- Notes on the Barberini Armour and some Allied Armours. London: Privately Published, 1924. One of 350 (this copy unnumbered). Lge sq 8vo. 37 pp. 2 plates. Orig bds. *(Hollett)* **£25 [≈$38]**

Beard, Geoffrey

- Craftsmen and Interior Decoration in England 1660-1820. Edinburgh: J. Bartholomew, 1981. xxiv,312 pp. 16 cold plates, 145 ills. Orig cloth. Slipcase. *(Fine Art)* **£40 [≈$60]**
- Georgian Craftsmen and their Work. London: Country Life, 1966. 1st edn. 4to. 207 pp. Frontis, 123 plates. Orig cloth. Dw (sl worn). *(Spelman)* **£30 [≈$45]**
- International Modern Glass. US: Scribner, 1976. 4to. 264 pp. 344 plates. Dw (closed tear). *(Paul Brown)* **£32 [≈$48]**

Beardsley, Aubrey

- A Book of Fifty Drawings. London: Leonard Smithers, 1897. 1st edn [one of 500]. 50 ills. Orig gilt dec cloth, spine sl darkened, few marks to cvrs. *(Words Etcetera)* **£165 [≈$248]**
- Letters from Aubrey Beardsley to Leonard Smithers. Edited with Introduction and Notes by R.A. Walker. London: The First Edition Club, 1937. Sq 8vo. 2 ports, pict title. Orig gilt dec cloth. *(David Slade)* **£45 [≈$68]**
- The Letters. London: Cassell, 1971. 1st edn. Lge 8vo. [6],472 pp. Ills. Dw (sl soiled). *(Spelman)* **£30 [≈$45]**
- The Uncollected Work. Introduction by C. Lewis Hind. London: John Lane; The Bodley Head, 1925. 1st edn. 4to. 155 plates, ports, photo ills. Orig dec cloth. Dw. *(First Folio)* **$250 [≈£167]**

Beaton, Cecil

- Chinese Album. London: 1945. 1st edn. Photo ills. Dw (sl marked, torn & rubbed). *(Susan Wood)* **£20 [≈$30]**
- The Face of the World. London: 1957. Numbered edn Signed by the author. Num photos & ills by the author. Orig buckram backed cloth, hd of spine bumped. Price-clipped dw (rubbed, frayed & nicked). *(Ulysses Bookshop)* **£350 [≈$525]**
- Photobiography. Garden City: Doubleday, 1951. 1st edn. 255 pp. 100 b/w photo ills. Orig cloth. Dw (chipped). *(Clarice Davis)* **$65 [≈£43]**

Beattie, William

- The Castles and Abbeys of England from the National Records ... London: George Virtue, n.d. 4to. xvi,352 pp. 11 plates, num text w'cuts. Orig cloth gilt, spine faded, recased. *(Hollett)* **£40 [≈$60]**

Beaumont, Cyril W.

- Ballet Design Past and Present. London: The Studio, 1946. 1st edn. 4to. xxxii,216 pp. Ills. Orig cloth, upper cvr sl marked. *(Claude Cox)* **£35 [≈$53]**

Beaumont, Roberts

- Carpets and Rugs. London: Scott, Greenwood, 1924. Tall 8vo. xvi,410 pp. 14 cold plates, num ills. Stamp on free endpaper. Orig cloth gilt. Dw (chipped & stained). *(Hollett)* **£30 [≈$45]**

Beckett, Oliver

- J.F. Herring & Sons. London: J. Allen, 1981. 176 pp. 52 cold & 56 b/w plates. Orig cloth. Dw. *(Fine Art)* **£35 [≈$53]**

Beckett, R.B.

- Hogarth. London: 1949. Sm 4to. vii,79 pp. 202 plates. Orig cloth. *(Washton)* **$75 [≈£50]**
- Hogarth. London: Routledge, 1949. vii,80 pp. 202 plates. Orig cloth. *(Leicester Art Books)* **£65 [≈$98]**
- Lely. London: Routledge, 1951. viii,70 pp. 129 plates. Orig cloth. *(Fine Art)* **£80 [≈$120]**
- Lely. London: Routledge, 1951. viii,70 pp. 127 ills. Orig buckram. *(Leicester Art Books)* **£70 [≈$105]**

Beddingham, Philip, Carter, Will & Stone, Reynolds

- Concerning Booklabels. Private Libraries Association: 1963. 1st edn. Ills. Orig wraps (sl creased). *(Ulysses Bookshop)* **£25 [≈$375]**

Beddoes, Thomas Lovell

- The Complete Works ... Edited with a Memoir by Sir Edmund Gosse ... London: Fanfrolico Press, 1928. One of 750. 2 vols. Port frontis, w'cut ills. Orig canvas backed bds, uncut. *(Claude Cox)* **£135 [≈$203]**

Bedford, Arthur

- The Temple Musick: or, an Essay concerning the Method of singing the Psalms of David, in the Temple ... London: Mortlock ..., 1706. 1st edn. 8vo. [xvi],253,[iii] pp. Final blank. Some foxing & browning. Contemp calf, rebacked, crnrs sl worn. *(Clark)* **£160 [≈$240]**

Bedier, Joseph

- The Romance of Tristan & Iseult. Translated from the French by Hilaire Belloc and Paul Rosenfeld ... Illustrations by Serge Ivanoff. New York: Limited Editions Club, 1960. One of 1500 sgnd by Ivanoff. Sm 4to. Orig qtr leather (spine darkened, chip at ft). *(Oak Knoll)* **$35 [≈£23]**

Beedham, R. John

- Wood Engraving with an Introduction and Appendix by Eric Gill. Ditchling: S. Dominic's Press, 1920. 1st edn. Sm 8vo. viii,40 pp. 31 ills by Gill. Orig holland backed bds. *(Hollett)* **£150 [≈$225]**
- Wood Engraving. With an Introduction and Appendix by Eric Gill. Ditchling: S. Dominic's Press, 1925. Probable 2nd edn. [2], viii, 33,[3] pp. 41 w'engvs (10 by Gill). Orig holland backed bds, uncut, spine sl browned. *(Claude Cox)* **£100 [≈$150]**
- Wood Engraving. With Introduction and Appendix by Eric Gill. Ditchling: S. Dominic's Press, 1935. 4th edn. [2],viii, 39,[5] pp. W'engvs. Orig buckram backed bds. *(Bow Windows)* **£55 [≈$83]**

Beerbohm, Max

- Fifty Caricatures. London: Heinemann, 1913. Sm 4to. 49 mtd & 2 other plates. Orig dec cloth gilt, front bd faded & sl discold. *(Cooper Hay)* **£40 [≈$60]**
- Max's Nineties - Drawings 1892-1899. Introduced by Osbert Lancaster. London: 1958. 1st edn. 4to. 46 plates. Orig buckram backed bds. No dw issued. *(Ulysses Bookshop)* **£35 [≈$53]**
- Observations. London: Heinemann, 1925. 1st edn. 4to. Cold frontis, 51 plates. Orig cloth, sl dusty, hd of spine sl torn, crnrs bumped. *(Hermitage)* **$65 [≈£43]**
- The Philip Guedalla Collection of Caricatures [Catalogue]. London: Leicester Galleries, 1945. 1st edn. Ills. Orig wraps, browned. *(Words Etcetera)* **£55 [≈$83]**
- The Poet's Corner. London: Heinemann, 1904. 1st edn. Folio. 20 cold ills. Orig ptd wraps, foredge of upper cvr sl spotted. *(Sotheran's)* **£325 [≈$488]**
- Rossetti and his Circle. London: 1922. One of 380 signed by the author. Ills. Some offsetting tissue guards & endleaves. Orig bndg, upper bd bumped at ft. Dw (frayed). *(Adam Blakeney)* **£250 [≈$375]**
- Rossetti and his Circle. London: Heinemann, 1922. Sm 4to. 22 mtd cold plates. Orig cloth gilt, spine ends sl frayed, sm stain upper cvr. *(First Folio)* **$150 [≈£100]**
- "The Second Childhood of John Bull". London: Stephen Smith, [1911]. 1st edn. Folio. 15 cold ills. Orig cloth backed bds. *(Sotheran's)* **£325 [≈$488]**
- Zuleika Dobson or an Oxford Love Story. Illustrations by George Him. New York: Limited Editions Club, 1960. One of 1500 sgnd by Him. Tall 8vo. Orig cloth. Slipcase. *(Oak Knoll)* **$65 [≈£43]**
- Zuleika Dobson. The Limited Editions Club 1960. One of 1500 signed by the illustrator, George Him. Orig pict cloth. Tissue dw (frayed). Card slipcase. *(Ulysses Bookshop)* **£75 [≈$113]**
- Zuleika Dobson or, an Oxford Love Story. With a Foreword and Illustrations by Osbert Lancaster. Oxford: Shakespeare Head Press, 1975. One of 750 signed by the artist. Sm folio. 12 cold plates, ills. Orig qtr mor, t.e.g. *(Blackwell's)* **£95 [≈$143]**

Begbie, Harold

- The Struwwelpeter Alphabet. Illustrated by F. Carruthers Gould. London: Grant Richards, 1900. Ills. Few marks. Orig cloth backed pict bds. *(Jo Ann Reisler)* **$200 [≈£133]**
- Struwwelpeter Alphabet. Illustrated by F. Carruthers Gould. London: Grant Richards, 1900. Sm 4to. 27 cold ills. Orig pict bds, hinges reinforced. *(BookAdoption Agency)* **$100 [≈£67]**

Beilenson, Peter

- The Story of Frederic W. Goudy. Mount Vernon: Peter Pauper Press, 1965. One of 1950. Orig cloth gilt. Tissue dw. *(Hermitage)* **$35 [≈£23]**

Belcher, John & Macartney, Mervyn E. (editors)

- Later Renaissance Architecture in England. A Series of Examples of the Domestic Buildings ... London: Batsford, 1901. 1st edn. 2 vols. Atlas folio. 170 plates, 53 text ills. Contemp half mor, sl rubbed & flaked. *(Hollett)* **£180 [≈$270]**

Bell, C.F.

- A List of the Works contributed to Public Exhibitions by J.M.W. Turner, R.A. London: 1901. One of 350. 8vo. xv,184 pp. Orig cloth, backstrip worn. *(Washton)* **$90 [≈£60]**
- A List of the Works contributed to Public Exhibitions by J.M.W. Turner, R.A. London: Geo. Bell, 1901. One of 350.

xiv,184 pp. Orig cloth, t.e.g., hd of spine sl worn. *(Fine Art)* **£50 [≈$75]**

Bell, C.F. (editor)

- Annals of Thomas Banks, Sculptor, Royal Academician. With some Letters from Sir Thomas Lawrence ... Cambridge: UP, 1938. xviii, 230 pp. 43 plates. Orig cloth. *(Leicester Art Books)* **£55 [≈$83]**

Bell, Charles Dent

- The Four Seasons at the Lakes. Illuminated by Blanche de Montmorency Conyers Morrell. London: Marcus Ward, [ca 1880]. 4to. 16 pp. Cold lithos on thick card. Orig cloth gilt, a.e.g., extrs sl frayed. *(Hollett)* **£140 [≈$210]**

Bell, Henry

- The Perfect Painter: or, a Compleat History of the Original Progress and Improvement of Painting ... London: Printed in the Year, 1730. Lge 12mo. [iv],138,[iv] pp. Possibly lacks an advt leaf at end. Sl foxing. Contemp calf, rebacked. Anon. *(Rankin)* **£125 [≈$188]**

Bell, R.C.

- Copper Commercial Coins 1811-1819. Newcastle: 1964. 4to. xvii,238 pp. 4 plates, 405 ills. Orig cloth. Dw. *(Castle Bookshop)* **£22.50 [≈$35]**

Bellamy, B.E.

- Private Presses & Publishing in England since 1945. London: Saur & Bingley, (1980). 1st edn. 8vo. 168 pp. Orig cloth. Dw. *(Oak Knoll)* **$65 [≈£43]**

Bellows, Emma S.

- George Bellows. His Lithographs ... New York: Knopf, 1928. Rvsd edn. 278 pp. Frontis, 196 ills. Orig cloth. *(Leicester Art Books)* **£100 [≈$150]**

Bemelmans, Ludwig

- The Donkey Inside. New York: Viking, 1941. One of 175 signed by the author with an original drawing tipped-in. 8vo. Orig cloth. Slipcase. *(Dermont)* **$250 [≈£167]**
- Madeline and the Bad Hat. New York: Viking, [1956]. One of 985 signed by the author. 4to. Orig dec cloth. Slipcase (used). *(Dermont)* **$300 [≈£200]**

Bemrose, Geoffrey

- Nineteenth Century English Pottery and Porcelain. London: Faber, 1952. 1st edn. xi, 57 pp. 4 cold plates, 96 ills. Orig cloth gilt. Dw (spine faded). *(Hollett)* **£25 [≈$38]**

Bemrose, William

- The Life and Works of Joseph Wright, A.R.A. commonly called 'Wright of Derby'. London: 1885. Ltd edn. Folio. Port, 2 etched plates by Seymour Haden, 4 other plates. Orig cloth. *(Traylen)* **£40 [≈$60]**
- Mosaicon: or, Paper Mosaic. London: Bemrose, [ca 1870]. 2nd edn. 8vo. 16,8 pp. 3 cold plates. Upper tip of title torn. Orig cloth. *(Bookpress)* **$225 [≈£150]**

Benesch, Otto

- Collected Writings. Volume 1: Rembrandt. London: 1970. Sm 4to. xx,456 pp. 250 ills. Orig cloth. *(Washton)* **$50 [≈£33]**
- Collected Writings. Volume III. German and Austrian Art of the 15th and 16th Centuries. Edited by Eva Benesch. London: 1972. Sm 4to. xxi,667 pp. 442 ills on plates. Orig cloth. Dw. *(Washton)* **$50 [≈£33]**
- The Drawings of Rembrandt. First Complete Edition in Six Volumes. London: Phaidon, 1954-57. 6 vols. Over 1700 ills. Orig buckram. Dws (torn). *(Leicester Art Books)* **£400 [≈$600]**
- The Drawings of Rembrandt. London: Phaidon Press, (1954). 1st edn. 6 vols. Folio. Num ills. Inscrptns. Orig cloth. Dws (worn). Slipcases. *(Bookpress)* **$875 [≈£583]**
- Master Drawings in the Albertina. European Drawings from the 15th to the 18th Century. London: Evelyn, Adams, Mackay, 1967. 379 pp. Cold & b/w plates. Orig cloth. *(Clarice Davis)* **$125 [≈£83]**
- Rembrandt. Selected Drawings. Oxford & London: Phaidon, 1947. 255 pp. 292 ills. Orig cloth. *(Leicester Art Books)* **£35 [≈$53]**

Benezit, E.

- Dictionnaire Critique et Documentaire des Peintres, Sculpteurs, dessinateurs et Gravures ... Paris: Librairie Grund, 1966. 8 vols. 8vo. Orig cloth. *(Robert Frew)* **£250 [≈$375]**

Benjamin, Asher

- The Builders Guide or Complete System of Architecture ... Boston: 1838. 4to. 84 pp. 66 plates. Occas sl spots. New cloth. *(Clevedon Books)* **£275 [≈$413]**
- The Builder's Guide, Illustrated by Sixty-Six Engravings ... Boston: Perkins & Marvin, 1839. 4to. 83 pp. 66 plates. Lacks plate 7, with an extra copy of plate 5. Sl foxing. Later half calf. *(Bookpress)* **$875 [≈£583]**

Bennett, Arnold

- Elsie and the Child. Drawings by E. McKnight Kauffer. London: Cassell, (1929). One of 750. Sm 4to. [6],86,[2] pp. 7 plates & 3 vignettes (all pochoir). Orig cloth, sl soiled. Slipcase. *(Karmiole)* **$300 [≈£200]**
- The Old Wives' Tale. New York: Limited Editions Club, 1941. One of 1500 sgnd by the illustrator, John Austen. 2 vols. Thick 4to. Orig cloth-backed dec bds. Dws. Slipcase. *(Oak Knoll)* **$125 [≈£83]**

Bennett, Arnold, & others

- The Art of E.A. Rickards ... London: Technical Journals, 1920. 1st edn. Folio. xvii,[i],139 pp. Frontis, ills. Orig cloth, inner hinges cracked. *(Bookpress)* **$235 [≈£157]**

Bennett, Ian (editor)

- Rugs and Carpets of the World. London: Ferndale Editions, 1977. Sm folio. 352 pp. Num ills. Orig cloth gilt. Dw. *(Hollett)* **£30 [≈$45]**

Bennett, Paul A. (editor)

- Books and Printing, A Treasury for Typophiles. Cleveland & New York: World, (1951). 1st edn. 8vo. 418 pp. Ills. Orig cloth. Dw. *(Oak Knoll)* **$45 [≈£30]**

Bennett, Richard

- The Story of Bovril. London: Bovril Limited, 1953. 19 w'engvs by Robert Gibbings. Spine ends & crnrs sl bumped. Dw (sl rubbed, chipped & nicked). *(Ulysses Bookshop)* **£125 [≈$188]**
- The Story of Bovril. London: Bovril Ltd., 1953. 1st edn. 4to. 34 pp. 19 w'engvs by Robert Gibbings. Dw (sl torn). *(Waddington)* **£45 [≈$68]**

Bennett, Whitman

- A Practical Guide to American Nineteenth Century Color Plate Books. New York: Bennett Book Studios, 1949. 132, [supplement 1 133-140] pp. Mor gilt, a.e.g., minor wear. *(John K. King)* **$125 [≈£83]**
- A Practical Guide to American Nineteenth Century Color Plate Books. New York: Bennett Book Studios, 1949. 1st edn. 8vo. Errata slip. Orig cloth. *(Book Block)* **$70 [≈£47]**

Berenson, Bernard

- Caravaggio. His Incongruity and His Fame. London: Chapman & Hall, 1953. 122 pp. 88 plates. Orig cloth. *(Leicester Art Books)* **£24 [≈$36]**
- The Drawings of the Florentine Painters. Chicago: UP, (1970). 3 vols. 361; 388 pp. 1009 ills. Private lib card pockets. Orig cloth. *(Abacus)* **$125 [≈£83]**
- Homeless Paintings of the Renaissance. Bloomington: 1970. 4to. 256 pp. 422 ills. Orig cloth. Dw. *(Washton)* **$85 [≈£57]**
- Italian Pictures of the Renaissance. A List of the Principal Artists and their Works with an Index of Places. Central Italian and North Italian Schools. London: 1968. 3 vols. 4to. 1988 plates. Lib b'plates & deaccession stamps. Orig cloth. *(Washton)* **$900 [≈£600]**
- Lorenzo Lotto. London: Phaidon, 1956. xx, 486 pp. 400 ills. Orig buckram. *(Leicester Art Books)* **£60 [≈$90]**

Berger, Klaus

- Odilon Redon. Phantasy and Colour. London: Weidenfeld & Nicholson, [ca 1964]. 244 pp. 111 ills. Orig cloth. *(Leicester Art Books)* **£180 [≈$270]**

Berkovits, Ilona

- Illuminated Manuscripts from the Library of Matthias Corvinus. Budapest: 1964. Lge 4to. 147 pp. 48 cold plates, 31 text ills. Orig cloth. Dw (sl torn). *(Washton)* **$75 [≈£50]**

Berman, E.

- Art & Artists of South Africa. New Enlarged Edition. South Africa: 1983. 543 pp. Num ills. Dw. *(Trophy Room Books)* **$60 [≈£40]**

Berman, Eugene

- The Graphic Work of Eugene Berman. New York: Clarkson N. Potter, 1971. 1st edn. 4to. Ills. Remainder marks. Orig cloth. Dw (chipped). *(First Folio)* **$45 [≈£30]**

Berry, W. Turner, & others

- The Encyclopaedia of Type Faces. London: Blandford Press, 1962. 3rd edn, rvsd & enlgd. Sm 4to. 420 pp. Orig cloth. Dw (worn). *(Claude Cox)* **£28 [≈$42]**

Berry-Hill, Henry & Sidney

- Chinnery and China Coast Painting. Leigh-on-Sea: F. Lewis, 1970. One of 600. 64 pp. Cold frontis, 142 ills. Orig cloth. Dw. *(Leicester Art Books)* **£110 [≈$165]**
- George Chinnery 1774-1852. Artist of the China Coast. Leigh-on-Sea: F. Lewis, 1963. One of 600. 64 pp. 76 plates. Orig buckram, sl foxed. Dw. *(Leicester Art Books)* **£120 [≈$180]**

Bertram, Anthony

- Contemporary British Artists: Paul Nash. London: Ernest Benn, 1923. 32 pp. 35 plates. Orig cloth & bds. *(Leicester Art Books)* **£28 [≈$42]**
- Paul Nash. London: British Artists of Today, 1927. 17 plates. Orig dec bds. *(Fine Art)* **£18.50 [≈$29]**
- Paul Nash. The Portrait of an Artist. London: Faber, (1955). 1st edn. Lge 8vo. 336 pp. Cold frontis, 32 plates. Orig cloth. Dw (sl soiled). *(Karmiole)* **$40 [≈£27]**
- Paul Nash. The Portrait of an Artist. London: Faber, 1955. Ills. Dw. *(Mermaid Books)* **£28 [≈$42]**

Besterman, Theodore (editor and translator)

- The Travels and Sufferings of Father Jean de Brebeuf among the Hurons of Canada. Golden Cockerel Press: 1938. One of 300. Folio. 200 pp. W'engvd title by Eric Gill. Orig qtr canvas. *(Waddington)* **£250 [≈$375]**

Besterman, Theodore (editor)

- The Pilgrim fathers, a Journal of their coming in the Mayflower to New England and their Life and Adventures there. Golden Cockerel Press: 1939. One of 300. Tall 4to. 88 pp. 8 w'engvs by Geoffrey Wales. Orig qtr mor. *(Waddington)* **£100 [≈$150]**

Bewick, Thomas

- A Memoir of Thomas Bewick, written by himself. Newcastle & London: 1862. 8vo. xix, 344 pp. Frontis, plate, num w'cuts. Orig cloth. *(Wheldon & Wesley)* **£140 [≈$210]**
- Memoir of Thomas Bewick, written by himself with an Introduction by Selwyn Image. London: John Lane, 1924. xxxi,274 pp. 61 ills. Orig cloth. *(Leicester Art Books)* **£24 [≈$36]**
- A Memoir of Thomas Bewick written by himself. Edited and with an Introduction by Montague Weekley. London: Cresset Press, 1961. 18 w'engvs. Orig cloth, partly unopened. Dw (sl worn). *(Margaret Nangle)* **£19 [≈$29]**
- Select Fables. With Cuts Designed and Engraved by Thomas and John Bewick. Newcastle: Frank Graham, 1975. 332 pp. Orig cloth. Dw (spine sunned). *(Waddington)* **£16 [≈$24]**
- Thomas Bewick: Birds, being Impressions from Original Wood-Blocks. Newcastle: David Esslemont, 1984. One of 147 (of 250). [79] pp. Orig qtr cloth. Dw. Prospectus inserted. *(Michael Taylor)* **£100 [≈$150]**
- The Works. Newcastle: for Emerson Charnley, 1822. 5 vols. 8vo. 3 ports, 7 plates, num w'cuts. Contemp calf gilt extra, a.e.g., minor reprs. *(Wheldon & Wesley)* **£600 [≈$900]**

Bhushan, Jamila Brij

- Indian Jewellery, Ornaments and Decorative Designs. Bombay: Taraporevala Sons & Co., [ca 1950]. 1st edn. 4to. xviii,168 pp. 80 plates. Orig cloth over bds. *(Karmiole)* **$75 [≈£50]**

Bialostocki, Jan

- The Art of the Renaissance in Eastern Europe, Hungary, Bohemia, Poland. Ithaca, New York: Cornell UP, (1976). 1st edn. 4to. xxvi, 312 pp. 356 plates. Orig cloth, extrs sl rubbed. Dw. *(Karmiole)* **$40 [≈£27]**

Bibliographica ...

- Bibliographica. Papers on Books, their History and Art. London: Kegan Paul, 1895-97. 12 parts in 3 vols, complete. Thick 4to. 65 plates, num ills. Qtr mor by Zaehnsdorf. *(Traylen)* **£330 [≈$495]**

Bickell, L.

- Bookbindings from the Hessian Historical Exhibition illustrating the Art of Binding from the XVth to the XVIIIth Centuries. Leipzig: Hiersemann, 1893. One of 100 in English. 14 pp. 53 Heliotype prints on 42 plates. Minor lib stamps. Rec lib buckram. *(Hermitage)* **$900 [≈£600]**

Bickham, George

- The Universal Penman. London: Robert Sayer, (1741). 1st edn, 4th issue. Folio. Frontis, 212 plates. Later calf. *(Bookpress)* **$5,800 [≈£3,867]**
- The Universal Penman. London: H. Overton, 1743. 1st edn. Folio. Port frontis, engvd title, 211 plates. Some plates sl browned. Contemp calf, 19th c reback. *(Traylen)* **£620 [≈$930]**

Bielefeld, Charles Frederick

- On the Use of the Improved Papier-Mache in Furniture and in the Interior Decoration of Buildings and in Works of Art. London: Papier-Mache Works, [1840-42]. 1st edn. 4to. xi, [i], 2 pp. Frontis, 127 plates. Orig cloth, worn. *(Bookpress)* **$750 [≈£500]**

Bielfeld, H.

- A Guide to Painting on Glass. London:

George Rowney, 1855. 1st edn. 16mo. 33,[3],26 pp. Wrappers sunned, spine reprd with tape. *(Bookpress)* **$75 [≈£50]**

Bierce, Ambrose

- The Monk and the Hangman's Daughter. Illustrations by Michel Ciry. New York: Limited Editions Club, 1967. One of 1500 sgnd by Ciry. Sm 4to. Orig cloth. Board wrapper. Slipcase. *(Oak Knoll)* **$55 [≈£37]**

Bigmore, E.C. & Wyman, C.W.H.

- A Bibliography of Printing. London: Holland Press, 1969. Reprint of 1880 edn. Thick 8vo. 412,115 pp. Orig cloth. Dw. *(First Folio)* **$55 [≈£37]**

Bill, Max

- Wassily Kandinsky. Boston: Institute of Contemporary Art; Paris: Maeght, 1951. Sm 4to. 178 pp. Num ills. Orig bds. Dw. Glassine (sl chipped). Slipcase. *(Abacus)* **$100 [≈£67]**

Billings, Robert William

- Architectural Illustrations, History and Description of Carlisle Cathedral ... London: Thomas & William Boone, & the author, 1840. 1st edn. 4to. vi,92 pp. Frontis, 45 engvs. V sl marg spotting few ff. Orig cloth, crnrs sl bumped. *(Sotheran's)* **£45 [≈$68]**

Bindman, David

- The Complete Graphic Work of William Blake. London: Thames & Hudson, 1978. 492 pp. 765 ills. Orig cloth. Dw. *(Leicester Art Books)* **£70 [≈$105]**

Binyon, Laurence

- Brief Candles. Golden Cockerel Press: 1938. One of 100 signed by the author and the artist. 6 w'engvs by Helen Binyon. Orig bndg gilt. *(Waddington)* **£60 [≈$90]**
- A Catalogue of Japanese & Chinese Woodcuts ... in the British Museum. London: BM, 1916. Thick 4to. Cold & b/w ills. Orig cloth. *(Book Block)* **$250 [≈£167]**
- The Court Painters of the Grand Moguls. London: OUP, 1921. 1st edn. 4to. 87 pp. 40 plates. Orig cloth, spine faded, rear lower crnr reprd. *(Bookpress)* **$85 [≈£57]**
- The Drawings and Engravings of William Blake. London: The Studio, 1922. 1st edn. 4to. x,29 pp. 16 cold & 90 b/w plates. Orig japon backed bds. *(Claude Cox)* **£68 [≈$102]**
- Dutch Etchers of the Seventeenth Century. London: Seeley, 1895. 1st edn. Lge 8vo. 80 pp. 4 plates, 29 text ills. Orig cloth. *(Claude Cox)* **£20 [≈$30]**
- The Engraved Designs of William Blake. London: Benn, 1926. 1st edn. 4to. xiv,140 pp. 82 plates. Orig canvas backed bds, sl soiled. *(Claude Cox)* **£90 [≈$135]**
- The Followers of William Blake. Edward Calvert, Samuel Palmer, George Richmond and their Circle. London: Halton & Truscott Smith, 1925. One of 100 signed by the author. Lge 4to. 79 plates inc 8 mtd cold. Rec half leather gilt. *(First Folio)* **$275 [≈£183]**
- The Followers of William Blake: Edward Calvert, Samuel Palmer, George Richmond and their Circle. London: Halton & Truscott Smith, 1925. x,29 pp. 80 plates (8 mtd cold). Sm lib stamps on title. New cloth. *(Fine Art)* **£48 [≈$72]**
- Landscape in English Art and Poetry. Tokyo: 1930. xii,295 pp. 101 ills. Orig cloth, t.e.g. *(Fine Art)* **£30 [≈$45]**
- Painting in the Far East. London: Edward Arnold, 1908. 1st edn. 4to. xvi,287 pp. 30 plates. Orig silk cloth gilt, t.e.g., spine sl faded. *(Claude Cox)* **£32 [≈$48]**

Biographical Anecdotes of William Hogarth ...

- See Nichols, John

Birch, John

- Country Architecture: A Work Designed for the Use of the Nobility and Country Gentlemen ... Edinburgh: Blackwood, 1874. 4to. Half-title. 49 litho plates. Orig cloth, a.e.g., upper jnt worn, few plates loose in guttapercha. *(Rankin)* **£85 [≈$128]**

Birch, Walter De Gray & Jenner, Henry

- Early Drawings and Illuminations ... With a Dictionary of Subjects in the British Museum. London: Bagster, 1879. 8vo. Ills. Orig gilt dec bevelled cloth, sl worn, crnrs rubbed. *(First Folio)* **$75 [≈£50]**
- Early Drawings and Illuminations. An Introduction to the Study of Illustrated Manuscripts ... London: 1879. 8vo. 310 pp. 12 plates. Orig cloth, sl soiled. *(Washton)* **$75 [≈£50]**

Birkenhead, The Earl of

- The World in 2030 A.D. London: 1930. 1st edn. 8 b/w ills by McKnight Kauffer. Orig cloth. Dw. *(Margaret Nangle)* **£90 [≈$135]**

Birrell & Garnett

- Birrell & Garnett: Catalogue of Typefounders' Specimens ... London: 1928. 4to. viii,108 pp. Num ills. Orig wraps, sl soiled. *(Claude Cox)* **£35 [≈$53]**

- Birrell & Garnett: Catalogue of Typefounders' Specimens ... Brighton: Tony Appleton, 1972. One of 500. 4to. xii,108 pp. Orig cloth. Dw. *(Bookpress)* **£45 [≈$68]**

Birrell, Augustine

- An Appendix to the Rowfant Library. A Catalogue of the Printed Books, Manuscripts, Autograph letters etc. Collected since the Printing of the First Catalogue in 1886 ... London: Chiswick Press, 1910. One of 350. 8vo. Frontis. Orig qtr mor gilt, t.e.g. Anon. *(Cooper Hay)* **£55 [≈$83]**

The Birth of Christ ...

- The Birth of Christ from the Gospel according to Saint Luke. Golden Cockerel Press: 1925. One of 370. W'engvs by Noel Rooke. Orig qtr leather, hd of spine sl damaged, sides sl mottled. *(Waddington)* **£45 [≈$68]**
- The Birth of Christ from the Gospel according to Saint Luke. Golden Cockerel Press: 1925. W'engvs by Noel Rooke. Orig qtr leather. *(Michael Taylor)* **£95 [≈$143]**

Bishop, C.K.K.

- Notes on Church Organs. Their Position and the Materials used in their Construction. London: Rivingtons, 1873. Sq 8vo. 52 pp. 11 litho plates. Orig ptd bds, backstrip sl defective. *(Hollett)* **£75 [≈$113]**

Bishop, H.H.

- Pictorial Architecture in Greece and Italy. London: SPCK, 1887. 1st edn. Oblong 4to. 135 pp. Num w'cut ills. Orig pict cloth gilt. *(Hollett)* **£55 [≈$83]**
- Pictorial Architecture of France. London: SPCK, 1893. Sm oblong folio. [ii],175 pp. W'engvs. Orig pict cloth gilt, sl used. *(Clevedon Books)* **£26 [≈$39]**
- Pictorial Architecture of the British Isles. London: SPCK, 1885. 3rd edn. Oblong 4to. 123 pp. Num w'cut ills. Orig pict cloth gilt, sl marked, extrs sl rubbed. *(Hollett)* **£45 [≈$68]**
- Pictorial Architecture of the British Isles. London: SPCK, 1894. 14th thousand. Sm oblong folio. [ii],123 pp, advt leaf. W'engvs. Orig pict cloth gilt, some stains. *(Clevedon Books)* **£37 [≈$56]**

Bishop, John George

- The Brighton Chain Pier: In Memoriam. Its History from 1823 to 1896 ... Brighton: the author, 1897. 4to. [viii],74,[ii blank], xxv, [i blank] pp. 22 plates inc frontis. Orig dec cloth, edge of front cvr sl rubbed. *(Sotheran's)* **£98 [≈$147]**

Black, J. Anderson

- A History of Jewels. London: Orbis, 1974. Lge 4to. 400 pp. Num ills. Orig cloth gilt. Dw. Slipcase. *(Hollett)* **£45 [≈$68]**

Blackburn, Henry

- Randolph Caldecott. His Early Art Career. London: Routledge, 1886. 1st edn. 8vo. 172 ills. Orig cloth, a.e.g. Dw. *(Davidson)* **$150 [≈£100]**

Blacker, J.F.

- The A B C of Collecting Old Continental Pottery. London: Stanley Paul, n.d. 315,[4 advt] pp. Over 250 ills. Orig pict cloth gilt. *(Hollett)* **£35 [≈$53]**
- The A B C of Collecting Old English Pottery. London: Stanley Paul, n.d. 4th edn. 344 pp. Over 450 ills. Orig pict cloth gilt. *(Hollett)* **£35 [≈$53]**
- The A B C of Japanese Art. London: Stanley Paul, 1929. Cheap edn. 460 pp. Ills. Orig cloth. *(Hollett)* **£20 [≈$30]**
- The A B C of Nineteenth-century English Ceramic Art. London: Stanley, Paul, n.d. 534 pp. Cold frontis, num ills. Orig pict cloth gilt, uncut. *(Hollett)* **£40 [≈$60]**

Blades, William

- The Enemies of Books. London: Trubner, 1880. 2nd edn, with some addtns & crrctns. 8vo. 7 ills. Contemp qtr mor, orig parchment wraps bound in. *(Oak Knoll)* **$175 [≈£117]**
- The Enemies of Books. Revised and Enlarged. London: 1888. Fcap 8vo. 8 plates. Lacks fly-leaf. Orig qtr mor. *(Traylen)* **£15 [≈$23]**
- William Caxton. San Francisco: The Windsor Press, 1926. One of 200. Lge 4to. (28) pp. 6 text ills. Orig linen over bds, lower edge bumped. *(Karmiole)* **$125 [≈£83]**

Blake, William

- Blake's Pencil Drawings. Second Series. Edited by Geoffrey Keynes. London: Nonesuch Press, 1953. One of 1440. 12 pp. 112 pp plates. Orig cloth over bevelled bds, crnrs sl bruised. Dw (sm hole at spine, minor wear extrs). *(Bookworks)* **£78 [≈$117]**
- Catalogue of Original Works by William Blake the property of the late Graham Robertson ... July 22, 1949. London: Christie, Manson & Woods, 1949. 8vo. 44 pp. 17 plates. Orig ptd bds, spotted. *(Clark)* **£45 [≈$68]**

- A Cradle Song, The Divine Image, A Dream, Night. New York: Valenti Angelo, 1949. One of 125 signed by Angelo. [12] pp. Hand cold title & printer's device. Orig blue bds gilt. *(Argonaut)* **$175 [≈£117]**
- Engravings. Edited with an Introduction by Geoffrey Keynes. London: Faber, 1950. 1st edn. Sm 4to. 142 ills. Orig cloth. *(Spelman)* **£16 [≈$24]**
- Engravings. Edited with an Introduction by Geoffrey Keynes. Second Edition. New York: 1972. Sm 4to. 142 ills. Orig cloth. Inscrbd by Keynes. *(Spelman)* **£16 [≈$24]**
- Jerusalem. The Emanation of the Giant Albion. London: Trianon Press for the William Blake Trust, 1952. One of 2500. 124 pp. 102 pp plates. Orig cloth, t.e.g. Dw (spine sl chipped & browned). *(Bookworks)* **£48 [≈$72]**
- The Paintings and Drawings of William Blake. Edited by Martin Butlin. Yale: UP, 1981. 1st edn. 2 vols (text & plates). 4to. 1193 ills. Orig cloth. Dws. *(Spelman)* **£120 [≈$180]**
- Pencil Drawings. Edited by Geoffrey Keynes. London: Nonesuch Press, 1927. One of 1550. 4to. 16 pp. 82 plates. Orig half cloth, sl soiled. *(Abacus)* **$150 [≈£100]**
- Pencil Drawings. Edited by Geoffrey Keynes. London: The Nonesuch Press, 1927. One of 1550. Orig qtr cloth, uncut. *(Hermitage)* **$175 [≈£117]**
- The Prophetic Writings ... Edited by D.J. Sloss and J.P.R. Wallis. Oxford: Clarendon Press, 1926. 2 vols. 8vo. Lib b'plates. Orig cloth. *(Robert Frew)* **£45 [≈$68]**
- Songs of Experience. London: Benn, 1927. 8vo. Ills. Orig gilt dec cloth. *(Robert Frew)* **£50 [≈$75]**
- Songs of Innocence. Illustrated by Jacynth Parsons. Introduction by W.B. Yeats. London: Medici Society, 1927. 1st edn thus. Sm 4to. 12 cold plates, b/w ills. Orig cloth, sl worn. *(BookAdoption Agency)* **$85 [≈£57]**
- Vala or the Four Zoas. A Facsimile of the Manuscript. A Transcription of the Poem and a Study of its Growth and Significance. By G.E. Bentley. Oxford: 1963. Folio. 145 ills. Lacks front free endpaper. Cvrs sl marked. Dw (torn). *(Spelman)* **£160 [≈$240]**

Blanche, Jacques-Emile

- Portraits of a Lifetime [with] More Portraits of a Lifetime. London: Dent, 1937-39. 2 vols. 48 plates. Orig cloth, vol 2 spine faded. *(Leicester Art Books)* **£55 [≈$83]**

Bland, David

- A History of Book Illustration. The Illuminated Manuscript and the Printed Book. London: Faber, 1958. 4to. 448 pp. Mtd cold frontis, 395 ills. Orig cloth gilt. *(Cooper Hay)* **£60 [≈$90]**
- A History of Book Illustration. Cleveland: World, 1958. 1st edn. Sm 4to. 448 pp. Ills, inc mtd cold plates. Orig cloth, v sl shaken. Dw (chipped). *(First Folio)* **$85 [≈£57]**
- A History of Book Illustration. The Illuminated Manuscript and the Printed Book. London: Faber, 1958. 1st edn, 1st issue. 448 pp. 19 mtd cold plates, 376 ills. Orig buckram. Dw (frayed). *(Bookworks)* **£65 [≈$98]**

Blankert, Albert

- Ferdinand Bol (1616-1680) Rembrandt's Pupil. Holland: Davaco, 1982. 382 pp. Cold frontis, 204 ills. Orig cloth. Dw. *(Fine Art)* **£60 [≈$90]**
- Ferdinand Bol. Rembrandt's Pupil. Doomspijk: Davaco, 1982. 382 pp. 204 ills. Orig cloth. Dw. *(Leicester Art Books)* **£95 [≈$143]**

Blanshard, Frances

- Portraits of Wordsworth. London: Allen & Unwin, 1959. 1st edn. 208 pp. 48 plates. Orig cloth gilt. Dw (worn). *(Hollett)* **£35 [≈$53]**

Bles, Joseph

- Rare English Glass of the XVII & XVIII Centuries. Boston: Houghton, Mifflin 1925. 1st Amer edn. One of 250 (of 750) for America. 269 pp. Frontis, 100 plates. Orig cloth, scratch on front cvr, sl soiled. *(Hermitage)* **$225 [≈£150]**

Bliss, Douglas Percy

- Edward Bawden. London: Pendomer Press, [1979]. One of 200. 200 pp. 139 ills. Orig qtr mor, t.e.g., fine. Slipcase. Lacks the separate signed lithograph. *(Bookworks)* **£95 [≈$143]**
- A History of Wood-Engraving. London: Dent, 1928. 1st edn. 4to. Ills. Three qtr mor gilt, t.e.g., rear crnrs scuffed. *(First Folio)* **$250 [≈£167]**
- A History of Wood-Engraving. London: 1928. 1st edn. 4to. Num ills. Orig buckram. *(Words Etcetera)* **£60 [≈$90]**
- A History of Wood-Engraving. London: Spring Books, 1964. 4to. 120 ills. 263 pp. Dw. *(Michael Taylor)* **£20 [≈$30]**

Bloch, E. Maurice

- The Drawings of George Caleb Bingham with a Catalogue Raisonne. Columbia: Missouri UP, 1975. 272 pp. 183 ills. Orig cloth. Dw. Signed by the author. *(Clarice Davis)* **$350 [≈£233]**

Blomfield, Sir Reginald

- A History of French Architecture from the death of Mazarin till the death of Louis XV, 1661-1774. London: 1921. 2 vols. Roy 8vo. 200 plates & ills. Orig cloth. *(Traylen)* **£48 [≈$72]**
- A History of French Architecture from the Reign of Charles VIII till the death of Mazarin. London: 1911. 2 vols. Roy 8vo. 178 plates & ills. Orig cloth. *(Traylen)* **£45 [≈$68]**
- A History of French Architecture from the Reign of Charles VIII to the Death of Mazarin (1494-1661). London: G. Bell & Sons, 1911. 2 vols. 4to. 178 plates. Inscrptn. Orig cloth, sl soiled. *(Quest Books)* **£60 [≈$90]**
- A History of Renaissance Architecture in England, 1500 to 1800. London: 1897. 2 vols. Roy 8vo. Num plates & ills. Orig cloth. *(Traylen)* **£48 [≈$72]**
- A History of Renaissance Architecture in England 1500-1800. London: George Bell, 1897. 2 vols. Sm 4to. Num plates & ills. Orig cloth gilt, spines sl faded & rubbed. *(Hollett)* **£125 [≈$188]**
- Memoirs of an Architect. London: Macmillan, 1932. 8vo. xi,314,[2 advt] pp. Frontis, 3 plates. Orig cloth, somewhat worn & stained. *(Quest Books)* **£16 [≈$24]**
- A Short History of Renaissance Architecture in England 1500-1800. London: George Bell, 1900. 8vo. xii,323,[iv] pp. 27 plates, num text ills. Endpapers spotted. Orig cloth gilt, trifle rubbed. *(Hollett)* **£18 [≈$27]**
- Studies in Architecture. London: Macmillan, 1905. 8vo. xi,266,[2 advt] pp. Frontis, 35 plates, text ills. Orig cloth. *(Quest Books)* **£18 [≈$27]**

Bloom, J. Harvey

- English Seals. London: Methuen, The Antiquary's Books, (1906). 1st edn. 8vo. xvi,274 pp. 93 ills. Orig cloth gilt, sl soiled. *(Karmiole)* **$40 [≈£27]**

Bloomfield, Paul (compiler)

- The Mediterranean. An Anthology. Decorated by Edward Ardizzone. London: 1935. 8vo. 247 pp. Ills. Orig bndg. *(Zeno)* **£27.50 [≈$42]**

Blore, Edward

- The Monumental Remains of Noble and Eminent Persons ... The Sepulchral Antiquities of Great Britain. London: Harding, Lepard, [1824]-1826. 1st edn. Imperial 8vo. 24 sep paginated fascicles. 30 plates. Few sl marks. Contemp half roan, sl rubbed. *(Ash)* **£125 [≈$188]**
- The Monumental Remains of Noble and Eminent Persons comprising the Sepulchral Antiquities of Great Britain ... London: Harding, Lepard, 1826. 1st edn. Roy 8vo. 30 plates. Occas v sl marg spotting. Rec half mor. *(Sotheran's)* **£58 [≈$87]**

Bloxham, M.H.

- Principles of Gothic Ecclesiastical Architecture. London: Bell, 1882. 11th edn. 2 vols. 322; 324 pp. W'engvs by Jewitt. Rubbed, sl dusty. *(Monmouth)* **£20 [≈$30]**

Blumenthal, Walter Hart

- Book Gluttons and Book Gourmets, with a Digression on Hungry Authors. Chicago: The Black Cat Press, 1961. Ltd edn. Miniature book (2" x 2 3/4"). 84,[1] pp. Orig leather. *(Oak Knoll)* **$95 [≈£63]**
- Bookmen's Bedlam. An Olio of Literary Oddities. New Brunswick: Rutgers UP, 1955. 1st edn. Sm 4to. xi,[3],274 pp. Photo ills. Orig cloth & bds. *(Karmiole)* **$50 [≈£33]**
- Eccentric Typography, and Other Diversions in the Graphic Arts. Worcester: St. Onge, 1963. One of 500. Tall 8vo. 40 pp. Orig cloth. *(Oak Knoll)* **$85 [≈£57]**
- Heaven and Hades. Two Excursions for Bookmen. Worcester: Achille J. St. Onge, 1965. One of 200. Sm 8vo. 64 pp. 8 plates, text ills. Orig cloth gilt. *(Karmiole)* **$50 [≈£33]**

Blunt, Anthony

- The Drawings of G.B. Castiglioni and Stefano della Bella at Windsor Castle. London: Phaidon, 1954. viii,128 pp. 86 plates, 36 text ills. Orig buckram. *(Leicester Art Books)* **£55 [≈$83]**
- The Drawings of Poussin. Yale: UP, 1979. xiii,209 pp. 203 plates. Orig cloth. Dw. *(Fine Art)* **£28 [≈$42]**
- Nicolas Poussin. New York: 1967. 2 vols. 4to. 265 plates, 271 ills. Orig cloth. Slipcase. *(Washton)* **$200 [≈£133]**
- Nicolas Poussin. New York: Bollingen Foundation, 1967. 1st edn. 2 vols. 4to & oblong 4to. 265 plates, 271 text ills. Orig bndgs, no dws or slipcase. *(Bookpress)* **$375 [≈£250]**

Blunt, Wilfred

- The Art of Botanical Illustration. London: Collins, 1950. 1st edn. 8vo. xxxi,304 pp. Plates, ills. Orig cloth. Dw. *(Robert Frew)* **£75 [≈$113]**

Boalch, Donald H.

- Makers of the Harpsichord and Clavichord 1440 to 1840. London: (1956). 1st edn. 4to. 32 ills. Orig cloth. Dw (rubbed). *(Bookpress)* **$85 [≈£57]**
- Prints and Paintings of British Farm Livestock 1780-1910. A Record of the Rothamsted Collection, Harpenden. London: 1958. Cr 4to. xxxv,127 pp. Num ills. Orig ptd cvrs. *(Phenotype)* **£120 [≈$180]**

Boase, T.S.R.

- English Art 1100-1216. OUP: 1953. 331 pp. 96 plates, 19 text ills. Orig cloth. Dw. *(Fine Art)* **£30 [≈$45]**
- English Art 1800-1870. Oxford: 1959. Sm 4to. xxiv,352 pp. 96 plates. Orig cloth, spine sl sunned. *(Washton)* **$65 [≈£43]**
- St. Francis of Assisi. With 16 Lithographs by Arthur Boyd. London: Thames & Hudson, 1968. 120 pp. 16 ills. Orig cloth. Dw. *(Leicester Art Books)* **£25 [≈$38]**

Bobbin, Timothy

- The Human Passions Delineated in above 120 Figures, Droll, Satyrical, and Humorous ... Manchester: John Heywood, 1858. Folio. 6 ff. Frontis, title, 44 plates on 25 sheets. Occas spotting. Orig cloth, spotted, sl worn. *(Robert Frew)* **£120 [≈$180]**

Bober, Harry

- The St. Blasien Psalter. New York: Kraus, 1963. Sm folio. 80 pp. 5 plates, 76 ills on 24 plates. Orig cloth. *(Washton)* **$95 [≈£63]**

Bober, Phyllis

- Drawings after the Antique by Amico Aspertini. Sketchbook in the British Museum. London: Warburg Institute, 1967. 4to. xiv,108 pp. 148 ills on 64 plates. Orig cloth. *(Washton)* **$95 [≈£63]**
- Drawings after the Antique by Amico Aspertini. Sketchbooks in the British Museum. London: Warburg Institute, 1957. xiv,108 pp. 64 plates. Orig cloth. *(Leicester Art Books)* **£40 [≈$60]**

Boccacio, Giovanni

- The Decameron. Translated by Richard Aldington. Illustrated by Jean de Bosschere. New York: Covici Friede, 1930. 1st edn thus. One of 2500. 2 vols. 8vo. 16 cold ills. Orig cloth, faded. *(Stella Books)* **£100 [≈£67]**
- Life of Dante. Cambridge: Riverside Press, 1904. One of 265. 4to. Port. Orig vellum-backed bds, vellum sl foxed, crnrs v sl bumped. Designed by Bruce Rogers. *(The Veatchs)* **$275 [≈£183]**
- Pasquverella and Madonna Babetta, Two Hitherto Untranslated Stories. With Some Hitherto Unpublished Sketches by Aubrey Beardsley. New York: The Biblion Society, (1927). 4to. Orig cloth, paper label, hinges cracked. Paper slipcase (shows wear). *(Oak Knoll)* **$45 [≈£30]**

Bockwitz, Hans

- John Baskerville in the Judgement of German Contemporaries. Birmingham: Birmingham School of Printing, 1937. 8vo. 9,[1] pp. Orig stiff wraps, cord-tied. *(Oak Knoll)* **$55 [≈£37]**

Boeck, Wilhelm & Sabartes, Jaime

- Picasso. New York: Abrams, 1959. Lge 4to. 606 ills. Orig pict cloth. Dw (chipped). *(First Folio)* **$95 [≈£63]**
- Picasso. London: Readers Union and Thames & Hudson, 1961. 524 pp. 606 ills. Orig cloth. *(Leicester Art Books)* **£80 [≈$120]**

Boehn, Max von

- Dolls and Puppets. Translated by Josephine Nicoll with a Note on Puppets by George Bernard Shaw. London: Harrap, 1932. 522 pp. 30 cold plates, 464 ills. Orig cloth gilt, spine v sl faded. *(Hollett)* **£75 [≈$113]**

Boggs, Jean Sutherland

- Portraits by Degas. Berkeley: Calif UP, 1962. xv,142 pp. 145 plates. Orig cloth. Dw (chipped). *(Leicester Art Books)* **£60 [≈$90]**

Bohatec, Miloslav

- Illuminated Manuscripts. Prague: Artia, (1970). 4to. 72 pp. 203 ills. Orig dec cloth gilt. Dw (sl chipped). *(Karmiole)* **$35 [≈£23]**

Bohlin, Diane Degrazia

- Prints and Related Drawings by the Carracci Family. A Catalogue Raisonne. Washington, DC: 1979. 4to. 533 pp. Num ills. Orig wraps. *(Washton)* **$90 [≈£60]**
- Prints and Related Drawings by the Carracci Family: A Catalogue Raisonne. Bloomington: Indiana UP; Washington: National Gallery of Art, (1979). Thick 4to. 533 pp. Num ills. Orig cloth. Dw. *(Abacus)* **$85 [≈£57]**

Bol, L.J.

- The Bosschaert Dynasty. Painters of Flowers and Fruit. Leigh-on-Sea: F. Lewis, 1980. Reprint. 108 pp. 64 plates. Orig buckram. Dw. *(Leicester Art Books)* **£28 [≈$42]**

Bolliger, Hans

- Picasso's Vollard Suite. London: Thames & Hudson, 1956. xxii pp. 100 plates. Orig cloth. Dw. *(Leicester Art Books)* **£28 [≈$42]**

Bolten, Jaap

- Method and Practice. Dutch and Flemish Drawing Books 1600-1750. Landau-Pfalz: 1985. New edn, crrctd. Sm 4to. 373 pp. Num ills. Orig cloth. Dw. *(Washton)* **$85 [≈£57]**

Bolton, T.

- Early American Portrait Draughtsmen in Crayons. New York: Privately Printed, 1923. One of 325. xii,112 pp. Frontis, 12 plates. Orig qtr cloth, unopened. *(Clevedon Books)* **£80 [≈$120]**

Bonaparte, Marie

- Flyda of the Seas. Translated by John Rodker. London: Imago, 1950. 1st edn. 100 pp. 12 cold lithos by John Buckland Wright. Orig pict gilt cloth. Dw (sm closed tear). *(Bookworks)* **£28 [≈$42]**

Bond, Francis

- The Chancel of English Churches ... OUP: 1916. 8vo. ix,274,[18 advt] pp. 229 ills. Orig cloth. *(Taylor & Son)* **£30 [≈$45]**
- Dedications and Patron Saints of English Churches. OUP: 1914. 8vo. xvi,343,advt pp. 252 ills. Orig cloth. *(Taylor & Son)* **£35 [≈$53]**
- Gothic Architecture in England ... London: Batsford, 1906. Sm thick 4to. xv,782,24 pp. 785 ills, 469 plans. Orig cloth gilt, spine faded & sl marked. *(Hollett)* **£55 [≈$83]**
- Introduction to English Church Architecture, from the 11th to the 16th Century. OUP 1913. 1st edn. 2 vols. 4to. 1400 ills. Orig cloth gilt. *(Hollett)* **£85 [≈$128]**
- Screens and Galleries in English Churches. OUP: 1908. xi,192 pp. Num plates & figs. Orig cloth, rubbed & worn. *(Castle Bookshop)* **£24 [≈$36]**

Bonnardot, Alfred

- The Mirror of the Parisian Bibliophile. Translated and Edited by Theodore Wesley Koch. Illustrated by Jose Longoria. Chicago: Koch, 1931. One of 500 signed by the translator. xxxi,145 pp. Frontis, text ills. Orig cloth. Slipcase (somewhat worn). *(Argonaut)* **$60 [≈£40]**

Bonney, T.G. (editor)

- Abbeys and Churches of England and Wales. Descriptive, Historical, Pictorial. Second Series. London: Cassell, 1890. 4to. viii, 274, 8 pp. Num ills. Orig pict cloth gilt, extrs sl worn, upper jnt cracking. *(Hollett)* **£50 [≈$75]**
- Cathedrals, Abbeys and Churches of England and Wales. Descriptive, Historical, Pictorial. London: Cassell, 1891. 2 vols. 4to. xxvii,404; xvi,405-838 pp. Num ills. Orig pict cloth gilt, extrs sl worn, jnts cracked. *(Hollett)* **£85 [≈$128]**

Bony, Jean

- French Cathedrals. Photographs by Martin Hurlimann, Descriptive Notes by Peter Meyer. London: Thames & Hudson, 1954. 4to. 47 pp. 196 ills. Orig cloth. Dw. *(Hollett)* **£30 [≈$45]**

Book and Magazine Collector ...

- Book and Magazine Collector. London: 1984-90. Complete run from No. 1 to No. 72. 72 parts. 8vo. Num ills. Orig wraps. *(Traylen)* **£48 [≈$72]**

The Book of Ecclesiastes ...

- The Book of Ecclesiastes, in the Revised King James Version. Illustrations by Edgar Miller. New York: Limited Editions Club, 1968. One of 1500 signed by Miller. 4to. Orig calf (spine rubbed). Slipcase. *(Oak Knoll)* **$95 [≈£63]**

The Book of Job ...

- The Book of Job. With Thirty-Three Original Signed Etchings by Sir Frank Brangwyn. Leigh-on-Sea: F. Lewis, 1948. One of 110. Folio. (116) pp. Orig three qtr vellum, sl soiled. *(Karmiole)* **$1,500 [≈£1,000]**

The Book of Jonah ...

- The Book of Jonah. With Engravings on Wood by David Jones. Clover Hill Editions: Douglas Cleverdon, 1979. One of 300. 4to. Orig qtr cloth, pict bds. *(Barbara Stone)* **£135 [≈$203]**

The Book of Psalms ...

- The Book of Psalms, and the First Psalm of David; the Book of Proverbs; the Book of Ecclesiastes ... London: 1952. 1st edn thus. 26 w'engvs by Clare Leighton. Orig cloth gilt. *(Margaret Nangle)* **£38 [≈$57]**

The Book of Tobit ...

- The Book of Tobit and History of Susanna reprinted from the Revised Version of the Apocrypha with Introduction by M.R. James. Illustrated by Sir W. Russell Flint. London: 1929. One of 875. 4 mtd cold plates. Orig bds gilt, silk marker, 2 crnrs bumped. Dw worn *(Margaret Nangle)* **£100 [≈$150]**

The Book of Trade Secrets ...

- The Book of Trade Secrets, Receipts and Instructions for Renovating, Repairing, Improving and Preserving Old Books and Prints. By an Expert. London: J. Haslam, 1909. Sm 8vo. 48,[8] pp. Soiled, some wear. Orig wraps. Anon. *(Oak Knoll)* **$55 [≈£37]**

The Bookbinder ...

- The Bookbinder. An Illustrated Journal for Binders, Librarians, and all Lovers of Books. [Vols 1 & 2]. London: William Clowes, 1888-89. 2 vols. 4to. Cold & tinted plates, ills. Contemp half mor, jnts rubbed, orig wraps bound in. *(Claude Cox)* **£175 [≈$263]**

Boon, K.G.

- Rembrandt. The Complete Etchings. London: 1977. 2nd edn. [298] pp. 307 ills. Orig cloth. *(Leicester Art Books)* **£50 [≈$75]**
- Rembrandt: The Complete Etchings. New York: Abrams, (1963). Sm folio. 287 pp. Orig dec cloth gilt. Dw. *(First Folio)* **$85 [≈£57]**

Boot, William Henry James

- Trees, and How to Paint them in Water-Colours. London: Cassell, 1883. 1st edn. Oblong 8vo. 24,[4 advt] pp. 18 chromolitho plates, text engvs. Occas foxing. Orig cloth, recased, spine faded. *(Spelman)* **£25 [≈$38]**

Booth, Richard (editor)

- The Country Life Bookof Book Collecting. London: Country Life, 1976. Sm 4to. 192 pp. Num ills. Orig cloth gilt. Dw. *(Hollett)* **£25 [≈$38]**

Booth-Clibborn, Edward

- My Father and Edward Ardizzone: A Lasting Friendship. London: (1983). 1st edn. Cr 4to. 48 pp. Ills. Orig bds. Dw. *(Bow Windows)* **£30 [≈$45]**

Borden, John W. & Krueger, Janet S.

- Thomas Bewick & The Fables of Aesop ... With an Original Leaf from the First Edition (1818) of "The Fables of Aesop" ... San Francisco: The Book Club of California, 1983. One of 518. 4to. Frontis, 8 ills. Prospectus laid in. Orig bds, label. Dw. *(Karmiole)* **$165 [≈£110]**

Borenius, Tancred

- Four Early Italian Engravers ... Boston: The Medici Society, 1923. 4to. 114 pp. 84 ills. Orig cloth. *(Rona Schneider)* **$50 [≈£33]**
- The Painters of Vicenza, 1480-1550. London: Chatto & Windus, 1909. 1st edn. 8vo. xxi,[i],238 pp. Frontis, ills. Orig cloth, sl rubbed, spine sunned. *(Bookpress)* **$65 [≈£43]**

Borlase, William Copeland

- The Dolmens of Ireland: their Distribution, Structural Characteristics, and Affinities in Other Countries ... London: Chapman & Hall, 1897. One of 350. 3 vols. Sm 4to. 4 maps, 800 ills inc 2 cold plates. Orig cloth gilt. *(Emerald Isle)* **£650 [≈$975]**

Borsch-Supan, Helmut

- Caspar David Friedrich. London: Thames & Hudson, (1974). 4to. 184 pp. 120 ills. Orig cloth. *(Abacus)* **$75 [≈£50]**

Boskovits, Nikos, & others

- Christian Art in Hungary. Collections from the Esztergom Christian Museum. Budapest: 1965. Sm folio. 162 pp. 82 mtd cold plates, 152 ills. Front free endpaper creased. Orig cloth, hd of spine sl bumped. *(Washton)* **$65 [≈£43]**

Bossert, Helmuth

- An Encyclopaedia of Colour Decoration from the Earliest Times to the Middle of the XIXth Century. Berlin: 1928. 4to. 35 pp. 120 cold plates, sev text figs. Lib stamp on plate versos. Lib qtr mor, sl worn. *(Francis Edwards)* **£75 [≈$113]**
- Ornament: Two Thousand Decorative Motifs in Colour, forming a Survey of the Applied Art of All Ages and All Countries ... London: 1924. Lge 4to. [xii],36 pp. 120 cold plates. Name stamp, some crayon underlining of text. Orig cloth, dull. *(Bow Windows)* **£150 [≈$225]**

Boswell, Peyton Jr.

- George Bellows. Photo Research and Bibliography by Aimee Crane. New York: Crown, 1942. 4to. 29,[3] pp. 112 plates.

Orig cloth. *(Ars Libri)* **$50 [≈£33]**

Boudaille, Georges

- Expressionists. New York: Alpine Fine Arts Collection, 1981. Sm folio. 170 pp. 48 mtd cold plates, ills. Orig cloth. Dw. *(Ars Libri)* **$75 [≈£50]**

Boughton, Alice

- Photographing the Famous. [New York]: The Avondale Press, [1928]. 1st edn. Sm folio. 28 photo ills. Orig cloth backed bds, sl stain, a few bumps. *(Mac Donnell)* **$150 [≈£100]**

Bouillon, Jean-Paul

- Art Nouveau, 1870-1914. New York: Rizzoli, (1985). 1st edn. Sm folio. 247,[1] pp. 220 ills. Orig cloth. Dw (rear panel rubbed). *(Bookpress)* **$100 [≈£67]**

Bouquet, A.C.

- Church Brasses British & Continental, with some Notes on Incised Stone Slabs and Indents. London: Batsford, 1956. 8vo. xii,284 pp. Cold frontis, 129 ills. Orig cloth gilt. Dw (worn). *(Hollett)* **£18 [≈$27]**

Bourdon, David

- Christo. New York: Abrams, 1972. 321 pp. 320 ills (84 cold). Orig cloth. Dw. *(Leicester Art Books)* **£180 [≈$270]**
- Warhol. New York: Abrams, 1989. Thick sq 4to. 432 pp. Photo ills. Orig dec cloth, sl shaken. Dw. *(First Folio)* **$60 [≈£40]**

Boutell, Charles

- Arms and Armour in Antiquity and the Middle Ages; also a Descriptive Notice of Modern Weapons. London: 1874. xvi,296 pp. 71 figs. Orig bndg, sl scuffed, jnts sl weak. *(Whitehart)* **£35 [≈$53]**
- Arms and Armour in Antiquity and the Middle Ages ... London: Reeves & Turner, 1907. New edn. xx,296 pp. 22 plates, num text ills. Orig cloth gilt. *(Hollett)* **£30 [≈$45]**
- The Monumental Brasses of England: A Series of Engravings upon Wood ... London: George Bell, 1849. 8vo. [viii],xii, 53,[ix] pp. 150 w'engvs inc frontis. Contemp half mor, jnts rubbed, crnrs sl bumped. *(Sotheran's)* **£85 [≈$128]**
- The Monumental Brasses of England. London: George Bell, 1849. 1st edn. Cr 4to. xii,60 pp. 48 plates. Victorian half calf gilt, spine sl dulled. *(Ash)* **£100 [≈$150]**

Boutens, P.C.

- The Christ-Child. A Poem, translated from the Dutch ... with Wood Engravings by Tom Chadwick. London: The Samson Press, 1938. One of 150. Sm 4to. Orig cloth, edges sl browned. Glassine dw. *(Waddington)* **£55 [≈$83]**

Bouvet, Francis

- Bonnard. The Complete Graphic Work. London: Thames & Hudson, 1981. 351 pp. 536 ills. Orig cloth. Dw. *(Leicester Art Books)* **£32 [≈$48]**

Bowe, Nicola Gordon

- Harry Clarke: His Graphic Art. Mountrath, Ireland: Dolmen Press, 1983. 1st trade edn. Orig cloth gilt. Dw. *(First Folio)* **$85 [≈£57]**
- Harry Clarke: His Graphic Art. Mountrath, Ireland: Dolmen Press, 1983. One of 250 signed by the author, with 8 extra ills. 4to. [10],160 pp. Plates. Orig elab gilt cloth. Slipcase. *(Karmiole)* **$150 [≈£100]**
- The Life and Work of Harry Clarke. Irish Academic Press: 1989. 1st edn. 336 pp. Orig bds. Dw. *(Bookworks)* **£30 [≈$45]**

Bowers, Georgina

- Hunting in Hard Times. London: Chapman & Hall, [inscribed 1890]. Oblong 4to. 22 cold plates. Crease in front endpaper. Orig cloth, soiled, pict onlay (chipped). *(Barbara Stone)* **£55 [≈$83]**
- Mr Crop's Harriers. London: Day & Son, [ca 1880]. Oblong 4to. 20 mtd cold plates. Orig cloth gilt, darkened, sl spotted, top hinge cracked. *(Barbara Stone)* **£55 [≈$83]**

Bowley, M.

- Innovations in Building Materials: An Economic Study. London: Duckworth, 1960. 446 pp. Some edge foxing. Dw (worn). *(Monmouth)* **£20 [≈$30]**

Bowman, Russell

- Philip Pearlstein: The Complete Paintings. New York: Alpine Fine Arts, (1983). 4to. 363 pp. 120 cold plates, 508 b/w ills. Orig cloth. Dw. signed by the artist on a tipped-in b'plate. *(Abacus)* **$100 [≈£67]**

Bowness, Alan

- Ivon Hitchins. London: Lund Humphries, 1973. 62 pp. 120 plates, 69 ills. Orig cloth. Dw. *(Leicester Art Books)* **£140 [≈$210]**
- Recent British Painting. Peter Stuyvesant Foundation Collection. London: Lund Humphries, 1968. Oblong 4to. 161 pp. 98

ills. Orig cloth. Dw. *(Ars Libri)* **$35 [≈£23]**

Bowness, Henry (editor)

- Henry Moore: Sculpture and Drawings. With an Introduction by Herbert Read. Vol 3: Sculpture, 1955-64. New York: Wittenborn, 1965. Lge 4to. 32,[1] pp. 177 plates. Orig cloth. *(Ars Libri)* **$65 [≈£43]**

Boyd, James

- Drums. Illustrated by N.C. Wyeth. New York: Scribner, (1928). One of 525 signed by the author and illustrator. 4to. Cold title, 14 cold plates, b/w ills. Orig cloth, pict onlay, some fading to spine, tiny chip to onlay. *(Jo Ann Reisler)* **$850 [≈£567]**

Bozo, Dominique

- Jackson Pollock. Paris: Centre Georges Pompidou, 1982. Lge sq 4to. 420 pp. 76 cold ills. Orig wraps. *(Ars Libri)* **$200 [≈£133]**

Brackett, Oliver

- English Furniture Illustrated. A Pictorial Review of English Furniture from Chaucer to Queen Victoria. Revised and edited by H. Clifford Smith. London: Benn, 1950. Lge 4to. 300 pp. 240 plates. Orig cloth gilt. Dw. *(Hollett)* **£75 [≈$113]**
- Thomas Chippendale, a Study of his Life, Work and Influence. London: [ca 1930]. 4to. 62 plates, text ills. Orig cloth gilt. *(Traylen)* **£60 [≈$90]**

Bradbury, Frederick

- History of Old Sheffield Plate ... London: Macmillan, 1912. 1st edn. 4to. [xiii],539 pp. Frontis, num ills. Lib stamps on endpapers & title verso. Orig cloth gilt, sl worn. *(Hollett)* **£95 [≈$143]**

Bradfield, N.

- Historical Costumes of England from the Eleventh to the Twentieth Century. London:1938. 4to. 155 pp. 2 plates, num ills. Orig cloth, soiled, some extrs rubbed. *(Washton)* **$40 [≈£27]**

Bradford, Ernle

- Four Centuries of European Jewellery. London: Country Life, 1953. 1st edn. 4to. 226 pp. Ills. Orig cloth gilt. Dw. *(Hollett)* **£30 [≈$45]**

Bradley, H.G. (editor)

- Ceramics of Derbyshire 1750-1975. London: 1978. 4to. 338,advt pp. 470 ills. Orig cloth. Dw. *(Castle Bookshop)* **£28.50 [≈$44]**
- Ceramics of Derbyshire 1750-1975. London: Gilbert Bradley, 1978. Tall 4to. xvi,338,[xi] pp. 16 cold plates, 470 ills. Orig cloth gilt. Dw. *(Hollett)* **£60 [≈$90]**

Bradley, Helen

- And Miss Carter Wore Pink. Scenes from an Edwardian Childhood. London: Cape, 1971. 1st edn. Oblong 4to. 32 pp. Cold ills throughout. Orig cloth gilt. Dw. *(Hollett)* **£45 [≈$68]**
- "In the Beginning" said Great-Aunt Jane. London: Cape, 1975. 1st edn. Oblong 4to. 32 pp. Cold ills. Orig cloth. Price-clipped dw. *(Hollett)* **£45 [≈$68]**
- Miss Carter Came With Us. London: Cape, 1973. 1st edn. Oblong 4to. 32 pp. Cold ills. Orig cloth. Price-clipped dw. *(Hollett)* **£45 [≈$68]**
- The Queen Who Came To Tea. London: Cape, 1978. 1st edn. Oblong 4to. 32 pp. Cold ills. Orig cloth. Dw. *(Hollett)* **£48 [≈$72]**

Bradley, Van Allen

- The Book Collector's Handbook of Values. 4th Edition. New York: Putnam, (1982). 4th edn, rvsd & enlgd. 8vo. Dw (soiled). *(Oak Knoll)* **$100 [≈£67]**

Bradlow, E. & F.

- Thomas Bowler of the Cape of Good Hope: His Life and Works. With a Catalogue of Extant Paintings and a Commentary on the Bowler Prints by A. Gordon-Brown. Cape Town: 1955. Ltd edn. 248 pp. Ills. Dw. *(Trophy Room Books)* **$150 [≈£100]**

Bradshaw, A.E.

- Handmade Woodwork of the 20th Century. London: Murray, 1962. 1st edn. 123 pp. Ills. Lib stamp & label. Orig pict bds. *(Willow House)* **£15 [≈$23]**

Braham, Allan & Hager, Hellmut

- Carlo Fontana. The Drawings at Windsor Castle. London: Zwemmer, 1977. xxviii,222 pp. 570 ills. Orig buckram. *(Leicester Art Books)* **£50 [≈$75]**

Brake, Brian

- Art of the Pacific. Photographs by Brian Brake. Conversations by James McNeish. With Commentary by David Simmons. New York: Abrams, (1980). Lge 4to. 240 pp. 174 ills. Orig silk, blue spine. Dw. *(Karmiole)* **$65 [≈£43]**

Brandon, John Raphael & Brandon, Joshua Arthur
- An Analysis of Gothic Architecture. London: Pelham Richardson, 1847. 2 vols. 4to. 168 litho plates. Contemp half roan, scuffed, vol 1 case loose. *(Waterfield's)* **£125 [≈$188]**
- An Analysis of Gothic Architecture ... Edinburgh: John Grant, 1903. 2 vols. Lge 4to. viii,120; [2],x pp. 47 + 111 plates. Orig cloth, extrs sl rubbed & marked. *(Claude Cox)* **£80 [≈$120]**

Brandt, Bill
- Camera in London. London: Focal Press, 1948. 1st edn. 59 plates. Orig bndg, some staining. *(Sclanders)* **£30 [≈$45]**

Branner, Pierre
- St. Louis and the Court Style in Gothic Architecture. London: 1965. Lge 8vo. xvi,157 pp. 140 ills on plates, 14 figs. Orig cloth, somewhat bubbled, sl spotted. *(Washton)* **$250 [≈£167]**

Branner, Robert
- Manuscript Painting in Paris during the Reign of St. Louis. A Study of Styles. Berkeley: 1977. Lge 4to. xxiv,270 pp. 437 ills on plates (25 cold). Orig cloth. Dw. *(Washton)* **$95 [≈£63]**

Brassington, W. Salt
- A History of the Art of Bookbinding, with Some Account of the Books of the Ancients. London: Elliott Stock, 1894. 4to. 277 pp. Ills, inc cold plates. Three qtr crushed mor elab gilt, t.e.g. *(First Folio)* **$595 [≈£397]**

Braunfels, Wolfgang
- Monasteries of Western Europe. Princeton: UP, (1972). 1st Amer edn. 4to. 263 pp. Frontis, ills. Orig cloth. *(Bookpress)* **$75 [≈£50]**

Brears, P.C.D.
- The Collector's Book of English Country Pottery. David & Charles: 1974. 207 pp. Plates & figs. Orig cloth. Dw. *(Castle Bookshop)* **£35 [≈$53]**
- The English Country Pottery: Its History and Techniques. David & Charles: 1971. 266 pp. 16 plates, text figs. Ex-lib. Orig cloth. Dw. *(Castle Bookshop)* **£29.50 [≈$45]**

Bredius, Abraham (editor)
- The Paintings of Rembrandt. Oxford: Phaidon Press, (1942). One of 950. 630 ills. Loose plates in portfolio & slipcase. *(Leicester Art Books)* **£60 [≈$90]**

Breslauer, Bernard H. & Folter, Roland
- Bibliography Its History and Development. New York: The Grolier Club, 1984. One of 600. 8vo. 223,[1] pp. Ills. Orig cloth. *(Oak Knoll)* **$125 [≈£83]**

Bressey, C.H., & others
- British Bridges; An Illustrated Technical and Historical Record. London: 1933. 8vo. xxiv,498 pp. Num ills. Orig cloth backed bds gilt, spine sl crinkled. *(Clevedon Books)* **£58 [≈$87]**

Breton, Andre
- What is Surrealism. London: Faber, 1936. 1st edn. 4 plates. Orig card wraps. Dw (edges sl faded). *(Clearwater)* **£55 [≈$83]**

Breton, Nicholas
- The Twelve Months. Edited by Brian Rhys. Wood Engravings by Eric Ravilious. London: Golden Cockerel Press, 1927. One of 500. Sl offsetting on front free endpaper. Orig buckram gilt, touch of fraying spine ends. *(Hermitage)* **$150 [≈£100]**

Brett, Stanley
- The London Bookshop. Pinner: Private Libraries Association, 1971-77. 1st edn. 2 vols. Ills. Orig cloth. *(Words Etcetera)* **£35 [≈$53]**

Breuil, Henri
- Anibib & Omandumba and other Erongo Sites. Clairvaux, Jura, France: Trianon Press for the Calouste Gulbenkian Foundation, The Rock Paintings of Southern Africa Vol 4, 1960. 1st edn. Folio. 3 maps, 87 cold plates, 72 ills. Orig cloth gilt. Dw. *(Oriental and African)* **£125 [≈$188]**
- Philipp Cave. London: Abbe Breuil Publications, The Rock Paintings of Southern Africa Vol 2, 1957. 1st edn. Folio. 28 cold plates, 30 ills. Orig cloth gilt. Dw. *(Oriental and African)* **£85 [≈$128]**
- The Tisbab Ravine and other Brandberg Sites. Clairvaux, Jura, France: Trianon Press for the Calouste Gulbenkian Foundation, The Rock Paintings of Southern Africa Vol 3, 1959. 1st edn. Folio. 78 cold plates, 75 ills. Orig cloth gilt. Dw. *(Oriental and African)* **£125 [≈$188]**

Breviarium Aberdonense ...
- Breviarium Aberdonense. London: Bannantyne Club, 1854. One of 100. 2 vols. 4to. Contemp half mor, t.e.g. *(Traylen)* **£110 [≈$165]**

Bridges, Robert

- Peace. Ode Written upon the Conclusion of the Three Years' War. By R.B. Printed for the First Anniversary June 1st: 1903, by C.H.D[aniel]. [One of ca 100]. 4to. [8] pp. Orig wraps & later linen, uncut. *(Claude Cox)* **£95 [≈$143]**
- The Testament of Beauty. A Poem in Four Books. Oxford: Clarendon Press 1929. One of 250. 4to. [8],154,colophon pp. Orig cloth, uncut, sl rubbed. 2-leaf publisher's note laid in. *(Claude Cox)* **£45 [≈$68]**

Bridson, Gavin & Wakeman, Geoffrey

- Printmaking & Picture Printing. A Bibliographical Guide to Artistic & Industrial Techniques in Britain 1750-1900. Oxford & Williamsburg: The Plough Press & The Bookpress Ltd., 1984. 1st edn. 4to. 250 pp. Orig cloth. Dw. *(Bookpress)* **$55 [≈£37]**

Brieger, P., Meiss, M. & Singleton, C.S.

- Illuminated Manuscripts of the Divine Comedy. London: Routledge, 1969. 1st edn. 2 vols. 4to. Num ills. Dws. *(Spelman)* **£120 [≈$180]**

Briganti, Giuliano

- The View Painters of Europe. London: Phaidon, (1970). 1st edn in English. Sm folio. [vi],318 pp. Ills. Inscrptn. Orig cloth, sl shaken. *(Bookpress)* **$100 [≈£67]**

Briggs, M.S.

- Men of Taste, from Pharaoh to Ruskin. London: Batsford, 1947. 1st edn. 8vo. viii, 232 pp. Ills. Orig cloth, sl marked. Dw. *(Clevedon Books)* **£16 [≈$24]**

Briggs, Martin

- The Architect in History. Oxford: Clarendon Press, 1927. 1st edn. 12mo. xii,400 pp. 46 plates. Orig cloth, spine sunned, sl worn. *(Bookpress)* **$35 [≈£23]**
- The English Farmhouse. London: Batsford, The New Heritage Series, 1953. 1st edn. 8vo. 242 pp. Cold frontis, 131 ills. Orig cloth gilt. Dw. *(Hollett)* **£35 [≈$53]**

Briggs, Raymond

- Fungus the Bogeyman. London: 1977. 1st edn. 4to. Cold ills. Orig laminated cold bds, spine ends & crnrs sl bumped. *(Ulysses Bookshop)* **£30 [≈$45]**
- When the Wind Blows. London: 1982. 1st edn. 4to. Cold ills. Orig laminated pict bds, spine ends v sl bumped. *(Ulysses Bookshop)* **£25 [≈$38]**

Brigham, Clarence C.

- Paul Revere's Engravings. New York: Atheneum, 1969. 2nd edn. xx,262 pp. 77 plates. Orig cloth. Dw. *(Leicester Art Books)* **£25 [≈$38]**

Brigstocke, Hugh

- William Buchanan and the 19th Century Art Trade: 100 Letters to his Agents in London and Italy. Paul Mellon Centre: 1982. 8vo. x, 525 pp. Orig cloth. *(Spelman)* **£35 [≈$53]**

Bristowe, W.S.

- Victorian China Fairings. London: A. & C. Black, 1964. 1st edn. Lge 8vo. 108 pp. Cold frontis, 48 plates. Orig cloth gilt. Dw. *(Hollett)* **£30 [≈$45]**

The British Union Catalogue of Early Music ...

- The British Union-Catalogue of Early Music Printed before the year 1801 ... Editor: Edith B. Schnapper. London: Butterworths, 1957. 4to. Orig cloth. *(David Slade)* **£350 [≈$525]**

Britten, F.J.

- Old English Clocks (The Wetherfield Collection). Woodbridge: 1980. One of 1000. 4to. 131 ills. Orig cloth. *(Traylen)* **£17 [≈$26]**
- Old English Clocks and Watches and their Makers. Republished from the Sixth Edition (1932). S.R. Publishers: 1971. viii,891 pp. Num text ills. Orig cloth gilt. Dw. *(Hollett)* **£30 [≈$45]**
- The Watch & Clock Maker's Handbook, Dictionary and Guide. London: Spon, 1896. 460 pp. Ills. Orig cloth gilt. *(Hollett)* **£25 [≈$38]**
- The Watch & Clock Maker's Handbook, Dictionary and Guide. Fourteenth Edition, Revised by J.W. Player. London: Spon, 1938. Thick 8vo. vi,547 pp. Ills. Orig cloth gilt. *(Hollett)* **£40 [≈$60]**
- The Watch & Clock Maker's Handbook ... Antique Collectors Club: 1976. Facsimile of 11th edn. 499 pp. 400 ills. Orig cloth gilt. Dw. *(Hollett)* **£25 [≈$38]**

Britton, John

- The Architectural Antiquities of Great Britain ... London: Longman, 1807-26. 5 vols. 4to. 6 engvd titles (inc general title), 355 plates (4 dble page). Minimal foxing. Later 19th c half mor, t.e.g., gilt dec spines. *(Spelman)* **£480 [≈$720]**
- An Historical Account of Corsham House in Wiltshire: the Seat of Paul Cobb Methuen

Esq. with a Catalogue of his Celebrated Collection of Pictures ... Bath: Joseph Barrett, 1806. 108 pp. Frontis (browned), view, plan. Orig bds, rebacked in leather. *(Fine Art)* **£85 [≈$128]**

- The History and Antiquities of the Metropolitical Church of York ... London: Longman ..., 1819. 1st edn. 4to. vi,[i],8-96 pp. 34 plates. Contemp half calf, spine ends sl worn. *(Spelman)* **£100 [≈$150]**
- The Union of Architecture, Sculpture and Painting; Exemplified by a Series of Illustrations ... London: for the author, 1827. Lge 4to. xvi,60 pp. Hand cold aquatint frontis, 23 plates all in proof state. Plate V misnumbered as VII. Sl spots. Later half mor. *(Sotheran's)* **£625 [≈$938]**

Britwell Library

- Handlist or Short-title Catalogue of the Principal Volumes from the Time of Caxton to the Year 1800 formerly in the Library of Britwell Court Buckinghamshire. London: Quaritch, 1933. 2 vols. 4to. Frontis, 62 plates. Orig cloth gilt. *(Cooper Hay)* **£85 [≈$128]**

Broadley, A.M.

- Chats on Autographs. London: Fisher Unwin, 1910. 1st edn. 384 pp. 135 ills. Orig cloth. Dw (dusty, sl frayed). *(Hollett)* **£20 [≈$30]**

Brodsky, Horace

- Gaudier-Brzeska Drawings. London: 1946. Cold frontis, 92 plates & ills. Orig cloth, pict onlay. *(Fine Art)* **£40 [≈$60]**
- Henri Gaudier-Brzeska 1891-1915. London: 1933. 1st edn. 192 pp. Frontis, 55 ills. Orig cloth, spine faded. *(Fine Art)* **£25 [≈$38]**

Bromberg, Ruth

- Canaletto's Etchings. A Catalogue and Study illustrating and describing the Known States, including those hitherto unrecorded. London: 1974. Sm folio. xi,193 pp. Over 250 ills & plates. Orig cloth. Dw. *(Washton)* **$300 [≈£200]**
- Canaletto's Etchings. A Catalogue and Study ... London & New York: 1974. 194 pp. Ca 280 ills. Orig cloth. *(Leicester Art Books)* **£200 [≈$300]**

Bromley, Henry

- A Catalogue of Engraved British Portraits from Egbert the Great to the Present Time ... London: 1793. xiv,479,56 pp. Leather, rebacked. *(Fine Art)* **£45 [≈$68]**

Bronte, Charlotte

- Jane Eyre. Illustrated by Barnett Freedman. London: Collins, 1955. 1st edn thus. 456 pp. 16 cold lithos. Orig dec cloth, glassine dw, slipcase, fine. *(Bookworks)* **£32 [≈$48]**

Bronte, Emily

- Wuthering Heights. Illustrated by Barnett Freedman. London: Collins, 1955. 1st edn thus. 456 pp. 16 cold lithos. Orig dec cloth, glassine dw, slipcase, fine. *(Bookworks)* **£32 [≈$48]**

Brooke, George C.

- English Coins from the Seventh Century to the Present Day. London: Methuen, 1932. 1st edn. 8vo. 277 pp. 64 plates. Orig cloth. *(J &J House)* **$60 [≈£40]**
- English Coins from the Seventh Century to the Present Day. London: Methuen's Handbooks of Archaeology series, 1942. 2nd edn. xii,277 pp. 64 plates. Orig cloth gilt. Dw. *(Hollett)* **£20 [≈$30]**

Brooks, Alfred Mansfield

- From Holbein to Whistler. New Haven: Yale UP, 1920. 1st edn. 4to. 194 pp. 71 ills. Orig cloth. *(Rona Schneider)* **$90 [≈£60]**

Brooks, Charles Mattoon

- Vincent Van Gogh. A Bibliography. New York: MoMA, 1942. xviii,58 pp. Orig cloth. *(Leicester Art Books)* **£45 [≈$68]**

Brown, Christopher

- Carel Fabritius. Oxford: Phaidon, 1981. 168 pp. 100 ills. Orig cloth. Dw. Slipcase. *(Leicester Art Books)* **£27 [≈$41]**
- Van Dyck. London: Phaidon, 1982. 240 pp. Num plates. Orig cloth. Dw. *(Fine Art)* **£30 [≈$45]**

Brown, G. Baldwin

- The Arts in Early England Vol 1: The Life of Saxon England in its relation to the Arts. London: Murray, 1926. Rvsd edn. 2 tables, 28 maps & ills. Lib marks. Orig buckram. Dw (worn). *(Baker)* **£27 [≈$41]**

Brown, J.H.

- Water Colour Guidance. London: A. & C. Black, 1931. Med 8vo. 302 pp. 24 cold plates, 86 text diags. Orig cloth gilt. *(Stella Books)* **£24 [≈$36]**

Brown, Percy

- Indian Architecture (The Islamic Period). Bombay: Taraporevala, [ca 1940]. 2nd edn, rvsd & enlgd. 4to. xiv,146 pp. 100 plates. Sl marg spotting. Orig bds. Dw (sl rubbed). *(Worldwide)* **$65 [≈£43]**

Brown, R. Allen, & others

- The History of the King's Works. The Middle Ages. London: HMSO, 1963. 2 vols. 4to. 4 plans, 52 plates, 72 figs. Orig cloth gilt, sl marked. *(Taylor & Son)* **£74 [≈$111]**

Brown, Richard

- Sacred Architecture, its Rise, Progress, and Present State ... London: Fisher, Son & Co., [1845]. 1st edn. 4to. xxxvi,304 pp. Frontis, 62 plates, text ills. Contemp half calf. *(Fenning)* **£125 [≈$188]**

Browne, Gordon F.

- Proverbial Sayings. Being Some Old Friends in New Dresses. Printed by Edmund Evans. London: Wells, Gardner, Darton, [1901]. 1st edn. Oblong 4to. Cold title, 27 cold plates. Orig cloth backed pict bds. *(Fenning)* **£55 [≈$83]**

Browne, K.R.G.

- How to Make a Garden Grow. Illustrated by Heath Robinson. London: [1938]. 1st edn. Num b/w ills, dec endpapers. Edges and endpapers spotted, occas foxing. Orig cloth, ft of spine bumped. Dw (sl worn). *(Ulysses Bookshop)* **£45 [≈$68]**

Browning, Elizabeth Barrett

- Sonnets from the Portuguese. London: Riccardi Press for the Medici Society, (1914). One of 1000. Sm 4to. 27 pp. Orig cloth backed bds, sl dusty, faintly rubbed. *(Hermitage)* **$65 [≈£43]**

Browning, Robert

- DramatisPersonae and Dramatic Romances and Lyrics. Illustrated by Eleanor F. Brickdale. London: Chatto & Windus, 1909. 10 cold plates. Orig dec bds. *(Old Cathay)* **£29 [≈$44]**
- Dramatis Personae. Hammersmith: The Doves Press, 1910. One of 250. Orig limp vellum. *(First Folio)* **$475 [≈£317]**
- Dramatis Personae and Dramatic Romances and Tales. Illustrated by Eleanor Fortescue Brickdale. London: Chatto & Windus, 1919. One of 260. 4to. 10 mtd cold plates. Occas foxing. Orig vellum gilt, sl spotted. *(Barbara Stone)* **£65 [≈$98]**
- The Pied Piper of Hamelin. Illustrated by Arthur Rackham. London: Harrap, (1934). 1st British trade edn. 45 pp. 4 cold plates, text ills, pict endpapers. Orig pict wraps. Dw (sl soiled). *(Argonaut)* **$150 [≈£100]**
- The Poems of Robert Browning. Illustrated by Peter Reddick. New York: Limited Editions Club, 1969. One of 1500 sgnd by Reddick. Tall 8vo. Orig dec qtr leather. Slipcase. *(Oak Knoll)* **$95 [≈£63]**

Browse, Lillian

- Degas Dancers. London: Faber, 1949. 435 pp. 12 mtd cold plates, 256 b/w plates. Orig cloth. Dw (chipped). *(Leicester Art Books)* **£80 [≈$120]**
- Walter Sickert. London: Hart Davis, 1960. 1st edn. 4to. 124 pp. 96 ills. Dw (sl worn). *(Spelman)* **£50 [≈$75]**
- William Nicholson. London: Hart-Davis, 1956. 144 pp. Cold frontis, 54 plates. Orig cloth. Dw. *(Leicester Art Books)* **£55 [≈$83]**
- William Nicholson. London: 1956. 1st edn. 144 pp. Cold frontis, plates. Orig cloth. Dw. *(Fine Art)* **£85 [≈$128]**

Brumme, C. Ludwig

- Contemporary American Sculpture. New York: Crown, 1948. Lge 4to. 156 pp. 130 plates. Orig cloth. *(Ars Libri)* **$125 [≈£83]**

Brunel, Georges

- Boucher. London: Trefoil Books, 1986. 304 pp. 302 ills. Orig cloth. Dw. *(Leicester Art Books)* **£40 [≈$60]**

Brunner, A.W.

- Cottages or Hints on Economical Building ... New York: Comstock, 1884. 1st edn. 8vo. 77 pp. Frontis, 23 plates. Cloth, rubbed. *(Bookpress)* **$250 [≈£167]**

Brunner, Arnold & Tryon, Thomas

- Interior Decoration. New York: Comstock, 1887. 1st edn. 4to. [vi],65 pp. Frontis, 15 plates, 50 text ills. Orig cloth, sl worn. *(Bookpress)* **$495 [≈£330]**

Brunskill, R.W.

- Illustrated Handbook of Vernacular Architecture. London: Faber, 1974. 8vo. 230 pp. 148 ills. Orig cloth gilt. Dw. *(Hollett)* **£30 [≈$45]**

Brunton, Violet

- Ecclesiasticus or The Wisdom of Jesus the Son of Sirach. With Illustrations by Violet Brunton and an Illustration by C. Lewis Hind. London: John Lane; The Bodley Head, 1927. 1st edn thus. 8vo. 16 cold plates. Orig cloth gilt, t.e.g. *(Bow Windows)* **£35 [≈$53]**

Bryan, M.

- Dictionary of Painters and Engravers. New Edition, Revised and Enlarged by G.C. Williamson. London: 1909. 5 vols. 4to. 500 ills. Orig cloth. *(Traylen)* **£120 [≈$180]**

Bryant, Arthur

- Historian's Holiday. The Dropmore Press: 1946. One of 550. 4to. [6],84,colophon pp. Orig buckram, uncut, sl rubbed. *(Claude Cox)* **£28 [≈$42]**

Bryant, William Cullen

- The Story of the Fountain. New York: Appleton, 1872. 48 pp. 42 w'engvs. Orig dec cloth, shabby. *(Rona Schneider)* **$120 [≈£80]**

Buchanan, Briggs

- Early Near Eastern Seals in the Yale Collection. New Haven: Yale UP, 1981. 1st edn. 4to. xxiv,498 pp. 218 plates. Orig cloth. *(Worldwide)* **$80 [≈£53]**

Buckle, Richard

- Epstein Drawings. With Notes by Lady Epstein. Cleveland & New York: World, 1962. Lge 4to. 160 pp. 65 plates. Orig cloth. Dw. *(Ars Libri)* **$50 [≈£33]**

Buckley, Wilfred

- Aert Schouman and the Glasses that he engraved, with a supplementary note on glasses engraved by Frans Greenwood. London: 1931. One of 250. 4to. 50 pp. 32 plates. Orig cloth backed bds, hd of spine sl torn. Dw (torn with loss). *(Robertshaw)* **£75 [≈$113]**

Buechner, Thomas S.

- Norman Rockwell, Artist and Illustrator. New York: Abrams, (1970). 1st edn. Folio. 328 pp. Frontis, 614 ills Orig cloth. *(Bookpress)* **$150 [≈£100]**

Bulfinch, Thomas

- The Age of Fable or Stories of Gods and Heroes. Illustrated by Joe Mugnani. New York: Limited Editions Club, 1958. One of 1500 sgnd by the illustrator. Sm 4to. Orig parchment-backed cloth. Slipcase. *(Oak Knoll)* **$55 [≈£37]**

Bulloch, J.M.

- The Art of Extra-Illustration. London: Anthony Treherne, 1903. 61 pp. Ills. Some foxing. Qtr cloth, jnts cracked. *(Oak Knoll)* **$75 [≈£50]**

Bulloch, John

- George Jamesone. The Scottish Vandyck. Edinburgh: David Douglas, 1885. One of 250 initialled by the author. 201 pp. 2 etched ills by George Reid. Orig cloth gilt. *(Leicester Art Books)* **£85 [≈$128]**

Bulwer-Lytton, Edward George

- The Last Days of Pompeii. Illustrations by Kurt Craemer. New York: Limited Editions Club, 1956. One of 1500 sgnd by Craemer & Mardersteig. Sm 4to. Orig cloth (spine yellowed). Slipcase. *(Oak Knoll)* **$95 [≈£63]**
- The Last Days of Pompeii. New York: Limited Editions Club, 1956. One of 1500 signed by the artist Kurt Craemer and the printer. 4to. 512 pp. Occas v sl foxing. Orig cloth, faintly foxed & darkened on sides. Slipcase. *(Waddington)* **£48 [≈$72]**

Bumpus, T. Francis

- The Cathedrals and Churches of Italy. London: Werner Laurie, 1926. Lge 8vo. viii, 400 pp. 79 plates. Occas sl spotting. Orig cloth gilt. Dw. *(Hollett)* **£20 [≈$30]**
- A Guide to Gothic Architecture. London: Werner Laurie, [ca 1914]. xi,359 pp. 143 plates. 4 advt pp. Text sl foxed. Orig pict cloth. *(Willow House)* **£18 [≈$27]**

Bunt, Cyril G.E.

- The Water-Colours of Frank Brangwyn R.A. 1867-1956. Leigh-on-Sea: F. Lewis, [1958]. One of 500. 4to. 87 pp. 24 mtd cold plates, 16 b/w plates. Orig cloth. Dw. *(Cooper Hay)* **£55 [≈$83]**

Bunyan, John

- The Pilgrim's Progress. Illustrated by William Strang. London: Nimmo, 1895. 1st edn thus. 396 pp. Port frontis, pict title, 12 etched plates. Orig gilt dec calf, t.e.g., rubbed and marked, *(Bookworks)* **£65 [≈$98]**
- The Pilgrim's Progress from this World to that which is to come ... Essex House Press: 1899. One of 750. Sq 12mo. 426 pp. Orig vellum, sl soiled. *(Chapel Hill)* **$150 [≈£100]**
- The Pilgrim's Progress and the Life and Death of Mr. Badman ... London: Nonesuch Press, 1928. One of 1600. 8 cold (pochoir) w'cut ills by Karl Michel. Orig mrbld cloth bds, label. *(Michael Taylor)* **£75 [≈$113]**

Burchett, R.

- Linear Perspective for the Use of Schools of Art. London: Chapman & Hall, 1872. 2nd edn, 16th thousand. Cr 8vo. xii,102 pp. 24 fldg plates. Orig cloth gilt, uncut. *(Clevedon Books)* **£25 [≈$38]**

Burgess, Fred W.

- Antique Jewellery and Trinkets. London: Routledge, Home Connoisseur series, 1919. xiii,399 pp. 142 ills. Orig cloth gilt. *(Hollett)* **£30 [≈$45]**
- Antique Jewelry and Precious Stones. New York: Tudor, [1919]. xii,399 pp. 142 ills. Orig cloth gilt. Dw (sl worn). *(Hollett)* **£30 [≈$45]**
- Chats on Old Copper and Brass. London: Fisher Unwin, 1914. 1st edn. 400 pp. 91 ills. Orig pict cloth gilt, spine faded. *(Hollett)* **£25 [≈$38]**
- Chats on Old Copper and Brass. Edited and Revised by Cyril G.E. Bunt. London: Benn, 1954. 184 pp. Ills. Orig cloth gilt. Dw (sl rubbed). *(Hollett)* **£10 [≈$15]**
- Silver, Pewter, Sheffield Plate. London: Routledge, The Home Connoisseur series, 1921. xvi,304 pp. 85 ills. Orig cloth gilt, a few spots. *(Hollett)* **£12.50 [≈$20]**

Burke, Bernard

- Illuminated Heraldic Illustrations, with Annotations. London: Hurst, 1856. Roy 8vo. 16 cold plates, heightened with gold. Orig cloth, reprd. *(Emerald Isle)* **£50 [≈$75]**

Burke, Edmund

- A Philosophical Enquiry into the Origin of our Ideas of the Sublime and Beautiful. London: Dodsley, 1757. 1st edn. 8vo. viii, [8], 184 pp. Half-title. Contemp calf, backstrip relaid, new label. Anon. *(Spelman)* **£600 [≈$900]**

Burke, James D.

- Jan Both: Paintings, Drawings and Prints. New York: Garland, 1976. xxiv,359 pp. 40 plates, 12 ills. Orig buckram. *(Leicester Art Books)* **£45 [≈$68]**

Burl, Aubrey

- Rings of Stone. The Prehistoric Stone Circles of Britain and Ireland. London: Weidenfeld, 1979. 4to. Ills. Dw. *(Emerald Isle)* **£35 [≈$53]**
- The Stone Circles of the British Isles. New Haven: Yale, 1976. Sm 4to. 410 pp. Ills. Dw. *(Emerald Isle)* **£45 [≈$68]**

Burlin, Martin & Joll, Evelyn

- The Paintings of J.M.W. Turner. Yale: UP, 1977. 1st edn. 2 vols. 4to. 550 ills. Dws. *(Spelman)* **£100 [≈$150]**

Burne-Jones, Edward

- The Beginning of the World: Twenty Five Pictures by Edward Burne-Jones. London: Longman Green, 1903. new edn. 23 pp. Orig cloth backed bds, uncut, some wear. *(Willow House)* **£35 [≈$53]**

Burnett, David

- Longleat. The Story of an English Country Life. London: Collins, 1978. 1st edn. 208 pp. Ills. Orig cloth gilt. Dw. *(Hollett)* **£15 [≈$23]**

Burney, Charles

- A General History of Music, from the Earliest Ages to the Present Period. London: for the author ..., 1782-89. Vol 1 2nd edn, vols 2-4 1st edn. 4 vols. 4to. Contemp half calf, spines sl faded. *(Jarndyce)* **£550 [≈$825]**

Burnier, Raymond

- Hindu Medieval Sculpture. Paris: La Palme, (1950). 1st edn. Folio. 13 pp. 79 photo plates. Orig bds, sl worn. *(Bookpress)* **$110 [≈£73]**

Burns, Robert

- Songs from Robert Burns. Selected by A.E. Coppard. Golden Cockerel Press: 1925. One of 450. 112 pp. 18 w'engvs by Mabel M. Annesley. Orig qtr buckram. *(Waddington)* **£48 [≈$72]**

Burns, Thomas

- Old Scottish Communion Plate ... with ... Chronological Tables of Scottish hall-Marks prepared by Alexander J.S. Brook. Edinburgh: Clark, 1892. One of 500 signed by the author. Num plates. Mod qtr calf. *(Waterfield's)* **£65 [≈$98]**

Burr, Frederick

- Life and Works of Alexander Anderson, M.D. The First American Wood Engraver. New York: Burr Bros., 1893. One of 725 signed by the author. 210 pp. Contemp three qtr mor, t.e.g., edges & jnts rubbed, front hinge cracked, faint mark on spine. *(The Veatchs)* **$200 [≈£133]**

Burton, William

- A History and Description of English Earthenware and Stoneware (to the beginning of the 19th Century). London: Cassell, 1904. Cold frontis, 89 ills. Orig cloth gilt, trifle faded. *(Hollett)* **£25 [≈$38]**

Bury, Adrian

- Francis Towne: Lone Star of Water-Colour Painting. London: 1962. 157 pp. 45 plates. Orig cloth, sl marked. *(Fine Art)* **£38 [≈$57]**
- Joseph Crawhall. The Man and the Artist. London: Charles Skilton, [1958]. One of

975. 4to. 251 pp. Mtd cold frontis, 6 mtd cold plates, 32 b/w plates, 26 text ills. Orig cloth, pict onlay. *(Cooper Hay)* **£120 [≈$180]**

- Joseph Crawhall. The Man and the Artist. Foreword by Sir Alfred Munnings. London: Charles Skilton, 1958. One of 990. 251 pp. Mtd cold frontis, 65 ills. Orig buckram. *(Leicester Art Books)* **£60 [≈$90]**
- Shadow of Eros. A Biographical and Critical Study of the Life and Work of Sir Alfred Gilbert. Dropmore Press: 1952. One of 300. 4to. 8,[iv],108,colophon pp. 25 plates. Orig niger half mor. Dw. *(Claude Cox)* **£32 [≈$48]**

Bush, Martin

- Goodnough. New York: Abbeville, (1982). Sq 4to. 260 pp. 244 ills. Orig cloth. Dw. signed by the artist on a tipped-in b'plate. *(Abacus)* **$100 [≈£67]**

Bushell, S.W.

- Oriental Ceramic Art. Illustrated by Examples from the Collection of W.T. Walters. New York: Crown, (1980). Folio. 429 pp. Ills. Dw. *(Schoyer)* **$85 [≈£57]**

Buten, David

- 18th-Century Wedgwood. A Guide for Collectors and Connoisseurs ... New York: Methuen, 1980. 1st edn. Sm 4to. 192 pp. 20 cold plates, 198 ills. Orig cloth backed bds. Dw. *(Hollett)* **£35 [≈$53]**

Butler, A.S.G.

- The Architecture of Sir Edwin Lutyens ... London: Country Life, 1950. 1st edn. 3 vols. 4to. Num ills. Some sl marg damp damage. Orig cloth. *(Bow Windows)* **£365 [≈$548]**

Butler, A.S.G. & Hussey, Christopher

- The Architecture of Sir Edwin Lutyens. [With] The Life of Sir Edwin Lutyens. London: Country Life, 1950. 1st edn. 4 vols. 4to (text) & folio (plates). Num ills. Orig cloth. *(Bookpress)* **$1,750 [≈£1,167]**

Butler, Elizabeth

- From Sketch-Book and Diary ... London: Adam & Charles Black, 1909. 1st edn. 8vo. 28 cold plates by the author. Orig dec cloth, t.e.g. *(Claude Cox)* **£25 [≈$38]**

Butler, Samuel

- The Way of All Flesh. London: Collins, 1934. 1st edn thus. 512 pp. 14 w'engvs by John Farleigh. Orig cloth, jnts sl faded. Dw. *(Bookworks)* **£28 [≈$42]**

Butlin, Martin

- The Paintings and Drawings of William Blake. New Haven: Yale UP, 1981. 2 vols. 4to. 668 pp. 1193 ills. Orig cloth. Dws. *(Abacus)* **$250 [≈£167]**

Butlin, Martin & Joll, Evelyn

- The Paintings of J.M.W. Turner. New Haven: Yale UP, 1984. Rvsd edn. 2 vols. 4to. 572 plates. Orig cloth. Dws. *(Abacus)* **$150 [≈£100]**

Butlin, William

- The Paintings and Drawings of William Blake. New Haven: Yale UP, 1981. 2 vols. 1193 ills. Orig cloth. Dw. *(Leicester Art Books)* **£200 [≈$300]**

Butterfield, L.P. & Townsend, W.G.P.

- Floral Forms in Historic Design ... London: Batsford, 1922. 18 plates. Cloth backed bds portfolio, sl worn & spotted. *(Monmouth)* **£40 [≈$60]**

Byron, George Gordon, Lord

- The Prisoner of Chillon. Illuminated by W. & G. Audsley, Architects. Chromolithographed by W.R. Tymms. London: Day & Son, 1865. Sm folio. 20 ff. Few sl stains on blank versos. Rec three qtr mor. *(Wilkinson)* **£69 [≈$104]**

Byron, R.

- The Appreciation of Architecture. London: Wishart, 1932. Sm 4to. 64 pp. 16 plates. Sl foxed. Orig cloth backed bds. Remains of glassine dw. *(Monmouth)* **£50 [≈$75]**

Byron, Robert & Rice, David Talbot

- The Birth of Western Painting. London: 1930. One of 650. 4to. Plates. Inscrptn. V sl spotting. Dw (piece missing from hd of spine, few edge tears, some clumsy internal reprs). *(Blakeney)* **£175 [≈$263]**

Cabell, James Branch

- Domnei. A Comedy of Woman Worship. London: The Bodley Head, 1930. 1st edn. 272 pp. Frontis, 9 plates, 30 ills by Frank Cheyne Pape. Orig gilt dec cloth, unopened. Dw. *(Bookworks)* **£30 [≈$45]**
- Jurgen, a Comedy of Justice. With 16 Wood Engravings by John Buckland Wright. The Golden Cockerel Press: 1949. One of 500. Orig qtr leather, spine v sl faded. *(Michael Taylor)* **£125 [≈$188]**
- Jurgen. A Comedy of Justice. Illustrations by Virgil Burnett. Westport: The Limited Editions Club, (1976). One of 2000 signed

by Burnett. Tall 8vo. Orig cloth. Slipcase. *(Oak Knoll)* **$55 [≈£37]**

- The Line of Love. Illustrated by Howard Pyle. New York & London: Harper, 1905. 1st edn. 10 cold plates. Orig pict cloth, pict onlay. *(Barbara Stone)* **£55 [≈$83]**

The Cabinet of Useful Arts ...

- The Cabinet of Useful Arts and Manufactures: designed for the perusal of Young Persons. London: W. Welton, [advts dated 1831]. 12mo. 180,[10 advt] pp. 10 full-page w'cuts. Contemp qtr roan. *(Robertshaw)* **£75 [≈$113]**

Cadman, S. Parkes

- The Parables of Jesus. Illustrated by N.C. Wyeth. Phila: David McKay, (1931). 1st edn. 4to. 8 cold plates. Orig cloth, pict onlay (v sl edge wear). Dw (sl worn, sl dusty). *(Jo Ann Reisler)* **$800 [≈£533]**

Caesar, Julius

- The Gallic Wars. Illustrated with Engravings by Bruno Bramanti. New York: The Limited Editions Club, 1954. One of 1500 sgnd by Mardersteig & Bramanti. Sm 4to. Orig cloth-backed bds. Dw (spine darkened). Slipcase. *(Oak Knoll)* **$150 [≈£100]**

Cage, John

- Silence. Lectures and Writings. Middletown: Wesleyan UP, 1967. 4to. xii,276 pp. Orig cloth. Dw. *(Ars Libri)* **$75 [≈£50]**
- A Year from Monday. New Lectures and Writings. Middletown: Wesleyan UP, [1967]. 4to. xi,167 pp. Orig cloth. Dw. *(Ars Libri)* **$50 [≈£33]**

Cahill, Holger

- George O. 'Pop' Hart. Twenty-four Selections from his Work. New York: The Downtown Gallery, 1928. One of 250 with orig litho frontis signed by the artist. Sm 4to. [2],25,[3] pp. 24 plates. Orig bds, spine chipped. *(Ars Libri)* **$150 [≈£100]**

Cahill, James

- Treasures of Asia: Chinese Painting. Lausanne: Skira, (1960). 4to. 214 pp. Num mtd cold plates. Dw. *(Schoyer)* **$50 [≈£33]**

Caiger, G.

- Japan: Dolls on Display. Japan in Miniature. Being an Illustrated Commentary on the Girls Festival and the Boys Festival. Tokyo: Hokuseido Press, (1933). Sm 4to. Cold & b/w ills. Pict endpapers. Orig silk cvrd bds, silk ties. *(Barbara Stone)* **£55 [≈$83]**

Caiger-Smith, A.

- Lustre Pottery: Technique, Tradition and Innovation in Islam and the Western World. London: Faber, 1985. 4to. 246 pp. 105 plates, 33 cold plates, 12 figs. Orig cloth. Dw. *(Castle Bookshop)* **£25 [≈$38]**

Cain, Julien

- The Lithographs of Chagall 1962-1968. Boston: Boston Book and Art Shop, (1969). 4to. 179 pp. Num ills. Orig cloth. Dw. Vol 3 of the Lithographs. *(Abacus)* **$450 [≈£300]**
- The Lithographs of Chagall 1962-1968. Notes and Catalogue by Fernand Mourlot, Charles Sorlier. Boston: Boston Book and Art Shop, [1969]. 4to. 179,[3] pp. Orig litho frontis & dw, 155 cold ills, 45 b/w ills. Dw. *(Cooper Hay)* **£250 [≈$375]**
- The Lithographs of Chagall 1969-1973. Notes and Catalogue by Fernand Mourlot, Charles Sorlier. New York: Crown, [1974]. 179,[3] pp. Orig litho frontis & dw, 134 cold ills, 27 b/w ills. Dw. *(Cooper Hay)* **£200 [≈$300]**
- The Lithographs of Chagall, 1962-1968. Vol III. Notes and Catalogue: Fernand Mourlot, Charles Sorlier. Boston: Boston Book and Art Shop, 1969. Lge 4to. 179,[3] pp. Orig cold litho frontis, 195 ills. Orig cloth, worn. *(Ars Libri)* **$450 [≈£300]**

Caldecott, Randolph

- Aesop's Fables with Modern Instances. London: Macmillan, 1883. Demy 4to. 20 ills. Some pp detached. Orig pict cloth, soiled. *(Stella Books)* **£20 [≈$30]**
- Randolph Caldecott's Graphic Pictures. Complete Edition. London: Routledge, 1898. Oblong folio. Cold & b/w ills. Orig pict cloth gilt, fine. *(Barbara Stone)* **£135 [≈$203]**

Calder, Alexander

- Three Young Rats and Other Rhymes. Drawings by Alexander Calder. Edited with an Introduction by J.J. Sweeney. New York: Curt Valentin, 1944. One of 700. Lge 4to. xviii, [3], 130,[6] pp. 85 ills. Orig cloth backed bds. *(Ars Libri)* **$400 [≈£267]**

Calderon, V.G.

- The Lottery Ticket. Golden Cockerel Press: 1945. One of 100. Tall 8vo. 12 pp. Engvd title & 5 w'engvs by Dorothea Braby. Orig qtr mor, t.e.g. *(Waddington)* **£62 [≈$93]**
- The Lottery Ticket. Golden Cockerel Press: 1945. One of 400. Tall 8vo. 12 pp. Engvd

title & 5 w'engvs by Dorothea Braby. B'plate. Orig cloth, sl thumbed.
(Waddington) **£42 [≈$63]**

Calloway, Stephen

- English Prints for the Collector. London: Lutterworth, 1980. 232 pp. Dw.
(Carol Howard) **£18 [≈$27]**

Calthrop, Dion Clayton

- English Costume. London: A. & C. Black, Twenty Shilling Series, 1923. Reprint. 61 cold plates by the author. Orig cloth.
(Old Cathay) **£29 [≈$44]**

Calvesi, Maurizio

- Alberto Burri. New York: Abrams, (1975). 4to, 163 pp. 82 cold & 81 b/w plates. Orig cloth. Dw. *(Abacus)* **$100 [≈£67]**

Campos, Jules

- Jose de Creeft. New York: Erich S. Herrmann, 1945. One of 700. Lge 4to. 32,[4] pp. 42 plates, text ills. Orig cloth.
(Ars Libri) **$150 [≈£100]**
- The Sculpture of Jose de Creeft. With a 'Statement on Sculpture' by the Artist. New York: 1972. 4to. [4],227 pp. 284 ills. Orig cloth. Dw. *(Ars Libri)* **$50 [≈£33]**

Camus, Albert

- The Stranger. Translated by Stuart Gilbert. Paintings by Daniel Maffia. N.p.: The Limited Editions Club, 1971. One of 1500 sgnd by Maffia. Sq 8vo. Orig leather, t.e.g. Slipcase. *(Oak Knoll)* **$65 [≈£43]**

Candee, Helen Churchill

- The Tapestry Book. New York: Tudor, 1935. Lge 8vo. xvi,275 pp. 103 plates (4 cold). Occas sl spotting. Orig cloth, spine sl mottled. *(Hollett)* **£30 [≈$45]**

Caplan, H.H.

- The Classified Directory of Artist's Signatures, Symbols and Monograms. London: Paul Grahame, 1982. 888 pp. Orig cloth. *(Fine Art)* **£65 [≈$98]**

Carls, Carl Dietrich

- Ernst Barlach. London: Pall Mall, 1969. 216 pp. 123 ills. Orig cloth.
(Leicester Art Books) **£32 [≈$48]**

Carmel, James H.

- Exhibition Techniques. Travelling and Temporary. New York: Reinhold, 1963. Lge 8vo. 216 pp. Num photo ills. orig bndg.
(Mendelsohn) **$50 [≈£33]**

Carmichael, J.W.

- The Art of Marine Painting in Water-Colours. London: Winsor & Newton, 1862. 6th edn. Sm 8vo. 50,2,48 advt pp. Frontis, 10 plates. Rec cloth.
(Clevedon Books) **£45 [≈$68]**

Carpenter, Edward

- Westminster Abbey. Illustrated by David Gentleman. London: 1987. 1st edn. 4to. Ills. Orig cloth. Dw.
(Margaret Nangle) **£20 [≈$30]**

Carrington, Fitzroy

- Prints and their Makers. New York: Century, 1912. 1st edn. Lge 8vo. xvi,268 pp. 200 plates. Orig cloth, sl worn.
(Bookpress) **$65 [≈£43]**

Carroll, Lewis (C.L. Dodgson)

- The Hunting of the Snark. Illustrated by Ralph Steadman. London: 1975. 1st edn thus. Num ills. Orig bndg, spine ends sl bumped, ft of spine sl stained. Price-clipped dw (sl creased).
(Ulysses Bookshop) **£55 [≈$83]**

Carter, Frederick

- D.H. Lawrence and the Body Mystical. London: Denis Archer, (1932). One of 75 with a signed artist's proof of the port of Lawrence. 63 pp. Orig bds gilt.
(Argonaut) **$300 [≈£200]**

Carter, Harry

- Orlando Jewitt. London: OUP, 1962. 1st edn. Sq 8vo. Ills. [vi],50 pp. Orig cloth. Dw.
(Oak Knoll) **$40 [≈£27]**

Carter, Huntly

- The New Spirit in the Cinema ... London: Harold Shaylor, 1930. 1st edn. 8vo. xxxvi,403 pp. 32 plates. Orig cloth, spine faded. *(Claude Cox)* **£30 [≈$45]**

Carter, John

- More Binding Variants. London: 1938. Sm 8vo. Orig wraps. *(Traylen)* **£40 [≈$60]**
- Specimens of the Ancient Sculpture & Painting now remaining in England ... New & Improved Edition ... London: Bohn, 1887. Lge folio. 120 plates inc chromolithos. Orig half mor, elab gilt spine.
(Mermaid Books) **£145 [≈$218]**

Carter, John & Muir, Percy H.

- Printing and the Mind of Man. A Descriptive Catalogue ... Great Britain: the authors,

1967. 1st edn. 4to. xxxiii,280 pp. Ills. Orig cloth. Dw (spine darkened). *(Argonaut)* **$250 [≈£167]**

Carter, John (editor)

- New Paths in Book Collecting. Essays by Various Hands. London: Constable, (1934). 1st edn. 8vo. vi,294 pp. Orig cloth. Dw (sm tear). *(Oak Knoll)* **$125 [≈£83]**
- New Paths in Book Collecting. London: 1934. Sm 8vo. Orig cloth, spine sl faded. *(Traylen)* **£18 [≈$27]**

Carter, Thomas

- Medals of the British Army, and how they were won. Egypt, Peninsula, and South Africa ... London: Groombridge, 1861. 3 vols in one. viii,185; x,185; viii,192 pp. 19 cold plates, 5 text ills. Three qtr mor gilt. *(Hollett)* **£325 [≈$488]**

Carter, Thomas Francis

- The Invention of Printing in China. New York: Columbia UP, (1931). 2nd edn, rvsd. 8vo. xxxvi,283 pp. Num plates, text ills. Orig cloth. Dw. *(Bookpress)* **$135 [≈£90]**

Cartier-Bresson, Henri

- The Decisive Moment. New York: Simon & Schuster with Editions Verve, (1952). Pamphlet of captions laid in. B'plate. Dw (sl worn). *(Hermitage)* **$600 [≈£400]**
- The People of Moscow, seen by Henri Cartier-Bresson. New York: Simon & Schuster, 1955. 1st edn. 4to. 163 plates. Orig burlap. Dw (sl chipped & soiled). *(Karmiole)* **$75 [≈£50]**
- The People of Moscow. New York: Simon & Schuster, 1955. 163 photo ills. Orig cloth, spine browned. *(Clarice Davis)* **$100 [≈£67]**

Casanova de Seingalt, Jacques

- The Memoirs. Translated by Arthur Machen. New York: The Limited Editions Club, 1940. One of 1500. 8 vols. Orig cloth-backed bds. 2 slipcases (broken). *(Oak Knoll)* **$150 [≈£100]**

Caskey, L.D.

- Museum of Fine Arts, Boston: Catalogue of Greek and Roman Sculpture. Cambridge, MA: Museum of Fine Arts, Boston, 1925. 1st edn. Tall 4to. x,234 pp. Num ills. Orig cloth & bds, crnrs sl rubbed. *(Karmiole)* **$75 [≈£50]**

Casson, Stanley

- Sculpture of To-day. London & New York: The Studio, 1939. Lge 4to. 144 pp. 112 plates. Orig cloth. *(Ars Libri)* **$75 [≈£50]**
- Some Modern Sculptors. OUP: 1928. 1st edn. Lge 8vo. x,119 pp. Frontis, 39 plates. Orig cloth gilt, spine faded. *(Hollett)* **£15 [≈$23]**
- Some Modern Sculptors. London: OUP, 1929. 4to. x,119 pp. 40 plates. Orig cloth. *(Ars Libri)* **$40 [≈£27]**

Castelfranco, Giorgio

- Donatello. New York: [ca 1965]. Lge 4to. 118 pp. 40 cold plates, 209 ills. Orig cloth. Dw. *(Washton)* **$100 [≈£67]**

Castillejo, Jose Luis

- The Book of Eighteen Letters. Madrid: Privately Printed, 1972. One of 350. 4to. (352) pp. Orig cloth. Dw. *(Ars Libri)* **$50 [≈£33]**

Cathedrals of England and Wales ...

- The Cathedrals of England and Wales. Their History, Architecture and Associations. London: Cassell, 1906. 1st edn. 2 vols. 4to. 2 frontis, 18 plates. Orig cloth, t.e.g., minor wear. *(Bookpress)* **$125 [≈£83]**

Cats, Jacob & Farlie, Robert

- Moral Emblems with Aphorisms, Adages and Proverbs of All Ages and All Nations. Translated and Edited by Richard Pigot. London: Longman ..., 1862. 2nd edn. xvi,241 pp. Frontis, 120 ills by Leighton. Orig gilt dec cloth, a.e.g., sl worn. *(Holtom)* **£17.50 [≈$27]**

Cattaneo, Raffaele

- Architecture in Italy from the Sixth to the Eleventh Century ... London: Fisher Unwin, 1896. 4to. 363 pp. 170 ills. Orig cloth gilt, soiled & stained. *(Hollett)* **£20 [≈$30]**

Catullus, Gaius Valerius

- The Complete Poetry of Gaius Catullus. Translated by Jack Lindsay. With Decorations Engraved on Wood by Lionel Ellis ... London: Fanfrolico Press, (1929). One of 325. Lge 8vo. (250) pp. Ills. Orig mor, extrs sl rubbed. *(Karmiole)* **$150 [≈£100]**

Caulfield, James

- Memoirs of the Celebrated Persons composing the Kit-Kat Club ... London: for Hurst, Robinson, 1821. Large Paper. Folio. [iv], x, 262 pp. Errata slip. 48 plates after Kneller. Some foxing. 2 sm marg tears. Qtr mor, uncut, inner jnts strengthened. Anon. *(Rankin)* **£125 [≈$188]**

Caulfield, S.F.A. & Saward, Blanche C.
- Encyclopaedia of Victorian Needlework. 1882. New York: Dover, 1972. 697 pp. 83 + 159 plates, over 800 text figs. Orig pict bndg. *(Willow House)* **£18 [≈$27]**

Cautley, H.M.
- Suffolk Churches and their Treasures. London: Batsford, 1938. 2nd edn. 4to. 363 pp. Plates, plans. Ex-lib. Orig cloth. *(Castle Bookshop)* **£22 [≈$33]**
- Suffolk Churches and their Treasures. Ipswich: Norman Adlard, 1954. 3rd edn. Sm 4to. ix,363 pp. 3 cold plates, 415 photo ills. Orig cloth gilt. Dw (sl worn). *(Hollett)* **£75 [≈$113]**

Cave, Roderick
- The Private Press. London: Faber, (1971). 1st edn. 4to. 376 pp. 72 plates, 83 text ills. Orig cloth. *(Bookpress)* **$85 [≈£57]**

Cave, Roderick & Wakeman, Geoffrey
- Typographia Naturalis. Wymondham: Brewhouse Press, 1967. One of 333. 4to. 37 pp. 5 tipped-in plates. Orig qtr leather & bds. Prospectus inserted. *(Oak Knoll)* **$375 [≈£250]**

Cavendish, George
- The Life of Thomas Wolsey Archbishop of York. Hammersmith: Kelmscott Press, 1893. One of 260 (of 256). 8vo. [i],iv,287 pp. Few trivial creases. Orig limp vellum, silk ties, sl soiling. *(Finch)* **£550 [≈$825]**

Caw, James L.
- Scottish Painting Past and Present 1620-1908. Edinburgh: T.C. & E.C. Jack, 1908. 4to. xiii,503 pp. Frontis, 75 b/w plates. Some foxing. Orig cloth gilt. *(Cooper Hay)* **£135 [≈$203]**
- Sir James Guthrie. A Biography. London: Macmillan, 1932. xv,244 pp. 47 plates, 10 ills. Orig cloth, t.e.g. Dw. *(Leicester Art Books)* **£60 [≈$90]**
- William McTaggart, R.S.A. A Biography and an Appreciation. Glasgow: Maclehose, 1917. xiv,302 pp. Frontis, 50 plates. Orig cloth. *(Leicester Art Books)* **£100 [≈$150]**

Caxton Club
- Catalogue of an Exhibition of Nineteenth Century Bookbinding. By the Caxton Club (in the Arts Institute). Chicago: The Caxton Club, (1898). One of 127. Sm 8vo. 84 pp. 24 plates. Orig cloth, leather label. Slipcase. *(Karmiole)* **$175 [≈£117]**

Cecil, Lord David
- Augustus John. Fifty Two Drawings. London: George Rainbird, 1957. 15 pp. 52 plates. Orig cloth. Dw (worn). *(Leicester Art Books)* **£50 [≈$75]**

Cellini, Benvenuto
- The Autobiography. Translated by J. Addington Symonds. New York: 1946. Ltd edn sgnd by the illustrator, Salvador Dali. Cold plates, b/w ills. Orig pict gilt bndg, spine sl darkened. *(Rob Warren)* **$275 [≈£183]**
- The Life of Benvenuto Cellini translated by John Addington Symonds. London: The Vale Press, [1900]. 1st edn thus. 2 vols. 4to. Lib stamp on one endpaper. Orig cloth backed bds, sl soiled, labels chipped. *(Sotheran's)* **£125 [≈$188]**
- The Treatises on Goldsmithing and Sculpture. Translated by C.R. Ashbee. London: Edward Arnold, Essex House Press, 1898. One of 600. xiv,164 pp. 11 plates, 7 text ills. Orig buckram. *(Leicester Art Books)* **£95 [≈$143]**

Cervantes, Miguel de
- Don Quixote ... With Twenty-One Illustrations by E. McKnight Kauffer. London: Nonesuch Press, 1930. One of 1475. 2 vols. 21 stencil-coloured plates. Orig niger mor, spines darkened, 2 sm holes in leather on one side. *(Claude Cox)* **£135 [≈$203]**
- The History of Don Quixote de la Mancha ... With Illustrations by Jean de Bosschere ... London: Constable, 1922. 1st edn with these illustrations. 4to. xxiv,311 pp. Cold frontis, 24 plates, decs. Orig cloth gilt, sl soiled, sl faded. *(Robert Frew)* **£50 [≈$75]**
- The History of Don Quixote de la Mancha ... With Illustrations by Jean de Bosschere ... London: Constable, 1922. 1st edn with these illustrations. 4to. Cold frontis, 24 plates, decs. Orig buckram gilt, sl rubbed & marked. *(Claude Cox)* **£30 [≈$45]**

Cescinsky, Herbert
- The Old English Master Clockmakers and their Clocks 1670-1820. London: Routledge, 1938. 1st edn. Lge 8vo. xii,182 pp. 275 ills. Orig cloth. *(Claude Cox)* **£70 [≈$105]**
- The Old World House, its Furniture and Decoration. London: A. & C. Black, 1924. 2 vols. Sm 4to. Frontises, num text ills. Orig leather backed cloth, t.e.g. *(Traylen)* **£50 [≈$75]**
- The Old-World House, Its Furniture &

Decoration. London: A. & C. Black, 1924. 1st edn. 2 vols. 4to. 2 frontis, photo ills. Orig cloth, t.e.g., rubbed.
(Bookpress) **$225 [≈£150]**

Cescinsky, Herbert & Gribble, E.R.

- Early English Furniture & Woodwork. London: 1922. 2 vols. Folio. Cold frontises, over 700 ills. Mor gilt.
(Traylen) **£125 [≈$188]**
- Early English Furniture & Woodwork. London: Routledge, 1922. 1st edn. 2 vols. Lge thick 4to. 2 cold frontises, 527 ills. Orig buckram backed cloth gilt.
(Hollett) **£150 [≈$225]**

Chaffers, William

- Hall Marks on Gold and Silver Plate ... Extended and enlarged ... London: Reeves & Turner, 1905. 9th edn. Tall 8vo. 299,[4] pp. Fldg facsimile, plate. Occas sl spotting. Orig cloth gilt. *(Hollett)* **£40 [≈$60]**
- Marks and Monograms on Pottery and Porcelain, of the Renaissance and Modern Periods ... London: Bickers, 1872. 3rd edn. Lge thick 8vo. viii,778,[vi] pp. 2200 ills. Orig cloth gilt, extrs sl worn. *(Hollett)* **£40 [≈$60]**

Chagall, Marc

- Chagall by Chagall. New York: Harrison House, (1982). Reprint edn. 4to. 263 pp. 285 ills. Orig buckram. Dw.
(Abacus) **$50 [≈£33]**

Chalmers, Patrick R.

- A Dozen Dogs or So. Illustrated by Cecil Aldin. London: 1928. 2nd edn. 12 cold plates. Orig bndg. *(Old Cathay)* **£39 [≈$59]**
- Forty Fine Ladies. Illustrated by Cecil Aldin. London: Eyre & Spottiswoode, 1929. 1st edn. Slim 4to. 62 pp. Ills. Orig cloth.
(Sotheran's) **£68 [≈$102]**

Chamberlain, Arthur B.

- George Romney. London: Methuen, 1910. xvii,422 pp. 73 plates. Orig cloth.
(Leicester Art Books) **£28 [≈$42]**
- Hans Holbein the Younger. London: George Allen, 1913. 1st edn. 2 vols. 4to. 24 cold & 228 b/w ills. Orig cloth gilt.
(Traylen) **£65 [≈$98]**

Chancellor, E.B.

- The Private Palaces of London. London: Kegan Paul, 1908. 1st edn. 4to. 390 pp. 44 plates. Sl dusty. Orig cloth, spine faded, ink number at ft of spine, soiled.
(Monmouth) **£35 [≈$53]**

Chanticleer

- Chanticleer. A Bibliography of the Golden Cockerel Press, April 1921 - August 1936. Golden Cockerel Press: 1936. One of 300 signed by Christopher Sandford. 48 pp. 34 w'engvs. Orig qtr mor.
(Waddington) **£150 [≈$225]**

Chapel, C.E. & Hunter, George Leland

- English and American Furniture. A Pictorial Handbook ... New York: Garden City Publishing, 1929. Lge 8vo. 311 pp. Ills. Sl spotting. Orig cloth gilt. Dw (trifle worn).
(Hollett) **£45 [≈$68]**

Chapman, R.W.

- Cancels. London: 1930. One of 500. 8vo. Vellum backed bds. *(Traylen)* **£80 [≈$120]**

Chappuis, Adrien

- The Drawings of Paul Cezanne. A Catalogue Raisonne. New York: New York Graphic Society, 1973. 2 vols. 168 + 1223 ills. Orig cloth gilt. Slipcase.
(Leicester Art Books) **£300 [≈$450]**

Chapuis, Alfred & Jaquet, Eugene

- The History of the Self-Winding Watch 1770-1931. Neuchatel: Editions du Griffon, (1956). 1st edn in English. Demy 4to. 246 pp. Num ills. Dw (torn & reprd).
(Ash) **£85 [≈$128]**

Charles, C.J.

- Elizabethan Interiors. London: Newnes, n.d. One of 800. Folio. 40 pp. 32 plates. Rubber stamp on title. Half leather, rubbed.
(Bookpress) **$150 [≈£100]**

Charlot, Jean

- Picture Book II. Los Angeles: Zeitlin & Ver Brugge, 1973. One of 1000 signed by the artist and the printer. Lge 4to. [14] pp. 32 cold lithos. Orig wraps. Slipcase.
(Ars Libri) **$500 [≈£333]**

Chastel, Andre

- Studios and Styles of the Italian Renaissance. Translated by Jonathan Griffin. New York: Odyssey, (1966). 4to. xvi,418 pp. 300 plates. Orig cloth gilt. Dw. *(Karmiole)* **$75 [≈£50]**

Chatterton, Edward Keble

- Old Sea Paintings. The Story of Maritime Art ... London: Bodley Head, 1928. 1st edn. 4to. xiii,179 pp. 15 cold & 95 b/w ills. Sm lib stamps on plate versos. Rec half mor.
(Clevedon Books) **£85 [≈$128]**

- Old Sea Paintings. The Story of Maritime Art ... London: John Lane; New York: Dodd, Mead, (1928). 1st edn. 4to. xv,179,[4 advt] pp. 15 cold & 95 b/w ills. Orig pict cloth, some wear extrs. *(J & J House)* **$90 [≈£60]**
- Ship-Models. Edited by Geoffrey Holme. London: The Studio, 1923. 1st edn. One of 1000. 4to. ix,53 pp. 142 plates. Name. Orig cloth, sl faded. Dw. *(Argonaut)* **$300 [≈£200]**

Chatterton, Thomas

- The Rowley Poems. London: Vale Press, 1898. One of 210. 2 vols. Orig bndgs, sl worn. *(Ulysses Bookshop)* **£195 [≈$293]**

Chatto, William Andrew

- A Treatise on Wood Engraving, Historical and Practical ... New Edition. London: Chatto & Windus, [1861]. 664 pp. Ills. Half mor gilt. *(Waddington)* **£95 [≈$143]**

Chatzidakis, Manolis

- Byzantine Monuments in Attica and Boeotia. Architecture, Mosaics, Wallpaintings. Athens: 1956. 4to. 28 pp. 21 plates. Folder. *(Zeno)* **£35 [≈$53]**

Chaucer, Geoffrey

- A.B.C. Called la priere de Notre Dame. Translated by Dave Haslewood. San Francisco: Grabhorn-Hoyem, 1967. One of 1000. 12mo. 52 pp. Orig dec bds. *(Argonaut)* **$45 [≈£30]**
- The Canterbury Tales. Illustrated after Drawings by W. Russell Flint. London: Philip Lee Warner, Medici Society, 1913. One of 500 (of 512). 3 vols. 4to. 36 mtd cold plates. Orig qtr holland, t.e.g., silk markers, sl soiled, sl stain vol 1, crnrs sl rubbed. *(Finch)* **£500 [≈$750]**
- The Canterbury Tales. Illustrated by W. Russell Flint. London: 1928. 1st edn thus. Sm cr 4to. 21 cold plates. Orig bndg, t.e.g., spine darkened. *(Margaret Nangle)* **£45 [≈$68]**
- The Canterbury Tales. Rendered into Modern English Verse by Frank Ernest Hill. London: Limited Editions Club, 1934. One of 1500 signed by the designer-printer, George W. Jones. 3 vols. 4to. Orig buckram over bds (some soiling). Slipcase (wear to edges). *(Oak Knoll)* **$125 [≈£83]**
- Canterbury Tales. Illustrated by Rockwell Kent. London: Harrap, 1935. 1st trade edn, with addtnl ills. 25 2-colour plates, head & tail pieces. V sl foxing, few pp crnrs turned. Dw. *(Waddington)* **£20 [≈$30]**
- The Complete Poetical Works. Illustrated by Warwick Goble. New York: Macmillan, 1912. 1st edn. Thick 4to. 32 cold plates. Sm hole in blank prelim. 1st gathering sl loose. Orig elab gilt cloth, t.e.g., edges sl worn. *(Jo Ann Reisler)* **$250 [≈£167]**
- The Nun Priest's Tale ... Newly rendered into modern English by Nevill Coghill. London: Allen & Richard Lane, Christmas, 1950. One of 1000. 8vo. 30 pp. W'engvd ills by Lynton Lamb. Orig vellum backed bds. *(Robert Frew)* **£25 [≈$38]**
- The Parlement of Foules. [Boston: Houghton Mifflin] 1904. One of 325. 8vo. Hand cold intls. Note present. Name & date. Orig vellum-paper bds. Slipcase (v worn). Designed by Bruce Rogers. *(The Veatchs)* **$175 [≈£117]**
- Troilus and Cressida. (New York): The Limited Editions Club, 1939. One of 1500 signed by the printer-designer, George W. Jones. Sm 4to. Orig cloth-backed bds. Slipcase (sm crack along hinge). *(Oak Knoll)* **$85 [≈£57]**

Cheesman, T.

- Rudiments of Drawing the Human Figure, from Cipriani, Guido, Poussin, Rubens, &c. Drawn and Engraved by T. Cheesman. London: T. Cheesman, to be had of R. Ackermann, 1816. Oblong folio. Engvd title, 10 plates. Some foxing & sl use. Contemp wraps, spine reprd. *(Spelman)* **£120 [≈$180]**

Chekhov, Anton

- The Short Stories. Illustrated by Lajos Szalay. Avon, CT: The Limited Editions Club, 1973. One of 2000 signed by Szalay. Tall 8vo. Orig cloth, leather label. Slipcase. *(Oak Knoll)* **$45 [≈£30]**
- Two Plays. The Cherry Orchard, Three Sisters. Illustrated by Lajos Szalay. New York: The Limited Editions Club, 1966. One of 1500 signed by Szalay. 8vo. Orig qtr leather. Slipcase. *(Oak Knoll)* **$55 [≈£37]**

Chevreul, M.E.

- The Laws of Contrast of Colours: and their Application to the Arts of Painting, Decoration of Buildings ... Translated from the French by John Spanton. New Edition ... London: Routledge ..., 1859. 8vo. 17 plates (16 cold). Orig dec cloth gilt, inner jnts strained. *(Rankin)* **£100 [≈$150]**

Chignell, Robert

- The Life and Painting of Vicat Cole, R.A. London: Cassell, 1898. 3 vols in one. 45 plates, 89 text ills. Orig dec cloth, worn, v faded. *(Leicester Art Books)* **£30 [≈$45]**

Child, Peter

- The Craftsman Woodturner. London: G. Bell, 1973. 2nd printing. 238 pp. Ills. Orig bds. Dw (worn). Signed by the author. *(Willow House)* **£15 [≈$23]**

The Children of the Bible ...

- The Children of the Bible. London: RTS, [ca 1850s]. 1st edn. Sm 4to. [vi],76 pp. 6 cold Kronheim plates. Orig cloth, sl rubbed. *(Bookpress)* **$150 [≈£100]**

Childs, George

- English Landscape Scenery; an Advanced Drawing Book. Twenty-four Sketches from Nature. London: David Bogue, [ca 1860]. Oblong 4to. Title, 24 litho plates. Advt labels on pastedowns. Minor marg browning. Orig cloth, sl marked. *(Spelman)* **£90 [≈$135]**

Chinese Nursery Rhymes ...

- Chinese Nursery Rhymes. Put into English Verse by Alan Ayling from Translations by Duncan Mackintosh. Andoversford: The Whittington Press, 1976. [One of 500]. [24] pp. Ills by Judy Ling Wong. Orig dec wraps. *(Bookworks)* **£32 [≈$48]**

Chipp, Herschel B. (editor)

- Theories of Modern Art. A Source Book by Artists and Critics. Berkeley & Los Angeles: Calif UP, 1968. 4to. 664 pp. Num ills. Orig cloth. *(Ars Libri)* **$75 [≈£50]**

Choice Observations ...

- Choice Observations upon the Art of Painting ... see Aglionby, William

Christ-Janer, Albert & Foley, Mary Mix

- Modern Church Architecture. New York: McGraw-Hill, 1962. 1st edn. 4to. [vi],333 pp. Ills. Orig cloth, sl rubbed. *(Bookpress)* **$50 [≈£33]**

Christie, Mrs Archibald

- Samplers and Stitches: A Handbook of the Embroiderer's Art. London: Batsford, 1934. 3rd edn, enlgd. 152 pp. 37 plates, 243 ills. Orig cloth backed bds. Dw (sl torn). *(Willow House)* **£30 [≈$45]**

Chubb, Ralph

- A Fable of Love and War. Curridge, Berkshire: Chubb, 1925. One of 200 initialled by the author. 2 w'engvs. (Original?) white paper dw. *(Any Amount)* **£200 [≈$300]**

Church, A.H.

- Josiah Wedgwood, Master-Potter. London: Seeley & Co., The Portfolio Monographs, 1894. Tall 8vo. 103,[i] pp. 4 plates, 28 text ills. Orig buckram gilt, leather label, orig wraps bound in. *(Hollett)* **£25 [≈$38]**

Church, Richard

- Mereside Chronicle. London: Country Life, 1948. 1st edn. 200 pp. Num ills by the author. Orig (1st issue) cloth, sl bruised. Dw (sl chipped, long closed tear and creased rear panel). *(Bookworks)* **£68 [≈$102]**

Cibber, Colley

- An Apology for the Life of Colley Cibber ... Written by Himself. London: Golden Cockerel Press, 1925. One of 450. 2 vols. Orig cloth backed bds, trifle dusty. *(Hermitage)* **$150 [≈£100]**

Clapham, Sir Alfred W.

- English Romanesque Architecture. Oxford: 1930. 2 vols. xx,168; xvi,180 pp. 112 plates, 95 figs. Ex-lib. Orig cloth, sl faded. *(Castle Bookshop)* **£46 [≈$69]**
- English Romanesque Architecture before the Conquest. Oxford: Clarendon Press 1930. 1st edn. Tall 8vo. xx,168 pp. Frontis, 65 plates. Orig buckram gilt, spine faded. *(Hollett)* **£15 [≈$23]**
- English Romanesque Architecture. Oxford: Clarendon Press, 1930-69. 2 vols. Plates. Orig cloth. Dws. *(Peter Bell)* **£65 [≈$98]**

Clapp, Frederick Mortimer

- Jacopo Carucci da Pontormo. His Life and Work. New Haven: Yale UP, 1916. xxviii,355 pp. 153 ills. Orig cloth & bds. Slipcase. *(Leicester Art Books)* **£110 [≈$165]**

Clark, Anthony M.

- Pompeo Batoni. A Complete Catalogue of his Works with an Introductory Text. London: Phaidon, 1985. 414 pp. 431 ills. Orig cloth. Dw. *(Fine Art)* **£60 [≈$90]**

Clark, John

- The Amateur's Assistant; or, a Series of Instructions in Sketching from Nature, the Application of Perspective ... To accompany the subjects which form the Portable Diorama. London: 1826. 4to. vi,[2],66 pp, advt leaf. 10 plates. Orig bds, paper label, rebacked. *(Spelman)* **£180 [≈$270]**

Clark, Kenneth

- The Drawings of Leonardo da Vinci in the

Collection of Her Majesty the Queen at Windsor Castle. Second Edition. Revised with the assistance of Carlo Pedretti. London: Phaidon, 1968. Vol 1 only. lxvii,220 pp. Orig cloth, sl soiled.
(Clarice Davis) **$100 [≈£67]**

- Piero della Francesca. London: Phaidon, (1951). 1st edn. Folio. 212 pp. Frontis, ills. Orig cloth, spine sunned.
(Bookpress) **$165 [≈£110]**

Clark, Leonard

- An Intimate Landscape. With Wood Engravings by Miriam MacGregor. Whittington Press for Nottingham Court Press, 1981. One of 500 (this copy unnumbered). Orig qtr buckram. Slipcase.
(Michael Taylor) **£45 [≈$68]**

Clarke, A.D.

- Modern Farm Buildings. Their Construction and Arrangement. Winchester: 1891. Cr 8vo. viii, 167 pp. Plans, ills, text figs. Orig cloth.
(Phenotype) **£29 [≈$44]**

Clarke, H.G. & Wrench, F.

- Colour Pictures on Pot Lids and other forms of 19th Century Staffordshire Pottery ... London: Courier Press, 1924. 1st edn. 18 plates (2 cold). Orig cloth gilt.
(Hollett) **£30 [≈$45]**

Claudin, A.

- The First Paris Press. An Account of the Books printed for G. Fichet and J. Heynlin in the Sorbonne, 1470-1472. London: Bibl Soc., 1898 for 1897. 4to. Corrigenda slip. Frontis, 10 facs. Orig canvas backed bds.
(Traylen) **£90 [≈$135]**

Clay, Enid

- The Constant Mistress. Golden Cockerel Press: 1934. One of 300 signed by the author and the artist, Eric Gill. 6 w'engvs. Orig cloth backed bds, edges sl worn, crnrs sl bumped, spine ends sl rubbed, label torn.
(Ulysses Bookshop) **£450 [≈$675]**
- Sonnets and Verses. Golden Cockerel Press: 1925. One of 450. 56 pp. W'engvs by Eric Gill. V few spots to deckle edges. Orig qtr linen, uncut, partly unopened, label trifle chipped. *(Bookworks)* **£390 [≈$585]**
- Sonnets and Verses. Golden Cockerel Press: 1925. One of 450. 35 pp. W'engvs by Eric Gill. Orig qtr linen, unopened.
(Waddington) **£240 [≈$360]**

Clay, Jean

- Romanticism. New York: Vendome Press, 1981. Lge sq 4to. 320 pp. Cold ills. Orig cloth. Dw. *(First Folio)* **$75 [≈£50]**

Clay, Rotha Mary

- Julius Caesar Ibbetson 1759-1817. London: Country Life, 1948. xx,156 pp. 128 plates. Orig cloth. *(Leicester Art Books)* **£60 [≈$90]**
- The Mediaeval Hospitals of England ... London: Methuen, The Antiquary's Books, 1909. 1st edn. 8vo. xxii,357,48 pp. 78 ills on 30 plates. Occas sl spotting. Orig cloth gilt, sl faded, sl frayed at ft. *(Hollett)* **£45 [≈$68]**
- Samuel Hieronymus Grimm of Burgdorf, Switzerland. London: Faber, 1941. xxxii,112 pp. 76 plates. Orig cloth.
(Leicester Art Books) **£40 [≈$60]**

Clayton, Ellen C.

- English Female Artists. London: Tinsley Bros., 1876. 1st edn. 2 vols. 8vo. viii, 427, [4 advt]; [4],438,[2 advt] pp. Occas v sl marg waterstain. Orig cloth, inner jnts tender.
(Fenning) **£85 [≈$128]**

Clephan, Robert Coltman

- The Defensive Armour and Weapons of War of Mediaeval Times, and of the 'Renaissance'. London: Walter Scott, 1900. 1st edn. 8vo. xv,15-237 pp. 51 plates. Orig cloth gilt, t.e.g., rubbed. Author's presentation copy. *(Sotheran's)* **£90 [≈$135]**

Clifford, Derek

- Collecting English Watercolours. London: 1970. 1st edn. 4to. 143 pp. 13 cold & 243 b/w plates. Lib stamp on title & last page. Sellotape marks on pastedowns. Dw (v sl chipped). *(Francis Edwards)* **£25 [≈$38]**

Clifford, Derek & Timothy

- John Crome. London: Faber, 1963. 301 pp. 6 cold plates, 173 plates. Orig cloth. Dw.
(Leicester Art Books) **£28 [≈$42]**

Clouston, K. Warren

- The Chippendale Period in English Furniture. London: 1897. xvi,224 pp. 200 ills. Orig cloth backed buckram gilt, sl scratched, sm tears to hinges.
(Hollett) **£30 [≈$45]**

Coats, Alice

- The Book of Flowers. Four Centuries of Flower Illustrations. London: Phaidon, 1973. 1st edn. Folio. 208 pp. 40 cold & 86 b/w plates. Orig cloth gilt. Dw.
(Hollett) **£60 [≈$90]**

Cobbett, William

- Life and Adventures of Peter Porcupine with Other Records of his Early Career in England and America. London: Nonesuch Press, 1927. One of 1800. Cold frontis. Rear endpapers foxed. Foredges browned. Orig cloth backed bds. *(Margaret Nangle)* **£12 [≈$18]**
- Life and Adventures of Peter Porcupine with Other Records of his Early Career in England and America. London: Nonesuch Press, 1927. One of 1800. Orig cloth backed bds. Slipcase. *(Lamb)* **£30 [≈$45]**
- Rural Rides ... Edited ... by G.D.H. and Margaret Cole. With numerous Vignettes by John Nash. London: Peter Davies, 1930. One of 1000 (this unnumbered). 3 vols. xl,1064 pp. Orig buckram backed mrbld bds, extrs sl worn. *(Claude Cox)* **£140 [≈$210]**

Cobden-Sanderson, T.J.

- The Closing of the Doves Press ... With a Preface by David Magee. Stanford University Libraries: 1969. One of 102. 8vo. [16] pp. Orig stiff wraps. *(Oak Knoll)* **$65 [≈£43]**

Cockerell, Charles Robert

- Iconography of the West Front of Wells Cathedral, with an Appendix on the Sculptures of other Mediaeval Churches in England. London: John Henry Parker, 1851. 4to. xxiii, 126, 115 pp. Fldg frontis, 8 plates, 2 plans. Orig cloth gilt, reprd. *(Hollett)* **£65 [≈$98]**

Cockerell, Douglas

- Bookbinding, and the Care of Books. Fourth Edition. London: Pitman, 1927. 8vo. Orig bndg, sl marked. *(Limestone Hills)* **$55 [≈£37]**

Cockerell, Sydney C.

- Old Testament Miniatures: A Medieval Picture Book with 283 Paintings from the Creation to the Story of David. New York: George Braziller, n.d. Folio. 209 pp. Cold plates. Orig cloth. Dw. *(Abacus)* **$85 [≈£57]**

Coen, Luciano & Duncan, Louise

- The Oriental Rug. London: Harper & Row, 1978. 1st edn. 4to. xiv,192 pp. 102 cold plates, num ills. Orig cloth gilt. Dw. *(Hollett)* **£45 [≈£30]**

Cogniat, Raymond

- XXth Century Drawings & Watercolors. Translated from the French by Anne Ross. New York: Crown, n.d. 224 pp. 114 cold & 84 2-toned plates. Orig cloth. Dw. *(Clarice Davis)* **$75 [≈£50]**

Cohen, Arthur A.

- Sonia Delaunay. New York: Abrams, 1975. Sm oblong folio. 206 pp. 217 ills. Orig cloth. Dw. *(Ars Libri)* **$150 [≈£100]**

Cohn, Albert M.

- A Few Notes upon some Rare Cruikshankiana. London: Karslake, 1915. One of 250. Tall 4to. 24 pp. Ills. Orig wraps, minor dusting, edge wear rear wrapper. *(Jo Ann Reisler)* **$100 [≈£67]**
- George Cruikshank. A Catalogue Raisonne of the Works executed during the years 1806-1877 ... London: The Bookman's Journal, 1924. One of 500. xvi,375 pp. 31 plates. Orig cloth, t.e.g. *(Leicester Art Books)* **£200 [≈$300]**

Cohn, William

- Chinese Painting. New York: Hacker, 1978. 4to. (238) pp. B/w ills. *(Schoyer)* **$40 [≈£27]**

Colahan, Colin

- Max Meldrum. His Art and Views. Melbourne: Alexander McCubbin, [ca 1920]. 117 pp. 48 ills. Orig bds. Wraps torn. *(Leicester Art Books)* **£50 [≈$75]**

Cole, Alphaeus P. & Cole, Margaret Ward

- Timothy Cole, Wood-Engraver. New York: The Pioneer Association, 1935. One of 750 signed & numbered. Tall 8vo. 19 w'cut ills. Orig cloth (sm mark). *(Oak Knoll)* **$75 [≈£50]**

Cole, Bruce

- Giotto and Florentine Painting, 1280-1375. New York: Harper & Row, (1976). 1st edn. 8vo. x,[ii],209 pp. Ills. Orig cloth, rear cvr sl soiled. *(Bookpress)* **$45 [≈£30]**

Cole, Sir Henry

- The Veritable History of Whittington and his Cat. London: Chapman & Hall, & Joseph Cundall, 1847. 1st edn thus. Sm 8vo. [16] pp. 3 cold plates. Orig dec card cvrs, fine. Anon. *(Sotheran's)* **£148 [≈$222]**
- See also Summerly, Felix

Cole, Vicat

- The Artistic Anatomy of Trees. London: Seeley Service, 1941. Reprint. 347 pp. Num ills. Orig cloth gilt. Dw. *(Willow House)* **£25 [≈$38]**

Coleridge, Samuel Taylor

- The Rime of the Ancient Mariner. Illustrated by Gustave Dore. London: Dore Gallery, 1875. Lge folio. 12 pp. Engvd title vignette,

frontis, 38 plates. Orig gilt dec cloth, sometime rebacked, sl soiled.
(Robert Frew) **£175 [≈$263]**

- Coleridge's Ancient Mariner Illustrated by David Scott, R.S.A. with Life of the Artist and Descriptive Notices of the Plates by the Rev. A.L. Simpson. London: Nelson, 1885. Sm 4to. 160 pp. 25 plates. Orig pict cloth gilt. *(Claude Cox)* **£25 [≈$38]**
- The Rime of the Ancient Mariner. Campden: Essex House Press, 1903. One of 150 on vellum. 8vo. 30,[2] pp. Frontis. Inscrptn. Orig parchment, uncut, somewhat soiled. *(Finch)* **£385 [≈$578]**
- The Rime of the Ancient Mariner. OUP: 1930. One of 750. 8vo. Prospectus. Orig cloth backed mrbld bds. Dw. Designed by Bruce Rogers. *(The Veatchs)* **$175 [≈£117]**
- The Rime of the Ancient Mariner. London: Allen & Richard Lane, 1945. One of 700. 40 pp. 5 lithos by Duncan Grant. Orig niger leather gilt, t.e.g., spine sunned, extrs sl darkened. *(Bookworks)* **£290 [≈$435]**

Collier, John

- The Devil and All. Six Short Stories. London: Nonesuch Press, 1934. One of 1000 signed by the author. 123 pp. W'engvd frontis by Blair Hughes-Stanton. Top edge dusty, gilt labels sl tarnished. Glassine & gold dw. *(Waddington)* **£48 [≈$72]**

Colling, James K.

- Details of Gothic Architecture. Measured and Drawn ... London: Batsford, [1856]. 1st edn in book form. 2 vols. 4to. 8; 27 pp. 95 + 85 litho plates. Orig cloth, sl rubbed, inner hinges reinforced. *(Claude Cox)* **£85 [≈$128]**

Collingwood, R.G.

- The Principles of Art. Oxford: 1946. 1st edn. 8vo. Orig cloth. *(Waterfield's)* **£25 [≈$38]**

Collins, Wilkie

- The Moonstone. Illustrated by Dignimont. New York: The Limited Editions Club, 1959. One of 1500 signed by the illustrator. Tall 8vo. Orig cloth (spine soiled). Slipcase. *(Oak Knoll)* **$25 [≈£17]**
- The Woman in White. Illustrated by Leonard Rosoman. New York: The Limited Editions Club, 1964. One of 1500 signed by the illustrator. Tall 8vo. Orig cloth-backed bds (hd of spine darkened). Slipcase. *(Oak Knoll)* **$65 [≈£43]**

The Colophon

- The Colophon, A Book Collector's Quarterly. New York: 1930-50-68. 48 vols, complete. 4to & 8vo. Orig bds & glassine or cloth. Original Series (1930-35, 20 vols); New Series (1935-38, 12 vols); The Annual of Bookmaking (1938, 1 vol); New Graphic Series (1939, 4 vols); New Colophon (1948-50, 9 vols), & 2 Indexes. *(The Veatchs)* **$950 [≈£633]**

Colt, C.F. & Miall, Antony

- The Early Piano. London: Stainer & Bell, 1981. 1st edn. 160 pp. Cold ills. Orig bds gilt. Dw. *(Willow House)* **£20 [≈$30]**

Colvin, F.F. & Gordon, E.R.

- Diary of the 9th (Q.R.) Lancers during the South African Campaign 1899 to 1902. South Kensington: Cecil Roy, 1904. 1st edn. 8vo. xvi,304 pp. Pocket map, ills. Orig pict cloth, soiled & rubbed, shaken, hd of spine nicked. *(Sotheran's)* **£88 [≈$132]**

Comini, Alessandra

- Egon Schiele's Portraits. Berkeley: Calif UP, 1974. xxxii,272 pp. 335 ills. Orig buckram. *(Leicester Art Books)* **£95 [≈$143]**

Compton-Rickett, Arthur

- William Morris: A Study in Personality. London: Jenkins, 1913. xxii,325 pp. 2 plates. B'plate. Orig cloth, worn. *(Fine Art)* **£20 [≈$30]**

Comstock, Francis & Fletcher, William D.

- The Work of Thomas W. Nason. Boston: Boston Public Library, 1977. One of 1000. Folio. 279,[1] pp. Orig cloth. Dw. *(Bookpress)* **$135 [≈£90]**

Comstock, Francis Adams

- A Gothic Vision. F.L. Griggs and his Work. Boston & Oxford: 1978. 2nd edn. One of 500. 370 pp. 150 ills. Orig cloth. *(Leicester Art Books)* **£55 [≈$83]**

Conant, Kenneth John

- Carolingian and Romanesque Art. Baltimore: Penguin, (1959). 1st edn. 8vo. xxxviii, [ii], 343 pp. 176 plates. Orig cloth. *(Bookpress)* **$85 [≈£57]**

Congreve, William

- The Way of the World. With Illustrations by T.M. Cleland. New York: The Limited Editions Club, 1959. One of 1500 signed by Cleland. Sm 4to. Sm ink mark on front endpaper. Orig cloth. Slipcase (spotted). *(Oak Knoll)* **$5 [≈£37]**
- The Way of the World. An Unexpurgated

Edition, Including an original signed Etching by A.R. Middleton Todd. London: The Haymarket Press, 1928. One of 875. Lge 8vo. xxii,82 pp. Orig cloth, spine extrs sl frayed. *(Karmiole)* **$100 [≈£67]**

Conner, Patrick

- Oriental Architecture in the West. London: Thames & Hudson, 1979. Roy 8vo. 14 cold & 140 other ills. Dw. *(David Slade)* **£25 [≈$38]**
- Oriental Architecture in the West. London: Thames & Hudson, (1979). 1st edn. Sm 4to. 200 pp. 154 ills. Orig cloth. Dw. *(Bookpress)* **$45 [≈£30]**

Conrad, Joseph

- An Outcast of the Islands. Illustrations by Robert Shore. Avon, CT: The Limited Editions Club, 1975. One of 2000 signed by Shore. Sm 4to. Orig cloth. Slipcase. *(Oak Knoll)* **$55 [≈£37]**

Conrads, Ulrich & Sperlich, Hans G.

- The Architecture of Fantasy. Utopian Building and Planning in Modern Times. New York: Praeger, 1962. Sm 4to. 187 pp. Num ills. Orig cloth. Dw. *(Mendelsohn)* **$50 [≈£33]**

Constable, Freda & Simon, Sue

- The England of Eric Ravilious. London: Scolar Press, 1982. 96 pp. 64 plates, 12 engvs. Orig cloth. Dw. *(Fine Art)* **£25 [≈$38]**

Constable, John

- The Letters of John Constable, R.A., to C.R. Leslie, R.A. 1826-1837. Edited by Peter Leslie. London: 1931. Lge 8vo. ix,174 pp. Few plates. Orig cloth, sl sunned. *(Washton)* **$40 [≈£27]**

Constantini, Angelo

- The Birth, Life and Death of Scaramouch. ... Rendered into English Verse by Edmund Blunden. London: C.W. Beaumont, 1924. One of 80 signed by Beaumont & Blunden. 4 plates. Orig vellum & dec bds gilt, sl soiled. *(Karmiole)* **$150 [≈£100]**

Conway, William Martin

- The Woodcutters of the Netherlands in the Fifteenth Century. In Three Parts ... Cambridge: UP, 1884. 8vo. Orig cloth, lower crnrs bumped. *(David Slade)* **£50 [≈$75]**

Cook, Clarence

- Art and Artists of Our Time. New York: Selmar Hess, 1888. 3 vols. 4to. 286; 352; 336 pp. 198 ills. Orig cloth. *(Rona Schneider)* **$400 [≈£267]**

Cook, G.H.

- Mediaeval Chantries and Chantry Chapels. London: Phoenix House, 1947. 1st edn. 8vo. xii,196 pp. 26 plans, 59 plates. Lib label removed from rear pastedown. Orig cloth. *(Hollett)* **£20 [≈$30]**

Cook, John W. & Klotz, Heinrich

- Conversations with Architects. New York: Praeger, (1973). 1st edn. 8vo. 272 pp. Ills. Orig cloth. Dw. *(Bookpress)* **$45 [≈£30]**

Cooke, H. Lester

- Fletcher Martin. New York: Abrams, (1977). Oblong folio. 232 pp. 202 ills (51 cold). Orig cloth. Dw. *(Abacus)* **$55 [≈£37]**

Cooke, William

- The Medallic History of Imperial Rome ... London: Dodsley, 1781. 2 vols. 4to. xxxix, 507; [ii],502 pp. 51 plates. Tree calf gilt, hinges cracked, crnrs bumped. *(Hollett)* **£150 [≈$225]**

Coomaraswamy, Ananda K.

- Bronzes from Ceylon, chiefly in the Colombo Museum. Ceylon: for the Colombo Museum, 1914. 1st edn. Lge 4to. 32 pp. 189 ills on 28 plates. Calf & cloth. *(Karmiole)* **$85 [≈£57]**
- The Origin of the Buddha Image. New Delhi: (1972). 1st Indian edn. 4to. [iv],42 pp. Frontis, 73 text ills. Name. Orig cloth. Dw (torn). *(Bookpress)* **$85 [≈£57]**

Cooper, Douglas

- The Work of Graham Sutherland. London: Lund Humphries, 1962. 2nd printing. Tall 4to. Orig dec bds, sl warped. *(First Folio)* **$75 [≈£50]**

Cooper, James Fenimore

- The Deerslayer. Illustrations by Edward A. Wilson. New York: The Limited Editions Club, 1961. One of 1500 signed by Wilson. Thick 8vo. Orig leather-backed bds. Slipcase (hinge partially cracked). *(Oak Knoll)* **$55 [≈£37]**
- The Last of the Mohicans. Illustrations by Edward Wilson. New York: The Limited Editions Club, 1932. One of 1500 signed by Wilson. Tall 8vo. Orig qtr leather (spine faded). Slipcase. *(Oak Knoll)* **$85 [≈£57]**
- The Pilot. Illustrated with Woodcuts by Robert M. Quackenbush. New York: The

Limited Editions Club, 1968. One of 1500 signed by Quackenbush. Sm 4to. Orig cloth. Slipcase. *(Oak Knoll)* **$55 [≈£37]**

- The Spy, A Tale of the Neutral Ground. With Illustrations by Henry C. Pitz. New York: The Limited Editions Club, 1963. One of 1500 signed by Pitz. Thick 8vo. Orig cloth, leather label. Slipcase (cracked). *(Oak Knoll)* **$55 [≈£37]**

Cooper, W. Heaton

- Mountain Painter. An Autobiography. Kendal: Frank Peters, 1984. 1st edn. 4to. vi,148 pp. Cold ills. Orig cloth gilt. Dw. *(Hollett)* **£25 [≈$38]**

Copeland, R. Morris

- Country Life. Boston: Crosby & Nichols, 1863. 2nd edn. 8vo. x,814 pp. Frontis, 8 plates. Orig cloth, sl worn, faint water stain lower edge. *(Bookpress)* **$195 [≈£130]**

Coplans, John

- Andy Warhol. Greenwich: New York Graphic Society, [1970]. Lge 4to. 160 pp. Num ills. Orig wraps. *(Ars Libri)* **$65 [≈£43]**

Coppard, A.E.

- Clorinda Walks in Heaven. London: The Golden Cockerel Press, 1922. One of 1200. Bds mildly shelfworn, one crnr bumped. Dw (sl chipped & rubbed). *(Hermitage)* **$90 [≈£60]**
- Count Stefan. Golden Cockerel Press: 1928. One of 600. 60 pp. Engvs by Robert Gibbings. Inscrptn. Orig qtr buckram. Dw (soiled & rubbed). *(Waddington)* **£80 [≈$120]**
- Crotty Shinkwin [with] The Beauty Spot. Golden Cockerel Press: (1932). One of 500. W'engvs by Robert Gibbings. Sm label rear pastedown. Orig qtr mor, spine v sl worn. *(Hermitage)* **$100 [≈£67]**
- The Hundredth Story. Golden Cockerel Press: 1931. One of 1000. 72 pp. 4 w'engvs by Robert Gibbings. Orig qtr leather, t.e.g., spine sunned. *(Bookworks)* **£68 [≈$102]**
- The Hundredth Story. Golden Cockerel Press: 1931. One of 1000. 4 w'engvs by Robert Gibbings. Orig morocco backed bds, t.e.g., spine sunned & v sl worn at hd. *(Waddington)* **£75 [≈$113]**
- The Hundredth Story. Golden Cockerel Press: 1931. One of 1000. W'engvs by Robert Gibbings. Orig morocco backed bds, top edges of bds v sl browned, spine sl faded. The 1st book from the press. *(Margaret Nangle)* **£65 [≈$98]**
- Pelagea and Other Poems. Golden Cockerel Press: 1926. One of 425. 44 pp. Engvs by Robert Gibbings. Inscrptn. Orig qtr buckram, faintest wear to one crnr. *(Waddington)* **£80 [≈$120]**

Copplestone, Trewin (editor)

- World Architecture. An Illustrated History. London: Hamlyn, 1968. Folio. 348 pp. Ills. Orig cloth gilt. Dw. *(Hollett)* **£40 [≈$60]**

Corbett, M. & Lightbrown, R.W.

- The Comely Frontispiece: The Emblematic Titlepage in England 1550-1660. London: Routledge, 1979. 1st edn. 224 pp. 20 ills. Sm lib marks. Orig cloth gilt. *(Willow House)* **£15 [≈$23]**

Core, Philip

- The Original Eye. Arbiters of Twentieth-Century Taste. Englewood Cliffs: Prentice-Hall, 1984. Tall 4to. 189,[3] pp. 197 ills. Orig cloth. Dw. *(Ars Libri)* **$50 [≈£33]**

Cork, Richard

- David Bomberg. New Haven: Yale UP, 1987. 1st edn. 356 pp. 60 cold plates, 357 ills. Orig cloth. Dw. *(Bookworks)* **£60 [≈$90]**
- David Bomberg. Yale: UP, 1987. 1st edn. 4to. 65 cold & 375 b/w ills. Dw. *(Spelman)* **£40 [≈$60]**

Corner, Sidney

- Rural Churches, Their Histories, Architecture, and Antiquities. London: Groombridge, [1869]. 1st edn. Sm folio. viii,72 pp. 18 cold plates. Orig purple cloth gilt, a.e.g., faded & torn. *(Bookpress)* **$325 [≈£217]**

Cornforth, J.

- English Interiors 1790-1848: The Quest for Comfort. London: 1978. Sm folio. 144 pp. 175 plates. Dw. *(Monmouth)* **£45 [≈$68]**

The Cornhill Gallery ...

- The Cornhill Gallery: 100 Engravings from Drawings on Wood: Being Designs for the Illustrations of "The Cornhill Magazine". London: Smith, Elder, 1865. 4to. 100 sheets. Portfolio, broken. *(Rona Schneider)* **$75 [≈£50]**

Corroyer, Edouard

- Gothic Architecture. Edited by Walter Armstrong. London: Seeley, 1893. 8vo. xvi, 388,[iv] pp. 236 ills. Orig cloth gilt, spine sl faded. *(Hollett)* **£12.50 [≈$20]**

Cortissoz, Royal, & others

- The Book of Alexander Shilling. New York: The Paisley Press, 1937. 4to. 72 pp. 21 plates. Orig cloth. *(Rona Schneider)* **$50 [≈£33]**

Cotchett, Lucretia Eddy

- The Evolution of Furniture. London: Batsford, 1938. 1st edn. Lge 8vo. x,118 pp. 94 plates. A few spots. Orig cloth gilt. Dw (damaged). *(Hollett)* **£25 [≈$38]**

Cotterell, H.H.

- Old Pewter, Its Makers and Marks in England, Scotland and Ireland. London: Batsford, 1929. 1st edn. Thick 4to. xv,432 pp. 7 fldg & 76 other plates. Orig cloth gilt. Dw (reprd). *(Hollett)* **£150 [≈$225]**
- Old Pewter, Its Makers and Marks in England, Scotland and Ireland. London: Batsford, 1969. Thick 4to. xxii,432 pp. 7 fldg & 76 other plates. Orig cloth gilt. Dw. Slipcase. *(Hollett)* **£65 [≈$98]**

Coulton, G.T.

- Art and the Reformation. Cambridge: 1953. 2nd edn. 8vo. xxii,622 pp. Num plates. Orig cloth, edges sl soiled. *(Washton)* **$85 [≈£57]**

Courthion, Pierre

- Edouard Manet. New York: Abrams, n.d. 4to. 152 pp. 131 ills (48 mtd cold plates). Orig cloth. Dw. *(Abacus)* **$40 [≈£27]**
- Georges Rouault. New York: Abrams, [1961]. 1st edn. 489 pp. Dw (v sl soiled). *(Hermitage)* **$125 [≈£83]**
- Georges Rouault. New York: Abrams, n.d. 490 pp. 832 ills. Orig cloth. Dw. *(Leicester Art Books)* **£80 [≈$120]**
- Georges Rouault. New York: Abrams, n.d. Stout 4to. 490 pp. 832 ills (49 mtd cold plates). Orig cloth. *(Abacus)* **$75 [≈£50]**

Cousens, Henry

- The Architectural Antiquities of Western India. London: The India Society, 1926. 1st edn. 8vo. xi,[i],86,[2] pp. 57 plates. Cloth backed bds, crnrs bumped. *(Bookpress)* **$110 [≈£73]**

Covarrubias, Miguel

- Indian Art of Mexico and Central America. New York: Knopf, 1957. 1st edn. 4to. Cold plates, ills. Orig cloth over linen gilt, crnrs sl bumped. Dw. *(First Folio)* **$85 [≈£57]**

Coventry, Francis

- The History of Pompey the Little, or the Life and Adventures of a Lap-Dog. Golden Cockerel Press: 1926. One of 400. W'engvd frontis by David Jones. Orig qtr buckram, unopened. *(Waddington)* **£110 [≈$165]**

Cowham, Hilda

- Blacklegs and Others. London: Kegan Paul, 1911. 1st edn. 4to. Cold & b/w ills. Orig dec cloth gilt, t.e.g., sl rubbed. *(Jo Ann Reisler)* **$200 [≈£133]**

Cowper, William

- John Gilpin. Illustrated by Ronald Searle. London: Chiswick Press for Sir Allen Lane, Christmas 1952. One of 1600. 4to. 44 ills. Orig pict wraps, fine. *(Barbara Stone)* **£48 [≈$72]**

Cox, Alwyn & Cox, Angela

- Rockingham Pottery and Porcelain 1745-1842. London: Faber, 1983. 1st edn. 262 pp. 10 cold plates, map, 15o ills. Orig cloth gilt. Dw. *(Hollett)* **£40 [≈$60]**

Cox, David

- A Series of Progressive Lessons Intended to Elucidate the Art of Landscape Painting in Water Colours. London: T. Clay, 1811. 1st edn. Oblong 4to. 30 pp, directions to binder leaf. 13 plates (6 hand cold), 8 cold squares in text. Contemp half roan, mor label. Anon. *(Spelman)* **£600 [≈$900]**
- A Series of Progressive Lessons Intended to Elucidate the Art of Landscape Painting in Water Colours. Second Edition. London: T. Clay, 1812. Oblong 4to. 30 pp, directions to binder leaf. 13 plates (6 hand cold), 8 cold squares in text. Sl soil. Later half mor. *(Spelman)* **£360 [≈$540]**
- A Treatise on Landscape Painting and Effect in Water Colours ... London: Fuller, 1814. 1st edn. 2nd issue, with harvesting scene plate. Oblong 4to. [ii],32 pp. 56 plates (16 hand cold). Some imprints cropped. Occas v sl spotting. Later half mor, a.e.g. *(Sotheran's)* **£1,850 [≈$2,775]**
- A Treatise on Landscape Painting in Water Colours. With a Foreword by A.L. Baldry. Edited by Geoffrey Holme. London: The Studio, 1922. 4to. 72 plates (15 mtd cold). Orig cloth. *(Lamb)* **£25 [≈$38]**
- A Treatise on Landscape Painting in Water-Colours ... Edited by Geoffrey Holme. London: The Studio, 1922. One of 250. Sm folio. 72 plates. Orig japon vellum, t.e.g., sl rubbed & soiled. *(Claude Cox)* **£40 [≈$60]**

Cox, J. Charles

- English Church Fittings, Furniture and Accessories. New York: 1923. Sm 4to. ix,320 pp. Ca 275 ills. Orig cloth, spine sl sunned & sl frayed at hd. *(Washton)* **$40 [≈£27]**

Cox, Morris

- An Abstract of Nature. London: The Gogmagog Press, 1968. One of 26 signed by the author. Tall 8vo. (43) pp. Prospectus laid in. Orig cloth, paper label. *(Bookpress)* **$900 [≈£600]**
- Crash, An Experiment in Blockmaking and Printing. London: The Gogmagog Press, 1963. One of 80. 8vo. (26) pp. 8 ills. Orig cloth. *(Bookpress)* **$675 [≈£450]**
- 14 Triads. London: The Gogmagog Press, 1967. One of 60 (of 100). 8vo. (28) pp. 3 cold plates. Orig bds, paper label. Signed by the author. *(Bookpress)* **$400 [≈£267]**
- An Impression of (Winter, Spring, Summer, Autumn). London: The Gogmagog Press, 1965-66. One of 100 signed by the author. 4 vols. 8vo. Ills. Orig nature-printed paper over bds. *(Bookpress)* **$2,500 [≈£1,667]**
- Mummers' Fool. London: Gogmagog Press, 1965. One of 60 signed by the author. 4to. (22) pp. 7 ills. Orig cloth backed dec bds. *(Bookpress)* **$750 [≈£500]**
- The Warrior and the Maiden. London: The Gogmagog Press, 1967 (1968). One of 65 signed by the author. 8vo. (24) pp. 10 engvs. Orig dec bds. Slipcase. Prospectus laid in. *(Bookpress)* **$850 [≈£567]**

Cox, P. & Stacey, W.

- The Australian Homestead. Lansdowne: 1972. 1st edn. Oblong 4to. Num ills. Orig cloth. Dw (sl worn). *(Monmouth)* **£25 [≈$38]**

Cox, Warren E.

- Chinese Ivory Sculpture. New York: Bonanza Books, (1946). 1st edn. Folio. 112,[6] pp. 75 ills. Orig cloth backed bds. Dw (torn). *(Bookpress)* **$50 [≈£33]**

Coxe, William

- Sketches of the Lives of Correggio and Parmegiano. London: 1823. 1st edn. 8vo. 276,index pp. Port. Contemp half mor. Anon. *(Robertshaw)* **£35 [≈$53]**

Craddock, Harry

- The Savoy Cocktail Book ... London: Constable, 1930. 1st edn. 287 pp. Ills by Gilbert Rumbold. Orig pict metallic bds, cloth spine gilt. *(Gough)* **£100 [≈$150]**

Craig, Edward Gordon

- Index to the Story of My Days. Some Memoirs of the Years 1872-1907. London: 1957. 1st edn. 31 ills. Orig half leather gilt. Dw. *(Margaret Nangle)* **£45 [≈$68]**
- Nothing or the Bookplate. With a Handlist by E. Carrick [ie Edward Anthony Craig]. London: Chatto & Windus, 1924. One of 280. Roy 8vo. 51 mtd specimens of bookplates, one bookplate also signed by him in pencil. Orig dec buckram gilt. Dw (sl soiled, internal reprs). *(Blackwell's)* **£200 [≈$300]**
- Paris Diary, 1932-1933. Edited with a Prologue by Colin Franklin. North Hills: Bird & Bull Press, 1982. One of 350. 8vo. Ills. Orig calf & rice paper over bds. Acetate dw. *(Dermont)* **$250 [≈£167]**
- Woodcuts and Some Words. London: Dent, 1924. 1st edn. 122 pp. 59 w'engvs by the author. Endpapers browned. Orig bds, a few marks, tips sl worn. *(Waddington)* **£40 [≈$60]**
- Woodcuts and Some Words. With an Introduction by Campbell Dodgson. London: 1924. 1st edn. Sq 8vo. 59 ills. Some marg stains. Orig cloth, worn. *(Margaret Nangle)* **£35 [≈$53]**

Craig, Maurice

- Irish Book Bindings 1600-1800. London: Cassell, (1954). 1st edn. 4to. 47 pp. Cold frontis, 58 plates. Dw (sl soiled). *(Hermitage)* **$350 [≈£233]**
- Irish Bookbindings, 1600-1800. London: Cassell, 1954. 1st edn. Folio. 60 pp. 58 plates. Orig cloth, one tip bruised. *(Bookpress)* **$385 [≈£257]**

Craighead, Meinrad

- The Mother's Birds. Images for a Death and a Birth. Worcester: Stanbrook Abbey Press, 1976. One of 30 specially bound signed by the author. 40 pp inc 20 pp ills. Orig mor. Slipcase. Prospectus laid in. *(Claude Cox)* **£110 [≈$165]**

Craik, Dinah Maria Mulock, Mrs.

- John Halifax, Gentleman. London: A. & C. Black, 1912. One of 250 signed by the publishers. Cold plates by Oswald Moser and G.F. Nicholls. Orig cloth. *(Old Cathay)* **£75 [≈$113]**
- John Halifax, Gentleman. London: A. & C. Black, 1912. One of 250 signed by the publishers. Cold plates by Oswald Moser and G.F. Nicholls. Orig cloth, sl worn. *(Old Cathay)* **£39 [≈$59]**

Cramer, Gerald, & others

- Henry Moore. Catalogue of Graphic Work. Volume II: 1973-1975 ... Geneva: Gerald Cramer, 1976. Lge 4to. 209 ills. Orig cloth. Dw. Slipcase. *(Ars Libri)* **$325 [≈£217]**

Crane, Stephen

- Maggie. A Girl of the Streets. With Gravures from Etchings by Sigmund Abeles. New York: The Limited Editions Club, 1974. One of 2000 signed by Abeles. Tall 8vo. Orig qtr leather. Slipcase. *(Oak Knoll)* **$55 [≈£37]**

Crane, Walter

- The Bases of Design. London: George Bell & Sons, 1898. 1st edn. 8vo. xix,[i blank], 365, [i imprint],[10 advt] pp. Ills. 2 sm blind stamps. Orig dec cloth gilt, t.e.g., spine sl rubbed. *(Sotheran's)* **£70 [≈$105]**
- The Bases of Design. London: George Bell, 1902. 2nd edn. 8vo. xviii,381 pp. Text ills. Endpapers browned. Orig cloth, t.e.g., rather worn, spine faded. *(Hollett)* **£30 [≈$45]**
- Flora's Feast a Masque of Flowers. London: Cassell, 1889. 1st edn. 4to. 40 pp, french-folded & unopened. Orig cloth backed pict bds. *(Claude Cox)* **£65 [≈$98]**
- Flora's Feast. London: Cassell, 1889. 1st edn. 4to. 40 pp. Cold ills. Orig cloth backed dec bds, lower cvr darkened & soiled, crnrs sl worn. *(Claude Cox)* **£55 [≈$83]**
- India Impressions. New York: Macmillan, 1907. 1st edn. 8vo. 325 pp. Cold frontis, 16 plates, text ills by the author. Orig pict cloth. *(J &J House)* **$50 [≈£33]**
- India Impressions. With Some Notes of Ceylon during a Winter Tour, 1906-07. London: Methuen, 1907. 1st edn. 8vo. Cold frontis, num b/w ills. Occas pale foxing. Orig pict cloth. *(Barbara Stone)* **£85 [≈$128]**
- Line & Form. London: George Bell & Sons, 1900. 1st edn. 8vo. xv,[i],282,[1] pp. Ills. Sl foxed. Orig cloth gilt, t.e.g., sunned. *(Bookpress)* **$265 [≈£177]**
- A Masque of Days. London: Cassell, 1901. 1st edn. Sm folio. 44 pp. Cold ills. Orig pict cloth backed bds, edges & crnrs sl rubbed. *(Sotheran's)* **£138 [≈$207]**
- Of the Decorative Illustration of Books Old and New. London: George Bell, 1921. 3rd edn, rvsd. 8vo. xiv,341 pp. Ills. Orig cloth, inner hinges cracked. *(Oak Knoll)* **$35 [≈£23]**
- Of the Decorative Illustration of Books Old and New. London: George Bell & Sons, 1896. One of 130 on japanese vellum. Lge 8vo. Orig ptd wraps over flexible bds, unopened. *(Book Block)* **$375 [≈£250]**
- William Morris to Whistler. Papers and Addresses on Art & Craft and The Commonwealth. London: George Bell & Co., 1911. 1st edn. 8vo. x,277,[ii] pp. Ills. Orig dec cloth, uncut, white lettering sl rubbed, inner hinges strengthened. *(Sotheran's)* **£148 [≈$222]**

Craven, Thomas

- A Treasury of American Prints. New York: Simon & Schuster, 1939. 4to. Orig cloth over bds, spiral bound. Dw. Slipcase. *(First Folio)* **$50 [≈£33]**

Crawford, John M.

- Chinese Calligraphy & Painting in the Collection of John M. Crawford. New York: Pierpont Morgan Library, 1962. 1st edn. Folio. 302 pp. Plates. Orig dec cloth. *(Terramedia)* **$100 [≈£67]**

Crawhall, Joseph

- Chorographia, or a Survey of Newcastle upon Tyne. Newcastle: Andrew Reid, 1883. 4to. 121,[3] pp. Hand cold w'cut ills. Orig qtr vellum gilt by A. Reid Newcastle, fine. Anon. *(Cooper Hay)* **£165 [≈$248]**
- A Collection of right merrie garlands for North Country Anglers. Edited by Joseph Crawhall ... Newcastle-on-Tyne: George Rutland, 1864. 1st edn. xvi,312 pp, advt leaf. Ills. Orig morocco backed cloth, t.e.g., hd of spine & crnrs rubbed. *(Claude Cox)* **£65 [≈$98]**
- Crawhall's Chap-Book Chaplets. London: Field & Tuer, 1883. 8 titles. 4to. Sep paginations. Hand cold ills. Orig dec paper spine & bds, orig wraps bound in, sl rubbed & faded. *(Cooper Hay)* **£145 [≈$218]**
- Isaak Walton: His Wallet Book. London: Field & Tuer, The Leadenhall Press, 1885. One of 500. 120 pp. Hand cold w'cut ills. Orig vellum backed blue bds, spine darkened & sl rubbed. *(Barbara Stone)* **£225 [≈$338]**
- A Jubilee Thought Imagined & Adorn'd by Joseph Crawhall. Newcastle-on-Tyne: Mawson, Swan & Morgan, 1887. One of 50 Large Paper. 4to. [2],77 pp. Hand cold ills. 1 leaf loose, few page edges chipped. Orig half parchment, spine chipped. Author's presentation copy. *(Cooper Hay)* **£150 [≈$225]**
- Old Tayles Newlye related Enryched with all ye Ancyente Embellyshments. London: Leadenhall Press, [1883]. 14 items. 4to. Sep paginations. W'cuts. Orig dec cloth. Anon. *(Cooper Hay)* **£95 [≈$143]**

Crichton, G.H.

- Romanesque Sculpture in Italy. London: 1954. 8vo. xx,172 pp. 92 plates. Orig cloth, sm reprs. *(Quest Books)* **£35 [≈$53]**

Crichton, G.H. & E.R.

- Nicola Pisano and the Revival of Sculpture in Italy. Cambridge: 1938. 8vo. 126 pp. 79 plates. Orig cloth. *(Washton)* **$65 [≈£43]**

Crick-Kuntziger, Martha, & others

- Bernard Van Orley. The Apocalypse Tapestries. Antwerp: 1956. Folio. 75 pp. 20 cold plates, 8 ills. Bds sl soiled, extrs & spine sl rubbed. *(Washton)* **$100 [≈£67]**

Cripps, Wilfred Joseph

- Old English Plate ... Its Makers and Marks. London: Murray, 1878. 1st edn. 8vo. xvi,432 pp. 70 ills. Sl spotting. Orig cloth, edges sl rubbed. *(Young's)* **£35 [≈$53]**
- Old English Plate. Ecclesiastical, Decorative and Domestic: its Makers and Marks. London: Murray, 1901. Library edn. Lge 8vo. xx,519 pp. 122 text w'cuts. Orig half parchment gilt, sl spotted. *(Hollett)* **£40 [≈$60]**
- Old English Plate ... London: Murray, 1903. 8th edn. xxvi,540 pp. 133 ills, over 2700 marks. Orig cloth gilt. *(Hollett)* **£20 [≈$30]**
- Old English Plate ... London: Murray, 1906. 9th edn. xxiv,524 pp. 131 ills, over 2600 marks. Orig cloth gilt. *(Hollett)* **£20 [≈$30]**
- Old English Plate ... London: Murray, 1926. 11h edn. xxvi,540 pp. 133 ills, over 2700 marks. Orig cloth gilt, spine lettering sl dulled. *(Hollett)* **£25 [≈$38]**

Critical Observations ...

- Critical Observations on the Buildings and Improvements of London ... see Stuart, James

Cross, A.W.S.

- Public Baths and Wash-Houses: A Treatise on their Planning, Design, Arrangement and Fitting ... London: Batsford, 1906. 4to. 281 pp. Lib stamps on free endpaper. Cvrs rubbed & bumped, sl shaken. *(Monmouth)* **£50 [≈$75]**

Crossley, Fred H.

- English Church Monuments A.D. 1150-1550 ... London: Batsford, 1933. 2nd edn. Sm 4to. x,274 pp. Num ills. Orig cloth gilt. Price-clipped dw (top edge trifle rubbed). *(Hollett)* **£85 [≈$128]**

Crow, Gerald H.

- William Morris Designer. London: Studio, 1934. 120 pp. 4 mtd cold plates, port frontis, 67 plates. One plate sl marked. Orig cloth, sl faded. *(Fine Art)* **£50 [≈$75]**
- William Morris. Designer. London: The Studio Special Winter Number, 1934. 120 pp. 72 ills. Orig cloth. *(Leicester Art Books)* **£45 [≈$68]**

Croydon, Michael

- Ivan Albright. New York: Abbeville, n.d. Folio. 308 pp. 170 plates. Orig cloth. Dw. signed by the artist on pasted-in b'plate. *(Abacus)* **$125 [≈£83]**

Cruikshank, George

- The Comic Almanack, 1835-1847. London: for Charles Tilt, 1835-47. 13 years bound in 3 vols. 8vo. Ills. Orig green cloth, hd of 2 spines v sl worn. *(Spelman)* **£140 [≈$210]**
- Cruikshankiana. An Assemblage of the Most Celebrated Works of George Cruikshank ... London: Mclean, (1835). 1st edn. 1st issue, with McLean imprint on title & plates. Tall folio. Title, 81 ills. Foxed. Orig cloth backed ptd bds, rebacked, edges worn. *(Argonaut)* **$400 [≈£267]**
- Illustrations of Time. London: Published May 1st 1827 by the Artist, sold by Js. Robins. Oblong folio. Etched title, 6 plates. Plate edges dusty & some chipped. Orig ptd wraps, edges frayed, spotted. *(Clark)* **£150 [≈$225]**
- Omnibus ... Edited by Laman Blanchard. London: Bell & Daldy, 1870. 8vo. viii,300 pp. Half mor gilt, t.e.g. *(Robert Frew)* **£60 [≈$90]**

Cruikshank, Isaac Robert

- Lessons of Thrift. Published for general benefit, by a Member of the Save-All Club. London: Thomas Boys, 1820. 1st edn. 8vo. xvi,240 (without the suppressed ff 39-42, 87-110, 163-178, as in all copies). 13 hand cold plates inc frontis & title. Levant mor gilt, a.e.g. Anon. *(Sotheran's)* **£798 [≈$1,197]**

Cruikshank, Robert

- Cruikshank at Home. London: Bohn, 1845. 1st edn thus. 2 vols in one. 319 pp. Num w'engvs. Some foxing. Orig cloth, gilt dec spine. *(Carol Howard)* **£25 [≈$38]**

Crunden, John

- Convenient and Ornamental Architecture, consisting of Original Designs ... London: Taylor, 1791. New edn. 4to. vi,26 pp. 70 plates on 57 sheets. 4 pp ctlg bound in at end. Sl browning & soiling. Contemp calf, rebacked. *(Spelman)* **£380 [≈$570]**

Crutchley, Brooke

- The Cambridge Christmas Books. Brighton: (Cambridge: Rampant Lions Press) 1976. One of 200 (of 220) signed by the author. Orig wraps, spine ends v sl bumped. *(Ulysses Bookshop)* **£45 [≈$68]**
- Two Men. Walter Lewis and Stanley Morison at Cambridge. Cambridge: Christmas, 1968. One of 500. vi,48 pp. Ills, 7 mtd pages from books. Orig buckram backed dec bds. Slipcase. *(Claude Cox)* **£55 [≈$83]**
- The University Printing Houses at Cambridge from the Sixteenth to the Twentieth Century. Cambridge: Christmas, 1962. One of 500. [2],16 pp. Num ills. Orig gilt cloth. Slipcase. *(Claude Cox)* **£32£ [≈$48]**

Crutchley, E.A.

- A History and Description of the Pitt Press ... Cambridge: 1938. Trade edn. Sm 4to. v,36 pp. Fldg frontis, 6 plates. Orig cloth. Dw (sl frayed & soiled). *(Claude Cox)* **£20 [≈$30]**

The Crystal Palace Described and Illustrated ...

- See Tallis, John

Cuevas, Jose Luis

- The Worlds of Kafka & Cuevas. Phila: Falcon Press, 1959. One of 600 (this copy unnumbered). Folio. Ills. Orig bds, sl worn. *(First Folio)* **$285 [≈£190]**

Cummins, D. Duane

- William Robinson Leigh, Western Artist. Norman: Oklahoma UP, 1980. 4to. xvi,204 pp. Num ills. Orig cloth. *(Ars Libri)* **$32.50 [≈£22]**

Cundall, H.M.

- Birket Foster, R.W.S. London: A. & C. Black, 1906. 1st edn. 8vo. xx,216 pp. 73 cold & 20 b/w plates, 58 ills. Orig cloth. *(Lamb)* **£45 [≈$68]**
- Birket Foster. London: 1906. xx,216 pp. 73 cold & 20 b/w plates, 58 text ills. Orig dec cloth, t.e.g., spine sl faded. *(Fine Art)* **£45 [≈$68]**

Cundall, Joseph (editor)

- On Bookbindings, Ancient and Modern. London: 1881. Sm 4to. 28 plates. Some foxing. Morocco backed cloth. *(Traylen)* **£150 [≈$225]**

Cunnington, Phillis

- Costume of Household Servants from the Middle Ages to 1900. London: A. & C. Black, 1974. 1st edn. ix,165 pp. Cold frontis, 48 plates. Orig cloth gilt. Dw. *(Hollett)* **£30 [≈$45]**

Cursiter, Stanley

- Peploe. An Intimate Memoir of an Artist and of his Work. London: Nelson, 1947. 100 pp. 64 plates, 5 text ills. Orig cloth. *(Leicester Art Books)* **£42 [≈$63]**

Curtis, Charles B.

- Velazquez and Murillo. A Descriptive and Historical Catalogue ... London & New York: 1983. Sm 4to. xxxvii,424 pp. 4 plates. Orig cloth. *(Washton)* **$125 [≈£83]**

Curtis, W.J.R.

- Modern Architecture since 1900. London: Phaidon, 1982. Sm 4to. 416 pp. Ills. Dw. *(Monmouth)* **£30 [≈$45]**

Cushion, J.P.

- Pottery & Porcelain Tablewares. London: Studio Vista, 1976. 1st edn. Lge 8vo. 240 pp. Ills. Orig cloth. Dw. *(Hollett)* **£30 [≈$45]**

Cust, A.M.

- The Ivory Workers of the Middle Ages. London: George Bell & Sons, 1902. 1st edn. Sm 8vo. xix,170 pp. 37 plates. Free endpapers browned. Orig cloth gilt, spine lettering sl faded. *(Hollett)* **£22.50 [≈$35]**

Cutler, Thomas W.

- A Grammar of Japanese Ornament and Design ... London: Batsford, 1880. 1st edn. Folio. xi,[1],31,[1] pp. 58 plates. Orig pict cloth, sl soiled. *(Bookpress)* **$1,250 [≈£833]**

Cutts, Edward L.

- A Manual for the Study of the Sepulchral Slabs and Crosses of the Middle Ages. London: John Henry Parker, 1849. 8vo. vi,[ii],93 pp. 84 plates. Occas spotting. Orig cloth gilt, reprd, edges sl rubbed. *(Hollett)* **£35 [≈$53]**

Czwiklitzer, Christopher

- Picasso's Posters. New York: Random House, 1970-71. 1st Amer edn. Folio. 365

pp. Num ills. Orig cloth. Dw (chipped). *(First Folio)* **$285 [≈£190]**

Dafforne, James

- Pictures by Sir A.W. Callcott. London: Virtue, Spalding, (1878). 74 pp. 11 engvd plates. Orig dec cloth gilt, t.e.g., v sl worn. *(Fine Art)* **£90 [≈$135]**

Dahl, George Leighton

- Portals, Doorways and Windows of France. New York: Architectural Book Co., 1925. 4to. 209 plates. Orig cloth. Dw. *(Sotheran's)* **£55 [≈$83]**

Daix, Pierre & Rosselet, Joan

- Picasso. The Cubist Years 1907-1916. A Catalogue Raisonne of the Paintings and related Works. London: Thames & Hudson, 1979. 376 pp. 1059 ills. Orig cloth. Dw. *(Leicester Art Books)* **£65 [≈$98]**

Dali, Salvador

- Dali, 50 Secrets of Magic Craftsmanship. New York: Dial Press, 1948. 1st edn in English. 4to. 192 pp. Frontis, ills. Orig cloth, sl rubbed. *(Bookpress)* **$150 [≈£100]**
- Salvador Dali. New York: Julian Levy Gallery, 1939. 4to. Ills. Orig pict wraps, centre crease. *(Black Sun)* **$550 [≈£367]**

Dalton, O.M.

- Byzantine Art and Archaeology. Oxford: Clarendon Press 1911. 8vo. xix,727 pp. Frontis, 457 ills. Orig cloth gilt, t.e.g., spine sl rubbed & reprd. *(Quest Books)* **£85 [≈$128]**

Dalziel, George & Edward

- The Brothers Dalziel. A Record of Fifty Years' Work ... London: Methuen, 1901. xii,360 pp. 143 plates. Orig cloth gilt, t.e.g. Signed by Edward Dalziel. *(Leicester Art Books)* **£60 [≈$90]**

Damase, Jacques & Delaunay, Sonia

- Rhythms and Colours. London: Thames & Hudson, 1972. 412 pp. 338 ills. Orig cloth. Dw. *(Leicester Art Books)* **£110 [≈$165]**

Damaz, Paul

- Art in European Architecture. New York: Reinhold, (1956). 1st edn. 4to. xii,228 pp. Frontis, ills. Orig cloth. Dw (used). *(Bookpress)* **$45 [≈£30]**

Damjan, Mischa

- The False Flamingoes. Illustrated by Ralph Steadman. London: 1968. 1st edn. 4to. Ills. Orig bndg, spine ends bumped. Dw (sl rubbed and creased). Sgnd by Steadman. *(Ulysses Bookshop)* **£65 [≈$98]**

Damon, Bertha

- Green Corners. London: Michael Joseph, 1947. 1st edn. 191 pp. 6 cold ills by Clare Leighton. Orig cloth. Dw (hd of spine trifle frayed). *(Hollett)* **£18 [≈$27]**

Dana, Charles A. & Johnson, Rossiter

- Fifty Perfect Poems. New York: Appleton, 1882. 4to. 203 pp. 72 ills. Orig red silk gilt. *(Rona Schneider)* **$50 [≈£33]**

d'Ancona, P. & Aeschlimann, E.

- The Art of Illumination. An Anthology of Manuscripts from the Sixth to the Sixteenth Century. London: 1969. Lge 4to. 235 pp. 146 plates (24 mtd cold). Orig cloth. Dw. *(Washton)* **$85 [≈£57]**

Daniel, Glyn E.

- The Prehistoric Chamber Tombs of England and Wales. Cambridge: UP, 1950. 16 plates, 33 figs. Orig cloth. Dw (torn). *(Peter Bell)* **£25 [≈$38]**

Daniel, W.B.

- Rural Sports. London: 1801-13. 3 vols. Roy 8vo. 10,535; 4,378; 6,356 pp. 68 plates inc titles, 2 tables (1 dble-page). Occas sl foxing. Orig calf, rebacked. *(Phenotype)* **£188 [≈$282]**

Daniell, A.E.

- London City Churches. London: Constable, 1907. 2nd edn. 8vo. 394 pp. Map, 14 plates. Orig cloth gilt, spine sl faded. *(Hollett)* **£25 [≈$38]**

Daniell, Frederick B.

- Richard Cosway. A Catalogue Raisonne of the Engraved Works. London: Frederick Daniel, 1890. xvi,68 pp. Frontis. Orig bds, t.e.g., some wear spine. *(Leicester Art Books)* **£40 [≈$60]**

Daniels, Jeffery

- Sebastiano Ricci. Hove: Wayland, 1976. xx,172 pp. 379 ills. Orig cloth. Dw. Slipcase. *(Leicester Art Books)* **£80 [≈$120]**

Dante Alighieri

- The Vision of Hell. Translated by the Rev Henry Francis Cary, and Illustrated with the Designs of M. Gustave Dore. New Edition ... London: Cassell Petter & Galpin, 1866. Folio. W'cut frontis, 75 w'cut ills. Contemp three qtr mor gilt, spine sl rubbed. *(Wilkinson)* **£65 [≈$98]**

- The Vision of Purgatory and Paradise. Translated by the Rev Henry Francis Cary, and Illustrated with the Designs of M. Gustave Dore. New Edition ... London: Cassell & Co., [ca 1900]. 4to. W'cut frontis, 59 w'cut ills. Orig dec cloth gilt, dusty, extrs worn. *(Wilkinson)* **£19 [≈$29]**

Darracott, Joseph

- The First World War in Posters, from the Imperial War Museum, London. New York: Dover, (1974). 4to. xxiii,72 pp. 71 ills. Orig cloth. Dw (sl torn). *(Oak Knoll)* **$45 [≈£30]**

Darton, F.J. Harvey

- Children's Books in England: Five Centuries of Social Life. Second Edition, with Introduction by Kathleen Lines. Cambridge: UP, 1960. 367 pp. 8 plates. Orig cloth. Dw (soiled). *(Peter Bell)* **£36 [≈$54]**
- Modern Book Illustration in Great Britain and America. London: The Studio, 1931. 1st edn. Sm folio. Num plates, ills. Orig cloth gilt. Dw (sl faded & foxed). *(Words Etcetera)* **£65 [≈$98]**
- Modern Book Illustration in Great Britain and America. London: The Studio, 1931. 1st edn. 4to. 144 pp. Num ills. Occas foxing. Crnrs bumped. Dw (frayed). *(Waddington)* **£36 [≈$54]**

Darwin, Charles

- On the Origin of Species ... Illustrated with Wood Engravings by Paul Landacre. New York: The Limited Editions Club, 1963. One of 1500 signed by Landacre. Sm 4to. Orig qtr leather. Slipcase. *(Oak Knoll)* **$95 [≈£63]**

Daudet, Alphonse

- Tartarin of Tarascon. With Drawings by W.A. Dwiggins. New York: The Limited Editions Club, 1930. One of 1500 signed by Dwiggins. 12mo. Orig cloth & bds (hd of spine sl worn). *(Oak Knoll)* **$95 [≈£63]**

Daulby, Daniel

- A Descriptive Catalogue of the Works of Rembrandt, and of his Scholars, Bol, Livens, and Van Vliet, compiled from the Original Etchings, and from the Catalogues. Liverpool: M'Creery, 1796. 1st edn. 8vo. Errata leaf. Frontis. Contemp half mor, spine sl rubbed. *(Spelman)* **£140 [≈$210]**

Daulte, Francois

- Auguste Renoir: Watercolours and Pastels. New York: Abrams, (1959). Folio. 24 mtd cold plates. Orig qtr cloth. *(Abacus)* **$60 [≈£40]**

Daval, Jean-Luc

- Avant-Garde Art, 1914-1939. New York: Skira, Rizzoli, 1980. Folio. 223 pp. 345 ills. Orig cloth. Dw. *(Ars Libri)* **$85 [≈£57]**

Davenport, C.

- Cameos. London: Seeley & Co., 1900. Cr 4to. viii,66,[6 ctlg] pp. Cold frontis, 7 plates, 20 ills. Lacks front free endpaper. Orig cloth gilt. *(Clevedon Books)* **£75 [≈$113]**

Davidson, Ellis A.

- A Practical Manual of House Painting, Graining, Marbling and Sign Writing. London: Crosby & Lockwood, 1896. 7th edn. 394 pp. 8 cold plates, ills. Orig cloth, spine snagged, worn. *(Willow House)* **£40 [≈$60]**

Davidson, Hugh Coleman (editor)

- The Book of the Home. London: Gresham Publishing, 1905. 1st edn. 8 vols. Cold plates, ills. Orig cloth, sl worn. *(Bookpress)* **$375 [≈£250]**
- The Book of the Home: a Practical Guide to Household Management. London: Gresham Publishing Co., 1908. 8 vols. Tall 8vo. Half-titles. Frontis, cold & other plates, ills. Orig dec cloth, sl dulled. *(Jarndyce)* **£150 [≈$225]**

Davidson, Marshall B.

- The Drawing of America. Eyewitness to History. New York: Abrams, 1983. 256 pp. 308 plates, ills. Orig cloth. Dw. *(Clarice Davis)* **$85 [≈£57]**

Davie, Alan

- Alan Davie. Edited by Alan Bowness. London: Lund Humphries, 1967. 1st edn. Lge 4to. Num cold & b/w plates. Orig pict bds. *(Clearwater)* **£120 [≈$180]**

Davie, W. Galsworthy

- Old English Doorways. A Series of Historical Examples from Tudor Times ... London: Batsford, 1903. 1st edn. Lge 8vo. xii,44 pp. 70 plates, 34 ills. Endpapers spotted. Orig cloth gilt, sl marked & stained. *(Hollett)* **£65 [≈$98]**
- Old English Doorways. A Series of Historical Examples from Tudor Times to the End of the XVIII Century ... Notes ... by H. Tanner. London: Batsford, 1903. 1st edn. Lge 8vo. xii,44,[24 ctlg] pp. 70 plates, 34 ills. Occas spots. Orig cloth. *(Bow Windows)* **£50 [≈$75]**

Davies, Gerald S.

- Frans Hals. London: George Bell, 1902. 1st

edn. 4to. Frontis (spotted), dec title, plates, ills. Few plates sl spotted. Orig vellum backed cloth bds, t.e.g., v sl rubbed. *(Wilkinson)* **£29 [≈$44]**

Davies, Hugh William

- Catalogue of a Collection of Early French Books in the Library of C. Fairfax Murray. London: The Holland Press, 1961. 4to. xvi, 600; [iv],601-1096 pp. Orig cloth. Dws. *(Bookpress)* **$375 [≈£250]**

Davies, Martin

- Rogier van der Weyden. An Essay, with a Critical Catalogue of Paintings assigned to him and to Robert Campin. London: 1972. Lge 4to. 272 pp. Num plates. Orig cloth. *(Washton)* **$250 [≈£167]**

Da Vinci, Leonardo

- The Drawings. With an Introduction and Notes by A.E. Popham. London: 1946. Sm 4to. 320 plates. Orig buckram. *(Traylen)* **£25 [≈$38]**
- The Notebooks. Arranged, rendered into English and Introduced by Edward MacCurdy. London: 1945. 2 vols. Sm 4to. Num plates. Orig buckram. *(Traylen)* **£40 [≈$60]**

Davis, Charles H.S.

- The Egyptian Book of the Dead ... New York & London: Putnam, 1895. Folio. 186,xx,lxxix pp. 99 plates. Orig cloth, sl rubbed & dulled. *(Terramedia)* **$250 [≈£167]**

Davis, Derek C. & Middlemas, Keith

- Coloured Glass. London: Jenkins, 1968. 4to. 119 pp. 96 cold plates. Dw. *(Paul Brown)* **£20 [≈$30]**

Davis, Hubert

- The Symbolic Drawings of Hubert Davis for An American Tragedy by Theodore Dreiser. New York: Horace Liveright, 1930. One of 525. Folio. 4 pp. 20 litho ills. Orig dec bds. *(Rona Schneider)* **$40 [≈£27]**

Dawe, George

- The Life of George Morland. With an Introduction and Notes by J.J. Foster. London: Dickinsons, 1904. One of 500. xxxiv,196 pp. 52 plates. Orig cloth, spine worn. *(Leicester Art Books)* **£80 [≈$120]**

Dawson, Nelson

- Goldsmiths' and Silversmiths' Work. London: Methuen, Connoisseur's Library, 1907. 4to. xx,267,[4 advt] pp. Frontis, 127 plates, 4 text figs. Endpapers & advts foxed. Orig cloth gilt. *(Hollett)* **£90 [≈$135]**

Day, Lal Behair

- Folk Tales of Bengal. Illustrated by Warwick Goble. London: Macmillan, 1912. 1st edn. Lge 8vo. 247 pp. 32 cold ills. Orig elab gilt cloth. *(Davidson)* **$285 [≈£190]**

Day, Langston

- The Life and Art of W. Heath Robinson. London: Joseph, 1947. 270 pp. 18 plates, 24 ills. Orig cloth. *(Leicester Art Books)* **£25 [≈$38]**

Day, Lewis F.

- Nature and Ornament ... London: Batsford, 1909. xv,284,[24 advt] pp. Over 300 ills. Half-title sl browned. Orig cloth, t.e.g., hinges cracked, spine sl discold. *(Francis Edwards)* **£45 [≈$68]**
- Nature in Ornament. London: Batsford, 1902. 8vo. xxiii,[i],260 pp. 123 plates. Orig cloth gilt, t.e.g., sl edgewear. *(Bookpress)* **$225 [≈£150]**
- Ornamental Design ... London: Batsford, 1897. 4th edn, rvsd. 12mo. Orig cloth gilt, sl worn. *(Bookpress)* **$210 [≈£140]**
- Pattern Design. A Book for Students ... London: Batsford, 1903. 1st edn. 8vo. xx,267 pp. Errata slip. 285 ills. Orig cloth gilt. *(Fenning)* **£24.50 [≈$38]**

Day, Lewis F. & Buckle, Mary

- Art in Needlework, a Book about Embroidery. London: Batsford, 1900. 1st edn. 12mo. xxi,[i], 262,[12] pp. 30 ills. Occas foxing. Orig cloth, front inner hinge cracked. *(Bookpress)* **$125 [≈£83]**

De Baye, The Baron J.

- The Industrial Arts of the Anglo-Saxons. Translated by T.B. Harbottle. London: Swan Sonnenschein, 1893. 4to. xii,135 pp. 17 litho plates. Orig dec cloth gilt, extrs trifle worn, sl shaken. *(Hollett)* **£75 [≈$113]**

De Bock, Th.

- Jacob Maris. London: Alexander Moring, The De La More Press; Amsterdam: Scheltema & Holkema, (1904). One of 100. 182 pp. Port frontis, 90 plates. Orig vellum cvrd bds gilt. *(Leicester Art Books)* **£110 [≈$165]**

De Bosschere, Jean

- The Closed Door. London: John Lane; The Bodley Head, 1917. 1st edn. Ills by the

author. Some foxing. Orig bndg.
(Alphabet) **$40 [≈£27]**

- Marthe and the Madman. New York: Covici, Friede, 1928. One of 275 signed by the author. 8vo. Cold frontis, ills. Orig cloth backed dec bds, uncut, extrs rubbed, orig crease to paper of lower bd. *(Sotheran's)* **£168 [≈$252]**

Defoe, Daniel

- A Journal of the Plague Year ... Embellish'd with notable Illustrations by Signor Domenico Gnoli, of Rome. Bloomfield: The Limited Editions Club, 1968. One of 1500 signed by Gnoli. Tall 8vo. Orig cloth, leather label. Slipcase. *(Oak Knoll)* **$55 [≈£37]**
- The Life and Strange Adventures of Robinson Crusoe of York. Introduced by Edward A. Craig. Illustrated by Edward Gordon Craig. London: Basilisk Press, 1979. One of 25 (of 515) with 10 orig prints bound in. 4to. 180 pp. Orig gilt dec mor. Orig box. *(Cooper Hay)* **£580 [≈$870]**
- Roxana, The Fortunate Mistress. Woodcuts by Bernard Kroeber. Avon, CT: The Limited Editions Club, 1976. One of 2000 signed by Kroeber. 4to. Orig cloth. Slipcase. *(Oak Knoll)* **$55 [≈£37]**

Degenhardt, R.K.

- Belleek. The Complete Collector's Guide and Illustrated Reference. New York: 1978. Lge 4to. Ills. Dw. *(Emerald Isle)* **£45 [≈$68]**

De Guillebon, Regine de Plinval

- Porcelain of Paris, 1770-1850. Translated by Robin R. Charleston. New York: Walker, (1972). 4to. 362 pp. 242 ills. Orig cloth gilt. Dw. *(Karmiole)* **$150 [≈£100]**

de la Faille, J.-B.

- The Works of Vincent Van Gogh: His Paintings and Drawings. New York: Reynal, Morrow, (1970). Folio. 703 pp. 56 cold plates, num ills. Orig cloth. Dw (sl chipped). *(Abacus)* **$100 [≈£67]**

Delafield, E.M.

- The Diary of a Provincial Lady. Illustrated by Nicholas Bentley. London: Folio Society, 1979. Ills. Orig pict cloth. Slipcase. *(Margaret Nangle)* **£25 [≈$38]**

Delaisse, L.M.J.

- A Century of Dutch Manuscript Illumination. Berkeley: Calif UP, 1968. 1st edn. Folio. xii,102 pp. Num ills. Orig cloth gilt. *(Karmiole)* **$65 [≈£43]**

Delamotte, Phillip H.

- The Art of Sketching from Nature. London: G. Bell, 1888. 2nd edn. 69 pp. 20 mtd chromolitho plates, engvs. Orig cloth gilt, crnrs sl rubbed. *(Willow House)* **£65 [≈$98]**

Delaney, Paul

- The Lithographs of Charles Shannon. London: 1978. One of 400. 56 pp. 15 plates. Orig wraps. *(Leicester Art Books)* **£36 [≈$54]**

Delvaux, Paul

- The Drawings of Paul Delvaux. New York: Grove Press, (1968). 1st edn. Lge 4to. 112,[8] pp. 112 ills. Orig cloth. Dw. *(Karmiole)* **$85 [≈£57]**

De Mare, Eric

- The Victorian Woodblock Illustrators. London: Gordon Fraser, 1980. 1st edn. Oblong 4to. 200 pp. Num ills. Orig cloth backed bds. Dw (torn). *(Waddington)* **£30 [≈$45]**

De Morant, G.S.

- A History of Chinese Art from Ancient Times to the Present Day. Translated by G.C. Wheeler. London: Harrap, 1931. Sm 4to. 296 pp. 80 plates, 73 text ills. Orig cloth gilt. *(Clevedon Books)* **£25 [≈$38]**

Demus, Otto

- Byzantine Art and the West. London: Weidenfeld & Nicholson, (1970). 4to. xxi,274 pp. Errata slip. Num ills. Orig cloth. *(Schoyer)* **$50 [≈£33]**
- Byzantine Art and the West. New York: 1970. 4to. xxi,274 pp. 272 ills (8 cold). Orig cloth. *(Washton)* **$85 [≈£57]**
- Romanesque Mural Painting. New York: 1970. Lge 4to. 654 pp. 324 plates (102 cold mtd). Orig cloth. Dw. *(Washton)* **$165 [≈£110]**

De Musset, Alfred

- Fantasio. A Comedy in Two Acts. Translated by Maurice Baring. The Pleiad: 1929. One of 550. 4to. 58 pp. 2 hand cold & 10 litho ills by Fernand Giauque. Orig silk, spine faded. *(Claude Cox)* **£85 [≈$128]**

De Nerval, Gerard

- Dreams & Life. La Reve et la Vie. Translated by Vyvyan Holland. London: The First Edition Club; Manaton, Devon: The Boar's Head Press, 1933. One of 450 (this unnumbered). [6],88 pp. Ills by Lettice Sandford. Orig dec cloth, t.e.g. *(Claude Cox)* **£45 [≈$68]**

Dening, C.F.W.

- The Eighteenth Century Architecture of Bristol. Bristol: Arrowsmith, 1923. Lge 4to. xxiv,192 pp. 69 mtd photo plates, text ills. Orig cloth. *(Sotheran's)* **£90 [≈$135]**
- The Eighteenth Century Architecture of Bristol. London: Arrowsmith, 1923. 1st edn. Lge 4to. 69 plates. Lib stamps. Sl dusty & fingered. Lib bndg. *(Monmouth)* **£50 [≈$75]**

Denton, J.B.

- The Farm Homesteads of England. A Collection of Plans of English Homesteads ... London: 1864. Lge folio. xv,186 pp. Frontis, 68 plates & plans. Occas foxing. Orig calf, gilt spine. *(Phenotype)* **£295 [≈$443]**

de Palol, Pedro

- Paleochristian Art in Spain. New York: 1969. Sq 4to. 377 pp. Num ills. Orig cloth. Dw. *(Washton)* **$90 [≈£60]**

De Quincey, Thomas

- Confessions of an English Opium-Eater. With Twelve Lithographs drawn on the Stone by Zhenya Gay. New York: The Limited Editions Club, 1930. One of 1520 signed by Gay & by the printer, B.H. Newdigate. Tall 4to. Orig cloth-backed bds, t.e.g. (worn & spotted). *(Oak Knoll)* **$35 [≈£23]**

De Ricci, Seymour

- English Collectors of Books & Manuscripts (1530-1930) and their marks of Ownership. London: 1960. 8vo. 8 plates, text ills. Orig cloth. Dw. *(Traylen)* **£18 [≈$27]**
- French Signed Bindings in the Mortimer L. Schiff Collection. New York: 1935. 4 vols. 613; 161 pp. 413 plates. Few sm lib marks. Orig buckram. *(Hermitage)* **$1,750 [≈£1,167]**

Derrick, Thomas

- The Prodigal Son and Other Parables shown in Pictures. Shakespeare Head Press: 1931. 1st edn. Ills. Orig leather backed pict bds. Dw (worn). *(Margaret Nangle)* **£16 [≈$24]**

Derry, Georges

- The Lithographs of Charles Shannon: with a Catalogue of Lithographs issued between the years 1904-1918. London: R.A. Walker, 1920. One of 100. Orig card wraps, spine strengthened. *(Fine Art)* **£20 [≈$30]**

De Sausmarez, Maurice

- Bridget Riley. London: Studio Vista, 1970. One of 110 specially bound & signed by the artist. 128 pp. 90 ills. Orig PVC cvrd bds. Glassine dw. *(Leicester Art Books)* **£90 [≈$135]**

Descargues, Pierre

- Picasso. New York: Felicie, 1974. 4to. Ills. Orig dec cloth. Dw. *(First Folio)* **$90 [≈£60]**

Descharnes, Robert

- Salvador Dali. New York: Abrams, 1976. Sm folio. 175 pp. 199 ills. Orig cloth. Dw. *(Ars Libri)* **$45 [≈£30]**
- The World of Salvador Dali. London: Macmillan, 1962. 1st edn. 4to. 228 pp. Mtd cold plates, ills. Dw (sl worn). *(Spelman)* **£45 [≈$68]**

Descharnes, Robert & Chabrun, Jean-Francois

- Auguste Rodin. New York: Viking, (1967). 4to. 283 pp. Num mtd cold plates, ills. Orig cloth. *(Abacus)* **$75 [≈£50]**

Descriptive ...

- A Descriptive Catalogue of the Prints of Rembrandt ... see Wilson, Thomas

Deuchler, Florens, & others

- The Cloisters Apocalypse. An Early 14th Century Manuscript in Facsimile. New York: Metropolitan Museum of Art, (1971). 1st edn. 2 vols. 4to. Ills. Orig buckram. Slipcase (sl worn). *(J &J House)* **$50 [≈£33]**

Devinne, Theodore L.

- Modern Methods of Book Composition. New York: Century, 1904. 1st edn. 8vo. Orig cloth, leather label. *(Book Block)* **$70 [≈£47]**
- Plain Printing Types. New York: Century Co., 1900. 1st edn. 8vo. 403 pp. Cloth, leather label dry, extrs sl worn. *(The Veatchs)* **$50 [≈£33]**

De Vries, Leonard

- Victorian Advertisements, compiled in collaboration with Ilonka Van Amstel ... Text by James Laver. London: Murray, (1968). 4to. 136 pp. Ills. Orig cloth. Dw (some tears). *(Oak Knoll)* **$65 [≈£43]**

d'Hulst, R.-A.

- Jacob Jordaens. London: Sotheby, (1982). Folio. 375 pp. 252 ills. Orig cloth. Dw. *(Abacus)* **$50 [≈£33]**

Dibdin, Thomas Frognall

- Bibliomania: or Book-Madness; a Bibliographical Romance ... New and

Improved Edition ... London: Chatto & Windus, 1876. 8vo. xviii,618,xxxiv pp. Plates, ills inc mtd photos. Orig roan backed cloth, hd of spine reprd.
(Claude Cox) **£75 [≈$113]**

Dickens, Charles

- American Notes for General Circulation. With an Introduction by Angus Wilson. Illustrations by Raymond F. Houlihan. Avon, CT: The Limited Editions Club, 1975. One of 2000 signed by Houlihan. 8vo. Orig qtr leather. Slipcase. *(Oak Knoll)* **$55 [≈£37]**
- The Chimes. Illustrated by Arthur Rackham. London: George W. Jones for the Limited Editions Club, 1931. 1st edn thus. One of 1500 sgnd by Rackham. Prospectus laid in. Orig pict buckram gilt, t.e.g., spine sl worn. Pict box (sl worn). *(Mac Donnell)* **$675 [≈£450]**
- The Chimes. Introduction by Edward Wagenknecht. Illustrated by Arthur Rackham. London: for the Limited Editions Club, 1931. One of 1500 signed by Rackham. B/w ills. Orig dec cloth, spine darkened. Slipcase (sl worn). *(Argonaut)* **$375 [≈£250]**
- A Christmas Carol. Illustrated by Arthur Rackham. London: Heinemann, (1915). One of 525 signed by the author. Sm folio. 12 mtd cold plates, b/w ills. Orig vellum gilt, lacks ties, few tiny spots rear cvr. *(Jo Ann Reisler)* **$2,750 [≈£1,833]**
- Dickens's Children. Illustrated by Jessie W. Smith. New York: Scribner, 1912. 1st edn. 8vo. 10 cold ills. Orig cloth, pict onlay, crnrs bumped, spine ends v sl defective. *(Davidson)* **$150 [≈£100]**
- Hard Times for These Times. Illustrated by Charles Raymond. New York: The Limited Editions Club, 1966. One of 1500 signed by Raymond. 8vo. Orig cloth & bds. Slipcase. *(Oak Knoll)* **$55 [≈£37]**
- The Humour of Dickens. Chosen by R.J. Cruikshank with Illustrations by Modern Artists. London: [1952]. 1st edn. Ills. Orig wraps. Dw (sl marked & torn). *(Blakeney)* **£25 [≈$38]**
- The Life and Adventures of Martin Chuzzlewit. Illustrated by C.E. Brock. London: Harrap, 1932. 8vo. 752 pp. 16 cold plates. Orig cloth, sl faded. *(Sotheran's)* **£36 [≈$54]**
- The Old Curiosity Shop. Illustrated by Frank Reynolds. London: Hodder & Stoughton, [ca 1900-10]. One of 350 sgnd by Reynolds. Cold plates. Orig vellum. *(Old Cathay)* **£175 [≈$263]**
- The Personal History of David Copperfield. Illustrated by Frank Reynolds. London: Westminster Press, [ca 1910]. 20 cold plates. Orig dec cloth gilt. *(Old Cathay)* **£60 [≈$90]**
- The Personal History of David Copperfield. Illustrated by Frank Reynolds. London: Westminster Press, [ca 1911]. 4to. 572 pp. 20 mtd cold plates, pict endpapers. Orig pict cloth gilt. Dw. *(Carol Howard)* **£55 [≈$83]**

Dickson, Robert & Edmond, J.P.

- Annals of Scottish Printing ... to the Beginning of the Seventeenth Century. Cambridge: 1890. One of 500 signed by the author. 4to. 73 ills. Orig cloth gilt. *(Traylen)* **£85 [≈$128]**

Diehl, Edith

- Bookbinding, Its Background and Technique. New York: Rinehart, 1946. 1st edn. 2 vols. 8vo. Orig cloth. Slipcase (broken). *(Bookpress)* **$200 [≈£133]**

Digby, George Wingfield

- Meaning and Symbol in Three Modern Artists: Edvard Munch, Henry Moore and Paul Nash. London: Faber, 1955. 204 pp. 57 plates. Orig cloth. Dw (sl worn). *(Fine Art)* **£30 [≈$45]**

Dilley, Arthur Urban

- Oriental Rugs and Carpets. A Comprehensive Study. Revised by Maurice S. Mimmand. Philadelphia & New York: 1959. Rvsd edn. 4to. xxi,289 pp. Cold frontis, 74 plates, 7 maps. Sev lib stamps. Orig cloth, spine v sl faded. *(Francis Edwards)* **£55 [≈$83]**

Dillon, Edward

- Glass. London: Methuen, 1907. Cr 4to. 374 pp. 49 plates (11 cold inc frontis). Foxed. Orig bndg. *(Paul Brown)* **£95 [≈$143]**

Diringer, David

- The Hand-Produced Book. London: 1953. 8vo. x,603 pp. Num ills. Orig cloth. Dw (worn). *(Washton)* **$50 [≈£33]**

Ditchfield, P.H.

- The Manor Houses of England. Illustrated by Sydney R. Jones. London: Batsford, 1910. 1st edn. Lge 8vo. viii,211,[iv] pp. Cold frontis, num ills. Few spots to endpapers. Orig pict cloth, rubbed. *(Hollett)* **£25 [≈$38]**

Dobson, Austin

- The Story of Rosina and Other Verses. Illustrated by Hugh Thomson. London:

Kegan Paul ..., 1895. 1st edn. Sm 8vo. Orig dec red cloth, t.e.g., minor wear & darkening. *(Antic Hay)* **$45 [≈£30]**

- The Story of Rosina and Other Verses. Illustrated by Hugh Thomson. London: Kegan Paul, 1895. 1st edn thus. 8vo. 115 pp. Frontis, 14 plates, num ills. Orig elab gilt cloth, t.e.g. *(Marjorie James)* **£18 [≈$27]**
- Thomas Bewick and His Pupils. Boston: Osgood, 1884. One of 90 (of 200 deluxe) for America. 4to. 232 pp. Num ills. Orig cloth, paper labels. *(First Folio)* **$250 [≈£167]**
- Thomas Bewick and his Pupils. London: 1899. Cr 8vo. xviii,232 pp. 95 ills. Orig cloth, spine faded. *(Wheldon & Wesley)* **£45 [≈$68]**
- William Hogarth. London: Sampson Low, 1891. 1st edn. Lge 8vo. xiv,368 pp. Frontis, 11 plates, 47 ills. Orig cloth gilt, hd of spine worn. *(Spelman)* **£16 [≈$24]**
- William Hogarth. With an Introduction on Hogarth's Workmanship by Sir Walter Armstrong. London: Heinemann, 1902. 1st edn. Lge 4to. xiii,[i],248 pp. 77 plates, text ills. Orig cloth, faded. *(Spelman)* **£40 [≈$60]**
- William Hogarth. London: Heinemann, 1907. New & enlgd edn. xix,310 pp. 76 ills. Orig cloth. *(Leicester Art Books)* **£26 [≈$39]**

Dockstader, Frederick

- Indian Art of Central America. London: Cory, Adams & Mackay, 1964. 4to. 221 pp. Cold & bw ills. Orig cloth. Dw. *(Cooper Hay)* **£30 [≈$45]**

Dr Comicus ...

- Dr Comicus or the Frolics of Fortune. A Comic, Satirical Poem for the Squeamish and the Queer in Twelve Cantos. By a Surgeon. London: Jaques and Wright, 1828. 8vo. Title & 14 aquatint plates, all hand cold. Sl spotting. 2 sm reprs. Three qtr calf gilt, rubbed. *(Barbara Stone)* **£175 [≈$263]**

Dodgson, Campbell

- A Catalogue of Etchings by Augustus John, 1901-1914. London: Charles Chenil, 1920. One of 325. xii,152 pp. 152 ills. Orig cloth. *(Leicester Art Books)* **£200 [≈$300]**
- The Etchings of Charles Meryon. London: The Studio, 1921. vii,28 pp. 47 plates. Orig vellum backed bds, t.e.g. *(Leicester Art Books)* **£55 [≈$83]**
- The Etchings of Sir David Wilkie and Andrew Geddes: A Catalogue. London: Print Collectors' Club, 1936. One of 425. 52 pp. 43 ills. Orig cloth & bds, sl worn. *(Fine Art)* **£40 [≈$60]**
- An Iconography of the Engravings of Stephen Gooden. With Preface and Introduction ... London: Elkin Mathews, 1944. One of 500. 4to. Errata slip. 191 plates. Orig buckram gilt. *(Claude Cox)* **£80 [≈$120]**
- An Iconography of the Engravings of Stephen Gooden. London: Elkin Mathews, 1944. One of 500. xvi,198 pp. 200 ills. Orig cloth gilt. *(Leicester Art Books)* **£70 [≈$105]**
- The Masters of Engraving and Etching. Albrecht Durer. London & Boston: Medici Society, 1926. xii,145 pp. 121 ills. Orig cloth. *(Leicester Art Books)* **£25 [≈$38]**
- Prints in the Dotted Manner and other Metal-Cuts of the XV Century in the Department of Prints and Drawings, British Museum. London: BM, 1937. Imperial 4to. Cold frontis, 130 ills on 43 plates. Orig buckram gilt. *(Blackwell's)* **£100 [≈$150]**
- Some Drawings of the English School. London: Print Collectors' Club, 1948. One of 400. ix,13 pp. 40 plates. Orig cloth. *(Clarice Davis)* **$40 [≈£27]**

Doesburg, Theo Van

- Principles of Neo-Plastic Art. Greenwich: New York Graphic Society, 1968. 4to. x,73 pp. 33 ills. Orig cloth. *(Ars Libri)* **$60 [≈£40]**

Doggett, Kate Newell

- The Grammar of Painting and Engraving. New York: Hurd & Houghton, 1875. 8vo. 330 pp. 43 ills. Red & green leather, silk endpapers. *(Rona Schneider)* **$120 [≈£80]**

Dolez, Albane

- Glass Animals. 3,500 Years of Artistry and Design. New York: Abrams, 1988. 4to. 224 pp. 100 cold & 200 b/w plates. Dw, fine. *(Paul Brown)* **£32 [≈$48]**

Dollman, Francis T.

- Examples of Antient Pulpits existing in England ... London: George Bell & the Author, 1849. 4to. 32 pp. 30 plates (3 printed in colour). Some foxing. Orig cloth, sl worn & darkened. *(Spelman)* **£45 [≈$68]**

Dolman, Bernard (editor)

- A Dictionary of Contemporary British Artists 1929. Antique Collectors' Club: 1984. 561 pp. Orig cloth. Dw. *(Fine Art)* **£25 [≈$38]**

The Dolphin

- The Dolphin. A Journal of the Making of Books. Volume I. New York: Limited Editions Club, 1933. 4to. [viii], 363, [19] pp. Orig cloth. *(Oak Knoll)* **$125 [≈£83]**

- The Dolphin. A Journal of the Making of Books. Volume IV. Nos 1-3. New York: Limited Editions Club, 1940. Complete set of vol 4. 4to. Orig cloth, spine ends sl worn. *(Oak Knoll)* **$100 [≈£67]**
- The Dolphin. A Journal of the Making of Books. Volume II. New York: Limited Editions Club, 1935. 4to. 329, [20] pp. Orig cloth. *(Oak Knoll)* **$100 [≈£67]**
- The Dolphin, Number One [to Number Four]. New York: Limited Editions Club, 1933-41. 6 vols, complete. 4to. Orig cloth, vol 1 cvrs foxed. *(The Veatchs)* **$650 [≈£433]**

Donaldson, Thomas Leverton

- Architectural Maxims and Theorems ... London: J. Weale, 1847. 1st edn. 8vo. xii,105,9 pp. Endpapers spotted. Orig cloth gilt, faded. *(Hollett)* **£55 [≈$83]**

Donne, John

- The Flea. With a Design in Relief by Willow Legge. Guildford: Circle Press [Ron King], 1977. One of 75 signed by the artist. Orig stiff wraps, back cvr v sl faded. *(Michael Taylor)* **£30 [≈$45]**

Donovan, Richard E. & Murdoch, Joseph S.F.

- The Game of Golf and the Printed Word 1566-1985. Endicott, New York: Castalio Press, 1987. Lge 8vo. 658 pp. Orig cloth. Dw. *(First Folio)* **$45 [≈£30]**

Dore, Gustave

- Cassell's Dore Gallery ... With Memoir of Dore, Critical Essay and Descriptive Letterpress by Edmund Ollier. London: Cassell & Co., [ca 1865]. Thick folio. 250 engvs. Occas spotting. Contemp three qtr mor, worn, jnts cracked. *(Wilkinson)* **£19 [≈$29]**
- Cassell's Dore Gallery ... With Memoir of Dore, Critical Essay and Descriptive Letterpress by Edmund Ollier. London: Cassell, Petter, Galpin, [ca 1880]. Folio. lxviii,152 pp. 250 engvs. Contemp half mor, a.e.g., extrs rubbed & worn. *(Claude Cox)* **£55 [≈$83]**

Dormer, Peter & Cripps, David

- Elizabeth Fritsch. London: Bellew, 1985. 96 pp. Num cold plates. Orig cloth. Dw. *(Fine Art)* **£16 [≈$24]**

Dostoevsky, Feodor

- The House of the Dead. Wood Engravings by Fritz Eichenberg. New York: The Limited Editions Club, 1982. One of 2000 signed by Eichenberg & by Michael Bixler. Tall 8vo. Orig cloth. Slipcase. *(Oak Knoll)* **$185 [≈£123]**
- A Raw Youth. Illustrated with Wood Engravings by Fritz Eichenberg. New York: The Limited Editions Club, 1974. One of 2000 signed by Eichenberg. 2 vols. 4to. Orig cloth (sl bumped). Slipcase. *(Oak Knoll)* **$125 [≈£83]**

Doughty, Charles M.

- Travels in Arabia Deserta ... General Introduction by T.E. Lawrence. Illustrations by Edy Legrand. New York: The Limited Editions Club, 1953. One of 1500. Tall 8vo. Orig wraparound cloth bndg with flap (sl darkened). *(Oak Knoll)* **$75 [≈£50]**

Dow, Helen J.

- The Art of Alex Colville. Toronto: McGraw Hill, (1972). 4to. 232 pp. Port frontis, 104 ills. Orig cloth. Dw (sl chipped and soiled). *(Karmiole)* **$40 [≈£27]**

Dowding, Geoffrey

- An Introduction to the History of Printing Types ... London: Wace & Co., 1961. 1st edn. Lge 8vo. xxiv,278 pp. 117 ills. Orig cloth. Dw. *(Claude Cox)* **£18 [≈$27]**

Dowling, Henry G.

- A Survey of British Industrial Arts. London: F. Lewis, 1935. 1st edn. 4to. 57 pp. Frontis, 100 plates. Orig buckram. *(Spelman)* **£45 [≈$68]**
- A Survey of British Industrial Arts. Benfleet: F. Lewis, [1935]. 4to. 57,[7] pp. Frontis, 100 b/w plates. Orig cloth gilt. Dw. *(Cooper Hay)* **£60 [≈$90]**

Downes, Kerry

- Hawksmoor. London: Zwemmer, 1979. 2nd edn, rvsd. xvi,298 pp. 96 plates, 46 ills. Orig cloth. Dw. *(Leicester Art Books)* **£40 [≈$60]**
- Vanbrugh. London: Zwemmer, 1977. 1st edn. 4to. xiv,291 pp. 182 ills. Dw (v sl worn). *(Spelman)* **£60 [≈$90]**

Downes, William Howe

- John S. Sargent, His Life and Work. Boston: Little, Brown, 1925. 1st edn. 4to. Orig cloth, t.e.g., spine sl faded. *(First Folio)* **$50 [≈£33]**
- The Life and Works of Winslow Homer. Boston: Houghton, Mifflin 1911. 1st edn. 306 pp. 266 ills on 69 plates. Orig cloth backed bds. *(Hermitage)* **$60 [≈£40]**
- The Life and Works of Winslow Homer.

Boston: Houghton, Mifflin 1911. xxviii,306 pp. 67 plates. Orig cloth & bds, t.e.g. *(Leicester Art Books)* **£85 [≈$128]**

Downing, A.J.

- The Architecture of Country Houses. New York: Appleton, 1856. 8vo. x,[ii],484 pp. 31 plates. Text foxed. B'plate. Orig cloth, spine sunned, tips worn. *(Bookpress)* **$210 [≈£140]**
- A Treatise on the Theory and Practice of Landscape Gardening, adapted to North America ... Enlarged, revised and newly illustrated. Fourth Edition. New York: Putnam, 1849. 8vo. xiv,532,[iv] pp. Frontis (sl offset), 18 plates, text ills. Sl spotting. Mod half calf gilt. *(Hollett)* **£175 [≈$263]**

Downing, Antoinette F. & Scully, Vincent J., Jr.

- The Architectural Heritage of Newport Rhode Island 1640-1915. Harvard: UP, 1952. 4to. Fldg plan, 230 plates. Orig buckram. *(David Slade)* **£50 [≈$75]**

Downsbrough, Peter

- Notes on Location II. New York: The Vanishing Rotating Triangle, 1973. Lge 8vo. (44) pp. Orig self-wraps. *(Ars Libri)* **$65 [≈£43]**
- Notes on Location. New York: The Vanishing Rotating Triangle, [1972?]. Lge 8vo. (44) pp. Orig self-wraps. *(Ars Libri)* **$65 [≈£43]**
- Two Lines. Six Sections. Paris: Gallery 9, 1973. [64] pp. Orig self wraps. *(Ars Libri)* **$45 [≈£30]**

Dowson, Ernest

- New Letters from Ernest Dowson. Edited & with a Preface by Desmond Flower. Andoversford: The Whittington Press, 1984. One of 180 (of 200) signed by the editor. 8vo. Port frontis. Orig qtr canvas, untrimmed. *(Blackwell's)* **£30 [≈$45]**
- The Pierrot of the Minute. New York: Grolier Club, Eminent American Printers series, 1923. One of 300. 16mo. 49 pp. Orig mrbld bds, label, fine. Chipped glassine. Slipcase (dusty). Designed by Bruce Rogers. *(The Veatchs)* **$200 [≈£133]**

Doyle, Richard

- A Journal kept by Richard Doyle in the year 1840. Illustrated ... by the Author. London: Smith, Elder, 1885. 1st edn. 4to. xii,[ii],152 pp. Litho port frontis, ills. Orig pict cloth, a.e.g., sl marked, spine ends reprd. *(Clark)* **£40 [≈$60]**
- A Journal kept by Richard Doyle in the year 1840 ... With an Introduction by J. Hungerford Pollen. London: 1885. 1st edn. 4to. xii,[2],152 pp. Port, ills. Orig cloth gilt, a.e.g., recased. *(Fenning)* **£35 [≈$53]**

Drake, Maurice

- A History of English Glass-Painting ... London: Werner Laurie, 1912. 1st edn. Tall 4to. x,226 pp. 36 mtd plates. Sm stamp title verso. Orig bds, soiled, edges worn. *(Hollett)* **£65 [≈$98]**

Drayton, Michael

- Endimion & Phoebe. Edited by J. William Hebel ... Oxford: Shakespeare Head Press for Blackwell, 1925. One of 100 (of 1050). 4to. Postscript tipped in after page xviii. Orig limp vellum, silk ties, silk marker. *(Blackwell's)* **£75 [≈$113]**
- Nymphidia and the Muse's Elyzium. Edited by John Gray. London: Vale Press, 1896. One of 210. Frontis by Charles Ricketts. Orig cloth backed bds, sl worn. *(Ulysses Bookshop)* **£95 [≈$143]**

Dreier, Katherine S.

- Western Art and the New Era. An Introduction to Modern Art. New York: Brentano's, 1923. 4to. xii,139 pp. 60 ills. Orig cloth, sl dusty. *(Ars Libri)* **$150 [≈£100]**

Dreiser, Theodore

- An American Tragedy. Illustrations by Reginald Marsh. New York: The Limited Editions Club, 1954. One of 1500 (not signed by Marsh). Thick 8vo. Orig cloth. Slipcase. *(Oak Knoll)* **$85 [≈£57]**

Dresser, Christopher

- The Principles of Decorative Design. London: Cassell, Petter & Galpin, (1878). 3rd edn. Sm 4to. 2 chromolitho plates, num b/w ills. Orig pict cloth gilt. *(Barbara Stone)* **£110 [≈$165]**

Dreyfus, John

- A History of the Nonesuch Press ... London: Nonesuch Press, 1981. One of 950. 4to. xv,319,[3] pp. Orig cloth. Dw. *(Oak Knoll)* **$325 [≈£217]**
- Italic Quartet: a Record of the Collaboration between Karry Kessler, Edward Johnston, Emery Walker and Edward Prince in making the Cranach Press Italic. [Cambridge: Christmas, 1966]. One of 500. vii,50 pp. 10 plates. Orig dec cloth. Slipcase. *(Claude Cox)* **£85 [≈$128]**

Driberg, J.H.

- Initiation. Translations from Poems of the Didinga and Lango Tribes. Golden Cockerel Press: 1932. One of 325 signed by the translator. Tall 8vo. 30 pp. 11 w'engvs by Robert Gibbings. Endpapers & spine darkened, buckram sides spotted. *(Waddington)* **£75 [≈$113]**
- Initiation; Translations from Poems of the Didinga & Lango Tribes. With Wood Engravings by Robert Gibbings. Golden Cockerel Press: 1932. One of 325 signed by the author. Tall 8vo. Orig buckram gilt, spine trifle darkened. *(Words Etcetera)* **£75 [≈$113]**

Drinkwater, John & Rutherston, Albert

- Claude Lovat Fraser with representative Examples of his Work ... London: Heinemann, 1923. One of 430 signed by the authors. Lge 4to. 40 plates. Orig buckram. *(Mermaid Books)* **£140 [≈$210]**

Driver, David

- The Art of Radio Times. The First Sixty Years. London: BBC, 1981. 4to. Num ills. Dw. *(David Slade)* **£35 [≈$53]**

Druitt, Herbert

- A Manual of Costume as Illustrated by Monumental Brasses. London: Moring, 1906. 1st edn. Frontis, 110 ills. Orig cloth, sl rubbed. *(Baker)* **£55 [≈$83]**
- A Manual of Costume as Illustrated by Monumental Brasses. London: De La More Press, 1906. 8vo. 110 ills. Occas sl foxing. Orig cloth. *(David Slade)* **£28 [≈$42]**

Drummond, James

- Archaeologia Scotica: Sculptured Monuments in Iona & the West Highlands. Edinburgh: Archaeologia Scotica, 1881. Ltd edn. 100 tinted litho plates. New qtr calf. *(Baker)* **£195 [≈$293]**
- Ancient Scottish Weapons &c. A Series of Drawings ... With Introduction & Descriptive Notes by Joseph Anderson. London: George Waterston & Sons, 1881. One of 500. Folio. 26 pp. 54 cold lithos. Orig morocco backed bds gilt, sl worn & spotted. *(Hollett)* **£295 [≈$443]**
- Scottish Market-Crosses. Edinburgh: Neill & Co., 1861. One of 50. 4to. 40 pp. 7 tinted lithos, 14 text w'cuts. Faint damp stain through text. Mod half mor gilt. *(Hollett)* **£140 [≈$210]**

Dry, G.

- Robert Bevan 1865-1925. Catalogue Raisonne of the Lithographs and other Prints. London: The Maltzahn Gallery, 1968. 24 pp. 40 ills. Orig buckram. Dw. *(Leicester Art Books)* **£40 [≈$60]**

Dubon, David

- Tapestries from the Samuel H. Kress Collection at the Philadelphia Museum of Art. The History of Constantine the Great Designed by Peter Paul Rubens and Pietro da Cortona. London: 1964. 4to. 152 pp. 75 plates, 22 figs. Orig cloth. *(Washton)* **$65 [≈£43]**

Dubreuil, Jean

- The Practice of Perspective: or, an Easy Method of representing Natural Objects according to the Rules of Art ... The Third Edition. London: T. & J. Bowles, 1743. 4to. xviii,150 pp. 2 fldg & 150 full-page plans. Period calf, sl worn. Anon. *(Rankin)* **£200 [≈$300]**

Dubuisson, A.

- Richard Parkes Bonington: His Life and Work. Translated with Annotations by C.E. Hughes. London: John Lane; The Bodley Head, 1924. One of 1000. xv,217 pp. 88 plates. Dw (chipped). *(Leicester Art Books)* **£115 [≈$173]**

Duby, G.

- The Europe of the Cathedrals. London: Skira, 1966. 1st edn. 4to. 220 pp. Num mtd cold plates. Orig cloth. Dw. *(Monmouth)* **£40 [≈$60]**

Du Cane, Florence

- Flowers & Gardens of Japan. London: A. & C. Black, Twenty Shilling Series, 1908. 1st edn. 50 cold plates by Ella Du Cane. Orig green cloth. *(Old Cathay)* **£59 [≈$89]**
- Flowers & Gardens of Japan. London: A. & C. Black, Twenty Shilling Series, 1908. 1st edn. 50 cold plates by Ella Du Cane. Orig cream cloth. *(Old Cathay)* **£59 [≈$89]**

Duchamp, Marcel

- The Almost Complete Works of Marcel Duchamp. Introduction by Richard Hamilton. London: Tate Gallery, 1966. Lge 4to. 109,[1] pp. Num ills. Orig wraps. *(Ars Libri)* **$150 [≈£100]**

Duff, E. Gordon

- Early Printed Books. London: 1893. Sm 8vo. 11 plates. Orig buckram. *(Traylen)* **£20 [≈$30]**

Du Fresnoy, Charles Alphonse

- The Art of Painting ... with Remarks. Translated into English, with an Original Preface ... by Mr Dryden. The Second Edition, corrected, and enlarg'd. London: sold by William Taylor, 1716. Fcap 8vo. [16],lxviii, [4] ,397,[7] pp. Frontis. Contemp calf, sm crack in jnt. *(Spelman)* **£120 [≈$180]**

Dufty, Arthur Richard

- European Swords and Daggers in the Tower of London. London: HMSO, 1974. 4to. 35 pp. Cold frontis, 109 plates. Orig cloth gilt. Dw. *(Hollett)* **£50 [≈$75]**

Dulac, Edmund

- Edmund Dulac's Picture Book for the French Red Cross. London: for The Daily Telegraph by Hodder & Stoughton, [1915]. 4to. 20 mtd cold plates. Orig pict cloth. *(Barbara Stone)* **£65 [≈$98]**
- Edmund Dulac's Picture Book for the French Red Cross. London: Hodder & Stoughton for the Daily Telegraph, (1915). 4to. 20 mtd cold plates. Crease in front endpaper. Orig pict cloth. *(Barbara Stone)* **£75 [≈$113]**
- Edmund Dulac's Picture-Book for the French Red Cross. London: Hodder & Stoughton, [ca 1915]. 1st edn. Orig cloth, sl darkened. *(Old Cathay)* **£49 [≈$74]**
- Lyrics Pathetic & Humorous from A to Z. London: Warne, 1908. 1st edn. 4to. Title, 24 cold plates, pict endpapers. Inscrptn on title. Occas sl soiling. Orig cloth backed pict bds, dulled. *(Robert Frew)* **£225 [≈$338]**
- Picture Book for the French Red Cross. London: [ca 1915]. Port, 19 mtd cold plates. Few crnrs creased. Orig pict bds, sl marked, spine bumped, crnrs worn. *(Stella Books)* **£65 [≈$98]**

Dumas, Alexandre

- The Man in the Iron Mask. With Hand-Colored Illustrations by Edy Legrand. New York: The Limited Editions Club, 1965. One of 1500 signed by Legrand. Tall 8vo. Orig cloth. Slipcase. *(Oak Knoll)* **$55 [≈£37]**
- Marguerite de Valois. With Hand-Colored Illustrations by Edy Legrand. New York: The Limited Editions Club, 1969. One of 1500 signed by Legrand. Tall 8vo. Orig cloth. Slipcase. *(Oak Knoll)* **$55 [≈£37]**
- The Queen's Necklace. Illustrations by Cyril Arnstam. New York: The Limited Editions Club, 1973. One of 1500 signed by Arnstam. Thick 8vo. Orig cloth, t.e.g. Slipcase. *(Oak Knoll)* **$55 [≈£37]**

Du Maurier, George

- Peter Ibbetson. With a Preface by Daphne Du Maurier. Illustrated by the Author. New York: The Limited Editions Club, 1963. One of 1600. Sm 4to. Orig leather-backed bds. Slipcase. *(Oak Knoll)* **$55 [≈£37]**

Dunbar, Pamela

- William Blake's Illustrations to the Poetry of Milton. Oxford: 1980. 1st edn. Lge 8vo. Frontis, 92 plates. Dw. *(Spelman)* **£20 [≈$30]**

Duncan, Alastair

- American Art Deco. New York: Abrams, 1986. Lge 4to. 288 pp. 502 ills. Orig cloth. Dw. *(Ars Libri)* **$55 [≈£37]**
- Art Nouveau and Art Deco Lighting. New York: Simon & Schuster, (1978). 4to. 208 pp. Num ills. Orig cloth. Dw. *(Abacus)* **$55 [≈£37]**

Duncan, Alastair & de Bartha, Georges

- Art Nouveau and Art Deco Bookbinding. New York: Abrams, (1989). 1st edn. Sm folio. 200 pp. 252 ills. Orig cloth. Dw. *(Bookpress)* **$110 [≈£73]**

Duncan, David Douglas

- Goodbye Picasso. New York: Grosset & Dunlap, [1974]. Folio. Orig cloth. Dw (some indent marks). *(First Folio)* **$95 [≈£63]**
- Picasso's Picassos. New York: Harper & Row, n.d. 4to. 271 pp. Num ills. Orig cloth. Dw. *(Abacus)* **$90 [≈£60]**
- Picasso's Picassos. The Treasures of La Californie. London: Macmillan, 1961. 271 pp. 116 cold plates, 708 sm ills. Orig cloth. *(Leicester Art Books)* **£606 [≈$90]**

Dunlap, Jack

- American, British & Continental Pepperbox Firearms. California: H.J. Dunlap, 1964. 1st edn. 4to. [iv],279 pp. Ills. Orig pict cloth gilt. Inscribed by the author. *(Hollett)* **£75 [≈$113]**

Dunsany, Lord

- Lord Adrian. Waltham St. Lawrence: Golden Cockerel Press, 1933. One of 325 numbered. Decs by Robert Gibbings. Free endpapers faintly browned. Orig leather backed cloth, t.e.g., v sl worn, spine sl faded. *(Ulysses Bookshop)* **£125 [≈$188]**

Dunthorne, Robert

- Illustrated Catalogue of Etchings by Hedley Fitton with Descriptions. London: R. Dunthorne, n.d. One of 300. 36 pp. 36 mtd plates. Orig qtr vellum. *(Leicester Art Books)* **£32 [≈$48]**

Dupin, Jacques

- Miro. New York: Abrams, 1962. 596 pp. 1158 ills. Orig cloth. Dw. *(Leicester Art Books)* **£220 [≈$330]**

Durfort, Claire de

- Ourika. Translated into English with an Introduction and Epilogue by John Fowles. Austin: Bird & Bull Press for W. Thomas Taylor, 1977. One of 500 sgnd by Fowles. 4to. 68 pp. Orig mor & bds. *(Karmiole)* **$125 [≈£83]**

Duruy, Victor

- History of Greece and of the Greek People. From the Earliest Times to the Roman Conquest. Translated and Edited by M.M. Ripley. London: 1898. 8 vols. 4to. Num ills. Orig cloth. *(Traylen)* **£90 [≈$135]**

Dussler, Luitpold

- Raphael. A Critical Catalogue of his Pictures, Wall Paintings and Tapestries. London: Phaidon, 1971. xxi,220 pp. 187 ills. Orig buckram. *(Leicester Art Books)* **£65 [≈$98]**

Duthuit, Georges

- The Fauvist Painters. New York: Wittenborn, Schultz, 1950. 4to. 28 plates. Orig wraps. *(Ars Libri)* **$50 [≈£33]**

Dutton, R.

- The English Interior. London: Batsford, 1948. 1st edn. 8vo. 192 pp. Photo plates. Orig cloth. Dw. *(Clevedon Books)* **£27 [≈$41]**
- A Hampshire Manor. London: Batsford, 1968. 8vo. 136 pp. Plates. Dw. *(Clevedon Books)* **£20 [≈$30]**

Duveen, Edward J.

- Colour in the Home. With Notes on Architecture, Sculpture, Painting, and upon Decoration and Good Taste. London: George Allen, 1911. Lge 4to. ix,168 pp. 44 plates. Occas sl spotting. Orig cloth gilt, extrs sl rubbed. *(Hollett)* **£35 [≈$53]**

Duveen, Sir Joseph

- Thirty Years of British Art. London: Studio Special Number, Autumn, 1930. 1st edn. Plates, ills. Hd of spine faded. Dw (spine browned). *(Words Etcetera)* **£35 [≈$53]**
- Thirty Years of British Art. With an Introduction by Sir Martin Conway. London: The Studio, 1930. 1st edn. Folio. 8 cold & 8 gravure ills. Orig cloth, edges sl faded. Dw (worn). *(Margaret Nangle)* **£25 [≈$38]**

Dvorakova, Vlasta, & others

- Gothic Mural Painting in Bohemia and Moravia, 1300-1378. London: OUP, 1964. 1st edn. 4to. 160 pp. 2 maps, 250 plates. Orig cloth. *(Karmiole)* **$50 [≈£33]**

Dyer, John

- Grongar Hill. Hackney: Stourton Press, 1982. One of 175 sgnd by the illustrator, John Piper. Lge 4to. Orig cloth backed bds. *(Barbara Stone)* **£145 [≈$218]**
- Grongar Hill. Illustrated by John Piper. Hackney: The Stourton Press, 1982. One of 175 signed by Piper. 4to. Orig cloth backed bds. *(Ulysses Bookshop)* **£125 [≈$188]**

Dyson, Anthony

- Pictures to Print. The Nineteenth-Century Engraving Trade. London: Farrand Press, 1984. Ltd edn, signed. Sm 4to. [2],xxx,234 pp. 95 ills inc cold engvd plate. Half mor gilt. *(Karmiole)* **$125 [≈£83]**

Eaglestone, A.A. & Lockett, T.A.

- The Rockingham Pottery. Rotherham Museum: 1964. 152 pp. 8 plates. Ex-lib. Orig cloth. Dw. *(Castle Bookshop)* **£24 [≈$36]**

Eames, Penelope

- Medieval Furniture. Furniture in England, France and the Netherlands from the Twelfth to the Fifteenth Century. London: 1977. Lge 8vo. xxiv,303 pp. 72 plates. Orig wraps. *(Washton)* **$40 [≈£27]**

Earland, Ada

- John Opie and His Circle. London: Hutchinson, 1911. xvi,376 pp. 45 plates. Orig cloth. *(Leicester Art Books)* **£40 [≈$60]**

Earle, Alice Morse

- China Collecting in America. New York: Scribner, 1892. 1st edn. 8vo. 429 pp. 66 ills. Orig dec bndg. *(Rona Schneider)* **$60 [≈£40]**

East, Sir Alfred

- The Art of Landscape Painting in Oil Colour. Phila: Lippincott, n.d. 1st edn. 4to. Frontis, 28 cold plates. Orig cloth. *(Bookpress)* **$75 [≈£50]**

Eastlake, C.L.

- Hints on Household Taste in Furniture, Upholstery and Other Details. London: Longmans, 1866. 269 pp. 33 plates, ills. Lib stamps. Binder's cloth. *(Monmouth)* **£45 [≈$68]**

Easton, Malcolm & Holroyd, Michael

- The Art of Augustus John. London: Secker & Warburg, 1974. 1st edn. 224 pp. 90 plates. Orig cloth, 2 crnrs bumped. Dw (creased). *(Bookworks)* **£25 [≈$38]**

Easton, Phoebe Jane

- Marbling. A History and a Bibliography. Los Angeles: Dawson's Book Shop, 1983. One of 850. 4to. xiv,190 pp. Mtd cold frontis, 6 mtd samples on 4 ff, 12 plates. Orig cloth. *(Karmiole)* **$125 [≈£83]**

Eaton, Allen H.

- Beauty Behind Barbed Wire: The Arts of the Japanese in Our War Relocation Camps. New York: Harper, (1952). 208 pp. Ills. Dw (chipped). *(Schoyer)* **$75 [≈£50]**

Eaton, D. Cady

- A Handbook of Modern French Sculpture. New York: Dodd, Mead, 1913. 1st edn. xviii,348 pp. 189 ills. Orig cloth gilt, spine faded, a few marks. *(Hollett)* **£15 [≈$23]**

Ebeling, Klaus

- Ragamala Painting. Basel, Paris & New Delhi: Ravi Kumar, (1973). 1st edn. Folio. 305 pp. Num cold plates, ills. Orig cloth. Dw. *(Terramedia)* **$50 [≈£33]**

Eckardt, A.

- A History of Korean Art. Translated by J.M. Kindersley. London: 1929. xxiv, 226, clxxiv pp. Map, cold & other plates, 506 figs. Orig bndg. *(Whitehart)* **£18 [≈$27]**

Ede, H.S.

- Savage Messiah: Gaudier-Brzeska. New York: Literary Guild, 1931. 1st US edn. 260 pp. 16 plates. Orig cloth, sl worn & marked. *(Fine Art)* **£20 [≈$30]**

Edmondson, Joseph

- A Complete Body of Heraldry. London: for the author by T. Spilsbury ..., 1780. 2 vols. Folio. Plates. Contemp tree calf, later gilt reback, crnrs sl bumped. *(Peter Bell)* **£300 [≈$450]**

Edmunds, Will H.

- Pointers and Clues to the Subjects of Chinese and Japanese Art. London: Sampson, Low, Marston, [ca 1934]. 1st edn. One of 1000. 725 pp. Dw (sl dusty). *(Hermitage)* **$100 [≈£67]**

Edwardes, Ernest L.

- The Grandfather Clock. An Archaeological and Descriptive Essay ... Altrincham: John Sherratt, 1952. Sm 4to. 253 pp. 55 plates. Orig cloth gilt. Dw. *(Hollett)* **£45 [≈$68]**
- The Grandfather Clock ... New Edition, Revised and Enlarged. Altrincham: 1952. 4to. 54 plates. Orig buckram. Dw. *(Traylen)* **£48 [≈$72]**

Edwards, A. Cecil

- The Persian Carpet, a Survey of the Carpet-Weaving Industry of Persia. London: 1960. 4to. 4 cold plates, 9 maps, 419 ills. Orig buckram gilt. *(Traylen)* **£80 [≈$120]**

Edwards, Cyril

- Seven Sonnets. London: Cyril Edwards, 1934. One of 250. 8vo. 40 pp. Polished tree calf gilt, gilt inner dentelles, by Birdsall, sides sl bowed, hd of spine sl tender. Inscribed by the author (1935). *(Robert Frew)* **£40 [≈$60]**

Edwards, Hugh

- Surrealism and its Affinities. The Mary Reynolds Collection. A Bibliography. Chicago: Art Institute of Chicago, 1973. 4to. 147,[1] pp. Orig wraps. *(Ars Libri)* **$50 [≈£33]**

Edwards, Ralph & Jourdain, Margaret

- Georgian Cabinet-Makers c. 1700-1800. London: Country Life, 1955. 3rd edn. 247 pp. 232 plates. Front free endpaper creased. Orig cloth. Dw (worn). *(Fine Art)* **£50 [≈$75]**

Edwards, Ralph & Ramsey, L.G.C.

- The Connoisseur Period Guides to the Houses, Decoration, Furnishing and Chattels of the Classic Periods. London: The Connoisseur, 1956-58. 1st edn. 6 vols. Num ills. Orig cloth gilt. Dws. *(Hollett)* **£95 [≈$143]**
- The Connoisseur Period Guides to the Houses, Decoration, Furnishing and Chattels of the Classic Periods. London: The Connoisseur, 1968. 1st complete one-vol edn. Lge thick 8vo. 1536 pp. 576 plates, num text figs. Orig cloth gilt. Dw (few sm edge chips). *(Hollett)* **£40 [≈$60]**

Egerton, Judy

- George Stubbs 1724-1806. London: Tate Gallery, 1984. 4to. 248 pp. 190 plates. Dw. *(Spelman)* **£45 [≈$68]**

Egerton, Judy & Snelgrove, Dudley

- British Sporting and Animal Drawings c.1500-1850. Sport in Art and Books - The Paul Mellon Collection. London: Tate

Gallery, 1978. 1st edn. 4to. xviii,126 pp. 121 plates. Orig cloth gilt. Dw.
(Hollett) **£95 [≈$143]**

Ehrlich, Frederic

- The New Typography & Modern Layouts. New York: Stokes, 1934. 4to. 120 pp, 70 pp ills. Orig cloth, soiled, sl worn.
(The Veatchs) **$45 [≈£30]**

Eichenberg, Fritz

- Dance of Death: A Graphic Commentary on the Danse Macabre through the Centuries. New York: Abbeville, (1983). 4to. 136 pp. Ills. Orig cloth. Dw. signed by the artist on a pasted-in b'plate. *(Abacus)* **$50 [≈£33]**

Eisler, Colin

- Paintings from the Samuel H. Kress Collection. European Schools excluding Italian. London: 1977. Lge 4to. xii,638 pp. 502 ills inc 16 cold plates. Orig cloth, 2 crnrs sl bumped. Dw. *(Washton)* **$475 [≈£317]**
- The Seeing Hand. A Treasury of Great Master Drawings. New York: Harper & Row, 1975. 1st edn. 263 pp. 132 cold & num b/w plates. Orig cloth. Dw.
(Clarice Davis) **$115 [≈£77]**

Eitner, Lorenz

- Gericault. His Life and Work. London: Orbis, 1982. 376 pp. 270 ills. Orig cloth. Dw.
(Leicester Art Books) **£55 [≈$83]**

Eliot, Alexander

- Three Hundred Years of American Painting. New York: Time Inc., 1957. 4to. 317 pp. 215 cold ills. Orig cloth.
(Rona Schneider) **$40 [≈£27]**

Eliot, John

- The Parlement of Pratlers ... London: Fanfrolico Press, 1928. One of 625. Sm 8vo. 120 pp. W'cut ills by Hal Collins. Orig cloth over bds. Dw (chipped).
(Karmiole) **$75 [≈£50]**

Ellenport, Samuel B.

- An Essay on the Development & Usage of Brass Plate Dies including a Catalogue Raisonne from the Collection of the Harcourt Bindery. Boston: Harcourt Bindery, 1980. One of 500. 4to. Plates, ills. Orig blind stamped cloth. *(Cooper Hay)* **£65 [≈$98]**

Ellis, Edwin J.

- The Real Blake. London: Chatto & Windus, 1907. 1st edn. 464 pp. Frontis, 12 plates. Endpapers sl browned. Orig buckram, t.e.g., sunned, crnr bruised.
(Bookworks) **£28 [≈$42]**

Ellis, H.J. & Bickley, F.B.

- Index to the Charters and Rolls in the Dept of Manuscripts, British Museum. London: 1965. 2 vols. Thick 8vo. Sm stamp on title versos. Orig cloth. *(Traylen)* **£25 [≈$38]**

Ellwood, G.M.

- English Furniture and Decoration 1680-1800. London: Batsford, n.d. 3rd edn. 4to. Num photo ills. Orig cloth, partly stained.
(Mendelsohn) **$45 [≈£30]**

Elmes, James

- The Arts and Artists. London: John Knight & Henry Lacey, 1825. 1st edn. 3 vols. Fcap 8vo. Engvd titles, 14 ports, fldg chart, fldg plate. Later half mor gilt, few sl marks.
(Ash) **£100 [≈$150]**

Elsam, Richard

- The Practical Builder's Perpetual Price Book ... London: Thomas Kelly, 1829. 4th edn. 4to. x,[ii],180 pp. Frontis, 7 plates. Lacks dedic leaf. Contemp half calf, hinges cracked.
(Bookpress) **$225 [≈£150]**

Elsen, Albert E.

- Paul Jenkins. New York: Abrams, [ca 1973]. 283 pp. 171 ills. Orig cloth. Dw.
(Leicester Art Books) **£90 [≈$135]**
- Paul Jenkins. New York: Abrams, n.d. Oblong 4to. 284 pp. 171 ills (56 mtd cold). Orig cloth. Dw. *(Abacus)* **$125 [≈£83]**
- Seymour Lipton. New York: Abrams, n.d. Oblong 4to. 244 pp. 215 ills (52 mtd cold). Orig cloth. Dw. *(Abacus)* **$100 [≈£67]**
- The Sculpture of Matisse. New York: Abrams, 1972. 229 pp. 284 ills. Orig cloth. Dw. *(Leicester Art Books)* **£95 [≈$143]**

Eluard, Paul

- Pablo Picasso. London: Secker & Warburg, 1947. 178 pp. 98 ills. Orig card wraps.
(Leicester Art Books) **£25 [≈$38]**

Elville, E.M.

- The Collector's Dictionary of Glass. London: Country Life, 1967. 4to. 192 pp. 275 plates. Dw. *(Paul Brown)* **£25 [≈$38]**

Elvin, Charles Norton

- A Hand-Book of the Orders of Chivalry, War Medals & Crosses, with their Clasps & Ribbons and Other Decorations ... London: Dean & Son, 1892. Lge 8vo. 26 chromolitho plates & title, 5 other plates. Orig dec cloth gilt, rebacked in mor gilt. *(Hollett)* **£285 [≈$428]**

Embury, Aymar

- One Hundred Country Houses. New York: Century, 1909. 1st edn. 4to. xvi,264 pp. Ills. Orig cloth, sl worn. *(Bookpress)* **$135 [≈£90]**

Emery, John

- European Spoons before 1700. London: John Donald, 1976. 1st edn. Lge 8vo. [vi],205 pp. 131 ills. Orig cloth gilt. Dw. *(Hollett)* **£35 [≈$53]**

Engel, Heinrich

- The Japanese House, A Tradition for Contemporary Architecture. Rutland: Tuttle, 1980. 9th printing. 4to. 495 pp. Ills. Orig dec cloth. Dw. Cardboard slipcase. *(First Folio)* **$85 [≈£57]**

Enschede, Charles

- Typefoundries in the Netherlands from the 15th to the 19th Century. An English Translation with Revisions and Notes by Harry Carter. Haarlem: 1978. Folio. xxviii,477 pp. 519 ills. Orig qtr calf, lower tips v sl bumped. *(The Veatchs)* **$425 [≈£283]**
- Typefoundries in the Netherlands from the Fifteenth to the Nineteenth Century ... An English Translation with Revisions and Notes by Harry Carter ... Haarlem: 1978. One of 1500. Folio. xxviii,477 pp. Frontis, 519 ills. Orig qtr calf. Slipcase. *(Claude Cox)* **£220 [≈$330]**

Epictetus

- The Discourses of Epictetus. Illustrated by Hans Erni. New York: The Limited Editions Club, 1966. One of 1500 signed by Erni. Thick 4to. Orig cloth, leather label, slipcase. *(Oak Knoll)* **$100 [≈£67]**

Epstein, Jacob

- An Autobiography. London: Hulton Press, 1955. 1st edn thus. 8vo. x,294 pp. Plates. Dw. *(Spelman)* **£25 [≈$38]**

Epstein, K.

- Epstein Drawings. With Notes by Lady Epstein and an Introduction by Richard Buckle. London: Faber, 1962. 65 pp. 65 plates. Orig cloth. Dw (torn). *(Leicester Art Books)* **£35 [≈$53]**

Erdman, David V.

- Blake. Prophet against Empire. Princeton: UP, 1954. xx,503 pp. 8 plates, 14 ills. Orig cloth. Dw. *(Leicester Art Books)* **£28 [≈$42]**
- The Illuminated Blake. Garden City: Anchor Press, Doubleday, 1974. Oblong 4to. 416 pp. Plates. Orig cloth, remainder spray bottom edge. Dw. *(Abacus)* **$75 [≈£50]**

Eriksen, Svend

- Early Neo-Classicism in France. The Creation of the Louis Seize Style ... in the Mid-Eighteenth Century. London: Faber, 1974. Sm 4to. 432 pp. 499 ills. Orig cloth. Dw. *(Mendelsohn)* **$225 [≈£150]**

Erskine, Mrs Steuart

- Lady Diane Beauclerk. Her Life and Work. London: Fisher Unwin, 1903. xvi,316 pp. 10 plates, 104 ills. Orig buckram gilt, t.e.g. *(Leicester Art Books)* **£34 [≈$51]**

Erte

- Erte at Ninety. The Complete Graphics. Edited by Marshall Lee, with Introduction and Selected Writings by Erte. New York: Dutton, (1982). One of 250 signed by Erte. Folio. 224 pp. Cold plates. Orig silk. Slipcase. *(Karmiole)* **$375 [≈£250]**

Escher, M.C.

- Escher. With a Complete Catalogue of the Graphic Works. Edited by J.L. Locher. London: Thames & Hudson, 1982. 349 pp. 606 ills. Orig cloth. Dw. *(Leicester Art Books)* **£100 [≈$150]**
- The Graphic Art. New, Revised and Expanded Edition. New York: Meredith Press, 1969. 4to. 22,[6] pp. 76 ills. Orig cloth. Dw. *(Ars Libri)* **$45 [≈£30]**

An Essay upon Prints ...

- An Essay upon Prints ... see Gilpin, William

Essick, Robert N.

- William Blake Printmaker. Princeton: UP, 1980. xxii,283 pp. 236 plates. Orig cloth. Dw. *(Leicester Art Books)* **£65 [≈$98]**

Estes, Louise Reid (editor)

- Nature and Art: Poems and Pictures from the Best Authors and Artists. Boston: Estes & Lauriat, 1882. 4to. 159 pp. 14 etchings (foxed), 50 ills. Orig dec cloth. *(Rona Schneider)* **$100 [≈£67]**

Etlin, Richard A.

- The Architecture of Death. Cambridge: MIT Press, (1984). 1st edn. 8vo. xiv,[ii],441 pp. 268 ills. Orig cloth. Dw. *(Bookpress)* **$65 [≈£43]**

Ettinghausen, Richard

- Arab Painting. Skira: (1962). Thick folio. 81 mtd cold plates. Slipcase. *(Rob Warren)* **$85 [≈£57]**

Ettlinger, Leopold D.

- Antonio and Piero Pollaiulo. Oxford: Phaidon, 1978. 184 pp. 162 ills. Orig cloth. Dw. *(Leicester Art Books)* **£48 [≈$72]**

Euripides

- Medea Hippolytus The Bacchae. Newly Translated by Philip Vellacott. Illustrated by Michael Ayrton. New York: The Limited Editions Club, 1967. One of 1500 signed by Ayrton. Sm 4to. Orig cloth-backed bds. Slipcase. *(Oak Knoll)* **$65 [≈£43]**
- The Plays of Euripides, translated into English Rhyming Verse by Gilbert Murray. Newtown: Gregynog Press, 1931. One of 500. 2 vols. Folio. Orig linen gilt. *(Traylen)* **£260 [≈$390]**
- The Plays of Euripides, translated into English Rhyming Verse by Gilbert Murray. Newtown: Gregynog Press, 1931. One of 500. 2 vols. Folio. Orig cloth gilt, spine ends v sl wrinkled. *(First Folio)* **$500 [≈£333]**

Evan-Thomas, O.

- Domestic Utensils of Wood 16th-19th Century. L; the author, 1932. 4to. 178 pp. 69 plates. Dw (worn & chipped). *(Monmouth)* **£50 [≈$75]**

Evans, J.T.

- The Church Plate of Cardiganshire ... Stow: 1914. 4to. xxiv,163 pp. 20 plates. Sl foxing. Orig bndg, t.e.g. *(Castle Bookshop)* **£50 [≈$75]**

Evans, Joan

- Art in Mediaeval France 987-1498. OUP: 1948. Imperial 8vo. xxviii,300 pp. 11 plans, 280 ills. Orig cloth gilt, sl faded. *(Taylor & Son)* **£45 [≈$68]**
- English Art 1307-1461. OUP: 1949. xxiv,272 pp. 96 plates, 13 ills. Orig cloth. Dw. *(Fine Art)* **£30 [≈$45]**
- Monastic Architecture in France from the Renaissance to the Revolution. Cambridge: 1964. 4to. xlii,187 pp. 822 ills. Orig cloth gilt. *(Hollett)* **£60 [≈$90]**
- Pattern. A Study of Ornament in Western Europe from 1180 to 1900. Oxford: Clarendon Press 1931. 2 vols. 4to. 435 ills. Orig cloth. Dws (partly soiled). *(David Slade)* **£75 [≈$113]**

Evans, Sir John

- The Ancient Stone Implements, Weapons and Ornaments of Great Britain. London: Longmans, Green, 1897. 2nd edn, rvsd. Thick 8vo. xviii, 747 pp. 477 w'cut text ills. Orig cloth gilt. *(Hollett)* **£85 [≈$128]**

Evans, Lady

- Lustre Pottery. London: Methuen, 1920. 1st edn. 4to. xvii,148 pp. 24 plates. Some spotting. Lib b'plate. Orig cloth, edges sl rubbed. *(Francis Edwards)* **£120 [≈$180]**

Evans, M.W.

- Medieval Drawings. London: 1969. Lge 4to. 44 pp. 132 plates. Orig cloth. Dw. *(Washton)* **$85 [≈£57]**

Evans, R.

- The Fabrication of Virtue: English Prison Architecture 1750-1840. Cambridge: UP, 1982. Sm 4to. 464 pp. Ills. Dw. *(Monmouth)* **£40 [≈$60]**

Evelyn, John

- Sculptura Historico-Technica: or, the History and Art of Engraving ... With Additions. London: for J. Marks, 1770. 4th edn. Tall 12mo. 10 plates. Title & 1st 2 ff sl spotted. Contemp three qtr calf, jnts cracked. *(Wilkinson)* **£135 [≈$203]**
- Sculptura: or, The History and Art of Chalcography and Engraving in Copper ... annexed, a new Manner of Engraving, or Mezzotinto ... London: J. Payne, 1755. xxxvi, 140 pp. Port frontis, 1 plate, fldg mezzotint. Leather, rebacked. *(Fine Art)* **£130 [≈$195]**

Every Woman's Encyclopaedia ...

- Every Woman's Encyclopaedia. London: [ca 1900]. 8 vols. 5856 pp. Ills. Orig cloth gilt, some wear & soiling. *(Willow House)* **£50 [≈$75]**

Ewing, Elizabeth

- History of Children's Costume. London: Bibliophile, 1982. Lge 8vo. 191 pp. 4 cold & 124 other plates. Orig cloth gilt. Dw. *(Hollett)* **£30 [≈$45]**

Ewing, John Cameron

- Brash and Reid Booksellers in Glasgow and their Collection of Poetry Original and Selected. Glasgow: Maclehose, 1934. One of 50. 4to. 20 pp. 2 plates. Orig cloth. Author's presentation copy. *(Cooper Hay)* **£55 [≈$83]**

Fabes, Gilbert H.

- Modern First Editions: Points and Values. London: 1929. One of 750. Cloth, uncut. *(Margaret Nangle)* **£40 [≈$60]**
- Modern First Editions: Points and Values. (Second Series). London: Foyle, [1931]. One of 1000. Orig cloth. Dw. *(Cooper Hay)* **£24 [≈$36]**
- Modern First Editions: Points and Values. (Third Series). London: Foyle, [1932]. One of 750. Dw (sl chipped and dusty). *(Cooper Hay)* **£24 [≈$36]**

Fabre, J.H.

- Book of Insects ... London: Hodder & Stoughton, [1921]. 4to. vi,[i],184 pp. 12 mtd cold plates by E.J. Detmold. Orig gilt dec cloth, sm mark upper cover. *(Robert Frew)* **£90 [≈$135]**

Fagg, William

- The Sculpture of Africa. New York: Hacker Books, 1978. 2nd printing. Lge folio. 256 pp. Num ills. Orig cloth. Dw (sl torn). *(Worldwide)* **$85 [≈£57]**

Fahy, Everett & Watson, F.J.B.

- The Wrightsman Collection. Volume V: Paintings, Drawings, Sculpture. New York: Metropolitan Museum of Art, 1973. xii,455 pp. 260 plates. Orig cloth. Dw. *(Fine Art)* **£50 [≈$75]**

Fairless, Michael

- The Roadmender and Other Writings. Illustrated by Lennox Patterson. London: Collins, 1950. 256 pp. 27 w'engvs. V sl browned. Orig cloth gilt, spine & crnrs bumped, spine v sl faded. Dw (sl browned & damaged). *(Stella Books)* **£25 [≈$38]**
- The Roadmender. London: Philip Lee Warner, Medici Society, 1920. One of 1000. Sq 8vo. ix, 107,[3] pp. Orig parchment, t.e.g., bowed. Dw (soiled & chipped). *(Oak Knoll)* **$45 [≈£30]**

Fales, Dean A.

- American Painted Furniture, 1660-1880. New York: Dutton, 1972. 1st edn. 4to. 299 pp. 511 ills. Orig cloth. Dw (hd of spine chipped). *(Bookpress)* **$85 [≈£57]**

Falk, Bernard

- Thomas Rowlandson: His Life and Art. A Documentary Record. London: Hutchinson, [1949]. 1st edn. 4to. 91 ills (21 cold). Orig cloth, spine faded. *(Spelman)* **£45 [≈$68]**
- Thomas Rowlandson: His Life and Art. A Documentary Record. London: Hutchinson, 1949. 236 pp. 91 ills. Orig cloth gilt. *(Leicester Art Books)* **£50 [≈$75]**

Far, Isabella

- De Chirico. New York: Abrams, 1968. Sm folio. [2],21,[1] pp. 172 plates. Orig cloth. *(Ars Libri)* **$60 [≈£40]**

Farington, Joseph

- The Farington Diaries. Edited by James Greig. London: Hutchinson, 1923-28. Vol 1 4th edn, others 1st edn. 8 vols. 112 ills. Orig cloth, few vols sl worn & marked. *(Leicester Art Books)* **£45 [≈$68]**

Faris, James C.

- Nuba Personal Art. London: Duckworth, 1972. 1st edn. Sm 4to. x,130 pp. Map, plates, ills. Orig bds gilt. Dw. *(Oriental and African)* **£20 [≈$30]**

Farleigh, John

- An Autobiographical Textbook. London: Macmillan, 1940. 1st edn. Num ills. Page edges browned. Name. Orig cloth, spine & cover edges browned. *(Virgo)* **£60 [≈$90]**
- Graven Image. An Autobiographical Textbook. London: Macmillan, 1940. 1st edn. Num ills. Orig pict bds. *(Mermaid Books)* **£58 [≈$87]**
- Graven Image. An Autobiographical Textbook. London: Macmillan, 1940. 1st edn. 388 pp. Num ills. Dw (sl frayed). *(Michael Taylor)* **£45 [≈$68]**

Farnol, Jeffrey

- The Broad Highway. Illustrated by C.E. Brock. London: Sampson Low, 1912. New edn. 24 cold plates. Orig gilt dec bndg, pict onlay, a.e.g. *(Old Cathay)* **£25 [≈$38]**

Farnsworth, S.

- Illumination and its Development in the Present Day. London: [1922]. 8vo. [4],267 pp. 21 plates (4 cold). Orig cloth gilt. *(Fenning)* **£45 [≈$68]**

Farquhar, George

- The Beaux Stratagem. With Seven Engravings on Copper by J. Laboureur ... Bristol: Douglas Cleverdon, 1929. One of 450 (of 527). xxvii,128 pp. Occas sl spotting. Orig qtr buckram, sl rubbed. *(Michael Taylor)* **£35 [≈$53]**
- The Recruiting Officer: A Comedy ... With a Note on the Author and the Play by Sir Edmund Gosse; and Embellish'd with

Designs by Vera Willoughby. London: for Peter Davies, 1926. One of 550. Folio. 12 cold plates. Orig vellum & bds gilt. Slipcase. *(Karmiole)* **$125 [≈£83]**

Farr, Dennis

- William Etty. London: Routledge, 1958. xiii,217 pp. Cold frontis, 96 plates. Orig cloth. Dw. *(Leicester Art Books)* **£60 [≈$90]**

Fath, Creekmore

- The Lithographs of Thomas Hart Benton. Austin: Texas UP, (1979). Oblong 4to. 223 pp. Plates. Orig cloth. Dw. *(Abacus)* **$40 [≈£27]**

Fedderson, Martin

- Japanese Decorative Art. New York: Thomas Yoseloff, 1962. 1st Amer edn. 8vo. 296 pp. Fldg table. Orig cloth. Dw. *(Bookpress)* **$75 [≈£50]**

Feld, Charles

- Picasso: His Recent Drawings 1966-1968. Preface by Rene Char. New York: Abrams, (1969). 4to. 254 pp. 405 ills. Orig dec cloth. Printed plastic dw. *(Abacus)* **$50 [≈£33]**

Ferguson, John C.

- Chinese Painting. Chicago: UP, (1927). 1st edn. 4to. ix,[i],199 pp. 59 plates. Lib marks. Orig cloth, minor rubbing. *(Bookpress)* **$65 [≈£43]**

Ferguson, Richard S. (editor

- Old Church Plate in the Diocese of Carlisle: with the Makers and Marks ... Carlisle: Thurnam, 1882. 8vo. viii,326 pp. 29 lithos. Orig cloth gilt, sm snags hd of spine. *(Hollett)* **£75 [≈$113]**

Fergusson, James

- An Essay on the Ancient Topography of Jerusalem, with Restored Plans of the Temple &c. ... London: John Weale, 1847. Roy 8vo. 7 plates, 11 w'cuts. Orig cloth. *(Traylen)* **£220 [≈$330]**
- A History of Architecture in all Countries, from the Earliest Times to the Present Day. London: Murray, 1873-74. 2nd edn. 4 vols. 8vo. 1740 ills. Contemp polished calf gilt, rebacked. *(Hollett)* **£225 [≈$338]**
- History of Indian and Eastern Architecture. London: Murray, 1899. New imp. 8vo. xviii,756 pp. 2 fldg maps, 397 ills. Few sm lib marks. Lib qtr leather. *(Bates & Hindmarch)* **£68 [≈$102]**
- Rude Stone Monuments in all Countries; their Age and Uses. London: Murray, 1872. 1st edn. Lge 8vo. xix,560,[32 advt] pp. Fldg map, 234 ills. Orig cloth gilt, recased, spine faded. *(Hollett)* **£60 [≈$90]**

Fergusson, Peter

- Architecture of Solitude. Cistercian Abbeys in Twelfth-Century England. Guildford: Princeton UP, 1984. 1st edn. 4to. xxv,188 pp. 140 plates. Orig cloth gilt. Dw. *(Hollett)* **£65 [≈$98]**

Festschrift

- Essays in the History of Art presented to Rudolf Wittkower. Edited by Douglas Fraser. London: Phaidon Press, 1967. 4to. x,248 pp. Port frontis, 128 plates. Orig cloth gilt. Dw. *(Cooper Hay)* **£40 [≈$60]**

Ffoulkes, Charles & Hopkinson, E.C.

- Sword, Lance and Bayonet. A Record of the Arms of the British Army and Navy. Cambridge: 1938. 1st edn. xvi,143 pp. 3 plates, 80 text figs. Orig cloth gilt, trifle worn. *(Hollett)* **£45 [≈$68]**

Ffoulkes, Charles J.

- Inventory and Survey of the Armouries of the Tower of London. London: HMSO, 1916. 2 vols. 4to. 38 plates, num text ills. Orig qtr buckram. *(Traylen)* **£220 [≈$330]**

Ffoulkes, Constantin Jocelyn & Maiocchi, Rodolfo

- Vincenzo Foppa of Brescia, Founder of the Lombard School. His Life and Work. London: John Lane, 1909. One of 340. xxii,421 pp. 90 plates. Lib label. Orig buckram gilt, t.e.g. *(Leicester Art Books)* **£250 [≈$375]**

Field, Eugene

- Poems of Childhood. Illustrated by Maxfield Parrish. New York: Scribner, 1904. 1st edn. 4to. Title & 8 cold plates. Crease in half-title. Orig cloth gilt, pict onlay, extrs rubbed, spine gilt faded. *(Barbara Stone)* **£55 [≈$83]**
- The Symbol & the Saint. New York: Rudge, 1921. One of 300. 16mo. Orig dec bds, label, top edge dusty. Designed by Bruce Rogers. *(The Veatchs)* **$55 [≈£37]**

Field, Horace & Bunney, Michael

- English Domestic Architecture of the XVII and XVIII Centuries a Selection of Smaller Buildings ... London: Geo. Bell & Sons, 1905. 4to. Plates, text ills. Orig qtr cloth gilt, spine sl dusty. *(Cooper Hay)* **£45 [≈$68]**

Field, Richard S.

- Paul Gauguin: Monotypes. Phila: Philadelphia Museum of Art, 1973. Sq 8vo. 148 pp. Num ills. Orig wraps. *(Washton)* **$75 [≈£50]**

Fielding, A.

- A Hunting We Will Go. Illustrated by J.P. Donne. London: Eyre & Spottiswoode, [ca 1894]. Num b/w ills. Orig pict bndg, worn. *(Stella Books)* **£20 [≈$30]**

Fielding, Henry

- The History of the Life of the late Mr. Jonathan Wild the Great. With Illustrations by T.M. Cleland. New York: The Limited Editions Club, 1943. One of 1500 signed by Cleland. Tall 8vo. Orig cloth-backed bds. Slipcase (worn). *(Oak Knoll)* **$65 [≈£43]**
- The History of Tom Jones, a Foundling. With Illustrations by T.M. Cleland. New York: The Limited Editions Club, 1952. One of 1500 signed by Cleland. 2 vols. Tall 8vo. Orig cloth (vol 1 hd of spine torn, labels foxed). Slipcase (sl worn). *(Oak Knoll)* **$75 [≈£50]**
- A Journey from this World to the Next. Golden Cockerel Press: 1930. One of 500. 175 pp. 6 copper engvs by Denis Tegetmeier. Inscrptn erased. Orig buckram gilt, spine & hd of front bd darkened. *(Waddington)* **£60 [≈$90]**
- Tom Jones, the History of a Foundling. With Illustrations by Alexander King. New York: The Limited Editions Club, 1931. One of 1500 signed by King. Sm 4to. Orig limp leather (sl rubbed). Slipcase. *(Oak Knoll)* **$125 [≈£83]**

Fielding, T.H.

- The Art of Engraving. London: Nattali, 1844. 2nd edn. Lge 8vo. viii,109,[1] pp, advt leaf. 10 plates, 8 text ills. Orig cloth, spine v rubbed. *(Spelman)* **£80 [≈$120]**
- Index of Colours and Mixed Tints, for the Use of Beginners in Landscape and Figure Painting. London: for the author, 1830. 1st edn. 4to. 40 pp. Half-title. 18 plates (one showing 28 colours, others showing 24 mixed tints each). Orig bds, uncut, rebacked. Pres copy. *(Spelman)* **£350 [≈$525]**
- On Painting in Oil and Water Colours, for Landscape and Portraits ... London: Ackermann, 1839. 4to. viii,159,[1 advt] pp. 10 plates (4 hand cold). Blank section of frontis reprd. Contemp bds, later mor spine. *(Spelman)* **£100 [≈$150]**
- On the Theory of Painting ... Third Edition, much enlarged. London: Ackermann, 1842. Roy 8vo. xi,[1],146 pp, advt leaf. Hand cold frontis, 8 plates with 26 engvd ills, 6 plates containing 90 hand cold examples. Some foxing. Orig cloth backed bds, reprd. *(Spelman)* **£100 [≈$150]**
- The Theory and Practice of Painting in Oil and Water Colours, for Landscape and Portraits ... Fifth Edition. London: David Bogue, 1852. Tall 8vo. xii,236 pp. 18 plates (9 cold). Orig cloth, rebacked. *(Robert Frew)* **£150 [≈$225]**

Figgis, Darrell

- The Paintings of William Blake. New York: Scribner, 1925. One of 1150. 4to. 117 pp. 100 plates. Orig cloth & bds, sl worn. *(Abacus)* **$85 [≈£57]**

Finberg, A.J.

- The Life of J.M.W. Turner, R.A. Oxford: Clarendon Press 1939. 8vo. 24 plates. Orig bndg, trifle marked & rubbed. *(David Slade)* **£50 [≈$75]**

Fine Print

- Fine Print, A Review for the Arts of the Book. Vol 1, No. 1 - Vol 16 no 3. San Francisco: 1975-90. Complete run, with inserts. *(The Veatchs)* **$650 [≈£433]**

Finlay, Ian

- Scottish Crafts. London: 1948. 4to. 127 pp. 84 ills on plates (16 cold). Orig cloth. *(Washton)* **$35 [≈£23]**
- Scottish Gold and Silver Work. London: Chatto & Windus, 1956. 1st edn. Lge 8vo. 178 pp. 96 plates. Orig cloth gilt. Dw. *(Karmiole)* **$75 [≈£50]**

Fischel, Oskar

- Raphael. London: 1948. 2 vols. 4to. 302 plates. Orig cloth, sl rubbed. *(Washton)* **$75 [≈£50]**
- Raphael. London: Kegan Paul, (1948). 1st edn. 2 vols. 4to. Frontis, 302 plates. Sl used. Orig cloth, spines sunned. *(Bookpress)* **$125 [≈£83]**

Fischer, Peter

- Mosaic: History and Technique. London: Thames & Hudson, 1971. 152 pp. 16 cold & 104 b/w plates, 16 ills. Errata slip. Orig cloth gilt. Dw. *(Willow House)* **£15 [≈$23]**

'Fish' (Anna Harriet Sefton)

- The New Eve. London: Bodley Head, 1917.

1st edn. 72 pp. Num ills. Orig dec bds, sl soiled & rubbed, upper jnt tender. *(Bookworks)* **£32 [≈$48]**

- The Third Eve Book. London: Bodley Head, 1919. 1st edn. 72 pp. Num ills. Orig dec bds, sl rubbed & soiled. *(Bookworks)* **£32 [≈$48]**

Fisher, Harrison

- American Belles. With Decorations by Bertha Stuart. New York: Dodd, Mead, 1911. 1st edn. Folio. 16 mtd cold plates. Tiny crnr fold to frontis. Orig cloth backed bds, pict onlay. Glassine dw. Box, pict label (sl darkened). *(Jo Ann Reisler)* **$675 [≈£450]**
- The Little Gift Book. New York: Scribner, 1913. 1st edn. 8vo. 32 ports. Dw. Box (edges v sl worn). *(Jo Ann Reisler)* **$450 [≈£300]**

Fisher, S.W.

- English Blue and White Porcelain of the 18th Century ... London: Batsford, 1947. 1st edn. 4to. 45 ills (3 cold). Orig cloth gilt. *(Hollett)* **£75 [≈$113]**

Fitzgibbon, Constantine

- Watcher in Florence. Hemingford Grey: The Vine Press, 1959. One of 150. 63,colophon pp. Engvd title by Reg Boulton. Orig black mor backstrip & foredge strips, mrbld paper sides, t.e.g. Prospectus laid in. *(Claude Cox)* **£45 [≈$68]**

Flannagan, John B.

- Letters. With an Introduction by W.R. Valentiner. New York: Curt Valentin, 1942. Sm 4to. 100 pp. 7 plates, text ills. Orig cloth. *(Ars Libri)* **$85 [≈£57]**

Flaubert, Gustave

- The First Temptation of St. Anthony. Translated by Rennie Francis ... Illustrated by Jean de Bosschere. London: Bodley Head, 1924. One of 3000. 20 cold plates, num b/w ills. Orig bndg. *(Old Cathay)* **£95 [≈$143]**
- The First Temptation of St. Anthony ... Illustrated by Jean de Bosschere. London: John Lane, 1924. One of 3000. 8vo. Plates, text ills. Sl spotting at ends. Orig cloth gilt, spine faded. *(Claude Cox)* **£28 [≈$42]**
- Salambo. Translated by E. Powys Mathers. Golden Cockerel Press: 1931. One of 500. 318 pp. W'engvs by Robert Gibbings. Endpapers browned. Orig qtr buckram, t.e.g., crnrs v sl bumped. *(Waddington)* **£140 [≈$210]**
- Salambo: A Story of Ancient Carthage. Illustrated by Alexander King. New York: The Brown House, 1930. One of 800. Orig leather. Slipcase (sl faded & chipped). *(Hermitage)* **$250 [≈£167]**
- Three Tales. Illustrated by Robert Diaz de Soria. London: Chatto & Windus, 1923. 1st edn. 132 pp. 12 mtd cold plates. Orig qtr cloth, top edge tinted, others uncut. Dw (spine ends chipped). *(Bookworks)* **£26 [≈$39]**
- Three Tales. With an Introduction by Guy de Maupassant. Illustrated by May Neama. New York: The Limited Editions Club, 1978. One of 1500 signed by Neama. Sm 4to. Orig cloth-backed bds (some spotting to spine). Slipcase. *(Oak Knoll)* **$55 [≈£37]**

Flaxman, John

- Anatomical Studies of the Bones and Muscles, for the Use of Artists ... Notes ... by William Robertson. London: Nattali, 1833. 1st edn. Lge folio. 13,[i] pp. Port frontis, 21 plates. Orig (late 19th c) red cloth, sl marked, extrs sl worn. *(Clark)* **£200 [≈$300]**

Flecker, James Elroy

- The Letters to Frank Savery. London: Beaumont Press, 1926. One of 80 (of 390) signed. 126 pp. Orig parchment backed dec bds. *(Claude Cox)* **£85 [≈$128]**

Fleming, John

- Robert Adam and his Circle in Edinburgh and Rome. London: Murray, 1962. 1st edn. 8vo. 93 plates, 14 text figs. Dw. *(Spelman)* **£25 [≈$38]**

Fletcher, B.F. & Fletcher, H.P.

- The English Home. London: Methuen, 1910. 1st edn. 392 pp. Edges foxed. Orig cloth, spine v faded, some fading. *(Monmouth)* **£25 [≈$38]**

Fletcher, Sir Banister

- A History of Architecture on the Comparative Method ... Sixth Edition, enlarged ... London: Batsford, 1921. Roy 8vo. xxiv,932,[2] pp. Orig cloth, rubbed, sl worn. *(Claude Cox)* **£18 [≈$27]**

Fletcher, John Gould

- Japanese Prints. Boston: The Four Seas Co., 1918. 1st edn. 8vo. Cold frontis, 3 plates, b/w decs by Dorothy Lathrop. Orig cloth. Dw (some wear to top edges, spine darkened). *(Jo Ann Reisler)* **$225 [≈£150]**
- Japanese Prints. With Illustrations by Dorothy Pulis Lathrop. Boston: The Four Seas Co., 1918. One of 1000. Sm 8vo. 96,[2] pp. 4 plates. Orig cloth gilt, sl rubbed. *(Karmiole)* **$75 [≈£50]**

Fletcher, William Younger

- Bookbindings in France. London: Seeley & Co., The Portfolio, 1895. 80 pp. 8 chromolitho plates, 31 text ills. Orig wraps, uncut, spine sl faded. *(Cooper Hay)* **£55 [≈$83]**
- English Book Collectors. Edited by Alfred Pollard. London: 1902. 1st edn. Sm 4to. Port, 45 plates & ills. Orig buckram. *(Traylen)* **£40 [≈$60]**
- Foreign Bookbindings in the British Museum ... London: Kegan Paul ..., 1896. One of 500. Lge 4to. 65 chromolithos by William Griggs. Traces of b'plate. Orig watered silk, sl worn. *(Hermitage)* **$450 [≈£300]**

The Fleuron

- The Fleuron. A Journal of Typography. No. 4. Edited by Oliver Simon. L : The Fleuron, 1925. One of 120 numbered, on handmade paper. 4to. [vii i],164,[18] pp. Orig cloth, t.e.g. *(Oak Knoll)* **$325 [≈£217]**

Flint, Janet

- The Prints of Louis Lozowick. A Catalogue Raisonne. New York: Hudson Hills, Press, 1982. Lge 4to. 223 pp. 330 ills. Orig cloth. Dw. *(Ars Libri)* **$125 [≈£83]**

Flint, Sir William Russell

- Breakfast in Perigord ... London: Privately Printed, 1968. One of 450 signed by the author. Folio. Plates, ills. Orig qtr mor. Boards case. *(Traylen)* **£375 [≈$563]**
- The Living Goddess. London: Privately Printed, 1968. One of 240 signed by the author. Folio. 17 plates (2 cold), 9 ills. Orig qtr mor, t.e.g. Slipcase. *(Traylen)* **£380 [≈$570]**
- Minxes Admonished or Beauty Reproved ... London: Golden Cockerel Press, 1955. One of 550. Sm 4to. Frontis, 51 ills. Orig qtr mor, spine sl darkened. Slipcase. Prospectus laid in. *(Argonaut)* **$300 [≈£200]**
- Models of Propriety ... London: Michael Joseph, 1951. 1st trade edn. Dw (sl rubbed). *(Piglit Books)* **£65 [≈$98]**
- Models of Propriety ... London: Michael Joseph, 1951. One of 500 signed by the author. Foxing to endpapers, faint marks to bds. *(Piglit Books)* **£130 [≈$195]**
- Models of Propriety ... London: Michael Joseph, 1951. 1st trade edn. Lge 8vo. 75 pp. 31 sepia ills. Orig orange cloth gilt. *(Clevedon Books)* **£40 [≈$60]**
- Pictures from the Artist's Studio. London: 1962. 1st edn. 20 cold plates, title vignette, 36 b/w & 5 sepia ills. Orig buckram. Signed by the author. *(Margaret Nangle)* **£130 [≈$195]**
- Shadows in Arcady. London: Charles Skilton, 1965. One of 500 signed by the author. Orig bndg. *(Piglit Books)* **£65 [≈$98]**

Flower Emblems ...

- Flower Emblems or the Seasons of Life. Selections in Prose and Verse from Various Authors ... London: Seeley, Jackson, & Halliday, 1871. Lge 8vo. [ii],75 pp. Hand cold vignette title, 12 hand cold plates. Orig elab gilt cloth, some reprs to hinges. *(Sotheran's)* **£138 [≈$207]**

Flower, Margaret

- Victorian Jewellery ... London: Cassell, 1951. 1st edn. Sm 4to. xxviii,271 pp. 10 cold plates, 118 ills. Orig cloth gilt. Dw. *(Hollett)* **£40 [≈$60]**

Focillon, Henri

- The Art of the West in the Middle Ages. I. Romanesque Art. II. Gothic Art. Edited by Jean Bony. London: 1963. 2 vols. Sm 4to. Num ills. Orig cloth. *(Washton)* **$65 [≈£43]**
- The Art of the West in the Middle Ages. Volume 1: Romanesque Art. London: Phaidon, 1963. 1st edn. Sm 4to. xxii,310,[ii] pp. 159 ills. Orig cloth gilt. Dw. *(Hollett)* **£25 [≈$38]**

Foley, Edwin

- The Book of Decorative Furniture - Its Form, Colour and History. London: [ca 1920]. 2 vols. 4to. xv,427; xii,420 pp. 100 cold ills, 1000 text ills. Orig cloth gilt, sl scratched. *(Hollett)* **£85 [≈$128]**

Fontenelle, Bernard de

- A Plurality of Worlds. Translated by John Glanvill, with a Prologue by David Garnett. London: Nonesuch Press, 1929. One of 1200. ix,138 pp. Orig limp vellum, t.e.g., spine sl darkened. Slipcase. *(Argonaut)* **$175 [≈£117]**

Foot, Mirjam M.

- The Henry Davis Gift; A Collection of Bookbindings. Volume I. Studies in the History of Bookbinding. London: British Library, (1978). 1st edn. 4to. 352 pp. Ills. Orig qtr leather. *(Bookpress)* **$200 [≈£133]**

Ford, Brinsley

- The Drawings of Richard Wilson. London: 1951. 69 pp. 88 plates. Orig cloth, dw. *(Fine Art)* **£35 [≈$53]**

Formaggio, Dino & Basso, Carlo

- A Book of Miniatures. New York: Tudor, (1962). 1st Amer edn. 132 mtd cold plates. Dw (sl worn & soiled). *(Hermitage)* **$125 [≈£83]**

Forrester, Harry

- The Timber-Framed Houses of Essex. A Short Review of their Types and Details. Chelmsford: The Tindal Press, 1968. 8vo. x,93 pp. 70 text figs. Orig cloth gilt. Dw. *(Hollett)* **£25 [≈$38]**

Forsyth, Gordon

- 20th Century Ceramics. An International Survey ... London: The Studio, [ca 1935]. Sm 4to. 128 pp. 8 cold plates, ills. Lib stamp title verso. Lib qtr mor. *(Hollett)* **£50 [≈$75]**

The Fortas Catalogue ...

- The Fortas Catalogue: A Facsimile, with an Introduction by Lessing J. Rosenwald. North Hills: Bird & Bull Press, 1970. One of 250. 4to. Facsimile in rear pocket. Orig cloth. *(Dermont)* **$300 [≈£200]**

Fortescue, Hon. J.W.

- The Story of a Red Deer with Decorations by Dorothy Burroughs. Gregynog Press: 1935. One of 250. [xiv],125 pp. 11 cold headpieces. Inscrptn. Final 8 pp rather spotted. Orig cloth bds, sl marked. *(Michael Taylor)* **£140 [≈$210]**

Foster, J.J.

- A Dictionary of Miniatures (1525-1850) with some account of Exhibitions, Collections, Sales etc. pertaining to them. London: 1926. xvi,330,advt pp. Port frontis. Orig cloth, sl marked, spine sl creased. *(Fine Art)* **£32 [≈$48]**
- A Dictionary of Painters of Miniatures (1525-1850). London: Philip Alan, 1926. 1st edn. Lge 8vo. xv,330,[6 advt] pp. Port frontis. Orig cloth gilt, edges sl spotted. *(Clevedon Books)* **£70 [≈$105]**
- Miniature Painters British and Foreign, with some Account of those who practised in America in the Eighteenth Century. Author's Edition. London: 1903. 2 vols. Folio. 123 ills. Orig cloth backed bds, crnrs sl rubbed. *(Traylen)* **£65 [≈$98]**

Fourest, H.P.

- Delftware: Faience Produced at Delft. London: Thames & Hudson, 1980. Lge 4to. 241 pp. 180 plates. Orig bndg. *(Castle Bookshop)* **£45 [≈$68]**

Fowler, Alfred

- The Romance of Fine Prints. Kansas City: Print Society, 1938. Lge 8vo. 194,advt pp. Ills inc an etching from the original plate by T.J. Cobden-Sanderson. Orig cloth. *(First Folio)* **$75 [≈£50]**

Fowler, John & Cornforth, John

- English Decoration in the 18th Century. London: Barrie & Jenkins, 1983. Tall 4to. 288 pp. Ills. Dw (sl worn). *(Monmouth)* **£40 [≈$60]**
- English Decoration in the 18th Century. London: Barrie & Jenkins, 1986. 4th edn. 288 pp. 40 cold plates, 234 ills. Orig cloth. Dw. *(Fine Art)* **£20 [≈$30]**

Fowlie, Wallace

- Age of Surrealism. New York: The Swallow Press & William Morrow, 1950. 203,[3] pp. Orig cloth. *(Ars Libri)* **$50 [≈£33]**

Fox, Sir Cyril

- Pattern and Purpose. A Survey of Early Celtic Art in Britain. Cardiff: 1958. 4to. 160 pp. 80 plates, ills. Dw. *(Emerald Isle)* **£55 [≈$83]**

Fox, John Jr.

- Little Shepherd of Kingdom Come. Illustrated by N.C. Wyeth. New York: Scribner, 1931. 1st edn. 4to. Cold title, 14 cold plates. Prelims sl foxed. Tiny hole in illustration list. Orig cloth, pict onlay. *(Jo Ann Reisler)* **$225 [≈£150]**

Fox-Davies, Arthur

- Armorial Families. A Directory of Coat-Armour. London: Hurst, 1929. 7th edn. 2 vols. 4to. Ills. Orig bndg. *(Emerald Isle)* **£110 [≈$165]**
- A Complete Guide to Heraldry. Revised Edition. London: T.C. & E.C. Jack, 1929. 8vo. xii,647 pp. Frontis, 24 plates, num text ills. Orig dec cloth. *(Cooper Hay)* **£35 [≈$53]**

France, Anatole

- At the Sign of the Queen Pedauque. Illustrations by Sylvain Sauvage. New York: The Limited Editions Club, 1933. One of 1500 signed by Sauvage. 4to. Orig cloth, t.e.g., cloth at ft of spine rubbed. Slipcase (spine spotted). *(Oak Knoll)* **$65 [≈£43]**
- Crainquebille. Illustrated by Bernard Lamotte. New York: The Limited Editions Club, 1949. One of 1500 signed by Lamotte. 4to. Orig cloth. Slipcase. *(Oak Knoll)* **$45 [≈£30]**

- The Gods Are Athirst. Illustrated by John Austen. London: Bodley Head, 1927. 1st edn. 285 pp. 12 cold plates, 19 w'engvs. Foredge & some plate margs foxed. Orig gilt dec buckram, spine v sl sunned. *(Waddington)* **£30 [≈$45]**
- Penguin Island. Drawings by Malcolm Cameron. New York: The Limited Editions Club, 1947. One of 1500 signed by Cameron. Tall 8vo. Orig parchment-backed bds. Slipcase. *(Oak Knoll)* **$45 [≈£30]**
- The Revolt of the Angels. Illustrations by Pierre Watrin. New York: The Limited Editions Club, 1953. One of 1500. Sm 4to. Ink name. Orig cloth. Slipcase. *(Oak Knoll)* **$55 [≈£37]**

Francis of Assisi, Saint

- Laudes Creaturam ... from the Ancient Italian Text ... English Translation by the late Matthew Arnold. Hammersmith: Doves Press, 1910. One of 250. [xvi] pp. 2 intl blank ff, blank leaf at end. Contemp brown mor, a.e.g., by the Doves Bindery. *(Clark)* **£225 [≈$338]**

Francis, Grant R.

- Old English Drinking Glasses: their Chronology and Sequence. London: 1926. Lge 4to. xxxii,214 pp. 72 plates. Name, minor spots. Orig cloth, t.e.g. *(Bow Windows)* **£195 [≈$293]**

Francis-Lewis, Cecile

- The Art & Craft of Leatherwork ... London: Seeley Service, 1928. 1st edn. 256 pp. Cold frontis, 2 cold plates, 85 b/w plates, 82 ills. Orig dec cloth. *(Willow House)* **£20 [≈$30]**

Franger, Wilhelm

- The Millenium of Hieronymus Bosch. Outlines of a New Interpretation. London: Faber, 1952. xiii,164 pp. 4 mtd cold & 23 b/w plates, 8 ills. Orig cloth. Dw (sl worn). *(Fine Art)* **£35 [≈$53]**

Frankau, Gilbert

- One of Us. A Novel in Verse. London: Chatto & Windus, 1917. One of 110 signed by the author and the illustrator, A.H. Fish. Sm 4to. 173 pp. Frontis, vignette title, 8 plates. Orig parchment, t.e.g., some soiling. *(Chapel Hill)* **$200 [≈£133]**

Franklin, Colin

- Fond of Printing. Gordon Craig as Typographer and Illustrator. San Francisco: Book Club of California, 1980. One of 400 (of 1025) for the Club. Ills. Orig cloth backed bds. Tissue dw. *(Hermitage)* **$50 [≈£33]**
- Fond of Printing. San Francisco: The Book Club of California, 1980. One of 450. 12mo. 90,[1] pp. Orig cloth backed bds. *(Bookpress)* **$45 [≈£30]**

Franklin, Colin & Charlotte

- A Catalogue of Early Colour Printing from Chiaroscuro to Aquatint. Culham: 1977. 1st edn. Lge 4to. [viii],73 pp. Frontis, 16 cold plates. Orig cloth. *(Bookpress)* **$85 [≈£57]**

Franklin, J.W.

- The Cathedrals of Italy. London: Batsford, 1958. 1st edn. 8vo. 280 pp. 119 ills. Orig cloth gilt. Dw. *(Hollett)* **£15 [≈$23]**

Franzke, Andreas

- Dubuffet. Translated by Robert Erich Wolf. New York: Abrams, (1981). 1st edn. Lge 4to. 282 pp. 376 ills. Orig cloth, sl soiled. Dw. *(Karmiole)* **$100 [≈£67]**

Frasconi, Antonio

- Frasconi: Against the Grain. The Woodcuts of Antonio Frasconi. With an Introduction by Nat Hentoff ... New York: Macmillan; London: Collier Macmillan, 1974. One of 130 signed by the artist. 4to. 159 pp. Orig w'cut signed, 216 ills. Orig cloth. Slipcase. *(Ars Libri)* **$375 [≈£250]**

Fraser, Claud Lovat

- Sixty-Three Unpublished Designs. With an Introduction by Holbrook Jackson. London: The First Edition Club, (1924). One of 500. 12mo. Ills. Orig cloth & bds. Prospectus laid in. *(Karmiole)* **$100 [≈£67]**

Freart, Roland, Sieur de Chambray

- An Idea of the Perfection of Painting ... rendred English by J.E. Esquire ... In the Savoy: for Henry Herringman, 1668. 1st English edn. 8vo. [xl],136 pp. Final blank K5. Lib stamp on endpaper. Few sm tears. Mod mor gilt. Wing C.1922. *(Finch)* **£3503 [≈$525]**

Freedberg, S.J.

- Painting of the High Renaissance in Rome and Florence. Cambridge: 1961. 2 vols. Sm 4to. 700 plates. Orig cloth. *(Washton)* **$175 [≈£117]**

Freedman, Jill

- Circus Days. New York: (1975). 1st edn. Tall 8vo. Over 100 photo ills. Orig pict wraps. *(Rob Warren)* **$60 [≈£40]**

Freeman, Margaret

- The Unicorn Tapestries. New York: Dutton, (1976). 1st edn. 4to. 244 pp. 305 ills. Orig cloth. Dw. *(J &J House)* **$60 [≈£40]**

Freeman, Rosemary

- English Emblem Books. London: 1948. 1st edn. 8vo. xiv,256 pp. Frontis, ills. Orig cloth. Dw. *(Bow Windows)* **£60 [≈$90]**

French, Cecil

- T. Sturge Moore: Modern Woodcutters No. 3. London: Herbert Furst, 1921. 14 ills. Orig wraps. *(Fine Art)* **£35 [≈$53]**

Frere-Cook, G. (editor)

- The Decorative Arts of the Mariner. London: Jupiter Books, 1974. 4to. 296 pp. Ills. Orig cloth. Dw. *(Gemmary)* **$75 [≈£50]**

Fried, Michael

- Morris Louis. New York: Abrams, [1979]. Lge oblong 4to. 220 pp. 177 ills. Orig cloth. *(Ars Libri)* **$300 [≈£200]**

Friedlaender, Walter

- Nicolas Poussin, a New Approach. New York: Abrams, (1965). 1st edn. Folio. 203,[1] pp. Frontis, 48 plates. Orig cloth. *(Bookpress)* **$75 [≈£50]**

Friedlander, Max J.

- Jan Gossart and Bernart van Orley. Early Netherlandish Painting Volume VIII. New York: Praeger, 1972. 134 pp. 142 plates. Orig cloth. Dw. *(Leicester Art Books)* **£100 [≈$150]**

Friedlander, Max J. & Rosenberg, Jakob

- The Paintings of Lucas Cranach. London: Sotheby Parke Bernet, 1978. 202 pp. 454 plates, 54 ills. Orig cloth. Dw (chipped). *(Leicester Art Books)* **£60 [≈$90]**

Friedlander, Walter

- Caravaggio Studies. Princeton: UP, 1955. xxviii,320 pp. 67 plates, 117 ills. Orig buckram. *(Leicester Art Books)* **£110 [≈$165]**

Friedman, Martin

- David Hockney Paints the Stage ... USA: 1983. 1st edn. 4to. Num ills. Orig cloth. Dw (sm nick centre spine). *(Margaret Nangle)* **£43 [≈$65]**
- Hockney Paints the Stage ... Minneapolis: Walker Art Center; New York: Abbeville Press, 1983. Lge oblong 4to. 227 pp. Num ills. Orig cloth. Dw. *(Ars Libri)* **$125 [≈£83]**

Friendship's Offering ...

- Friendship's Offering. Boston: Lewis & Sampson, 1845. 12mo. 340 pp. 8 mezzotints by John Sartain. Orig cloth. *(Rona Schneider)* **$80 [≈£53]**

Friswell, J. Hain

- Life Portraits of William Shakespeare... London: Sampson, Low .., 1864. 1st edn. 128 pp. 8 photo plates. Occas dampstains. Orig cloth gilt, a.e.g., sl marked, trifle shaken, guttapercha refixed. *(Hollett)* **£65 [≈$98]**

Frith, Jack

- Scottish Watercolour Painting. Edinburgh: Ramsay Head Press, 1979. Sm 4to. 96 pp. 15 cold & 45 b/w ills. Orig cloth. Dw. *(Cooper Hay)* **£18 [≈$27]**

Frith, James & Andrews, Ronald

- Antique Pistol Collecting (1400-1860). London: Holland Press, 1960. 1st edn. Sm 4to. 122 pp. Frontis, 24 plates. Orig cloth gilt. Dw. Inscribed by the author. *(Hollett)* **£40 [≈$60]**

Frothingham, Alice Wilson

- Spanish Glass. London: Faber, 1964. Roy 8vo. 96 pp. 4 cold & 130 b/w plates. Price-clipped dw. *(Paul Brown)* **£30 [≈$45]**

Fry, Edmund

- Pantographia; containing Accurate Copies of all Known Alphabets in the World ... London: Cooper & Wilson, 1799. 8vo. [iv], xxxvi,320 pp. 10 pp sl foxed. Contemp calf gilt, sm crack upper hinge, some fading, edges sl rubbed. *(Cooper Hay)* **£450 [≈$675]**

Fry, Frederick M.

- A Historical Catalogue of the Pictures, Horse-Cloths & Tapestry at Merchant Taylor's Hall. With a List of the Sculptures and Engravings. London: Chapman & Hall, 1907. xiv,167 pp. Frontis, 33 plates. Some foxing prelims. Orig cloth, t.e.g. *(Fine Art)* **£18 [≈$27]**

Fry, Roger

- Last Lectures. Introduction by Kenneth Clark. Cambridge: UP, 1939. xxix,370 pp. 346 ills. Orig cloth. *(Fine Art)* **£25 [≈$38]**
- Last Lectures. With an Introduction by Kenneth Clark. Cambridge: 1939. Sm 4to. xxix, 370 pp. 346 ills on plates. *(Washton)* **$65 [≈£43]**
- Letters. With an Introduction by Denys Sutton. New York: Random House, 1972. 2

vols. 4to. 117 ills. Orig cloth.
(Ars Libri) **$65 [≈£43]**

- Transformations. Critical and Speculative Essays on Art. London: 1926. 4to. viii,230 pp. 40 ills. Vellum backed bds, sl soiled, extrs sl rubbed. *(Washton)* **$65 [≈£43]**

Fuller, George W. (editor)

- A Bibliography of Bookplate Literature ... Spokane: Public Library, 1926. One of 500 signed by the author. Lge 8vo. 152 pp. Orig cloth gilt. *(Karmiole)* **$150 [≈£100]**

Fullerton, William

- Architectural Examples in Brick, Stone, Wood and Iron. London: Spon, 1895. 2nd edn. 4to. xxii,34,220,[i] pp. Few ff sl creased & soiled at edges. Orig dec cloth gilt, rubbed, recased. *(Hollett)* **£45 [≈$68]**

Furness, S.M.M.

- Georges de la Tour of Lorraine 1593-1652. London: Routledge, 1949. ix,175 pp. 29 plates. Orig cloth.
(Leicester Art Books) **£45 [≈$68]**

Furniss, Harry

- The Confessions of a Caricaturist. London: Fisher Unwin, 1901. 2 vols. 8vo. Ills. Three qtr leather, gilt dec spine, some wear.
(First Folio) **$185 [≈£123]**

Furst, Herbert

- Leonard Campbell Taylor, R.A.; His Place in Art. Leigh-on-Sea: F. Lewis, n.d. One of 500. 148 pp. Port frontis, 12 cold & 29 b/w plates. Orig cloth gilt, t.e.g.
(Clevedon Books) **£55 [≈$83]**
- The Modern Woodcut. London: John Lane; The Bodley Head, (1924). 1st edn. 4to. xxviii,271 pp. 201 plates. Stamp on endpapers. Orig cloth. Dw (chipped).
(Bookpress) **$85 [≈£57]**

Gablik, Suzi

- Magritte. London: Thames & Hudson, 1970. 208 pp. 176 plates. Orig cloth. Dw.
(Leicester Art Books) **£30 [≈$45]**

Gage, Edward

- The Eye in the Wind. Scottish Painting since 1945. London: Collins, 1977. Sm 4to. 160 pp. 12 cold plates. Orig cloth. Dw.
(Cooper Hay) **£25 [≈$38]**

Gainsborough, Thomas

- A Collection of Prints, illustrative of English Scenery, from the Sketches of Thos. Gainsborough, R.A. ... London: Boydell, [1821]. Sm folio. 60 plates (37 hand cold). Contemp mor gilt extra.
(Cooper Hay) **£950 [≈$1,425]qqr**

Gale, Stanley

- Modern Housing Estates. London: Batsford, (1949). 1st edn. 8vo. xii,277 pp. Fldg frontis, 17 fldg plates. Lib marks. Orig cloth.
(Bookpress) **$50 [≈£33]**

Gallet, M.

- Paris Domestic Architecture of the 18th Century. London: Barrie & Jenkins, 1972. 4to. 196 pp. 177 plates, ills. Name. Cvrs sl marked. Dw. *(Monmouth)* **£30 [≈$45]**

Gallwitz, Klaus

- Picasso at 90. The Late Work. London: Weidenfeld & Nicholson, 1971. 221 pp. 383 ills. Orig cloth. Dw (chipped).
(Leicester Art Books) **£70 [≈$105]**

Galsworthy, John

- The Man of Property. With an Introduction by Evelyn Waugh. Illustrations by Charles Mozley. New York: The Limited Editions Club, 1964. One of 1500 signed by Mozley. Sm 4to. Orig cloth. Slipcase (cracked).
(Oak Knoll) **$55 [≈£37]**

Galvin, John

- The Etchings of Edward Borein. A Catalogue of his Work. San Francisco: John Howell, 1971. vi,[264] pp. 318 ills. Orig cloth. Dw.
(Leicester Art Books) **£55 [≈$83]**

Gans-Rudein, E.

- Indian Carpets. Photos by Leo Hilber. New York: Rizzoli, (1984). 4to. 318 pp. Cold plates. Orig cloth. Dw.
(Terramedia) **$60 [≈£40]**

Gant, Roland

- Mountains in the Mind. Andoversford: The Whittington Press, 1987. One of 160 (of 200) signed by the author and the artist, Howard Phipps. Imperial 8vo. Orig canvas, dec label.
(Blackwell's) **£55 [≈$83]**

Gantillon, Simon

- Maya. Golden Cockerel Press: 1930. One of 500. 95 pp. W'engvs by Blair Hughes-Stanton. Orig buckram, t.e.g., spine & cvrs sl darkened. *(Waddington)* **£98 [≈$147]**

Ganz, Paul

- The Drawings of Henry Fuseli. Foreword by John Piper. London: Max Parrish, 1949. 79 pp. Cold frontis, 106 b/w plates, text ills. Orig cloth, faded. *(Clarice Davis)* **$65 [≈£43]**
- The Drawings of Henry Fuseli. With a Foreword by John Piper. London: Max Parrish, 1949. 79 pp. Plates, text ills. Orig cloth. Dw (browned). *(Fine Art)* **£38 [≈$57]**

Gardner, Arthur

- Alabaster Tombs of the Pre-Reformation Period in England. Cambridge: UP, 1940. Tall 8vo. xix,218 pp. 305 ills. Orig cloth, trifle scratched & marked. *(Hollett)* **£60 [≈$90]**
- English Medieval Sculpture. The Original Handbook Revised and Enlarged. Cambridge: UP, 1951. 4to. viii,352 pp. 683 photo ills. Orig cloth gilt. Dw (sl defective). *(Hollett)* **£65 [≈$98]**

Gardner, E.C.

- Home Interiors. Boston: Osgood, 1878. 1st edn. 12mo. [i],268 pp. Frontis, ills. Inner hinges strengthened. Orig cloth gilt. *(Bookpress)* **$225 [≈£150]**
- Homes and All About Them. Boston: Osgood, 1885. 12mo. 710 pp. Frontis, ills. Orig cloth, sl rubbed. *(Bookpress)* **$485 [≈£323]**
- Homes, and How to Make Them. Boston: Osgood, 1874. 1st edn. Sm 8vo. 324 pp. Ills. Orig dec cloth gilt, sl shaken. *(First Folio)* **$175 [≈£117]**

Gardner, J. Starkie

- Armour in England from the Earliest Times to the Reign of James the First. London: Seeley & Co., 1897. 8vo. 100 pp. 8 cold plates, num ills. Three qtr leather & cloth, worn. *(Mendelsohn)* **$40 [≈£27]**
- Armour in England from the Earliest Times to the Seventeenth Century. London: Seeley & Co., 1898. Tall 8vo. 96 pp. 16 cold plates, num ills. Orig cloth gilt, sl worn & marked, sl shaken, jnts cracked. *(Hollett)* **£20 [≈$30]**
- Foreign Armour in England. London: Seeley & Co., 1898. Tall 8vo. 96 pp. 8 cold plates, 44 text ills. Lacks front flyleaf. Orig cloth gilt, spine sl marked & faded. *(Hollett)* **£25 [≈$38]**
- Ironwork. From the Earliest Times to ... the End of the Eighteenth Century. London: 1896. 2 vols. x,152; xvi,202 pp. Ills. Vol 2 endpapers sl marked. Orig cloth, sl marked. *(Phenotype)* **£38 [≈$57]**

Gardner, Samuel

- A Guide to English Gothic Architecture. Cambridge: 1922. Roy 8vo. 180 plates, 56 text figs. Orig cloth. *(Traylen)* **£20 [≈$30]**
- A Guide to English Gothic Architecture. Cambridge: Up, 1925. 2nd edn. Sm 4to. xii,228 pp. 180 plates, 56 text figs. Orig pict cloth. *(Hollett)* **£30 [≈$45]**

Garlick, Kenneth

- Sir Thomas Lawrence. London: Routledge, 1954. viii,92 pp. 119 plates. Orig cloth. Dw (worn). *(Fine Art)* **£70 [≈$105]**

Garner, H.M. & Medley, M.

- Chinese Art in Three-Dimensional Colour. Portland, Oregon: 1969. 1st edn. One of 1000. [Ca 1350] pp. 180 stereo discs. Orig buckram. Slipcases. Battery/mains viewer. *(Bow Windows)* **£375 [≈$563]**

Garner, Thomas & Stratton, Arthur

- The Domestic Architecture of England during the Tudor Period. New York: (1929). 2nd edn, rvsd & enlgd. 2 vols. Ills. Orig cloth, two crnrs bumped. Dws (worn). *(John K. King)* **$200 [≈£133]**

Garrett, Albert

- British Wood Engraving of the 20th Century. A Personal View. London: Scolar Press, 1980. 1st edn. Sm 4to. 223 pp. Ills. Orig cloth gilt. Dw. *(Hollett)* **£40 [≈$60]**

Garve, Andrew

- The Long Short Cut. New York: Harper & Row, (1968). 1st edn. 8vo. [vi],166,[1] pp. Orig cloth backed bds. Dw. The 1st book to be electronically composed (Bookpress). *(Bookpress)* **$45 [≈£30]**

Gascoyne, David

- A Short History of Surrealism. London: Cobden-Sanderson, 1935. Lge 8vo. xv,[1],168 pp. 12 plates. Orig cloth. *(Ars Libri)* **$85 [≈£57]**

Gaskell, Elizabeth Cleghorn

- Cranford. London: Harrap, 1940. 1st edn thus. 265 pp. W'engvs by Joan Hassall. Qtr leather, crnrs bumped, edges of cloth browned, leather sl rubbed. *(Waddington)* **£24 [≈$36]**

Gaskell, Philip

- A Bibliography of the Foulis Press. London: St. Paul's Bibliographies, 1986. 2nd edn. One of 450. 8vo. 484 pp. Orig cloth. *(Oak Knoll)* **$90 [≈£60]**

Gasquet, Abbot

- The Greater Abbeys of England. London: Chatto & Windus, 1908. 1st edn. Num cold plates by Warwick Goble. Orig bndg. *(Old Cathay)* **£45 [≈$68]**
- The Greater Abbeys of England. London: Chatto & Windus, 1908. 1st edn. 8vo. xvi,268 pp. 60 cold plates by Warwick Goble. Occas sl spotting. Orig cloth gilt, upper jnt cracking. *(Hollett)* **£30 [≈$45]**

Gassier, Pierre

- The Drawings of Goya. The Complete Albums. London: Thames & Hudson, 1973. 656 pp. 482 ills. Orig cloth. Dw. *(Leicester Art Books)* **£80 [≈$120]**
- The Drawings of Goya. The Sketches, Studies and Individual Drawings. London: Thames & Hudson, 1975. 582 pp. 407 ills. Orig cloth. Dw. *(Leicester Art Books)* **£80 [≈$120]**

Gassier, Pierre & Wilson, Juliet

- The Life and Complete Work of Francisco Goya. 2nd Revised Edition. New York: Harrison House, 1981. 400 pp. 2148 ills (48 cold). Orig cloth. Dw. *(Leicester Art Books)* **£145 [≈$218]**

Gaunt, William

- The Etchings of Frank Brangwyn, R.A. A Catalogue Raisonne. London: The Studio, 1926. 236 pp. 331 ills. Orig vellum backed bds, t.e.g. *(Leicester Art Books)* **£110 [≈$165]**

Gautier, Theophile

- Mademoiselle de Maupin. Golden Cockerel Press: 1938. One of 500. Sm 4to. 284 pp. 8 copper engvs by John Buckland Wright. Name. Orig qtr vellum, t.e.g. *(Waddington)* **£130 [≈$195]**
- Mademoiselle de Maupin. Translated by Powys Mathers. Golden Cockerel Press: 1938. One of 500. 8 engvs by John Buckland-Wright. Decs by Eric Gill. Orig qtr vellum gilt, t.e.g. *(Carol Howard)* **£110 [≈$165]**
- Mademoiselle de Maupin. Hand-Colored Illustrations by Andre Dugo. New York: The Limited Editions Club, 1943. One of 1000 signed by Dugo. Sm 4to. Orig qtr leather. Slipcase (rubbed). *(Oak Knoll)* **$65 [≈£43]**

Gay, Eben Howard

- A Chippendale Romance. New York: Longmans, Green, 1915. One of 1050. Lge 8vo. 206 pp. Frontis, 56 plates. Orig cloth & bds gilt, t.e.g., sl soiled. *(Karmiole)* **$60 [≈£40]**

Gay, John

- The Beggar's Opera. Illustrated by C. Lovat-Fraser. London: Heinemann, 1922. Roy 8vo. 8 cold plates, b/w decs. Foxed. Orig cloth backed bds. Dw (chipped, spine torn). *(Stella Books)* **£24 [≈$36]**

Geddes, Norman Bel

- Horizons. Boston: Little, Brown, 1932. 4to. xx,293 pp. Ills. Orig cloth. Dw. *(Sotheran's)* **£110 [≈$165]**
- Magic Motorways. New York: Random House, (1940). 1st edn, 1st printing. 4to. 298 pp. Num ills. Orig cloth. *(Karmiole)* **$65 [≈£43]**

Geisberg, Max

- The German Single-Leaf Woodcut: 1500-1550. Revised and Edited by Walter L. Strauss. New York: Hacker, 1974. 4 vols. Lge 4to. Over 1000 ills. Orig cloth. *(Karmiole)* **$175 [≈£117]**

Geist, Sidney

- Brancusi: The Sculpture and Drawings. New York: Abrams, (1975). Oblong 4to. 200 pp. 292 ills (52 cold). Orig cloth. Dw. *(Abacus)* **$500 [≈£333]**

Gems from the Poets. Illustrated ...

- See Lydon, F.A.

Genauer, Emily

- Chagall at the "Met." New York: 1971. Sm folio. 149,[3] pp. Num ills. Orig cloth. *(Ars Libri)* **$125 [≈£83]**

General ...

- The General Contents of the British Museum: with Remarks, serving as a Directory in Viewing that Noble Cabinet. The Second Edition, with Additions and Improvements, and a complete Index. London: Dodsley, 1762. xxiii,210,[xxx] pp. Last page browned. Mod cloth. *(Hollett)* **£120 [≈$180]**

Gent, Thomas

- The Life of Mr. Thomas Gent, printer, of York; Written by Himself. London: for Thomas Thorpe, 1832. 1st edn. Thick Paper. 8vo. Port frontis on india paper. Later red mor gilt, a.e.g., by Bedford. *(David Slade)* **£225 [≈$338]**

Genthe, Arnold

- As I Remember. New York: Reynal & Hitchcock, (1936). 290 pp. 112 photo ills

Orig bndg. *(Hermitage)* **$125 [≈£83]**

Gentleman, David

- Bridges on the Backs. Introduction by Peter Eden. Cambridge: Brooke Crutchley, Christmas Book, 1961. One of 500. Ills. Orig cloth portfolio. Card slipcase (sl bumped). *(Ulysses Bookshop)* **£150 [≈$225]**

Gerard, Max (editor)

- Dali. New York: Abrams, 1968. Lge sq 4to. 242,[8] pp. 271 ills. Orig cloth. Dw. *(Ars Libri)* **$150 [≈£100]**

Gerdts, William H.

- The Great American Nude. New York: Praeger, 1974. 4to. 224 pp. 194 ills. Orig cloth. Dw. *(Rona Schneider)* **$70 [≈£47]**

German-Reed, T.

- Bibliographical Notes on T.E. Lawrence's Seven Pillars of Wisdom and Revolt in the Desert. London: Foyle, 1928. One of 375. 8vo. W'engvs by Paul Nash on title. Orig cloth. Dw, fine. *(Sotheran's)* **£148 [≈$222]**

Gernsheim, Helmut

- Julia Margaret Cameron. Her Life and Photographic Work. London: 1948. 1st edn. 54 b/w plates. Edges & endpapers spotted. Orig cloth, spine ends sl bumped, spine sl darkened. Dw (sl worn). *(Ulysses Bookshop)* **£60 [≈$90]**
- Lewis Carroll, Photographer. New York: Chanticleer Press, 1949. 1st edn. xi,121 pp. 64 plates. Top edge sl spotted. Orig cloth gilt. Price-clipped dw. *(Hollett)* **£120 [≈$180]**

Gersaint, M.

- A Catalogue and Description of the Etchings of Rembrandt Van-Rhyn with Some Account of his Life ... Translated from the French. London: T. Jeffreys, 1752. 12mo. [viii], 184 pp. Port frontis. A few spots. Calf, rebacked, trifle worn, crnrs bumped. *(Clevedon Books)* **£250 [≈$375]**

Gerson, Horst

- Rembrandt Paintings. London: Weidenfeld & Nicolson, 1968. 527 pp. 730 ills. Orig cloth. Dw. *(Leicester Art Books)* **£55 [≈$83]**

Gethyn-Jones, Eric

- The Dymock School of Sculpture. London: 1979. Lge 8vo. xvi,93 pp. Ca 200 ills on 62 plates. Orig cloth. Dw. *(Washton)* **$45 [≈£30]**

Getting, Fred

- Arthur Rackham. London: Macmillan, 1975. 192 pp. Num ills. Orig bndg. Dw. *(Carol Howard)* **£27 [≈$41]**

Getz, John

- The Woodward Collection of Jades and Other Hard Stones. Catalogue. (New York): Privately Printed, 1913. xxiv,108 pp. 170 photo ills. Orig cloth gilt, t.e.g. *(Karmiole)* **$75 [≈£50]**

Ghirshman, Roman

- The Arts of Ancient Iran. Translated by Stuart Gilbert and James Emmons. New York: Golden Press, (1964). 4to. 593 ills. Orig cloth. Dw (sl soiled). *(Karmiole)* **$85 [≈£57]**
- Persian Art, the Parthian and Sassanian Dynasties 249 B.C. - A.D. 651. New York: Golden Press, 1962. 1st edn in English. 4to. Maps, ills. Orig cloth. Dw. *(First Folio)* **$75 [≈£50]**
- Persian Art. The Parthian and Sassanian Dynasties 249 B.C. - A.D. 651. Translated by Stuart Gilbert and James Emmons. New York: Golden Press, (1962). 4to. 538 ills. Orig cloth. Dw (sl soiled & chipped). *(Karmiole)* **$85 [≈£57]**

Gibbings, Robert

- Fourteen Wood Engravings ... From Drawings made on Orient Line Cruises. (Golden Cockerel Press) [1932]. 1st edn. Folio. 14 full-page & 2 smaller engvs. Orig wraps, sl torn & marked. Without the Orient Line compliments slip. *(Bow Windows)* **£150 [≈$225]**
- Iorana! A Tahitian Journal. With Wood-Engravings by the Author. Boston: Houghton, Mifflin 1932. One of 385 signed by the author. Lge 8vo. 158 pp. Orig cloth & pict bds, spine sl faded. Slipcase. *(Karmiole)* **$125 [≈£83]**
- The 7th Man, a True Cannibal Tale of the South Sea Islands ... Golden Cockerel Press: 1930. One of 500. 14 pp. 16 w'engvs by the author. Endpapers browned. Orig qtr buckram. Tissue dw (chipped). *(Waddington)* **£120 [≈$180]**

Gibbons, Felton

- Dossi and Battista Dossi. Court Painters at Ferrara. Princeton: 1968. Lge 4to. xxi,320 pp. 105 plates. Orig cloth. Dw. *(Washton)* **$100 [≈£67]**
- Dosso and Battista Dossi. Court Painters at Ferrara. Princeton: UP, 1968. xxi,320 pp. Cold frontis, 237 ills. Orig cloth. *(Leicester Art Books)* **£90 [≈$135]**

Gibson, Charles Dana

- Drawings. New York: R.H. Russell & Son, 1894. 1st edn. Orig cloth backed pict bds. *(Hermitage)* **$250 [≈£167]**
- The Education of Mr Pipp. London: J. Lane, 1901. 1st edn. 75 pp. Num ills. Free endpaper marked by tape. Orig cloth backed pict bds, sl marked, edges rubbed. *(Stella Books)* **£50 [≈$75]**

Gibson, Frank

- The Art of Henri Fantin-Latour: His Life and Works. London: Drane's Ltd., 1924. 247 pp. 61 ills. Orig cloth. *(Leicester Art Books)* **£55 [≈$83]**
- Charles Conder, his Life and Work. London: John Lane, 1914. 1st edn. 121 ills inc 12 cold plates. Orig linen backed bds, sl worn. New slipcase. *(Hermitage)* **$400 [≈£267]**
- Charles Conder. His Life and Work. London: John Lane; The Bodley Head, 1914. 117 pp. 120 plates. Orig dec cloth, t.e.g. Dw (chipped). *(Leicester Art Books)* **£280 [≈$420]**

Gibson, Louis H.

- Convenient Houses with Fifty Plans for the Housekeeper. New York: Crowell, (1889). 1st edn. 8vo. iv,321 pp. Frontis, 5 plates. Orig cloth, spine sl sunned, front inner hinge cracked. *(Bookpress)* **$185 [≈£123]**

Giedion, Sigfried

- The Eternal Present: The Beginnings of Art. New York: Bollingen, 1962. 4to. Ills. Orig cloth. Dw. *(First Folio)* **$40 [≈£27]**
- Space, Time and Architecture: The Growth of a New Tradition. Cambridge: Harvard UP, 1956. 3rd edn. 8vo. xxii,778 pp. Ills. Orig cloth. Dw (sl worn). *(Bookpress)* **$50 [≈£33]**

Giedion-Welcker, Carola

- Contemporary Sculpture, an Evolution in Volume and Space. New York: George Wittenborn, 1955. Sm 4to. Ills. Orig cloth. Dw (rubbed). *(First Folio)* **$150 [≈£100]**
- Contemporary Sculpture. An Evolution in Volume and Space. Revised and Enlarged Edition ... New York: George Wittenborn, 1960. 4to. 371 ills. Orig cloth. *(Ars Libri)* **$100 [≈£67]**
- Jean Arp. Documentation Marguerite Hagenbach. New York: Abrams, n.d. Lge 4to. 122 pp. 101 plates. Orig cloth. *(Ars Libri)* **$400 [≈£267]**
- Jean Arp. London: Thames & Hudson, 1957. xliii,122 pp. 101 plates, 27 text ills. Orig dec cloth. *(Leicester Art Books)* **£220 [≈$330]**
- Paul Klee. New York: Viking, 1952. 4to. 156 pp. 164 ills. Orig cloth. *(Ars Libri)* **$40 [≈£27]**

Gieure, Maurice

- G. Braque. London: Zwemmer, 1956. 111 pp. 136 plates (36 mtd cold), 39 ills. Orig cloth. *(Leicester Art Books)* **£38 [≈$57]**
- G. Braque. Paris & New York: 1956. English-language edn. Lge 4to. 108,[4] pp. 148 plates. Orig cloth. *(Ars Libri)* **$60 [≈£40]**

Gilbert, Christopher

- The Life & Work of Thomas Chippendale. London: Studio Vista & Christies, 1978. 1st edn. 2 vols. 4to. 25 cold & 525 b/w ills. Orig cloth gilt. Slipcase. *(Hollett)* **£75 [≈$113]**

Gilbert, W.S.

- Iolanthe and Other Operas. Illustrated by W. Russell Flint. London: Bell, 1910. 4to. 32 cold plates. Orig cloth gilt, fine. *(Barbara Stone)* **£125 [≈$188]**
- The Mikado. Illustrated by W. Russell Flint. London: 1928. 1st edn thus. 8 cold plates, b/w ills by C.E. Brock. Orig elab gilt bndg. *(Margaret Nangle)* **£60 [≈$90]**
- The Savoy Operas. Illustrated by W. Russell Flint. London: Bell, 1909. Lge 4to. 32 cold plates. Orig cloth gilt, fine. *(Barbara Stone)* **£125 [≈$188]**
- The Story of the Mikado ... Illustrated by Alice B. Woodward. London: Chiswick Press, 1921. 1st edn thus. Lge 8vo. 6 cold plates, 10 ills. Inscrptn. Orig ptd bds. Dw (dusty). *(Bow Windows)* **£75 [≈$113]**

Gilbey, Sir Walter & Cuming, E.D.

- George Morland: His Life and Works. London: A. & C. Black, Twenty Shilling Series, 1907. 1st edn. 50 cold plates. Orig cloth. *(Old Cathay)* **£49 [≈$74]**

Giles Annual

- Giles Annual. No 1. Orig bndg, fine. *(D & M Books)* **£155 [≈$233]**
- Giles Annual. No 3. Orig bndg, fine. *(D & M Books)* **£145 [≈$218]**

Gilhespy, F. Brayshaw

- Derby Porcelain. London: Spring Books, 1965. 4to. 144 pp. 12 cold plates, 170 b/w ills. Orig cloth gilt. Dw. *(Hollett)* **£35 [≈$53]**

Gilhespy, F. Brayshaw & Budd, Dorothy M.

- Royal Crown Derby from 1876 to the Present Day. London: Charles Skilton, 1964. 1st edn. Sm 4to. 87 pp. Cold frontis, 86 ills. Orig cloth gilt. Price-clipped dw (trifle worn). *(Hollett)* **£40 [≈$60]**

Gill, Eric

- Art & Prudence an Essay ... London: Golden Cockerel Press, 1928. One of 500. 8vo. Orig buckram. Dw, fine. *(Sotheran's)* **£398 [≈$597]**
- Art-Nonsense and Other Essays. London: 1929. One of 100 signed by the author. 8vo. x,324,[i] pp. Orig buckram, t.e.g. *(Sotheran's)* **£450 [≈$675]**
- Christianity and the Machine Age. London: 1940. 1st edn. Free endpapers partly browned, edges spotted. Orig bndg, spotted. Dw (sl frayed, spine darkened). *(Ulysses Bookshop)* **£25 [≈$38]**
- Clothes. London: 1931. One of 160 signed by the author. 10 diags. Orig leather backed bds, t.e.g., edges v sl worn. *(Ulysses Bookshop)* **£450 [≈$675]**
- Clothing without Cloth. Golden Cockerel Press: 1931. One of 500. Tall 8vo. 20 pp. 4 w'engvs by Eric Gill. Orig buckram, top & foredge gilt. *(Waddington)* **£200 [≈$300]**
- Drawings from Life. London: 1940. 1st edn. 15 pp. 33 ills. Orig pict cloth. Dw. *(Margaret Nangle)* **£82 [≈$123]**
- Engravings by Eric Gill. A Selection ... With a Complete Chronological List and a Preface by the Artist. Bristol: Douglas Cleverdon, 1929. One of 490. Tall 4to. 103 plates. Orig cloth gilt, t.e.g., sl worn. *(Oak Knoll)* **$750 [≈£500]**
- The Engravings of Eric Gill. With an Introduction by Douglas Cleverdon. Wellingborough: Christopher Skelton, 1983. One of 85 special copies with separate portfolio of 8 prints. 2 vols & portfolio. Num ills. Orig half mor. Slipcase. *(Karmiole)* **$1,500 [≈£1,000]**
- An Essay on Typography. London: Dent, (1936). 2nd edn. Sm 8vo. [vi],133 pp. Name. *(Oak Knoll)* **$45 [≈£30]**
- First Nudes. New York: The Citadel Press, (1954). 1st Amer edn. Orig cloth gilt. *(Hermitage)* **$65 [≈£43]**
- The Future of Sculpture. Privately Printed: December 1928. One of 55. Bds v sl sprung, edges sl rubbed. *(Gekoski)* **£350 [≈$525]**
- Letters of Eric Gill. Edited by Walter Shewring. London: Cape, (1947). 8vo. 480 pp. Ills. Orig cloth. *(Oak Knoll)* **$55 [≈£37]**
- Wood-Engravings ... Ditchling: St. Dominic's Press, 1924. One of 150. Lge 4to. 37 w'engvs by Gill. Orig cream canvas, untrimmed, covers faintly foxed. *(Blackwell's)* **£1,350 [≈$2,025]**

Gill, Evan R.

- Bibliography of Eric Gill ... London: Cassell, 1953. One of 1000. 224 pp. Ills. Endpapers & frontis margs sl foxed. Inscrptn. Dw (foxed, sl chipped). *(Waddington)* **£60 [≈$90]**

Gilpin, William

- An Essay upon Prints; containing Remarks upon the Principles of Picturesque Beauty, the Different Kinds of Prints ... London: for J. Robson, 1768. 1st edn. 8vo. [2],iv, 4, [2], 249,[1 errata],[11] pp. Early 19th c qtr mor, backstrip relaid. Anon. *(Spelman)* **£120 [≈$180]**
- Gilpin's Forest Scenery. Edited by F.G. Heath. London: 1887. 8vo. xix,371 pp. Title vignette, 14 plates. Sl foxing at ends. Orig pict cloth gilt, a.e.g. *(Henly)* **£21 [≈$32]**

Gioia, Dana

- Journeys in Sunlight. Poems by Dana Gioia, Etchings by Fulvio Testa. [Cottondale, Alabama]: Ex Ophidia Press, 1986. One of 90 signed by the author and the artist. Folio. Orig leather backed dec bds. Cloth case. *(Black Sun)* **$450 [≈£300]**

Giraud, B.

- Stable Building & Stable Fittings. A Handbook for the Use of Architects, Builders and Horse Owners. London: 1891. 8vo. xvi,103 pp. 56 plates, 72 text figs. Orig cloth. *(Phenotype)* **£66 [≈$99]**

Girouard, Mark

- Cities and People ... New Haven: Yale UP, 1985. 1st edn. 4to. vii,[iii],397 pp. Num ills. Orig cloth. Dw. *(Bookpress)* **$55 [≈£37]**
- Life in the English Country House ... New Haven & London: Yale UP, 1978. 1st edn. Sm cr 4to. viii,344 pp. Num ills. Orig cloth. Dw. *(Bow Windows)* **£30 [≈$45]**
- Life in the English Country House. New Haven: Yale UP, 1978. 1st edn. 4to. 344 pp. Over 250 ills. Orig cloth, rubbed. *(Bookpress)* **$45 [≈£30]**
- Robert Smythson and the Architecture of the Elizabethan Era. London: Country Life, 1966. 4to. 232 pp. 198 plates. Orig cloth. Dw. *(Castle Bookshop)* **£29.50 [≈$45]**

- Robert Smythson and the Architecture of the Elizabethan Era. London: Country Life, 1966. 232 pp. 198 ills. Orig cloth. Dw. *(Fine Art)* **£22 [≈$33]**
- Robert Smythson and the Architecture of the Elizabethan Era. New York: A.S. Barnes, (1967). 1st Amer edn. 8vo. 232 pp. 198 ills. Orig cloth. Dw. *(Bookpress)* **$75 [≈£50]**
- The Victorian Country House. New Haven: Yale UP, 1979. 2nd edn. 4to. x,467 pp. Num ills. Orig cloth, sl rubbed. *(Bookpress)* **$65 [≈£43]**

Girtin, Thomas & Loshak, David

- The Art of Thomas Girtin. With a Catalogue. London: A. & C. Black, 1954. xiv, 232 pp. 45 plates. Orig cloth. Dw. *(Leicester Art Books)* **£65 [≈$98]**

Giry, Marcel

- Fauvism. Origins and Development. New York: Alpine Fine Arts Collection, 1982. Lge sq 4to. 275 pp. 130 plates. Orig cloth. Dw. *(Ars Libri)* **$100 [≈£67]**

Glass, Frederick J.

- Drawing, Design and Craftwork: for Teachers, Students etc. London: Batsford, 1920. 215 pp. Orig buckram. *(Carol Howard)* **£25 [≈$38]**

Glazier, R.

- Historic Textile Fabrics. London: Batsford, 1923. 1st edn. Tall 8vo. xiv,120 pp. 104 plates, text ills. Orig gilt dec cloth, spine sunned. *(Clevedon Books)* **£34 [≈$51]**

Glazier, Richard

- A Manual of Historic Ornament ... Prepared for the Use of Students and Craftsmen. London: Batsford, 1906. 2nd edn. Tall 8vo. 168,24 pp. 55 plates. Occas spotting, endpapers browned. Orig cloth gilt, rather worn. *(Hollett)* **£20 [≈$30]**

Gleadall, Eliza Eve

- The Beauties of Flora, with Botanic and Poetic Illustrations: being a Selection of Flowers drawn from Nature ... Heath Hall, near Wakefield: Eliza Eve Gleadall, 1834-36. 2 vols. 4to. 2 hand cold engvd titles, 41 hand cold plates. Orig gilt dec cloth. *(Spelman)* **£3,200 [≈$4,800]**

Gloag, John

- Architecture. New York: Hawthorn Books, (1964). 1st Amer edn. 4to. [vi],197,[1] pp. Num ills. Orig bds. Dw (sl soiled). *(Bookpress)* **$45 [≈£30]**
- The English Tradition in Design. London: Adam & Charles Black, (1959). Rvsd edn. 8vo. x,89 pp. 40 plates. Orig cloth. Dw (sl worn). *(Bookpress)* **$65 [≈£43]**
- Industrial Art Explained. London: Allen & Unwin, (1934). Rvsd & enlgd edn. 248 pp. Plates, ills. Orig cloth gilt. Dw (some loss at hd). *(Clevedon Books)* **£18 [≈$27]**
- Mr Loudon's England. London: Oriel Press, (1970). 1st edn. 8vo. 224 pp. Plates, text ills. Orig cloth gilt. Dw. *(Clevedon Books)* **£25 [≈$38]**
- A Short Dictionary of Furniture containing 1764 Terms used in Britain and America. London: Allen & Unwin, 1952. 1st edn. 566 pp. 630 ills. Orig cloth gilt. Dw. *(Hollett)* **£30 [≈$45]**
- A Social History of Furniture Design. New York: Bonanza Books, (1966). 1st edn. 4to. [vi],202 pp. 4 plates, 344 ills. Orig cloth. Dw. *(Bookpress)* **$45 [≈£30]**
- Victorian Taste: Some Social Aspects of Architecture and Industrial Design, from 1820-1900. London: Adam & Charles Black, 1962. 1st edn. 4to. xvi,175 pp. 24 plates, 117 ills. One marg torn, a few smudges. Orig cloth. Dw (worn). *(Bookpress)* **$65 [≈£43]**

Gloag, John (editor)

- Design in Modern Living. London: Allen & Unwin, 1934. 1st edn. Lge 8vo. 138 pp. 3 charts, 39 plates. Sl foxing. Orig cloth. *(Spelman)* **£20 [≈$30]**

Globe, Alexander

- Peter Stent: London Printseller c. 1642-1665: a Catalogue Raisonne of his Engraved Prints and Books with an Historical and Bibliographical Introduction. British Columbia UP: 1985. 268 pp. 315 ills. Orig cloth. Dw. *(Fine Art)* **£50 [≈$75]**

Glossary ...

- A Glossary of Terms used in Grecian, Roman, Italian and Gothic Architecture. Oxford: John Henry Parker, 1845. 2 vols. 8vo. ix,416,16; 23 pp. 1100 w'cuts on 164 plates (1 loose, edges sl chipped). Orig cloth gilt, recased, foredges damped. Anon. *(Hollett)* **£45 [≈$68]**
- A Glossary of Terms used in Grecian, Roman, Italian, and Gothic Architecture ... see also Parker, John Henry

Glover, Alan

- Gloriana's Glass. London: Nonesuch Press, 1953. One of 1250. 153 pp. Port by Joan Hassall. Orig dec cloth, sl faded & dull. *(Waddington)* **£26 [≈$39]**

Godden, Geoffrey A.

- An Illustrated Encyclopaedia of British Pottery and Porcelain. London: Jenkins, 1966. 1st edn. Sm thick 4to. xxvi,390 pp. 679 ills. Orig cloth gilt. Dw. *(Hollett)* **£40 [≈$60]**
- Lowestoft Porcelain. Antique Collectors' Club: 1985. 200 pp. 12 cold plates, 245 ills. Orig cloth. Dw. *(Fine Art)* **£25 [≈$38]**
- Ridgway Porcelain. Antique Collectors' Club: 1972. 1st edn. 257 pp. 16 cold plates, 218 ills. Orig cloth. Dw. *(Fine Art)* **£25 [≈$38]**
- Staffordshire Porcelain. London: Granada, 1983. Lge 4to. 592 pp. 737 ills. Orig cloth. Dw. *(Castle Bookshop)* **£58 [≈$87]**
- Stevengraphs and Other Victorian Silk Pictures. London: Barrie & Jenkins, (1971). 1st edn. 4to. 492 pp. 321 ills. Orig cloth. Dw. *(Karmiole)* **$75 [≈£50]**
- Victorian Porcelain. London: Jenkins, 1962. 222 pp. 102 plates. Orig cloth gilt. Dw. *(Hollett)* **£35 [≈$53]**

Godfrey, F.M.

- Early Italian Painting 1250-1500. Later Italian Painting 1500-1800. London: Tiranti, 1956. 2 vols. xiii,184; viii,185-408 pp. 294 ills. Dws (sl worn). *(Fine Art)* **£18 [≈$27]**

Godfrey, Walter H.

- The English Almshouse with some account of its predecessor, the Medieval Hospital. London: Faber, 1955. 1st edn. Lge 8vo. 95 pp. 48 plates. Orig cloth gilt. Dw. *(Hollett)* **£25 [≈$38]**

Goepper, Roger

- Essence of Chinese Painting. Boston: Boston Book and Art Shop, (1963). 1st Amer edn. 4to. 244 pp. Mtd cold plates, ills. Dw. *(Schoyer)* **$45 [≈£30]**

Goethe, Johann Wolfgang von

- Faust. Translated by John Anster. Illustrated by Harry Clarke. New York: Dingwall, Rock, [1925]. One of 1000 (of 2000) for America sgnd by Clarke. 4to. 22 cold & num other ills. Orig vellum backed bds, uncut. *(Jo Ann Reisler)* **$500 [≈£333]**
- Wilhelm Meister's Apprenticeship. The Thomas Carlyle Translation. Illustrations by William Sharp. New York: The Limited Editions Club, 1959. One of 1500 signed by Sharp. Sm 4to. Orig cloth, spine sl yellowed. Slipcase (soiled, edges cracked). *(Oak Knoll)* **$55 [≈£37]**

Gogol, Nikolai

- The Overcoat. The Government Inspector. Engravings by Sam Field. Westport, CT: The Limited Editions Club, 1976. One of 2000 signed by Field. 8vo. Orig cloth. Slipcase. *(Oak Knoll)* **$45 [≈£30]**

Goldberg, Norman L.

- John Crome the Elder. Oxford: Phaidon Press, 1978. 2 vols. 16 cold plates, 243 ills. Orig cloth. Dw. *(Leicester Art Books)* **£45 [≈$68]**

Goldman, Judith

- Windows at Tiffany's. The Art of Gene Moore. New York: Abrams, 1980. Folio. 223 pp. 213 ills. Orig cloth. Dw. *(Ars Libri)* **$75 [≈£50]**

Goldscheider, Ludwig

- Ghiberti. London: Phaidon, 1949. 154 pp. 233 ills. Orig cloth. *(Leicester Art Books)* **£24 [≈$36]**

Goldschmidt, Adolf

- German Illumination. Florence: Pantheon & Casa Editrice, (1928). 1st edn in English. 2 vols. Sm folio. 200 plates. Minor foxing. Half mor gilt, t.e.g., sl rubbed. *(Bookpress)* **$550 [≈£367]**
- German Illumination. New York: 1970. Reprint of 1928 edn. 2 vols in one. Lge 4to. 88 + 112 plates. Lib cloth, one crnr bumped. *(Washton)* **$150 [≈£100]**

Goldschmidt, E.P.

- Gothic & Renaissance Bookbindings exemplified and illustrated from the Author's Collection. London: Benn, 1928. 1st edn. 2 vols (text & plates). 4to. 110 plates. B'plates. Vol 1 spine sl faded. *(Hermitage)* **$500 [≈£333]**

Goldsmith, Oliver

- The Deserted Village. Illustrations by Charles Gregory, Frederick Hines and E. Wilson. London: Hildesheimer & Faulkner, [ca 1888]. 4to. Sepia ills. Lacks front free endpaper. Orig cloth backed pict bds, edges sl worn. *(Wilkinson)* **£27 [≈$41]**
- Poems. Edited by R.A. Willmott. London: Routledge Warne, 1860. 1st edn thus. Cold ills by Birket Foster & H.N. Humphreys. Orig prize bndg gilt, spine sl rubbed, hd of spine worn. *(Old Cathay)* **£75 [≈$113]**
- Poems. Edited by R.A. Willmott. London: Routledge, 1877. New edn. Cold ills by Birket Foster & H.N. Humphreys. Some

foxing. Orig elab dec cloth gilt. *(Old Cathay)* **£69 [≈$104]**

- She Stoops to Conquer. New York: The Limited Editions Club, 1964. One of 1500 signed by Cleland. Sm 4to. Orig cloth. Slipcase. *(Oak Knoll)* **$55 [≈£37]**
- The Vicar of Wakefield. Illustrated by V.A. Poirson. London: Nimmo, 1886. Cold ills. Sl foxing. Orig dec cloth. *(Old Cathay)* **£59 [≈$89]**
- The Vicar of Wakefield. Illustrated by John M. Wright. London: A. & C. Black, 1903. 1st edn thus. 260 pp. 13 cold plates. Some foxing. Orig dec cloth gilt, spine faded & rubbed, spine & crnrs sl bumped. *(Stella Books)* **£30 [≈$45]**
- The Vicar of Wakefield. Illustrated by Arthur Rackham. London: Harrap, 1929. 1st edn. 8vo. 232 pp. 12 cold & 22 b/w ills, pict endpapers. Orig pict gilt cloth. Dw (torn). *(Davidson)* **$250 [≈£167]**
- The Vicar of Wakefield. Illustrated by Arthur Rackham. London: Harrap, 1929. 1st edn thus. Num cold plates. Orig gilt dec cloth, fine. Dw (head of spine defective). *(Old Cathay)* **£149 [≈$224]**
- The Vicar of Wakefield. Illustrated by Arthur Rackham. London: Harrap, 1929. 1st Rackham edn. 4to. 12 cold plates, ills, pict endpapers. Orig cloth gilt, t.e.g., mostly unopened. *(Blackwell's)* **£80 [≈$120]**
- The Vicar of Wakefield. Illustrated by Arthur Rackham. Phila: David McKay, (1929). 1st Amer edn. 4to. 232 pp. 12 cold plates, num b/w ills. Orig cloth gilt. Dw (sl chipped). *(Karmiole)* **$125 [≈£83]**

Gombrich, E.H.

- Meditations on a Hobbyhorse: & Other Essays on the Theory of Art. London: Phaidon, 1971. 2nd edn. 252 pp.135 plates, text ills. Orig buckram gilt. Dw. *(Willow House)* **£15 [≈$23]**

Gomme, Andor, & others

- Bristol: an Architectural History. London: Lund Humphries, 1979. 4to. Frontis, 336 ills. Dw. *(David Slade)* **£85 [≈$128]**

Gomme, Laurence (editor)

- The Queen's Story Book. New York: Longman, 1898. 1st Amer edn. B/w ills by W. Heath Robinson. Few ff carelessly opened. Extrs v sl rubbed. *(Barbara Stone)* **£65 [≈$98]**

Gomringer, Eugen

- Josef Albers. His work as contribution to verbal articulation in the Twentieth Century. New York: Wittenborn, [1968]. Oblong folio. 198 pp. Num ills. Orig cloth, shaken. Dw. *(Ars Libri)* **$225 [≈£150]**

Goodison, J.W.

- Catalogue of Paintings: Fitzwilliam Museum, Cambridge. Volume III. The British School. Cambridge: UP, 1977. x,311 pp. 64 plates. Orig cloth. Dw. *(Fine Art)* **£30 [≈$45]**

Goodrich, Lloyd

- Edward Hopper. New York: Abrams, 1971. 306 pp. 246 ills. Orig cloth. Dw. *(Leicester Art Books)* **£100 [≈$150]**
- Edward Hopper. New York: Abrams, n.d. Oblong folio. 306 pp. 246 ills (88 cold). Orig cloth, tips worn. *(Abacus)* **$85 [≈£57]**
- Raphael Soyer. New York: Abrams, n.d. Folio. 349 pp. 290 ills (77 mtd cold plates). Orig cloth. Dw. *(Abacus)* **$250 [≈£167]**
- Reginald Marsh. New York: Abrams, n.d. Oblong folio. 307 pp. 239 ills (85 cold). Orig cloth. Dw. *(Abacus)* **$200 [≈£133]**
- Reginald Marsh. New York: Abrams, [1972]. 308 pp. 239 ills. Orig cloth. Dw. *(Leicester Art Books)* **£90 [≈$135]**

Goodwin, Gordon

- British Mezzotinters. James McArdell. London: A.H. Bullen, 1903. 168 pp. 6 plates. Orig buckram, t.e.g. *(Leicester Art Books)* **£28 [≈$42]**

Goodyear, Frank H., Jr.

- Welliver. New York: Rizzoli, (1985). Folio. 165 pp. 155 mtd cold plates. Orig cloth. Dw. signed by the artist on a tipped-in b'plate. *(Abacus)* **$100 [≈£67]**

Gordon, Donald E.

- Expressionism: Art and Idea. New Haven & London: Yale UP, 1987. Oblong 4to. xvii,[3], 263 pp. 201 ills. Orig qtr cloth. Dw. *(Ars Libri)* **$60 [≈£40]**

Gordon, Jan

- Modern French Painters. London: John Lane; The Bodley Head, 1929. 3rd printing. Lge 8vo. Ills. Orig cloth over bds. *(First Folio)* **$35 [≈£23]**

Gordon, John

- Jim Dine. New York: Whitney Museum of American Art, 1970. 4to. (96) pp. 55 ills. Orig dec wraps. *(Ars Libri)* **$65 [≈£43]**

Gordon, T. Crouther

- David Allan of Alloa 1744-1796. The Scottish Hogarth. Alva: R. Cunningham, [1951]. 4to. xi,100 pp. Cold frontis, 34 ills. Orig cloth. Dw (sl torn). *(Cooper Hay)* **£40 [≈$60]**

Gorham, Maurice

- Back to the Local. Illustrated by Edward Ardizzone. London: 1949. 1st edn. 21 b/w ills. Lacks free endpaper. Orig cloth, sl faded. *(Margaret Nangle)* **£12.50 [≈$20]**
- Londoners. Illustrated by Edward Ardizzone. London: Percival Marshall, 1951. 1st edn. 168 pp. Ills. Orig cloth. Dw (chipped, sl waterstained). *(Bookworks)* **£25 [≈$38]**

Gotch, J.A.

- Squires' Homes and other Old Buildings of Northamptonshire. London: Batsford, 1939. 4to. 52 pp. 133 plates. One plate worn & chipped at edges. Sl rubbed, lib mark on spine. *(Monmouth)* **£40 [≈$60]**

Gothein, Marie Louise

- A History of Garden Art. London: Dent, 1928. 1st edn. 2 vols. 4to. Over 600 ills. Orig cloth, some soiling. *(Bookpress)* **$550 [≈£367]**

Goudy, Frederic W.

- The Alphabet, Fifteen Interpretative Designs Drawn and Arranged ... New York: Mitchell Kennerley, 1922. 2nd edn. Tall 4to. 27 plates. Orig cloth gilt. signed by the author (1922). *(Oak Knoll)* **$100 [≈£67]**
- Elements of Lettering. New York: Mitchell Kennerley, 1922. 1st edn. 4to. [iv],48,[4] pp. 13 plates. Orig cloth. signed by the author. Orig cardboard slipcase (worn). *(Oak Knoll)* **$100 [≈£67]**
- A Half-Century of Type Design and Typography. New York: The Typophiles, 1946. One of 300 (of 825) for subscribers. 2 vols. Tall 12mo. Frontis, ills. Orig cloth, soiled. Slipcase, soiled. *(Oak Knoll)* **$100 [≈£67]**
- Typologia. Studies in Type Design & Type Making ... Berkeley: Calif UP, 1940. One of 300 signed by the author. Sm 4to. Orig qtr leather. Slipcase. *(Oak Knoll)* **$125 [≈£83]**

Goulburn, Edward Meyrick, & others

- The Ancient Scupltures in the Roof of Norwich Cathedral, which exhibit the Course of Scripture History ... London: The Autotype Fine Art Co., 1876. Thick folio. xxxiii,593 pp. 50 plates. Occas sl spotting. Orig mor gilt extra. *(Hollett)* **£220 [≈$330]**

Gould, Cecil

- The Paintings of Correggio. Ithaca: 1976. 4to. 307 pp. 204 plates, ills. Orig cloth. *(Washton)* **$100 [≈£67]**
- The Paintings of Correggio. London: Faber, 1976. 307 pp. 258 ills (12 cold). Orig cloth. Dw. *(Leicester Art Books)* **£65 [≈$98]**

Goulding, Richard W.

- The Welbeck Abbey Miniatures belonging to the Duke of Portland. A Catalogue Raisonne. OUP: 1916. viii,231 pp. Plates. V sl foxing. Orig cloth, t.e.g. *(Fine Art)* **£150 [≈$225]**

Gozzi, Carlo, Count

- The Memoirs ... Translated into English by John Addington Symonds. London: Nimmo, 1896. One of 520. 2 vols. Port frontis & 6 etchings by Adolphe Lalauze, 11 hand cold engvs by Maurice Sand. Leather gilt, t.e.g., jnts sl rubbed, spines sl faded. *(Argonaut)* **$350 [≈£233]**

Grabar, Andre

- The Beginnings of Christian Art 200-395. London: Thames & Hudson, 1967. 4to. 326 pp. Plan, map, ills. Orig cloth gilt. Dw (torn). *(Hollett)* **£30 [≈$45]**
- Early Christian Art. From the Rise of Christianity to the Death of Theodosius. New York: Odyssey Press, 1968. Sm 4to. 326 pp. 312 ills. Orig cloth. Dw. *(Mendelsohn)* **$85 [≈£57]**
- The Golden Age of Justinian. From the Death of Theodosius to the Rise of Islam. New York: Odyssey Press, (1967). 4to. [10],422 pp. Map, 464 ills. Orig cloth. Dw. *(Karmiole)* **$75 [≈£50]**

Grabhorn, Robert (compiler)

- A Commonplace Book of Cookery ... with a Preface by M.F.K. Fisher. San Francisco: The Arion Press, 1975. One of 425. viii,175 pp. Text ills. Orig cloth backed dec bds. *(Argonaut)* **$275 [≈£183]**

Grace, A.F.

- A Course of Lessons in Landscape Painting in Oils. London: Cassell, Petter & Galpin, 1881. 1st edn. Lge 4to. 93,[3 advt] pp. 9 mtd chromolithos inc frontis, w'cuts in text. Sl foxing. Orig cloth gilt, some marks, crnrs bumped. *(Clevedon Books)* **£68 [≈$102]**

Graham, Rigby

- Patterned Papers. Brewhouse Press: 1977. One of 80. Tipped-in papers. Orig cloth gilt. *(Words Etcetera)* **£75 [≈$113]**

- Patterned Papers. Wymondham: Brewhouse Press, 1977. One of 80. Sm 4to. [44] pp. 16 cold samples. Orig cloth. *(Bookpress)* **$275 [≈£183]**

Grant, M.H.

- Rachel Ruysch 1664-1750. Leigh-on-Sea: F. Lewis, n.d. One of 500. 46 pp. 46 plates. Orig cloth. *(Leicester Art Books)* **£95 [≈$143]**

Grant, Michael

- The Roman Forum. London: Weidenfeld & Nicolson, 1970. Lge 8vo. 240 pp. Num ills. Orig cloth gilt. Dw. *(Hollett)* **£30 [≈$45]**

Grant, R. Francis

- Old English drinking Glasses: Their Chronology and Sequence. London: Jenkins, 1926. Lge 4to. xxxi,214 pp. 72 plates. Orig cloth, t.e.g. *(Castle Bookshop)* **£120 [≈$180]**

Grassier, Pierre & Wilson, Juliet

- The Life and Complete Work of Francisco Goya. New York: 1981. 2nd English edn. Folio. 400 pp. 48 cold plates, 2148 ills. *(Washton)* **$250 [≈£167]**

Grassineau, James

- A Musical Dictionary: being a Collection of Terms and Characters, as well Ancient as Modern ... London: for J. Wilcox, 1740. Issue with 'A' of title over 'i' of Dictionary. Half-title. 3 fldg plates, music. Lib stamps. Rec half calf. *(Jarndyce)* **£180 [≈$270]**

Gray, Basil

- The English Print. London: A. & C. Black, 1937. 1st edn.8vo. xvi,225 pp. 24 plates, 8 text ills. Orig cloth gilt. *(Clevedon Books)* **£22 [≈$33]**
- The English Print. London: Adam & Charles Black, 1937. 1st edn. 8vo. xvi,225 pp. Orig cloth. Dw (rubbed). *(Claude Cox)* **£20 [≈$30]**

Gray, Camilla

- The Russian Experiment in Art, 1863-1922. New York: Abrams, (1962) 1970. Sm 4to. 296 pp. 256 ills. Orig cloth. Dw. *(Ars Libri)* **$65 [≈£43]**

Gray, Nicolette

- XIXth Century Ornamented Types and Title Pages. London: Faber, (1938). 1st edn. 8vo. 213 pp. Ills. Orig cloth. Dw (chipped, spine darkened). *(Oak Knoll)* **$55 [≈£37]**
- Nineteenth-century Ornamented Types and Title Pages. London: Faber, 1951. 213 pp. Ills. Dw (frayed). *(Claude Cox)* **£25 [≈$38]**
- The Painted Inscriptions of David Jones. London: Gordon Fraser, 1981. 1st edn. Lge 4to. 113 pp. 76 ills. Dw. *(Waddington)* **£30 [≈$45]**

Gray, Thomas

- Gray's Elegy. Illuminated by Lady Willoughby. London: Day & Son, [1866]. 1st edn. Folio. 11 ff. Orig cloth, a.e.g., minor spotting. *(Bookpress)* **$265 [≈£177]**
- Gray's Elegy: An Elegy Written in a Country Churchyard. Artists' Edition de Luxe. Phila: Lippincott, 1883. One of 500. 4to. 22 w'engvs. "Alligator" paper cvr. *(Rona Schneider)* **$40 [≈£27]**

Graziosi, P.

- Palaeolithic Art. London: Faber, 1960. Lge 4to. xi,278 pp. 306 plates. Endpapers damaged. Ex-lib. Orig cloth. *(Castle Bookshop)* **£60 [≈$90]**

Greard, Valery

- C.O. Meissonier. His Life and His Art. With Extracts from His Notebooks ... Collected by his Wife. London: Heinemann, 1897. xiv,395 pp. Port frontis, 18 plates, 19 gravures, 236 ills. Orig cloth gilt. *(Leicester Art Books)* **£70 [≈$105]**

Green, Bertha de Vere

- A Collector's Guide to Fans over the Ages. London: Muller, 1975. 1st edn. Lge 8vo. 332 pp. 40 cold plates, 64 b/w & 68 line ills. Orig cloth gilt. Price-clipped dw (trifle creased). *(Hollett)* **£45 [≈$68]**

Green, David

- Blenheim Palace. London: Country Life, 1951. 1st edn. 4to. 348 pp. 112 ills. Orig cloth gilt. Dw. *(Hollett)* **£140 [≈$210]**
- Grinling Gibbons. His Work as Carver and Statuary 1648-1721. London: Country Life, 1964. 1st edn. 4to. 207 pp. Port frontis, 248 ills. Sev sm lib stamps. Dw. *(Francis Edwards)* **£90 [≈$135]**

Green, Julian

- The Pilgrim on the Earth. Translated by C. Bruerton. Illustrated by Rene Ben Sussan. London: The Blackamore Press, 1929. One of 410. 126 pp. 12 w'engvs. Orig qtr vellum, t.e.g., deckle edges sl browned, trifling wear extrs. *(Bookworks)* **£48 [≈$72]**

Green, N.E.

- Hints on Sketching from Nature. London: George Rowney & Co., [ca 1870]. 7th edn. 3

parts in one vol. Sm 8vo. vi,40,68,[20 advt] pp. 40 plates on 36 ff. Orig cloth gilt, rebacked. *(Clevedon Books)* **£50 [≈$75]**

Greenberg, Clement

- Joan Miro. With a Memoir by Ernest Hemingway. New York: The Quadrangle Press, 1950. Rvsd edn. 4to. 134 pp. Num ills. Orig yellow bds stamped in black. Dw. *(Karmiole)* **$75 [≈£50]**

Greener, W.W.

- The Gun and its Development; with Notes on Shooting. London: Cassell, Petter & Galpin, 1881. Lge 8vo. [iv],674,xxi,8 pp. Frontis, 342 w'cuts in text. Orig pict cloth gilt, a.e.g., recased. *(Hollett)* **£130 [≈$195]**
- The Gun and its Development ... London: Cassell & Co., 1899. Lge 8vo. xvi,768,xii pp. Frontis, over 300 w'cut text ills. Orig pict cloth gilt, recased. *(Hollett)* **£145 [≈$218]**

Greenwell, William & Rolleston, George

- British Barrows. A Record of the Examination of Sepulchral Mounds in various parts of England ... Oxford: Clarendon Press 1877. 1st edn. Lge 8vo. xi,763 pp. 164 text figs. Orig cloth gilt, v sl worn. *(Hollett)* **£185 [≈$278]**

Greenwood, James

- Legends of Savage Life. London: John Camden Hotten, 1867. 1st edn. 4to. 36 hand cold ills by Ernest Griset. Orig cloth gilt, new endpapers, spine reinforced. *(Jo Ann Reisler)* **$300 [≈£200]**

Grego, Joseph

- Cruikshank's Water Colours. London: A. & C. Black, 20 Shilling Series, 1903. 1st edn. 328 pp. 67 plates. Orig dec cloth gilt, t.e.g., faded. *(Carol Howard)* **£60 [≈$90]**
- Cruikshank's Watercolours. London: A. & C. Black, 1903. xxvi,326 pp. 67 cold plates. Orig cloth gilt, t.e.g. *(Leicester Art Books)* **£35 [≈$53]**

Gregson, Wilfred

- A Student's Guide to Wood Engraving. London: Batsford, 1953. 1st edn. 79 pp. Ills. Dw. *(Michael Taylor)* **£18 [≈$27]**

Grehan, Ida

- Waterford: an Irish Art. The Collector's Guide. New York: Portfolio Press, 1981. Tall 4to. 256 pp. Cold ills. Orig cloth gilt. Dw. *(Hollett)* **£40 [≈$60]**

Gresham, C.A.

- Medieval Stone Carvings in North Wales: Sepulchral Slabs and Effigies of the 13th and 14th Centuries. Cardiff: 1968. 4to. xxiv,264 pp. 19 plates, 97 figs. Orig cloth. *(Castle Bookshop)* **£58 [≈$87]**

Griffith, William Pettit

- Ancient Gothic Churches, Their Proportions and Chromatics. London: the author, 1847. 4to. viii,10, 1-12,1-10 pp, 4 litho plates, 44 pp, 7 litho plates, 32 pp, 5 litho plates, [3 advt] pp. Errata slip, advt slip. Some spotting. Orig cloth. *(Sotheran's)* **£80 [≈$120]**

Grigson, Geoffrey

- Painted Caves. London: Phoenix House, 1957. 1st edn. 223 pp. Maps, plates, ills. Occas spots. Orig cloth gilt. Dw. *(Hollett)* **£25 [≈$38]**
- Samuel Palmer. The Visionary Years. London: Kegan Paul, 1947. xii,206 pp. 68 plates. Orig cloth. *(Leicester Art Books)* **£38 [≈$57]**
- Samuel Palmer: The Visionary Years. London: 1947. 1st edn. xi,203 pp. 2 cold & 68 other plates. Few pp crnrs creased. Orig cloth. *(Fine Art)* **£20 [≈$30]**
- Shell Guide to Flowers of the Countryside. Illustrated by Rowland and Edith Hilder. London: Phoenix House, 1955. Sm 4to. 12 cold ills. Orig pict glazed bds, crnrs rubbed. *(Barbara Stone)* **£35 [≈$53]**

Grimwade, A.G.

- The Queen's Silver. A Survey of Her Majesty's Personal Collection. London: The Connoisseur, 1953. 1st edn. Lge 8vo. vii,120 pp. 64 plates. Orig cloth backed bds gilt. Dw (trifle worn). *(Hollett)* **£65 [≈$98]**

Grinnell, Isabel Hoopes

- Greek Temples. New York: Metropolitan Museum of Art, 1943. 4to. xxi,60 pp. 54 plates. *(Zeno)* **£37.50 [≈$57]**

Gris, Juan

- Letters of Juan Gris [1913-1927]. Collected by Daniel-Henry Kahnweiler. Edited by Douglas Cooper. London: Privately Printed, 1956. One of 300. 8vo. xv,221 pp. Orig cloth. Dw (sl worn). ALS by Cooper inserted. *(Washton)* **$275 [≈£183]**

Grohmann, Will

- The Art of Henry Moore. New York: Abrams, [1960]. Lge 4to. 279 pp. 239 ills.

Orig cloth. *(Ars Libri)* **$150 [≈£100]**

- The Drawings of Paul Klee. New York: Curt Valentin, 1944. One of 700. Lge 4to. xiv,[9] pp. 72 plates. New cloth. *(Ars Libri)* **$200 [≈£133]**
- Paul Klee. London: Lund Humphries, 1954. 448 pp. 472 ills. Orig cloth, spine rubbed & worn. *(Leicester Art Books)* **£80 [≈$120]**
- Paul Klee. New York: Abrams, [1954]. Lge 4to. 448 pp. Num ills. Orig cloth. *(Ars Libri)* **$200 [≈£133]**
- Wassily Kandinsky. Life and Work. New York: Abrams, n.d. 4to. 428 pp. 920 ills (41 mtd cold plates). Orig cloth. Dw. *(Abacus)* **$225 [≈£150]**
- Wassily Kandinsky: Life and Work. New York: Abrams, [1958]. Sm folio. 428 pp. 920 ills. Orig cloth. *(Ars Libri)* **$250 [≈£167]**
- Willi Baumeister. Life and Work. New York: Abrams, n.d. Lge 4to. 360,[2] pp. 1143 ills (53 mtd cold). Orig cloth. *(Ars Libri)* **$375 [≈£250]**
- Willi Baumeister. Life and Work. London: Thames & Hudson, 1966. 362 pp. Ca 200 ills. Biro name. Orig cloth. Dw. *(Leicester Art Books)* **£190 [≈$285]**

Grolier Club

- Catalogue of an Exhibition of the Liber Studiorum of J.M.W. Turner. New York: The Grolier Club, 1888. 1st edn. Orig ptd wraps, uncut, some chips. *(Mac Donnell)* **$60 [≈£40]**

Gropius, Walter

- The New Architecture and the Bauhaus. Boston: Charles T. Branford, n.d. 12mo. 112 pp. Ills. Orig cloth. Dw (sm tear). *(Bookpress)* **$165 [≈£110]**
- The New Architecture and The Bauhaus ... Translated from the German by P. Morton Shand. New York: MoMA, 1936. 1st Amer edn. 8vo. 80 pp. 16 photo plates. Orig cloth, edges sl soiled. *(Sotheran's)* **£85 [≈$128]**

Gropper, William

- Gropper. New York: ACA Gallery Publications, 1938. 4to. (128) pp. 59 ills. Orig linen, sl stained. *(Karmiole)* **$65 [≈£43]**

Grosbois, Charles

- Shunga. Images of Spring. Essay on Erotic Elements in Japanese Art. Geneva: Nagel, 1966. Folio. Mtd cold plates. Orig linen gilt. Dw. *(First Folio)* **$155 [≈£103]**

Grose, Irving

- The Drypoints of Horace Mann Livens. London: Belgrave Gallery, 1979. One of 400. 72 pp. 65 ills. Orig cloth. Dw. *(Fine Art)* **£18 [≈$27]**

Grossman, F.

- Bruegel. The Paintings. Complete Edition. London: Phaidon, 1966. Rvsd edn. 206 pp. 155 ills. Orig buckram. *(Leicester Art Books)* **£35 [≈$53]**
- Pieter Bruegel. Complete Edition of the Paintings. London: 1973. 3rd edn, rvsd. 4to. 206 pp. 149 plates. Orig cloth. Dw. *(Washton)* **$85 [≈£57]**

Grosz, George

- Ecce Homo. Introduction by Henry Miller. New York: Grove Press, 1966. Lge 4to. xiv,[2] pp. 100 plates. Orig cloth. Dw. *(Ars Libri)* **$125 [≈£83]**

Grover, Ray & Grover, Lee

- Art Glass Nouveau. US: Tuttle, 1968. 3rd printing. 4to. 231 pp. 424 cold plates. Dw (damaged). *(Paul Brown)* **£58 [≈$87]**

Gruffydd, W.J.

- Caniadau. Gregynog Press: 1932. One of 250. 4 w'engvs by Blair Hughes-Stanton. Orig bndg, unopened, spine ends sl bumped, crnrs rubbed, sl soiled. *(Ulysses Bookshop)* **£250 [≈$375]**

Grundy, C.R. & Roe, F.G.

- Catalogue of the Paintings and Drawings in the Collection of Frederick John Nettlefold. London: 1933-38. [One of 100 deluxe]. 4 vols. Folio. 384 mtd cold plates. Orig mor gilt extra, silk endpapers & doublures. *(Traylen)* **£600 [≈$900]**

Gruner, Lewis

- Decorations and Stuccos of Churches & Palaces, in Italy ... London: Thomas McLean, 1854. Lge folio. [viii] pp. 56 plates. Lib marks, occas foxing. Contemp half mor, rebacked, worn. *(Bookpress)* **$1,250 [≈£833]**

Guerman, Mikhail

- Art of the October Revolution. New York: 1979. Lge 4to. 34,[8] pp. 384 ills. Orig cloth. Dw. *(Ars Libri)* **$100 [≈£67]**

Guidol, Jose

- Goya. 1746-1828. Biography, Analytical Study and Catalogue of his Paintings. New York: Tudor, 1971. 4 vols. 1295 plates (135

cold). Orig rexine cvrd bds. Dws.
(Leicester Art Books) **£310 [≈$465]**

Gullick, J.T. & Timbs, J.
- Painting Popularly Explained ... London: Kemp, 1859. 1st edn. 326 pp. Frontis. Orig cloth gilt, somewhat worn.
(Willow House) **£30 [≈$45]**

Gunnis, Rupert
- Dictionary of British Sculptors (1660-1851). London: Abbey Library, [ca 1964]. Rvsd edn. Lge thick 8vo. 514 pp. 30 plates. Orig cloth gilt. Dw. *(Hollett)* **£20 [≈$30]**

Gurney, George
- Sculpture and the Federal Triangle. Washington: Smithsonian, 1985. Lge 4to. 464 pp. 257 ills. Orig cloth. Dw.
(Ars Libri) **$50 [≈£33]**

Gwilt, Joseph
- The Architecture of Marcus Vitruvius Pollio, in Ten Books. London: Priestley & Weale, 1826. 1st edn. 4to. xl,413 pp. 10 plates. Occas foxing. Orig cloth, rebacked, rubbed, rebacked. *(Bookpress)* **$250 [≈£167]**

H., J.
- Three Treatises ... see Harris, James

Hackenbroch, Yvonne
- Meissen and Other Continental Porcelain, Faience and Enamel, in the Irwin Untermeyer Collection. London: Thames & Hudson, 1956. 1st edn. Lge 4to. xxix,264 pp. 146 plates. Orig buckram backed cloth gilt. Dw. Slipcase. *(Hollett)* **£120 [≈$180]**

Hackmack, Adolf
- Chinese Carpets and Rugs ... Authorised Translation by Miss L. Arnold. Tientsin: La Librairie Francaise, 1924. 4to. Cold frontis, map, 26 plates (2 cold). Orig cloth, sl stained.
(Rankin) **£65 [≈$98]**

Haesaerts, Paul
- James Ensor. London: Thames & Hudson, 1957. 386 pp. 457 ills. Orig cloth. Dw (torn).
(Leicester Art Books) **£165 [≈$248]**

Haftmann, Werner
- Marc Chagall. New York: Abrams, n.d. 4to. 162 pp. 140 ills (49 mtd cold). Orig cloth. Dw. *(Abacus)* **$60 [≈£40]**

Haggar, Reginald G.
- English Country Pottery. London: Phoenix House, 1950. 1st edn. 160 pp. 32 plates. Orig cloth gilt. Dw (sl worn & chipped).
(Hollett) **£40 [≈$60]**

Hagreen, Philip
- Philip Hagreen, the Artist and his Work. At the Sign of the Arrow: May, 1975. One of 200. 206 ills. Orig buckram bds.
(Michael Taylor) **£40 [≈$60]**

Hahn, Emily
- Mabel. A Biography of Mabel Dodge Luhan. Boston: Houghton, Mifflin 1977. 4to. [8],228 pp. 16 plates. Orig cloth. Dw.
(Ars Libri) **$35 [≈£23]**

Haining, Peter
- Movable Books, An Illustrated History. London: New English Library, 1979. Oblong 4to. 142 pp. Cold ills, fldg plates. Orig cloth. Dw. *(First Folio)* **$150 [≈£100]**

Hajek, L.
- Japanese Woodcuts. Early Periods. London: Spring Books, n.d. Sm 4to. 96 pp. 50 cold plates, b/w text ills. Japanese style bndg. Fldg box, peg fastenings. Slipcase.
(Clevedon Books) **£40 [≈$60]**
- Utamaro - Portraits in the Japanese Woodcut. London: Spring Books, n.d. Sm 4to. 86 pp. 58 cold plates, b/w text ills. Japanese style bndg. Fldg box, peg fastenings. Slipcase.
(Clevedon Books) **£40 [≈$60]**

Haldane, Duncan
- Islamic Bookbindings. London: Victoria & Albert Museum, (1983). 1st edn. 4to. 205 pp. Num ills. Orig cloth. Dw.
(Bookpress) **$150 [≈£100]**

Halfpenny, Joseph
- Gothic Ornaments in the Cathedral Church of York. York: J. Todd & Sons, 1795 [1800]. 1st edn. Imperial 4to. Engvd title, dedic, 21 ff dated 1800. 105 plates (2 cold). Contemp tree calf, flat spine gilt.
(Robert Frew) **£375 [≈$563]**

Hall, Julie
- Tradition and Change. The New American Craftsman. New York: Dutton, 1977. 4to. 192 pp. 233 ills. Orig cloth. Dw.
(Ars Libri) **$75 [≈£50]**

Hall, S.C.
- The Baronial Halls and Ancient Picturesque Edifices of England ... London: Sotheran, 1881. 2 vols. 71 tinted lithos, num w'engvs. Contemp three qtr mor, gilt spines, crnrs &

extrs worn. *(Hermitage)* **$1,200 [≈£800]**

- The Baronial Halls and Ancient Picturesque Edifices of England. London: Sotheran, 1881. 2 vols. Folio. 71 cold lithotints, num text ills. Half mor gilt, a.e.g. *(Traylen)* **£350 [≈$525]**

Hall, William

- A Biography of David Cox: with Remarks on his Works and Genius. London: Cassell, Petter, Galpin, 1881. xv,268 pp. Orig cloth, front hinge cracked, sl loose. *(Leicester Art Books)* **£40 [≈$60]**

Halton, Ernest G.

- Sketches by Samuel Prout in France, Belgium, Germany, Italy and Switzerland. London: The Studio, 1915. 26 pp. 65 plates, facs letter. Orig cloth, t.e.g. *(Leicester Art Books)* **£26 [≈$39]**

Hamburger, Michael

- In Suffolk. Madely: Five Seasons Press, 1981. One of 150 signed by the author and artist. 8vo. 66 pp. Etching by Derek Southall as frontis. Orig canvas & cloth. Slipcase. *(Lamb)* **£75 [≈$113]**

Hamel, Maurice

- Corot and his Work. Glasgow: 1905. One of 200. 2 vols. Lge thick 4to. Port, 100 mtd ills. Endpapers foxed. Orig qtr mor. *(Traylen)* **£95 [≈$143]**

Hamerton, Philip Gilbert

- The Etcher's Handbook. Boston: Roberts Bros., 1881. 3rd edn. 8vo. 129 pp. 6 orig etchings, 29 ills. Occas v sl foxing. Orig cloth. *(Rona Schneider)* **$50 [≈£33]**
- The Etcher's Handbook. London: Charles Robertson & Co., 1881. 3rd edn. 8vo. 129 pp. 6 orig etchings, 29 ills. Orig cloth. *(Rona Schneider)* **$50 [≈£33]**
- Etching & Etchers.London: Macmillan, 1868. 1st edn. xxvi,354 pp. 35 etchings. Orig bndg, spine rubbed, crnrs sl bumped. *(Rona Schneider)* **$1,500 [≈£1,000]**
- Etching & Etchers. Illustrated. Boston: Roberts Bros., 1876. xxxii,460 pp. 12 etched plates, port on title. Orig illust cloth, t.e.g., extrs sl frayed & chipped. *(Karmiole)* **$100 [≈£67]**
- Etching and Etchers. London: Macmillan, 1876. 8vo. 459 pp. 1 etching by Lalanne and 11 reproductive etchings by Hamerton. Orig dec bndg, shabby. *(Rona Schneider)* **$65 [≈£43]**
- The Graphic Arts: A Treatise on the Varieties of Drawing, Painting, & Engraving. London: Seeley, Jackson & Halliday, 1882. Large Paper. Folio. 384 pp. 54 ills. Orig white leather cloth. *(Rona Schneider)* **$250 [≈£167]**

Hamilton, Count Anthony

- Memoirs of the Count de Grammont. Translated by Horace Walpole. London: Bodley Head, 1928. One of 1000. 230 pp. 8 w'engvs by Wilfred Jones. Crnrs bumped. *(Waddington)* **£14 [≈$21]**

Hamilton, Edward

- A Catalogue Raisonne of the Engraved Works of Sir Joshua Reynolds from 1755 to 1822 .... London: Colnaghi, 1884. 196 pp. Few pp sl foxed. Orig cloth gilt. *(Leicester Art Books)* **£45 [≈$68]**

Hamilton, George Heard

- The Art and Architecture of Russia. Harmondsworth: Penguin Books, 1954. 4to. 480 pp. 180 plates. Dw. *(Bury Place)* **£40 [≈$60]**
- The Art and Architecture of Russia. Harmondsworth: Penguin, 1954. xxi,320 pp. Map, 180 plates, plans in text. Orig cloth. *(Quest Books)* **£28 [≈$42]**
- 19th and 20th Century Art. New York: Abrams, (1970). 1st edn. 4to. 481,[3] pp. Frontis, 417 ills. Few lib marks. Orig cloth. Dw (sl rubbed). *(Bookpress)* **$125 [≈£83]**
- Painting and Sculpture in Europe. 1880 to 1940. Baltimore: Penguin Books, 1967. Stout 4to. xxiv,443 pp. 193 plates. Orig cloth. *(Ars Libri)* **$100 [≈£67]**

Hamilton, Walter

- Dated Book-Plates (Ex Libris), with a Treatise on their Origin and Development ... London: A. & C. Black, 1895. 1st edn. 4to. [4],226,[20] pp. Num ills. Orig gilt dec cloth, t.e.g., hd of spine sl chipped. *(Karmiole)* **$100 [≈£67]**

Hamlin, Talbot

- Benjamin Henry Latrobe. New York: OUP, 1955. 1st edn. 8vo. xxxvi,633 pp. 40 plates. Orig cloth backed bds, tips sl bruised, front inner hinge cracked. *(Bookpress)* **$65 [≈£43]**
- Greek Revival Architecture in America. London: OUP, 1944. 1st edn. 8vo. xl,439 pp. 94 plates, 39 text ills. Orig cloth backed bds, rear cvr internally cracked, sl worn. *(Bookpress)* **$65 [≈£43]**

Hammacher, A.M.

- The Evolution of Modern Sculpture.

Tradition and Innovation. London: Thames & Hudson, (1969). 1st edn. Lge 4to. 384 pp. 404 plates. Orig cloth gilt. Dw. *(Karmiole)* **$65 [≈£43]**

- The Evolution of Modern Sculpture: Tradition and Innovation. New York: Abrams, 1969. 4to. 383 pp. 404 ills. Orig cloth. Dw. *(Ars Libri)* **$200 [≈£133]**
- Jacques Lipchitz. His Sculpture. New York: Abrams, [1960]. Lge 4to. 176 pp. 100 plates. Orig cloth. *(Ars Libri)* **$60 [≈£40]**

Hammon, H.J.

- The Architectural Antiquities and Present State of Crosby Place, London as lately restored by John Davies, Architect. London: Weale, 1844. 4to. 16 pp. Subscribers. 15 plates. Some foxing. Orig cloth, worn. *(Monmouth)* **£40 [≈$60]**

Hammond, Alex

- The Book of Chessmen. London: Arthur Barker, (1950). 1st edn. Sm 4to. 61 plates. Orig cloth gilt. Dw. *(Karmiole)* **$35 [≈£23]**

"Handasyde" (pseudonym)

- The Four Gardens. Illustrated by Charles Robinson. London: Heinemann, 1912. 161 pp. 8 mtd cold plates, text ills, pict endpapers. Orig gilt dec cloth. *(Carol Howard)* **£40 [≈$60]**

Handley-Read, Charles (editor)

- The Art of Wyndham Lewis. With an Essay ... London: Faber, 1951. 109 pp. 53 plates. Orig cloth. Dw. *(Leicester Art Books)* **£55 [≈$83]**

Haney, Kristine Edmondson

- The Winchester Psalter an Iconographic Study. Leicester: UP, 1986. 1st edn. xx,180 pp. 163 ills. Orig cloth. Dw. *(Claude Cox)* **£18 [≈$27]**

Hannan, Thomas

- Famous Scottish Houses. The Lowlands. London: A. & C. Black, 1938. 1st edn. Lge 8vo. viii,205,[ii] pp. 101 plates. Occas sl spotting. Orig cloth gilt. *(Hollett)* **£30 [≈$45]**

Hanneford-Smith, W.

- The Architectural Work of Sir Banister Fletcher. London: Batsford, 1934. One of 500 (this copy unnumbered). Lge 4to. xi,291,[i] pp, inc plates. Orig cloth. *(Sotheran's)* **£85 [≈$128]**

Hannover, Emil

- Pottery and Porcelain, a Handbook for Collectors ... London: Benn, 1925. 3 vols. Roy 8vo. 11 cold plates, 1944 ills. Orig buckram gilt. 2 vols in dws. *(Traylen)* **£120 [≈$180]**

Hansen, Al

- A Primer of Happenings & Time/Space Art. New York: Something Else Press, 1965. Lge 8vo. [6],145 pp. Num ills. Orig cloth. Dw. *(Ars Libri)* **$50 [≈£33]**

Harada, Jiro

- The Lesson of Japanese Architecture. London: The Studio, 1936. 1st edn. 4to. 192 pp. Num ills. Orig cloth gilt. *(Hollett)* **£40 [≈$60]**

Harbison, P.

- The Daggers and the Halberds of the Early Bronze Age in Ireland. Munich: Beck, 1969. 1st edn. 27 plates, 4 figs. Dw. *(Baker)* **£28.50 [≈$44]**

Hardie, Martin

- The British School of Etching. London: Print Collectors' Club, 1921. 33 pp. 12 plates. Sl foxing. V sl worn. *(Fine Art)* **£15 [≈$23]**
- English Coloured Books (1906). Bath: Kingsmead Reprints, 1966. xxiv,340 pp. 27 plates. Orig cloth. Dw. *(Fine Art)* **£38 [≈$57]**
- The Etched Work of W. Lee-Hankey, R.E. from 1904 to 1920. London: H. Lefevre, [1920]. One of 350. vi,98 pp. 94 plates. Orig cloth gilt. *(Leicester Art Books)* **£180 [≈$270]**
- Etchings and Drypoint from 1902 to 1924 by James McBey. A Catalogue. London: Colnaghi, 1925. One of 500 signed by the artist with an orig etching. Qtr calf, t.e.g., lacks backstrip. *(Leicester Art Books)* **£170 [≈$255]**
- John Pettie. London: Adam & Charles Black, 1908. Sm 4to. xxiv,278 pp. Cold frontis. Orig dec cloth gilt, t.e.g. *(Cooper Hay)* **£28 [≈$42]**
- John Pettie. London: Adam & Charles Black, 1908. 1st edn. Thick 4to. 278 pp. 50 cold plates, 8 ills. Orig pict cloth. *(Hermitage)* **$75 [≈£50]**
- Samuel Palmer. London: Print Collector's Club, 1928. One of 500. 22 pp. 12 plates. Orig cloth & bds, spine marked. *(Fine Art)* **£20 [≈$30]**
- Water-Colour Painting in Britain. London: Batsford, 1966. 3 vols. Orig cloth. One dw sl worn. *(Spelman)* **£150 [≈$225]**
- Water-Colour Painting in Britain. London:

Batsford, 1967-68. 1st edn vols 2 & 3. 3 vols. 4to. Num ills. Dws. *(Mermaid Books)* **£125 [≈$188]**

- Water-Colour Painting in Britain. London: Batsford, (1967-68). Vol 1 2nd edn, vols 2 & 3 1st edns. 3 vols. 4to. Num ills. Orig cloth. Dws. *(Bow Windows)* **£175 [≈$263]**
- Water-Colour Painting in Britain. London: Batsford, 1968-70. 3 vols. Folio. Num ills. Orig cloth. Dws. *(Robert Frew)* **£150 [≈$225]**

Hardie, Martin & Sabin, Arthur K.

- War Posters issued by Belligerent and Neutral Nations 1914-1919. London: A. & C. Black, 1920. 1st edn. Sm 4to. xvi,46 pp. 80 plates. Orig pict cloth gilt, rather cockled in places. *(Hollett)* **£95 [≈$143]**

Harding, Annaliese

- German Sculpture in New England Museums. Boston: 1972. Sm 4to. 95 pp. 148 ills. Orig cloth. Dw. *(Washton)* **$75 [≈£50]**
- German Sculpture in New England Museums. Boston: 1972. Sm 4to. 95 pp. 148 ills. Orig cloth. Dw. *(Washton)* **$75 [≈£50]**

Hardy, Thomas

- Far From the Madding Crowd. New York: The Limited Editions Club, 1958. One of 1500 signed by Parker. Thick 8vo. Orig qtr leather, wear to spine. Slipcase (spotted). *(Oak Knoll)* **$100 [≈£67]**
- Far From the Madding Crowd. New York: Heritage Press, 1958. 400 pp. W'engvs by Agnes Miller Parker. Orig linen. Slipcase. *(Waddington)* **£36 [≈$54]**
- Far From the Madding Crowd. With Wood Engravings by Agnes Miller Parker. New York: The Limited Editions Club 1958. One of 1500 signed by the artist. Orig leather backed pict bds. Slipcase, fine. *(Margaret Nangle)* **£135 [≈$203]**
- Jude the Obscure. New York: Heritage Press, 1969. 427 pp. W'engvs by Agnes Miller Parker. Orig dec linen, spine sl sunned. *(Waddington)* **£34 [≈$51]**
- The Mayor of Casterbridge. Illustrated with Wood Engravings by Agnes Miller Parker. New York: The Limited Editions Club, 1964. One of 1500 signed by Parker. Thick 8vo. Orig qtr leather. Slipcase. *(Oak Knoll)* **$95 [≈£63]**
- The Mayor of Casterbridge. New York: Heritage Press, (1964). 318 pp. W'engvs by Agnes Miller Parker. Orig dec linen, spine sunned. Slipcase (sl worn). *(Waddington)* **£32 [≈$48]**
- The Return of the Native. With Wood Engravings by Agnes Miller Parker. New York: Heritage Press, 1942. Orig cloth. Dw (upper edge v sl creased). *(Margaret Nangle)* **£95 [≈$143]**
- Tess of the D'Urbervilles. Illustrated by Vivien Gribble. London: Macmillan, 1926. 1st edn thus. One of 1500. 508 pp. 41 w'engvs. Orig buckram, t.e.g., spine sunned. *(Waddington)* **£40 [≈$60]**
- Tess of the D'Urbervilles. London: Macmillan, 1926. One of 1500. 524 pp. 41 w'engvs by Vivien Gribble, fldg map. Orig buckram, t.e.g., sl marked, spine sunned. *(Bookworks)* **£45 [≈$68]**
- Tess of the D'Urbervilles. New York: Heritage Press, 1956. 448 pp. W'engvs by Agnes Miller Parker. Orig qtr linen. Slipcase (broken). *(Waddington)* **£34 [≈$51]**

Hardy, W.J.

- Book-Plates. Second Edition. London: Kegan Paul, 1897. xvi,240 pp. 44 plates. Orig cloth gilt. *(Karmiole)* **$35 [≈£23]**

Harford, John S.

- The Life of Michael Angelo Buonarroti with Translations of his Poems and Letters ... Second Edition. London: Longmans, 1858. 2 vols. 8vo. 21 plates. Contemp calf, double mor labels, spines v sl rubbed. *(Waterfield's)* **£90 [≈$135]**

Harling, Robert

- Notes on the Wood Engravings of Eric Ravilious. London: Faber, 1947. Reprint. 72 pp. 90 ills. Endpapers v sl foxed. Dw. *(Waddington)* **£24 [≈$36]**

Harling, Robert (editor)

- "House and Garden" Dictionary of Design and Decoration. London: Collins, Conde Nast, 1974. 539 pp. Num ills. Dw. *(Fine Art)* **£45 [≈$68]**

Harrington, H. Nazeby

- The Engraved Work of Sir Francis Seymour Haden, P.R.E. An Illustrated and Descriptive Catalogue. Liverpool: Henry Young & Sons, 1910. One of 225. xxv,128 pp. 109 plates. Orig cloth gilt, t.e.g. *(Leicester Art Books)* **£250 [≈$375]**

Harris, Ann Sutherland

- Andrea Sacchi. Complete Edition of the Paintings with a Critical Catalogue. Princeton: 1977. 4to. 133 pp. 185 ills. Orig cloth. Dw. *(Washton)* **$90 [≈£60]**

- Andrea Sacchi. Complete Edition of the Paintings with a Critical Catalogue. Oxford: Phaidon, 1977. x,264 pp. 185 ills. Orig cloth. *(Leicester Art Books)* **£70 [≈$105]**

Harris, James

- Three Treatises. The First concerning Art. The Second Music, Painting and Poetry. The Third concerning Happiness. By J.H. London: for Nourse & Vaillant, 1744. 1st edn. Contemp calf gilt, spine dulled, jnts sl cracked. *(Jarndyce)* **£250 [≈$375]**
- Three Treatises. The First concerning Art. The Second Music, Painting and Poetry. The Third concerning Happiness. The Third Edition revised and Corrected. London: for Nourse & Vaillant, 1772. Contemp calf, later reback. *(Jarndyce)* **£60 [≈$90]**
- Three Treatises. The First concerning Art. The Second Music, Painting and Poetry. The Third concerning Happiness. The Fifth Edition revised and Corrected. London: for F. Wingrave, 1792. Sl marg worming. Contemp calf, jnts cracking. *(Jarndyce)* **£4 [≈$60]**

Harris, Joel Chandler

- Uncle Remus. His Songs and Sayings. New York: Limited Editions Club, 1957. One of 1500 signed by the artist, Seong Moy. Ills. Slipcase (worn). *(Waddington)* **£35 [≈$53]**

Harris, S. Hutchinson

- The Art of Anglada-Camarasa. A Study in Modern Art. London: The Leicester Galleries, 1929. One of 500. 88 pp. 57 ills on 48 plates. Orig parchment & bds. *(Leicester Art Books)* **£45 [≈$68]**

Harris, Tomas

- Goya Engravings and Lithographs. Oxford: Bruno Cassirer, 1964. 2 vols. 190 mtd plates, 292 ills. Orig buckram. Dws. *(Leicester A Books)* **£475 [≈$713]**

Harrison, Frederick

- Notes on Sussex Churches. Hove: Combridge's, 1911. 3rd edn, rvsd & enlgd. Sm 8vo. 186 pp. 40 ills. Foredge sl stained. Orig cloth gilt. *(Hollett)* **£25 [≈$38]**

Harrison, Kenneth

- The Windows of King's College Chapel, Cambridge. Notes on their History and Design. Cambridge: UP, 1952. 1st edn. Sq 8vo. ix,90 pp. Orig cloth backed bds. Dw. *(Hollett)* **£45 [≈$68]**

Harrison,, Martin & Waters, Bill

- Burne-Jones. London: Barrie & Jenkins, 1979. Reprint. 209 pp. 280 ills. Orig cloth. *(Leicester Art Books)* **£45 [≈$68]**

Harrop, Dorothy

- A History of the Gregynog Press. Pinner: PLA, 1980. 4to. xvi,266 pp. Plates. Orig cloth gilt. *(Cooper Hay)* **£40 [≈$60]**
- A History of the Gregynog Press. Pinner: PLA, 1980. Sm folio. Ills. Orig bndg. Acetate dw. *(Words Etcetera)* **£28 [≈$42]**

Hart, George

- The Violin: its Famous Makers and their Imitators. London: Dulau, 1885. xl,499 pp. 22 w'engvd plates. Orig pict cloth gilt, sl worn, spine v faded, jnts cracking. *(Hollett)* **£50 [≈$75]**

Hart, Horace

- Notes on a Century of Typography at the University Press Oxford 1693-1794. A Photographic Reprint of the Edition of 1900 with an Introduction and Additional Notes by Harry Carter. Oxford: Clarendon Press 1970. 4to. Orig cloth gilt. Dw. *(Cooper Hay)* **£45 [≈$68]**

Hart, J.

- A Practical Treatise on the Construction of Oblique Arches. London: 1839. 2nd edn, with addtns. Large Paper. 4to. vi,40 pp. 10 plates. Orig dec cloth, sl worn. *(Clevedon Books)* **£80 [≈$120]**

Hart, J. Coleman

- Designs for Parish Churches ... New York: Dana, 1857. 1st edn. 8vo. 108 pp. Frontis, 42 plates. Text foxed. Orig cloth, front inner hinge cracked. *(Bookpress)* **$425 [≈£283]**

Hart, John W.

- External Plumbing Work. A Treatise on Lead Work for Roofs. London: Scott, Greenwood, 1902. 2nd edn, rvsd & enlgd. viii,273,32 pp. 180 text ills. Orig cloth gilt, lower crnrs trifle damp marked. *(Hollett)* **£60 [≈$90]**

Hart-Davis, Rupert

- A Catalogue of the Caricatures of Max Beerbohm. Cambridge: Harvard UP, 1972. 1st edn. Sm 4to. 258 pp. 100plates. Orig cloth. Dw. *(Karmiole)* **$35 [≈£23]**
- A Catalogue of the Caricatures of Max Beerbohm. London: Macmillan, 1972. 258 pp. 100 ills. Orig cloth. Dw. *(Leicester Art Books)* **£45 [≈$68]**

Harte, Bret

- The Queen of the Pirate Isle. Illustrated by Kate Greenaway. London: Chatto & Windus, (1886). 1st edn. Cold ills. Orig pict cloth gilt. Schuster & Engen 1e. *(Barbara Stone)* **£135 [≈$203]**
- The Queen of the Pirate Isle. Illustrated by Kate Greenaway. London: Chatto & Windus, (1886). 1st edn. Cold ills. Orig pict cloth gilt, spine ends v sl worn. Schuster & Engen 1e. *(Barbara Stone)* **£125 [≈$188]**
- The Wild West. Paris: Harrison of Paris, 1930. One of 840. 8vo. [vi],187,[2] pp. Pochoir illustrations by Pierre Falke. Orig cloth. Slipcase. *(Bookpress)* **$150 [≈£100]**

Harthan, John

- Books of Hours and their Owners. London: 1977. 4to. 89 ills. Orig cloth. Dw. *(Traylen)* **£20 [≈$30]**

Hartmann, Sadakichi

- The Whistler Book. Boston: L.C. Page, 1910. 8vo. 271 pp. 57 ills. Orig cloth. *(Rona Schneider)* **$25 [≈£17]**

Hartnoll, Phyllis

- The Grecian Enchanted. With Eight Aquatints by John Buckland-Wright. (London): The Golden Cockerel Press, 1952. One of 320. Tall 4to. 80 pp. 8 plates. Orig cloth gilt. *(Karmiole)* **$200 [≈£133]qqr**

Hartt, Frederick, & others

- The Chapel of the Cardinal of Portugal 1434-1459 at San Miniato in Florence. Phila: 1964. 4to. 192 pp. 4 cold & 152 b/w plates. Orig cloth. Dw (sl worn). *(Washton)* **$85 [≈£57]**

Harvey, Alfred

- The Castles and Walled Towns of England. London: Methuen, The Antiquary's Books series, 1911. 1st edn. xix,276 pp. 46 ills. Half-title & foredge spotted. Orig cloth gilt. *(Hollett)* **£30 [≈$45]**
- The Castles and Walled Towns of England. London: Methuen, The Antiquary's Books, 1911. 1st edn. 8vo. xix,276 pp. 46 ills. Half-title & foredge spotted. Orig cloth gilt. *(Hollett)* **£30 [≈$45]**
- The Castles and Walled Towns of England. London: Methuen, The Antiquary's Books, 1925. 2nd edn. xix,276 pp. 46 ills. Foredge spotted. Orig cloth gilt, sm snag hd of spine. *(Hollett)* **£20 [≈$30]**

Harvey, J.R.

- Victorian Novelists and their Illustrators. New York: New York UP, 1971. 1st Amer edn. 4to. xii,240 pp. 76 ills. Orig cloth. Dw. *(Bookpress)* **$95 [≈£63]**

Harvey, John Hooper

- The Cathedrals of Spain. London: Batsford, 1957. 1st edn. 280 pp. 149 ills. Orig cloth gilt. Dw (worn). *(Hollett)* **£12.50 [≈$20]**
- The English Cathedrals. Revised and re-illustrated edition. London: Batsford, 1956. 2nd edn. 192 pp. 82 plates. Orig cloth gilt. Dw. *(Hollett)* **£15 [≈$23]**
- English Mediaeval Architects. A Biographical Dictionary down to 1550 ... London: Batsford, 1954. 1st edn. Lge 8vo. xxiii,412 pp. 16-page 1984 supplement inserted. Orig cloth gilt. Dw (sm chip). *(Hollett)* **£75 [≈$113]**
- Gothic England. A Survey of National Culture 1300-1550. London: Batsford, 1947. 1st edn. xiv,242 pp. Num ills. Orig cloth gilt. Dw (v sl rubbed). *(Hollett)* **£25 [≈$38]**
- Henry Yevele: The Life of an English Architect. London: Batsford, 1944. 1st edn. 8vo. x,86 pp. Cold frontis, plates, text ills. Orig cloth, faded. Dw (sl frayed). *(Clevedon Books)* **£20 [≈$30]**
- Henry Yevele, c.1320 to 1400. The Life of an English Architect. London: Batsford, 1946. 2nd edn. x,86 pp. Cold frontis, 71 ills. Orig cloth, spine faded. *(Hollett)* **£25 [≈$38]**

Harvey, Mary

- The Bronzes of Rembrandt Bugatti (1885-1916). An Illustrated Catalogue and Biography. Ascot, Berkshire: Palaquin Publishing, 1979. 4to. [6],112 pp. 142 ills. Orig wraps. *(Ars Libri)* **$40 [≈£27]**
- The Bronzes of Rembrandt Bugatti. An Illustrated Catalogue and Biography. Ascot: Palaquin Publishing, 1979. 112 pp. 163 ills. Orig wraps. *(Leicester Art Books)* **£35 [≈$53]**

Harvey, William

- The Anatomical Exercises of Dr. William Harvey. London: Nonesuch Press, 1928. One of 1450. xiv,202 pp. Fldg plate. Niger morocco. *(Goodrich)* **$175 [≈£117]**

Haskell, Arnold & Lewis, Min

- Infantalia, The Archaeology of the Nursery. London: Dennis Dobson, 1971. 1st edn. 4to. 120 pp. Ills by Stanley Lewis. Orig cloth gilt. Dw. *(Hollett)* **£25 [≈$38]**

Haskell, Arnold L.

- Some Studies in Ballet. London: Lamley & Co., 1928. One of 400 (this copy unnumbered). 4to. 16 mtd photos inc one on cover. Occas spotting. Orig wraps, sl worn. *(Robert Frew)* **£85 [≈$128]**

Haskell, Francis

- Patrons and Painters. A Study in the Relations between Italian Art and Society in the Age of Baroque. London: Chatto & Windus, 1963. 1st edn. 4to. xx,454 pp. 64 plates. Orig cloth. Dw (sl chipped). *(Karmiole)* **$50 [≈£33]**

Haslam, Malcolm

- The Real World of Surrealism. London: Weidenfeld & Nicholson, 1978. 264 pp. 32 cold plates, 200 b/w ills. Orig cloth. Dw. *(Fine Art)* **£25 [≈$38]**

Haslem, John

- The Old Derby China Factory; the Workmen and their Productions ... London: George Bell & Sons, 1876. 1st edn. Sm 4to. xvi,255 pp. Cold frontis, 12 plates (11 cold). Orig cloth gilt, t.e.g., lower bd sl marked, sl shaken. *(Hollett)* **£175 [≈$263]**

Hasluck, P.N.

- Printers' Oils, Colours and Varnishes. London: Cassell, 1913. Sm 8vo. 100 pp. 51 text ills. Orig cloth. *(Clevedon Books)* **£30 [≈$45]**

Hassell, J.

- The Camera; or, Art of Drawing in Water Colours. London: Simpkin & Marshall, 1823. 1st edn. 8vo. iv,5-32 pp. Fldg cold frontis, 2 fldg plates. Rather foxed. Orig bds, worn. *(Spelman)* **£50 [≈$75]**

Hastings, H. de C.

- Recent English Domestic Architecture 1929. London: The Architectural Press, [1929]. Lge 4to. viii,104 pp. Cold frontis, plates, plans. Orig cloth backed bds, crnrs sl rubbed. *(Sotheran's)* **£38 [≈$57]**

Hastings, Viscount

- The Golden Octopus. Legends of the South Seas. Illustrated by Blamire Young. London: Eveleigh Nash & Grayson, 1928. One of 700. 12 cold plates. Orig bndg, fine. Dw. *(Old Cathay)* **£95 [≈$143]**

Haudicquer de Blancourt, Francois

- The Art of Glass. Shewing, how to make all sorts of Glass, Crystal and Enamel ... Now first translated into English. With an Appendix ... London: for Dan. Brown, 1699. 8vo. [14],355,[13] pp. Half-title. 9 plates. Occas sl browning. Rec half calf. Wing H.1150. *(Spelman)* **£850 [≈$1,275]**

Havell, E.B.

- A Handbook of Indian Art. London: Murray, (1927). 2nd edn. 8vo. xvi,222 pp. Frontis, 79 plates. Orig cloth, some wear. *(Bookpress)* **$185 [≈£123]**

Haverkamp-Begemann, E. & Logan, Anne-Marie S.

- European Drawings & Watercolors in the Yale University Art Gallery. New Haven: 1970. 2 vols (text & plates). 400 plates & ills. Orig cloth. Dws. *(Clarice Davis)* **$150 [≈£100]**
- European Drawings and Watercolors in the Yale University Art Gallery, 1500-1900. New Haven: 1970. 2 parts. Sm 4to. xxii,391; xiv pp. 321 ills on plates, 69 figs. Orig cloth. Dw. *(Washton)* **$175 [≈£117]**

Haves, J.W.

- Late Roman Pottery. London: British School at Rome, 1972. 1st edn. 40 maps, 23 plates, 93 text figs. Orig cloth. Dw (chipped). *(Baker)* **£33 [≈$50]**

Hawcroft, Francis

- Edward Seago: A Review of the Years 1953-1964. London: Collins, 1965. Subscribers' edition, in cloth. 76 plates. Orig cloth. Dw (reprd). *(Fine Art)* **£95 [≈$143]**
- Edward Seago. A Review of the Years 1953-1964. London: Collins, 1965. 196 pp. 76 ills. Orig cloth. Dw. *(Leicester Art Books)* **£40 [≈$60]**

Haweis, H.R.

- Old Violins. Edinburgh: John Grant, 1905. 293 pp. Ills. Orig cloth gilt, sl rubbed, upper jnt strained. *(Hollett)* **£20 [≈$30]**

Haweis, Mrs H.R.

- The Art of Beauty. London: Chatto & Windus, 1883. 2nd edn. 8vo. xiv,298,[1] pp. Frontis, text ills. Endpapers browned. Orig cloth, front inner hinge cracked, spine sunned. *(Bookpress)* **$300 [≈£200]**

Hawkins, Edward & others

- Medallic Illustrations of the History of Great Britain and Ireland to the Death of George II. London: BM, 1885. 2 vols. Thick 8vo. xxxiv,724; 866 pp. 2 frontises, 454 text ills.

Lib stamps title versos. Mod half mor gilt. *(Hollett)* **£120 [≈$180]**

Hawkins, Sir John

- A General History of the Science and Practice of Music. London: for T. Payne & Son, 1776. 5 vols. 4to. Half-titles. Frontis vol 1. Sl spotting. Later bds, uncut, cloth spines, crnrs rubbed. *(Jarndyce)* **£450 [≈$675]**

Hawthorne, Nathaniel

- The Marble Faun. The Romance of Monte Beni. New York: The Limited Editions Club, 1931. One of 1500 signed by Carl Strauss, the illustrator. 2 vols. Sm 8vo. Orig limp cloth, t.e.g. Slipcase (rubbed). *(Oak Knoll)* **$65 [≈£43]**
- The Scarlet Letter. Illustrated by Barry Moser. West Hatfield: Pennyroyal Editions, 1984. Orig cloth. Slipcase. *(Hermitage)* **$125 [≈£83]**
- Twice-Told Tales. Selected and Edited by Wallace Stegner. New York: The Limited Editions Club, 1966. One of 1500 signed by Valenti Angelo, the illustrator. Sm 4to. Orig cloth. Slipcase. *(Oak Knoll)* **$65 [≈£43]**
- A Wonder Book. Illustrated by Arthur Rackham. London: Hodder & Stoughton, [1922]. 1st Rackham edn. 4to. 16 mtd cold plates, ills. V sl mark to preface. Orig cloth gilt. *(Sotheran's)* **£248 [≈$372]**

Hay, John

- The Pike County Ballads. Illustrated by N.C. Wyeth. Boston: Houghton, Mifflin (1912). 1st edn. 4to. Cold frontis, 6 cold plates, 26 b/w ills, dec endpapers. Orig cloth, pict onlay. *(Jo Ann Reisler)* **$135 [≈£90]**

Hayden, Arthur

- By-Paths in Curio Collecting. London: Fisher Unwin, 1919. 1st edn. 462 pp. Num ills. Orig pict cloth gilt, trifle faded. *(Hollett)* **£15 [≈$23]**
- Chats on Old Clocks. London: Fisher Unwin, 1917. 1st edn. 302,[i] pp. Frontis, 80 ills. Orig cloth, sl marked, sl shaken, jnts cracked. *(Hollett)* **£25 [≈$38]**
- Chats on Old Silver. Edited and Revised by Cyril G.E. Bunt. London: Benn, 1949. 306 pp. Ills. Orig cloth gilt. Dw. *(Hollett)* **£10 [≈$15]**
- Chats on Royal Copenhagen Porcelain. London: Fisher Unwin, 1928. 345 pp. 57 ills. Orig cloth gilt, hd of spine trifle frayed. *(Hollett)* **£30 [≈$45]**

Haydon, Benjamin Robert

- The Diary of Benjamin Robert Haydon. Edited by Willard Bissell Pope. Harvard: UP, 1960. 5 vols. Dws (chipped). *(Peter Bell)* **£120 [≈$180]**

Hayes, John

- Catalogue of the Oil Paintings in the London Museum. London: HMSO, 1970. 267 pp. 194 ills. Orig cloth. Dw. *(Fine Art)* **£40 [≈$60]**
- The Drawings of Thomas Gainsborough. London: Zwemmer, 1970. 2 vols. 462 ills. Orig cloth. Dw. *(Leicester Art Books)* **£150 [≈$225]**
- Gainsborough as Printmaker. London: 1971. xix,114 pp. 95 ills. Orig cloth. *(Leicester Art Books)* **£50 [≈$75]**
- Gainsborough as Printmaker. New Haven: 1972. 4to. xx,114 pp. 95 ills. Orig cloth. Dw. *(Washton)* **$50 [≈£33]**
- Gainsborough Paintings and Drawings. London: Phaidon, 1975. 232 pp. 186 ills. Orig cloth. Dw. *(Leicester Art Books)* **£28 [≈$42]**
- The Landscape Paintings of Thomas Gainsborough. A Critical Text and Catalogue Raisonne. London: Sotheby, 1982. 2 vols. 13 cold plates, 609 ills. Orig cloth. Dws. Slipcase. *(Leicester Art Books)* **£75 [≈$113]**
- Rowlandson's Watercolours and Drawings. London: Phaidon, 1972. 214 pp. 145 ills. Orig cloth. Dw. *(Leicester Art Books)* **£25 [≈$38]**

Hayter, Charles

- An Introduction to Perspective, Drawing, and Painting ... London: Kingsbury, Parbury, & Allen, (1825). 4th edn. 8vo. xxiv,300 pp. 21 plates. Some foxing, offsetting of frontis. Orig bds. *(Bookpress)* **$95 [≈£63]**

Hayter, Stanley William

- Jankel Adler. London & Paris: Nicholson & Watson, 1948. 4to. ix,[1] pp. 38 plates. Orig cloth, shaken. *(Ars Libri)* **$35 [≈£23]**
- New Ways of Gravure. London: Routledge, 1949. 1st edn. 280 pp. 4 cold plates, 96 ills, 25 figs. Orig cloth. Dw. *(Bookworks)* **£75 [≈$113]**

Hayward, Helena & Kirkham, Pat

- William and John Linnell, Eighteenth Century Furniture Makers. London: Studio Vista, 1980. 1st edn. 2 vols. 4to. 19 cold &

322 other plates. Orig cloth. Slipcase. *(Claude Cox)* **£35 [≈$53]**

- William and John Linnell. Eighteenth Century London Furniture Makers. London: Studio Vista & Christie's, 1980. 2 vols. 107 plates, 28 ills. Orig cloth. Slipcase. *(Leicester Art Books)* **£60 [≈$90]**

Hayward, Helena (editor)

- World Furniture. An Illustrated History. London: Hamlyn, 1967. 320 pp. 52 cold plates. Orig bndg, top crnr bumped. *(Carol Howard)* **£20 [≈$30]**

Hazen, Edward

- The Panorama of Professions and Trades; or, Every Man's Book. Phila: Uriah Hunt, 1841. Sm 4to. 320 pp. 82 engvs. Later qtr calf. *(Bookpress)* **$225 [≈£150]**

Head, Barclay V.

- A Guide to the Principal Coins of the Greeks from circa 700 B.B. to A.D. 270. New Edition. London: BM, 1932. 4to. [v],106 pp. 50 plates. Lib label & 2 blind-stamps. Orig cloth gilt. *(Hollett)* **£40 [≈$60]**

Heal, Sir Ambrose

- The English Writing-Masters and their Copy-Books 1570-1800. A Biographical Dictionary & a Bibliography ... Cambridge: UP, 1931. One of 300 signed by the author. Folio. Frontis, 81 plates. Orig qtr buckram, t.e.g., sl shelfworn. *(David Slade)* **£325 [≈$488]**
- The London Furniture Makers from the Restoration to the Victorian Era 1660-1840 ... London: Batsford, 1953. 1st edn. 4to. xx,376 pp. Ills. Orig cloth gilt. Dw. *(Hollett)* **£75 [≈$113]**
- The London Goldsmiths 1200-1800. A Record ... Cambridge: UP, 1935. Folio. Frontis, 80 plates. Orig buckram gilt, t.e.g. *(David Slade)* **£110 [≈$165]**
- London Tradesmen's Cards of the XVIIIth Century ... London: Batsford, 1925. One of 950. Sm 4to. vi,89 pp. 102 plates. Orig holland backed bds gilt, edges trifle rubbed. *(Hollett)* **£120 [≈$180]**

Heath, Ambrose

- The Country Life Cookery Book. London: Country Life, 1937. 1st edn. 253 pp. W'engvs by Eric Ravilious. Crnrs v sl bumped, spine sl dull. *(Waddington)* **£58 [≈$87]**

Heath Robinson, W.

- See Robinson, W. Heath

Heine, Heinrich

- Atta Troll. From the German by Herman Scheffauer. With Some Pen-and-Ink Sketches by Willy Pogany. New York: Huebsch, 1914. 1st Amer edn thus. 12mo. 185 pp. Orig bds gilt, spine trifle darkened. *(Chapel Hill)* **$45 [≈£30]**
- Florentine Nights. With Twelve Illustrations in Colour by Felix De Gray. London: Methuen, [1927]. 1st edn thus. 4to. 78,[1] pp. 12 mtd cold ills. Trace of foxing. Orig cloth. *(Chapel Hill)* **$50 [≈£33]**
- Poems. Illustrated by Fritz Kredel. New York: The Limited Editions Club, 1957. One of 1500 signed by Kredel. 8vo. Orig leather-backed bds (spine faded). Slipcase. *(Oak Knoll)* **$95 [≈£63]**

Held, Julius S.

- The Oil Sketches of Peter Paul Rubens. A Critical Catalogue. Princeton: UP, 1980. 2 vols. 599 ills. Orig cloth. Dws. *(Leicester Art Books)* **£110 [≈$165]**
- Rubens. Selected Drawings. With an Introduction and Critical Catalogue. London: Phaidon, 1959. 2 vols. 6 cold & 179 other plates, 61 ills. Orig buckram. *(Leicester Art Books)* **£65 [≈$98]**
- Rubens: Selected Drawings. London: Phaidon Press, (1959). 1st edn. 2 vols (text & plates). Plates, ills. Orig cloth. Plastic dws. Slipcase. *(Fine Art)* **£65 [≈$98]**

Heleniak, Katherine Moore

- William Mulready. Yale: UP, 1980. 288 pp. 8 cold plates, 192 ills. Dw (sl worn). *(Fine Art)* **£45 [≈$68]**
- William Mulready. New Haven: Yale UP, 1980. xiv,287 pp. 208 ills. Orig cloth. Dw. *(Leicester Art Books)* **£55 [≈$83]**

Helm, W.H.

- Homes of the Past - A Sketch of Domestic Buildings ... Norman to Georgian ... London: John Lane; Bodley Head, 1921. 1st edn. 4to. xix,155 pp. 59 plates. Orig qtr cloth gilt, crnrs sl bumped. *(Clevedon Books)* **£45 [≈$68]**

Hemans, Felicia Dorothea, nee Browne

- The Better Land. A Poem. Illuminated by Helen Baker. London: Day & Son, 1866. 4to. Title & 8 pp printed in colours and gold. Sl marg foxing. Orig pict cloth gilt. *(Barbara Stone)* **£55 [≈$83]**

Hendley, T.H.

- Asian Carpets, XVI and XVII Century Designs from the Jaipur Palaces, &c. &c. ... London: W. Griggs, 1905. Folio. (24) pp. 6 fascicles of loose plates, each in orig folder. 158 plates inc map & inc 12 dble plates. *(Karmiole)* **$2,000 [≈£1,333]**

Hendricks, Jon

- Fluxus Codex. With an Introduction by Robert Pincus-Witten. Detroit & New York: Abrams, 1988. Oblong 4to. 616 pp. 800 ills. Orig cloth. Dw. *(Ars Libri)* **$95 [≈£63]**

Hennell, Thomas

- The Countryman at Work. London: Architectural Press, 1947. 1st edn. 80 pp. Port, 51 ills. B'plate. prelims & edges sl spotted. Orig cloth. Dw (chipped). *(Bookworks)* **£28 [≈$42]**

Henry, Francoise

- Irish Art during the Viking Invasions (800-1020 AD). London: Methuen, 1967. 236 pp. 120 plates. Dw. *(Emerald Isle)* **£30 [≈$45]**
- Irish Art in the Romanesque Period, 1020-1170 AD. London: Methuen, 1970. Sm 4to. Ills. Dw. *(Emerald Isle)* **£30 [≈$45]**

Henslow, T.G.W.

- Ye Sundial Book. London: 1914. 1st edn. 8vo. [iv],422,[4 advt] pp. Port, 2 plates, ca 370 ills. Orig parchment gilt, spine sl dulled. *(Clevedon Books)* **£85 [≈$128]**
- Ye Sundial Book. London: 1914. 8vo. 422 pp. 2 photo ills, ca 350 figs. Orig bds, edges worn. *(Gemmary)* **$100 [≈£67]**

Hepworth, Barbara

- Carvings and Drawings. With an Introduction by Herbert Read. London: Lund Humphries, 1952. 1st edn. Lge 4to. 4 cold & 277 b/w plates. Dw (missing sm pieces). *(Clearwater)* **£160 [≈$240]**
- Drawings from a Sculptor's Landscape. With Introductory Essays by the Author and Alan Bowness. New York: Praeger, 1967. 1st Amer edn. Lge 4to. Cold & b/w plates. Dw (sl browned). *(Clearwater)* **£40 [≈$60]**

Herbert, George

- Poems. Newtown: Gregynog Press, 1923. One of 300. 8vo. xv,26,[1] pp. Orig linen backed bds, uncut. The first book from this press. *(Lamb)* **£75 [≈$113]**
- The Temple. Sacred Songs & Private Ejaculations. London: Nonesuch Press, 1927. One of 1500. x,214 pp. Port frontis (sl offset). Orig tapestry cloth, top edge gilt on the rough. *(Claude Cox)* **£55 [≈$83]**

Herberts, K.

- Oriental Lacquer: Art and Technique. New York: Abrams, (1963). 1st edn. Thick 4to. 513,[2] pp. 324 mtd plates, 2 maps. Orig cloth. Dw (chipped). *(Argonaut)* **$275 [≈£183]**

Hering, Oswald C.

- Concrete and Stucco Houses. New York: McBride, Nast, 1912. 1st edn. 8vo. xviii,105 pp. Frontis, 67 ills. Orig cloth, sl worn. *(Bookpress)* **$85 [≈£57]**
- Modern Dwellings in Town and Country. New York: Harper, (1878). 1st edn. 8vo. 219 pp. Frontis. 1 gathering sprung. Orig cloth gilt. *(Bookpress)* **$425 [≈£283]**

Herlitz-Gezelius, Ann Marie

- Orrefors. A Swedish Glassplant. Atlantis: 1984. Roy 4to. 144 pp. Ills. Orig ptd bds. *(Paul Brown)* **£48 [≈$72]**

Herodotus

- The Histories of Herodotus of Halicarnassus ... Translated for the Limited Editions Club by Harry Carter; Illustrated and Decorated by Edward Bawden. Limited Editions Club: 1958. One of 1500 signed by Bawden. xxviii,615 pp. Slipcase. *(Michael Taylor)* **£115 [≈$173]**

Heron, Patrick

- The Changing Forms of Art. London: 1955. 1st edn. 15 plates. Orig cloth, spine ends sl bumped. Price-clipped dw (sl rubbed, v sl creased). *(Ulysses Bookshop)* **£95 [≈$143]**

Herrick, Robert

- Poems. Hammersmith: Kelmscott Press, 1895. One of 250. 8vo. Hand cold dec borders & initials. Orig limp vellum, silk ties, sl rubbed. Morocco case. *(Heritage)* **$1,250 [≈£833]**

Herring, Robert

- Adam and Evelyn at Kew, or Revolt in the Gardens. London: Elkin Mathews & Marrot, 1930. One of 1060. Ills by Edward Bawden. Orig bndg, some discolouration to edges. *(Old Cathay)* **£59 [≈$89]**
- Adam and Evelyn at Kew. London: Elkin Mathews & Marrot, 1930. One of 1000. 168 pp. Hand cold ills by Edward Bawden. Orig 1st issue grey cloth, titled green, t.e.g., extrs rubbed & browned. *(Bookworks)* **£115 [≈$173]**

Herrman, Luke

- British Landscape Painting of the 18th Century. New York: OUP, 1974. 1st US edn. 151 pp. Plates. Orig cloth, v sl marked. *(Fine Art)* **£35 [≈$53]**

Herrmann, Frank

- The English as Collectors: A Documentary Chrestomathy. London: Chatto & Windus, 1972. xv,461 pp. 96 ills. Orig cloth. Dw. *(Fine Art)* **£40 [≈$60]**

Hersey, Carl Kenneth

- The Salamantine Lanterns. Their Origins and Development. Cambridge: Harvard UP, 1937. 4to. 238 pp. 86 ills. Orig cloth. *(Mendelsohn)* **$55 [≈£37]**

Hess, Hans

- George Grosz. London: Studio Vista, 1974. 272 pp. 237 ills. Orig cloth. Dw. *(Leicester Art Books)* **£30 [≈$45]**
- Lyonel Feininger. London: Thames & Hudson, 1961. xvi,354 pp. 540 ills. Orig cloth. Dw. *(Leicester Art Books)* **£320 [≈$480]**
- Lyonel Feininger. New York: Abrams, [1961]. Lge 4to. 354,[2] pp. 100 plates. Orig cloth. *(Ars Libri)* **$750 [≈£500]**

Hess, Thomas B.

- Abstract Painting. Background and American Phase. New York: Viking, 1951. Lge 4to. 164 pp. 106 plates. Orig cloth. *(Ars Libri)* **$65 [≈£43]**

Hetherington, A.L.

- The Pottery & Porcelain Factories of China. London: Kegan Paul, 1921. 1st edn. Sm 4to. Fldg map. A few spots. Orig cloth backed bds. *(Hollett)* **£35 [≈$53]**

Hettes, Karel

- Old Venetian Glass. London: Spring Books, 1960. 4to. 46 pp. Cold & b/w plates. Dw. Slipcase. *(Paul Brown)* **£25 [≈$38]**

Hey, Rebecca

- The Spirit of the Woods. London: Longmans, Rees ..., 1837. 8vo. 26 cold plates. Orig half mor gilt, t.e.g. *(Traylen)* **£350 [≈$525]**

Hiatt, Charles

- Picture Posters. A Short History of the Illustrated Placard ... London: George Bell; New York: Macmillan, 1895. 2nd edn. 4to. xvi,367 pp. Num ills. Orig cloth, sl worn. *(Ars Libri)* **$100 [≈£67]**

Hibbard, Howard

- Caravaggio. London: Thames & Hudson, 1983. xii,404 pp. 8 cold plates, 194 ills. Orig cloth. Dw. *(Leicester Art Books)* **£38 [≈$57]**

Higgins, Dick

- foew&ombwhnw [sic]. A grammar of the mind and a phenomenology of love and a science of the arts as seen by a stalker of wild mushroom. New York: Something Else Press, 1969. Sm 4to. 320 pp. Ills. Orig buckram. *(Ars Libri)* **$50 [≈£33]**

Higgins, Reynold

- Greek and Roman Jewellery. London: Methuen, 1980. 2nd edn. xliii,243 pp. 64 plates. Orig cloth gilt. Dw. *(Hollett)* **£25 [≈$38]**

Hiler, Hilaire & Hiler, Meyer

- Bibliography of Costume. New York: H.W. Wilson Co., 1939. 1st edn. 4to. 912 pp. Orig cloth, gilt spine. *(Karmiole)* **$150 [≈£100]**

Hill, D.

- Mr Gillray, the Caricaturist ... A Biography. London: Phaidon, 1965. 8vo. vii,266 pp. Frontis, num ills. Orig cloth gilt. *(Clevedon Books)* **£25 [≈$38]**

Hill, D. & Grabar, O.

- Islamic Architecture and its Decoration. London: Faber, 1964. Sm 4to. 88 pp. 527 ills. Few lib marks erased. Dw (sl worn). *(Monmouth)* **£35 [≈$53]**

Hill, Draper

- Fashionable Contrasts. London: Phaidon Press, (1966). 1st edn. 4to. 184,[1] pp. Frontis. Ex-lib. Orig cloth. Dw. Study of Gillray. *(Bookpress)* **$65 [≈£43]**

Hill, G.F.

- Renaissance Medals. From the Samuel H. Kress Collection at the National Gallery of Art ... Revised and Enlarged by Graham Pollard. London: Phaidon, 1967. 4to. x,307 pp. 1209 ills. Sev lib stamps. Dw (sellotape marks). *(Francis Edwards)* **£42 [≈$63]**

Hill, George F.

- Drawings by Pisanello. Paris: G. van Oest, 1929. 65 pp. 65 plates. Orig cloth, t.e.g., spine sl worn. *(Leicester Art Books)* **£110 [≈$165]**
- Pisanello. London: Duckworth, 1905. viii, 264 pp. 74 plates. Orig cloth. *(Leicester Art Books)* **£22 [≈$33]**

Hill, O.

- Scottish Castles of the 16th and 17th Centuries. London: Country Life, 1953. 1st edn. Folio. 280 pp. 3 maps, 140 photo plates. Text ills. Orig cloth gilt. *(Clevedon Books)* **£56 [≈$84]**

Hill, W.H., & others

- Antonio Stradivari. His Life and Work. London: 1902. Sm folio. 28 plates, 68 text ills. Half vellum. *(Traylen)* **£540 [≈$810]**
- The Violin Makers of the Guarneri Family (1626-1762). Their Life and Work ... London: 1931. Sm folio. Num plates, ills. Orig half vellum. *(Traylen)* **£495 [≈$743]**

Hiller, Bevis

- The Decorative Arts of the Forties and Fifties. Austerity / Binge. New York: Clarkson N. Potter, 1975. Lge 4to. 200 pp. 160 ills. Orig cloth. Dw. *(Ars Libri)* **[≈£40]**

Hillier, Jack

- Hokusai: Paintings, Drawings and Woodcuts. London: Phaidon, (1955). 4to. 134 pp. 18 mtd cold plates, 130 b/w ills. Orig cloth. Dw. *(Abacus)* **$65 [≈£43]**
- Japanese Prints & Drawings from the Vever Collection. London & New York: 1976. One of 2000. 3 vols. 4to. Num ills. Orig cloth. Dws. Slipcase. *(Bow Windows)* **£150 [≈$225]**
- Suzuki Harunobu. An Exhibition of his Colour-Prints and Illustrated Books on the Occasion of the Bicentenary of his Death in 1770 ... Philadelphia & Boston: (1970). 4to. 240 pp. 10 cold & 125 b/w plates. Orig cloth. Dw. *(Karmiole)* **$75 [≈£50]**

Hills, Chester

- The Builder's Guide; Or a Practical Treatise on the Several Orders of Grecian and Roman Architecture, Together with the Gothic Style of Building. Hartford: 1834. 1st edn. 2 vols in one. 20; 55 pp. 70 plates. Occas foxing. Old calf, v worn. *(John K. King)* **$650 [≈£433]**

Hinckley, F. Lewis

- A Directory of Antique Furniture. The Authentic Classification of European and American Designs for Professionals and Connoisseurs. New York: Crown, 1953. 4to. 1099 ills. Orig cloth gilt. Dw (trifle worn). *(Hollett)* **£60 [≈$90]**

Hind, Arthur M.

- The Drawings of Claud Lorrain. London: Halton & Truscott Smith, 1925. v,33 pp. 72 plates. Orig cloth backed bds, t.e.g. *(Leicester Art Books)* **£45 [≈$68]**
- The Etchings of D.Y. Cameron. London: 1924. One of 200. Folio. 4 plates, 95 ills of etchings. Leather backed cloth, t.e.g. *(Traylen)* **£130 [≈$195]**
- The Etchings of D.Y. Cameron. London: Halton & Truscott Smith, 1934. 4to. vii,43 pp. 95 plates. Orig bndg. Slipcase (broken). *(Corn Exchange)* **£60 [≈$90]**
- Giovanni Battista Piranesi. A Critical Study. With a List of his Published Works and detailed Catalogues of the Prisons and the Views of Rome. London: Cotswold Gallery, 1922. One of 500. xii,95 pp. 74 plates. Orig cloth & bds. *(Leicester Art Books)* **£120 [≈$180]**
- Giovanni Battista Piranesi. A Critical Study ... (1922). London: Holland Press, 1978. xii,95 pp. 74 plates. Orig cloth. Dw. *(Leicester Art Books)* **£55 [≈$83]**
- A History of Engraving and Etching, from the 15th Century to the Year 1914 ... Boston: Houghton, Mifflin 1923. 3rd edn, rvsd. 4to. xviii,[2],487 pp. 100 ills. Ex-lib, inner hinges reprd. Orig cloth. *(Bookpress)* **$110 [≈£73]**
- Rembrandt's Etchings. An Essay and a Catalogue. London: Methuen, 1912. 1st edn. 2 vols. Roy 8vo. 34 plates, 330 ills. Sl foxed. Orig cloth. *(Traylen)* **£80 [≈$120]**
- Rembrandt's Etchings. An Essay and a Catalogue. London: Methuen, [1912]. 2 vols. 4to. 34 plates, 330 ills. Sl foxed. Orig cloth gilt, gilt faded. *(Cooper Hay)* **£40 [≈$60]**

Hind, C. Lewis

- Adventures among Pictures. London: A. & C. Black, 1904. Only edn. 8 cold & 16 b/w plates. Orig cloth, spine worn at rear edge. *(Old Cathay)* **£35 [≈$53]**
- Hercules Brabazon Brabazon 1821-1906 His Art and Life. London: 1912. 103 pp. Mtd frontis, 24 mtd cold plates. Orig cloth, t.e.g., sl marked & worn. *(Fine Art)* **£95 [≈$143]**

Hindley, Charles

- The History of the Catnach Press ... London: Charles Hindley, 1886. One of 250 Large Paper. 8vo. xlii,[ii],308 pp. Num ills. Orig parchment backed bds, untrimmed, rubbed, crnrs & edges sl worn. Inscribed by the author. *(Clark)* **£165 [≈$248]**
- The Life and Times of James Catnach (late of Seven Dials), Ballad Monger. London: Reeves & Turner, 1878. One of 500. 8vo. xvi, 432,[12 ctlg] pp. Num ills, some hand cold. Browned, few edges chipped, sm hole in one

leaf. Orig cloth, paper label, sl worn. *(Clark)* **£75 [≈$113]**

Hindley, Charles (editor)

- The Old Book Collector's Miscellany ... London: 1871-73. 3 vols. 8vo. Num w'cut ills. Bds, new mor spines gilt. *(Traylen)* **£95 [≈$143]**

Hinkle, William M.

- The Portal of the Saints of Reims Cathedral. A Study in Mediaeval Iconography. New York: 1965. 4to. 85 pp. 94 ills. Orig cloth, crnrs sl bumped. *(Washton)* **$45 [≈£30]**

Hinz, Berthold

- Art in the Third Reich. New York: Pantheon Books, 1979. 4to. [12],268,[4] pp. Num ills. Orig cloth. *(Ars Libri)* **$50 [≈£33]**

Hipkins, A.J.

- Musical Instruments, Historic, Rare and Unique. London: A. & C. Black, 1921. 4to. xxiii,123 pp. 40 cold plates by William Gibb. Orig buckram backed cloth gilt, sl marked, upper hinge splitting. *(Hollett)* **£120 [≈$180]**

Hitchcock, Henry-Russell

- German Rococo: the Zimmerman Brothers. Baltimore: 1968. Sm 4to. 100 pp. 58 ills. Orig cloth. *(Washton)* **$75 [≈£50]**
- In the Nature of Materials. New York: Duell, Sloan & Pearce, 1942. 1st edn. Sq 8vo. xxxv,[i],143 pp. 413 ills. Name. Orig cloth, spine sl sunned. *(Bookpress)* **$150 [≈£100]**
- Painting toward Architecture. New York: Duell, Sloan & Pearce, 1948. 1st edn. 4to. 118 pp. Ills. Orig cloth. Dw (slightly used). *(Bookpress)* **$75 [≈£50]**

Hitchcock, J.R.

- Etching in America: With Lists of American Etchers and Notable Collections of Prints. New York: White, Stokes & Allen, 1886. 95 pp.Etched frontis. Orig cloth gilt, crnrs sl bumped. *(Rona Schneider)* **$190 [≈£127]**

Hitchcock, Ripley

- Notable Etchings by American Artists. New York: White, Stokes & Allen, 1886. Folio. 54 pp. 10 orig etchings. Orig dec bndg. *(Rona Schneider)* **$375 [≈£250]**

Hobbs, Richard

- Odilon Redon. Boston: New York Graphic Society, (1977). 4to. 192 pp. 19 cold plates, 100 ills. Orig cloth. Dw. *(Abacus)* **$45 [≈£30]**

Hobhouse, Christopher

- 1851 and the Crystal Palace. London: Murray, 1950. 8vo. xxiii,[iii],181 pp. Ills. Orig bds. *(Bookpress)* **$45 [≈£30]**

Hobson, Burton

- Historic Gold Coins of the World from Croesus to Elizabeth II. London: Blandford Press, 1971. 1st edn. 4to. 192 pp. Cold ills. Endpaper edges sl faded. Orig cloth gilt. Dw (sl worn). *(Hollett)* **£40 [≈$60]**

Hobson, G.D.

- Bindings in Cambridge Libraries. Cambridge: UP, 1929. One of 230. Lge 4to. 179 pp. 72 plates. Orig cloth gilt. Dw (sl dusty & torn). *(Hermitage)* **$1,750 [≈£1,167]**
- Thirty Bindings, selected from The First Edition Club's Seventh Edition. London: The First Edition Club, 1926. One of 600. 4to. 68 pp. 30 plates. Orig linen gilt. *(Hermitage)* **$250 [≈£167]**
- Thirty Bindings, selected from The First Edition Club's Seventh Edition. London: The First Edition Club, 1926. One of 600. 4to. 68 pp. 30 plates. Orig linen gilt, sl worn, spine sl faded. *(Hermitage)* **$175 [≈£117]**

Hobson, R.L.

- The Later Ceramic Wares of China ... London: Benn, 1925. 4to. 26 cold & 50 b/w plates. Orig cloth. *(Traylen)* **£75 [≈$113]**
- Worcester Porcelain. London: Quaritch, 1910. 1st edn. Folio. [xii],208 pp. 17 chromolitho & 92 collotype plates, 16 text ills. Frontis sl foxed. Orig cloth, sl edge wear. Dw (worn). *(Bookpress)* **$350 [≈£233]**

Hockney, David

- David Hockney. By David Hockney. London: 1976. 1st edn. 4to. 311 pp. Num ills. Orig cloth. Dw. *(Margaret Nangle)* **£38 [≈$57]**
- Martha's Vineyard and Other Places. My Third Sketchbook from the Summer of 1982. New York: Abrams, 1985. 2 vols (text & plates). Orig bndgs. Cardboard carton signed by the author. *(Clarice Davis)* **$195 [≈£130]**
- Martha's Vineyard and Other Places: My Third Sketchbook from the Summer of 1982. New York: Abrams, (1985). 2 vols. 4to. Ills. Half cloth & wraps. Slipcase. *(Abacus)* **$60 [≈£40]**
- Paper Pools. Edited by Nikos Stangos. London: 1980. 1st edn. 4to. 122 ills (87 cold). Orig cloth. Dw. *(Margaret Nangle)* **£40 [≈$60]**

- Travels with Pen, Pencil and Ink. Introduction by Edmund Pillsbury. London & New York: Petersburg Press, 1978. Cold & b/w plates, ills. Orig bndg. *(Clarice Davis)* **$65 [≈£43]**
- Travels with Pen, Pencil and Ink 1962-1977. With an Introduction by Edmund Pillsbury. London: 1978. 1st edn. Num ills. Orig pict card cvrs. *(Margaret Nangle)* **£22 [≈$33]**

Hockney, David & Posner, David

- A Rake's Progress. London: Lion and Unicorn Press, 1967. One of 400. Lge 4to. 16 ills. Orig black cloth bds. Plastic binder. *(Robert Frew)* **£250 [≈$375]**

Hoddinott, R.F.

- Early Byzantine Churches in Macedonia and Southern Serbia. A Study of the Origins and Initial Development of East Christian Art. London: Macmillan, 1963. xix,263 pp. Cold frontis, 3 fldg maps, 64 plates, ills. Dw (reprd). *(Quest Books)* **£75 [≈$113]**

Hodgkin, John Eliot

- Rariora. Being Notes of Some of the Printed Books, Manuscripts, Historical Documents, Medals, Engravings, Pottery, etc., etc., Collected (1858-1900) by John Eliot Hodgkin. London: Sampson Low, [ca 1900-02]. 3 vols. 4to. 65 plates. Orig cloth, t.e.g., sl soiled. *(Karmiole)* **$300 [≈£200]**

Hodgson, J.E. & Eaton, F.A.

- The Royal Academy and its Members 1768-1830. London: 1905. 410 pp. Frontis, 10 plates. Orig cloth, t.e.g., front hinge sl weak. *(Fine Art)* **£24 [≈$36]**

Hodgson, Ralph

- The Gipsy Girl. London: Flying Fame, [ca 1913]. Broadsheet. 2 hand cold ills by Claud Lovat Fraser. Signed by the author and artist. *(Bookworks)* **£21 [≈$32]**
- The Late, Last Rook. London: Flying Fame, [ca 1913]. Broadsheet. Uncold issue. *(Bookworks)* **£10 [≈$15]**
- The Late, Last Rook. London: Flying Fame, [ca 1913]. Broadsheet. 2 hand cold ills by Claud Lovat Fraser. Signed by the author and artist. *(Bookworks)* **£21 [≈$32]**
- A Song. London: Flying Fame, [ca 1913]. Broadsheet. 2nd imp. 2 hand cold ills. Signed by the author and the artist, Claud Lovat Fraser. *(Bookworks)* **£16 [≈$24]**

Hodgson, Mrs Willoughby

- The Quest of the Antique. London: Herbert Jenkins, 1924. 1st edn. 4to. 255 pp. Cold frontis, 63 plates. Orig cloth gilt. *(Hollett)* **£45 [≈$68]**

Hodin, J.P.

- Alan Reynolds. London: The Redfern Artists Series, [ca 1962]. 1st edn. [48] pp. Port frontis, 32 plates, 11 ills. Orig cloth backed laminated bds. *(Bookworks)* **£22 [≈$33]**
- Barbara Hepworth. Boston: Boston Book and Art Shop, 1961. Lge 4to. 171,[1] pp. 128 plates. Orig cloth. Dw. *(Ars Libri)* **$275 [≈£183]**
- Manessier. Bath: Adams & Dart, 1972. 243 pp. 150 ills. Orig cloth. *(Leicester Art Books)* **£60 [≈$90]**

Hodnett, Edward

- English Woodcuts 1480-1534. Oxford: Bibl Soc., 1973. 4to. 600 pp. Orig cloth. *(Lamb)* **£25 [≈$38]**
- Francis Barlow: First Master of English Book Illustration. London: Scolar Press, 1978. 237 pp. 107 plates. Orig cloth. Dw. *(Fine Art)* **£35 [≈$53]**

Hoe, Robert

- Catalogue of the Library of Robert Hoe of New York. New York: The Anderson Auction Co., 1911-12. 8 vols. 8vo. 120 plates. Lib stamps on title & front cvrs. Orig wraps. *(Oak Knoll)* **$250 [≈£167]**

Hoff, Ursula

- The Art of Arthur Boyd. London: Deutsch, 1986. 247 pp. 202 plates. Orig cloth. Dw. *(Fine Art)* **£30 [≈$45]**

Hoffman, Malvina

- Heads and Tales. New York: Scribner, 1936. 4to. xx,416 pp. Num ills. Orig cloth. *(Ars Libri)* **$40 [≈£27]**
- Sculpture Inside and Out. New York: Norton, 1939. 1st edn. 4to. 330 pp. 276 ills. Orig cloth. *(Rona Schneider)* **$40 [≈£27]**

Hofstatter, Hans H.

- Gustave Klimt. Erotic Drawings. London: Thames & Hudson, 1980. One of 1000. 88 pp. 36 ills. Orig cloth. Slipcase. *(Leicester Art Books)* **£55 [≈$83]**

Hogarth, Paul

- Paul Hogarth's American Album. Drawings 1962-65. With Notes from a Journal. London: Lion & Unicorn Press, 1973. One of 400. Folio. Ills. Orig pict bds. Dw, fine. *(Barbara Stone)* **£150 [≈$225]**

Hogarth, William

- The Analysis of Beauty. London: J. Reeves for the author, 1753. 4to. 2 plates. Early reprs to folds. Sm foredge water-stain 1st few ff. Contemp calf, sl rubbed, splits in jnts. *(Jarndyce)* **£320 [≈$480]**
- Biographical Anecdotes of William Hogarth; with a Catalogue of his Works chronologically arranged; and Occasional Remarks. The Third Edition, Enlarged and Corrected. London: John Nichols, 1785. 8vo. Engvd half-title (foxed). 19th c half mor. *(Spelman)* **£50 [≈$75]**
- Hogarth Moralized ... accompanied with Concise and Comprehensive Explanations of their Moral Tendency, by the late Rev Dr Trusler. London: The Shakespeare Press, 1832. 8vo. xxvi,293 pp. Engvd plates, text ills. 1 sm repr. Early half calf. *(Spelman)* **£65 [≈$98]**
- Hogarth's Peregrination. Edited with an Introduction by Charles Mitchell. Oxford: 1952. 8vo. 11 plates, text ills. Dw. *(Spelman)* **£20 [≈$30]**

Hogben, Carol & Watson, Rowan

- From Manet to Hockney: Modern Artists' Illustrated Books. London: V & A, 1985. 380 pp. 36 cold plates, ills. Orig cloth, pict onlays. *(Fine Art)* **£48 [≈$72]**

Hogben, Carol (editor)

- The Art of Bernard Leach. London: Faber, 1978. 1st edn. 4to. 192 pp. Num ills. Orig cloth gilt. Price-clipped dw. *(Hollett)* **£35 [≈$53]**

Hogg, James

- Kilmeny. Illustrated by Jessie M. King. Edinburgh: Foulis, 1911. Thin 12mo. Frontis, title, 4 cold plates. Orig pict wraps, pict onlay, sl dusty. *(Barbara Stone)* **£55 [≈$83]**

Hohl, Reinhold

- Alberto Giacometti. New York: Abrams, [1972]. Lge 4to. 328 pp. 270 plates. Orig cloth. Dw. *(Ars Libri)* **$950 [≈£633]**

Holbein, Hans

- The Celebrated Hans Holbein's Alphabet of Death ... selected by A. de Montaiglon. Paris: Edwin Tross, 1856. 1st edn in English. 8vo. Orig cloth gilt. *(Book Block)* **$220 [≈£147]**
- The Celebrated Hans Holbein's Alphabet of Death ... selected by A. de Montaiglon. Paris: Edwin Tross, 1856. 1st edn in English. 8vo. Orig pict wraps, untrimmed. *(Book Block)* **$425 [≈£283]**
- Icones Veteris Testamenti; Illustrations of the Old Testament, engraved on Wood, from Designs by Hans Holbein. [Edited by T.F. Dibdin]. London: William Pickering, 1830. 1st edn. 14 pp. [180] ff. Orig morocco backed bds, uncut, rubbed. *(Claude Cox)* **£110 [≈$165]**

Holden, Harold H.

- Art and Craft Education in the City of Birmingham. Birmingham: Birmingham School of Printing, 1942. Lge 8vo. 16 pp. 72 pp ills. Orig cloth. *(Claude Cox)* **£18 [≈$27]**

Holden, John Allan

- Private Book Collectors in the United States and Canada ... Revised Edition. New York: Bowker, 1931. 8vo. 304 pp. Some pencil notes. Orig qtr cloth. *(Cooper Hay)* **£24 [≈$36]**

Hole, James

- The Homes of the Working Classes with Suggestions for their Improvement. London: Longmans, Green, 1866. 1st edn. xvi,214 pp. 22 fldg plates. Occas sl spotting. Orig cloth gilt, front edges sl damped. *(Hollett)* **£140 [≈$210]**

Hole, William & Wilson, Thomas

- The Ornaments of Churches considered ... Oxford: R. & J. Dodsley ..., 1761. 1st edn. 4to. [iv],iv,[vi],v-143, 38,8 pp. 2 plates. Calf, edges v sl rubbed. *(Bookpress)* **$1,500 [≈£1,000]**

Holgate, D.

- New Hall and its Imitators. London: Faber, 1971. xvi,112 pp. 6 cold plates, 257 ills. Orig cloth. Dw. *(Castle Bookshop)* **£48 [≈$72]**
- New Hall. London: Faber, 1978. 2nd imp. xii,243 pp. 19 cold plates, 371 ills. Orig cloth. Dw. *(Castle Bookshop)* **£45 [≈$68]**

Holland, John

- Memorials of Sir Francis Chantrey, R.A. Sculptor, in Hallamshire and elsewhere. Sheffield: [ca 1851]. 1st edn. 8vo. [8],364 pp. Title vignette. Orig cloth, rebacked. *(Spelman)* **£50 [≈$75]**

Holland, Lord

- Eve's Legend. London: Etchells & Macdonald, Haslewood Books, 1928. One of 300. 4to. Hand cold w'engvs by Hester Sainsbury. Orig patterned bds. *(Barbara Stone)* **£125 [≈$188]**

Hollingworth, Jane

- Collecting Decanters. London: Studio Vista, Christies, 1980. 1st edn. Lge 8vo. 128 pp. Ills. Orig cloth gilt. Dw. *(Hollett)* **£30 [≈$45]**

Holme, Charles (editor)

- Art in Photography with Selected Examples of European and American Work. London: The Studio, Special Number, 1905. Mtd plates (few sl creased). Orig wraps (sl worn & marked). *(Words Etcetera)* **£45 [≈$68]**
- The Art of the Book. London: Studio Special Number, Spring, 1914. 1st edn. Sm folio. Num plates, ills. Orig wraps, sm ink blot on upper panel, tear reprd. *(Words Etcetera)* **£60 [≈$90]**
- The Art-Revival Austria. London: Studio, 1906. 1st edn. 4to. Num plates. Sl browned. Rec cloth, orig wraps bound in. *(Monmouth)* **£60 [≈$90]**
- The Art-Revival in Austria. London: Studio Special Summer Number, 1906. 4to. vii,(47) pp. 142 plates. Orig wraps (chipped). *(Ars Libri)* **$125 [≈£83]**
- Colour Photography and Other Recent Developments of the Art of the Camera. London: Studio Special Number, 1908. Folio. Num mtd & other plates. Orig wraps. *(Words Etcetera)* **£65 [≈$98]**
- Corot and Millet. London: The Studio, Special Winter Number, 1902. 4to. Lib cloth, orig wraps bound in. *(First Folio)* **$50 [≈£33]**
- English Water-Colour with reproductions of Drawings by Eminent Painters. London: The Studio, 1902. 1st edn. Folio. 8 parts. 74 pp. 66 mtd cold plates, 25 ports (only, of 26). Orig wraps, sm splits in a few folds. *(Claude Cox)* **£65 [≈$98]**
- The Genius of J.M.W. Turner, R.A. London: Studio Special Number, Winter 1903. [Ca 200] pp. Num plates. Some margs flaking. New buckram. *(Willow House)* **£30 [≈$45]**
- Masters of English Landscape Painting: J.S. Cotman, David Cox, Peter Dewint. London: Studio Special Number, Summer 1903. 48pp. Num plates. Few stamps, sl foxing. Orig cloth gilt, sl worn. *(Willow House)* **£30 [≈$45]**
- Modern Etching and Engraving. London: The Studio, Special Number 1902. 4to. Lib cloth, orig wraps bound in. *(First Folio)* **$60 [≈£40]**
- Modern Etching and Engraving. London: The Studio, 1902. 4to. 220 ills. Orig cloth. *(Rona Schneider)* **$130 [≈£87]**
- Modern Etching and Engraving. London: The Studio, 1902. Num ills. Orig wraps. *(Fine Art)* **£25 [≈$38]**
- Modern Etching and Engraving. London: The Studio, 1902. 4to. xx,[64] pp. 224 ills. Orig wraps. *(Ars Libri)* **$40 [≈£27]**
- Modern Pen Drawings ... London: The Studio, 1901. One of 300. 4to. [ii],216 pp. Num ills. Orig 'parchment antique' bds, green cloth ties and page marker, t.e.g. *(Bow Windows)* **£125 [≈$188]**
- Modern Pen Drawings: European and American. London: The Studio, 1901. 4to. 216 pp. Lib cloth. *(First Folio)* **$60 [≈£40]**
- Modern Pen Drawings: European and American. London: The Studio, Special Winter Number, 1901. Lge 4to. [16],215,[1] pp. Num ills. Orig cloth. *(Ars Libri)* **$40 [≈£27]**
- The "Old" Water-Colour Society 1804-1904. London: Studio Special Number, Spring 1905. 46 pp. 39 cold plates. Sl foxing. Rec buckram retaining orig front bd. *(Willow House)* **£45 [≈$68]**
- The 'Old' Water-Colour Society 1804-1904. London: The Studio, 1905. 4to. [8],46 pp. 40 cold plates (inc one by Arthur Rackham). Orig cloth gilt, sl soiled. *(Karmiole)* **$60 [≈£40]**
- Pen, Pencil and Chalk. A Series of Drawings by Contemporary European Artists. London: The Studio, Special Winter Number, 1911. 4to. 246 pp. Num ills. Orig wraps (worn). *(Ars Libri)* **$40 [≈£27]**
- Pen, Pencil and Chalk. A Series of Drawings by Contemporary European Artists. London: The Studio, 1911. viii,246 pp. Cold & b/w plates. Some foxing. A few brittle pp. Orig cloth gilt, crnrs rubbed. *(Clarice Davis)* **$125 [≈£83]**
- Pen, Pencil and Chalk. A Series of Drawings by Contemporary European Artists. London: The Studio, 1911. viii,246 pp. Cold & b/w plates. Orig wraps, sm tear to spine. *(Clarice Davis)* **$90 [≈£60]**
- Portrait Miniatures. English and French, 17th and 19th Centuries. London: The Studio, 1910. 4to. 88,advt pp. 81 ills. Orig wraps. *(Rona Schneider)* **$35 [≈£23]**
- The War depicted by Distinguished British

Artists. London: The Studio, 1918. 4to. v, [3], 98 pp. Num ills. Orig cloth. *(Ars Libri)* **$30 [≈£20]**

Holme, Geoffrey (editor)

- British Water-Colour Painting of Today. London: The Studio, Winter Special 1921. Sm folio. viii,48 pp. 24 mtd cold plates. Orig wraps, trifle stained & rubbed. *(Clevedon Books)* **£25 [≈$38]**
- The Children's Art Book. London: The Studio, 1942. 96 pp. 8 cold & 17 b/w plates, num ills. *(Holtom)* **£20 [≈$30]**

Holmes, Oliver Wendell

- The Autocrat of the Breakfast-Table. Illustrations by R.J. Holden. New York: The Limited Editions Club, 1955. One of 1500 signed by Holden. Sm 4to. Orig cloth, leather label. Slipcase. *(Oak Knoll)* **$45 [≈£30]**

Holt, Claire

- Art in Indonesia: Continuities and Change. Ithaca: Cornell, [ca 1967]. 1st edn. Lge 8vo. xvii,355 pp. Photo ills. Dw. *(McBlain)* **$50 [≈£33]**

The Holy Bible ...

- The Holy Bible. The Authorized or King James Version of 1611 Now Reprinted with the Apocrypha ... London: Nonesuch Press, 1963. 3 vols. Tall 8vo. Num ills. Orig cloth gilt. *(Karmiole)* **$125 [≈£83]**

Homer

- Homer's Hymns to Aphrodite. Translated by Jack Lindsay. London: The Fanfrolico Press, [ca 1930]. One of 500. [32] pp. Plates. Orig dec cloth, t.e.g., extrs sl bruised, label sl spotted. *(Bookworks)* **£45 [≈$68]**
- The Homeric Hymn to Aphrodite ... With Ten Engravings by Mark Severin. Golden Cockerel Press: 1948. One of 750. Thin folio. Orig morocco backed bds. *(Sotheran's)* **£198 [≈$297]**
- The Odyssey of Homer. Done into English Prose by S.H. Butcher & Andrew Lang. Illustrated by W. Russell Flint. London: The Medici Society, 1924. One of 530. Sm folio. 20 mtd cold plates. Orig cloth, 2 labels (sl chipped), spine sl darkened. *(Jo Ann Reisler)* **$650 [≈£433]**

Homer, William Inness

- Robert Henri and his Circle. Ithaca & London: Cornell UP, 1969. 4to. xvii,[3],308 pp. 4 cold plates, 66 ills. Orig cloth. Dw. *(Ars Libri)* **$75 [≈£50]**

Honce, Charles

- Books and Ghosts. Mount Vernon: The Golden Eagle Press, 1948. One of 111. Lge 8vo. xv,[i],102,[1] pp. Orig bds. Author's presentation copy. *(Bookpress)* **$235 [≈£157]**

Honey, W.B.

- The Art of the Potter. A Book for the Collector and the Connoisseur. London: Faber, 1955. Tall 8vo. xvi,111 pp. 160 plates. Orig cloth gilt, trifle rubbed. *(Hollett)* **£16.50 [≈$26]**
- The Ceramic Art of China and other Countries of the Far East. London: 1954. 4to. 3 cold & 192 other plates. Orig cloth. *(Traylen)* **£35 [≈$53]**
- English Pottery & Porcelain. Revised by R.J. Charleston. London: A. & C. Black, 1962. 5th edn. xvi,285 pp. 24 plates. Orig cloth gilt. Sm dent upper bd. Dw. *(Hollett)* **£15 [≈$23]**
- European Ceramic Art from the End of the Middle Ages to about 1815. A Dictionary of Factories, Artists, Technical Terms ... [with] Illustrated Historical Survey. London: Theodore Brun, 1949-52. One of 150, one of 300. 2 vols. Sm 4to. Plates, ills. Orig mor gilt. *(Hollett)* **£450 [≈$675]**
- Old English Porcelain. A Handbook for Collectors. London: Faber, 1949. 292 pp. 112 plates. Orig cloth gilt. Dw (top edge chipped with some loss). *(Hollett)* **£25 [≈$38]**
- Wedgwood Ware. London: Faber, 1951. Tall 8vo. xv,35 pp. Cold frontis, 96 plates. Orig cloth gilt. Dw (lower panel spotted). *(Hollett)* **£25 [≈$38]**

Honeyman, Tom John

- Introducing Leslie Hunter. London: Faber, 1937. 223 pp. Port frontis, 42 plates. Orig cloth. Dw. *(Leicester Art Books)* **£45 [≈$68]**
- Introducing Leslie Hunter. London: Faber, [1937]. 8vo. 223 pp. 16 cold & 27 b/w plates. Orig cloth. Dw. *(Cooper Hay)* **£65 [≈$98]**

Honour, Hugh

- Chinoiserie. The Vision of Cathay. London: Murray, 1951. 1st edn. Lge 8vo. viii,294 pp. 144 plates. Orig cloth gilt. Dw. *(Hollett)* **£55 [≈$83]**

Hood, Thomas

- Miss Kilmansegg and Her Precious Leg. A Golden Legend. London: E. Moxon, 1870. Sm 4to. 150 pp, ptd on card. 60 ills by Thomas S. Seccombe. Sl spotting. Contemp half mor gilt, a.e.g., extrs sl rubbed. *(Robert Frew)* **£20 [≈$30]**

- Miss Kilmansegg and her Precious Leg a Golden Legend with 60 Illustrations by Thomas S. Seccombe, R.A.... London: Moxon, 1870. 1st edn. Folio. 150 ff on india paper. Occas sl marg spotting. Rebound retaining orig cloth of backstrip & cvrs, a.e.g. *(Claude Cox)* **£35 [≈$53]**
- Poems. London: Moxon, 1871. 22 b/w plates by Birket Foster. Sl foxed. Orig cloth gilt, a.e.g., faded, split in jnt, edges worn. *(Stella Books)* **£70 [≈$105]**
- Poems. London: Moxon, (1878). 1st & 2nd series complete in one vol. Large Paper. Lge 4to. 44 engvd plates by Birket Foster, w'engvd decs. V occas pale spotting. Three qtr mor gilt, sl rubbed. *(Barbara Stone)* **£85 [≈$128]**
- The Serious Poems. Illustrated by Granville Fell. London: Newnes, 1901. One of 105 signed by Fell. 12mo. Ills. Endpapers sl browned. Spine darkened with sl wear. *(Jo Ann Reisler)* **$150 [≈£100]**

Hope, Thomas

- Costume of the Ancients. London: for William Miller, by W. Bulmer, 1809. 8vo. 200 plates. Contemp half calf, rebacked. *(Waterfield's)* **£150 [≈$225]**

Hope, William St. John

- The Architectural History of the Cathedral Church and Monastery of St. Andrew at Rochester. London: Mitchell & Hughes, 1900. vi,220 pp. 6 fldg plans, cold plate, 43 text ills. Orig cloth gilt. *(Hollett)* **£85 [≈$128]**

Hope, William St. John & Atchley, E.G. Cuthbert

- English Liturgical Colours. London: SPCK, 1918. 1st edn. Sm 4to. xiii,273,[1] pp. Frontis. Cloth, sl rubbed, spine sl sunned. *(Bookpress)* **$65 [≈£43]**

Hopkins, R. Thurston

- Moated Houses of England. London: Country Life, 1935. 1st edn. viii,236 pp. 47 ills. A few spots. Orig cloth gilt, jnts trifle rubbed. *(Hollett)* **£30 [≈$45]**
- Moated Houses of England. London: Country Life, 1935. 1st edn. 8vo. viii,236 pp. 47 ills. A few spots. Orig cloth gilt, hinges trifle rubbed. *(Hollett)* **£30 [≈$45]**

Hoppus, E.

- The Gentleman's and Builder's Repository; or, Architecture Display'd ... London: James Hodges, 1737. 1st edn. Sm 4to. 86 plates engvd by B. Cole. Sl staining at start. Contemp calf, sometime rebacked. *(Traylen)* **£380 [≈$570]**

Horace

- Carmina Sapphica. Chelsea: Ashendene Press, 1903. One of 150 (of 175). 8vo. 46,[i] pp. Orig limp vellum, sl soiled. *(Finch)* **£600 [≈$900]**

Horne, H.P.

- The Binding of Books. An Essay in the History of Gold-Tooled Bindings. Second Edition. London: 1915. 8vo. 9 plates. Orig cloth, paper label. *(Traylen)* **£15 [≈$23]**

Horodisch, Abraham

- Picasso as a Book Artist. London: Faber, 1962. Enlgd edn. Lge 8vo. 2 cold plates, 66 ills. Dw (sl marked). *(Spelman)* **£30 [≈$45]**

Horswell, Jane

- Bronze Sculpture of "Les Animaliers" Reference and Price Guide. Antique Collectors' Club: 1971. 239 pp. Num ills. Orig cloth. *(Fine Art)* **£40 [≈$60]**

Houart, Victor

- Easter Eggs. A Collector's Guide. London: Souvenir Press, 1978. 1st edn. 128 pp. Ills. Orig cloth gilt. Dw. *(Hollett)* **£30 [≈$45]**

Houfe, Simon

- The Dictionary of British Book Illustrators and Caricaturists 1800-1914. N.p.: Antique Collectors' Club, (1981). 2nd edn, rvsd. 4to. 520 pp. Frontis. Orig cloth. Dw. *(Bookpress)* **$79.50 [≈£53]**
- John Leech and the Victorian Scene. Antique Collectors' Club: 1984. 1st edn. 4to. 265 pp. Frontis, 40 cold plates, num ills. Orig cloth. Dw. *(Claude Cox)* **£25 [≈$38]**

Housman, A.E.

- A Shropshire Lad. London: Harrap, 1940. 1st edn thus. 98 pp. 56 w'engvs by Agnes Miller Parker. Sm mark to one marg. Dw (chipped). *(Waddington)* **£28 [≈$42]**
- A Shropshire Lad. London: The Riccardi Press for The Medici Society, 1914. One of 1000. Dw (sl sunned, chip at ft of spine). *(Hermitage)* **$125 [≈£83]**

Housman, Laurence

- Arthur Boyd Houghton. A Selection from his Work ... London: Kegan Paul, 1896. 32 pp. 89 plates. Orig cloth, t.e.g., spine sl faded. *(Leicester Art Books)* **£60 [≈$90]**
- Mendicant Rhymes. [Chipping Camden:

Essex House Press, 1906]. One of 300. 4to. 56 pp. Orig vellum backed bds, uncut. *(Claude Cox)* **£110 [≈$165]**

Houston, Mary G.

- Medieval Costume in England and France. The 13th, 14th and 15th Centuries. London: 1939. Sm 4to. xi,228 pp. 8 cold plates, 350 ills. Orig cloth. *(Washton)* **$45 [≈£30]**

Houston, Mary G. & Hornblower, F.S.

- Ancient Egyptian, Assyrian and Persian Costumes. London: A. & C. Black, 1920. 1st edn. 89 pp. 16 mtd cold plates, 46 figs. Orig pict cloth, extrs sl worn. *(Willow House)* **£30 [≈$45]**

How, George Evelyn Paget

- English and Scottish Silver Spoons: Mediaeval to Late Stuart ... London: 1952-57. One of 550. 3 vols. Folio. Num plates. Orig buckram, t.e.g. Dws (torn). *(David Slade)* **£400 [≈$600]**

Howard, Ebenezer

- Garden Cities of Tomorrow. London: Swan Sonnenschein, 1902. 1st edn thus. 12mo. 191 pp. Frontis, 5 plates. Some ink notes. Occas marg foxing. Orig wraps, rebacked. Cloth slipcase. *(Bookpress)* **$175 [≈£117]**

Howard, Frank

- Colour as a Means of Art ... London: Joseph Thomas, 1838. 1st edn. Cr 8vo. [2], 106 pp, advt leaf. Cold frontis, 17 chromolitho plates. Minor foxing. Orig cloth, spine faded & sl worn. *(Spelman)* **£70 [≈$105]**
- Colour as a Means of Art ... London: Bohn, 1849. 8vo. 106 pp. 18 hand cold plates. Orig cloth, partly unopened, sl faded. *(Clark)* **£100 [≈$150]**

Howe, E.

- A List of London Bookbinders 1648-1815. London: 1950. xxxviii,104 pp. Cloth bound hard boards. *(Whitehart)* **£35 [≈$53]**

Howells, John Mead

- The Architectural Heritage of the Piscataqua. New York: Architectural Book Publishing Co., (1937). 1st edn. Folio. (iii)-xxvi,217 pp. 301 ills. Orig cloth, sl edge wear. *(Bookpress)* **$100 [≈£67]**

Howells, William Dean

- The Rise of Silas Lapham. Illustrations by Mimi Korach. New York: The Limited Editions Club, 1961. One of 1500 signed by Korach. Tall 8vo. Orig cloth. Slipcase (minor fading). *(Oak Knoll)* **$55 [≈£37]**

Howgrave-Graham, R.P.

- The Cathedrals of France. London: Batsford, 1959. 1st edn. 280 pp. 121 ills. Orig cloth gilt. Dw. *(Hollett)* **£20 [≈$30]**

Howitt, S.

- British Preserve, with Etchings from Drawings by Samuel Howitt. London: Sherwood, Gilbert & Piper, (1824). 1st edn. Title engv, 36 plates. Occas foxing. Orig cloth, spotted, sl faded. *(Argonaut)* **$300 [≈£200]**

Hoy, Peter

- Silence at Midnight. N.p.: Brewhouse Press, 1967. One of 200. 2 lge broadsides, folded in paper portfolio. *(Oak Knoll)* **$45 [≈£30]**

Hoyle, John

- A Complete Dictionary of Music. Containing a full and clear Explanation ... London: for H.D. Symonds, 1791. Title sl spotted. Lib stamps. Rec half calf. *(Jarndyce)* **£140 [≈$210]**

Hubert, J., & others

- The Carolingian Renaissance. New York: Braziller, (1970). 1st Amer edn. 4to. 380 pp. Fldg map, frontis, ills. Orig cloth. *(Bookpress)* **$125 [≈£83]**

Huddleston, Sisley

- Paris Salons, Cafes, Studios. Being Social, Artistic and Literary Memories. Philadelphia & London: Lippincott, 1928. Sm 4to. 366 pp. 48 plates. Orig cloth. *(Ars Libri)* **$50 [≈£33]**

Hudson, Derek

- Arthur Rackham His Life and Work. New York: Scribner, 1975. 4to. 181 pp. Orig cloth. *(Davidson)* **$125 [≈£83]**
- James Pryde 1866-1941. London: Constable, 1949. 1st edn. 99 pp. Plates. Orig buckram, sm mark on cvr. Dw (chipped, water marked). *(Bookworks)* **£32 [≈$48]**
- James Pryde 1886-1941. London: Constable, 1949. 99 pp. 5 cold & 32 b/w plates, 8 text ills. Orig cloth. *(Leicester Art Books)* **£30 [≈$45]**

Hudson, Stephen

- Celeste and Other Sketches. Wood Engravings by John Nash. Blackamore Press: 1930. One of 700. 102 pp. 6 engvs. Orig cloth gilt. *(Claude Cox)* **£45 [≈$68]**

Hudson, W.H.

- Green Mansions. Illustrated by Keith Henderson. London: 1926. One of 165 signed by the artist. 35 engvs. Orig buckram, spine ends sl bumped. *(Ulysses Bookshop)* **£125 [≈$188]**
- Green Mansions. Illustrations by Edward A. Wilson. New York: The Limited Editions Club, 1935. One of 1500 signed by Wilson. Tall 8vo. Orig cloth-backed bds. Slipcase. *(Oak Knoll)* **$75 [≈£50]**
- 153 Letters ... Edited with an Introduction and Notes by Edward Garnett. London: Nonesuch Press, 1923. One of 1000. [2],191 pp. Port vignette. Orig buckram, uncut. Dw (sl frayed). *(Claude Cox)* **£35 [≈$53]**

Hughes, G. Bernard

- Collecting Antiques. London: Country Life, 1951. Sm 4to. 351 pp. Num ills (10 cold plates). Orig cloth gilt. *(Hollett)* **£20 [≈$30]**
- Collecting Antiques. London: Country Life, 1960. 2nd edn. Lge 8vo. 391 pp. 19 cold & 72 b/w plates. Orig cloth gilt. Dw (edges sl torn & frayed). *(Hollett)* **£25 [≈$38]**
- Collecting Miniature Antiques. A Guide for Collectors. London: Heinemann, 1973. Lge 8vo. 184 pp. 8 cold plates, 250 ills. Orig cloth gilt. Dw. *(Hollett)* **£25 [≈$38]**
- English and Scottish Earthenware 1660-1860. London: Abbey Fine Arts, n.d. 238 pp. 4 cold & 46 b/w plates. Orig cloth gilt. Dw. *(Hollett)* **£30 [≈$45]**
- English Glass for the Collector 1660-1860. London: Lutterworth, 1969. 3rd imp. 251 pp. 47 plates. Dw (edgeworn). *(Paul Brown)* **£20 [≈$30]**
- English Painted Enamels. Illustrated from the Collections of Her Majesty Queen Mary and the Hon. Mrs. Ionides. London: Country Life, 1951. 156 pp. Cold frontis, 90 plates. Orig cloth gilt. *(Hollett)* **£35 [≈$53]**
- English, Scottish and Irish Table Glass from the 16th Century to 1820. London: Batsford, 1956. 4to. 410 pp. Dw (sl chipped). *(Corn Exchange)* **£40 [≈$60]**
- Horse Brasses and Other Small Items for the Collector. London: Country Life, 1956. 1st edn. 104 pp. Cold frontis, 42 plates. Orig cloth gilt. Dw. *(Hollett)* **£20 [≈$30]**
- Small Antique Silverware. London: Batsford, 1957. 1st edn. Lge 8vo. 224 pp. 249 ills. Orig cloth gilt. Dw. *(Hollett)* **£25 [≈$38]**
- Three Centuries of English Domestic Silver 1450-1820. London: Lutterworth Press, 1963. 248 pp. 47 plates. Orig cloth gilt. Dw (sl worn & marked). *(Hollett)* **£10 [≈$15]**
- Victorian Pottery and Porcelain. London: Country Life, 1959. 1st edn. Lge 8vo. 184 pp. Cold frontis, 88 plates. Orig cloth gilt. Dw. *(Hollett)* **£20 [≈$30]**
- Victorian Pottery and Porcelain. London: Spring Books, 1967. Lge 8vo. 184 pp. 89 ills. Orig cloth gilt. Dw (sl torn & chipped). *(Hollett)* **£20 [≈$30]**

Hughes, Spencer Leigh

- The English Character. London: T.N. Foulis, 1912. 1st edn. 16 mtd cold plates by Frederick Gardner. Orig bndg. *(Old Cathay)* **£23 [≈$35]**

Hugo, Thomas

- The Bewick Collector. A Descriptive Catalogue of the Works of Thomas and John bewick (1866). New York: Burt Franklin, 1970. 2 vols. 8vo. 562; 353 pp. Text ills. Orig cloth. *(Robertshaw)* **£35 [≈$53]**

Hugo, Victor

- Notre-Dame de Paris. Illustrations by Bernard Lamotte. New York: The Limited Editions Club, 1955. One of 1500 signed by Lamotte. Sm 4to. Orig cloth. Slipcase. *(Oak Knoll)* **$55 [≈£37]**
- The Toilers of the Sea. Wood-Engravings by Tranquillo Marangoni. New York: The Limited Editions Club, 1960. One of 1500 signed by Marangoni. Sm 4to. Orig cloth-backed bds. Dw (spine yellowed). Slipcase (wear to top edge). *(Oak Knoll)* **$125 [≈£83]**

Huish, Marcus B.

- Japan and Its Art. London: Fine Art Society, 1889. 1st edn. Sm 8vo. xii,254,[2],4 pp. Frontis, 121 text ills. Orig cloth, worn. *(Bookpress)* **$325 [≈£217]**
- Japan and Its Art. London: Fine Art Society, 1899. 1st edn. Sm 8vo. xii,254,[2],4 pp. Frontis, 121 text ills. Orig cloth, worn. *(Bookpress)* **$325 [≈£217]**

Hulme, F.E.

- Suggestions in Floral Design. London: Cassell, Petter & Galpin, [ca 1870-75]. Folio. 52 pp. Addtnl cold title, 50 chromolitho plates heightened in gold. Orig dec cloth gilt, sl marked. *(Clevedon Books)* **£275 [≈$413]**

Hume, Frances

- The Story of the Circle of Chalk. A Drama from the Old Chinese. The Rodale Press: (1953). One of 1000. 6 copper engvs by John

Buckland Wright. Orig qtr buckram. Slipcase (sl worn). *(Waddington)* **£36 [≈$54]**

Humphrey, Lizbeth B.

- Child Life. A Souvenir of Lizbeth B. Humphrey. Boston: Louis Prang, 1890. Oblong folio. 22 mtd chromolitho ills on 14 card sheets. Orig pict cloth, crnrs sl bumped. *(Barbara Stone)* **£95 [≈$143]**

Humphreys, Henry Noel

- Ancient Coins and Medals ... London: Grant & Griffith, 1850 [1849]. 1st edn. Sm 4to. [4],iv,208 pp, advt leaf. Errata slip. 114 facs coins set in sunken panels on 10 card mounts. Some browning & sl damage. Rec buckram retaining 'relievo' cvrs. *(Claude Cox)* **£220 [≈$330]**
- Masterpieces of the Early Printers and Engravers. London: Sotheran, 1870. 1st edn. Folio. 81 ills. Occas foxing. Orig cloth. *(Bookpress)* **$350 [≈£233]**
- The Origin and Progress of the Art of Writing ... Second Edition. London: Day & Son, 1855. Folio. vi,178 pp. 28 litho plates (of 30, lacks plates 10 & 11). Orig black monastic papier mache bndg, sl worn, rebacked in buckram. *(Claude Cox)* **£65 [≈$98]**
- A Record of the Black Prince ... Embellished with Highly Wrought Miniatures and Borderings selected from Various Illuminated MSS ... London: Longman ..., 1849. 6 chromolithos. Orig papier-mache bndg, a.e.g., rebacked in leather, one crnr sl damaged. *(Mermaid Books)* **£125 [≈$188]**

Humphries, Sydney

- Oriental Carpets, Runners & Rugs & Some Jacquard Reproductions. London: A. & C. Black, (1910). Only edn. 4to. Cold plates. Orig elab gilt cream cloth, fine. *(Old Cathay)* **£275 [≈$413]**
- Oriental Carpets, Runners and Rugs and some Jacquard Reproductions. London: A. & C. Black, 1910. 1st edn. 8vo. 428 pp. Plates (24 cold). Foredge sl spotted. Orig dec cloth gilt, t.e.g. *(Robertshaw)* **£115 [≈$173]**

Hunt, J. Eric

- English and Welsh Crucifixes 670-1550. London: SPCK, 1956. Lge 8vo. [viii],92 pp. Cold frontis, 39 plates. Orig cloth gilt. Dw. *(Hollett)* **£30 [≈$45]**

Hunt, W. Holman

- Pre-Raphaelitism and the Pre-Raphaelite Brotherhood. London: 1905. 1st edn. 2 vols. 40 plates, ills. Lib b'plates. Orig cloth, t.e.g., sl rubbed, bottom edges shelfworn, vol 1 hinges cracked. *(Ulysses Bookshop)* **£150 [≈$225]**
- Pre-Raphaelitism and the Pre-Raphaelite Brotherhood. London: Macmillan, 1905. 2 vols. xxviii,512; xiv,493 pp. 40 plates, num text ills. New half leather, t.e.g. *(Fine Art)* **£90 [≈$135]**

Hunter, Dard

- My Life with Paper. New York: Knopf, 1958. 1st edn. With paper sample. Orig cloth gilt. Dw (sl used). *(Mac Donnell)* **$100 [≈£67]**
- Papermaking in Pioneer America. Phila: Pennsylvania UP, 1952. 1st edn. 8vo. xii,178 pp. Plates. Orig cloth-backed bds. *(Oak Knoll)* **$125 [≈£83]**
- Papermaking through Eighteen Centuries. New York: William Edwin Rudge, 1930. 1st edn. Thick 8vo. xviii,358 pp. 214 ills. Orig buckram, leather label, t.e.g. Dw (v sl spotting). *(Oak Knoll)* **$250 [≈£167]**
- Romance of Watermarks ... And a Biographical Sketch of the Author by Katherine Fisher. Cincinnati: Stratford Press, [ca 1940]. 1st edn. One of 210. Sm 8vo. 34 pp. Orig cloth-backed bds. Slipcase. *(Oak Knoll)* **$300 [≈£200]**

Hunter, George Leland

- Decorative Furniture. Phila: Lippincott, 1923. 1st edn. Lge 4to. xxiv,480 pp. 23 cold plates, 900 ills. Orig cloth, sl rubbed, spine sunned. *(Bookpress)* **$110 [≈£73]**

Hunter, Sam

- Hans Hofmann. With an Introduction by Sam Hunter and Five Essays by Hans Hofmann. New York: Abrams, [1963]. Lge sq 4to. 227 pp. 168 plates. Orig cloth. *(Ars Libri)* **$750 [≈£500]**
- Isamu Noguchi. London: Thames & Hudson, 1979. 334 pp. 316 ills. Orig cloth. Dw. *(Leicester Art Books)* **£85 [≈$128]**
- Larry Rivers. New York: Abrams, 1969. Lge oblong 4to. 261,[1] pp. 220 plates. Orig cloth. Dw. *(Ars Libri)* **$600 [≈£400]**
- Larry Rivers. New York: Rizzoli, 1989. Lge sq 4to. 358 pp. 400 ills. Orig cloth. Dw. *(Ars Libri)* **$75 [≈£50]**

Hunter, Sam, & others

- New Art around the World. Painting and Sculpture. New York: Abrams, [ca 1965]. Lge 8vo. 510 pp. 478 ills. Orig cloth. Dw. *(Karmiole)* **$45 [≈£30]**

Huntington Library

- Guide to American Historical Manuscripts in the Huntington Library. San Marino: 1979. 8vo. Dec title. Orig cloth gilt. *(Traylen)* **£18 [≈$27]**
- Guide to Literary Manuscripts in the Huntington Library. San Marino: 1979. 8vo. Dec title. Orig cloth gilt. *(Traylen)* **£25 [≈$38]**

Hurlbutt, Frank

- Bow Porcelain. London: G. Bell & Sons, 1926. Sm folio. xviii,160 pp. 64 plates (8 cold). Orig cloth gilt, spine dulled, edges sl rubbed, sm snags to spine. *(Clevedon Books)* **£90 [≈$135]**
- Bow Porcelain. London: G. Bell & Sons, 1926. Lge 4to. xiv,463 pp. 64 plates (8 cold). Orig cloth gilt, sl bumped. *(Hollett)* **£85 [≈$128]**
- Bristol Porcelain. London: Medici Society, 1928. 1st edn. 4to. xx,164 pp. 64 plates (sm marg blind stamps). Orig cloth gilt, sl soiled, lib marks. *(Hollett)* **£150 [≈$225]**

Hurlimann, Bettina

- Three Centuries of Children's Books in Europe. Translated and Edited by Brian Alderson. OUP: 1967. 297 pp. 28 plates. Dw. *(Peter Bell)* **£30 [≈$45]**

Hurlimann, Martin & Clemen, Paul

- Gothic Cathedrals. Paris, Chartres, Amiens, Reims. Oxford: Blackwell, 1958. 4to. 52 pp. 160 plates. Orig cloth. Dw (extrs chipped). Slipcase. *(Hollett)* **£25 [≈$38]**

Hurlimann, Martin & Meyer, Peter

- English Cathedrals. With a Foreword by Geoffrey Grigson. London: Thames & Hudson, 1951. 4to. 48 pp. 166 plates. Orig cloth. Dw (torn). *(Hollett)* **£25 [≈$38]**

Husey, E.C.

- Home Building, a Reliable Book of Facts, relative to Building, Living, Materials, Costs ... New York: Leader & Van Hoesen, 1876. 1st edn. 4to. viii,416 pp. 42 plates, 45 ills. Perf stamp on title. Cloth, front inner hinge cracked. *(Bookpress)* **$385 [≈£257]**

Hussey, Christopher

- Clarence House. London: Country Life, 1949. 1st edn. 4to. 136 pp. 66 plates. Foredge sl spotted. Orig cloth gilt. Dw. *(Hollett)* **£50 [≈$75]**
- English Country Houses. Early, Mid and Late Georgian. London: Country Life, 1955-58. 1st edns. 3 vols. 4to. 1444 ills. Orig cloth gilt. Dws. *(Hollett)* **£550 [≈$825]**
- English Country Houses. Early, Mid and Late Georgian. Antique Collectors Club: 1986. 3 vols. Lge 8vo. 1444 ills. Orig pict wraps. *(Hollett)* **£65 [≈$98]**
- English Country Houses open to the Public. London: Country Life, 1957. 3rd edn. 4to. 240 pp. 389 ills. Orig cloth gilt. Dw. *(Hollett)* **£40 [≈$60]**
- The Life of Sir Edwin Lutyens. London: Country Life, 1953. Special edn. 4to. xxii,602 pp. 178 plates. Orig cloth gilt. *(Hollett)* **£60 [≈$90]**
- The Life of Sir Edwin Lutyens ... see also Butler, A.S.G.
- Tait McKenzie. A Sculptor of Youth. London: Country Life, 1929. xii,108 pp. 93 plates. Orig cloth. *(Leicester Art Books)* **£38 [≈$57]**

Hutchinson, F.E.

- Mediaeval Glass at All Souls College. A History and Description ... London: Faber, 1949. 1st edn. Tall 8vo. 67 pp. Cold frontis, 31 plates. Orig cloth gilt. Dw (sm edge tear). *(Hollett)* **£30 [≈$45]**

Hutchison, Harold F.

- London Transport Posters. London: London Transport Board, 1963. Roy 8vo. 124 plates. Orig buckram. Dw. *(David Slade)* **£65 [≈$98]**
- The Poster: An Illustrated History from 1860. New York: Viking, (1968). 4to. 216 pp. 218 ills (40 cold). Orig cloth. Dw. *(Abacus)* **$50 [≈£33]**
- Sir Christopher Wren. New York: Stein & Day, (1976). 1st edn. 8vo. 191 pp. 35 ills. Orig cloth backed bds. Dw (minor wear). *(Bookpress)* **$45 [≈£30]**

Huth Bequest

- Catalogue of the Fifty Manuscripts and Printed Books bequeathed to the British Museum by Alfred H. Huth. London: 1912. Lge 4to. Port, 18 plates, ills. Orig buckram. *(Traylen)* **£48 [≈$72]**

Hutton, C.A.

- Greek Terracotta Statuettes. London: Seeley & Co., 1899. Sm 4to. xvi,78 pp. 8 cold & 36 other plates. Orig cloth gilt. *(Hollett)* **£40 [≈$60]**

Hutton, E.

- The Cosmati: The Roman Marble Workers of the XIIth and XIIIth Centuries. London:

Routledge, 1950. 4to. xii,62 pp. 64 plates. Ex-lib. Orig cloth. *(Castle Bookshop)* **£25 [≈$38]**

Hutton, W.R.

- The Washington Bridge over the Harlem River. New York: 1890. 1st edn. 4to. [4],90,[6],[1,[21 advt] pp. 26 Albertype plates, 37 litho plates, text figs, tables. Sm lib stamps, occas sl dusting. Orig cloth gilt, rubbed, some snags. Inscribed by the author. *(Clevedon Books)* **£185 [≈$278]**

Huxley, Aldous

- Brave New World. Illustrated with Gravures by Mara McAfee. Avon, CT: The Limited Editions Club, 1974. One of 2000 signed by McAfee. Sm 4to. Orig blue vinyl cloth. Slipcase. *(Oak Knoll)* **$55 [≈£37]**

Huyghe, Rene

- Delacroix. London: Thames & Hudson, 1963. 564 pp. 461 ills. Orig cloth. *(Leicester Art Books)* **£95 [≈$143]**

Hyams, E.

- Capability Brown and Humphry Repton. London: 1971. 8vo. viii,248 pp. 49 ills. Ex-lib. Cloth. *(Wheldon & Wesley)* **£25 [≈$38]**

Ibbett, W.J.

- Ibbett's Jessie. Flansham, Sussex: Pear Tree Press, [1923]. One of 100. Roy 8vo. Orig wraps, unopened. *(Blackwell's)* **£90 [≈$135]**

Ibsen, Henrik

- Peer Gynt. A Dramatic Poem. Illustrated by Arthur Rackham. Phila: [1936]. 1st Amer trade edn. 4to. 12 cold plates, num b/w ills. B'plate removed. Orig cloth, sl bowed. Dw. *(Heritage)* **$300 [≈£200]**
- Peer Gynt. Illustrated by Per Krohg. New York: The Limited Editions Club, 1955. One of 1500 signed by Krohg. Sm 4to. Orig cloth-backed bds. Slipcase (sl worn). *(Oak Knoll)* **$55 [≈£37]**
- Three Plays. Illustrated by Frederik Matheson. New York: The Limited Editions Club, 1964. One of 1500 signed by Matheson. 8vo. Orig qtr leather. Slipcase. *(Oak Knoll)* **$60 [≈£40]**

Ideas for Rustic Furniture ...

- Ideas for Rustic Furniture proper for Garden Seats, Summer Houses, Hermitages, Cottages, &c. London: for I. & J. Taylor, [ca 1795]. 8vo. 25 plates. Rec qtr mor. Often attributed to William Wrighte. *(Spelman)* **£480 [≈$720]**

The Illustrated Exhibitor ...

- The Illustrated Exhibitor ... comprising Sketches by Pen and Pencil of the Principal Objects of the Great Exhibition ... 1851. London: John Cassell, [1851]. Lge 8vo. xliv, 556 pp. 10 fldg plates, text ills. Contemp half calf, gilt spine. *(Claude Cox)* **£65 [≈$98]**

Illustrations ...

- Illustrations of Shakespeare; comprised in Two Hundred and Thirty Vignette Engravings, by Thompson ... adapted to all Editions. London: Sherwood, Gilbert & Piper, 1825. 8vo. [lxxx] pp. Frontis, 6 engvs per leaf throughout. Disbound. *(Clark)* **£32 [≈$48]**
- Illustrations of the Anglo-French Coinage ... see Ainslie, G.R.

Image, Selwyn

- Thomas Bewick. London: The Print Collectors' Club, 1932. One of 500. 61 pp. 39 ills. Orig cloth & bds. *(Leicester Art Books)* **£22 [=$33]**

Ingoldsby, Thomas

- See Barham, R.H.

Inn, Henry

- Chinese Houses and Gardens. Honolulu: Fong Inn's Ltd., 1940. One of 2000 signed by the author. Lge 4to. xii,140 pp. Num ills. Orig linen gilt. *(Karmiole)* **$85 [≈£57]**

International ...

- International Exhibition Glasgow 1901. Official Catalogue of the Fine Art Section. Glasgow: Watson, 1901. xx,234, xxi-lxviii, advt pp. Orig wraps, sl dusty. *(Cooper Hay)* **£35 [≈$53]**
- The International Society of Sculptors, Painters and Gravers. Exhibition 1905. Manchester: Manchester Art Gallery, 1905. 64 pp. Orig wraps. *(Cooper Hay)* **£35 [≈$53]**
- The International Society of Sculptors, Painters and Gravers. Art Congress ... Inaugurated May, 1898, London. [Chelsea: Shield, 1898]. 95 pp. Orig cloth, sl dusty, few stains. *(Cooper Hay)* **£85 [≈$128]**

Ireland, Alexander

- The Book-Lover's Enchiridion ... London: 1888. Large Paper. 4to. Orig cloth, spine rubbed. *(Traylen)* **£20 [≈$30]**

Ireland, Geoffrey

- Epstein. A Camera Study of the Sculptor at Work. Introduction by Laurie Lee. London:

Lion & Unicorn Press, [1956]. One of 200 signed by Epstein & Lee. 8 pp. 31 plates. Orig cloth. *(Leicester Art Books)* **£100 [≈$150]**

Irving, Washington

- The Alhambra. Illustrated by Lima de Freitas. New York: The Limited Editions Club, 1969. One of 1500 signed by de Freitas. Sm 4to. Orig cloth. Slipcase. *(Oak Knoll)* **$65 [≈£43]**
- The Legend of Sleepy Hollow. Illustrated by Arthur Rackham. London: Harrap, 1928. 103 pp. Ills, pict endpapers. Name. Orig green silk gilt. *(Carol Howard)* **£120 [≈$180]**
- The Legend of Sleepy Hollow. Illustrated by Arthur Rackham. Phila: [1928]. One of 125 (of 375) for the US signed by Rackham. 4to. 8 mtd cold plates, 30 b/w ills. Orig vellum gilt, sl soiled, sl bowed. *(Heritage)* **$1,850 [≈£1,233]**
- Rip Van Winkle and the Legend of Sleepy Hollow. Illustrated by Barry Moser. West Hatfield: Pennyroyal Editions, 1985. Orig cloth. Slipcase. *(Hermitage)* **$125 [≈£83]**
- Rip Van Winkle. Illustrated by Arthur Rackham. London: Heinemann, 1905. 1st edn, 2nd imp. 4to. 51 mtd cold plates. Orig elab gilt cloth. *(Sotheran's)* **£198 [≈$297]**
- The Sketchbook of Geoffrey Crayon. New York: Putnam, 1895. Van Tassel Edition. 2 vols. 8vo. Num plates inc 4 by Arthur Rackham. Orig elab dec cloth gilt, t.e.g. Dws. *(Argonaut)* **$250 [≈£167]**

Irwin, David

- John Flaxman 1755-1826. Sculptor, Illustrator, Designer. London: Studio Vista & Christie's, 1979. xviii,250 pp. 282 ills. Orig cloth. Dw. *(Leicester Art Books)* **£25 [≈$38]**

Irwin, David & Francina

- Scottish Painters at Home and Abroad 1700-1900. London: 1975. 508 pp. 8 cold plates, 220 ills. Orig cloth. Dw. *(Fine Art)* **£40 [≈$60]**

Irwin, John & Brett, K.B.

- Origins of Chintz. London: HMSO, 1970. 1st edn. 4to. viii,134 pp. 164 plates. Front free endpaper creased, a few marks. Orig cloth, soiled. *(Hollett)* **£30 [≈$45]**

Irwin, Raymond

- The Origins of the English Library. London: Allen & Unwin, (1958). 1st edn. 8vo. 255,[1] pp. Orig cloth. Dw (sl soiled). *(Oak Knoll)* **$55 [≈£37]**

Isaac, Frank

- English & Scottish Printing Types 1501-35, 1508-41. OUP: Bibl Soc, 1930. 4to. 98 ills. Occas sl foxing. One crnr sl worn. *(Clark)* **£50 [≈$75]**
- English Printers' Types of the Sixteenth Century. London: OUP, 1936. 1st edn. Lge 8vo. xix,[i],60 pp. 80 plates. Orig cloth backed bds. *(Bookpress)* **$135 [≈£90]**

Isham, Samuel

- The History of American Painting. New York: Macmillan, 1910. 4to. 573 pp. 133 ills. Orig cloth gilt. *(Rona Schneider)* **$65 [≈£43]**

Ivins, William M.

- Prints and Visual Communication. London: Routledge, 1953. xxv,190 pp. 84 plates. Orig cloth. *(Fine Art)* **£22 [≈$33]**

Jackson, A.W.

- The Half-Timber House; Its Origin, Design, Modern Plan and Construction ... With American Adaptations of the Style. New York: McBride, (1912) 1919. Sm 4to. xviii,115 pp. Frontis, 65 ills. Orig pict cloth, spine title faded. *(Clevedon Books)* **£38 [≈$57]**

Jackson, Sir Charles

- English Goldsmiths and their Marks ... London: Macmillan, 1921. 2nd edn. 4to. xvi, 748 pp. Num ills. Flyleaves sl browned. Orig cloth gilt, sl marked. *(Hollett)* **£65 [≈$98]**
- English Goldsmiths and their Marks ... London: Batsford, 1949. Thick 4to. xvi,747 pp. Orig cloth gilt. Dw. *(Hollett)* **£55 [≈$83]**

Jackson, Mrs E. Nevill

- History of Hand-Made Lace ... London: Upcott Gill; New York: Scribner, 1900. Sm 4to. [xii],245,[2 advt] pp. 19 plates, over 200 engvs. Orig dec cloth. *(Schoyer)* **$125 [≈£83]**
- Silhouette. New York: Scribner, 1938. 4to. 10 cold & 93 other plates. Orig cloth gilt. *(Barbara Stone)* **£55 [≈$83]**
- Silhouette: Notes and Dictionary. London: Methuen, 1938. 1st edn. 154 pp. 10 cold & 93 b/w plates. Orig cloth. Dw (worn). *(Willow House)* **£65 [≈$98]**

Jackson, Holbrook

- The Anatomy of Bibliomania. London: The Soncino Press, (1930). 2nd edn. 2 vols. 8vo. Prelims & foredges sl foxed. Orig cloth, t.e.g., spines sl faded. *(Bookpress)* **$100 [≈£67]**
- A Cross-Section of English Printing. The Curwen Press, 1918-1934. London: The

Curwen Press, 1935. One of 75. 24 pp. Ills. Orig cloth, v sm wrinkle front cvr. Slipcase. *(Argonaut)* **$175 [≈£117]**

Jackson, John

- A Treatise on Wood Engraving, Historical and Practical. London: Charles Knight, 1839. 1st edn. Lge 8vo. xvi,749,[3] pp. Num ills inc 7 plates (2 cold, 1 tinted). Occas marks. Contemp half roan, rubbed, jnts sl weak. *(Bow Windows)* **£105 [≈$158]**

Jackson, T.G.

- Byzantine and Romanesque Architecture. Cambridge: UP, 1920. 2nd edn. 2 vols. Roy 8vo. 165 plates, 148 text figs. Qtr vellum, gilt dec cloth, leather labels. *(Quest Books)* **£58 [≈$87]**
- The Church of St. Mary the Virgin, Oxford. Oxford: Clarendon Press 1897. 1st edn. 4to. 220,index pp. Plates, ills. B'plate. Orig cloth, t.e.g., sl dusty, crnrs worn. *(Hermitage)* **$125 [≈£83]**

Jackson, W.A.

- Records of a Bibliographer. Selected Papers of William Alexander Jackson. Edited with an Introduction and Bibliography by William H. Bond. Cambridge, MA: 1967. 4to. 95 ills. Orig linen backed bds. Inscrbd by the editor. *(Traylen)* **£48 [≈$72]**

Jackson, William Henry

- Time Exposure. New York: Putnam, (1940). 341 pp. Photo ills. B'plate. Dw (sl chipped & frayed). signed by the author. *(Hermitage)* **$200 [≈£133]**

Jackson-Stops, Gervase

- The Treasure Houses of Britain. Five Hundred Years of Private Patronage and Art Collecting. Washington: National Gallery of Art, 1985. Thick 4to. 680 pp. Cold ills. Orig cloth gilt. Dw. *(Hollett)* **£45 [≈$68]**

Jacobs, Flora G.

- A History of Dolls' Houses. London: Cassell, 1954. 1st edn. 320 pp. 116 ills. Lacks front free endpaper. Orig cloth. *(Willow House)* **£20 [≈$30]**

Jacobus, John

- Henri Matisse. New York: Abrams, n.d. 4to. 184 pp. 168 ills (48 mtd cold plates). Orig cloth. Dw. *(Abacus)* **$50 [≈£33]**

Jacquet, Eugene & Chapuis, Alfred

- Technique and History of the Swiss Watch. London: Spring Books, 1970. 4to. 272 pp. 46 cold & 190 b/w plates, 30 text figs. Orig cloth. *(Mendelsohn)* **$60 [≈£40]**

Jaffe, Hans L.

- Piet Mondrian. London: Thames & Hudson, 1970. 164 pp. 139 ills. Orig cloth. Dw. *(Leicester Art Books)* **£50 [≈$75]**

Jaffe, Irma B.

- The Sculpture of Leonard Baskin. New York: Viking, 1980. Lge 4to. 224 pp. 142 ills. Orig cloth. Dw. *(Ars Libri)* **$60 [≈£40]**

Jaffe, Michael

- Rubens and Italy. Ithaca: 1977. 4to. 128 pp. 16 cold plates, 346 ills. Orig cloth. Dw. *(Washton)* **$75 [≈£50]**
- Rubens and Italy. London: Phaidon, 1977. 128 pp. 346 plates. Orig cloth. Dw. *(Fine Art)* **£65 [≈$98]**
- Van Dyck's Antwerp Sketchbook. London: Macdonald, 1966. 2 vols. 316; 290 pp. Frontis, 171 plates, 181 ills. Orig cloth. *(Leicester Art Books)* **£85 [≈$128]**
- Van Dyke's Antwerp Notebook. London: Macdonald, 1966. 2 vols. 4to. Ills. Orig cloth gilt. Dws. *(Cooper Hay)* **£60 [≈$90]**

Jaggard, Walter R. & Drury, Francis E.

- Architectural Building Construction. Cambridge Technical Series. Cambridge: UP, 1916-27. 2 vols in 3. 8 pocket plans, ills. Orig cloth gilt. *(Hollett)* **£45 [≈$68]**

Jahss, Melvin & Betty

- Inro and other Miniature Forms of Japanese Lacquer Art. London: Kegan Paul, n.d. 4to. 488 pp. 256 plates (76 cold). Dw. *(Francis Edwards)* **£75 [≈$113]**

Jalovec, Karel

- Italian Violin Makers. Revised Edition. London: 1964. 4to. 445 pp. 32 plans, 404 ills. Lib stamps. Dw (sl torn). *(Francis Edwards)* **£75 [≈$113]**

James I, King of Scotland

- The King's Quair. London: Printed at the Caradoc Press, Bedford Park, and published by Grafton & Co., 1914. (One of 350). [4],78, colophon pp. Decs. Orig cloth gilt, uncut. *(Claude Cox)* **£25 [≈$38]**

James, Henry

- The Ambassadors. Illustrations by Leslie Saalburg. New York: The Limited Editions Club, 1963. One of 1500 signed by Saalburg. Orig cloth. Slipcase (sm spot on spine). *(Oak Knoll)* **$55 [≈£37]**

- Daisy Miller. Illustrations by Gustave Nebel. New York: The Limited Editions Club, 1969. One of 1500 signed by Nebel. Orig leather, t.e.g. Slipcase. *(Oak Knoll)* **$95 [≈£63]**

James, M.R.

- Abbeys. London: Great Western Railway, 1926. Lge 8vo. x,154 pp. 7 cold plates, 100 ills, 56 drawings, 13 plans, map. Orig cloth backed bds gilt, trifle marked & scratched. *(Hollett)* **£15 [≈$23]**
- The Sculptured Bosses in the Roof of the Bauchun Chapel of Our Lady of Pity in Norwich Cathedral ... Norwich: Goose & Son ..., 1908. Sm folio. 7 pp. Ills. Orig ptd bds, sl soiled, rebacked. *(Hollett)* **£65 [≈$98]**

Janis, Harriet & Blesh, Rudi

- Collage. Personalities, Concepts, Techniques. Philadelphia & New York: Chilton, 1962. 4to. [8],302 pp. 427 ills. Orig cloth. Dw. *(Ars Libri)* **$75 [≈£50]**

Janis, Sidney

- Abstract & Surrealist Art in America. New York: Reynal & Hitchcock, 1944. 4to. [6],146 pp. 100 plates. Orig cloth. *(Ars Libri)* **$125 [≈£83]**

Janneau, Guillaume

- Modern Glass. London: Studio, 1931. 4to. 184 pp. 128 b/w plates. Dw (minor damage front panel). *(Paul Brown)* **£125 [≈$188]**

Japanese Paper Balloon Bombs ...

- Japanese Paper Balloon Bombs: The First ICMB. North Hills: Bird & Bull Press, 1982. One of 375. 16mo. Orig bds gilt. In paper slipcase with folder containing a drawing. *(Dermont)* **$75 [≈£50]**

Jarves, James Jackson

- A Glimpse at the Art of Japan. New York: Hurd & Houghton, 1876. 1st edn. 12mo. [iv], 216 pp. Frontis, ills. 1 gathering sprung. Occas foxing. Orig cloth, sl worm. *(Bookpress)* **$225 [≈£150]**

Jay, Leonard

- Modern Linotype Typography. Birmingham: Birmingham School of Printing, 1931. 4to. 11,[53] pp. Orig cloth. *(Oak Knoll)* **$65 [≈£43]**
- Modern Typography. Birmingham: Birmingham School of Printing, 1930. 8vo. 8 pp. 8 plates. Orig stiff wraps, cord-tied. *(Oak Knoll)* **$45 [≈£30]**
- Of Making Many Books There is no End. Birmingham: Birmingham School of Printing, 1931. Sm 4to. 19,[45] pp. Orig cloth. *(Oak Knoll)* **$85 [≈£57]**
- Si Monumentum requiris, circumspice. Notes on the Libraries of George W. Jones. Birmingham: Birmingham School of Printing, 1942. Sm 4to. 15,[1] pp. Orig stiff wraps, cord-tied. *(Oak Knoll)* **$55 [≈£37]**
- Tribute to the Work of George W. Jones, Master Printer on the Occasion of his Eightieth Birthday. Birmingham: Birmingham School of Printing, 1940. 4to. 13,[3] pp. Orig stiff wraps, cord-tied. *(Oak Knoll)* **$75 [≈£50]**

Jean, Marcel

- The History of Surrealist Painting. London: Weidenfeld & Nicholson, 1960. 384 pp. 36 cold plates, 384 ills. Orig dec cloth. Dw. *(Fine Art)* **£50 [≈$75]**
- The History of Surrealist Painting. New York: Grove Press, 1967. Sq 4to. 383 pp. Num ills. Orig cloth. Dw. *(Ars Libri)* **$100 [≈£67]**

Jefferies, Richard

- By the Brook. Edited with an Introduction by George Miller. Eric & Joan Stevens: 1981. 1st edn. One of 170. Etched frontis by Arthur Neal, signed by him. Orig cloth backed mrbld bds. *(Claude Cox)* **£18 [≈$27]**
- The Old House at Coate and Other Hitherto Unpublished Essays. With Wood-Engravings by Agnes Miller Parker. London: 1948. 1st edn. Orig cloth. Dw. *(Margaret Nangle)* **£25 [≈$38]**
- The Story of My Heart. London: Duckworth, 1923. One of 225 signed by the illustrator, Ethelbert White. 4to. 145 pp. 36 w'engvs. Orig buckram, t.e.g., label v sl rubbed. *(Waddington)* **£60 [≈$90]**

Jekyll, Gertrude

- Old West Surrey. Some Notes and Memories. London: 1904. 1st edn. 330 photo ills. Foredge sl foxed. Occas v sl loose stitching. Orig dec cloth, uncut, spine ends sl bumped. *(Margaret Nangle)* **£75 [≈$113]**

Jekyll, Gertrude & Hussey, Christopher

- Garden Ornament. London: Country Life, 1927. 2nd edn, rvsd. Folio. 438 pp. Ills. Few faint spots. Orig buckram backed cloth gilt. *(Hollett)* **£225 [≈$338]**
- Garden Ornament. London: Country Life, (1927). 2nd edn, rvsd. Folio. x,438 pp. 690 ills, 23 text ills. Inscrptn. Orig 2-toned cloth. *(Bow Windows)* **£165 [≈$248]**

Jekyll, Gertrude & Weaver, Lawrence

- Gardens for Small Country Houses. London: Country Life, (1912). 1st edn. [iv],xvi, 260, [16 advt] pp. Cold frontis, 1 plate, num ills. Orig cloth gilt, t.e.g., crnrs bumped, spine snagged. *(Clevedon Books)* **£125 [≈$188]**

Jencks, Charles

- Post-Modernism. The New Classicism in Art and Architecture. New York: Rizzoli, 1987. Lge 4to. 360 pp. 350 ills. Orig cloth. Dw. *(Ars Libri)* **$100 [≈£67]**

Jenkinson, Hilary

- Mediaeval Tallies Public and Private. London: Society of Antiquaries, 1925. Lge 4to. 62 pp. 8 plates. Mod half mor gilt, orig wraps bound in. *(Hollett)* **£45 [≈$68]**

Jennings, David

- An Introduction to the Knowledge of Medals. The Second Edition. London: Sarah Baskerville, sold by Joseph Johnson, 1775. 8vo. [4],49 pp, errata leaf. Title washed but dust soiled. Contemp calf, rebacked. *(Claude Cox)* **£75 [≈$113]**

Jennings, H.J.

- Our Homes and How to Beautify Them. Second Edition. London: Harrison & Sons, 1902. 4to. 254,[2] pp. Num ills. Orig qtr vellum. *(Claude Cox)* **£25 [≈$38]**

Jermsawatdi, Promsal

- Thai Art with Indian Influences. New Delhi: 1979. 4to. 160 pp. Plates. Orig pict hessian. *(Bury Place)* **£45 [≈$68]**

Jerome, Jerome K.

- Three Men in a Boat. To Say Nothing of the Dog! With an Introduction by Stella Gibbons and Drawings by John Griffiths. Ipswich: W.S. Cowell for The Limited Editions Club, 1975. One of 2000 sgnd by Griffiths. Oblong 4to. Orig cloth & bds. Slipcase. *(Karmiole)* **$35 [≈£23]**

Jerrold, Blanchard

- The Life of Gustave Dore. London: W.H. Allen, 1891. viii,415 pp. 138 ills. Orig cloth, worn, spine faded. *(Leicester Art Books)* **£28 [≈$42]**

Jervis, Marian, Lady

- Painting and Celebrated Painters, Ancient and Modern; including Historical and Critical Notices of the Schools of Italy, Spain, France, Germany, and the Netherlands. London: Hurst & Blackett, 1854. 1st edn. 2 vols. 24 ctlg pp vol 1. Orig cloth, spines faded. *(Jarndyce)* **£30 [≈$45]**

Jervoise, E.

- The Ancient Bridges of Mid and Eastern England. London: Architectural Press, 1932. 1st edn. xi,164 pp. Frontis, 80 ills. Orig cloth. Dw (sl frayed). *(Clevedon Books)* **£25 [≈$38]**
- The Ancient Bridges of Mid and Eastern England. London: Architectural Press, 1932. Sm 8vo. xi,164 pp. 80 ills. Orig cloth. Dw (faded, sl chipped). *(Hollett)* **£15 [≈$23]**
- The Ancient Bridges of the South of England. London: Architectural Press, 1930. 1st edn. xvi,128 pp. Frontis, 78 ills. Orig cloth. *(Clevedon Books)* **£23 [≈$35]**
- The Ancient Bridges of Wales and Western England. London: Architectural Press, 1936. Sm 8vo. xi,180 pp. 90 ills. Edges spotted. Orig cloth. *(Hollett)* **£15 [≈$23]**

Jewitt, Edwin

- Manual of Illuminated Missal Painting. London: J. Barnard, (1860). 1st edn. Sm 8vo. [4 advt],47,2,[32 advt] pp. 8 cold plates. Orig cloth gilt, a.e.g., sl stained, recased. *(Clevedon Books)* **£80 [≈$120]**

Jianou, Ionel

- Lardera. Paris: Arted, Editions d'Art, 1968. English-language Text. 4to. 183 pp. 88 plates. Orig cloth. Dw. Slipcase. *(Ars Libri)* **$60 [≈£40]**

Joannides, Paul

- The Drawings of Raphael with a Complete Catalogue. Berkeley: California UP, 1983. 271 pp. Num plates & ills. Orig cloth. Dw. *(Clarice Davis)* **$125 [≈£83]**

Joad, C.E.M.

- The Adventures of the Young Soldier in Search of a Better World. Illustrated by Mervyn Peake. London: Faber, 1943. 1st edn. 8vo. Orig cloth. Dw (darkened). *(Barbara Stone)* **£45 [≈$68]**

John Cheap the Chapman's Library ...

- John Cheap the Chapman's Library: the Scottish Chap Literature of the last Century, classified. With Life of Dougal Graham. London: Robert Lindsay, 1877-78. 3 vols. 8vo. Num w'cut ills. Contemp qtr roan, rubbed, 2 spines chipped at ends. *(Clark)* **£100 [≈$150]**

John of the Cross, Saint

- The Song of the Soul. Translated by John

O'Connor. Capel-y-Ffin, Abergavenny: Francis Walterson, 1927. One of 105 signed by the illustrator, Eric Gill. Orig buckram backed bds, worn & partly faded, buckram sl bubbled, spine ends sl rubbed.
(Ulysses Bookshop) **£425 [≈$638]**

John, Augustus

- Drawings. London: 1941. 1st edn. Sm folio. 64 plates. Orig bndg. Dw (torn, sl chipped). *(Words Etcetera)* **£18 [≈$27]**
- Fifty-Two Drawings. With an Introduction by Lord David Cecil. London: George Rainbird, 1967. One of 150 signed by the author & by cecil. Folio. Orig half vellum, sl worn. Slipcase. *(Dermont)* **$750 [≈£500]**

John, W.D.

- Swansea Porcelain. Newport: Ceramic Books Co., (1958) 1978. 2nd edn. Roy 4to. 118 pp. 97 plates. Orig cloth. *(Castle Bookshop)* **£70 [≈$105]**

John, W.D. & Coombes, K.

- Paktong: The Non-Tarnishable Chinese 'Silver' Alloy used for 'Adam' Firegrates and Early Georgian Candlesticks. Newport: Ceramic Book Co., 1970. One of 500. 4to. ix,25 pp. 51 plates. Orig cloth, sl spotted. *(Castle Bookshop)* **£38 [≈$57]**

John, W.D. & Simcox, A.

- Pontypool and Usk Japanned Wares: With the Early History of the Iron and Tinplate Industries at Pontypool. Newport: Ceramic Book Co., 1966. 2nd imp. Lge 4to. xi,88 pp. 27 plates. Orig cloth. *(Castle Bookshop)* **£38 [≈$57]**

Johnson, Alfred Forbes

- A Catalogue of Engraved & Etched English Title-Pages down to the Death of William Faithorne. OUP: Bibl Soc., 1934 (for 1933). 4to. 95 plates. Orig qtr buckram. *(Clark)* **£90 [≈$135]**
- A Catalogue of Engraved and Etched English Title-Pages down to the Death of William Faithorne. London: Bibl Soc., 1934 (for 1933). 4to. 95 ills. Orig linen backed bds. *(Traylen)* **£65 [≈$98]**
- The First Century of Printing at Basle. London: Benn, 1926. 1st edn. Lge 8vo. 27,[2] pp. 50 plates. Orig dec bds. *(Claude Cox)* **£30 [≈$45]**
- German Renaissance Title-Borders. OUP: Bibl Soc, 1929. 4to. 86 ills. Orig qtr buckram. *(Clark)* **£65 [≈$98]**
- Selected Essays on Books and Printing. Edited by Percy H. Muir. Amsterdam: 1971. Folio. 180 ills. Orig cloth., Dw. *(Traylen)* **£60 [≈$90]**
- The Italian Sixteenth Century. London: Benn, Periods of Typography Series, 1926. 1st edn. Lge 8vo. 34,[2] pp. 50 plates. Orig dec bds. *(Claude Cox)* **£30 [≈$45]**
- One Hundred Title-Pages 1500-1800. London: John Lane; The Bodley Head, 1928. One of 100. 4to. Collotype plates. Orig qtr vellum, t.e.g. *(First Folio)* **$285 [≈£190]**
- Selected Essays on Books and Printing. Edited by Percy H. Muir. Amsterdam: Van Gendt, 1970. 1st edn. Sm folio. xiv,489 pp. Ills. Dw (sl soiled). *(Claude Cox)* **£50 [≈$75]**
- Selected Essays on Books and Printing. Edited by Percy H. Muir. Amsterdam: 1970. Sm folio. xiv,489 pp. Ills. Orig cloth. Dw. *(Bow Windows)* **£90 [≈$135]**

Johnson, Cecil & Johnson, James

- A Printer's Garland. Being a Miscellany of Typographic Fancies. N.p.: The Book Club of California, 1935. One of 300. 12mo. [ii],35, [1] pp. Ills. Orig qtr vellum. *(Oak Knoll)* **$55 [≈£37]**

Johnson, Edward Mead

- Francis Cotes. Complete Edition with a Critical Essay and a Catalogue. London: Phaidon Press, 1976. 1st edn. 4to. 178 pp. 115 ills (4 cold plates). Dw. *(Spelman)* **£50 [≈$75]**
- Francis Cotes: Complete Edition with a Critical Essay and Catalogue. London: 1976. 178 pp. 4 cold & 110 b/w plates. Orig cloth. Dw. *(Fine Art)* **£30 [≈$45]**

Johnson, G.Y. & Bramwell, F.H.

- A Catalogue of Masonic Pottery in the Freemasons' Hall, Duncombe Place, York ... York: 1951. 60 pp. 12 plates. Orig cloth gilt, sl spotted. *(Hollett)* **£45 [≈$68]**

Johnson, Lee

- The Paintings of Eugene Delacroix. A Critical Catalogue. Oxford: Clarendon Press 1981. 1st edn. 2 vols. 4to. Cold frontis, plates. Orig cloth gilt. Dws. *(Hollett)* **£95 [≈$143]**

Johnson, Peter & Money, Ernle

- The Nasmyth Family of Painters. Leigh-on-Sea: F. Lewis, 1977. One of 500. 64 pp. 35 plates. Orig cloth. Dw. *(Leicester Art Books)* **£55 [≈$83]**

Johnson, Ray

- The Paper Snake. New York: Something Else Press, 1965. Oblong 4to. [44] pp. Num ills. Orig cloth. Dw. *(Ars Libri)* **$50 [≈£33]**

Johnson, Samuel, M.A.

- The New London Letter Writer containing the Complete Art of Correspondence ... Golden Cockerel Press: 1948. One of 500. Num ills. Orig cloth backed bds. *(Margaret Nangle)* **£52 [≈$78]**
- The New London Letter Writer containing the Compleat Art of Corresponding ... Golden Cockerel Press: 1948. One of 500. Frontis, w'cut ills. Orig half buckram, spine sl faded. *(Jarndyce)* **£20 [≈$30]**

Johnson, Stanley C.

- Chats on Military Curios. London: Fisher Unwin, 1915. 1st edn. 342 pp. 80 ills. Orig pict cloth. *(Hollett)* **£20 [≈$30]**
- The Medal Collector. A Guide to Naval Military and Air Force Awards. London: Jenkins, 1921. 1st edn. 320 pp. 24 cold & other plates. Orig cloth. Dw (sl chipped). *(Hollett)* **£25 [≈$38]**
- The Medals of Our Fighting Men. London: A. & C. Black, 1917. 2nd edn. [iv],120 pp. 4 cold & 12 other plates. Occas sl spotting. Orig cloth gilt, spine faded, few faint spots. *(Hollett)* **£45 [≈$68]**

Johnson, William

- The Practical Draughtsman's Book of Industrial Design ... New York: Stringer & Townsend, (1857). 2nd edn. 4to. 196 pp. 55 plates. Occas foxing & marg stains. Orig cloth, crnrs & spine worn. *(Bookpress)* **$150 [≈£100]**

Johnston, Frederick

- Terracina Cloud. The Verona Press: 1936. 1st edn. 8vo. x,[89],colophon pp. Orig linen, uncut. *(Claude Cox)* **£18 [≈$27]**

Johnston, Paul

- Biblio-Typographica, A Survey of Contemporary Fine Printing Style. New York: Covici-Friede, 1930. One of 1050. Tall 8vo. 303 pp. Orig cloth, paper label. Dw (spine ends chipped). *(Oak Knoll)* **$175 [≈£117]**
- Biblio-Typographica. A Survey of Contemporary Fine Printing Style. New York: Covici Friede, 1930. One of 1050. Tall 8vo. 303 pp. Orig cloth, paper label, sl shaken, sl worn. *(First Folio)* **$75 [≈£50]**

Johnston, Priscilla

- Edward Johnston [calligrapher]. London: Faber, (1959). 1st edn. 8vo. 316 pp. Orig cloth. Dw (sl rubbed). *(Oak Knoll)* **$55 [≈£37]**

Johnstone, William

- Creative Art in England from the Earliest Times to the Present. London: Art Book Club, [1936]. 4to. 276 pp. Ills. Orig qtr cloth. *(Cooper Hay)* **£40 [≈$60]**

Joly, Henri L.

- Japanese Sword Fittings. A Descriptive Catalogue of the Collection of G.H. Naunton ... Reading: Privately Printed, 1912. One of 300. 4to. xxix,317 pp. 88 plates. Orig buckram, rebacked in mor. *(Robert Frew)* **£350 [≈$525]**

Jones, Barbara

- Follies and Grottoes. London: Constable, 1974. 2nd edn, rvsd & enlgd. xviii,459 pp. 442 ills. Orig cloth. Dw. *(Fine Art)* **£20 [≈$30]**

Jones, Dan Burne

- The Prints of Rockwell Kent. A Catalogue Raisonne. Chicago: UP, 1975. 1st edn. Lge 4to. Num b/w ills. Orig cloth gilt. Dw. *(Barbara Stone)* **£65 [≈$98]**

Jones, David

- An Introduction to the Rime of the Ancient Mariner. Clover Hill Editions: 1972. One of 115 (of 330) signed by the author. Lge 4to. Orig parchment backed buckram, t.e.g. Slipcase. Prospectus laid in. *(Claude Cox)* **£250 [≈$375]**

Jones, George W.

- Catalogue of the Library of George W. Jones at The Sign of the Dolphin next to Dr. Johnson's House in Gough Square. [Printed for Private Circulation only, 1938]. 1st edn. Folio. xii,132 pp. Ills, inc inserted specimens. Orig bds, sl rubbed. *(Claude Cox)* **£120 [≈$180]**

Jones, Gwyn

- The Green Island. Engravings by John Petts. Golden Cockerel Press: 1946. 8vo. 84 pp. 11 ills. Orig cloth. *(Bow Windows)* **£85 [≈$128]**
- The Green Island. Golden Cockerel Press: 1946. One of 500. W'engvs by John Petts. Orig dec canvas. *(Waddington)* **£75 [≈$113]**

Jones, Mrs Herbert
- The Princess Charlotte of Wales. An Illustrated Monograph. London: Quaritch, 1885. 1st edn. One of 250. 4to. xxiii,173 pp. 16 ills. Qtr mor, uncut, sl worn. *(Young's)* **£45 [≈$68]**

Jones, Ifano
- Printing and Printers in Wales and Monmouthshire. Cardiff: 1925. 366 pp. Orig cloth, uncut. *(Castle Bookshop)* **£85 [≈$128]**

Jones, Mary Eirwen
- British Samplers. London: 1948. 1st edn. 85 pp. Frontis, 37 plates. Orig cloth. Dw (chipped). *(Willow House)* **£15 [≈$23]**

Jones, Owen
- The Grammar of Ornament ... London: Day & Son, 1856. 1st edn. Folio. Chromolitho frontis, 100 chromolitho plates, text ills. Few marg tears, occas marg soiling. Orig half mor gilt, gilt label, a.e.g., recased. *(Robert Frew)* **£1,650 [≈$2,475]**
- The Grammar of Ornament ... London: 1987. 4to. 157 pp. 112 cold plates, num text ills. Dw. *(Francis Edwards)* **£25 [≈$38]**

Jones, S.R.
- The Village Homes of England. Edited by Charles Holme. London: The Studio, 1912. Sm folio. viii,163 pp. Cold frontis, 11 cold plates, ills. Orig wraps, sl worn. *(Clevedon Books)* **£35 [≈$53]**

Jones, William
- Poikilographia, or Various Specimens of Ornamental Penmanship comprising Twenty Two Different Alphabets. London: W. Jones, [ca 1830]. Thin folio. Port, title vignette, vignette in intro, 22 plates in all. Sl foxing. Later qtr calf, orig label preserved. *(Traylen)* **£280 [≈$420]**

Jonson, Ben
- Volpone, or the Fox. Illustrations by Rene Ben Sussan. New York: The Limited Editions Club, 1952. One of 1500 signed by Ben Sussan. Sm 4to. Orig cloth-backed bds (spine sl rubbed). Slipcase (spine spotted). *(Oak Knoll)* **$50 [≈£33]**
- Volpone: or, the Foxe. A New Edition with a Critical Essay on the Author by Vincent O'Sullivan. Illustrated by Aubrey Beardsley. London: Leonard Smithers, 1898. One of 1000. 4to. xlv,193 pp. Orig gilt dec cloth, spine sl faded. *(Robert Frew)* **£200 [≈$300]**

Jordan, Jim & Goldwater, Robert
- The Paintings of Arshile Gorky. A Critical Catalogue. New York & London: New York UP, 1982. Lge 4to. 576 pp. Num ills. Orig cloth. Dw. *(Ars Libri)* **$275 [≈£183]**
- The Paintings of Arshile Gorky. A Critical Catalogue. New York: 1982. xxix,576 pp. 366 ills. Orig cloth. Dw. *(Leicester Art Books)* **£120 [≈$180]**

Jorg, C.J.A.
- Porcelain and the Dutch China Trade. The Hague: 1982. 4to. 372 pp. 87 plates. Orig cloth. Dw. *(Castle Bookshop)* **£32 [≈$48]**

Josephson, Matthew
- Life among the Surrealists. A Memoir. New York: Holt, Rinehart & Winston, 1962. 4to. xi,[1],403,[1] pp. 16 plates. Orig cloth. *(Ars Libri)* **$35 [≈£23]**

Jourdain, Margaret
- English Decorative Plasterwork of the Renaissance. New York: Scribner, [1926]. 4to. xiii,258 pp. 200 ills. Orig cloth, sm tear hd of spine. *(Mendelsohn)* **$150 [≈£100]**
- English Decorative Plasterwork of the Renaissance. Second Issue. London: Batsford, 1933. 4to. 258 pp. Frontis, 200 ills. Endpapers foxed. Orig cloth. *(Spelman)* **£80 [≈$120]**
- English Interior Decoration 1500 to 1830. A Study in the Development of Design. London: Batsford, 1950. 1st edn. 4to. xii,84 pp. Cold frontis, 194 figs. Lib b'plate. Orig cloth, sl rubbed & worn. *(Francis Edwards)* **£25 [≈$38]**
- The History of English Secular Embroidery. London: Kegan Paul, 1910. 1st edn. xiv,203 pp. Fldg cold frontis, 62 plates. Orig cloth gilt, sl marked & dulled. *(Hollett)* **£95 [≈$143]**
- Regency Furniture 1795-1820. London: Country Life, 1948. Rvsd & enlgd edn. 4to. xv,188 pp. 235 ills. Orig cloth gilt. Dw. *(Hollett)* **£75 [≈$113]**
- Regency Furniture 1795-1820. London: Country Life, 1948. 4to. 235 ills. Orig cloth. *(Traylen)* **£18 [≈$27]**
- The Work of William Kent ... London: Country Life, 1948. 1st edn. 4to. 184 pp. Errata slip. Frontis, 150 ills. Some foxing at end. Orig cloth, spine faded. *(Spelman)* **£75 [≈$113]**
- The Work of William Kent. Artist, Painter, Designer and Landscape Gardener. London: Country Life, 1948. xiv,184 pp. Frontis, 150

ills. Orig cloth.
(Leicester Art Books) **£90 [≈$135]**

- The Work of William Kent. London: Country Life, (1948). 1st edn. 4to. 184 pp. Frontis, 150 ills. Name. Orig cloth, sl rubbed. *(Bookpress)* **$185 [≈£123]**

Jourdain, Margaret & Rose, F.

- English Furniture. The Georgian Period (1750-1839). London: Batsford, 1953. 1st edn. 4to. 210 pp. 172 ills inc cold frontis. Orig cloth gilt. Dw. *(Hollett)* **£120 [≈$180]**
- English Furniture. The Georgian Period (1750-1830) ... London: Batsford, 1953. 1st edn. 4to. 210 pp. Cold frontis, 171 ills. Lib b'plate. Orig cloth, spine faded. *(Francis Edwards)* **£45 [≈$68]**

Judson, J. Richard

- The Drawings of Jacob de Gheyn II. New York: Grossman, 1973. 46 pp. 111 plates. Orig cloth. Dw. *(Leicester Art Books)* **£32 [≈$48]**

Jugaku, Bunsho

- A Bibliographical Study of William Blake's Notebook. Tokyo: Hokuseido Press, 1953. 1st edn. Lge 8vo. 176 pp. 4 plates. Orig cloth. Dw (chipped). *(Karmiole)* **$45 [≈£30]**
- Paper-Making by Hand in Japan. Tokyo: Meiji-Shobo, 1959. 1st edn. 24 mtd paper samples, photo ills. Dw (worn). *(Hermitage)* **$500 [≈£333]**

Jullian, Philippe

- The Symbolists. London: Phaidon, 1973. 1st edn. 4to. Cold ills. Orig cloth. Dw. *(First Folio)* **$75 [≈£50]**
- The Triumph of Art Nouveau, Paris Exhibition 1900. New York: Larousse, 1974. 4to. Ills. Orig cloth. Dw. *(First Folio)* **$55 [≈£37]**
- The Triumph of Art Nouveau, Paris Exhibition, 1900. New York: Larousse, (1974). 1st Amer edn. 8vo. 216 pp. Frontis, 143 ills. Orig cloth. Dw (sl rubbed). *(Bookpress)* **$35 [≈£23]**

Justice, Jean

- Dictionary of Marks and Monograms of Delft Pottery. London: Herbert Jenkins, 1930. 1st edn. Sm 4to. 171 pp. Ills. Few sl lib stamps. Orig cloth gilt, sl lib marks. *(Hollett)* **£95 [≈$143]**

Kafka, Franz

- The Trial. Illustrations by Alan E. Cober. Avon, CT: The Limited Editions Club, 1975. One of 2000 signed by Cober. Sm 4to. Orig leather gilt. Slipcase. *(Oak Knoll)* **$55 [≈£37]**

Kahnweiler, Daniel-Henry

- Juan Gris. His Life and Work. Translated by Douglas Cooper. Revised Edition. New York: Abrams, [1969]. Lge 4to. 347,[1] pp. 184 ills. Orig cloth. Dw. *(Ars Libri)* **$225 [≈£150]**
- The Rise of Cubism. Translated by Henry Aronson. New York: Wittenborn, Schulz, 1949. 4to. 24 ills. Orig wraps. *(Ars Libri)* **$65 [≈£43]**
- The Sculpture of Henri Laurens. New York: Abrams, 1970. 228 pp. 186 plates. Orig cloth. Dw. *(Fine Art)* **£25 [≈$38]**

Kallir, Otto

- Egon Schiele. The Graphic Work. New York: Crown, 1970. 207 pp. 66 ills. Orig cloth. Dw. *(Leicester Art Books)* **£280 [≈$420]**

Kandinsky, Wassily

- Concerning the Spiritual in Art, and Painting in Particular (1912). New York: Wittenborn, Schultz, 1947. 4to. 95 pp. 5 plates, text ills. Orig wraps. *(Ars Libri)* **$65 [≈£43]**
- Sounds. Translated and with an Introduction by Elizabeth R. Napier. New Haven & London: Yale UP, 1981. Sm sq 4to. vi,[2],136 pp. Ills. Orig cloth. *(Ars Libri)* **$40 [≈£27]**

Kanos, I.

- Forty-Four Turkish Tales ... With Illustrations by Willy Pogany. London: Harrap, [1913]. 1st edn. Lge 8vo. [xii],364 pp. 16 mtd cold plates, num b/w ills. Occas minor spots. Orig dec linen, t.e.g. Dw (hd of spine v sl chipped). *(Bow Windows)* **£195 [≈$293]**

Kapp, Edmond X.

- Reflections. A Second Series of Drawings. London: Cape, 1922. One of 50 signed. Sm 4to. 24 mtd plates. Occas foxing. Orig cloth gilt, sl soiled. Dw panel laid in. *(First Folio)* **$50 [≈£33]**

Kaprow, Allan

- Assemblage, Environments & Happenings ... New York: Abrams, [1966]. Oblong folio. 341, [3] pp. Num ills. Orig burlap over bds. *(Ars Libri)* **$700 [≈£467]**

Karginov, German

- Rodchenko. London: Thames & Hudson,

1979. 263 pp. 211 ills. Orig cloth. Dw. *(Leicester Art Books)* **£70 [≈$105]**

Karolik, M.

- Karolik Collection of American Paintings 1815 to 1865. Boston: Museum of Fine Arts, 1949. 1st edn. 4to. 544 pp. Num ills. Orig cloth. *(Robertshaw)* **£50 [≈$75]**
- M. & M. Karolik Collection of American Water Colors and Drawings, 1800-1875. Boston: Museum of Fine Arts, 1962. 2 vols. 4to. 337; 352 pp. 24 cold plates, 407 ills. Orig cloth. Slipcase. *(Rona Schneider)* **$160 [≈£107]**

Karsson, Lennart

- Medieval Ironwork in Sweden. Stockholm, 1988. 2 vols. 4to. 290 + 1120 ills. Orig bds, some crnrs sl bumped. *(Washton)* **$200 [≈£133]**

Kaufmann, C.M.

- A Survey of Manuscripts Illuminated in the British Isles. Vol. 3. Romanesque Manuscripts 1066-1190. London: 1975. Sm folio. 235 pp. 350 ills (inc 4 cold mtd). Orig cloth, spine ends sl splayed. Dw. *(Washton)* **$145 [≈£97]**

Kavanagh, P.J.

- Real Sky. With Wood Engravings by Miriam MacGregor. Whittington Press: 1980. One of 500. Orig wraps. signed by the author. *(Michael Taylor)* **£20 [≈$30]**

Keats, John

- Endymion. A Poetic Romance. Golden Cockerel Press: 1947. One of 500. 156 pp. 58 w'engvs by John Buckland Wright. Orig qtr vellum, t.e.g., fine. *(Bookworks)* **£390 [≈$585]**
- Endymion. A Poetic Romance. Golden Cockerel Press: 1947. One of 100 (of 500). Folio. 152 pp. 58 w'engvs by John Buckland Wright. 5 margs sl foxed, 2 pp browned. Orig vellum gilt, t.e.g. *(Waddington)* **£585 [≈$878]**
- Lamia, Isabella, The Eve of Saint Agnes & Other Poems ... With Engravings by Robert Gibbings. Golden Cockerel Press: 1928. One of 500. Folio. [ii],101,[i blank],[i colophon] pp. Orig qtr sharkskin, t.e.g., by Sangorski & Sutcliffe. *(Sotheran's)* **£698 [≈$1,047]**
- Odes by John Keats, Decorated by Vivien Gribble. London: Duckworth, 1923. One of 170 signed by the artist. 20 pp. Glassine dw. *(Michael Taylor)* **£28 [≈$42]**
- Poems. Edited by John Middleton Murry. London: 1958. 1st edn thus. Decs by Michael Ayrton. Dw (sl nicked & rubbed). *(Blakeney)* **£35 [≈$53]**
- The Poems. Hammersmith: Kelmscott Press, 1894. One of 300 (of 307). 8vo. 384 pp. Orig vellum, silk ties, fine. *(Finch)* **£1,350 [≈$2,025]**
- The Poems. Illustrated by David Gentleman. New York: The Limited Editions Club, 1966. One of 1500 signed by Gentleman. Tall 8vo. Orig qtr leather. Slipcase. *(Oak Knoll)* **$125 [≈£83]**

Kelemen, Pal

- Medieval American Art. New York: Macmillan, 1956. One-vol edn. 4to. 414 pp. Plates. Orig cloth. *(First Folio)* **$60 [≈£40]**

Kelley, Austin P.

- The Anatomy of Antiques. A Collector's Guide. New York: Viking Press, 1974. 1st edn. 4to. 189 pp. 19 cold plates, ills. Orig cloth gilt. Dw. *(Hollett)* **£25 [≈$38]**

Kelly, Alison

- The Story of Wedgwood. London: Faber, 1975. Lge 8vo. 91 pp. Cold frontis, 62 plates. Orig cloth gilt. Dw. *(Hollett)* **£30 [≈$45]**

Kelly, Rob Roy

- American Wood Type 1828-1900. Notes on the Evolution of Decorated and Large Types and Comments on Related Trades of the Period. New York: Van Nostrand Reinhold, 1969. 4to. 350 pp. Ills. Orig cloth. Dw. *(Cooper Hay)* **£50 [≈$75]**

Kemble, Edward W.

- Comical Coons. London: Kegan Paul, 1898. 1st English edn. Oblong 4to. B/w ills. Foxing to endpapers. Spotting to tissue guard frontis. Orig cloth backed pict bds, edge wear & spots. *(Jo Ann Reisler)* **$375 [≈£250]**

Kempf, Franz

- Contemporary Australian Printmakers. Melbourne: Lansdowne Editions, 1976. 1st edn. 4to. 100,32 pp. Num ills. Orig cloth. Dw. *(Karmiole)* **$40 [≈£27]**

Kendrick, A.F.

- English Needlework. London: A. & C. Black, Library of English Art series, 1933. 1st edn. xii,193 pp. 24 plates. Orig cloth gilt, faded. Dw. *(Hollett)* **£30 [≈$45]**

Kendrick, T.D.

- Anglo-Saxon Art to A.D. 900. New York: 1972. Reprint of 1938 edn. Lge 8vo. xxi,228 pp. 104 plates, 25 text ills. Orig cloth, spine sl sunned. *(Washton)* **$45 [≈£30]**

- Late Saxon and Viking Art. London: Methuen, 1949. 1st edn. xv,152 pp. 96 plates, 21 ills. Orig cloth gilt. Dw (sl worn). *(Hollett)* **£15 [≈$23]**

Kennedy, H.A.

- Early English Portrait Miniatures in the Collection of the Duke of Buccleuch. London: The Studio, 1916. 43 pp. 68 plates. Orig cloth. *(Fine Art)* **£20 [≈$30]**

Kent, Nathaniel

- Hints to Gentlemen of Landed Property ... London: for J. Dodsley, 1776. 2nd edn. 8vo. vii,282 pp. 9 fldg plates. Sm worm-hole. Rec half calf. *(Young's)* **£120 [≈$180]**

Kent, Norman

- Drawings by American Artists. With an Introduction by Rockwell Kent. New York: Watson-Guptil, 1947. Lge 4to. 158,[2] pp. 72 plates. Orig cloth. *(Ars Libri)* **$45 [≈£30]**

Kent, Rockwell

- How I Make a Wood Cut. Pasadena: Esto Publishing Co., 1934. One of 1000. 12mo. 22 pp. Title w'cut, 4 w'cuts. Orig bds, sl rubbed. *(Argonaut)* **$90 [≈£60]**
- It's Me O Lord. New York: Dodd, Mead, 1955. 1st edn. 632 pp. Num plates, ills. Orig gilt dec cloth, minor marks & wear. Dw (frayed & defective). *(Bookworks)* **£29 [≈$44]**

Keppel, Frederick

- The Golden Age of Engraving. New York: The Baker & Taylor Co., 1910. One of 300 signed by the author. 8vo. 314 pp. 262 ills. Orig bds. Slipcase. *(Rona Schneider)* **$120 [≈£80]**
- The Golden Age of Engraving. New York: The Baker & Taylor Co., 1910. 8vo. 314 pp. 262 ills. Orig cloth. *(Rona Schneider)* **$40 [≈£27]**

Keppler, Victor

- The Eighth Art: A Life of Color Photography. London: 1939. 1st edn. 4to. 266 pp. 31 cold ills. Frontis marked on reverse, some other marks. Orig cloth. Dw (reprd). signed by the author. *(Bow Windows)* **£65 [≈$98]**

Kerr, R.

- The Gentleman's House or How to Plan English Residences from the Parsonage to the Palace ... London: Murray, 1865. 2nd edn. 464 pp. 45 plans, num w'engvs. Sl dusty. Rec cloth. *(Monmouth)* **£60 [≈$90]**

Kershaw, S.W.

- Art Treasures of the Lambeth Library. A Description of the Illuminated Manuscripts &c ... London: Basil Montagu Pickering, 1873. 1st edn. [One of 225]. 8vo. x,108 pp. 8 plates. Orig cloth. *(Claude Cox)* **£55 [≈$83]**

Kessel, Dmitri

- Splendors of Christendom. Great Art and Architecture in European Churches. Switzerland: Edita Lausanne, 1964. Sq folio. Mtd cold plates. Orig cloth gilt. *(First Folio)* **$50 [≈£33]**

Ketterer, Roman N. (editor)

- Ernst Ludwig Kirchner. Drawings and Pastels. New York: Alpine, 1982. 315 pp. Num cold & b/w plates. Orig cloth. Dw. Cardboard slipcase. *(Clarice Davis)* **$85 [≈£57]**

Keynes, Geoffrey

- A Study of the Illuminated Books of William Blake. Trianon Press: 1964. One of 525 signed by the author. 4to. 32 cold plates. Orig morocco backed bds. *(Traylen)* **£175 [≈$263]**

Killanin, Lord

- Sir Godfrey Kneller and his Times (Being a Review of the Portraiture of the Period 1646-1723). London: 1948. x,118 pp. Fldg chart, 86 plates. Orig cloth. *(Fine Art)* **£24 [≈$36]**

Kimball, Fiske

- The Creation of the Rococo. Phila: Museum of Art, 1943. 4to. xviii,244 pp. 54 plates. Orig cloth over bds, crnrs sl rubbed. *(Karmiole)* **$100 [≈£67]**

King, A. Hyatt

- Some British Collectors of Music c.1600-1900. Cambridge: 1963. 4to. 8 plates. Orig cloth. Dw. *(Traylen)* **£12 [≈$18]**

King, A.W.

- An Aubrey Beardsley Lecture. London: R.A. Walker, 1924. One of 500. 4to. 103 pp. Ills. Prospectus laid in. Orig cloth. *(Bookpress)* **$125 [≈£83]**

King, Henry

- The Poems of Bishop Henry King. Edited by John Sparrow. London: Nonesuch Press, 1925. One of 900. Lge 8vo. xxx,197 pp. Orig parchment bds, upper hinges splitting with sl loss. *(Claude Cox)* **£30 [≈$45]**

King, Jessie M.

- A Carol Good King Wenceslas. London: Leopold B. Hill, [1920]. 1st edn thus. 4to. [26] pp. 12 mtd cold plates. Orig wraps, pict onlays, some wear to spine.
  (Jo Ann Reisler) **$500 [≈£333]**
- Kirkcudbright. A Royal Burgh. A Book of Drawings. London & Glasgow: Gowans & Gray, 1934. 40 pp. 18 ills. Rec cloth & bds.
  (Clarice Davis) **$125 [≈£83]**
- Seven Happy Days: A Series of Drawings with Quotations from John Davidson & Others. London: Studio, New Year's Supplement, 1914. Lge 4to. 13 plates, dec title. Minor wear to text.
  (Jo Ann Reisler) **$450 [≈£300]**

King, William

- Chelsea Porcelain. London: Benn, 1922. 4to. 171 ills (7 cold). Orig cloth gilt.
  (Traylen) **£50 [≈$75]**

Kingsley, Charles

- The Heroes, or Greek Fairy Tales for my Children. Illustrated by W. Russell Flint. London: Philip Lee Warner for the Medici Society, 1912. 1st edn thus. One of 500. 12 cold plates. Orig limp vellum, silk ties. Dw, plain outer wrapper, sl used.
  (Hermitage) **$375 [≈£250]**
- Westward Ho! New York: The Limited Editions Club, 1947. One of 1500 signed by the illustrator. Sm 4to. Orig cloth-backed bds. Slipcase. *(Oak Knoll)* **$75 [≈£50]**

Kinney, Peter

- The Early Sculpture of Bartolomeo Ammanati. New York: Garland, 1976. xx,356 pp. 273 ills. Orig buckram.
  (Leicester Art Books) **£35 [≈$53]**

Kinney, Troy

- The Etchings of Troy Kinney. Garden City: Doubleday, Doran, 1929. One of 990 signed by Kinney. Sm folio. 80 pp. 25 plates. Orig cloth backed bds, sl soiled.
  (Karmiole) **$100 [≈£67]**

Kinsella, Thomas (translator)

- The Tain. Illustrated by Louis le Brocquy. Dublin: Dolmen Press, 1969. One of 50 signed by the translator, illustrator and publisher, with 3 extra plates. Orig calf gilt (sl bumped). *(Blakeney)* **£2,000 [≈$3,000]**

Kipling, Rudyard

- An Almanac of Twelve Sports. New York: R.H. Russell, 1898. 1st Amer edn. 12 cold w'cuts by William Nicholson. Sl soiling. Orig cloth, edges worn, front bd sl soiled.
  (Davidson) **$500 [≈£333]**
- Collected Verse. Illustrated by W. Heath Robinson. New York: Doubleday, Page, 1910. 1st edn. 4to. 9 mtd cold plates, b/w ills. 4to. Orig cloth gilt, t.e.g., spine v sl worn.
  (Jo Ann Reisler) **$175 [≈£117]**
- The Jungle Books. Illustrated by David Gentleman. Luxenburg, VT: Limited Edition Club, 1968. One of 1500 sgnd by David Gentleman. 4to. Glassine dw. Slipcase. *(Antic Hay)* **$125 [≈£83]**
- Kim. Illustrations by Robin Jacques. New York: The Limited Editions Club, 1962. One of 1500 signed by Jacques. Orig qtr leather.
  (Oak Knoll) **$55 [≈£37]**
- Sea and Sussex from Rudyard Kipling's Verse. Illustrated by Donald Maxwell. London: Macmillan, 1926. 1st edn. Num cold plates. New free endpaper. Orig blue cloth. *(Old Cathay)* **£35 [≈$53]**
- Sea and Sussex. Illustrated by Donald Maxwell. Garden City: 1926. One of 150 signed by the author. 95 pp. Orig vellum backed bds, t.e.g., spine sl spotted, extrs fraying. *(John K. King)* **$350 [≈£233]**
- A Song of the English. Illustrated by W. Heath Robinson. London: Hodder & Stoughton, n.d. 16 cold plates. Orig dec cloth. *(Old Cathay)* **£39 [≈$59]**
- Songs of the Sea. Illustrated by Donald Maxwell. London: Macmillan, 1927. One of 500 signed by the author. 12 mtd cold plates, text ills. Vellum spine, bds re-cvrd with paper to style, t.e.g. *(Carol Howard)* **£100 [≈$150]**
- Tales of East and West. Illustrated by Charles Raymond. Avon, CT: The Limited Editions Club, 1973. One of 1500 signed by Raymond. Orig cloth . Slipcase.
  (Oak Knoll) **$55 [≈£37]**

Kirby, Michael

- Happenings. An Illustrated Anthology. New York: Dutton, 1965. 4to. 287,[1] pp. Num ills. Orig cloth. Dw. *(Ars Libri)* **$65 [≈£43]**

Kirkus, A. Mary

- Robert Gibbings. A Bibliography. Edited by Patience Empson and John Harris, with a Chronological Check List and Notes on the Golden Cockerel Press. London: Dent, 1962. One of 975. 8vo. xiii,170 pp. Port frontis, text engv. Orig cloth. Dw.
  (Cooper Hay) **£35 [≈$53]**
- Robert Gibbings. A Bibliography. Edited by Patience Empson and John Harris, with a

Chronological Check List and Notes on the Golden Cockerel Press. London: Dent, 1962. One of 975. 8vo. Ills. Orig cloth. Dw (sl soiled). *(First Folio)* **$125 [≈£83]**

Kirschenbaum, Baruch

- The Religious and Historical Paintings of Jan Steen. New York: 1977. 4to. 261 pp. Cold frontis, 132 ills. Orig cloth, crnrs sl bumped. *(Washton)* **$125 [≈£83]**

Kitson, Sydney D.

- The Life of John Sell Cotman. London: Faber, 1937. xx,144 pp. Cold frontis, 156 ills. Orig cloth. *(Leicester Art Books)* **£60 [≈$90]**

Klee, Felix

- Paul Klee. His Life and Work in Documents ... New York: Braziller, 1962. 4to. x,212 pp. 121 ills. Orig qtr cloth. Dw. *(Ars Libri)* **$35 [≈£23]**

Klee, Paul

- The Diaries of Paul Klee 1898-1918. Edited with an Introduction by Felix Klee. London: Peter Owen, 1965. xx,424 pp. Ills. Orig cloth. Dw (chipped). *(Leicester Art Books)* **£55 [≈$83]**

Klein, Dan & Lloyd, Ward

- The History of Glass. London: Orbis, 1984. 4to. 288 pp. Ills. Tail edge marks. Dw. *(Paul Brown)* **£25 [≈$38]**

Klingender, Francis D.

- Art and the Industrial Revolution. London: Carrington, 1947. 1st edn. Sm 4to. xv,232 pp. Cold frontis, 14 cold plates, 116 ills. Orig cloth gilt. Dw. *(Clevedon Books)* **£32 [≈$48]**
- Art and the Industrial Revolution. London: Noel Carrington, 1947. Cold & b/w ills. Orig bndg, sl soiled & worn. *(Mermaid Books)* **£15 [≈$23]**

Knecht, Edmund & Fothergill, James Best

- The Principles and Practice of Textile Printing. London: Charles Griffin, 1924. 2nd edn, rvsd. Thick 8vo. xix,731 pp. Ills inc mtd samples. Part of free endpaper torn away. Orig cloth. *(Oak Knoll)* **$275 [≈£183]**

Knight, Charles

- Old England: A Pictorial Museum of ... Antiquities. London: Charles Knight & Co., 1845. 2 vols. Folio. Cold title, 24 cold plates, num w'engvs. Sm lib stamps at ft of titles & back of cold plates. New endpapers. Old half calf gilt, rebacked, bds scraped. *(Hollett)* **£140 [≈$210]**
- The Popular History of England. An Illustrated History ... London: James Sangster, [ca 1888]. 9 vols. Tall 8vo. 67 steel engvd plates, num w'engvs. Three qtr mor, gilt spines, t.e.g. *(J &J House)* **$1,000 [≈£667]**

Knight, Laura

- A Book of Drawings. With a Foreword by Charles Marriott and Descriptive Notes. London: John Lane, (1923). One of 500. 4to. Frontis, 20 plates. Prize inscrptn. Orig holland backed bds, crnr tips sl worn. *(Bow Windows)* **£150 [≈$225]**
- The Magic of a Line: Autobiography. London: William Kimber, 1965. 348 pp. 60 plates, 22 text ills. Inscrptn. Dw (torn). *(Fine Art)* **£20 [≈$30]**

Knight, William

- Knight's Pictorial Gallery of Arts. London: London Printing and Publishing Co., [ca 1860]. 2 vols in one. 388; 404 pp. Steel engvs, nearly 4000 w'engvd ills. Mor gilt, a.e.g., edges scuffed, some darkening. *(Willow House)* **£120 [≈$180]**

Knox, George

- Catalogue of the Tiepolo Drawings in the Victoria & Albert Museum. London: HMSO, 1960. xi,[i],111 pp. 326 ills. Orig cloth. Dw. *(Clarice Davis)* **$135 [≈£90]**

Knuttel, Gerard

- Adriaen Brouwer. The Master and his Work. The Hague: L.J.C. Boucher, 1962. 195 pp. 13 cold plates, 120 ills. Orig cloth. Dw. *(Leicester Art Books)* **£180 [≈$270]**

Koch, Robert

- Louis C. Tiffany, Rebel in Glass. New York: Crown, 1974. 2nd edn, 6th printing. 4to. 246 pp. 350 ills. Price-clipped dw. *(Paul Brown)* **£32 [≈$48]**

Koch, Rudolf

- The Book of Signs, which contains all manner of Symbols used from the Earliest times to the Middle Ages ... London: The First Edition Club, 1930. One of 500. [4],104 pp. 493 ills. Orig linen, sl soiled. *(Karmiole)* **$150 [≈£100]**

Koch, Stephen

- Andy Warhol Photographs. New York: Robert Miller, n.d. 4to. [12] pp. 78 plates.

Orig cloth. *(Ars Libri)* **$75 [≈£50]**

Kochno, Boris

- Diaghilev and the Ballets Russes. New York: Harper & Row, 1970. Lge 4to. 258,[2] pp. 312 ills. Orig cloth. Dw. *(Ars Libri)* **$65 [≈£43]**

Koechlin, R. & Migeon, G.

- Oriental Art. Ceramics, Fabrics, Carpets. Translated by Florence Heywood. New York: Macmillan, [ca 1930]. 1st edn. 4to. 20 pp. 100 cold plates. Few lib marks. Orig cloth, sl rubbed, spine ends frayed. *(Worldwide)* **$125 [≈£83]**

Koehler, Sylvester Rosa

- Etching: An Outline of Its Technical Processes and Its History, with Some Remarks on Collections and Collecting ... New York: Cassell, 1885. Folio. xiv,238 pp. 30 etchings, 95 ills. Orig cloth gilt, stained, scuffed, spine ends worn, 2 vertical splits in spine. *(Rona Schneider)* **$1,600 [≈£1,067]**
- Twenty American Etchings. Troy, New York: Nims & Knight, 1887. One of 40 (of 350). Folio. 40 pp. 19 "india paper" etchings (of 20, lacks one Farrer etching). Orig cloth.. *(Rona Schneider)* **$1,000 [≈£667]**

Koehn, Alfred

- Japanese Tray Landscapes. Peking: Lotus Court Pub., 1937. One of 500 signed by the author. 12mo. (51) pp. Frontis, cold ills. Oriental-style bndg. *(McBlain)* **$200 [≈£133]**

Kohler, Carl

- A History of Costume. London: Harrap, 1929. 464 pp. 578 ills. Orig cloth gilt, ft of spine sl faded. *(Willow House)* **£30 [≈$45]**

Konody, P.G.

- The Painter of Victorian Life. A Study of Constantin Guys ... Edited by C. Geoffrey Holme. London: The Studio, 1930. x,172 pp. Frontis, 146 ills. Orig cloth gilt, t.e.g., sl faded. *(Leicester Art Books)* **£36 [≈$54]**

Konody, P.G. & Dark, Sydney

- Sir William Orpen. Artist and Man. London: Seeley Service, 1932. 288 pp. Cold frontis, 64 plates, 5 ills. Orig cloth. *(Leicester Art Books)* **£35 [≈$53]**

Kootz, Samuel M.

- New Frontiers in American Painting. New York: Hastings House, 1943. Lge 4to. xix, [1], 65 pp. 89 plates. Orig cloth. *(Ars Libri)* **$50 [≈£33]**

Koschatzky, Walter

- Albrecht Durer. The Landscape Water-Colours. London: Academy Editions, 1973. 112 pp. 61 ills. Orig cloth. Dw (torn). *(Leicester Art Books)* **£36 [≈$54]**
- Italian Drawings in the Albertina. Greenwich: 1971. 322 pp. 100 cold plates, 56 text ills. Orig cloth. Dw. *(Clarice Davis)* **$100 [≈£67]**

Koshiro, Onchi

- Prints of Onchi Koshiro. Tokyo: Keishosha, 1975. One of 170 'Overseas Edition'. Folio. 327 pp. Orig cloth. Slipcase. Box. *(Bookpress)* **$300 [≈£200]**

Kostof, Spiro T.

- The Orthodox Baptistery of Ravenna. New Haven: 1965. 4to. xviii,171 pp. 147 ills on plates. Orig cloth. Dw. *(Washton)* **$65 [≈£43]**

Kowalczyk, Georg (editor)

- Decorative Sculpture. With an Introduction by August Koster. London: 1927. 4to. 26 pp. 320 plates. Occas lib stamps. Occas foxing of text. Orig cloth, lib mark on spine. *(Francis Edwards)* **£48 [≈$72]**
- Decorative Sculpture. London: 1927. Lge 4to. 320 plates. Some foxing. Orig cloth, extrs sl rubbed. *(Washton)* **$85 [≈£57]**

Kozakiewicz, Stefan

- Bernardo Bellotto. Translated by Mary Whittall. London: Paul Elek, 1972. 2 vols. 896 ills. Orig cloth. Dws. Slipcase. *(Leicester Art Books)* **£220 [≈$330]**

Kozloff, Max

- Cubism / Futurism. New York: Charterhouse, 1973. 4to. xix,[1],234,[2] pp. 92 ills. Orig cloth. Dw. *(Ars Libri)* **$35 [≈£23]**
- Jasper Johns. New York: Abrams, [1967]. Sm oblong folio. 195,[1] pp. 143 ills. Orig cloth. Dw. *(Ars Libri)* **$1,250 [≈£833]**

Kraemer-Noble, Magdelena

- Abraham Mignon 1640-1679. Leigh-on-Sea: F. Lewis, 1973. One of 500. 83 pp. 41 plates. Orig buckram. Dw. *(Leicester Art Books)* **£45 [≈$68]**

Kramer, Hilton

- Milton Avery: Paintings, 1930-1960. New York: Thomas Yoseloff, 1962. Lge 4to. 112 plates. Orig cloth. *(Ars Libri)* **$300 [≈£200]**
- Richard Lindner. Boston: New York Graphic Society, 1975. Lge sq 4to. 254,[2] pp. 171 ills. Orig cloth. *(Ars Libri)* **$300 [≈£200]**

Kramrisch, Stella

- The Art of India: Traditions of Indian Sculpture, Painting and Architecture. London: Phaidon, 1955. 2nd edn. 4to. 231 pp. 180 ills. Orig cloth. Dw. *(Abacus)* **$75 [≈£50]**
- The Hindu Temple. Delhi: Motilal Banarsidass, (1976). 2nd edn. 2 vols. 4to. 80 plates. Orig cloth. Box. *(Bookpress)* **$225 [≈£150]**

Kraus, H.F.

- A Rare Book Saga. New York: 1978. 8vo. Port, 32 plates. Orig cloth. Dw. *(Traylen)* **£16 [≈$24]**

Krauss, Rosalind E.

- Passages in Modern Sculpture. New York: Viking, 1977. 4to. ix,[3],308 pp. 212 ills. Orig qtr cloth. Dw. *(Ars Libri)* **$5 [≈£33]**
- Terminal Iron Works: The Sculpture of David Smith. Cambridge: MIT Press, (1971). 4to. 200 pp. 148 ills. Orig cloth. Dw. *(Abacus)* **$75 [≈£50]**

Kredel, Fritz

- Dolls and Puppets of the Eighteenth Century, as delineated in Twenty-Four Drawings ... Lexington: Gravesend Press, 1958. One of 500 signed by Kredel. 16mo. 24 stencil-coloured plates. Orig blue silk gilt. Slipcase. *(Karmiole)* **$150 [≈£100]**

Krens, Thomas

- Jim Dine. Prints: 1970-1977. New York: Harper & Row, 1977. Lge 4to. 134 pp. Num ills. Orig wraps. *(Ars Libri)* **$125 [≈£83]**

Kristeller, Paul

- Early Florentine Woodcuts. With an Annotated List of Florentine Illustrated Books. London: Kegan Paul, 1897. One of 300. Tall 4to. 193 ills. Some text foxing. Orig morocco over cloth, t.e.g., spine sl rubbed. *(Karmiole)* **$200 [≈£133]**

Krumbhaar, E.B.

- Isaac Cruikshank. A Catalogue Raisonne with a Sketch of his Life and Work. Phila: UP, 1966. 178 pp. 131 plates. Orig cloth. Dw. *(Leicester Art Books)* **£45 [≈$68]**

Krummel, D.W.

- English Music Printing, 1553-1700. London: 1975. 4to. Num ills. Orig cloth. *(Traylen)* **£18 [≈$27]**

Kuh, Katherine

- Break-Up: The Core of Modern Art. Greenwich: New York Graphic Society, 1965. Lge 4to. 136 pp. 95 ills. Orig cloth. Dw. *(Ars Libri)* **$40 [≈£27]**
- Leger. Urbana: Illinois UP, 1953. 4to. 121 pp. Num ills. Orig cloth. *(Ars Libri)* **$60 [≈£40]**

Kultermann, Udo

- Art and Life. New York & Washington: Praeger, 1971. Sq 4to. 210 pp. 173 plates. Orig cloth. *(Ars Libri)* **$75 [≈£50]**
- The New Painting. Revised and Updated Edition. Boulder: Westview Press, 1976. 4to. 73,[1] pp. 196 plates. Orig cloth. Dw. *(Ars Libri)* **$85 [≈£57]**

Kuretsky, Susan Donahue

- The Paintings of Jacob Ochtervelt (1534-1682) with a Catalogue Raisonne. London: Phaidon, 1979. 245 pp. 199 ills. Orig cloth. Dw. *(Fine Art)* **£40 [≈$60]**
- The Paintings of Jacob Ochtervelt (1634-1682). Oxford: Phaidon, 1979. xv,245 pp. 199 ills. Orig cloth. Dw. *(Leicester Art Books)* **£55 [≈$83]**

Kurz, Otto

- Fakes. A Handbook for Collectors and Students. London: Faber, 1948. 1st edn. 328 pp. 95 ills. Orig cloth gilt. Dw. *(Hollett)* **£35 [≈$53]**

Kuspit, Donald

- The Critic is Artist. The Intentionality of Art. Ann Arbor: UMI Research Press, 1984. 4to. xx,398 pp. Orig cloth. Dw. *(Ars Libri)* **$110 [≈£73]**

Kutal, Albert

- Gothic Art in Bohemia and Moravia. London: 1971. Sq 4to. 212 pp. Num ills. Orig cloth. Dw. *(Washton)* **$50 [≈£33]**

'Kyd' (pseudonym of Joseph Clayton Clarke)

- The Characters of Charles Dickens, Portrayed in a Series of Original Water Colour Sketches. London: Raphael Tuck, [ca 1889]. 4to. Uncold litho title & endpiece, 24 chromolitho plates. Occas sl spotting. Orig cloth gilt, shaken. *(Clevedon Books)* **£180 [≈$270]**

La Motte Fouque, Friedrich Heinrich Carl de, Baron

- Undine ... With a Critical Introduction by

Edmund Gosse. London: Lawrence & Bullen, 1896. 1st edn thus. 4to. vii,189 pp. 10 plates by W.F. Britten. Orig cloth gilt, t.e.g. *(Fenning)* **£35 [≈$53]**

- Undine. Illustrated by Arthur Rackham. London: Heinemann, 1909. One of 1000 signed by Rackham. 4to. 15 mtd cold plates. Half-title & 2 ff of text browned. Rec mor gilt, t.e.g. *(Sotheran's)* **£650 [≈$975]**
- Undine. Illustrated by Arthur Rackham. London: Heinemann, 1909. 1st Rackham edn. 4to. 15 mtd cold plates. Illustrated endpapers (browned). Orig blue cloth, gilt vignette. *(Sotheran's)* **£158 [≈$237]**
- Undine. Illustrated by Arthur Rackham. London: Heinemann, 1909. 1st Rackham edn. 4to. 15 mtd cold plates, decs, pict endpapers. Endpapers sl foxed. Orig gilt dec cloth, extrs sl rubbed. *(Blackwell's)* **£60 [≈$90]**
- Undine. Adapted from the German by W.L. Courtney. Illustrated by Arthur Rackham. London: Heinemann, 1911. 4to. 136 pp. 15 mtd cold plates, decs, illust endpapers. Orig pict cloth gilt. *(Carol Howard)* **£80 [≈$120]**

Labarre, E.J.

- A Dictionary of Paper and Paper-Making Terms, With Equivalents in French, German, Dutch and Italian. Amsterdam: 1937. 1st edn. 8vo. 315 pp. 45 paper specimens. Orig cloth (sl foxed). Dw. *(The Veatchs)* **$225 [≈£150]**

Labarte, Jules

- Handbook of the Arts of the Middle Ages and Renaissance, as applied to the Decoration of Furniture, Arms, Jewels, &c. &c. Translated from the French. London: Murray, 1855. xxxvi,443 pp. 200 engvd text ills. Old half calf gilt, spine trifle scuffed. *(Hollett)* **£75 [≈$113]**

Lacroix, Paul

- The XVIIIth Century. Its Institutions, Customs, and Costumes. France 1700-1789. London: Chapman & Hall, 1876. 4to. xvi,489 pp. 21 chromolithos, 851 w'engvs. Three qtr levant, elab gilt spine, t.e.g., by Tout. *(J &J House)* **$300 [≈£200]**

La Fontaine, Jean de

- The Fables of Jean de la Fontaine. Translated by Edward Marsh. London: Heinemann, 1933. 1st edn thus. 542 pp. 12 collotype plates by Stephen Gooden. Edges sl spotted. Orig cloth, crnrs sl worn, nick at hd. *(Bookworks)* **£25 [≈$38]**

Laidlay, William James

- The Royal Academy: Its Uses and Abuses. London: Simpkin, Marshall ..., 1898. 229 pp. New cloth, t.e.g., orig wraps bound in. *(Fine Art)* **£30 [≈$45]**

Laing, Allan M.

- More Prayers and Graces. Illustrated by Mervyn Peake. London: Gollancz, 1957. 1st edn. Sm 8vo. 64 pp. Ills. Orig cloth. Dw (lower spine torn). *(Bookmark)* **£12 [≈$18]**

Laing, Donald A.

- Clive Bell: An Annotated Bibliography of the Published Writings. US: Garland, 1983. 154 pp. Orig cloth. *(Fine Art)* **£35 [≈$53]**

Lajoux, Jean-Dominique

- The Rock Paintings of Tassili. Cleveland: 1963. Ills. Price-clipped dw (v sl worn). *(Rob Warren)* **$60 [≈£40]**

Laking, Guy Francis

- The Armoury of Windsor Castle. European Section. London: Bradbury, Agnew, 1904. 1st edn. 4to. xiv,284 pp. 39 plates. Orig qtr pigskin gilt. Dw (reprd). Slipcase (worn). *(Hollett)* **£285 [≈$428]**

Lal, Kanwar

- Temples and Sculptures of Bhubaneswar. Delhi: Arts & Letters, (1970). 1st edn. 4to. vii,[ii] 124 pp. 103 ills. Orig cloth. Dw (worn). *(Bookpress)* **$110 [≈£73]**

Lalande, Jme. de

- The Art of Making Paper taken from The Universal Magazine of Knowledge and Pleasure. Loughborough: Plough Press, (1978). One of 200. 8vo. 31 pp. 6 plates. Orig cloth. *(Oak Knoll)* **$75 [≈£50]**

Lalanne, Maxime

- Lalanne on Etching. Translated by S.R. Koehler. London: W. & G. Foyle, 1880. 8vo. 79 pp. 14 orig etchings, 2 ills. Orig cloth. Dw (torn). *(Rona Schneider)* **$100 [≈£67]**
- Lalanne on Etching. Translated by S.R. Koehler. Boston: The Page Co., 1880. 8vo. 79 pp. 14 orig etchings, 2 ills. Orig cloth. *(Rona Schneider)* **$100 [≈£67]**

Lamartine, A. De

- Graziella. Translated by Ralph Wright with 30 Illustrations by Jacquier. London: Nonesuch Press, 1929. One of 1600. Colour-stencilled ills. Orig dec cloth, t.e.g. on the rough. *(Claude Cox)* **£18 [≈$27]**

Lamb, Charles

- Essays of Elia. The Temple Edition. New York: Putnam, 1884. 501 pp. Port frontis, 8 orig etchings. Orig maroon cloth gilt, sl scuffed, spine ends torn. *(Rona Schneider)* **$300 [≈£200]**
- A Tale of Rosamund Gray and Old Blind Margaret. Golden Cockerel Press: 1928. One of 500. Orig parchment backed cloth gilt, extreme ft of front cvr stained. *(Words Etcetera)* **£35 [≈$53]**

Lamb, Charles & Mary

- Tales from Shakespeare. Illustrated by Arthur Rackham. London: Dent, n.d. Early Reprint. 12 cold plates. Orig gilt dec green cloth. *(Old Cathay)* **£69 [≈$104]**

Lamb, Martha J.

- The Homes of America. New York: Appleton, 1879. 4to. 256 pp. 103 ills. Orig pict cloth gilt, a.e.g., sl worn. *(First Folio)* **$145 [≈£97]**

The Lamentations of Jeremiah ...

- The Lamentations of Jeremiah. Gregynog Press: 1933. One of 250. Folio. W'engvs by Blair Hughes-Stanton. B'plate removed. Orig blue calf. Card slipcase. *(Spelman)* **£500 [≈$750]**

Lancaster, Osbert

- Classical Landscape with Figures. London: 1947. One of 100 signed by the author. Plates, ills, dec endpapers. Orig cloth backed bds, t.e.g., v sl worn. *(Ulysses Bookshop)* **£175 [≈$263]**
- Draynflete Revealed. London: 1949. 1st edn. Num ills. Orig bndg. Dw (rubbed, frayed & chipped). *(Ulysses Bookshop)* **£25 [≈$38]**
- Progress at Pelvis Bay. London: 1936. 1st edn. Ills by the author. Orig cloth backed pict bds, 2 crnrs bumped. Price-clipped dw (rubbed, dusty, sl torn). Author's 1st book. *(Ulysses Bookshop)* **£28 [≈$42]**

Landor, Walter Savage

- Imaginary Conversations. (New York): The Limited Editions Club, 1936. One of 1500 signed by the printer, hans Mardersteig. Tall 8vo. Occas foxing. Orig cloth. Dw (piece missing at ft of spine). Slipcase. *(Oak Knoll)* **$100 [≈£67]**
- The Sculptured Garland. A Selection from the Lyrical Poems. [With Wood-Engravings by Iain MacNab]. Dropmore Press: 1948. One of 300. 4to. 16 w'engvs. Orig deluxe half mor, unopened. *(Claude Cox)* **£55 [≈$83]**

Landseer, John

- Lectures on the Art of Engraving, delivered at the Royal Institution of Great Britain. London: Longman, Hurst, 1807. 1st edn. 8vo. xxxviii,341,[1] pp, advt leaf. Some foxing. Contemp half roan, rubbed. *(Spelman)* **£160 [≈$240]**

Landwehr, John

- Romeyn de Hooghe the Etcher. Contemporary Portrayal of Europe 1662-1707. Leiden: A.W. Sijthoff, 1973. One of 1000. 406 pp. 320 ills. Orig cloth. Slipcase. *(Leicester Art Books)* **£140 [≈$210]**
- Splendid Ceremonies. State Entries and Royal Funerals in the Low Countries, 1515-1791. A Bibliography. Nieuwkoop & Leiden: De Graaf, 1971. Roy 8vo. Ills. Dw (sl frayed). *(David Slade)* **£40 [≈$60]**

Lane, Arthur

- French Faience. London: Faber, 1948. 1st edn. xi,49 pp. 96 plates. Orig cloth gilt. Dw (chipped). *(Hollett)* **£30 [≈$45]**
- A Guide to the Collection of Tiles [in the] Victoria and Albert Museum. London: HMSO, 1960. Lge 8vo. xi,88 pp. 48 plates. Orig cloth gilt. Dw. *(Hollett)* **£40 [≈$60]**

Lanes, Selma G.

- The Art of Maurice Sendak. New York: Abrams, (1980). Oblong 4to. 278 pp. 261 ills (94 cold plates), pop-up. Orig dec cloth. Printed plastic dw. *(Abacus)* **$85 [≈£57]**

Lang, Andrew

- Aucassin and Nicolette. New York: The Limited Editions Club, 1931. One of 1500 signed by the illustrator, Vojtech Preissig. 4to. Orig cloth. Dw. Slipcase. *(Oak Knoll)* **$65 [≈£43]**
- The True Story Book. London: Longmans, Green, 1893. 1st edn. 8vo. Frontis, num ills. Orig elab dec cloth gilt, a.e.g., minor marks rear bd. *(Cooper Hay)* **£38 [≈$57]**

Langley, Batty

- The Builder's Director, or Bench-Mate: being a Pocket-Treasury of the Grecian, Roman, and Gothic Orders of Architecture ... London: for A. Webley, 1763. Introduction & 184 plates. Rec calf. *(Jarndyce)* **£320 [≈$480]**

Langley, Batty & Langley, Thomas

- Gothic Architecture, improved by Rules and Proportions in many Grand Designs ... London: I. & J. Taylor, [ca 1787]. 3rd edn.

Lge 4to. Engvd title,7,[1] pp. 64 plates. Sm marg tear title. Old sheep, recased. *(Bookpress)* **$1,350 [≈£900]**

Langui, Emile

- Frits van den Berghe. 1883-1939. The Man and his Work. Antwerp: Mercatorfonds, 1968. 325 pp. 229 ills. Orig cloth. Dw. *(Leicester Art Books)* **£90 [≈$135]**

Larkin, David (editor)

- The Fantastic Paintings of Charles & William Heath Robinson. Introduction by Leo John de Freitas. London: Bantam Books, 1976. 1st edn. 4to. 40 cold plates. Orig pict wraps. *(Hollett)* **£30 [≈$45]**

Larsen, Erik

- 17th Century Flemish Painting. Freren: 1985. Lge 4to. 364 pp. 44 cold plates, 255 b/w ills. Orig cloth. Dw. *(Washton)* **$100 [≈£67]**

Larsen, Sofus & Kyster, Anker

- Danish Eighteenth Century Bindings, 1730-1780. Copenhagen: Levin & Munkgaard, 1930. 1st edn. 4to. 52,[3],[6] pp. 102 plates. Orig half calf, sl edge wear. *(Bookpress)* **$485 [≈£323]**

Lartigue, J.H.

- Boyhood Photos of J.H. Lartigue. The Family Album of a Gilded Age. Lausanne: Ami Guichard, (1966). 1st edn. Oblong 4to. 128 pp. Num mtd photos. Orig elab gilt cloth. *(Karmiole)* **$300 [≈£200]**

Larwood, Jacob & Hotten, J.C.

- The History of Signboards, from the Earliest Times to the Present Day. London: John Camden Hotten, [ca 1866]. 5th edn. 8vo. x,536 pp. Hand cold frontis, 19 plates. Three qtr calf, gilt spine, t.e.g., by Lauriat, front jnt tender. *(J &J House)* **$150 [≈£100]**

Lascaris, Evadine

- The Golden Bed of Kydno. Translated from the Modern Greek by P.M. (Powys Mathers). Golden Cockerel Press: 1935. One of 60 signed by the translator. Folio. Ills by Lettice Sandford. Orig gilt dec mor, t.e.g., lower bd sl spotted. Lacks the extra set of engvs. *(Waddington)* **£200 [≈$300]**

Lasdun, Susan

- Victorians at Home. New York: Viking Press, (1981). Oblong 4to. 160 pp. Frontis, ills. Orig cloth. Dw. *(Bookpress)* **$45 [≈£30]**

Lasko, Peter

- Ars Sacra: 800-1200. Harmondsworth: Penguin Books, (1972). 1st edn. 4to. 338 pp. Frontis, 296 ills. Orig cloth. Dw, rubbed. Slipcase. *(Bookpress)* **$100 [≈£67]**

Lassaigne, Jacques

- Flemish Painting. The Century of Van Eyck. (Volume 2) Flemish Painting from Bosch to Rubens. London: Albert Skira, 1957-58. 2 vols. Folio. Cold ills. Orig cloth. *(Traylen)* **£60 [≈$90]**

Lassaigne, Jacques & Argan, Giulio Carlo

- The Great Centuries of Painting: the Fifteenth Century from Van Eyck to Botticelli. London: Skira, 1955. Num mtd cold plates. Dw. *(Mermaid Books)* **£18 [≈$27]**

Latham, Charles

- In English Homes. London: Country Life, 1908-09. 3rd edn vol 1, 2nd edn vol 2. 2 vols. Sm folio. Frontis, ills. Orig dec cloth, a.e.g., sl worn, ex-lib. *(Bookpress)* **$250 [≈£167]**

Latimore, Sarah Briggs & Haskell, Grace Clark

- Arthur Rackham: A Bibliography. Los Angeles: Suttonhouse, 1936. One of 550. xii,111 pp. Cold frontis, port, ills. Orig cloth backed dec bds. Slipcase. The Doheny copy. *(Argonaut)* **$350 [≈£233]**
- Arthur Rackham: A Bibliography. Jacksonville, FL: 1987. Reprint of 1936 edn. Orig cloth, hd of spine sl bumped. Dw. *(Ulysses Bookshop)* **£35 [≈$53]**

Laufer, Berthold

- Paper and Printing in Ancient China. Chicago: The Caxton Club, 1931. One of 250. 8vo. 33,[3] pp. Orig cloth backed bds, partly uncut, tips bruised, sl sunned. *(Bookpress)* **$75 [≈£50]**

Laurie, A.P.

- The Brush-Work of Rembrandt and his School Illustrated by Photomicrographs. Oxford: UP; London: Milford, 1932. xviii,44 pp. 127 plates. Orig cloth. *(Leicester Art Books)* **£45 [≈$68]**

Lauts, Jan

- Carpaccio. Paintings and Drawings. Complete Edition. London: Phaidon, 1962. 310 pp. 230 ills (18 cold). Orig cloth. *(Leicester Art Books)* **£100 [≈$150]**

Lavalleye, Jacques

- Bruegel and Lucas Van Leyden. Complete Engravings, Etchings, and Woodcuts. London: Thames & Hudson, 1967. 1st edn. Lge 4to. 205 pp. 491 plates. Dw. *(Spelman)* **£60 [≈$90]**

Laver, James

- French Painting and the Nineteenth Century. London: Batsford, 1937. 1st edn. 4to. viii,120 pp. 141 plates. Orig cloth. *(Claude Cox)* **£18 [≈$27]**

Lawrence, A.W.

- Classical Sculpture. London: Cape, 1929. 1st edn. 419 pp. 160 plates. Orig cloth. Dw. *(Hollett)* **£15 [≈$23]**

Lawrence, D.H.

- Birds, Beasts and Flowers. Wood-Engravings by Blair Hughes-Stanton. London: Cresset Press, 1930. One of 500. Folio. Orig vellum backed bds, t.e.g. *(Sotheran's)* **£348 [≈$522]**

Lawrence, T.E.

- Letters to E.T. Leeds with a Commentary by E.T. Leeds. Edited by J.M. Wilson. The Whittington Press: (1988). One of 650 (of 750). 4to. xxiii ,141 pp. Orig qtr cloth. Slipcase. *(Oak Knoll)* **$175 [≈£117]**
- Men in Print. Golden Cockerel Press: [1940]. One of 500. Lge 8vo. 59,[i] pp. Endpapers sl spotted, sm inkstain to marg on verso of title & contents ff. Orig morocco backed bds, t.e.g., spine sl faded. *(Sotheran's)* **£498 [≈$747]**
- T.E. Lawrence's Letters to H.S. Ede 1927-1935. Golden Cockerel Press: [1942]. One of 500. Lge 8vo. 62,[2 blank] pp. Orig morocco backed boards, t.e.g. With notice to purchasers concerning alleged inaccuracies in text. *(Sotheran's)* **£498 [≈$747]**

Layard, George Soames

- The Life and Letters of Charles Samuel Keene. London: Sampson Low, 1892. xxii,463 pp. 83 ills. Orig cloth, t.e.g., worn & faded. *(Leicester Art Books)* **£35 [≈$53]**

Leach, Bernard

- A Potter's Portfolio. A Selection of Fine Pots. New York: 1951. 28 pp. 60 plates. Orig cloth, minor spot on spine., Slipcase (splitting). *(John K. King)* **$125 [≈£83]**

Leadbetter, J.

- The Gentleman and Tradesman's Compleat Assistant ... Third Edition. London: for A. Webley, & W. Todd, 1770. 8vo. viii,263,[5] pp. Frontis, 2 fldg plates. Sl soiling. Rec qtr calf. *(Spelman)* **£280 [≈$420]**

Lebel, Robert

- Marcel Duchamp. New York: Grove Press, 1959. 1st Grove Press edn. 4to. 192 pp. Ills. Endpapers & prelims foxed. Orig cloth. Dw. *(First Folio)* **$300 [≈£200]**

Le Camus, Antoine

- Abdeker: or, the Art of Preserving Beauty. Translated from an Arabic Manuscript. London: for A. Millar, 1754. 12mo. vii,[1],220 pp. Contemp calf, hd of spine reprd. Anon. *(Spelman)* **£160 [≈$240]**

Le Corbusier, (Charles Jeanneret-Gris)

- Towards a New Architecture. London: 1927. 1st English edn. 289 pp. Ills. Orig cloth, hd of spine frayed, crnrs sl bumped. *(John K. King)* **$65 [≈£43]**

Lee, Ruth Webb & Rose, James H.

- American Glass Cup Plates. US: Tuttle, 1985. 8vo. 445 pp. 131 plates. Orig wraps. *(Paul Brown)* **£20 [≈$30]**

Lee-Elliot, Theyre

- Paintings of the Ballet. Introduction by Arnold L. Haskell. London: Collins, (1947). 1st edn. Sm 4to. (94) pp. 91 ills. Orig cloth. *(Karmiole)* **$30 [≈£20]**

Leemhardt, Maurice

- Folk Art of Oceania. Paris: Les Editions du Chene; New York: Tudor, (1950). Sm 4to. 124 pp. 11 maps, 4 cold plates, 124 b/w ills. Orig cloth. *(Abacus)* **$45 [≈£30]**

Leepa, Allen

- Abraham Rattner. New York: Abrams, 1974. 235 pp. 212 ills. Orig cloth. Dw. *(Leicester Art Books)* **£40 [≈$60]**

Lees-Milne, J.

- The Age of Adam. London: Batsford, 1947. 1st edn. 8vo. vii,184 pp. Num photo ills. V sl spotting. Orig cloth gilt. Dw (reprd). *(Clevedon Books)* **£24 [≈$36]**

Lees-Milne, James

- Saint Peter's. The Story of Saint Peter's

Basilica in Rome. London: Hamish Hamilton, 1967. 1st edn. Lge 8vo. 336 pp. 47 cold plates, 250 ills. Orig cloth gilt. Dw. *(Hollett)* **£25 [≈$38]**

Lehmann-Haupt, Hellmut

- Gutenberg and the Master of Playing Cards. New Haven: Yale UP, 1966. 1st edn. Tall 4to. xii,84 pp. Pocket table, 38 ills. Orig cloth gilt. *(Karmiole)* **$85 [≈£57]**
- Peter Schoeffer of Gernsheim and Mainz, with a List of his Surviving Books and Broadsides. Rochester: Leo Hart, (1950). 1st edn. 8vo. xv,146 pp. 19 plates, 25 figs. Orig cloth. Dw. *(Oak Knoll)* **$55 [≈£37]**

Leigh, Mabel Constance

- Love Songs and Verses. Illustrated by W. Graham Robertson. London: 1913. 1st edn. 8vo. 4 b/w plates. Free endpapers browned. Inscrptn. Orig cloth, t.e.g., ft of spine & 2 crnrs bumped. *(Ulysses Bookshop)* **£45 [≈$68]**

Leighton, Clare

- The Farmer's Year. A Calendar of English Husbandry. London: Collins, 1933. 1st edn. Oblong folio. W'engvs by the author. Dw. *(Waddington)* **£120 [≈$180]**
- Where Land Meets Sea. The Tide Line of Cape Cod. London: 1954. 1st edn. Num w'engvs. Orig bndg. *(Margaret Nangle)* **£80 [≈$120]**
- Wood Engraving of the 1930's, reviewed by Clare Leighton. London: The Studio, Special Winter Number, 1936. 192 pp. Num ills. Occas sl foxing. Orig cloth bds, sl soiled. *(Michael Taylor)* **£65 [≈$98]**

Leipnik, F.L.

- A History of French Etching, from the Sixteenth Century to the Present Day ... London: John Lane; The Bodley Head, (1924). 1st edn. Lge 4to. xviii,214,[2 advt] pp. Num ills. Orig cloth over bds, leather label. Dw (sl chipped). *(Karmiole)* **$125 [≈£83]**

Leiris, Michel

- Andre Masson Drawings. London: Thames & Hudson, 1972. [26] pp. 90 plates. Orig cloth. Dw. *(Leicester Art Books)* **£40 [≈$60]**

Leisinger, Hermann

- Romanesque Bronzes. Church Portals in Mediaeval Europe. London: Phoenix House, 1956. 1st English edn. Lge 4to. 160 plates. Orig cloth gilt. Dw (sl creased & chipped). *(Hollett)* **£75 [≈$113]**

Leitch, R.P.

- A Course of Painting in Neutral Tint. London: Cassell Petter & Galpin, [ca 1860]. 8 pp. 24 chromolitho plates. Orig cloth gilt, worn & shaken. *(Willow House)* **£25 [≈$38]**
- A Course of Water-Colour Painting. London: Cassell, [ca 1880]. 10th edn, rvsd. 11 pp. 24 mtd chromolitho plates. Prize label. Foxed. Orig cloth gilt, darkened, crnrs sl rubbed. *(Willow House)* **£25 [≈$38]**

Lejard, Andre

- The Art of the French Book. Paris: Editions du Chene, (1947). 1st edn. Sm folio. [iv],166 pp. Orig cloth. Dw (chipped). *(Bookpress)* **$100 [≈£67]**

Lejeune, Rita & Stiennon, Jacques

- The Legend of Roland in the Middle Ages. London: 1971. 1st edn. 2 vols. 4to. 63 cold plates, 510 ills. Price-clipped dws (v sl rubbed & nicked). *(Adam Blakeney)* **£85 [≈$128]**

Leng, Kyrle

- Juvenilia. Stanford Dingley: The Mill House Press, 1931. One of 35. 8vo. 26,[2] pp. Orig linen backed bds. Tissue dw. *(Young's)* **£75 [≈$113]**

Lenygon, F.

- The Decoration and Furniture of English Mansions during the Seventeenth and Eighteenth Centuries. London: Werner Laurie, 1909. 1st edn. Folio. 216 pp. Num photo ills. Orig cloth, t.e.g. *(Monmouth)* **£60 [≈$90]**

Leroi-Gourhan, Andre

- Treasures of Prehistoric Art. New York: Abrams, [ca 1967]. Lge thick 4to. 543 pp. Ills. Orig cloth. Dw. *(First Folio)* **$75 [≈£50]**

Leroy, L. Archier

- Wagner's Music Drama of the Ring. Illustrated by Paul Nash. London: n.d. 1st edn. Ills. Orig cloth backed bds, hd of spine & 3 crnrs sl bumped. Dw (chipped, sl rubbed and creased). *(Ulysses Bookshop)* **£75 [≈$113]**

Lesage, Alain Rene

- The Adventures of Gil Blas de Santillane. Translated by Tobias Smollett. Illustrations by John Austen. New York: The Limited Editions Club, 1937. One of 1500 signed by Austen. 2 vols. Sm 4to. Orig cloth. Dws (sl yellowed). Slipcase (sl worn). *(Oak Knoll)* **$150 [≈£100]**

- The Adventures of Gil Blas de Santillane. Translated by Tobias Smollett. Illustrations by John Austen. New York: The Limited Editions Club, 1937. One of 1500 signed by Austen. 2 vols. Sm 4to. Orig cloth. Slipcase (partly broken). *(Oak Knoll)* **$100 [≈£67]**

Leslie, Charles Robert & Taylor, Tom

- Life and Times of Sir Joshua Reynolds ... London: Murray, 1865. 1st edn. 2 vols. 8vo. [xviii],532,[32 ctlg]; [viii],646 pp. 2 errata ff. Advt slip. 2 ports, 9 plates. Orig cloth, minor wear extrs. *(Clark)* **£65 [≈$98]**

Lessons of Thrift ...

- See Cruikshank, Isaac Robert

Levey, Michael

- Giambattista Tiepolo: His Life and Art. Yale: UP, 1986. 301 pp. 238 plates. Orig cloth. Dw. *(Fine Art)* **£45 [≈$68]**
- Later Georgian Pictures in the Royal Collection. London: Phaidon, 1969. 2 vols (text & plates). Orig cloth. Dws. *(Fine Art)* **£85 [≈$128]**
- The Later Italian Pictures in the Collection of Her Majesty the Queen. London: Phaidon, 1964. 282 pp. 205 plates, 41 text ills. Orig cloth. Dw. *(Fine Art)* **£55 [≈$83]**
- Painting at Court. London: Weidenfeld & Nicholson, 1971. 4to. 228 pp. Over 200 ills. Orig cloth. Dw. *(Cooper Hay)* **£18 [≈$27]**

Levy, Julien

- Arshile Gorky. New York: Abrams, [1966]. Sm oblong folio. 235,[1] pp. 208 plates. Orig cloth. *(Ars Libri)* **$600 [≈£400]**

Levy, Julien (editor)

- Eugene Berman. New York & London: American Studio Books, n.d. Lge 4to. xv pp. 81 plates, 6 text ills. Orig cloth. *(Ars Libri)* **$45 [≈£30]**

Levy, Marvyn

- Drawings of L.S. Lowry. London: Cory, Adams & Mackay, 1963. 1st edn. 22 pp. Erratum pasted on contents page. 84 plates. Orig cloth. Dw. *(Clarice Davis)* **$75 [≈£50]**

Lewis, C.T. Courtney

- George Baxter, the Picture Printer. London: Sampson Low ..., [ca 1924]. One of 1000. Sm 4to. xxxvi,608 pp. 80 plates. Orig cloth, t.e.g. Dw (soiled & defective). *(Oak Knoll)* **$325 [≈£217]**

Lewis, Frank

- Edward Ladell 1821-1886. Leigh-on-Sea: F. Lewis, 1976. 48 pp. 48 plates. Orig buckram. *(Leicester Art Books)* **£30 [≈$45]**
- Edward Ladell, 1821-1886. Leigh-on-Sea: 1976. One of 500. 48 plates. Orig cloth. *(Lamb)* **£25 [≈$38]**
- Myles Birket Foster 1825-1899. Leigh-on-Sea: F. Lewis, 1973. One of 600. 47 pp. 44 plates. Orig buckram. *(Leicester Art Books)* **£30 [≈$45]**

Lewis, George R.

- The Ancient Font of Little Walsingham, in Norfolk, Drawn and Illustrated, with a Descriptive Interpretation. London: G.R. Lewis, 1843. Folio. 8 pp. 7 litho plates. Occas spotting & staining. Orig half parchment, spine ends sl defective. *(Hollett)* **£140 [≈$210]**
- Illustrations of Kilpeck Church, Herefordshire ... With an Essay on Ecclesiastical Design ... London: G.R. Lewis & William Pickering, 1842. Sm folio. 40 pp. 28 litho plates. Mod half mor gilt. *(Hollett)* **£175 [≈$263]**

Lewis, Griselda

- English Pottery. A Picture History. London: Hulton Press, 1956. 1st edn. 4to. Cold frontis, 418 ills. Orig cloth gilt. *(Hollett)* **£45 [≈$68]**

Lewis, J.M.

- John Frederick Lewis, R.A. 1805-1876. Leigh-on-Sea: F. Lewis, 1978. One of 500. 102 pp. 38 plates. Orig cloth. *(Leicester Art Books)* **£55 [≈$83]**

Lewis, John

- Collecting Printed Ephemera. London: Studio Vista, 1976. 1st edn. Folio. 160 pp. 16 cold plates, ills. Orig cloth. Dw. *(Claude Cox)* **£15 [≈$23]**
- A Handbook of Type and Illustration ... London: 1956. 8vo. 21 plates. Orig cloth. *(Traylen)* **£15 [≈$23]**
- John Nash. The Painter as Illustrator. With a Foreword by Wilfred Blunt. Godalming: The Pendomer Press, 1978. 136 pp. 126 ills. Orig cloth. Dw. *(Leicester Art Books)* **£35 [≈$53]**
- Printed Ephemera. Ipswich: Cowell, 1962. 1st edn. Folio. 288 pp. 713 ills. Orig cloth. Dw. *(Lamb)* **£25 [≈$38]**
- Printed Ephemera. London: Faber, 1969. Sm folio. 127 pp. 713 ills. Orig card cvrs. *(Lamb)* **£10 [≈$15]**

- The Twentieth Century Book. Its Illustrations and Design. New York: Reinhold, 1967. 4to. 269 pp. Num ills. Ex-lib. Orig cloth. Dw. *(Ars Libri)* **$75 [≈£50]**
- Typography: Design and Practice. London: Barrie & Jenkins, 1978. 1st edn. 4to. 144 pp. Ills. Orig cloth. Dw. *(Claude Cox)* **£12 [≈$18]**

Lewis, John & Brinkley, John

- Graphic Design. With Special Reference to Letterpress, Typography and Illustration. London: 1954. 4to. 198 pp. 40 plates. Orig cloth. Dw. *(Lamb)* **£20 [≈$30]**

Lewis, M.J.T.

- Temples in Roman Britain. Cambridge: UP, 1966. 1st edn. 4 plates, 9 tables, 130 text figs. Ex-lib. Lib cloth. *(Baker)* **£32 [≈$48]**

Lewis, Ralph

- Sir William Russell Flint, 1880-1969. Edinburgh: Charles Skilton, [1980]. 4to. 122 pp. 20 cold ills, other ills. Orig cloth gilt. *(Cooper Hay)* **£24 [≈$36]**

Lewis, Wyndham & Fergusson, Louis F.

- Harold Gilman. An Appreciation. London: Chatto & Windus, 1919. 95 pp. 34 ills. Orig cloth. *(Leicester Art Books)* **£150 [≈$225]**

Leymarie, Jean

- Balthus. New York: Rizzoli, 1979. Sq folio. [46] pp. 63 plates. Orig cloth. Dw. *(Ars Libri)* **$200 [≈£133]**
- Dutch Painting. London: Albert Skira, 1956. Folio. Num cold plates. Orig cloth. *(Traylen)* **£30 [≈$45]**
- Paul Gaugin: Watercolors and Pastels. New York: Abrams, 91962). Folio. 24 mtd cold plates. Orig qtr cloth. *(Abacus)* **$60 [≈£40]**

Lichten, Frances

- Decorative Art of Victoria's Era. New York: 1950. 273 pp. 14 cold plates, 96 ills. Orig cloth. *(Fine Art)* **£20 [≈$30]**

Lieberman, William S.

- Henri Matisse. Fifty Years of Graphic Art. New York: Braziller, 1956. 150 pp. 132 ills. Orig cloth. *(Leicester Art Books)* **£32 [≈$48]**

Liebmann, Michael

- Western European Sculpture from Soviet Museums. 15th and 16th Centuries. Leningrad: 1988. Folio. 262 pp. 168 plates. Orig cloth. Dw. *(Washton)* **$85 [≈£57]**

Lindley, Kenneth

- Of Graves and Epitaphs. London: Hutchinson, 1965. 1st edn. 176 pp. Ills by the author. Orig pict gilt cloth, 2 tiny bruises. Dw. *(Bookworks)* **£32 [≈$48]**
- Seamarks. Designed, Written, Engraved and Printed by Kenneth Lindley. Hereford: Pointing Finger Press, 1975. One of 45 signed by the artist. Orig qtr leather gilt, v sl rubbed. *(Michael Taylor)* **£38 [≈$57]**

Lindsay, J. Seymour

- Iron and Brass Implements of the English House. London: 1927. 4to. xii,212 pp. Num ills. Orig cloth. *(Phenotype)* **£36 [≈$54]**
- Iron and Brass Implements of the English Home. London: Tiranti, (1927) 1964. 4to. vii,88 pp. 473 figs. Ex-lib. Orig cloth. Dw. *(Castle Bookshop)* **£28 [≈$42]**

Lindsay, Jack

- Helen Comes of Age. Three Plays. London: The Fanfrolico Press, 1927. One of 500 signed by the author. 4to. Orig cloth, sl rubbed. *(Black Sun)* **$125 [≈£83]**

Lindsay, John

- A View of the Coinage of Ireland from the Invasion of the Danes to the Reign of Geo. IV ... Cork: Bolster, 1839. 4to. Plates inc supplementary plates. Orig cloth backed bds. *(Emerald Isle)* **£150 [≈$225]**

Lindsay, Lady

- About Robins. London: Routledge, [ca 1880]. Med 4to. 115 pp. 7 chromolithos, num ills. Orig gilt dec bndg, spine & crnrs v worn. *(Stella Books)* **£48 [≈$72]**

Lindsay, Lionel

- A.J. Munnings, R.A. Pictures of Horses and English Life. London: Eyre & Spottiswoode, 1939. 2nd edn, rvsd. x,216 pp. 114 plates, 2 ills. Orig cloth. *(Leicester Art Books)* **£110 [≈$165]**
- Charles Keene. The Artist's Artist. London: Colnaghi, 1934. One of 130 signed by the author. 15 pp. Port frontis, 55 plates. Orig buckram & bds. *(Leicester Art Books)* **£65 [≈$98]**
- Conrad Martens. The Man and His Art. Sydney: Angus & Robertson, 1920. 33 pp. 61 plates, 3 ills. Orig cloth & bds. *(Leicester Art Books)* **£60 [≈$90]**

Lindsay, Norman

- Pen Drawings. Sydney: Arthur McQuitty, 1924. One of 500 signed by the author. Folio.

12 ills. Rec half mor.
(Robert Frew) **£120 [≈$180]**

Lindsay, Philip

- An Account Biographical and Informative of the Later Days of Sir Henry Morgan Admiral of Buccaneers ... London: Fanfrolico Press, 1930. One of 450 signed by the author. [20] ff. Ports by Raymond Lindsay. Orig cloth. *(Hermitage)* **$200 [≈£133]**

Links, J.G.

- Canaletto and his Patrons. London: Paul Elek, 1977. xvi,112 pp. 152 ills. Orig cloth. *(Leicester Art Books)* **£38 [≈$57]**

Linton, W.J.

- The History of Wood Engraving in America. London: George Bell, 1882. One of 1000 signed by the author. Folio. 72 pp. 20 w'engvs, num text engvs. B'plate. Cloth backed wood veneered bds, hd of spine split, edges rubbed. *(Waddington)* **£52 [≈$78]**

Lipke, William

- David Bomberg. A Critical Study of his Life and Work. London: 1967. 1st edn. Lge 8vo. 132 pp. 14 cold plates, b/w ills. Dw (torn). *(Spelman)* **£25 [≈$38]**
- David Bomberg: A Critical Study of his Life and Work. London: 1967. 132 pp. 14 cold plates, plates, ills. Orig cloth. Dw. *(Fine Art)* **£22 [≈$33]**

Lipman, Jean

- Calder's Universe. New York: Harrison House, 1980. Hardback edn. Thick 4to. 457 ills. Dw (sl chipped). *(Clearwater)* **£45 [≈$68]**

Lippmann, F.

- Drawings by Sandro Botticelli for Dante's Divina Commedia ... London: Lawrence & Bullen, 1896. One of 500. 80 pp. 92 plates. Orig cloth gilt, t.e.g., spine ends worn. *(Leicester Art Books)* **£35 [≈$53]**

Lister, R.

- Decorative Iron Work in Great Britain. London: 1957. 8vo. xii,265 pp. Ills. Orig cloth. *(Phenotype)* **£24 [≈$36]**

Lister, Raymond

- Catalogue Raisonne of the Works of Samuel Palmer. Cambridge: 1988. 4to. viii,279 pp. Num ills. Orig cloth. *(Washton)* **$95 [≈£63]**
- Edward Calvert. London: G. Bell & Sons, 1962. xii,116 pp. 59 plates. Orig cloth. Dw. *(Leicester Art Books)* **£32 [≈$48]**
- George Richmond. London: Robin Garton, 1981. 1st edn. 184 pp. 69 ills. Orig bds. Dw. *(Bookworks)* **£22 [≈$33]**
- Samuel Palmer and his Etchings. New York: Watson-Guptil, (1969). 1st edn. Sm 4to. 131 pp. Frontis, 39 ills. Orig cloth. *(Bookpress)* **$65 [≈£43]**
- Samuel Palmer and his Etchings. London: 1969. 131 pp. 39 plates. Orig cloth. Dw (torn). *(Fine Art)* **£35 [≈$53]**
- Samuel Palmer and His Etchings. New York: Watson-Guptil, 1969. 131 pp. Cold frontis, 39 ills. Orig cloth. Dw. *(Leicester Art Books)* **£32 [≈$48]**

Lister, Reginald

- Jean Goujon. His Life and Work. London: Duckworth, 1903. One of 250. 78 pp. 19 plates. Some foxing. Orig cloth & bds. *(Leicester Art Books)* **£30 [≈$45]**

Litchfield, Frederick

- Antiques Genuine and Spurious. An Art Expert's Recollections and Cautions. London: Bell & Sons, 1921. Tall 8vo. Cold frontis, num ills. Orig cloth gilt. *(Hollett)* **£25 [≈$38]**
- How to Collect Old Furniture. London: George Bell & Sons, 1906. xiv,169,[v] pp. Ills. Orig dec cloth gilt. *(Hollett)* **£18 [≈$27]**
- Illustrated History of Furniture: from the Earliest to the Present Time. London: 1893. 3rd edn. 4to. xx,280 pp. Num ills. Orig cloth gilt, t.e.g., front jnt tender. *(Hollett)* **£35 [≈$53]**
- Pottery and Porcelain. A Guide to Collectors. London: Truslove, Hanson & Comba, 1900. 1st edn. Lge 8vo. xv,362 pp. Ills. Endpapers spotted. Orig pict cloth gilt, extrs worn, spine ends frayed, shaken. *(Hollett)* **£30 [≈$45]**
- Pottery & Porcelain. A Guide to Collectors. New Edition Revised and Enlarged. London: 1905. Lge 8vo. xii,399,[1] pp. 7 cold & 35 other plates, num text ills. Minor marks. Orig cloth, t.e.g., sl rubbed & marked. *(Bow Windows)* **£30 [≈$45]**

Little, James Stanley

- The Life and Work of William Q. Orchardson, R.A. London: The Art Annual, The Art Journal, 1897. 32,[18 advt] pp. 4 plates, 59 text ills. Orig cloth. *(Leicester Art Books)* **£26 [≈$39]**

Little, W.L.

- Staffordshire Blue: Underglaze Blue-

Transfer Printed Earthenware. London: Batsford, 1987. 2nd imp. 4to. 160 pp. 119 plates. Orig bndg.
(Castle Bookshop) **£15 [≈$23]**

Livingston, Luther S.

- Auction Prices of Books ... from the Commencement of the English Book-Prices Current in 1886 ... New York: Dodd, Mead, 1905. One of 750. 4 vols. 4 to. Lib stamps on title. Orig cloth, lib nos on spine.
(Oak Knoll) **$175 [≈£117]**

Livy

- The History of Early Rome. Illustrated by Raffaele Scorzelli. New York: The Limited Editions Club, 1970. One of 1500 signed by Scorzelli & Mardersteig. Sm thick 4to. Orig cloth-backed bds. Slipcase (sl defective).
(Oak Knoll) **$100 [≈£67]**

Lloyd, H. Alan

- Some Outstanding Clocks over seven hundred years 1250-1950. London: Leonard Hill, 1958. 1st edn. Tall 8vo. xx,160 pp. Cold frontis, 173 ills. Orig cloth gilt. Dw.
(Hollett) **£65 [≈$98]**

Lloyd, Nathaniel

- Building Craftsmanship in Brick and Tile and in Stone Slates. Cambridge: UP, 1929. 4to. 99 pp. Ills. Stamp on free endpaper. Calf backed bds. *(Monmouth)* **£40 [≈$60]**
- A History of the English House from Primitive Times to the Victorian Period. London: The Architectural Press, 1931. 1st edn. xvii,487 pp. Subscribers. Num ills. Orig cloth gilt, t.e.g., spine sl dull.
(Taylor & Son) **£78] [≈$117]**
- A History of the English House from Primitive Times to the Victorian Period. London: The Architectural Press, 1949. 4to. ix,487 pp. 888 figs. Occas lib stamp. Orig cloth, sl soiled, spine faded.
(Francis Edwards) **£50 [≈$75]**
- A History of the English House from Primitive Times to the Victorian Period. London: Architectural Press, 1949. 487 pp. Ills. Orig bndg, sl marked.
(Carol Howard) **£55 [≈$83]**

Lloyd, Robert

- The Actor, a Poem. To which is prefix'd an Essay by Edmund Blunden ... Embellished ... by Randolph Schwabe. London: C.W. Beaumont, 1926. One of 270. Cold title, 5 plates. Orig buckram backed dec bds.
(Claude Cox) **£28 [≈$42]**

Lloyd, Ward

- Investing in Georgian Glass. London: Barrie & Jenkins, Corgi, 1971. 4to. 160 pp. Cold & b/w ills. Dw. *(Paul Brown)* **£20 [≈$30]**

Locke, W.J.

- The Beloved Vagabond. Illustrated by Jean Dulac. London: John Lane; The Bodley Head, 1922. 1st edn thus. 8vo. 16 cold plates, text ills. Orig cloth, extrs v sl rubbed.
(Claude Cox) **£25 [≈$38]**

Lockwood, Margo

- Bare Elegy. Poem by Margo Lockwood. Color Xerox Print by Ray K. Metzker. Vermont: Janus Press, 1980. One of 150 signed by the author and the artist. Tall thin 4to. Orig cloth, paper label.
(Black Sun) **$155 [≈£103]**

Lodwick, R.W.

- Humorous Sketches of the World We Live In. London: 1856. 1st edn. Roy 4to. 40 pp. Ills. Orig cloth, pict onlay, marked & worn.
(Stella Books) **£65 [≈$98]**

Loeffler, Fritz

- Otto Dix. Life and Work. New York & London: Holmes & Meier, 1982. Lge 4to. 418,[2] pp. Num ills. Orig cloth. Dw.
(Ars Libri) **$95 [≈£63]**

Loehr, Max

- Chinese Landscape Woodcuts from an Imperial Commentary to the Tenth-Century Printed Edition of the Buddhist Canon. Cambridge: Harvard UP, 1968. 4to. 144 pp. 40 plates. Dw. *(Schoyer)* **$45 [≈£30]**

Lomazzo, Giovanni Paolo

- A Tracte containing the Artes of Curious Paintinge, Carvinge and Buildinge. Translated by Richard Haydocke. Gregg Press: 1970. Lge 8vo. [24],217 pp. Orig cloth. *(Spelman)* **£30 [≈$45]**

The London Aphrodite ...

- The London Aphrodite. A Miscellany of Poems, Stories and Essays by Various Hands, Eminent or Rebellious. Edited by Jack Lindsay and P.R. Stephensen. London: Fanfrolico Press, (1929). 1st edn. 496 pp. 2 plates. Orig cloth gilt. *(Karmiole)* **$75 [≈£50]**

London, Jack

- The Sea-Wolf. With Illustrations by Fletcher Martin. New York: The Limited Editions Club, 1961. One of 1500 signed by Martin. 4to. Sm ink mark on endpaper. Orig cloth.

Slipcase. *(Oak Knoll)* **$65 [≈£43]**

- White Fang. With Illustrations by Lydia Dabcovich. New York: The Limited Editions Club, 1973. One of 1500 signed by Dabcovich. Tall 8vo. Orig cloth. Slipcase. *(Oak Knoll)* **$85 [≈£57]**

Lone, E. Miriam

- Some Noteworthy Firsts in Europe during the Fifteenth Century. With Illustrations. New York: Lathrop Harper, 1930. One of 425 signed. 8vo. xiv,73 pp. Orig cloth backed bds, spine sl darkened, tiny split in cloth. Slipcase (worn). *(The Veatchs)* **$85 [≈£57]**

Long, Basil

- British Miniaturists 1520-1860. Second Edition. London: Holland Press, 1966. 4to. xxxiii,[i],475,addenda pp. 153 ills. Dw (sl worn). *(Spelman)* **£50 [≈$75]**
- British Miniaturists. London: Holland Press, 1966. xxxii,475,addenda pp. 153 ills. Orig cloth. Dw. *(Fine Art)* **£45 [≈$68]**

Long, Richard

- Two sheepdogs cross in and out of the passing shadows The clouds drift over the hill with a storm. London: Lisson Publications, 1971. 4to. [12] pp. 8 ills. Orig self-wraps. *(Ars Libri)* **$150 [≈£100]**

Longhurst, M.H.

- English Ivories. London: 1926. 1st edn. 4to. 123 pp. Frontis, 56 plates, 10 text ills. Orig cloth, t.e.g., sl marked. *(Robertshaw)* **£36 [≈$54]**

Longman, W.

- Tokens of the Eighteenth Century connected with Booksellers & Bookmakers ... London: LOngmans, Green, 1916. 1st edn. 90 pp. 14 plates. Faint lib marks on title verso. Orig cloth gilt. *(Hollett)* **£50 [≈$75]**

Longus

- Daphnis and Chloe. New Rochelle, New York: The Elston Press, 1904. One of 160. 4to. Ills by H.M. O'Kane. Orig vellum, with ties. *(Black Sun)* **$300 [≈£200]**

Loomes, Brian

- Westmorland Clocks and Clockmakers. David & Charles: 1974. 1st edn. 8vo. 120 pp. 16 plates, 3 ills. Orig cloth gilt. Dw. *(Hollett)* **£30 [≈$45]**
- Yorkshire Clockmakers. Clapham: Dalesman Books, 1972. 1st edn. 192 pp. Ills. Orig cloth gilt. Price-clipped dw (sl rubbed). *(Hollett)* **£30 [≈$45]**

Lopez-Rey, Jose

- A Cycle of Goya's Drawings. The Expression of Truth and Liberty. London: 1956. Sm 4to. 159 pp. 134 ills on plates. Orig cloth, sl shelfworn. *(Washton)* **$45 [≈£30]**
- Goya's Caprichos. Beauty, Reason and Caricature. Princeton: UP, 1953. 2 vols. 265 plates. Slipcase. *(Leicester Art Books)* **£60 [≈$90]**

Lord, Albert B. (editor)

- Russian Folk Tales. Illustrated by Teje Etchemendy. New York: The Limited Editions Club, 1970. One of 1500 signed by the illustrator. Sm 4to. Orig cloth. Slipcase. *(Oak Knoll)* **$55 [≈£37]**

Lord, James

- Alberto Giacometti Drawings. Greenwich: New York Graphic Society, 1971. Lge 4to. 266 pp. 117 plates. Orig cloth. *(Ars Libri)* **$500 [≈£333]**

Loudon, J.C.

- The Architectural Magazine, and Journal ... London: Longmans, Orme ..., 1838. 1st edn. 8vo. ix,[i],728 pp. Ills. Half leather, worn. *(Bookpress)* **$250 [≈£167]**
- An Encyclopaedia of Cottage, Farm and Villa Architecture and Furniture ... London: 1833. 1st edn. 8vo. xx,1138 pp. Litho plates, num text engvs. Lacks 2 plates. Orig calf, gilt spine. *(Phenotype)* **£95 [≈$143]**
- An Encyclopaedia of Gardening ... A New Edition, Considerably Improved & Enlarged. London: Longman, 1835. Thick 8vo. [16 ctlg], xl,1270,[i errata],[32 ctlg] pp. Advts dated 1845. 981 text ills. Orig cloth, recased, hd of spine reprd. *(Clevedon Books)* **£135 [≈$203]**
- An Encyclopedia of Cottage, Farm, and Villa Architecture ... A New Edition with a Supplement. London: Longman, Brown ..., 1842. 4th edn, enlgd. 8vo. xx,i,306 pp. 2321 figs. Later cloth. *(Bookpress)* **$985 [≈£657]**
- The Villa Gardener ... Edited by Mrs. Loudon. London: W.S. Orr, 1850. 2nd edn. 8vo. xii,516 pp. 378 engvs. Rec half calf gilt. *(Clevedon Books)* **£215 [≈$323]**

Loudon, J.H.

- James Scott and William Scott Bookbinders. Edinburgh: Scolar Press & National Library of Scotland, 1980. 1st edn. xxvi,414 pp. Cold frontis, 170 plates. Dw. *(Claude Cox)* **£30 [≈$45]**

Lough, John & Merson, Elizabeth

- John Graham Lough, 1798-1876: A Northumbrian Sculptor. Woodbridge: Boydell Press, 1987. xi,95 pp. 40 plates. Orig cloth. Dw. *(Fine Art)* **£25 [≈$38]**

Low, David

- Twelve Biographies. London: New Statesman & Nation, December, 1933. One of 100 signed by the artist. Folio. 12 pp. 12 plates, each signed by Low. Orig canvas backed portfolio, silk ties, sl soiled & faded. *(Claude Cox)* **£55 [≈$83]**
- Years of Wrath. A Cartoon History 1932-1945. London: Gollancz, 1949. 1st edn. 4to. 325 pp. Ills. Orig cloth. *(Claude Cox)* **£20 [≈$30]**

Lowbury, Edward

- Flowering Cypress. Hereford: Pointing Finger Press, 1986. One of 50 signed by the author and the artist, Kenneth Lindley. Orig qtr leather. *(Michael Taylor)* **£35 [≈$53]**

Lowe, Alfred

- Six Cartoons. Introduction by Liam O'Flaherty. London: Foyle, 1930. One of 750. Folio. Orig bndg. *(Emerald Isle)* **£50 [≈$75]**

Lowell, Guy

- More Small Italian Villas and Farmhouses. New York: (1920). 140 pp. Ills. Orig cloth, sl rubbed, stained & worn. *(John K. King)* **$125 [≈£83]**
- Smaller Italian Villas & Farmhouses. New York: 1916. 1st edn. Sm folio. [xii],viii,[i] pp. 124 plates. Half cloth, rubbed. *(Bookpress)* **$125 [≈£83]**

Lower, Mark Anthony

- The Curiosities of Heraldry. London: John Russell Smith, 1845. 1st edn. Demy 8vo. xvi,(320) pp. Addtnl chromolitho title, ills. Orig dec cloth gilt, reprd. *(Ash)* **£60 [≈$90]**

Lowrie, Walter

- Art in the Early Church. New York: 1947. Sm 4to. xviii,268 pp. 500 ills on 150 plates. Orig cloth. *(Washton)* **$40 [≈£27]**

Lubbock, J.G.

- From Garden to Galaxy. London: Bertram Rota, 1980. One of 80 signed by the author. Sm folio. Orig gilt dec mor, t.e.g. Glassine dw. Slipcase. *(Claude Cox)* **£220 [≈$330]**
- Light and the Mind's Eye. London: Rota, 1974. One of 70 signed by the artist. Folio. Orig gilt dec mor. Slipcase. *(Lamb)* **£250 [≈$375]**
- Reflections from the Sea. Leicester: The Twelve by Eight Press, 1971. One of 85 signed by the author. Folio. Orig niger mor gilt, t.e.g. Glassine dw. Slipcase. Prospectus laid in. *(Claude Cox)* **£220 [≈$330]**
- Reflections from the Sea. Leicester: Twelve by Eight Press, 1971. One of 85 signed by the author. Orig gilt dec mor. Slipcase. *(Lamb)* **£250 [≈$375]**
- Reflections from the Sea. Original Prints & Text by J.G. Lubbock. Leicester: The Twelve by Eight Press, 1971. One of 85 signed by the author. Orig gilt dec mor. Slipcase. *(Lamb)* **£200 [≈$300]**

Lubke, Wilhelm

- Ecclesiastical Art in Germany during the Middle Ages. Translated from the Fifth German Edition with Appendix by L.A. Wheatley. London: Jack, 1870. Lge 8vo. 184 engvs. Orig cloth, spine sl faded. *(Spelman)* **£30 [≈$45]**

Lucas, E.V.

- Edwin Austin Abbey, Royal Academician. The Record of his Life and Work. London: Methuen, 1921. 2 vols. xii,268; 269-518 pp. 200 plates. Orig cloth backed bds, spine worn. *(Leicester Art Books)* **£70 [≈$105]**
- Edwin Austin Abbey. New York: Scribner, 1921. 1st edn. 2 vols. Orig qtr linen, uncut. *(Mac Donnell)* **$100 [≈£67]**
- John Constable the Painter. London: Halton & Truscott Smith, 1924. ix,78 pp. 64 plates. Orig cloth gilt, t.e.g., sl wrinkled. *(Leicester Art Books)* **£40 [≈$60]**
- The Open Road. A Book for Wayfarers. Illustrated by Claude Shepperson. London: Methuen, 1913. 1st edn thus. 16 mtd cold plates, dec endpapers. Orig elab gilt blue cloth, fine. *(Old Cathay)* **£49 [≈$74]**

Lucas, F.L.

- Gilgamesh, King of Erech. Golden Cockerel Press: 1948. One of 60 signed by the author and the artist, Dorothea Braby. Orig half mor gilt, t.e.g. *(Waddington)* **£110 [≈$165]**

Lucian

- Lucian's True History. Translated by Francis Hickes. Illustrated by Aubrey Beardsley, William Strang and J.B. Clark. London: Privately Printed, 1894. One of 50 on vellum. Sm 4to. 16 b/w ills. Mor gilt by Donnelly, Chicago, spine reprd. *(Barbara Stone)* **£225 [≈$338]**

Lucie-Smith, Edward

- Art Now: From Abstract Expressionism to Superrealism. New York: Morrow, 1977. Stout 4to. 504 pp. 384 cold plates. Orig buckram. Dw. *(Abacus)* **$45 [≈£30]**

Luhan, Mabel Dodge

- Taos and its Artists. New York: Duell, Sloan & Pearce, 1947. 4to. 168 pp. 56 plates, text ills. Orig cloth. Dw. *(Ars Libri)* **$250 [≈£167]**

Lullies, R.

- Greek Sculpture. Photographs by M. Hirmer. New York: Abrams, (1957). 4to. 88 pp. 264 plates. Orig cloth. Dw. Slipcase. *(Abacus)* **$85 [≈£57]**

Lumsden, E.S.

- The Art of Etching ... London: Seeley, Service, 1925. 8vo. 376,[14 ctlg] pp. 208 ills. Orig cloth, sl faded, lower inner hinge cracked. *(Cooper Hay)* **£14 [≈$21]**

Lust, Herbert C.

- Giacometti. The Complete Graphics and 15 Drawings. New York: Tudor, 1970. 224 pp. 368 ills. Orig cloth. *(Leicester Art Books)* **£180 [≈$270]**
- Giacometti: The Complete Graphics and 15 Drawings. New York: Tudor, (1970). 4to. 224 pp. 368 ills. Orig cloth. Dw. *(Abacus)* **$325 [≈£217]**

Lydon, F.A.

- Gems from the Poets Illustrated. The Designs by A.F. Lydon Printed in Colours from Wood Blocks. London: Groombridge, 1860. Cold frontis & 28 cold plates. Publisher's (?) half mor, a.e.g., sl scuffed, contents separating from guttapercha. *(Waterfield's)* **£145 [≈$218]**

Lyell, James P.R.

- Early Book Illustration in Spain. London: Grafton, 1926. One of 500. 4to. xxvi,331 pp. Frontis, 247 ills & plates. Orig cloth, front hinge starting. *(Bookpress)* **$235 [≈£157]**

Lyle, R.C.

- Royal Newmarket. London: 1945. 1st edn. 4to. 10 cold plates, 31 ills by Lionel Edwards. Orig cloth. Dw (sl worn). *(Margaret Nangle)* **£32 [≈$48]**

Lynch, Bohun

- A History of Caricature. London: Faber & Gwyer, 1926. 1st edn. Lge 8vo. Frontis, 20 plates, 12 text ills. Orig dec cloth. Glassine dw. *(Spelman)* **£40 [≈$60]**
- A History of Caricature. Boston: Little, Brown, 1927. 1st edn. 4to. Frontis, 20 plates. Orig cloth & bds, some what darkened. *(Karmiole)* **$50 [≈£33]**

Lysons, Samuel

- An Account of Roman Antiquities discovered at Woodchester in the County of Gloucester. London: Cadell & Davies, 1797. 1st edn. Lge folio. [vi],20,[4],21 pp. 40 plates. Some foxing. Orig half mor. *(Bookpress)* **$9,500 [≈£6,333]**

A Lyttel Book of Nonsense ...

- A Lyttel Book of Nonsense. Kensington: Cayme Press, 1925. 155 pp. 76 ills. Sl browning. Inscrptn. Orig illust bds, deckle edges. *(Carol Howard)* **£30 [≈$45]**

Maaskamp, E.

- Representations of Dresses, Morals and Customs, in the Kingdom of Holland, at the beginning of the Nineteenth Century. Amsterdam: 1808 [plates dated 1805-11]. 4to. 7 pp. 21 hand cold plates. Some spotting of ptd title. Rec calf. *(Spelman)* **£480 [≈$720]**

Maberly, J.

- The Print Collector ... Edited ... by Robert Hoe. New York: Dodd, Mead, 1880. One of 50 Large Paper. 4to. 350 pp. Unsewn sheets laid into a vellum and bds folder. Cvrs worn, soiled & chipped. *(Rona Schneider)* **$150 [≈£100]**

Mabie, Hamilton Wright

- The Writers of Knickerbocker New York. Illustrations Engraved by Walworth Stilson. New York: The Grolier Club, 1912. One of 303. Sm 8vo. viii,121 pp. Orig cloth gilt, a.e.g. Slipcase. *(Oak Knoll)* **$75 [≈£50]**

McCausland, Hugh

- Snuff and Snuff-Boxes. London: Batchworth Press, 1951. 1st edn. viii,144 pp. Frontis, 12 plates. Orig cloth gilt. *(Hollett)* **£25 [≈$38]**

McCawley, Patricia K.

- Antique Glass Paperweights from France. London: Spink & Son, 1968. Lge 8vo. xi,92 pp. 30 plates. Orig cloth gilt. Dw. signed by the author. *(Hollett)* **£35 [≈$53]**

McClure, Michael & Tanner, Wesley B.

- The Book of Benjamin. Berkeley: The Ary Press, 1982. One of 125. 4to. 21 printed cards in accordion binder. Bds. *(Bookpress)* **$150 [≈£100]**

McConathy, Dale & Vreeland, Diana

- Hollywood Costume. New York: Abrams, (1976). 1st edn. 317 pp. Photos by Keith Trumbo. Orig padded cloth. Acetate dw. *(Hermitage)* **$250 [≈£167]**

McCormack, John

- Channel Island Churches. London: Phillimore, 1986. 1st edn. 4to. xvi,346 pp. 92 plates. Orig cloth gilt. Dw. *(Hollett)* **£40 [≈$60]**
- The Guernsey House. London: Phillimore, 1980. 1st edn. Sm 4to. xii,405 pp. 97 plates, ills. Orig cloth gilt. Dw. *(Hollett)* **£35 [≈$53]**

McCrae, Hugh

- Colombine. Sydney: Angus & Robertson, 1920. One of 1000. 72 pp. 11 plates by Norman Lindsay. Orig cloth backed bds, sl browned. *(Bookworks)* **£65 [≈$98]**

McCraken, Harold

- Frederic Remington. Artist of the Old West. Phila: Lippincott, 1947. 158 pp. 48 plates, 29 text ills. Orig buckram. *(Leicester Art Books)* **£24 [≈$36]**

M'Cready, C.T. & Strickland, W.G.

- List of Oil Paintings, Mezzotints, Seal Matrices, Manuscripts etc. of the Church of Ireland. Dublin: UP, 1916. 44 pp. Orig wraps. *(Emerald Isle)* **£35 [≈$53]**

McCulloch, Alan

- Encyclopaedia of Australian Art. London: Hutchinson, 1968. 1st edn. 668 pp. Num ills. Orig cloth. Dw. *(Bookworks)* **£35 [≈$53]**

McCune, Evelyn

- The Arts of Korea; An Illustrated History. Rutland: Tuttle, [ca 1962]. 1st edn. Lge 8vo. 452 pp. Ills. Dw. *(McBlain)* **$70 [≈£47]**

Macdonald, John Denis

- Sound & Colour, their Relations, Analogies & Harmonies. Gosport: 1869. 1st edn. 8vo. [6], 86 pp, imprint leaf. 2 plates ptd in mauve, 16 text diags (13 hand cold), 4 tables (1 hand cold). Orig cloth. *(Spelman)* **£120 [≈$180]**

McDonnell, J. & Healy, P.

- Gold Tooled Bookbindings commissioned by Trinity College Dublin in the Eighteenth Century. Dublin: 1987. 4to. 340 pp. 106 plates. Dw. *(Emerald Isle)* **£65 [≈$98]**

McDowall, Roddy

- Double Exposure. New York: Delacorte Press, (1966). 1st edn. 4to. 251,[2] pp. Photo ills. Orig cloth. Dw (sl rubbed). *(Argonaut)* **$75 [≈£50]**

Macfall, Haldane

- Aubrey Beardsley the Clown, the Harlequin, the Pierrot of his Age. New York: Simon & Schuster, 1927. 1st edn. Ills. Orig cloth gilt, spine sl worn. *(First Folio)* **$115 [≈£77]**
- Aubrey Beardsley. New York: 1927. 1st edn. Lge 8vo. 270 pp. 54 ills. Orig cloth gilt, sl marked. *(Spelman)* **£40 [≈$60]**
- The Book of Lovat Claud Fraser. London: Dent, 1923. 1st edn. 4to. 184 pp. 3 ports, 18 plates, num text ills. Orig cloth backed pict bds, rubbed, sl soiled, spine faded, label rubbed. *(Claude Cox)* **£45 [≈$68]**
- The French Pastellists of the Eighteenth Century ... London: Macmillan, 1909. 4to. 52 ills. Orig gilt dec cloth, t.e.g. *(First Folio)* **$75 [≈£50]**
- A History of Painting. With a Preface by Frank Brangwyn. London: Caxton, n.d. 2nd edn. 8 vols. 4to. 200 cold plates. Orig cloth. *(Young's)* **£65 [≈$98]**
- The Splendid Wayfaring. Decorated by Lovat Fraser, Gaudier Brzeska, the Author and Gordon Craig. London: Simpkin, Marshall, 1913. 1st edn. 4to. xiii,202 pp. Frontis, ills. Orig gilt dec linen, t.e.g., spine faded. *(Blackwell's)* **£100 [≈$150]**

McFarlane, K.B.

- Hans Memling. Edited by Edgar Wind with the assistance of G.L. Harris. Oxford: 1971. Lge 4to. xv,74 pp. 153 plates. Orig cloth. Dw. *(Washton)* **$95 [≈£63]**
- Hans Memling. Edited by Edgar Wind. Oxford: Clarendon Press 1971. xv,74 pp. 152 plates. Lib stamps. Orig cloth. *(Leicester Art Books)* **£70 [≈$105]**

MacGeorge, A.

- Flags: Some Account of their History and Uses. London: Blackie, 1881. 1st edn. 8vo. 122 pp. 6 cold litho plates, 32 text figs. Orig cloth, t.e.g., snag hd of spine, lower cvr faded. *(Claude Cox)* **£18 [≈$27]**
- Wm. Leighton Leitch Landscape Painter. A Memoir. London: Blackie, 1884. viii,128 pp. 15 ills. Orig cloth gilt, t.e.g. *(Leicester Art Books)* **£35 [≈$53]**

MacGibbon, David

- Jean Bourdichon. A Court Painter of the

Fifteenth Century. Glasgow: UP for the author, 1933. xv,191 pp. Frontis, 33 plates. Orig cloth. Dw.
(Leicester Art Books) **£32 [≈$48]**

McGrandle, Leith

- Europe. The Quest for Unity. London: [Officina Bodoni for] Ranelagh Editions, [1975]. One of 475. Folio. xxiv,87,[1] pp. Frontis by Annigoni. Orig leather gilt, t.e.g. Slipcase. Includes contributions by Sir Winston Churchill.
(Sotheran's) **£350 [≈$525]**

McGrath, R.

- Twentieth Century Houses. London: Faber, 1934. 232 pp. Ills. Cvrs sl rubbed & soiled.
(Monmouth) **£60 [≈$90]**

MacGregor, Morna

- Early Celtic Art in North Britain ... from the Third Century B.C. to the Third Century A.D. Leicester: UP, 1976. 2 vols. Ills. Boxed.
(Emerald Isle) **£55 [≈$83]**

McGrew, Charles B.

- Italian Doorways. Measured Drawings and Photographs ... Cleveland, Ohio: Jansen, 1929. 4to. Frontis, 194 plates. Orig cloth. Dw (sl sunned). *(Sotheran's)* **£85 [≈$128]**
- Italian Doorways. Measured Drawings and Photographs ... Cleveland: J.H. Jansen, 1929. Folio. 195 plates. Orig cloth gilt, sl soiled. *(Karmiole)* **$125 [≈£83]**

McHardy, George

- Catalogue of the Drawings Collection of the Royal Institute of British Architecture. London: RIBA, (1977). 1st edn. Folio. [ii], 143,[1] pp. 123 ills. Orig cloth, sl soiled.
(Bookpress) **$65 [≈£43]**

Mackay, Agnes

- Arthur Melville, R.W.S., A.R.S.A., 1855-1904. Leigh-on-Sea: F. Lewis, 1951. One of 500. 151 pp. 46 plates. Orig cloth. Dw.
(Leicester Art Books) **£55 [≈$83]**

McKay, Barry

- Marbling Methods and Receipts from Four Centuries. With Other Instructions Useful to Bookbinders. Oxford: Plough Press, 1990. One of 500. 8vo. [vi],85,[14] pp. 18 samples. Orig cloth. *(The Veatchs)* **$125 [≈£83]**
- Patterns and Pigments in English Marbled Papers. Oxford: Plough Press, 1988. One of 160. 93 pp. 14 mtd samples. Orig cloth backed mrbld bds.
(The Veatchs) **$255 [≈£170]**

McKearin, George & Helen

- American Glass. New York: Crown, 1945. 6th printing. 4to. xvi,622 pp. 300 ills. Dw (torn). *(Young's)* **£45 [≈$68]**

Mackenzie, Colin

- Five Thousand Receipts in all the Useful and Domestic Arts ... New Edition. London: for Sir Richard Phillips, 1829. Sm sq 8vo. iv,[1],6-827 double column text,[1 advt] pp. Minor soiling. Contemp calf, rebacked.
(Spelman) **£95 [≈$143]**

Mackenzie, Compton

- The House of Coalport 1750-1950. London: Collins, 1953. 2nd edn. 127 pp. 33 plates (15 cold). Orig cloth gilt. Dw.
(Hollett) **£35 [≈$53]**

McKerrow, Ronald B.

- An Introduction to Bibliography for Literary Students. Oxford: 1928. 8vo. Orig cloth, unopened. Dw. *(Traylen)* **£20 [≈$30]**

McKerrow, Ronald B. & Ferguson, F.S.

- Title-page Borders used in England & Scotland 1485-1640. OUP: Bibl Soc, 1932 (for 1931). 4to. 314 ills. Orig qtr buckram, t.e.g., crnrs sl worn, spine darkened.
(Clark) **£60 [≈$90]**

Mackie, George

- Lynton Lamb, Illustrator, a Selection of his Work ... London: Scolar Press, 1978. Sm 4to. xxxi,104 pp. 96 plates. Orig cloth. Dw.
(Clevedon Books) **£26 [≈$39]**

McKitterick, David

- A New Specimen of Curwen Pattern Papers. Gloucestershire: Whittington Press, 1987. One of 335. Lge 8vo. xii,105 pp, inc 32 specimens. 8 plates. Orig qtr cloth. Slipcase.
(The Veatchs) **$250 [≈£167]**

Macklin, H.W.

- The Brasses of England. London: Methuen, Antiquary's Books, 1907. 2nd edn. xx,336,advt pp. 3 plates, ills. Orig cloth, spine sl rubbed. *(Quest Books)* **£26 [≈$39]**

Mackray, William Dunn

- Annals of the Bodleian Library, Oxford, A.D. 1598 - A.D. 1867 ... Oxford: Rivingtons, 1868. Orig cloth, hd of spine rubbed.
(Peter Bell) **£36 [≈$54]**

Maclean, Frank

- Henry Moore R.A. London: 1905. xvi,215 pp. Port frontis, 20 plates. Orig cloth, t.e.g.
(Fine Art) **£18 [≈$27]**

McLean, Ruari

- George Cruikshank. London: Art & Technics, 1948. 1st edn. Sm 4to. 100 pp. Num ills. Orig cloth gilt. Dw (a few snags). *(Clevedon Books)* **£24 [≈$36]**
- Joseph Cundall, a Victorian Publisher. Pinner: PLA, 1976. 8vo. viii,96 pp. Ills. B'plate removed. Orig cloth gilt. *(Cooper Hay)* **£14 [≈$21]**
- Joseph Cundall. A Victorian Publisher. Notes on his Life and a Check List of his Books. Pinner: PLA, 1976. 1st edn. 8vo. viii,96 pp. Num ills. Dw. *(Claude Cox)* **£15 [≈$23]**
- Modern Book Design. From William Morris to the Present Day. London: Faber, 1958. 1st edn. xii,116 pp. 32 plates, text ills. Dw. *(Claude Cox)* **£20 [≈$30]**
- Victorian Book Design and Colour Printing. London: Faber, 1972. 2nd edn, rvsd & enlgd. 4to. 16 cold plates, num b/w ills. Dw. *(Spelman)* **£60 [≈$90]**

McMullen, R.

- Degas; His Life, Times & Work. London: Secker & Warburg, 1984. Sm 4to. ix,517 pp. Ills. Orig cloth. Dw. *(Clevedon Books)* **£20 [≈$30]**

McMurtrie, Douglas C.

- Plantin's Index Characterum of 1567, Facsimile Reprint with an Introduction. New York: (Pynson Printers), 1924. One of 300 numbered. Sm 4to. Orig parchment-backed bds. Slipcase (cracked). *(Oak Knoll)* **$95 [≈£63]**

MacOrlan, Pierre

- Vlaminck. New York: 1958. 1st English edn. One of 2000. Folio. 5 orig lithos by Vlaminck, port, 34 cold plates. Orig stiff wraps. Slipcase. *(Robertshaw)* **£135 [≈$203]**

Macquoid, Percy

- A History of English Furniture. The Age of Mahogany. London & New York: 1906. 1st edn. Folio. 271 pp. Cold plates, ills. Lib stamp title verso. Orig cloth, sl worn. *(Francis Edwards)* **£50 [≈$75]**
- A History of English Furniture. London: 1925-28. 4 vols. Folio. Cold plates, ills. Orig pink cloth gilt. *(Traylen)* **£280 [≈$420]**

MacQuoid, Percy & Edwards, Ralph

- The Dictionary of English Furniture, from the Middle Ages to the late Georgian Period. London: 1953. 2nd edn, rvsd & enlgd. 3 vols. Folio. 43 cold plates, ca 3000 ills. Sm lib stamp on fly-leaves. Orig buckram gilt, t.e.g. Dws (worn). *(Traylen)* **£550 [≈$825]**

McRae, John Findlay

- Two Centuries of Typefounding; Annals of the Letter Foundry established by William Caslon in Chiswell Street, London, in the Year 1720. London: George W. Jones, 1920. 4to. xvi,93 pp. Fldg sheet, 66 ills. Orig wraps, edges chipped. *(Oak Knoll)* **$65 [≈£43]**

Macsporran, Fiona

- Edward Arthur Walton 1860 to 1922. Glasgow: Glasgow School of Art, Foulis Archive press, 1987. One of 300. 4to. 22 mtd cold plates, 70 b/w plates. Orig cloth. Dw. *(Cooper Hay)* **£55 [≈$83]**

Madan, Falconer

- The Daniel Press. Memorials of C.H.O. Daniel with a Bibliography of the Press 1845-1919. Oxford: Printed on the Daniel Press in the Bodleian Library, 1921. One of 500. 4to. [viii],(200) pp. 15 plates & facs. Minor foxing. Orig buckram backed bds, sl marked. *(Clark)* **£65 [≈$98]**

Maeterlinck, Maurice

- Hours of Gladness. Illustrated by E.J. Detmold. London: George Allen, [1912]. 1st edn. 4to. x,181 pp. 20 mtd cold plates. Orig cloth gilt, uncut, v sl soiled. *(Sotheran's)* **£168 [≈$252]**
- The Life of the Bee ... Translated by Alfred Suto. Illustrated by Edward J. Detmold. New York: Dodd, Mead, 1912. 4to. 265 pp. 13 mtd cold plates. Orig pict gilt cloth. *(Robert Frew)* **£75 [≈$113]**

Magee, David

- The Hundredth Book. A Bibliography of the Publications of the Book Club of California & A History of the Club. The Grabhorn Press for The Book Club of California: 1958. Folio. Orig linen backed dec bds. *(Black Sun)* **$300 [≈£200]**

Maillard, Elisa

- Old French Furniture and its Surroundings (1610-1815). New York: Scribner, 1925. 1st edn. Lge 8vo. xx,128 pp. 89 plates, 64 text figs. Orig cloth. *(Karmiole)* **$35 [≈£23]**

Mais, S.P.B.

- England of the Windmills. Drawings by F.L. Bussell. London: Dent, 1931. 1st edn. Sm 8vo. xxx,268 pp. 72 ills. Orig cloth gilt. *(Clevedon Books)* **£27 [≈$41]**

Major, Howard

- The Domestic Architecture of the Early American Republic. The Greek Revival. Philadelphia & London: 1926. 4to. 256 ills. Orig cloth gilt. Dw. *(First Folio)* **$140 [≈£93]**
- The Domestic Architecture of the Early American Republic. The Greek Revival. Phila: Lippincott, 1926. Sm 4to. xxii,237 pp. 256 ills. Orig cloth. Dw. *(Mendelsohn)* **$80 [≈£53]**

Malan, A.H.

- Famous Homes of Great Britain and their Stories, with More Famous Homes ... New York: Putnam, 1902. 2 vols. 4to. Frontises, ills. Orig cloth, sl rubbed, one inner hinge cracked. *(Bookpress)* **$110 [≈£73]**

Malcolm, Alexander

- A Treatise of Music, Speculative, Practical, and Historical. Edinburgh: for the author, 1721. 2nd issue, with new signature b containing lengthy corrigenda. 3 fldg plates (edges sl frayed). Lib stamps on title. Tear reprd. Rec half calf. *(Jarndyce)* **£280 [≈$420]**

Malcolm, J.P.

- An Historical Sketch of the Art of Caricaturing with Graphic Illustrations. London: Longmans, Hurst ..., 1813. 1st edn. 4to. vi,158,[2] pp. 21 plates. Three qtr calf. *(Bookpress)* **$550 [≈£367]**

Malcolmson, Anne

- The Song of Robin Hood. Designed and illustrated by Virginia Lee Burton. New York: Houghton Mifflin, 1947. 4to. Ills. Orig silver dec cloth, fine. *(Barbara Stone)* **£85 [≈$128]**

Male, Emile

- The Early Churches of Rome. London: Benn, 1960. 253 pp. 64 ills. Orig cloth. *(Quest Books)* **£32 [≈$48]**
- Religious Art in France XIII Century: A Study in Mediaeval Iconography ... London: Dent, 1913. 4to. 415 pp. Ills. Endpapers sl foxed. Orig cloth. Dw (worn). *(Monmouth)* **£60 [≈$90]**

Malory, Sir Thomas

- Sir Thomas Malory's Chronicles of King Arthur. Foreword by Kevin Crossley-Holland. London: Folio Society, 1982. 3 vols. Linocuts by Edward Bawden. Slipcase. *(Mermaid Books)* **£44 [≈$66]**

Malraux, Andre

- The Psychology of Art. New York: Pantheon, (1949-50). 3 vols. 4to. Num mtd cold plates, ills. Orig cloth. Dws (sl chipped). Slipcase (sl worn). *(Abacus)* **$125 [≈£83]**

Malton, James

- The Young Painter's Maulstick; being a Practical Treatise on Perspective ... London: V. Griffiths, 1800. 1st edn, title watermarked 1798. 4to. [4],ii,xiv,71 pp. 23 plates (1 fldg, 2 with overslips), 10 figs. 19th c half calf, some rubbing. *(Spelman)* **£320 [≈$480]**
- The Young Painter's Maulstick; being a Practical Treatise on Perspective ... London: the author, 1800. 1st edn. Sm folio. [iv], xiv, 71 pp. 23 plates. Some offsetting from plates. Contemp half calf. *(Bookpress)* **$200 [≈£133]**
- The Young Painter's Maulstick ... London: J. Barfield for Carpenter & Co., 1800. 1st edn, 2nd issue, title & dedic watermarked 1803. 4to. [4],ii, xiv,71 pp. 23 plates (1 fldg, 2 with overslips), 10 figs. Orig bds, uncut, rebacked, crnrs sl bumped. *(Spelman)* **£360 [≈$540]**

Maltzahn, Imre von

- Arthur Boyd. Etchings and Lithographs. London: Lund Humphries, 1971. 144 pp. 120 ills. Orig cloth. Dw. *(Leicester Art Books)* **£25 [≈$38]**

Manheim, Frank J.

- A Garland of Weights. Some Notes on Collecting Antique French Paperweights for Those who Don't. New York: Farrar, Straus, (1967). One of 1000. 45 cold plates. Orig cloth, sl soiled. Dw. *(Karmiole)* **$35 [≈£23]**

Mankowitz, Wolf

- Wedgwood. New York: Dutton, 1953. One of 1500 signed. 4to. xx,284 pp. 124 plates. Orig cloth gilt. Dw. *(Hollett)* **£85 [≈$128]**

Mann, A.J.

- The Salonika Front. Painted by William T. Wood. London: 1920. 1st edn. 8vo. 195 pp. Fldg map. Orig bndg. *(Zeno)* **£69.50 [≈$105]**

Mann, Sir James

- European Arms and Armour. Wallace Collection Catalogue. London: 1962. 2 vols. Cold frontis, 104 plates. Orig cloth gilt. *(Hollett)* **£35 [≈$53]**

Mann, Kathleen

- Peasant Costume in Europe. Book II. London: 1936. 4to. 109 pp. 8 cold plates, ills. *(Zeno)* **£45 [≈$68]**

- Peasant Costume in Europe. London: Adam & Charles Black, 1950. Sm 4to. 191 pp. 16 cold plates, 136 ills. Orig cloth gilt. Dw. *(Hollett)* **£35 [≈$53]**

Mann, Thomas
- Death in Venice. Illustrated with Wood-Engravings by Felix Hoffmann. New York: The Limited Editions Club, 1972. One of 1500 signed by Hoffmann. Sm 4to. Orig qtr leather. Slipcase. *(Oak Knoll)* **$65 [≈£43]**
- Nocturnes. New York: Equinox Cooperative Press, 1934. One of 1000 signed by the author. 7 b/w lithos by Lynd Ward. Orig dec cloth. Slipcase (sl worn & marked). *(Ulysses Bookshop)* **£350 [≈$525]**

Manners, Lady Victoria & Williamson, G.C.
- Angelica Kaufmann, R.A. Her Life and her Works. London: 1924. One of 1000. xiii,268 pp. Cold frontis, 9 cold & 69 b/w plates. Orig cloth, top edge of bds sl rubbed. *(Fine Art)* **£100 [≈$150]**

Manson, J.B.
- The Life and Work of Edgar Degas. London: The Studio, 1927. 1st edn. 4to. viii,54,[2] pp. 8 mtd cold & 74 b/w plates. Orig vellum backed bds, t.e.g., partly unopened, edges rubbed, sm split hd of spine. *(Claude Cox)* **£45 [≈$68]**

Manwaring, Elizabeth Wheeler
- Italian Landscape in Eighteenth Century England: a Study chiefly of the Influence of Claude Lorrain and Salvator Rosa on English Taste 1700-1800. New York: OUP, 1925. xi,243 pp. 9 plates. Orig cloth, sl worn. *(Fine Art)* **£50 [≈$75]**

Mapplethorpe, Robert & Fabre, Jan
- The Power of Theatrical Madness. London: (1986). 1st edn. Tall 8vo. Drawings by Fabre, photos by Mapplethorpe. No dw issued. *(Rob Warren)* **$95 [≈£63]**

Marchini, G.
- Italian Stained Glass Windows. London: Thames & Hudson, 1957. Lge 4to. 264 pp. Plates, ills. Orig cloth gilt. Dw. *(Fenning)* **£45 [≈$68]**

Mardersteig, Giovanni
- Officina Bodoni. The Work of a Hand Press. Verona: Officina Bodoni, 1980. One of 500 for America. 4to. lxi,292 pp. Orig cloth. Cardboard slipcase. *(Oak Knoll)* **$225 [≈£150]**
- On G.B. Bodoni's Type Faces. Verona: (Officina Bodoni), 1968. One of 200. Tall 8vo. 34 pp. Orig stiff paper wraps. *(Oak Knoll)* **$225 [≈£150]**

Margolin, Victor
- American Poster Renaissance. New Jersey: Castle Books, 1975. 4to. 224 pp. 250 ills. Orig cloth. Dw. *(Rona Schneider)* **$60 [≈£40]**

Marin, John
- The Selected Writings. Edited by Dorothy Norman. New York: Pellegrini & Cudahy, (1949). One of 1500. 8vo. 241 pp. Ills. Orig cloth. Dw. *(Abacus)* **$50 [≈£33]**

Markham, Christopher A.
- Pewter Marks and Old Pewter Ware. Domestic and Ecclesiastical ... London: Reeves & Turner, 1909. 1st edn. Tall 8vo. xv,316 pp. Ills. Orig cloth gilt, t.e.g., trifle rubbed & marked. *(Hollett)* **£48 [≈$72]**

Markham, V.R.
- Paxton and the Bachelor Duke. London: Hodder & Stoughton, 1935. 1st edn. 8vo. xii, 350 pp. 14 plates. Orig cloth gilt, t.e.g., new endpapers. *(Clevedon Books)* **£38 [≈$57]**

Marlowe, Christopher
- Hero and Leander ... Stourton Press: 1934. One of 200. 8vo. Orig qtr cloth. *(Blackwell's)* **£50 [≈$75]**

Marquand, Allan
- Robbia Heraldry. Princeton: UP, 1919. xviii, 310 pp. 277 ills. Orig bds, t.e.g. *(Leicester Art Books)* **£40 [≈$60]**

Marriage, Margaret & Ernest
- The Sculptures of Chartres Cathedral. Cambridge: Up, 1909. xv,270 pp. 120 plates. Orig cloth gilt, spine sl faded. *(Hollett)* **£25 [≈$38]**

Marrilier, H.C.
- English Tapestries of the Eighteenth Century: a Handbook to the Post-Mortlake Productions of English Weavers. London: Medici Society, 1930. xxiii,128 pp. 48 plates. B'plate. Orig cloth, front hinge sl weak. *(Fine Art)* **£30 [≈$45]**

Marriott, Charles
- Laura Knight. A Book of Drawings. London: John Lane; The Bodley Head, 1923. One of 500 signed by the artist. [72] pp. Frontis, 20 plates. Orig cloth backed bds, extrs rubbed & darkened. *(Bookworks)* **£130 [≈$195]**

Marryat, Frederick, Captain

- Jacob Faithful. Illustrated by R.W. Buss. London: Constable, 1928. One of 750. 2 vols. Med 8vo. 12 cold plates. Orig cloth, spines sl bumped. *(Stella Books)* **£30 [≈$45]**

Marryat, Joseph

- Collections towards a History of Pottery and Porcelain, in the 15th [to] 18th Centuries ... London: Murray, 1850. 1st edn. xxiii,381 pp. 11 cold plates. Mod cloth. *(Hollett)* **£75 [≈$113]**

Marshall, G.

- A View of the Silver Coin and Coinage of Great Britain from the year 1662 to 1837 ... London: 1838. Oblong 8vo. xxvii,160 pp. Traces of label removal. Cloth, leather label, stained. *(Whitehart)* **£35 [≈$53]**

Marshall, John

- Anatomy for Artists. London: 1883. 2nd edn. 436 pp. 199 ills. Occas pencil notes. Lib b'plate. Orig bndg. *(Fye)* **$150 [≈£100]**

Marston, E.

- Sketches of Some Booksellers of the Time of Dr. Samuel Johnson. London: Sampson Low, 1902. 1st edn. 12mo. xviii,127,[8] pp. 9 ports. Orig parchment-backed cloth, t.e.g. *(Oak Knoll)* **$65 [≈£43]**

Marston, John

- Metamorphosis of Pigmalion's Image. Golden Cockerel Press: 1926. One of 325. W'engvs by Rene Ben Sussan. Orig qtr buckram, spine sl darkened. *(Waddington)* **£70 [≈$105]**

Martin, A.R.

- Franciscan Architecture in England. British Society of Franciscan Studies: 1937. Only edn. xxi,306,[i] pp. 10 fldg plans, 28 plates, 19 text figs. Orig buckram gilt, spine spotted. *(Hollett)* **£75 [≈$113]**

Martin, David

- The Glasgow School of Painting. London: Geo. Bell, 1897. 8vo. xiii,72,[2] pp. Frontis, 57 b/w plates. Prelims sl foxed. Orig dec cloth gilt, extrs rubbed, front inner hinge cracked. *(Cooper Hay)* **£65 [≈$98]**

Martindale, Percy H.

- Engraving, Old and Modern. London: Heath Cranton, 1928. 1st edn. Lge 8vo. xiv,208 pp. Frontis, 6 plates, 8 text figs. Orig cloth. *(Karmiole)* **$30 [≈£20]**

Martinet, J. (editor)

- Hot Printing: Catalogue of the 'Druksel' Prints and Interim Catalogues of General Printed Matter - Lithographs, Etchings, Woodcuts, Typewriter Compositions and Paintings by Hendrik Nicolas Werkman. Amsterdam: 1963. 4to. 218 pp. Num ills. Orig wraps. *(Abacus)* **$175 [≈£117]**

Marx, Claude Roger

- Rembrandt. New York: Universe Books, 1960. 368 pp. 304 ills. Orig cloth. *(Leicester Art Books)* **£25 [≈$38]**

Marzials, Theo

- Pan Pipes. A Book of Old Songs. Illustrated by Walter Crane. Printed by Edmund Evans. London: Routledge, 1883. Inscrptn Christmas 1882. Orig pict bds, crnrs chipped & worn. *(Old Cathay)* **£75 [≈$113]**

Marzio, Peter C.

- Chromolithography 1840-1900; The Democratic Art. Boston: Godine, 1979. 1st edn. 4to. xvi,657 pp. 128 plates, num text ills. Orig cloth. Dw (rubbed). *(Oak Knoll)* **$75 [≈£50]**

Masefield, John

- The Country Scene. London: Collins, 1937. One of 50 signed by the author and the artist, Edward Seago. 4to. 98 pp. 42 cold plates. Orig qtr mor gilt, spine faded. *(Hollett)* **£450 [≈$675]**

Masheck, Joseph

- Historical Present: Essays of the 1970s. Ann Arbor, UMI Press, 1984. 4to. 294 pp. Orig cloth. Dw. *(Ars Libri)* **$125 [≈£83]**

Maskell, Alfred

- Ivories. London: Methuen, Connoisseur's Library, 1905. 1st edn. Lge thick 8vo. xiii,443 pp. 88 plates. Orig cloth gilt, sl worn & marked. *(Hollett)* **£75 [≈$113]**

Mason, George C.

- The Old House Altered. New York: Putnam, 1878. 1st edn. 8vo. x,179 pp. 37 text ills. Orig cloth, sl worn. *(Bookpress)* **$495 [≈£330]**

Mason, George Henry

- The Costume of China Illustrated by Sixty Engravings: with Explanations in English and French. London: Miller, 1800. Folio. 60 cold plates. Contemp leather, rebacked. *(McBlain)* **$1,250 [≈£833]**
- The Punishments of China. Illustrated by

Twenty-Two Engravings with Explanations in English and French. London: Bulmer, 1804. Folio. [73] pp. Frontis, 22 cold plates. Contemp leather, scuffed, jnts tender. *(McBlain)* **$800 [≈£533]**

Mason, Lauris

- The Lithographs of George Bellows. Milwood: 1977. 264 pp. 223 ills. Orig cloth gilt. *(Leicester Art Books)* **£45 [≈$68]**

Masse, H.J.L.J.

- Pewter Plate. A Historical & Descriptive Handbook. London: George Bell & Sons, 1904. Sm 4to. xxi,299 pp. Ills. Lib stamps on title. Orig cloth gilt, sl worn. *(Hollett)* **£30 [≈$45]**

Masson, G.

- Italian Villas and Palaces. London: Thames & Hudson, (1959). Lge 4to. 244 pp. Ills. Orig cloth. Dw. *(Bow Windows)* **£85 [≈$128]**

Masson, Sir Irvine

- The Mainz and Canon Missae, 1457-59. London: Bibl Soc, 1954. Lge folio. 6 fldg plates, 8 tables on 6 fldg sheets. Orig linen backed bds. *(Traylen)* **£28 [≈$42]**

Masters, E.L. & Houston, Jean

- Psychedelic Art. New York: Grove Press, 1968. 1st edn. Ills. Dw (sl torn, minor edgewear). *(The Associates)* **$125 [≈£83]**

Mathers, E. Powys

- Procreant Hymn. Golden Cockerel Press: 1926. One of 175 (of 200). 32 pp. 5 copper engvs by Eric Gill. Orig buckram, t.e.g. Dw (defective but essentially complete). *(Bookworks)* **£630 [≈$945]**
- Red Wise. Golden Cockerel Press: 1926. One of 500. 112 pp. 8 w'engvs by Robert Gibbings. Orig qtr buckram, upper bd faintly marked. *(Bookworks)* **£80 [≈$120]**

Mathieu, Pierre-Louis

- Gustave Moreau. Catalogue Raisonne of the Finished Paintings, Watercolours and Drawings. Oxford: Phaidon, 1977. 400 pp. 486 ills. Orig cloth. *(Leicester Art Books)* **£60 [≈$90]**

Matisse, Henri

- Catalogue of an Exhibition of Pictures by Henry Matisse and Sculpture by Maillol. London: Ernest Brown & Phillips, 1919. 12mo. 10 pp. Errata slip. Port frontis. Orig ptd wraps. *(Spelman)* **£90 [≈$135]**

Matrix

- Matrix Nine. (Manor Farm: The Whittington Press, 1989). One of 820 (of 925). Sm 4to. [viii], 200,[2] pp. Orig wraps. *(Oak Knoll)* **$200 [≈£133]**

Matthews, T.

- The Biography of John Gibson, R.A., Sculptor, Rome. London: 1911. xiv,255 pp. 27 plates inc cold frontis. Orig cloth gilt, t.e.g., front hinge sl weak. *(Fine Art)* **£30 [≈$45]**

Mattingly, Harold

- The Coins of the Roman Empire in the British Museum. Augustus to Commodus. London: 1965-68. 5 vols. Thick 8vo. 360 plates. Orig cloth. Dws. *(Traylen)* **£150 [≈$225]**

Matusow, Marshall

- The Art Collector's Almanac. No. 1. Introduction by Brian O'Doherty. New York: Privately Printed, 1965. Lge 4to. 672 pp. Num ills. Orig cloth, sl shaken. *(Ars Libri)* **$40 [≈£27]**

Maupassant, Guy de

- Bel-Ami. Illustrations by Bernard Lamotte. New York: The Limited Editions Club, 1968. One of 1500 signed by Lamotte. Sm 4to. Orig cloth. Slipcase. *(Oak Knoll)* **$45 [≈£30]**
- The Tales of Guy de Maupassant, 1850-1893. The Illustrations from Water-Colours by Gunter Bohmer. New York: The Limited Editions Club, 1963. One of 1500 signed by Bohmer. Thick 8vo. Orig cloth (spine yellowed). Slipcase. *(Oak Knoll)* **$50 [≈£33]**

Maxwell, Donald

- The Enchanted Road. London: Methuen, 1927. 1st edn. 99 ills by Maxwell. Orig cloth backed bds, spine sl darkened. *(Old Cathay)* **£29 [≈$44]**
- Excursions in Colour. London: Cassell, 1927. 1st edn. Sm 4to. xv,118 pp. Cold ills. Orig cloth gilt, spine sl darkened & rubbed. *(Hollett)* **£25 [≈$38]**
- The Landscape of Thomas Hardy. London: Cassell, 1928. 1st edn. 13 cold plates, b/w ills, pict endpapers. Orig bndg. *(Old Cathay)* **£39 [≈$59]**
- The Landscape of Thomas Hardy. London: Cassell, 1928. 1st edn. Sm 4to. xii,80 pp. 12 cold plates, text ills, endpaper maps. Orig cloth, trifle faded. *(Hollett)* **£30 [≈$45]**
- The New Lights o' London. London:

Herbert Jenkins, 1926. 1st edn. Lge 8vo. xvi,158 pp. Cold ills. Orig cloth gilt, rather worn. *(Hollett)* **£30 [≈$45]**

- Unknown Essex. London: John Lane; The Bodley Head, 1925. 1st edn. Lge 8vo. xiii,204 pp. 30 plates, num text ills. Orig cloth gilt, spine ends trifle rubbed. *(Hollett)* **£30 [≈$45]**
- Wembley in Colour. London: Longmans, Green, 1924. 1st edn. 4to. 112 pp. Ills. Orig cloth backed bds. Dw (few edge chips & tears). *(Hollett)* **£35 [≈$53]**

Maxwell, Sir Herbert

- Scottish Gardens ... London: Arnold, 1908. 1st edn. Large Paper. 8vo. x,252 pp. 32 cold plates. Orig dec cloth gilt, t.e.g., sm tear front jnt, crnrs sl bumped. *(Clevedon Books)* **£45 [≈$68]**

Maxwell, Stuart & Hutchison, Robin

- Scottish Costume 1550-1850. London: Adam & Charles Black, 1958. Lge 8vo. viii,184 pp. 4 cold plates, 24 ills. Orig cloth gilt. Dw. *(Hollett)* **£25 [≈$38]**

May, W.E. & Annis, P.G.W.

- Swords for Sea Service. National Maritime Museum, Greenwich. London: HMSO, 1970. 2 vols. 4to. 5 cold, 140 plain plates, 32 figs. Orig cloth gilt. Dws. *(Hollett)* **£120 [≈$180]**

Mayer, August L.

- Old Spain (Architecture and Applied Arts in Old Spain). New York: 1921. 176 pp. 310 ills. Orig cloth, soiled, inner hinges cracked. *(John K. King)* **$60 [≈£40]**

Mayer, Dorothy Moulton

- Angelica Kauffmann R.A., 1741-1807. London: 1972. 191 pp. 14 cold & 64 b/w plates. Orig cloth. Dw. *(Fine Art)* **£20 [≈$30]**

Mayeux, Henri

- A Manual of Decorative Composition for Designers, Decorators, Architects, and Industrial Artists. Translated by J. Gonino. London: Virtue, 1889. 1st edn in English. 8vo. ix,310 pp. 267 ills. Orig cloth gilt. *(Fenning)* **£48.50 [≈$74]**

Mayne, William

- The Mouldy. Illustrated by Nicola Bayley. London: Cape, 1983. 1st edn. Num cold ills. Orig laminated illust bds. *(Words Etcetera)* **£25 [≈$38]**
- The Patchwork Cat. Illustrated by Nicola Bayley. London: Cape, 1981. 1st edn. Num cold ills. Orig laminated illust bds. *(Words Etcetera)* **£25 [≈$38]**

Mayo, John Horsley

- Medals and Decorations of the British Army and Navy. London: Constable, 1897. 2 vols. Lge 8vo. lxxxviii,278; 279-616 pp. 55 plates (many cold & tinted). Occas spotting. Orig cloth gilt, sl fingered, spines faded & trifle frayed at ends. *(Hollett)* **£140 [≈$210]**

Mayor, A. Hyatt

- Artists & Anatomists. New York: 1984. 1st edn. 4to. 132 pp. Ills. Dw. *(Fye)* **$40 [≈£27]**
- The Bibiena Family. New York: H. Bittner, 1945. One of 1000. Tall 4to. 37,[3] pp. 53 plates. Orig buckram. *(Karmiole)* **$100 [≈£67]**
- Giovanni Battista Piranesi. New York: Bittner, 1952. 1st edn. 4to. [4],42 pp. 138 plates. Orig cloth gilt. Dw. *(Karmiole)* **$45 [≈£30]**
- Giovanni Battista Piranesi. New York: H. Bittner, 1952. 1st edn. 4to. [vi],41,[1] pp. Frontis, 138 plates. Orig cloth. Dw (sl rubbed, spine extrs chipped). *(Bookpress)* **$75 [≈£50]**
- Prints & People. New York: Metropolitan Museum of Art, 1971. 4to. 752 ills. 1st 6 pp creased. Orig cloth. Dw. *(Rona Schneider)* **$50 [≈£33]**

Mayor, S.

- Collecting Fans. Christies South Kensington Collectors Series. London: Studio Vista, 1980. 1st edn. Lge 8vo. 120 pp. Ills. Orig cloth gilt. Dw. *(Hollett)* **£30 [≈$45]**

Meadows, Lindon (pseudonym of Charles Butler Greatrex

- Dame Perkins and her Grey Mare; or, a Mount for Market. With Coloured Illustrations by Phiz. London: Sampson Low, 1866. 1st edn. 4to. 48 pp. 8 cold ills. Orig cloth gilt, a.e.g. *(Claude Cox)* **£30 [≈$45]**

Medley, Margaret

- T'Ang Pottery and Porcelain. London: Faber, 1981. 151 pp. Map, 18 cold plates. Orig cloth gilt. Dw. *(Hollett)* **£30 [≈$45]**

Meier-Graefe, Julius

- Modern Art: being a Contribution to a New System of Aesthetics. London: Heinemann, 1908. 2 vols. 237 plates, 58 text ills. Orig cloth, t.e.g., some wear. *(Fine Art)* **£45 [≈$68]**

Meinertzhagen, Frederick

- The Art of the Netsuke Carver. London: [ca 1956]. 1st edn. 4to. viii,80 pp. Ills. Dw (worn). *(McBlain)* **$85 [≈£57]**

Meirion-Jones, G.I.

- The Vernacular Architecture of Britanny. Edinburgh: Donald, 1982. 4to. 407 pp. 240 ills. Dw. *(Castle Bookshop)* **£28 [≈$42]**

Meiss, Millard

- The Great Age of Fresco: Discoveries, Recoveries and Survivals. New York: Braziller, 1970. 4to. 251 pp. 118 cold plates, 8 b/w ills. Orig cloth. Dw. *(Abacus)* **$45 [≈£30]**

Mellen, Peter

- Jean Clouet. Complete Edition of the Drawings Miniatures and Paintings. London: Phaidon, 1971. 1st edn. 4to. 262 pp. Cold port frontis, 192 plates (3 cold). Lib b'plate. Dw (sl chipped, spine sl faded). *(Francis Edwards)* **£60 [≈$90]**
- Jean Clouet. London: Phaidon, 1971. 8,262 pp. 193 ills. Orig cloth. Dw. *(Leicester Art Books)* **£110 [≈$165]**

Melville, Herman

- Benito Cereno. Illustrated by E. McKnight Kauffer. London: Nonesuch Press, 1926. One of 1650. Orig cloth, gilt spine. Dw (sl chipped). *(Hermitage)* **$150 [≈£100]**
- Billy Budd. Benito Cereno. Paintings by Robert Shore. New York: The Limited Editions Club, 1965. One of 1500 signed by Shore. Sm 4to. Orig cloth. Slipcase. *(Oak Knoll)* **$55 [≈£37]**
- Moby Dick or the Whale. Paintings by LeRoy Neiman. Preface by Jacques-Yves Cousteau. New York: 1975. One of 1500. Preface sgnd by Cousteau. Folio. xvi,274 pp. Frontis sgnd by Neimann, 12 cold plates. Orig mor gilt. Slipcase. *(Karmiole)* **$1,000 [≈£667]**

Melville, Robert

- Graham Sutherland. London: Ambassador Editions, 1950. Frontis, 69 plates, text ills. Orig cloth. Dw. *(Fine Art)* **£48 [≈$72]**
- Henry Moore. Sculpture and Drawings 1921-1969. London: Thames & Hudson, 1970. 368 pp. 846 ills. Orig cloth., Dw. *(Leicester Art Books)* **£60 [≈$90]**

Memoirs ...

- Memoirs of the Celebrated Persons composing the Kit-Kat Club ... see Caulfield, James

Mendelsohn, Erich

- Amerika. Berlin: Rudolf Mosse, 1926. 1st edn. Sm folio. ix,[ii],82,[1] pp. 77 photo plates. Orig cloth & bds, sl chipped & rubbed, edges worn. *(Bookpress)* **$325 [≈£217]**

Mendelssohn, Joanna

- The Life and Works of Sydney Long. Copperfield Art Collection: 1979. 284 pp. 38 cold plates, 150 ills. Orig rexine cvrd bds. Dw. *(Leicester Art Books)* **£80 [≈$120]**

Mercer, Eric

- English Art 1553-1625. OUP: 1962. 287 pp. 96 plates, 11 text ills. Orig cloth. Dw. *(Fine Art)* **£30 [≈$45]**

Merchant, W. Moelwyn

- Shakespeare and the Artist. OUP: 1959. 4to. xxx,254 pp. 88 plates, 56 figs. Few lib marks. Dw (reprd). *(Francis Edwards)* **£48 [≈$72]**

Meredith, George

- Jump to Glory Jane. Edited and arranged by Harry Quilter. London: Swan, Sonnenschein, 1892. One of 1000. 44 ills by Laurence Housman. Orig dec bds, sl faded, spine ends sl bumped. *(First Folio)* **$2202 [≈£147]**
- The Shaving of Shagpat. Illustrations by Honore Guilbeau. New York: The Limited Editions Club, 1955. One of 1500 signed by Guilbeau. 8vo. Orig half leather (chip hd of spine). Slipcase. *(Oak Knoll)* **$65 [≈£43]**

Merne, John G.

- A Handbook of Celtic Ornament ... Dublin: The Educational Co., (1930). 1st edn. 4to. 108 pp. Over 700 ills. Orig cloth backed bds. Dw (worn). *(Fenning)* **£38.50 [≈$59]**

Meryman, Richard

- Andrew Wyeth. Boston: Houghton, Mifflin 1968. Oblong folio. 174 pp. Num plates. Orig cloth. Dw. *(Abacus)* **$225 [≈£150]**

Messenger, M.

- Pottery and Tiles of the Severn Valley. London: 1979. 4to. 317 pp. Plates. Orig cloth. Dw. *(Castle Bookshop)* **£28 [≈$42]**

Messer, Thomas M.

- The Emergent Decade. Latin American Painters and Painting in the 1960s ... BY: 1966. Sm folio. 172 pp. Num ills. Orig cloth. *(Ars Libri)* **$45 [≈£30]**

Metcalf, Priscilla

- James Knowles, Victorian Editor and Architect. Oxford: Clarendon Press 1980. 1st edn. 8vo. xvi,382 pp. Frontis, 16 plates. Orig cloth. Dw (minor rubbing). *(Bookpress)* **$65 [≈£43]**

Metro ...

- Metro. An International Review of Contemporary Art. Milan & Venice: 1960-65. Vols 1-9. Folio. Orig wraps. *(Ars Libri)* **$850 [≈£567]**

Metz, Peter

- The Golden Gospels of Echternach. Codex Aureus Epternacensis. New York: 1957. Lge 4to. 96 pp. 109 plates (13 cold). Orig cloth. Dw. Slipcase. *(Washton)* **$95 [≈£63]**

Meyer, Franz

- Marc Chagall. New York: Abrams, 1964. 776 pp. 615 ills (53 mtd cold), text ills. Orig cloth. *(Leicester Art Books)* **£145 [≈$218]**
- Marc Chagall. New York: Abrams, n.d. Stout 4to. 775 pp. Over 1250 ills (53 mtd cold). Orig cloth. Dw. *(Abacus)* **$125 [≈£83]**
- Marc Chagall. New York: Abrams, [1961]. Sm stout folio. 775,[1] pp. Num ills. Orig cloth. *(Ars Libri)* **$200 [≈£133]**
- Marc Chagall: Life and Work. New York: Abrams, [ca 1964]. 775 pp. Over 1250 ills inc 53 mtd cold plates. Dw. *(Hermitage)* **$175 [≈£117]**

Meyer, Susan E.

- James Montgomery Flagg. New York: Watson-Guptil, 1974. Lge 4to. 207,[1] pp. 245 ills. Orig cloth. Dw. *(Ars Libri)* **$50 [≈£33]**

Meynell, Francis & Simon, Herbert

- Fleuron Anthology. London: 1973. 1st edn. 4to. Ills. Orig bndg. Dw (sm tear ft of spine). *(Words Etcetera)* **£45 [≈$68]**

Meyrick, Sir Samuel Rush

- A Critical Enquiry into Ancient Armour ... London: Robert Jennings, 1824. 1st edn. 3 vols. Folio. 80 cold plates, 27 hand cold initial letters. Contemp qtr mor, uncut. *(Traylen)* **£1,250 [≈$1,875]**

Meyrick, Sir Samuel Rush & Skelton, Joseph

- Engraved Illustrations of Antient Armour. From the Collection of Goodrich Court, Herefordshire. London: Bohn, 1854. 2 vols. Sm folio. 150 plates. Occas foxing. Contemp half mor gilt, a.e.g., rubbed & scraped. *(Hollett)* **£275 [≈$413]**

Michalowski, Kazimierz

- Art of Ancient Egypt. New York: Abrams, (1968). 1st edn. 4to. 600 pp. Num ills. Orig cloth. Dw. Slipcase. *(J &J House)* **$200 [≈£133]**

Michel, Emile

- Rembrandt: His Life, His Work, and His Times. London: Heinemann, 1903. 3rd edn. Stout 4to. 484 pp. 326 ills. Orig cloth. *(Abacus)* **$45 [≈£30]**
- Rubens His Life, His Work, and His Time. Translated by Elizabeth Lee. London: Heinemann, 1899. 2 vols. 4to. 40 cold plates, 40 gravures, 272 text ills. Occas sl spotting. Orig dec cloth gilt, sl worn & faded. *(Wilkinson)* **£25 [≈$38]**

Michel, Walter

- Wyndham Lewis, Paintings and Drawings. Toronto: McClelland & Stewart, 1971. 455 pp. 781 ills. Orig cloth. Dw. *(Leicester Art Books)* **£150 [≈$225]**

Michener, James A.

- The Floating World. New York: Random House, [ca 1954]. 1st edn. 8vo. xii,403 pp. Ills. Dw (worn). *(McBlain)* **$65 [≈£43]**
- Japanese Prints from the Early Masters to the Modern. Rutland: Tuttle, (1959). 4to. 287 pp. 257 ills (55 cold). Orig cloth. Dw. Slipcase. *(Abacus)* **$85 [≈£57]**

Middlemass, Keith

- Antique Coloured Glass. London: Ferndale Editions, 1979. 4to. 120 pp. Ills. Orig cloth gilt. Dw. *(Hollett)* **£20 [≈$30]**
- Antigua Coloured Glass. Ferndale: 1971. 120 pp. Cold plates. Dw. *(Paul Brown)* **£18 [≈$27]**

Middleton, C.

- Designs for Gates and Rails suitable to Parks, Pleasure Grounds, Balconys &c., also some Designs for Trellis Work on 27 Plates. London: J. Taylor, [ca 1799]. 8vo. Engvd title, 26 plates. Marg browning, sl foxing. Rec qtr mor. *(Spelman)* **£500 [≈$750]**

Middleton, G.A.T.

- The Drainage of Town and Country Houses. A Practical Account of Modern Sanitary Arrangements & Fittings. London: Batsford, 1903. 1st edn. vi,150,18 pp. 6 plates, 87 diags. Orig cloth gilt. *(Hollett)* **£25 [≈$38]**

Migeon, G.

- In Japan: Pilgrimages to the Shrines of Art. Translated from the French ... London: 1908. 1st edn in English. 8vo. xxii,207,[1] pp. 60 ills. Sl foxing. Orig cloth. *(Bow Windows)* **£55 [≈$83]**

Millais, John Guille

- The Life & Letters of Sir John Everett Millais. London: Methuen, 1899. One of 360. 2 vols. 8vo. 24 plates, 9 facs letters, 310 ills. Orig buckram gilt, uncut, spines faded. *(Claude Cox)* **£50 [≈$75]**
- The Life and Letters of Sir John Everett Millais. London: Methuen, 1899. 1st edn. 2 vols. 8vo. 319 ills. Orig cloth gilt, t.e.g. *(Jarndyce)* **£120 [≈$180]**
- The Life and Letters of Sir John Everett Millais. London: Methuen, 1899. 2 vols. 342 ills. Orig cloth, spines sl worn. *(Leicester Art Books)* **£55 [≈$83]**

Millar, Oliver

- The Tudor, Stuart and Early Georgian Pictures in the Collection of Her Majesty the Queen. London: Phaidon, 1963. 2 vols (text & plates). Orig cloth. Dw. Slipcase. *(Fine Art)* **£70 [≈$105]**
- The Tudor, Stuart and Early Georgian Pictures in the Collection of Her Majesty the Queen. London: Phaidon, 1963. 2 vols (text & plates). Orig cloth. Dws (torn). *(Fine Art)* **£60 [≈$90]**

Miller, Fred

- The Training of a Craftsman. London: Virtue, 1901. 1st edn. 12mo. x,249 pp. Orig cloth, sl worn. *(Bookpress)* **$185 [≈£123]**

Miller, Liam

- Dolmen XXV. An Illustrated Bibliography of the Dolmen Press 1951-1976. Dublin: Dolmen Editions, 1976. 1st edn. Port frontis, ills. Orig buckram gilt, ft of spine & one crnr bumped. Dw (v sl creased, spine sl faded). *(Ulysses Bookshop)* **£110 [≈$165]**
- Dolmen XXV. An Illustrated Bibliography of the Dolmen Press 1951-1976. Dolmen Editions: 1976. One of 650 for sale. Sm 4to. 95,[1] pp. Ills. Orig cloth. Dw (sl marked). *(Cooper Hay)* **£45 [≈$68]**

Miller, Patrick

- Ana the Runner. Golden Cockerel Press: 1937. 1st edn. 108 pp. 6 w'engvs by Clifford Webb. B'plate. Orig card cvrs, backstrip worn. *(Waddington)* **£20 [≈$30]**

Miller, Thomas

- Common Wayside Flowers. Illustrated by Birket Foster. London: Routledge, 1863. 1st edn. 24 chromolithos. Prelims foxed. Orig bndg, a.e.g. *(Old Cathay)* **£79 [≈$119]**

Millett, Robert W.

- The Vultures and the Phoenix: Paintings of D.H. Lawrence. USA: 1983. 167 pp. 16 cold plates, 20 ills. Orig cloth. Dw. *(Fine Art)* **£24 [≈$36]**

Milton, John

- Areopagitica, A Speech of Mr. John Milton for the Liberty of Unlicensed Printing ... Cambridge: Rampant Lions Press for Deighton, Bell, 1973. One of 100 (of 500). Mor. Slipcase. *(Meyer Boswell)* **$450 [≈£300]**
- Areopagitica. A Speech of Mr. John Milton for The Liberty of Unlicensed Printing. London: The Rampant Lions Press, 1973. One of 100 deluxe. Lge 4to. Orig morocco. Slipcase. *(Black Sun)* **$400 [≈£267]**
- A Brief History of Moscovia and of other less-known Countries lying eastwards of Russia ... Illustrations by A. Brodovitch. The Blackamore Press: 1929. One of 600. 120 pp. Frontis, 6 ills. Orig buckram, spotted, t.e.g. Dw (defective). *(Claude Cox)* **£45 [≈$68]**
- L'Allegro and Il Penseroso. London: Art-Union of London, 1848. 4to. 30 ills. Occas v sl spotting of text. Sl marg waterstain at end. Mor gilt. *(Mermaid Books)* **£30 [≈$45]**
- L'Allegro. With the Paintings by William Blake ... [bound dos-a-dos with] Il Penseroso. New York: The Limited Editions Club, 1954. One of 1500 (of 1780). Tall 8vo. Orig cloth. Slipcase (soiled). *(Oak Knoll)* **$55 [≈£37]**
- The Masque of Comus. Illustrated with Water-Colors by Edmund Dulac. New York: The Limited Editions Club, 1954. One of 1500 numbered, as issued. Sm 4to. Orig parchment -backed mrbld bds (some soiling to spine). Slipcase (worn). Not signed by Dulac as he died shortly after finishing the illustrations. *(Oak Knoll)* **$55 [≈£37]**
- Ode on the Morning of Christ's Nativity. (Oxford: H. Daniel, Christmas, 1894). One of 200. Sm 4to. Orig wraps, overlapping edges sl frayed. Prospectus inserted. *(Waterfield's)* **£215 [≈$323]**
- The Paradise Lost. With Illustrations by John Martin. London: Charles Tilt, 1838. Sm folio. 24 plates. Early Victorian calf gilt, a.e.g. *(Traylen)* **£620 [≈$930]**
- The Paradise Lost of Milton, with

Illustrations, Designed and Engraved by John Martin. London: Henry Washbourne, 1850. Lge 8vo. 373 pp. 24 mezzotints. Contemp black mor gilt, a.e.g., extrs sl rubbed. *(Robert Frew)* **£500 [≈$750]**
- Paradise Regained. Decorated by Thomas Lowinsky. London: The Fleuron, 1924. One of 350. Sq 8vo. [8],80 pp. 3 pocket plates, ills. Orig cloth & bds gilt. *(Karmiole)* **$100 [≈£67]**
- Poems in English. With Illustrations by William Blake. Paradise Lost. London: Nonesuch Press, 1926. One of 1450. Lge 8vo. [12],352,[8] pp. 15 plates. Orig qtr parchment. Cloth slipcase. *(Karmiole)* **$175 [≈£117]**

Mindlin, Henrique E.
- Modern Architecture in Brazil. New York: Reinhold, (1956). 1st edn in English. 4to. xiii,[i],256 pp. Num ills. Orig cloth. Dw (sl used). *(Bookpress)* **$65 [≈£43]**

Minghetti, Marco
- The Masters of Raffaello. London: Field & Tuer, 1882. One of 100. 8vo. 77,[2] pp. Name. Half leather. *(Bookpress)* **$100 [≈£67]**

Minkoff, George Robert
- A Bibliography of The Black Sun Press. With an Introduction by Caresse Crosby. Great Neck, New York: Minkoff, 1970. One of 1250. 4to. 72 pp. Frontis. Orig cloth gilt. *(Karmiole)* **$35 [≈£23]**

Minton, John
- London. A Brief Account of its Many Beautiful and Interesting Sights. London: The British Travel and Holidays Association, [ca 1949]. 1st edn. 80 pp. 10 ills by Minton, photo ills. Orig wraps. *(Bookworks)* **£75 [≈$113]**

Miro, Joan
- Miro: Paintings, Gouaches, Sobreteixims, Sculpture, Etchings. New York: Pierre Matisse Gallery, 1973. 4to. Plates. Orig stiff wraps. Orig litho dw. *(Abacus)* **$100 [≈£67]**

Mitchell, C.H.
- The Illustrated Books of the Nanga, Maruyama, Shijo and Other Related Schools of Japan. A Biobibliography ... LA: Dawson's Book Shop, 1972. 4to. 624 pp. 30 ills. Orig cloth. *(Karmiole)* **$250 [≈£167]**

Mitchell, Peter
- European Flower Painters. London: A. & C. Black, 1973. 272 pp. 388 ills. Orig cloth. *(Fine Art)* **£30 [≈$45]**

Mitford, Mary Russell
- Our Village. With an Introduction by Anne Thackeray Ritchie. Illustrated by Hugh Thomson. London: Macmillan, 1910. 1st edn thus. 16 cold plates by Alfred Fawlings, 100 b/w ills by Hugh Thomson. Orig bndg. *(Old Cathay)* **£59 [≈$89]**

Mizuno, Seiichi
- Bronzes and Jades of Ancient China. Tokyo: The Nihon Keizai, 1959. 1st edn. 4to. [iv], 35, [2],101 pp. 168 plates. Orig cloth. Slipcase. Box. *(Bookpress)* **$250 [≈£167]**

Mody, N.H.N.
- Japanese Clocks. Rutland: Charles E. Tuttle, (1967). 1st edn. 135 plates. Orig cloth, one crnr bumped. Price-clipped dw. *(Hermitage)* **$85 [≈£57]**

Moholy-Nagy, Sibyl
- Laszlo Moholy-Nagy. A Biography. New York: Harper, 1950. 1st edn. 81 ills (4 cold). Inscrptn. Dw (sm piece missing hd of back panel). *(Clearwater)* **£80 [≈$120]**
- Moholy-Nagy, Experiment in Totality. New York: Harper, (1950). 1st edn. 8vo. 253 pp. 81 ills (4 cold). Orig cloth. Dw (worn). Author's presentation copy. *(Bookpress)* **$50 [≈£33]**

Molesworth, H.D.
- Sculpture in England: Medieval. London: The British Council, 1951. 1st edn. 4to. 19 pp. 56 plates. Orig wraps. Dw. *(Hollett)* **£15 [≈$23]**

Moleville, Bertrand de
- Costume of the Hereditary States of the House of Austria. Displayed in Fifty Coloured Engravings. London: for William Miller, 1804. 1st edn. Large Paper. Sm folio. 50 hand cold plates. Contemp russia gilt, ft of spine sl chipped. *(Terramedia)* **$1,000 [≈£667]**

Moliere, Jean B.P. de
- Tartuffe & The Would-Be Gentleman. Illustrations by Serge Ivanoff. New York: The Limited Editions Club, 1963. One of 1500 signed by the illustrator. Sm 4to. Orig cloth. Slipcase. *(Oak Knoll)* **$45 [≈£30]**

Molimenti, Pompeo & Ludwig, Gustave
- The Life and Works of Vittorio Carpaccio. London: Murray, 1907. xxxi,248 pp. 248

plates, 34 text ills. Orig cloth, v sm tear spine. *(Leicester Art Books)* **£50 [≈$75]**

Mongan, Elizabeth & Hofer, P.

- Jean Sezenec. Drawings for Ariosto. London: Kegan Paul, 1945. 80 pp. 137 plates. Orig cloth. *(Leicester Art Books)* **£50 [≈$75]**

Mongan, Elizabeth, & others

- Fragonard. Drawings for Ariosto. New York: 1945. One of 1200. 4to. 80 pp. 135 plates. Orig cloth. Dw. *(Washton)* **$75 [≈£50]**

Monkhouse, W. Cosmo

- Pictures by William Etty, R.A. London: Virtue, Spalding, 1874. 45 pp. 9 engvd plates. Endpapers reinforced with cloth tape. Orig dec cloth, a.e.g., spine rubbed & worn. *(Leicester Art Books)* **£42 [≈$63]**

Montagu, J.A.

- A Guide to the Study of Heraldry. London: William Pickering, 1840. 4to. [4],76 pp. Lacks fldg frontis. Orig cloth, uncut, rebacked. *(Claude Cox)* **£35 [≈$53]**

Montagu, Jennifer

- Alessandro Algardi. New Haven: Yale UP, 1985. 2 vols. 493 ills. Orig cloth. Dws. *(Leicester Art Books)* **£90 [≈$135]**

Montgomery, Walter (editor)

- American Art and American Art Collections. Boston: E.W. Walker, 1889. 2 vols. 4to. 528; 475 pp. 759 ills. Vol 1 contents page supplied in xerox. Orig cloth, 1 front bd detached, shabby. *(Rona Schneider)* **$250 [≈£167]**

Moorat, Joseph

- The Snow Lay on the Ground. With the Christmas Greetings of the Essex House Press. 1902. 8 pp. Unopened. In orig envelope (rather worn) of the Guild of Handicraft. *(Michael Taylor)* **£45 [≈$68]**

Moore, George

- Ulick and Soracha. London: Nonesuch Press, 1926. One of 1250 signed by the author. [4], 286 pp. Copper engv by Stephen Gooden. Orig buckram. Parchment dw (cracked, sl chipped). *(Claude Cox)* **£35 [≈$53]**

Moore, George (editor)

- Pure Poetry. An Anthology. London: Nonesuch Press, 1924. One of 1250. Orig parchment backed bds, partly unopened. Dw (sl soiled & frayed). *(Claude Cox)* **£25 [≈$38]**

Moore, Henry

- Energy in Space. Photos: John Hedgecoe. Greenwich: New York Graphic Society, [1974]. Sq 4to. 88 pp. Num ills. Orig cloth. Dw. *(Ars Libri)* **$50 [≈£33]**
- Henry Moore at the British Museum. Photographs by David Finn. New York: Abrams, 1981. 4to. 128 pp. 150 ills. Orig cloth. Dw. *(Ars Libri)* **$40 [≈£27]**
- Henry Moore's Sheep Sketchbook. Comments by Henry Moore and Kenneth Clark. London: Thames & Hudson, [1980]. Oblong 4to. [10] pp. 96 plates. Orig cloth. Dw. *(Ars Libri)* **$50 [≈£33]**
- Henry Moore. Photographed and Edited by John Hedgecoe; Words by Henry Moore. New York: Simon & Schuster, 1968. Lge 4to. 524,[8] pp. Num ills. Orig cloth. Slipcase. *(Ars Libri)* **$225 [≈£150]**
- Henry Moore. Photographed and Edited by John Hedgecoe; Words by Henry Moore. New York: 1968. Folio. 532 pp. Num ills. Orig cloth. Slipcase. *(Abacus)* **$100 [≈£67]**
- Henry Moore. Sculpture and Drawings. Introduction by Herbert Read. New York: Curt Valentin, 1944. Lge 4to. xliv pp. 229 plates. Orig cloth. *(Ars Libri)* **$175 [≈£117]**
- Henry Moore. Volume Two: Sculpture and Drawings, 1949-1954. Second Edition, Revised. London: Lund Humphries, 1965. Lge 4to. 116 plates. Orig cloth. Dw. *(Ars Libri)* **$65 [≈£43]**

Moore, Henry & Clark, Kenneth

- Henry Moore's Sheep Sketch Book. London: 1980. 112 pp. Num ills. Orig cloth. Dw (sl torn). *(Phenotype)* **£28 [≈$42]**

Moore, N. Hudson

- Old Glass, European and American. New York: Tudor, 1946. xvi,394 pp. 265 ills. Orig cloth gilt, trifle scratched. *(Hollett)* **£30 [≈$45]**

Moore, T. Sturge (editor)

- The Passionate Pilgrim & The Songs in Shakespeare's Plays. London: The Vale Press, 1896. One of 310. 79 pp. Decs by Charles Ricketts. Orig bds, hd of spine chipped, rubbed, hinges splitting, darkened. *(John K. King)* **$495 [≈£330]**

Moran, James

- Heraldic Influence on Early Printers' Devices. Leeds: Elmete Press, 1978. One of 475, this one of about 35 specially bound copies. Cr 4to. xv,107 pp. 63 ills. Orig dark brown calf gilt, t.e.g. *(Blackwell's)* **£60 [≈$90]**

- Printing Presses. History and Development from the Fifteenth Century to Modern Times. California UP: 1973. Imperial 8vo. 64 plates, 109 ills. Dw (sl frayed). *(David Slade)* **£28 [≈$42]**
- Stanley Morison: His Typographic Achievement. London: (1971). 1st edn. Lge 8vo. 184 pp. Num ills. Orig bds. Dw. *(Bow Windows)* **£35 [≈$53]**

Mores, Edward Rowe

- A Dissertation upon English Typographical Founders ... Edited by Harry Carter and Christopher Ricks. Oxford: Bibl. Soc., 1961. 1st edn. 8vo. lxxx,145 pp. 13 plates, ills. 48 pp facsimile. Orig holland backed bds. *(Claude Cox)* **£25 [≈$38]**

Morgan, Lady

- The Life and Times of Salvator Rosa. London: Colburn, 1824. 2 vols. xvi,405; vii,380 pp. Vol 1 title foxed. Orig bds, worn. *(Leicester Art Books)* **£55 [≈$83]**

Morgan, Gwenda

- The Wood Engravings of Gwenda Morgan with an Introduction by John Randle. The Whittington Press: 1985. One of 300 (of 335). Orig oatmeal linen bds. Signed by the artist. *(Michael Taylor)* **£100 [≈$150]**

Morgan, Thomas

- Romano-British Mosaic Pavements: A History of their Discovery and a Record of their Interpretation and Designs. London: 1886. xxxiv,323 pp. Fldg map, 33 plates. Orig gilt dec cloth. *(Castle Bookshop)* **£75 [≈$113]**
- Romano-British Mosaic Pavements: A History of their Discovery and a Record and Interpretation of their Designs. London: Whiting & Co., 1886. Lge 8vo. xxxiv,323 pp. 15 cold plates, 116 other plates, 4 fldg plans. Orig dec cloth gilt, extrs trifle rubbed. *(Hollett)* **£220 [≈$330]**

Morice, Charles

- Paul Gauguin. Paris: H. Floury, 1919. 1st edn. 4to. 240 pp. Num ills. Rec buckram gilt, orig wraps bound in. *(Karmiole)* **$125 [≈£83]**

Morison, Stanley

- Four Centuries of Fine Printing ... New York: (1949). 2nd rvsd 8vo edn. 8vo. 342 pp. Ills. Orig cloth. Dw (spine sl yellowed). *(Oak Knoll)* **$45 [≈£30]**
- Type Designs of the Past and Present. London: The Fleuron, 1926. 1st edn. 8vo. [8],70,[2] pp. 64 ills. Orig cloth, uncut, paper label browned. *(Claude Cox)* **£20 [≈$30]**
- The Typographic Arts. Two Lectures. London: The Sylvan Press, 1949. 106 pp. 16 plates. Dw (defective). *(Claude Cox)* **£18 [≈$27]**
- The Typographic Book 1450-1935. A Study of Fine Typography through Five Centuries. London & USA: 1963. Folio. Ills. Orig cloth. *(Traylen)* **£95 [≈$143]**

Morison, Stanley & Carter, Harry

- John Fell, the University Press and the 'Fell' Types. Oxford: Clarendon Press 1967. One of 1000. Folio. 22 plates, text ills. Orig cloth. Dw (soiled & defective). *(Clark)* **£200 [≈$300]**

Morison, Stanley & Ruzicka, Rudolph

- Recollections of Daniel Berkeley Updike. Boston: Merrymount Press for The Club of Odd Volumes, 1943. One of 210. 12mo. xiv,29 pp. 4 plates. Orig cloth backed pastepaper bds, t.e.g., sl edge wear. *(The Veatchs)* **$175 [≈£117]**

Morley, Christopher

- Where the Blue Begins. New York: Doubleday & Page, 1922 [but 1925]. 1st Amer trade edn. 227 pp. 4 cold & 16 b/w ills. Name. Orig pict cloth gilt. *(Argonaut)* **$175 [≈£117]**

Morphet, Richard

- William Turnbull. Sculpture and Painting. London: Tate Gallery, 1973. Lge 4to. 76 pp. Num ills. Orig wraps. *(Ars Libri)* **$45 [≈£30]**

Morrell, J.B.

- The Arts and Crafts in York. York Monuments. London: Batsford for The Yorkshire Gazette, n.d. Demy 4to. viii,131 pp. 90 plates. Orig buckram. *(Taylor & Son)* **£35 [≈$53]**

Morris, Alice Talwyn

- My Book about New Zealand. Illustrated by Charles Robinson. London: Blackie, [ca 1913]. Sm 4to. 4 cold plates & b/w ills. Occas sl fingering. Orig cloth backed pict bds, sl rubbed. *(Barbara Stone)* **£65 [≈$98]**

Morris, Barbara

- Victorian Table Glass & Ornaments. London: Barrie & Jenkins, 1978. 8vo. 256 pp. 8 cold & 165 b/w plates. Dw. *(Paul Brown)* **£20 [≈$30]**

Morris, Margaret

- The Art of J.D. Fergusson. A Biased Biography. Glasgow & London: Blackie, 1974. 223 pp. 60 ills. Orig cloth. Dw. *(Leicester Art Books)* **£28 [≈$42]**
- The Art of J.D. Fergusson. Glasgow: Blackie, [1974]. 8vo. 223 pp. Frontis, 8 cold plates, 10 text ills. Orig cloth. Dw. *(Cooper Hay)* **£35 [≈$53]**
- The Art of J.D. Fergusson. London: Blackie, 1974. 223 pp. 69 plates. Orig cloth. Dw. *(Fine Art)* **£18 [≈$27]**

Morris, Robert

- Rural Architecture ... Facsimile Reprint of the 1750 Edition. Gregg Press: 1971. 8vo. [12],8.2,2 pp. 50 plates. Orig cloth. *(Spelman)* **£20 [≈$30]**

Morris, William

- The Early Poems. Illustrated by Florence Harrison. London: Blackie, 1914. 1st edn. 4to. 16 mtd cold & b/w plates & ills. Orig elab gilt cloth, t.e.g. *(Jo Ann Reisler)* **$225 [≈£150]**
- The Letters of William Morris to his Family and Friends. Edited by Philip Henderson. London: Longmans, Green, 1950. lxvii,406 pp. 7 plates, 4 text ills. Orig cloth. *(Fine Art)* **£32 [≈$48]**
- Some Thoughts on the Ornamented MSS. of the Middle Ages. New York: Press of the Woolly Whale, 1934. Ltd edn. Lge 8vo. [vi], 20,[2] pp. Orig qtr vellum, t.e.g. *(Oak Knoll)* **$125 [≈£83]**
- The Story of the Glittering Plain ... Hammersmith: Kelmscott Press, 1894. One of 250. Lge 4to. 23 w'engvs by Walter Crane, dec borders & intls. Orig limp vellum, silk ties (broken), some staining back cvr. *(Heritage)* **$4,000 [≈£2,667]**

Morrison, Arthur

- The Painters of Japan. London & Edinburgh: T.C. & E.C. Jack, 1911. One of 150 signed by the publisher. 2 vols. Folio. xiv,153; x,127 pp. Num plates. Orig cloth gilt. *(Terramedia)* **$450 [≈£300]**

Morrow, Bradford & Cooney, Seamus

- A Bibliography of the Black Sparrow Press 1966-1978. Santa Barbara: Black Sparrow Press, 1981. One of 1500. 8vo. 302 pp. Ills. Orig cloth & bds, paper label. Prospectus laid in. *(First Folio)* **$50 [≈£33]**

Morse, A. Reynolds

- Dali. A Study of His Life and Work. Greenwich: New York Graphic Society, (1958). 1st US edn. 94 ills. Orig pict bds. *(Rob Warren)* **$95 [≈£63]**
- Dali. A Study of his Life and Work. Greenwich: New York Graphic Society, 1958. Oblong folio. 96 pp. 111 plates. Orig dec bds. *(Ars Libri)* **$175 [≈£117]**

Morse, Edward S.

- Japanese Homes and their Surroundings. Boston: Ticknor, 1886. 2nd edn. Sm 4to. xxxiii,[i],372 pp. Ills. Inner hinges cracked. Orig cloth gilt, t.e.g., sl worn. *(Bookpress)* **$385 [≈£257]**
- Japanese Homes and their Surroundings. Boston: Ticknor, 1886. 1st edn. Sm 4to. xxxiv,372 pp. 307 ills. Orig dec cloth, t.e.g. *(Karmiole)* **$175 [≈£117]**

Morse, Frances Clary

- Furniture of the Olden Time. New York: Macmillan, 1905. xvii,371 pp. 296 ills. Orig cloth gilt, sl rubbed, upper jnt cracking. *(Hollett)* **£30 [≈$45]**

Morse, H.K.

- Elizabethan Pageantry: A Pictorial Survey of Costume and its Commentators from c.1560-1620. London: Studio Special Number, 1934. 1st edn. Cold frontis, 79 plates. Some foxing to title. Orig cloth, sl faded. *(Baker)* **£22.75 [≈$35]**

Morse, Willard S. & Brinckle, Gertrude

- Howard Pyle: A Record of his Illustrations and Writings. Wilmington: 1921. One of 500. x,242 pp. Port frontis, 23 ills. Orig bds, crnr of label torn. *(Karmiole)* **$75 [≈£50]**

Moschini, Vittorio

- Canaletto. London: Heinemann; Milan: Martello, 1954. 70,[6] pp. 26 mtd cold plates, 278 ills. Orig cloth. *(Leicester Art Books)* **£45 [≈$68]**

Moule, Thomas

- Architectural and Picturesque Illustrations of the Cathedral Churches of England and Wales ... see Winkles, H. & E.

Mountford, A.

- The Illustrated Guide to Staffordshire Salt-Glazed Stone Ware. London: Barrie & Jenkins, 1971. xiv,88 pp. 244 plates. Orig cloth. Dw laminated on. *(Castle Bookshop)* **£38 [≈$57]**

Moxey, Keith

- Pieter Aertsen, Joachim Beuckelaer, and the

Rise of Secular Painting in the Context of the Reformation. New York: 1977. 8vo. xii,284 pp. 72 plates. Orig cloth.
(Washton) **$60 [≈£40]**

Moxon, Joseph

- Mechanick Exercises or the Whole Art of Printing (1683-4). London: OUP, 1958. 1st edn thus. Tall 8vo. lxiv,480 pp. 2 fldg plates. Orig cloth. Dw (sl marked).
(Oak Knoll) **$95 [≈£63]**

Muir, Percy H.

- Catnachery. San Francisco: Book Club of California, 1955. One of 325. Sm 4to. 27 pp. Dec title, 5 fldg facsimiles, tinted ills. Orig cloth backed dec bds.
(Argonaut) **$100 [≈£67]**
- Points 1874-1930. Being Extracts from a Bibliographer's Note Book. London: 1931. One of 500. 8vo. 4 plates, 6 ills. Orig vellum backed bds. *(Traylen)* **£95 [≈$143]**
- Points. Second Series, 1866-1934. London: 1934. One of 750. 8vo. 7 plates, 6 ills. Orig vellum backed bds. *(Traylen)* **£85 [≈$128]**

Mumey, Nolie

- A Study of Rare Books with special reference to Colophons, Press Devices and Title Pages ... Denver: 1930. One of 1000 signed by the author. Thick 4to. xi,572 pp. Num ills. Orig cloth backed bds. *(Oak Knoll)* **$250 [≈£167]**

Mumford, John Kimberly

- Oriental Rugs. New York: Scribner, 1923. 4th edn. 4to. xxiv,278 pp. 2 fldg maps, 32 plates. Orig dec cloth, extrs sl rubbed.
(Karmiole) **$60 [≈£40]**

Munby, A.N.L.

- The Family Affairs of Sir Thomas Phillipps. London: 1952. 1st edn. 8vo. 11 plates. Edges spotted. Orig cloth, spine ends & one crnr sl bumped. Dw (sl worn).
(Ulysses Bookshop) **£55 [≈$83]**
- Some Caricatures of Book-Collectors. An Essay. London: Privately Printed for William H. Robinson, 1948. 17 pp. 8 mtd plates. Orig wraps (sl dusty, edges sl bumped).
(Ulysses Bookshop) **£85 [≈$128]**

Munnings, Sir Alfred

- The Autobiography. London: Museum Press, 1951-52. 1st edn vols 2 & 3, 2nd edn vol 1. 3 vols. 8vo. Ills. Orig cloth. Dws (sl frayed & rubbed). *(Claude Cox)* **£85 [≈$128]**

Munro, Robert

- Ancient Scottish Lake-Dwellings or Crannogs, with a Supplementary Chapter on remains of Lake-Dwellings in England. Edinburgh: David Douglas, 1882. 1st edn. xx,326 pp. 4 plates, 264 text ills. Orig cloth gilt, sl worn. *(Hollett)* **£85 [≈$128]**
- Archaeology and False Antiquities. London: Methuen, The Antiquary's Books series, 1905. 1st edn. xiii,292 pp. Plan, 18 plates, 63 ills. Occas spotting. Orig cloth gilt.
(Hollett) **£30 [≈$45]**
- The Lake-Dwellings of Europe ... London: Cassell, 1890. Lge 8vo. xl,600,[14 advt] pp. Num plans, ills. Qtr mor gilt, rubbed, crnrs sl bumped. Inscribed by the author.
(Hollett) **£150 [≈$225]**

Munz, Ludwig

- Bruegel. The Drawings. London: Phaidon, 1961. 247 pp. 240 ills. Orig cloth.
(Leicester Art Books) **£55 [≈$83]**

Muratoff, Paul

- Thirty-Five Russian Primitives. Jacques Zolotnitzky's Collection. Paris: 1931. 4to. 116 pp. 35 ills on 21 plates. Orig wraps, trifle rubbed. *(Washton)* **$45 [≈£30]**

Murdock, Harold

- Earl Percy's Dinner-Table. Boston 1774-5. Boston: Houghton, Mifflin: 1907. One of 55o. Frontis. 77 pp. Prospectus. Orig cloth, paper label, some finger marks. Slipcase (worn). Designed by Bruce Rogers.
(The Veatchs) **$75 [≈£50]**

Murphy, Bailey Scott

- English and Scottish Wrought Ironwork. A Series of Examples ... London: Batsford, 1904. 1st edn. Atlas folio. 14 pp. 80 photolitho ills. Flyleaves sl browned. Orig cloth gilt. *(Hollett)* **£185 [≈$278]**

Murphy, Shirley Foster (editor)

- Our Homes, and How to Make Them Healthy. London: Cassell, 1885. Thick 8vo. xii,948, [xvi] pp. Cold litho frontis, num plans, over 400 ills. Orig cloth gilt, spine sl rubbed & darkened, hd of spine chipped.
(Hollett) **£140 [≈$210]**

Murray, A.S.

- Designs from Greek Vases in the British Museum. London: Longmans, 1894. Folio. [iv], 17 pp. 62 plates on 15 sheets. Orig cloth over paper cvrd bds, crnrs v sl bumped.
(Sotheran's) **£98 [≈$147]**

- The Sculptures of the Parthenon. London: Murray, 1903. Sm 4to. viii,173 pp. Frontis, 17 plates, 1 pocket plate. Prelims sl foxed. Inscrptn. Qtr mor & cloth gilt, t.e.g. *(Quest Books)* **£38 [≈$57]**

Murray, C. Fairfax

- Catalogue of the Pictures belonging to His Grace the Duke of Portland at Welbeck Abbey, and in London. London: Chiswick Press, 1894. xvi,222 pp. 56 plates. Rec qtr leather. *(Fine Art)* **£150 [≈$225]**

Murtagh, William J.

- Moravian Architecture and Town Planning. Chapel Hill: North Carolina UP, (1967). 1st edn. 4to. xiv,145 pp. Orig cloth. Dw. *(Bookpress)* **$95 [≈£63]**

Musaeus

- Hero and Leander. Translated by F.L. Lucas. Golden Cockerel Press: 1949. One of 500. 56 pp. 11 copper engvs by John Buckland Wright. Orig dec buckram, t.e.g., spine sl sunned, extrs sl bruised. *(Bookworks)* **£95 [≈$143]**
- Hero and Leander. Translated by F.L. Lucas. Golden Cockerel Press: 1949. One of 500. 48 pp. 11 copper engvs by John Buckland Wright. Orig dec buckram, t.e.g. *(Waddington)* **£90 [≈$135]**

Mylne, Robert Scott

- The Master Masons to the Crown of Scotland and their Works. Edinburgh: 1893. 4to. Plans, ills. Orig dec cloth, t.e.g. Inscribed by the author. *(Sotheran's)* **£90 [≈$135]**
- The Master Masons to the Crown of Scotland and their Works. Edinburgh: Scott & Ferguson, Burness & Co., 1893. Folio. xviii,308 pp. Cold frontis, num photos, tinted plates, text ills. Orig buckram gilt, t.e.g., sl rubbed & faded, lower bd sl creased. *(Hollett)* **£125 [≈$188]**

Nadeau, Maurice

- The History of Surrealism. London: Cape, 1968. 351 pp. Orig cloth. Dw. *(Fine Art)* **£20 [≈$30]**

Nagaraju, I.

- Buddhist Architecture of Western India 250 B.C. to 300 A.D. Delhi: 1981. 4to. 400 pp. Num plates. Orig bndg. *(Bury Place)* **£45 [≈$68]**

Nanavati, J.M. & Dhaky, M.A.

- The Maitraka and the Saindhava Temples of Gujarat. Ascona: Artibus Asiae, 1969. 1st edn. 4to. 83,[1] pp. 106 ills. Orig cloth. Dw. Slipcase. *(Bookpress)* **$75 [≈£50]**

Nares, Gordon

- Royal Homes. Buckingham Palace, Windsor Castle ... London: Country Life, 1953. 4to. 112 pp. Ills. Orig cloth gilt. Dw. *(Hollett)* **£20 [≈$30]**

Nash, John

- English Garden Flowers. London: 1948. 1st edn. 4to. 12 cold plates. Orig cloth backed dec bds. Dw. *(Margaret Nangle)* **£38 [≈$57]**
- The Wood Engravings. Liverpool: Lea Press, 1987. One of 61, specially bound and with extra suite of 12 w'engvs. Folio. Orig mor backed bds. Box (sl used). *(Words Etcetera)* **£200 [≈$300]**

Nash, Joseph

- The Mansions of England in the Olden Time. Edited by Charles Holme ... London: The Studio, 1906. New edn. 4to. 104 plates. Orig cloth gilt, t.e.g., sl shaken, extrs worn. *(Hollett)* **£20 [≈$30]**

Nash, Paul

- Aerial Flowers. Oxford: Counterpoint Publications, 1947. One of 1000. Slim 4to. 8 pp. Mtd cold plate, 5 b/w ills. Orig stiff wraps, port onlay. *(Spelman)* **£35 [≈$53]**
- Fertile Image. London: 1951. 1st edn. 64 photo ills. Crnr of one plate sl creased. Free endpaper sl browned. Orig cloth, ft of spine sl bumped. Dw (chipped, torn, sl dusty & rubbed). *(Ulysses Bookshop)* **£95 [≈$143]**
- Outline, an Autobiography and other Writings. London: 1949. 271 pp. 2 cold & 51 b/w plates. Orig cloth. Dw. *(Fine Art)* **£65 [≈$98]**
- Outline. An Autobiography. London: Faber, 1949. 1st edn. 8vo. 271 pp. 2 cold plates, 51 b/w ills. Orig buckram, spine almost completely unmarked. Dw (rear panel worn). *(Spelman)* **£50 [≈$75]**
- Paintings, Drawings and Illustrations. Edited by Margot Eates. London: Lund Humphries, 1948. One of 1500. 4to. Port frontis, 20 mtd cold plates, 112 ills. Orig cloth. Dw. Order form inserted. *(Spelman)* **£90 [≈$135]**

Nash, Ray

- American Penmanship, 1800-1850. A History of Writing and a Bibliography of Copybooks from Jenkins to Spencer. Worcester: American Antiquarian Society, 1969. 8vo. xii,303 pp. Orig cloth. *(Oak Knoll)* **$65 [≈£43]**

Nash, Thomas

- The Unfortunate Traveller. Edited by Philip Henderson. Illustrated by Haydn Mackey. London: The Verona Society, 1930. One of 1000. 8vo. xxvi,[6],162 pp. Num ills. Orig cloth. *(Karmiole)* **$30 [≈£20]**

Nathan, Maude

- The Decoration of Leather. From the French of Georges De Recy. London: Constable, 1905. 1st English edn. 8vo. 104 pp. 20 plates, 34 text ills. Orig dec cloth, t.e.g. *(Claude Cox)* **£45 [≈$68]**

The National Portrait Gallery ...

- The National Portrait Gallery. London: Cassell, Petter & Galpin, [ca 1880]. 4 series in 2 vols. 4to. 80 ports. Orig half mor gilt, jnts & edges rubbed, fore edges of sides damp faded. *(Claude Cox)* **£35 [≈$53]**

Nature and Art ...

- 'Nature and Art' Magazine. London: Day & Son, 1866-67. 2 vols in one, all published. Cold & b/w ills. Orig pict cloth gilt, rather worn, some reprs, shaken. *(Willow House)* **£60 [≈$90]**

Neale, John Preston & Le Keux, John

- Views of the most interesting Collegiate and Parochial Churches of Great Britain ... With Historical and Architectural Descriptions. London: Longman ..., 1824. Large Paper. 2 vols in one. 4to. 2 frontises, 94 plates on India paper. Contemp half mor gilt, a.e.g. *(Traylen)* **£160 [≈$240]**

Nelson, G. & Wright, H.

- Tomorrow's House: A Complete Guide for the Home-Builder. New York: Simon & Schuster, 1945. 2nd edn. 214 pp. 232 ills. Orig cloth, sl shaken. *(Willow House)* **£18 [≈$27]**

Nelson, I.

- The Parliamentary and Forensic Short-Hand Writer ... London: 1836. 32 pp. 4 plates. Plates stained. Cloth, worn. *(Whitehart)* **£25 [≈$38]**

Nesfield, W. Eden

- Specimens of Mediaeval Architecture ... London: Day & Son, 1862. 1st edn. Folio. Dec title, 6 text ff, 100 litho plates (1 cold). Orig gilt dec cloth, mor spine (chipped at hd), guttapercha replaced. *(Claude Cox)* **£90 [≈$135]**
- Specimens of Mediaeval Architecture chiefly selected from Examples of the 12th and13th Centuries in France and Italy. London: Day & Son, 1862. 1st edn. Folio. [x] pp. Litho title, 100 litho plates (1 chromolitho). 1 sm repr, few sm marks. Orig cloth, rebacked with morocco. *(Hollett)* **£125 [≈$188]**

Neve, Christopher

- Leon Underwood. London: Thames & Hudson, 1974. 1st edn. 224 pp. 180 ills. Orig cloth. Dw. *(Bookworks)* **£22 [≈$33]**

Nevill, Ralph

- British Military Prints. London: Connoisseur, 1909. 1st edn. 4to. 102,[28 advt] pp. Num cold & other plates. Orig dec cloth gilt, spine dulled with 2 sm snags. *(Clevedon Books)* **£40 [≈$60]**
- Old French Line Engravings. London: Halton & Truscott Smith, 1924. One of 1250. 4to. viii, 23 pp. 86 plates. Orig cloth, t.e.g., sm spot on front cvr. *(Bookpress)* **$125 [≈£83]**

Nevinson, C.R.W.

- Paint and Prejudice. New York: 1938. 1st US edn. vii,285 pp. 32 plates. Some foxing. Orig cloth, sl worn. *(Fine Art)* **£24 [≈$36]**

The New Leader Book ...

- The New Leader Book. London: 1924. 1st edn. Folio. 12 ills. Orig card portfolio, detached. Includes ills by Gwen Raverat and Clare Leighton. *(Margaret Nangle)* **£100 [≈$150]**
- The New Leader Book. London: 1925. 1st edn. Folio. 15 ills. Orig card portfolio, shabby. Includes ills by Gwen Raverat. *(Margaret Nangle)* **£110 [≈$165]**

Newdigate, Bernard

- Book Production Notes. Foreword by Ruari Mclean. [Printed at the Whittington Press for the] Tabard Press, Oxford, 1986. One of 250 (of 270). Roy 8vo. Ills. Orig qtr canvas. *(Blackwell's)* **£48 [≈$72]**

Newhall, Beaumont

- The History of Photography, from 1839 to the Present Day. New York: MoMA,

(1964?). Revsd & enlgd edn. 4to. 215 pp. 210 ills. Orig cloth. Dw (some discoloration of edges). *(Bookpress)* **$65 [≈£43]**

Newlands, James

- The Carpenter and Joiner's Assistant ... Glasgow: Blackie, 1860. Folio. Engvd title, 110 plates + 3'A' plates. Contemp half calf, some rubbing. *(Traylen)* **£90 [≈$135]**

Newman, John Henry

- The Dream of Gerontius. London: Burnt Wood Press, 1976. One of 50 signed by the printer, Eileen Hogan. Orig morocco over printed wood veneer bds. *(Karmiole)* **$100 [≈£67]**

Newton, A. Edward

- A. Edward Newton on Books and Business. N.p.: Appellicon Press, 1930. One of 325 signed by the author. 8vo. [vi],16,[iv] pp. Orig cloth backed bds, t.e.g. *(Oak Knoll)* **$65 [≈£43]**
- The Amenities of Book-Collecting and Kindred Affections. Boston: Atlantic Monthly Press, 1918. 1st edn. 8vo. xxi,356 pp. No errata slip.. Orig cloth backed bds, t.e.g. Inscribed by the author (1925). *(Oak Knoll)* **$45 [≈£30]**
- The Greatest Book in the World and Other Papers. Boston: Little, Brown, (1925). 1st edn. 2nd issue, with Cruikshank signature listed as being on p 334. 8vo. Ills. Orig cloth backed bds, t.e.g. Inscribed by the author. *(Oak Knoll)* **$55 [≈£37]**
- A Magnificent Farce and Other Diversions of a Book-Collector. London: 1921. 1st edn. 8vo. Num plates. Orig linen backed bds. *(Traylen)* **£20 [≈$30]**

Newton, Charles Thomas

- Essays on Art and Archaeology. London: Macmillan, 1880. 8vo. [iii],472 pp. Map, 4 fldg plates. Orig cloth, sl worn. *(Quest Books)* **£24 [≈$36]**

Newton, Peter A.

- The County of Oxford. A Catalogue of Medieval Stained Glass. Oxford: 1979. Lge 4to. xviii,246 pp. 50 plates 933 cold). Orig cloth. *(Washton)* **$150 [≈£100]**

Nichols, Beverley (editor)

- A Book of Old Ballads. Selected with an Introduction by Beverley Nichols & Illustrated by H.M. Brock. London: Hutchinson, 1934. 1st edn thus. 4to. xl,280 pp. 16 cold plates, decs. Orig cloth gilt, partly unopened (one leaf badly opened). *(Claude Cox)* **£25 [≈$38]**

Nichols, John

- Biographical Anecdotes of William Hogarth; with a Catalogue of his Works ... Second Edition, enlarged and corrected. London: J. Nichols, 1782. 8v o. v,474,[2 advt] pp. Prelims sl foxed. Period calf, backstrip relaid. Anon. *(Rankin)* **£100 [≈$150]**

Nichols, John Gough

- Examples of Decorative Tiles, sometimes called Encaustic. London: J.B. Nichols, 1845. 1st edn. 4to. [ii],22 pp. 101 ills on 96 plates. Contemp half calf. *(Bookpress)* **$1,250 [≈£833]**

Nichols, Rose Standish

- Spanish and Portuguese Gardens. Boston: Houghton, Mifflin 1924. 1st edn. Lge 8vo. xxxii,304 pp. Num ills. Orig cloth. *(Karmiole)* **$45 [≈£30]**

Nichols, T.

- A Handy Book of the British Museum for Every-Day Readers. London: Cassell, Petter & Galpin, 1870. 8vo. viii,426,[16 advt] pp. Frontis, 15 plates, num text ills. Orig cloth, backstrip reprd. *(Quest Books)* **£18 [≈$27]**

Nicholson, Ben

- Ben Nicholson. Paintings, Reliefs, Drawings. Introduction by Herbert Read. London: Lund Humphries, (1948) 1955. 2nd printing, rvsd. Lge 4to. Num plates. Dw (chipped). *(Clearwater)* **£250 [≈]**

Nicholson, Francis

- The Practice of Drawing and Painting Landscape from Nature, in Water Colours. London: Booth & Clay, 1820. 1st edn. 4to. [4],iv,91,[1 blank] pp. 5 plates. Calf gilt, worn & rubbed. *(Spelman)* **£65 [≈$98]**

Nicholson, James B.

- A Manual of the Art of Bookbinding ... Also the Art of Marbling Book-edges and Paper. Phila: Baird, 1887. 3rd printing. 8vo. 310,[31 ctlg] pp. 12 plates, 7 samples of marbled paper, text ills. Some smudges. Orig cloth, sl worn. *(The Veatchs)* **$415 [≈£277]**

Nicholson, John

- The Operative Mechanic, and British Machinist ... With a Supplement ... London: for Sherwood, Gilbert & Piper, 1830. Lge 8vo. xxviii,902 pp. Frontis, 117 plates on 112 sheets (1-36, 36*, 37-77*, 78-95, I-XX).

Contemp diced russia gilt, upper jnt reprd. *(Spelman)* **£140 [≈$210]**

Nicholson, Peter

- The Carpenter's New Guide. Being a Complete Book of Lines for Carpentry and Joinery ... London: J. Taylor, 1808. 2nd edn. 4to. x,76 pp. 78 plates. Few spots on prelims. Contemp calf. *(Bookpress)* **$850 [≈£567]**
- The Carpenter's New Guide. Being a Complete Book of Lines for Carpentry and Joinery ... Phila: Lippincott, 1860. 16th edn. 4to. 107 pp. Frontis, 80 plates. Later qtr mor. *(Bookpress)* **$450 [≈£300]**

Nicholson, William

- An Almanac of Twelve Sports. London: Heinemann, 1897. 1st edn. 4to. 12 ills. Orig bds, spine worn. *(Robert Frew)* **£260 [≈$390]**
- An Almanac of Twelve Sports. London: Heinemann, 1898. Library edition on Japanese vellum. 4to. 12 ills. Orig pict vellum. *(Robert Frew)* **£400 [≈$600]**
- An Alphabet. London: Heinemann, 1898. 4to. Title, 26 plates. Orig cloth backed pict bds. *(Robert Frew)* **£600 [≈$900]**
- Characters of Romance. New York: R.H. Russell, 1900. Title, 16 plates. Orig portfolio, spine extrs sl chafed, lacks ties. *(Robert Frew)* **£920 [≈$1,380]**
- London Types. London: Heinemann, 1898. 1st edn. 4to. 12 ills. Lib b'plates, 3 lib stamps. Orig pict bds. *(Robert Frew)* **£200 [≈$300]**
- Nicholson's Practical Builder: A Theoretical and Practical Treatise on the Five Orders of Architecture. London: T. Kelly, [ca 1850]. 168 pp. 105 plates. Orig cloth gilt, sl worn & soiled, hinges cracking. *(Willow House)* **£65 [≈$98]**

Nicolson, Benedict

- Joseph Wright of Derby. Paul Mellon: 1968. 1st edn. 2 vols. 4to. 495 ills. Dws. *(Spelman)* **£80 [≈$120]**
- The Treasures of the Foundling Hospitals. With a Catalogue Raisonne .. Oxford: 1972. Sm 4to. xiv,98 pp. 99 ills on plates. Orig cloth. Dw. Author's presentation copy. *(Washton)* **$45 [≈£30]**
- The Treasures of the Foundling Hospital. With a Catalogue Raisonne based on a Draft Catalogue by John Kerslake. OUP: 1972. xiv,98 pp. 100 plates. Orig cloth. Dw (worn). *(Fine Art)* **£38 [≈$57]**

Nicolson, Benedict & Wright, Christopher

- Georges de la Tour. London: Phaidon, 1974. vi,234 pp. 242 ills. Orig cloth. Dw. *(Leicester Art Books)* **£190 [≈$285]**

Nietzsche, Friedrich

- Thus Spake Zarathustra. Decorations by Alan Bank. New York: The Limited Editions Club, 1964. One of 1500 numbered. Sm 4to. Orig qtr parchment & cloth. Slipcase. *(Oak Knoll)* **$55 [≈£37]**

Nikulin, N.

- Fragments of Some Hermitage Paintings. Italy, Spain, France, Germany, The Netherlands. Leningrad: 1970. 4to. Over 100 plates. Orig cloth. *(Washton)* **$50 [≈£33]**

Nixon, Howard M.

- British Bookbindings presented by Kenneth H. Oldaker to the Chapter Library of Westminster Abbey. London: Maggs Bros., 1982. One of 1000. 8vo. 159 pp. 3 cold plates, 68 ills. Orig cloth. *(Oak Knoll)* **$65 [≈£43]**

Noakes, Aubrey

- Ben Marshall 1768-1835. Leigh-on-Sea: F. Lewis, 1978. One of 500. 80 pp. 50 plates. Orig cloth. Dw. *(Leicester Art Books)* **£28 [≈$42]**
- Charles Spencelayh and his Paintings. London: (1978). 1st edn. 4to. 190 pp. 8 cold & 61 b/w plates, ills. Orig cloth. Dw. *(Bow Windows)* **£40 [≈$60]**

Norbury, James

- Traditional Knitting Patterns. London: Batsford, 1962. 1st edn. 240 pp. 263 ills. Orig cloth gilt. Dw (sl worn & reprd). *(Willow House)* **£25 [≈$38]**

Nordland, Gerald

- Gaston Lachaise: The Man and his Work. New York: Braziller, 1974. 4to. viii,184 pp. 95 ills. Orig cloth. Dw. *(Ars Libri)* **$100 [≈£67]**

North, S. Kennedy

- Mr North's Maggot. English Folk Dances Pictured by S.K. North. With an Introduction by Cecil Sharp. London: [ca 1921]. Oblong 8vo. 12 cold plates on thick card. Orig pict card wraps, edges worn, silk ribbon tie perished. *(Margaret Nangle)* **£45 [≈$68]**

Northcote, James

- The Life of Titian; with Anecdotes of the Distinguished Persons of his Time. London: 1830. 2 vols. 8vo. Lib half cloth. *(Traylen)* **£15 [≈$23]**

Norton, Bettina A.

- Edwin Whitefield: Nineteenth Century North American Scenery. Barre: Barre Publishing, 1977. 4to. 158 pp. 10 ills. Orig cloth. Dw. *(Rona Schneider)* **$50 [≈£33]**

Novotny, F.

- Paul Cezanne. London: Phaidon, 1937. 1st edn. Lge 4to. 24 pp. 126 plates. Orig cloth, sl marked. *(Clevedon Books)* **£25 [≈$38]**

Nuno, J.A. Gaya

- Juan Gris. London: Secker & Warburg, 1975. 268 pp. 722 ills. Orig cloth. Dw (torn). *(Leicester Art Books)* **£50 [≈$75]**

Nurnberg, Walter

- Words in their Hands. A Series of Photographs with a Commentary by Beatrice Ward. Cambridge: Privately Printed, 1964. One of 500. Sm 4to. 15 plates. Orig cloth. *(Traylen)* **£48 [≈$72]**

Nutt, David

- Good Queen Bess. Illustrated by John Hassall. London: n.d. Pict title, 23 cold plates. Orig cloth backed pict bds, extrs worn, soiled, front jnt cracked. *(Stella Books)* **£25 [≈$38]**

O'Brien, Donough

- Miniatures in the XVIIIth and XIXth Centuries: an Historical and Descriptive Record. London: Batsford for the author, 1951. xiv,198 pp. Errata slip. Frontis, 385 ills. Sl foxing. Orig cloth. Dw (foxed). *(Fine Art)* **£25 [≈$38]**

O'Connor, John

- A Pattern of People. London: Hutchinson, 1959. 1st edn. 80 pp. 37 w'engvs. Orig cloth. Dw. *(Bookworks)* **£45 [≈$68]**

O'Donoghue, Freeman

- A Descriptive and Classified Catalogue of Portraits of Queen Elizabeth. London: Quaritch, 1894. xviii,121 pp. Frontis, 7 plates. B'plate. New qtr leather. *(Fine Art)* **£40 [≈$60]**

O'Keefe, Georgia

- Georgia O'Keefe. New York: Viking Press, (1976). 1st edn. Folio. 108 plates. Orig cloth. Dw. *(Bookpress)* **$325 [≈£217]**
- Georgia O'Keefe. New York: Viking, (1976). 1st edn. Folio. Port, 108 cold plates. Orig cloth. Dw. *(Abacus)* **$200 [≈£133]**

O'Meara, Carra Ferguson

- The Iconography of the Facade of Saint-Gilles-du Gard. New York: 1977. 8vo. 222 pp. 9 plans, 95 ills. Orig cloth. *(Washton)* **$75 [≈£50]**

O'Neill, Eugene

- Ah, Wilderness! Illustrations by Shannon Stirnweis. New York: The Limited Editions Club, 1972. One of 1500 signed by the illustrator. Sm 4to. Orig cloth-backed bds, paper label. Slipcase *(Oak Knoll)* **$65 [≈£43]**

Oakeshott, Walter

- The Artists of the Winchester Bible (English Paintings of the Twelfth Century). London: 1945. Sm 4to. x,21 pp. 44 plates. Cloth. *(Washton)* **$40 [≈£27]**

October ...

- October. Editors: Douglas Crimp, Rosalind Krauss, Annette Nicholson. Cambridge: 1976-1981. Nos 1-16. 4to. Ills. Orig wraps. *(Ars Libri)* **$850 [≈£567]**

Ogden, Henry V.S. & Ogden, Margaret S.

- English Taste in Landscape in the Seventeenth Century. Ann Arbor: Michigan UP, 1955. 1st edn. 4to. xii,224 pp. 165 ills. Orig cloth gilt. Dw (soiled). *(Karmiole)* **$40 [≈£27]**

Ogston, Sir Alexander

- The Prehistoric Antiquities of the Howe of Cromar. Aberdeen: Spalding Club, 1921. 4to. xxvi,128 pp. 86 ills. Orig cloth gilt. *(Hollett)* **£50 [≈$75]**

Oistros (pseudonym)

- Truffle Eater by Oistros Illustrated by Archie Savoy. London: Arthur Barker, [1933]. 1st edn. 4to. Orig pict bds, fine. *(Jo Ann Reisler)* **$335 [≈£223]**

Oka, Hideyuki

- How to Wrap Five Eggs. Japanese Design in Traditional Packaging. New York: Harper & Row, (1967). 1st edn. 4to. 204 pp. 222 plates. Orig cloth over bds. Dw. *(Karmiole)* **$85 [≈£57]**

Okakura, Kakuzo

- The Ideals of the East, with Special reference

to the Art of Japan. London: 1905. 8vo. [ii],xxii,244,[4 advt] pp. Orig cloth. *(Bow Windows)* **£40 [≈$60]**

Oldenburg, Claes

- Notes in Hand. New York: Dutton, (1971). 1st Amer edn. 12mo. Num ills. Orig pict wraps. *(Wilder Books)* **$40 [≈£27]**
- Notes in Hand. N.p.: Petersburg Press, (1971). 12mo. 50 cold plates. Orig cloth. Dw. *(Abacus)* **$45 [≈£30]**
- Notes in Hand. New York: Dutton & Petersburg, 1971. 50 cold plates, 2 photo ills. Orig stiff wraps. *(Clarice Davis)* **$55 [≈£37]**
- Proposals for Monuments and Buildings 1965-69. Chicago: Big Table Publishing Co., (1969). Oblong 4to. 196 pp. 16 cold plates, num b/w ills. Orig cloth. Dw. *(Abacus)* **$50 [≈£33]**

Oldenburg, Claes & Emmett, Williams

- Store Days: Documents from the Store (1961) and Ray Gun Theatre (1962). New York: Something Else Press, 1967. 4to. 152 pp. Ills. Store business card in glassine envelope. Orig cloth. Dw. *(Abacus)* **$75 [≈£50]**

Oldham, J. Basil

- Blind Panels of English Binders. Cambridge: UP, 1958. 1st edn. Cr folio. [xvi],(56) pp. 67 plates. Few faint marks. Dw. *(Ash)* **£100 [≈$150]**

Oliver, Anthony

- The Victorian Staffordshire Figure. A Guide for Collectors. London: Heinemann, 1978. Sm 4to. [viii],179 pp. 8 cold plates, 250 ills. Orig cloth gilt. Dw. *(Hollett)* **£40 [≈$60]**

Ollier, Edmund

- Cassell's Dore Gallery ... see under Dore, Gustave

Olney, Clarke

- Benjamin Robert Haydon: Historical Painter. Georgia UP: 1952. xiv,309 pp. 27 plates. Orig cloth. Dw. *(Fine Art)* **£20 [≈$30]**

Olsen, D.J.

- Town Planning in London. The Eighteenth and Nineteenth Centuries. Second Edition. Yale: UP, 1982. 4to. 245 pp. 83 ills. Dw. *(Spelman)* **£20 [≈$30]**

Oman, Charles

- Castles. London: Great Western Railway, 1926. Lge 8vo. xii,232 pp. 2 maps, 5 plans, 2 cold plates, 105 ills, 67 drawings. Orig cloth backed bds gilt, sl worn & marked. *(Hollett)* **£20 [≈$30]**
- English Engraved Silver 1150-1900. London: Faber, 1978. 158 pp. 159 plates. Orig cloth. Dw. *(Castle Bookshop)* **£18 [≈$27]**
- English Silversmith's Work. Civil and Domestic. Am Introduction. London: HMSO, 1965. Sm 4to. 15 pp. 212 plates. Orig cloth gilt. Dw. *(Hollett)* **£35 [≈$53]**

Omar Khayyam

- Rubaiyat of Omar Khayyam. Rendered into English Verse by Edward FitzGerald. Illustrated by Gilbert James. London: Adam & Charles Black, 1909. 1st edn thus. Roy 8vo. viii,202 pp. Endpapers browned. Orig dec cloth gilt, t.e.g., edges v sl speckled. *(Sotheran's)* **£88 [≈$132]**
- Rubaiyat of Omar Khayyam. Rendered into English Verse by Edward FitzGerald. With Illustrations by Edmund Dulac. New York: Hodder & Stoughton, [ca 1910]. 2nd trade edn. 4to. (112) pp. 20 mtd cold plates. Orig elab gilt dec cloth. *(Karmiole)* **$175 [≈£117]**
- Rubaiyat of Omar Khayyam. Rendered into English Verse by Edward FitzGerald. With Illustrations by Edmund Dulac. London: Hodder & Stoughton, [ca 1910]. 20 mtd cold plates. Orig dec buckram gilt, sl marked, ft of spine worn. *(Stella Books)* **£95 [≈$143]**
- Rubaiyat of Omar Khayyam. Rendered into English Verse by Edward FitzGerald. With Drawings by Edmund J. Sullivan. London: Methuen, (1913). 4to. xvi,(150) pp. Cold frontis, 75 plates. Orig gilt dec cloth, a.e.g. Dw (chipped & reprd). *(Karmiole)* **$175 [≈£117]**
- Rubaiyat of Omar Khayyam. Rendered into English Verse by Edward FitzGerald. Illustrated by Willy Pogany. London: Harrap, [ca 1918]. 8vo. [112] pp. 16 mtd cold plates. Orig elab gilt black leather, pict onlays, t.e.g., fine. *(Sotheran's)* **£128 [≈$192]**
- Rubaiyat of Omar Khayyam. Rendered into English Verse by Edward FitzGerald. Illustrated by Willy Pogany. London: Harrap, 1930. 4to. 12 mtd cold plates, num mtd vignettes, decs. Orig gilt dec mor, t.e.g., spine sl faded. Orig etching sgnd by Pogany inserted. *(Sotheran's)* **£398 [≈$597]**

Ono, Yoko

- Grapefruit. A Book of Instructions. Introduction by John Lennon. New York: Simon & Schuster, 1970. (286) pp. Ills. Orig cloth. Dw (sl worn). *(Ars Libri)* **$100 [≈£67]**

Oppe, A.P.

- Alexander & John Robert Cozens ... London: Black, 1952. xii,196 pp. 69 plates, text ills. Orig cloth. Dw. *(Clarice Davis)* **$55 [≈£37]**
- Alexander and John Robert Cozens. London: A. & C. Black, 1952. 1st edn. 8vo. xii,196 pp. 48 plates, 16 text ills. Orig cloth, spine faded.. *(Spelman)* **£20 [≈$30]**
- The Drawings of William Hogarth. With an Introduction and a Complete Illustrated Catalogue. London: Phaidon, 1948. 4to. 65 pp. 120 ills. Dw (worn). *(Spelman)* **£20 [≈$30]**
- The Drawings of William Hogarth. London: Phaidon Press, 1948. 70 pp. 64 plates, 50 text ills. Orig cloth. *(Leicester Art Books)* **£32 [≈$48]**
- Raphael. Edited with an Introduction by Charles Mitchell. New York: 1970. Rvsd edn. 4to. xxiii,130 pp. 287 plates. Orig cloth. Dw. *(Washton)* **$100 [≈£67]**
- The Water-Colour Drawings of John Sell Cotman. London: The Studio, 1923. xvi pp. 24 cold plates. Orig wraps. *(Leicester Art Books)* **£35 [≈$53]**

Orcutt, William Dana

- The Book in Italy during the Fifteenth and Sixteenth Centuries shown in Facsimile Reproductions ... London: Harrap, (1928). One of 750. 4to. 220 pp. 128 plates. B'plate. Orig qtr vellum, t.e.g., tips sl bumped. Dw (worn & chipped). *(The Veatchs)* **$150 [≈£100]**
- The Magic of the Book. More Reminiscences and Adventures of a Bookman. Boston: Little, Brown, 1930. 1st edn. xi,314 pp. Cold frontis, 48 plates. 21 ills. Orig elab gilt cloth, t.e.g. Dw. *(Argonaut)* **$75 [≈£50]**

Oriental Ceramic Society

- Oriental Ceramic Society. Transactions. London: 1945-74. Vols 29-37, 39. 19 vols. 4to. Num photo plates. Orig buckram. *(Traylen)* **£190 [≈$285]**

Orme, William

- Rudiments of Landscape Drawing and Perspective. London: Edward Orme, 1801. Etched title, 1st part with 18 plates, 2nd part with 4 plates. Some soiling. Hd of title reprd. Orig bds, oval ptd label on upper bd, rebacked & reprd. *(Spelman)* **£360 [≈$540]**

Ormond, Leonee & Richard

- Lord Leighton. London: Studies in British Art, 1975. 216 pp. 10 cold plates, 197 ills. Orig cloth. *(Fine Art)* **£170 [≈$255]**
- Lord Leighton. New Haven: Yale UP, 1975. xvi,200 pp. 204 ills. Orig cloth. Dw. *(Leicester Art Books)* **£150 [≈$225]**

Ormond, Richard

- Early Victorian Portraits (Catalogue of the National Portrait Gallery Collection). London: HMSO, 1973. 2 vols (text & plates). 2 frontis, 6 cold plates, 1047 b/w ills. Lib labels removed. Dws. *(Quest Books)* **£55 [≈$83]**
- John Singer Sargent. Paintings, Drawings, Watercolours. London: Phaidon, 1970. 264 pp. 203 ills. Orig cloth. Dw. *(Leicester Art Books)* **£125 [≈$188]**

Orpen, William

- An Onlooker in France 1917-1919. Revised and Enlarged Edition. London: Williams & Norgate, 1924. x,127 pp. 97 plates. Orig cloth. *(Leicester Art Books)* **£26 [≈$39]**

Osten, Hans Henning von der

- Ancient Oriental Seals in the Collection of Mrs. Agnes Baldwin Brett. Chicago: UP, (1936). 1st edn. 4to. xii,76 pp. 12 plates, 20 text ills. Orig cloth. *(Bookpress)* **$165 [≈£110]**

Oswald, A., & others

- English Brown Stoneware 1670-1900. London: Faber, 1982. 308 pp. Num plates. Orig cloth. Dw. *(Castle Bookshop)* **£25 [≈$38]**

Ould, E.A.

- Old Cottages, Farm-Houses, and other half-Timber Buildings in Shropshire, Herefordshire and Cheshire ... London: Batsford, 1904. 1st edn. Lge 8vo. xi,39,24 pp. 101 collotype plates. Orig dec cloth gilt, rather damped. *(Hollett)* **£75 [≈$113]**

Our National Cathedrals ...

- Our National Cathedrals - Their History and Architecture from their Foundation to Modern Times. London: Ward Lock, 1887-89. 3 vols. 162 cold plates & ground plans, num w'engvs. Orig cold bndgs, fine. *(Old Cathay)* **£295 [≈$443]**
- Our National Cathedrals ... Their History and Architecture from their Foundation to Modern Times. London: Ward Lock, 1887-89. 3 vols. Sm 4to. 190 cold plates, num ills. Occas sl spotting. A few plates refixed. Orig dec cloth gilt. *(Hollett)* **£175 [≈$263]**

Ovid

- The Amores ... Newly Translated by E.

Powys Mathers. With Five Engravings by J.E. Laboureur. Golden Cockerel Press: 1932. One of 350. [6],82,colophon pp. 5 copper engvs. Orig niger half mor, t.e.g., cloth sides sl soiled & rubbed.
(Claude Cox) **£180 [≈$270]**

- The Metamorphoses of Publius Ovidus Naso. Golden Cockerel Press, 1959. One of 200. 4to. 264 pp. Ills by John Y. Bateman. Edges of frontis sl thumbed. Orig cloth, sl spotted. *(Waddington)* **£55 [≈$83]**
- Ovid's Elegies. Translated by Christopher Marlowe, together with Epigrams of Sir John Davies. London: Etchells & Macdonald, 1925. One of 650. Frontis & 6' full-page w'engvs by John Nash. Three qtr dove grey calf, gilt spine, by Bayntun. *(Barbara Stone)* **£110 [≈$165]**

Owen, Robert Dale

- Hints on Public Architecture. New York: Putnam, 1849. Sm folio. xvii,[1],119 pp. W'engvd tinted title, 7 w'engvd plates, 6 tinted litho plates, 99 w'engvd text ills. Orig dec cloth gilt, sm nick lower edge. *(Black Sun)* **$1,250 [≈£833]**

Oyred, Moyshed

- The Book of Affinity. Coloured Illustrations by Jacob Epstein. London: Heinemann, 1933. One of 525. Folio. 111 pp. Orig cloth, paper label, uncut. Author's presentation copy. *(Lamb)* **£80 [≈$120]**

Paas, John & Cook, James

- Provincial Book Binding in the Eighteen Thirties. The Plough Press: 1978. One of 200. Sq 8vo. 26 pp. 10 plates. Orig cloth. *(Oak Knoll)* **$55 [≈£37]**

Paccagnini, Giovanni

- Pisanello. London: Phaidon, 1973. 298 pp. 280 ills. Orig cloth. *(Leicester Art Books)* **£65 [≈$98]**

Pacht, Otto & Alexander, J.J.G.

- Illuminated Manuscripts in the Bodleian Library, Oxford. Oxford: 1969-73. 3 vols. Roy 8vo. 3 cold frontis, 274 b/w plates. Orig cloth. Dws. *(Traylen)* **£75 [≈$113]**

Page, Richard Charles

- The Page Memorial. A Series of Fac-simile Reproductions of Drawings made as a Pugin Student in the Year 1874. London: Batsford, 1884. Lge 4to. Port frontis, 26 plates. Orig cloth gilt, sl scratched. *(Hollett)* **£35 [≈$53]**

Pain, William

- The Practical House Carpenter; or, Youth's Instructor ... Phila: Thomas Dobson, 1797. 2nd Amer edn. 4to. v,15 pp. 148 plates. Lower edge of title reprd. Few marg tears. Occas foxing. Contemp calf, rebacked. *(Bookpress)* **$1,850 [≈£1,233]**

Painter, William

- The Palace of Pleasure. With an Introduction by Hamish Miles and Illustrations by Douglas Percy-Bliss. OUP for The Cresset Press: 1929. One of 500. 4 vols. 4to. Cold frontises. Orig canvas backed dec bds. *(Mermaid Books)* **£150 [≈$225]**

Paley, F.A.

- A Manual of Gothic Mouldings: with Directions for Copying them and for determining their dates ... Fifth Edition. London: Gurney & Jackson, 1891. 8vo. 100 pp. 21 plates, text ills. Orig cloth gilt, spine sl worn. *(Hollett)* **£25 [≈$38]**

Palladio, Andrea

- The Architecture of A. Palladio, in Four Books ... With Notes and Remarks of Inigo Jones ... London: A. Ward ..., 1742. 3rd edn. 2 vols in one. Lge folio. viii,104,100 pp. Frontis, port, 230 plates. Occas foxing. Contemp reversed sheep, cover wear, rebacked. *(Bookpress)* **$2,850 [≈£1,900]**

Palmer, A.

- More Than Shadows: a Biography of W. Russell Flint ... London: Studio, July 1943. 1st reprint. [xii],148 pp. 8 cold plates, 128 ills. Orig cloth gilt. *(Clevedon Books)* **£26 [≈$39]**

Palmer, A.H.

- The Life & Letters of Samuel Palmer, Painter & Etcher. London: Seeley, 1892. Lge 8vo. Erratum slip. Ills, inc orig etching 'The Willow' (marg v sl foxed). Orig cloth gilt, ft of spine reprd. *(Mermaid Books)* **£140 [≈$210]**
- The Life and Letters of Samuel Palmer, Painter and Etcher. London: 1892. One of 130 Large Paper. Lge 4to. xiii,422 pp. 22 plates. Lacks the original etching. Bds, extrs scuffed, rec rebacked. *(Washton)* **$85 [≈£57]**
- The Life of Joseph Wolf, Animal Painter. London: Longmans Green, 1895. 1st edn. 8vo. xviii,328 pp. Sm stains. Orig cloth gilt, t.e.g., recased. *(Clevedon Books)* **£95 [≈$143]**

Palmer, R. Liddesdale

- English Monasteries in the Middle Ages. An

Outline of Monastic Architecture and Custom ... London: Constable, 1930. 4to. xv,233 pp. 74 ills. Few marg lib blind stamps. Orig cloth gilt, crnrs sl bumped, lib marks on spine. *(Hollett)* **£38 [≈$57]**

Palmer, R.L.

- English Monasteries in the Middle Ages: an Outline of Monastic Architecture and Custom ... London: Constable, 1930. 1st edn. 4to. 233 pp. Plans, photo ills. Orig cloth. Dw (worn). *(Monmouth)* **£25 [≈$38]**

Palmer, S.

- A General History of Printing ... London: Bettesworth ..., 1733. 2nd edn. 4to. vii,[v], 400 pp. Contemp calf, backstrip relaid, rubbed. *(Bookpress)* **$725 [≈£483]**

Palmer, Samuel

- The Eclogues of Virgil, An English Version by Samuel Palmer. With Illustrations by the Author. London: Seeley, 1883. 14 ills, inc 5 etched plates. Orig dec cloth, spine reprd. *(Mermaid Books)* **£425 [≈$638]**

Panofsky, Erwin

- Durer. London: OUP, 1945. 2nd edn, rvsd. 2 vols. 149 plates. Orig buckram. *(Leicester Art Books)* **£120 [≈$180]**
- The Life and Art of Albrecht Durer. Princeton: UP, 1955. 4th edn, rvsd. 4to. 317 pp. 327 b/w ills. Orig cloth. Dw. *(Abacus)* **$50 [≈£33]**
- Problems in Titian, mostly Iconographic. New York: New York UP, (1969). 1st edn. 8vo. xv,[i],208 pp. Frontis, 199 ills on plates. Orig cloth. Dw (sl sunned). *(Bookpress)* **$125 [≈£83]**
- Problems in Titian. Mostly Iconographic. New York: 1969. 4to. xv,208 pp. 199 ills. Orig cloth. Dw. *(Washton)* **$110 [≈£73]**
- Renaissance & Renascence in Western Art. Stockholm: 1965. 2nd edn, in one vol. Sm 4to. 242 pp. 157 ills on plates. Orig cloth. Dw (worn). *(Washton)* **$100 [≈£67]**

Papadaki, Stamo

- Le Corbusier, Architect, Painter, Writer. New York: Macmillan, 1948. Sm 4to. 152 pp. Ills. Endpapers sl foxed. Orig cloth. Dw (foxed & chipped). *(First Folio)* **$85 [≈£57]**

Papworth, John Buonarotti

- Hints on Ornamental Gardening ... London: Ackermann, 1823. 1st edn. Roy 8vo. 110,[ii index] pp. 28 hand cold aquatints (one with overslip). Contemp half calf, rebacked. *(Sotheran's)* **£2,200 [≈$3,300]**

The Paradise and the Peri ...

- The Paradise and the Peri. Illuminated in Gold and Colours by Owen Jones and Albert Warren. London: Day & Son, 1860. Tall 4to. 54 pp. Unfoxed. Orig pict cloth gilt, sl spotted, extrs v sl rubbed, recased. *(Barbara Stone)* **£195 [≈$293]**

Parker, John Henry

- A Glossary of Terms used in Grecian, Roman, Italian, and Gothic Architecture. Fourth Edition. Oxford: John Henry Parker, 1845. [With] A Companion to the Fourth Edition of A Glossary of Terms (Oxford, 1846). 3 vols. Roy 8vo. Frontises, 206 plates. Half mor. *(Ash)* **£125 [≈$188]**
- Some Account of Domestic Architecture in England: From Richard II to Henry VIII. Oxford: Parker, 1859. 1st edn. 2 vols. viii,491 pp. Plates. Ex-lib. Orig cloth, t.e.g. *(Castle Bookshop)* **£28 [≈$42]**

Parker, K.T.

- The Drawings of Antonio Canaletto in the Collection of His Majesty the King at Windsor Castle. Oxford & London: Phaidon, 1948. 126 pp. Cold frontis, 96 plates. Orig buckram. *(Leicester Art Books)* **£30 [≈$45]**

Parmelin, Helene

- Picasso Plain. New York: St. Martin's, (1963). 1st edn. Inscrptn. Dw (spine sl faded). *(Between the Covers)* **$45 [≈£30]**
- Picasso. Intimate Secrets of a Studio at Notre Dame de Vie. New York: Abrams, [ca 1966]. Lge sq 4to. 189 pp. Mtd cold plates. Orig dec cloth. Dw. *(First Folio)* **$125 [≈£83]**

Parsons, Arthur Jeffrey

- Catalog of the Gardiner Greene Hubbard Collection of Engravings at the Library of Congress. Washington: GPO, 1905. 4to. 517 pp. 12 plates. Orig etching frontis. Orig cloth. *(Rona Schneider)* **$80 [≈£53]**

Pascal, Blaise

- Les Pensees. Translated by Martin Turnell. Illustrations by Ismar David. New York: The Limited Editions Club, 1971. One of 1500 signed by the illustrator. Sm 4to. Orig cloth. Slipcase. *(Oak Knoll)* **$55 [≈£37]**

Passeron, Roger

- Daumier. Oxford: Phaidon, 1981. 329 pp. 226 ills. Orig cloth. Dw. *(Leicester Art Books)* **£45 [≈$68]**

Pater, Walter

- The Marriage of Cupid and Psyche.

Illustrated by Edmund Dulac. New York: The Limited Editions Club 1951. One of 1500 signed by Dulac. 6 cold plates. Orig vellum. Slipcase (sl dusty).
(Ulysses Bookshop) **£250 [≈$375]**

Paterson, Arthur

- The Homes of Tennyson. Illustrated by Helen Allingham. London: A. & C. Black, 1905. 1st edn. Sm 4to. 20 cold plates. Orig dec cloth gilt, hint of rubbing to extrs.
(Barbara Stone) **£110 [≈$165]**

Paul, Leslie

- Exile and Other Poems. Caravel Press: 1951. One of 200. 39 pp. 2 w'engvs by Guy Wordsell. Orig canvas gilt, t.e.g.
(Waddington) **£22 [≈$33]**

Paul, R.W.

- An Account of the Incised & Sepulchral Slabs of North-West Somersetshire ... London: Provost & Co., 1882. Sm folio. [viii],35,[i], iii,[iii] pp. Errata slip. Litho frontis, 33 plates. Occas sl spotting. Orig dec cloth.
(Sotheran's) **£65 [≈$98]**

Paulson, Ronald

- Hogarth's Graphic Works. Revised Edition. Yale: UP, 1970. 2 vols. Oblong 4to. Ills. Dws (sl worn). *(Spelman)* **£140 [≈$210]**
- Hogarth: His Life, Art, and Times. Yale: UP, 1971. 1st edn. 2 vols. 4to. Cold frontis, 314 ills. Dws (sl worn). *(Spelman)* **£160 [≈$240]**

Paviere, Sydney H.

- The Devis Family of Painters ... Leigh-on-Sea: F. Lewis, 1950. One of 500. 148 pp. 52 plates. Orig buckram. Dw.
(Leicester Art Books) **£80 [≈$120]**

Payne, A.A.

- A Handbook of British and Foreign Orders, War Medals and Decorations awarded to the Army and Navy ... Sheffield, J.W. Northend for subscribers only, 1911. Lge thick 8vo. lxix,812 pp. Port frontis, ills. Orig cloth gilt, spine sl scratched, recased.
(Hollett) **£180] [≈$270]**

Payne, Albert Henry

- Payne's Book of Art, with the Celebrated Galleries of Munich ... With Descriptive Text ... Dresden: A.H. Payne; London: W. French, [ca 1850]. 3 vols. 4to. [2],166; [2],180; [2],164 pp. 2 addtnl engvd titles, 182 plates. Occas foxing. Contemp deluxe mor gilt, a.e.g. *(Karmiole)* **$350 [≈£233]**

Payne, Humfry & Mackworth-Young, Gerard

- Archaic Marble Sculpture from the Acropolis. London: 1950. 2nd edn, rvsd. 4to. xiii,79 pp. Frontis, 140 plates. Lib stamp title verso. Orig cloth, faded, crnrs sl bumped.
(Francis Edwards) **£45 [≈$68]**

Paz, Octavio & Lassaigne, Jacques

- Rufino Tamayo. New York: Rizzoli, 1982. Lge sq 4to. 299 pp. 309 ills. Orig cloth. Dw.
(Ars Libri) **$100 [≈£67]**

Peacock, Carlos

- Painters and Writers. An Anthology. London: 1949. 1st edn. 96 cold plates. Orig dec cloth. *(Margaret Nangle)* **£36 [≈$54]**
- Samuel Palmer. Shoreham and After. London: John Baker, 1968. 1st edn. 144 pp. 35 plates, 23 text ills. Orig cloth, crnrs sl bruised. Dw (sl chipped & soiled).
(Bookworks) **£45 [≈$68]**

Peacock, Edward

- English Church Furniture. Ornaments and Decorations at the Period of the Reformation ... London: 1866. 8vo. 271 pp. Charts, engvs, cold frontis. Orig cloth, sl worn.
(Washton) **$100 [≈£67]**

Pearce, Helen

- The Enchanted Barn. With a Woodcut by Asa Cheffetz. New York: The Watch Hill Press, 1929. One of 100 containing an original woodcut, signed by Cheffetz. 8vo. Orig dec bds, sl worn.
(Black Sun) **$225 [≈£150]**

Pearce, Walter J.

- Painting and Decorating. London: Chas. Griffin, 1902. 2nd edn, rvsd & enlgd. 8vo. 3 cold plates, num ills. Orig dec cloth, fine.
(Book Block) **$225 [≈£150]**

The Pearl ...

- The Pearl or Affection's Gift for 1840. A Christmas and New Year's Present. Phila: Henry F. Anners, 1840. 12mo. 222 pp. 6 engvs (inc 4 mezzotints by John Sartain). Orig cloth. *(Rona Schneider)* **$60 [≈£40]**

Pearsall, Ronald

- Victorian Sheet Music Covers. Newton Abbott: David & Charles, 1972. 1st edn. Lge 8vo. 112 pp. Ills. Orig cloth gilt. Dw.
(Hollett) **£20 [≈$30]**

Pedretti, Carlo

- Leonardo da Vinci. The Royal Palace at Romorantin. Cambridge: 1972. 4to. xvii,354 pp. 175 ills. Orig cloth. *(Washton)* **$45 [≈£30]**

Pembroke, 16th Earl of

- A Catalogue of the Paintings and Drawings at Wilton House, Salisbury, Wiltshire. London: Phaidon Press, 1968. 98 pp. 149 plates. Dw. *(Fine Art)* **£45 [≈$68]**

Pendred, Mary L.

- John Martin, Painter, His Life and Times ... London: Hurst & Blackett, 1923. 318 pp. Port frontis, 20 plates. Orig cloth. *(Leicester Art Books)* **£33 [≈$50]**

Penkala, Maria

- European Porcelain. A Handbook for the Collector. Amsterdam: 1947. 1st edn. Ills. Orig cloth gilt. *(Hollett)* **£20 [≈$30]**

Penley, Aaron

- Sketching from Nature in Water-Colours ... London: John Camden Hotten, [1869]. 1st edn. Folio. Chromolitho half-title, 13 chromolitho plates, 2 litho plates (1 hand cold). Some spotting to prelims. Orig cloth gilt, rebacked. *(Sotheran's)* **£58 [≈$87]**
- Sketching from Nature in Water Colours. London: Cassell, Petter & Galpin, [ca 1875]. Folio. Chromolitho title,13 chromolitho plates, 2 litho plans. Sl foxing. Period prize half mor gilt, upper jnt cracked. *(Rankin)* **£65 [≈$98]**

Penn, William

- Some Fruits of Solitude, in Reflections and Maxims, relating to the Conduct of Human Life. Essex House Press: 1901. Sq 12mo. 257 pp. Orig vellum gilt, uncut. Anon. *(Peter Bell)* **£25 [≈$38]**

Pennell, Elizabeth Robins

- French Cathedrals. New York: Century, 1909. 4to. [xxxii],424 pp. 183 ills by Joseph Pennell, plans, diags. Orig cloth gilt. *(Schoyer)* **$50 [≈£33]**

Pennell, Elizabeth Robins & Pennell, Joseph

- The Life of James Mcneill Whistler. Phila: Lippincott, 1908. 1st Amer edn. 2 vols. 4to. Num plates, ills. Orig cloth over bds, extrs sl rubbed. *(Karmiole)* **$75 [≈£50]**
- The Life of James McNeill Whistler. Phila: Lippincott, 1911. 5th edn. 8vo. 449 pp. 100 ills. Orig cloth. *(Rona Schneider)* **$110 [≈£73]**

Pennell, Joseph

- Etchers and Etching. New York: Macmillan, 1919. 1st edn. 4to. 342 pp. 54 ills. Orig cloth. *(Rona Schneider)* **$50 [≈£33]**
- Etchers and Etching. Chapters in the History of the Art together with Technical Explanations of Modern Artistic Methods. New York: 1929. 4th edn. 343 pp. Plates. Orig cloth, sl worn. *(John K. King)* **$100 [≈£67]**
- Etchers and Etching. New York: Macmillan, 1936. 4th edn. 4to. 342 pp. 54 ills. Orig cloth. *(Rona Schneider)* **$40 [≈£27]**
- The Work of Charles Keene. London: Fisher Unwin, 1897. Large Paper. Lge 4to. 290 pp. Ills. Occas foxing. Orig cloth gilt, t.e.g., spine dull. *(Clevedon Books)* **£48 [≈$72]**
- The Work of Charles Keene. With an Introduction and Comments on the Drawings ... London: Fisher Unwin & Bradbury, Agnew, 1897. iv,290 pp. Frontis, 133 plates, 8 text ills. Orig cloth. *(Leicester Art Books)* **£80 [≈$120]**

Penrose, F.C.

- An Investigation of the Principles of Athenian Architecture ... Washington (1888) 1973. Folio. xii,128 pp. 47 plates, ills. Orig cloth, crnrs sl bumped. *(Quest Books)* **£65 [≈$98]**

Penrose, Roland

- Scrapbook 1900-1981. London: Thames & Hudson, 1981. 300 pp. 696 ills. Orig cloth. Dw. *(Fine Art)* **£35 [≈$53]**

Penty, Arthur J.

- The Elements of Domestic Design. London: The Architectural Press, 1930. 4to. vi,102 pp. 45 plates. Free endpapers spotted. Orig cloth, worn & soiled. *(Hollett)* **£20 [≈$30]**

Penzer, N.M.

- The Book of the Wine-Label. With a Foreword by Andre L. Simon. London: Home & Van Thal, 1947. 1st edn. 4to. 144 pp. 28 plates. Orig cloth, rubbed. *(Gough)* **£48 [≈$72]**
- Paul Storr. The Last of the Goldsmiths. With a Foreword by Charles Oman. London: Batsford, 1954. 1st edn. 4to. 292 pp. 81 plates. Orig buckram gilt. Dw. *(Hollett)* **£220 [≈$330]**

Pepler, H.D.C.

- The Hand Press: an Essay Written and

Printed by Hand for the Society of Typographic Arts, Chicago. Ditchling: St. Dominic's Press, 1934. One of 250 signed by the author. 8vo. [i],79,[1] pp. Ills. Free endpapers v sl browned. Orig canvas, cloth label. *(Blackwell's)* **£400 [≈$600]**

Pepper, Adeline

- The Glass Gaffers of New Jersey & their Creations from 1739 to the Present. New York: Scribner, 1971. Cr 4to. 332 pp. 19 cold & 240 b/w ills. Edges rubbed. Dw. *(Paul Brown)* **£28 [≈$42]**

Pepper, D. Stephen

- Guido Reni. A Complete Catalogue of His Work. Oxford: Phaidon, 1984. 336 pp. 327 ills. Orig cloth. Dw. *(Leicester Art Books)* **£70 [≈$105]**

Peppin, Brigid & Micklethwait, Lucy

- Dictionary of British Book Illustrators. The Twentieth Century. London: Murray, 1983. 1st edn. 4to. 336 pp. Ills. Orig cloth gilt. Dw. *(Hollett)* **£40 [≈$60]**

Perceval, MacIver

- The Glass Collector. London: Jenkins, [ca 1920s]. 331 pp. 30 plates, 95 text ills. Orig cloth, spine soiled. *(Paul Brown)* **£30 [≈$45]**

The Perfect Painter ...

- See Bell, Henry

Perrot, Georges & Chipiez, Charles

- A History of Art in Chaldaea and Assyria. Translated and Edited by Walter Armstrong. London: 1884. 2 vols. Sm 4to. xiii,398; xii,420 pp. 14 plates inc 4 chromolithos, 452 ills. Lib stamps & marks. Orig dec cloth, t.e.g., sl worn. *(Francis Edwards)* **£85 [≈$128]**
- A History of Art in Chaldaea and Assyria. London: 1884. 2 vols. 14 plates (4 cold), ills. *(Quest Books)* **£70 [≈$105]**
- A History of Art in Primitive Greece. Mycenian Art. London: Chapman & Hall, 1894. 2 vols. 8vo. 3 fldg plans, 7 fldg plates, 7 cold plates, 4 plates, ills. Orig dec cloth, spines sl faded. *(Quest Books)* **£95 [≈$143]**

Perry, Walter Copland

- Greek and Roman Sculpture: a Popular Introduction ... London: Longman, 1882. 8vo.268 w'engvs. Contemp prize calf. *(Waterfield's)* **£50 [≈$75]**

Perry-Gore, Noel

- Coherence through the Eyes of Mary. A Christmas Sermon with Designs by the Author rendered as Wood Engravings by Simon Brett. Paulinus Press: 1985. One of 250 signed by the author and artist. 4to. 16 pp. Orig wraps. *(Waddington)* **£20 [≈$30]**

Pertelote ...

- Pertelote. A Sequel to Chanticleer, being a Bibliography of the Golden Cockerel Press October 1936 - April 1943. London: 1943. 1st edn. Num w'engvs. Orig cloth, soiled. *(Margaret Nangle)* **£42 [≈$63]**

Pesatova, Zuzana

- Bohemian Engraved Glass. London: Hamlyn, 1968. 4to. 61 pp. 132 plates. Dw (edges damaged). *(Paul Brown)* **£32 [≈$48]**

Peters, Harry Twyford

- America on Stone. New York: Arno Press, 1976. 8vo. 415 pp. 173 ills. Orig cloth. *(Rona Schneider)* **$180 [≈£120]**

Peterson, William

- A Bibliography of the Kelmscott Press. Oxford: Clarendon Press 1985. xliv,220. 23 ills. Orig cloth. Dw. *(Claude Cox)* **£35 [≈$53]**
- The Kelmscott Press. A History of William Morris's Typographical Adventure. Oxford: Clarendon Press 1991. Roy 8vo. 97 ills. Dw. *(David Slade)* **£35 [≈$53]**

Petit, J.L.

- Remarks on Architectural Character. Read before the Lichfield Architectural Society, at their General Meeting in 1845. Oxford: John Henry Parker, 1846. Folio. 15,[1] pp. 44 litho plates. Text foxed. Orig cloth, rebacked. *(Spelman)* **£50 [≈$75]**
- Remarks on Church Architecture. London: John Petheram, 1841. 1st edn. 2 vols. 8vo. Num lithos. Contemp mor gilt extra, a.e.g., by Hayday. *(Traylen)* **£150 [≈$225]**

Petrarch

- Fifteen Sonnets of Petrarch. Boston: Houghton, Mifflin 1903. One of 430. 16mo. xiv,31 pp. Orig vellum-backed bds. Glassine. Slipcase (sl worn). Designed by Bruce Rogers. *(The Veatchs)* **$175 [≈£117]**

Petrie, George

- The Ecclesiastical Architecture of Ireland anterior to the Anglo-Norman Invasion ... and the Origin and Uses of Round Towers of Ireland. Dublin: Hodges Smith, 1845. 4to.

Orig cloth. *(Emerald Isle)* **£125 [≈$188]**

Petronius Arbiter

- A Revised Latin Text of the Satyricon ... Together with One Hundred Illustrations by Norman Lindsay. London: Privately Printed by Ralph Straus, 1910. One of 250 signed by the artist and the publisher. Lge 4to. xv,303 pp. Rec half mor, t.e.g. *(Robert Frew)* **£145 [≈$218]**
- The Satyricon of Petronius. Illustrated by Antonio Sotomayor. New York: The Limited Editions Club , 1964. One of 1500 signed by the illustrator. Sm 4to. Orig parchment-backed cloth. Slipcase. *(Oak Knoll)* **$65 [≈£43]**

Pevsner, Nikolaus

- An Enquiry into Industrial Art in England. Cambridge: 1937. 1st edn. Lge 8vo. 24 ills. Orig cloth. *(Spelman)* **£40 [≈$60]**
- Pioneers of the Modern Movement from William Morris to Walter Gropius. London: Faber, 1936. 1st edn. 80 ills. Front endpapers sl browned. Dw (rubbed, sm pieces missing spine ends). *(Clearwater)* **£45 [≈$68]**

Philby, H. St. John

- A Pilgrim in Arabia. London: The Golden Cockerel Press, 1943. One of 350. Sm 4to. 191 pp. Port frontis. Orig qtr mor & cream cloth bds, minor soil. *(Trophy Room Books)* **$1,000 [≈£667]**

Philipp, Franz

- Arthur Boyd. London: Thames & Hudson, 1967. 288 pp. 178 ills. Orig cloth. *(Leicester Art Books)* **£65 [≈$98]**

Phillips, Duncan

- The Leadership of Giorgione. With a Note by H.G. Dwight. Washington: The American Federation of Arts, 1937. 1st edn. 4to. [16], 198 pp. Num ills. Orig cloth. *(Karmiole)* **$50 [≈£33]**

Phillips, Euan (editor)

- Tributes to Brooke Crutchley on his Retirement as University Printer. Cambridge: 1975. One of 650. 4to. Orig cloth backed bds, v sl bumped. *(Ulysses Bookshop)* **£85 [≈$128]**

Phillips, G.F.

- The Art of Drawing and Painting simplified in a Series of Examples of Parts of the Human Figure ... London: 1840. 8vo. vi,[2],59,[1] pp. Hand cold frontis & title, 19 plates (5 hand cold). Marg spotting & browning. Orig cloth gilt, hd of spine reprd. *(Spelman)* **£120 [≈$180]**
- A Practical Treatise on Drawing and on Painting in Water Colours. London: A. & H. Bailey, 1839. 1st edn. 8vo. vi,48 pp. Engvd title with hand cold vignette, colour chart, 5 cold aquatints, 14 soft-ground etchings. Occas foxing. Orig cloth gilt, spine ends sl worn. *(Spelman)* **£120 [≈$180]**
- A Practical Treatise on Drawing and on painting in Water Colours with Illustrative Examples ... London: A.H. Bailey, 1839. 1st edn. 8vo. vi,48 pp. Engvd title with hand cold aquatint, 5 hand cold aquatints, colour chart, 14 soft ground etchings. Orig cloth. *(Clevedon Books)* **£170 [≈$255]**
- The Theory and Practice of Painting in Water Colours, as connected with the Study of Landscape. London: Charles Tilt, 1838. 1st edn. Oblong 4to. 34 pp, advt leaf. 4 hand cold & 10 sepia plates. Minor foxing & offsetting. Orig half mor gilt. *(Spelman)* **£280 [≈$420]**

Phillips, J.B.

- St Luke's Life of Christ. Illustrated by Edward Ardizzone. London: 1956. One of 150 signed by translator and illustrator. Orig mor backed cloth. Slipcase. *(Words Etcetera)* **£65 [≈$98]**

Phillips, Philip

- The Forth Bridge in its Various Stages of Construction ... Edinburgh: Grant, [1899]. 1st edn. Oblong folio. [x],233 pp. 52 plates. Later qtr mor, orig pict cvr laid down. *(Bookpress)* **$2,500 [≈£1,667]**

Phillips, R.R.

- Small Family Houses. London: Country Life, 1924. 1st edn. 8vo. 159 pp. Num ills. Orig cloth gilt, stained, shaken. *(Clevedon Books)* **£25 [≈$38]**

Phillpotts, Eden

- A Dish of Apples. Illustrated by Arthur Rackham. London: 1921. One of 575 signed by the author and the artist. 3 mtd cold plates, 7 b/w ills, decs. Endpapers v sl spotted. Orig pict gilt buckram, t.e.g., v sl soiled and scratched, spine ends sl bumped. *(Ulysses Bookshop)* **£575 [≈$863]**
- A Dish of Apples. Illustrated by Arthur Rackham. London & New York: Hodder & Stoughton, (1921). One of 500 signed by the author and by Rackham. 75 pp. 3 mtd cold

plates, 23 b/w ills, pict endpapers. B'plate. Orig pict cloth gilt. *(Argonaut)* **$700 [≈£467]**

Phipson, Emma

- Choir Stalls and their Carvings. Examples of Misericords from English Cathedrals and Churches ... London: Batsford, 1896. 4to. v, 121 pp. Frontis, 101 plates. Orig pict cloth gilt, sm snag hd of spine. *(Hollett)* **£85 [≈$128]**

Physick, John

- Catalogue of the Engraved Work of Eric Gill. London: Victoria & Albert Museum, 1963. vii,266 pp. Orig cloth. *(Leicester Art Books)* **£30 [≈$45]**

Picasso, Pablo

- Graphic Works. 1899-1955; 1955-1965. London: Thames & Hudson, 1966-67. 2 vols. 4to. 6 cold plates, 286 ills. Dws. *(Spelman)* **£70 [≈$105]**
- Picasso 347. New York: Random House & Maecenas Press, (1970). 1st edn. 2 vols. Oblong 4to. 347 plates. Orig linen over cloth. Box. *(Karmiole)* **$300 [≈£200]**
- Picasso's Vollard Suite. Introduction by Hans Bollinger. London: Thames & Hudson, 1956. 1st edn. 4to. Ills. Dw (hd of spine torn). *(Spelman)* **£35 [≈$53]**
- Posters of Picasso. New York: Crown, 1957. Folio. Dw. Inscribed by the editor, Joseph Foster, and signed by Picasso. *(Lame Duck Books)* **$2,500 [≈£1,667]**

Picon, Gaetan

- Joan Miro, Catalan Notebooks. New York: Rizzoli, (1977). 1st edn. 4to. 157,[1] pp. Frontis, 180 ills. Orig cloth. Dw. Slipcase. *(Bookpress)* **$65 [≈£43]**
- Joan Miro: Catalan Notebooks. New York: Skira/Rizzoli, (1977). 4to. 157 pp. 30 cold & 150 b/w ills. Orig cloth. Dw. Slipcase. *(Abacus)* **$50 [≈£33]**

Piene, Otto

- More Sky 1. Part 1: Things to Do, A-M. Part II: Wind Manual I, II, III. Cambridge: Migrant Apparition, 1970. Lge 4to. 142 ff. Num ills. Orig spiral-bound wraps. *(Ars Libri)* **$100 [≈£67]**

Piggott, F.T.

- Studies in the Decorative Art of Japan. London: Batsford, 1910. 1st edn. 4to. 130 pp. 33 plates. Name. Orig cloth. *(Bookpress)* **$225 [≈£150]**

Pignatti, Terisio

- The Doges Palace. New York: n.d. Folio. 11 pp. Num plates (42 cold). Orig cloth. Dw (worn). *(Washton)* **$85 [≈£57]**
- Giorgione. Complete Edition. London: Phaidon, 1971. 1st English edn. 4to. 369 pp. 24 cold plates, 331 b/w ills. Dw (sl worn). *(Spelman)* **£65 [≈$98]**
- Giorgione. London: Phaidon, 1971. 369 pp. 24 mtd cold plates, 331 ills. Orig cloth. Dw. *(Leicester Art Books)* **£85 [≈$128]**
- Giorgione: Complete Edition. London: Phaidon, 1971. 369 pp. 24 cold & 331 b/w plates. Orig cloth. Dw. *(Fine Art)* **£65 [≈$98]**
- Pietro Longhi. Paintings and Drawings. London: Phaidon, 1969. 419 pp. 24 mtd cold plates, 550 ills. Orig cloth. Dw. *(Leicester Art Books)* **£50 [≈$75]**

Pilkington, Matthew

- A General Dictionary of Painters ... London: Thomas Tegg, 1829. 2 vols. Demy 8vo. [xxxii],(528); [ii],(602) pp. Contemp half calf, v sl rubbed. *(Ash)* **£95 [≈$143]**
- The Gentleman's and Connoisseur's Dictionary of Painters ... London: for T. Cadell, 1770. 1st edn. 4to. xxxiv,723,[3] pp. Final errata leaf. Contemp calf, sm reprs. *(Spelman)* **£140 [≈$210]**
- The Gentleman's and Connoisseur's Dictionary of Painters ... A New Edition [with] A Supplement ... by James Barry. London: Walker & Robinson, 1798. Lge 4to. xii,840,xxiv pp. 1st few ff sl spotted. Contemp calf, backstrip relaid. *(Claude Cox)* **£55 [≈$83]**

Pincus-Witten, Robert

- Jedd Garet. Pasadena: Twelvetree Press, 1984. 4to. 167,[3] pp. 65 cold plates. Orig cloth. Dw. *(Ars Libri)* **$45 [≈£30]**

Pindborg, J.J. & Marvitz, L.

- The Dentist in Art. London: George Proffer, 1961. 1st English edn. Lge 8vo. 144 pp. Mtd cold plates, ills. Orig bds. Dw (sl marked). *(Hollett)* **£40 [≈$60]**

Pinder-Wilson, R. (editor)

- Paintings from Islamic Lands. Oxford: Bruno Cassirer, 1969. Roy 8vo. 204 pp. Orig cloth gilt. Dw. *(Gray)* **£20 [≈$30]**

Piper, David

- Catalogue of Seventeenth Century Portraits in the National Portrait Gallery 1625-1714. Cambridge: UP, 1963. xxvii,410 pp. 33

plates. Cloth. *(Fine Art)* **£60 [≈$90]**

- The Image of the Poet. British Poets and their Portraits. London: 1982. 1st edn. 225 ills. Orig bndg, ft of spine sl bumped. Dw (creased). *(Ulysses Bookshop)* **£30 [≈$45]**

Piper, Myfanwy

- The Wood-Engravings of Reynolds Stone. London: Art & Technics, 1951. 1st edn. Ills. Orig bndg, spine ends sl bumped. Dw (frayed and nicked, sl rubbed). *(Ulysses Bookshop)* **£55 [≈$83]**

Pitt, George H.

- The Press in South Australia, 1836 to 1850. Adelaide: The Wakefield Press, 1946. 8vo. [v],60,[1] pp. Ills. Orig cloth. Dw. *(Oak Knoll)* **$65 [≈£43]**

Pitt-Rivers, Augustus

- Antique Works of Art from Benin. With a New Introduction by Bernard Fagg. Dover: 1976. 4to. vi,100 pp. 50 plates. Orig pict wraps. *(Hollett)* **£35 [≈$53]**

Pivar, Stuart

- The Barye Bronzes. A Catalogue Raisonne. Woodbridge: Antique Collectors Club, 1981. 284 pp. 282 ills. Orig cloth. *(Leicester Art Books)* **£22 [≈$33]**

Plato

- Crito. A Socratic Dialogue. Translated by Henry Cary. [Printed at the Officina Bodoni, Montagnola, for] The Pleiad, Paris, 1926. One of 470. Orig mrbld bds, paper label, paper caps at spine ends, uncut. *(Claude Cox)* **£250 [≈$375]**
- Lysis, or Friendship, The Symposium Phaedrus. Illustrations by Eugene Karlin. New York: The Limited Editions Club, 1968. One of 1500 signed by the illustrator. Tall 8vo. Orig qtr vellum. Slipcase. *(Oak Knoll)* **$75 [≈£50]**
- The Phaedo ... Translated into English by Benjamin Jowett. Waltham Saint Lawrence: Golden Cockerel Press, 1930. One of 500. Lge 8vo. Decs by Eric Gill. Orig buckram gilt, t.e.g., spine faded, crnrs bumped. *(Claude Cox)* **£55 [≈$83]**
- Plato's Symposium or Supper. Newly translated by Francis Birrell & Shane Leslie. London: Nonesuch Press, [1924]. One of 1050. Orig buckram backed bds, uncut. Dw (sl soiled & frayed). *(Claude Cox)* **£28 [≈$42]**
- The Trial and Death of Socrates. Illustrations by Hans Erni. New York: The Limited Editions Club, 1962. One of 1500 signed by the illustrator & by Mardersteig. Sm 4to. Orig cloth. Dw. Slipcase. *(Oak Knoll)* **$150 [≈£100]**

Plaw, John

- Sketches for Country Houses, Villas and Rural Dwellings ... also some Designs for Cottages ... London: J. Taylor, 1800. 1st edn. 4to. 18,[2 advt] pp. 42 sepia plates. Few sm marg marks. Contemp half calf, rebacked, rubbed, crnrs sl worn. *(Sotheran's)* **£438 [≈$657]**

Players of the Day ...

- Players of the Day. A Series of Portraits in Colour of Theatrical Celebrities of the Present Time. Based on Photographs. London: Newnes, [ca 1905]. Folio. 48 mtd plates. Orig pict cloth, worn, shaken. *(Carol Howard)* **£70 [≈$105]**

Plenderleith, H.J. & Werner, A.E.A.

- The Conservation of Antiquities and Works of Art, Treatment, Repair and Restoration. London: OUP, (1974). 2nd edn, rvsd, reprint. 8vo. xix,394 pp . 46 plates. Orig cloth. *(Oak Knoll)* **$65 [≈£43]**
- The Conversation of Antiquities and Works of Art: Treatment, Repair and Restoration. OUP: 1979. 2nd edn. 394 pp. 46 plates, 10 text figs. Orig cloth. Dw. *(Fine Art)* **£38.50 [≈$59]**

Plomer, Henry R.

- A Short History of English Printing, 1476-1898. London: Kegan Paul ..., 1900. 1st edn. Sq 8vo. xvi,330 pp. 4 plates, 39 text ills. Later buckram, t.e.g. *(Oak Knoll)* **$75 [≈£50]**
- Wynkyn De Worde, and His Contemporaries from the Death of Caxton to 1535. London: 1925. 4to. Frontis, 13 ills. Orig cloth backed bds. *(Traylen)* **£48 [≈$72]**

Plowman, George T.

- Etching and Other Graphic Arts. London: John Lane; The Bodley Head, 1914. One of 350. 8vo. 154 pp. 27 ills. Orig etching frontis signed by Plowman. Orig dec cloth. *(Rona Schneider)* **$50 [≈£33]**

Plummer, John (compiler)

- The Glazier Collection of Illuminated Manuscripts. New York: Pierpont Morgan Library, 1968. 1st edn. Sm 4to. 50 pp. 57 plates. Minor underlinings. Orig cloth. *(Karmiole)* **$35 [≈£23]**

Plutarch

- The Lives of the Noble Grecians & Romans ... London: Nonesuch Press, 1929-30. One of 1550. 5 vols. Folio. Ports. Orig buckram, t.e.g. on the rough. *(Claude Cox)* **£130 [≈$195]**

Poe, Edgar Allan

- The Bells and Other Poems. Illustrated by Edmund Dulac. London: Hodder & Stoughton, [1912]. 1st Dulac edn. 4to. [xii],174 pp. 28 cold plates. Occas v sl speckling of prelims & edges. Orig elab gilt cloth, 2 sm scratches lower bd. *(Sotheran's)* **£220 [≈$330]**
- The Bells and Other Poems. Illustrated by Edmund Dulac. London: Hodder & Stoughton, [1912]. 1st Dulac edn. Lge 4to. 28 mtd cold plates, port, 10 text ills. Orig pict gilt cloth, two marks lower cvr. *(Barbara Stone)* **£175 [≈$263]**
- The Mask of the Red Death. Baltimore: Aquarius Press, 1969. One of 500 signed by the artist, Frederico Castellon. Folio. 16 cold lithos. Orig cloth gilt. Slipcase. *(First Folio)* **$250 [≈£167]**
- The Murders in the Rue Morgue. Antibes, France: Allen Press, (1958). One of 150. 8vo. 81 pp. Ills. Orig cold bds, spine crnrs sl worn. *(The Veatchs)* **$400 [≈£267]**
- The Narrative of Arthur Gordon Pym. With Designs by Rene Clarke. New York: The Limited Editions Club, 1930. One of 1500 signed by the illustrator. 4to. Orig parchment-backed cloth. Slipcase (soiled & rubbed). *(Oak Knoll)* **$125 [≈£83]**
- The Poems. Illustrated by W. Heath Robinson. London: Bell, 1910. Dec title, 27 full-page & 76 smaller ills, dec endpapers. Orig dec cloth gilt, spine sl darkened, spine ends reprd. *(Barbara Stone)* **£110 [≈$165]**
- The Raven. With a Comment upon the Poem by Edmund Clarence Stedman. London: 1883. Folio. 23pp. 26 plates by Gustave Dore. Few sl marks. Orig cloth, a.e.g., sl worn & shaken. *(Francis Edwards)* **£125 [≈$188]**
- Tales of Mystery and Imagination. Illustrated by Harry Clarke. New York: Tudor, 1933. 1st edn thus. 4to. 412,[1] pp. Frontis, 31 plates. Orig cloth, sl rubbed. Box. *(Bookpress)* **$225 [≈£150]**
- Tales of Mystery and Imagination. Illustrated by Harry Clarke. London: Harrap, (1928). Sm cr 4to. 384 pp. 24 b/w plates. Orig simulated leather-cloth, gilt spine. *(Bow Windows)* **£115 [≈$173]**
- Tales of Mystery and Imagination. Illustrated by Arthur Rackham. London: Harrap, 1935. 1st edn. 4to. 318 pp. 12 cold plates, dec endpapers. Orig cloth gilt. Dw. *(Robert Frew)* **£300 [≈$450]**

Poetry of the Year ...

- Poetry of the Year, or Pastorals from Our Poets. (Illustrative of the Seasons). New Edition. London: Charles Griffin, [ca 1870s]. 16 chromolithos by Birket Foster & others. Prelims foxed. Orig dec cloth gilt, a.e.g. *(Old Cathay)* **£89 [≈$134]**

Pointon, Marcia

- William Dyce 1806-1864. OUP: 1979. 1st edn. 256 pp. 163 plates. Orig cloth. Dw. *(Bookworks)* **£18 [≈$27]**

Poling, Clark V.

- Kandinsky: Russian and Bauhaus Years, 1915-1933. New York: Guggenheim Museum, 1983. Sq 4to. 360 pp. Num ills. Orig wraps. *(Ars Libri)* **$45 [≈£30]**

Political ...

- A Political and Satyrical History of the Years 1756, 1757, 1758, and 1759. In a Series of One Hundred Humorous and Entertaining Prints ... London: for E. Morris, [1760]. Sm sq 8vo. 15,8 pp. 100 plates. Sl browning & spotting. Contemp calf, backstrip relaid. *(Spelman)* **£650 [≈$975]**

Pollard, Alfred W.

- Early Illustrated Books. London: Kegan Paul, 1943. One of 150. Large Paper. xvi,256 pp. Orig qtr vellum, spine darkened. *(Bookpress)* **$85 [≈£57]**
- Early Illustrated Books. London: Kegan Paul ..., Books About Books Series, 1943. One of 150. Lge 8vo. xvi,256 pp. Orig qtr vellum, spine darkened. *(Bookpress)* **$85 [≈£57]**
- Fine Books. London: EP Publishing, 1973. Sm 4to. xviii,332 pp. 40 plates. Orig cloth. Dw. *(Oak Knoll)* **$40 [≈£27]**
- Italian Book Illustrations chiefly of the Fifteenth Century. London: Seeley & Co., 1894. 1st edn. Lge 8vo. 80 pp. 9 plates, 28 text ills. Orig cloth, faded. *(Claude Cox)* **£22 [≈$33]**
- Italian Book Illustrations chiefly of the Fifteenth Century. London: Seeley & Co., 1894. 1st edn. Sm 4to. 80 pp. 37 ills. Orig parchment backed bds (spine rubbed). *(Oak Knoll)* **$85 [≈£57]**

Pollard, Alfred W. & Redgrave, G.R.

- A Short-title Catalogue of Books Printed in England, Scotland & Ireland and of English Books Printed Abroad 1475-1640. London: 1926. 4to. Orig linen backed bds. *(Traylen)* **£40 [≈$60]**

Pollen, John Hungerford

- A Description of the Trajan Column. London: Eyre & Spottiswoode, 1874. 8vo. 181 pp. Frontis, 45 w'cut ills. Orig cloth gilt. *(Hollett)* **£35 [≈$53]**

Pollen, Mrs John Hungerford

- Seven Centuries of Lace ... London: Heinemann, 1908. Lge 4to. xvi,59 pp. 120 plates. Lib stamps on title. Orig pict cloth gilt, t.e.g., trifle rubbed, sm label removed from spine. *(Hollett)* **£95 [≈$143]**

Pomeroy, Ralph

- Stamos. New York: Abrams, n.d. Lge oblong 4to. 271,[1] pp. 214 ills. Orig cloth. Dw. *(Ars Libri)* **$250 [≈£167]**

Ponente, Nello

- The Structures of the Modern World 1850-1900. Geneva: Skira, (1965). 4to. 210 pp. 66 mtd cold plates, ills. Orig cloth. Dw. Slipcase. *(Abacus)* **$65 [≈£43]**

Ponge, Francis, & others

- G. Braque. New York: Abrams, [1971]. Lge sq 4to. 261,[7] pp. Num ills. Orig cloth. Dw. *(Ars Libri)* **$250 [≈£167]**

Poole, Monica

- The Wood Engravings of John Farleigh. London: Gresham, 1985. 1st edn. 122 pp. Num ills. Orig buckram gilt. Dw. Box. *(Willow House)* **£35 [≈$53]**

Poole, Phoebe (compiler)

- Poems of Death. Chosen by Phoebe Pool. London: Muller, New Excursions into English Poetry Series, 1945. 1st edn. 16 lithos by Michael Ayrton. Dw. *(Mermaid Books)* **£26 [≈$39]**

Pooley, Charles

- An Historical and Descriptive Account of the Old Stone Crosses of Somerset. London: Longmans, Green, 1877. 4to. xvi,188 pp. 4 pp subscribers inserted. Map, 20 plates. Orig cloth. *(Sotheran's)* **£55 [≈$83]**

Pope, Alexander, & others

- Pope's Own Miscellany. Edited by Norman Ault. London: Nonesuch Press, 1935. One of 750. Orig gilt dec buckram, gilt on top edge worn, spine ends v sl bumped. Dw (nicked and creased). *(Ulysses Bookshop)* **£95 [≈$143]**

Pope, Arthur Upham

- Persian Architecture. The Triumph of Form and Color. New York: Braziller, (1965). Sm 4to. 288 pp. 23 cold plates, 364 ills. Sm tear in title. Orig cloth. Dw (sl torn). *(Mendelsohn)* **$50 [≈£33]**

Pope, John Alexander

- Chinese Porcelains from the Ardebil Shrine. Washington: Freer Gallery of Art, 1956. 4to. 194 pp. 142 plates. Orig cloth. Dw. *(Abacus)* **$100 [≈£67]**

Pope-Hennessy, John

- Cellini. Principal Photography by David Finn. London: Macmillan, 1985. 324 pp. 258 ills. Orig cloth. Dw. *(Leicester Art Books)* **£70 [≈$105]**
- The Complete Work of Paolo Uccello. London: 1950. 4to. 173 pp. 175 ills on plates. Orig cloth, spine ends sl frayed. Dw (worn). *(Washton)* **$40 [≈£27]**
- The Drawings of Domenichino in the Collection of His Majesty the King at Windsor Castle. London: Phaidon Press, 1948. 188 pp. 141 ills. Orig buckram. *(Leicester Art Books)* **£85 [≈$128]**
- Fra Angelico. Ithaca: 1974. 2nd edn, rvsd. 4to. 242 pp. 15 cold plates, 272 ills. Orig cloth. Dw. *(Washton)* **$125 [≈£83]**
- Italian Gothic Sculpture. London: Phaidon, 1955. 1st edn. 4to. [vi],224,[4] pp. 108 plates. Orig cloth. Dw (torn). *(Bookpress)* **$45 [≈£30]**
- Italian Renaissance Sculpture. London: Phaidon, (1971). 2nd edn, rvsd. 4to. [6],366 pp. 144 plates, 165 text figs. Orig cloth. Dw. *(Karmiole)* **$75 [≈£50]**
- Luca della Robbia. Oxford: Phaidon, 1980. 288 pp. 232 ills. Orig cloth. Dw. *(Leicester Art Books)* **£52 [≈$78]**
- The Portrait in the Renaissance. London: Phaidon, 1966. 348,xxxii pp. 330 plates. Orig cloth. Dw. *(Fine Art)* **£40 [≈$60]**
- Raphael. The Wrightsman Lectures. London: Phaidon, 1970. 304 pp. 246 ills. Orig cloth. *(Leicester Art Books)* **£32 [≈$48]**
- Sienese Quattrocento Painting. Oxford: Phaidon Press, (1947). 1st edn. 4to. 33,[6] pp. Frontis, 93 plates. Lib marks. Orig cloth, sl worn. *(Bookpress)* **$65 [≈£43]**

Pope-Hennessy, Una

- Early Chinese Jades. London: Benn, 1923. 4to. 64 plates. Orig cloth. *(Traylen)* **£80 [≈$120]**

Popham, A.E.

- Correggio's Drawings. London: OUP, 1957. xx,218 pp. 110 plates, 72 text ills. Orig buckram. *(Leicester Art Books)* **£125 [≈$188]**

Popham, A.E. & Pouncey, Philip

- Italian Drawings in the Department of Prints and Drawings in the British Museum. The Fourteenth and Fifteenth Centuries. London: BM, 1950. 2 vols. Sm 4to. Frontis, 286 plates. Dw (sl worn & soiled). *(Francis Edwards)* **£60 [≈$90]**

Porcher, Jean

- Medieval French Miniatures. New York: 1959. Lge 4to. 276 pp. 90 mtd cold plates. Orig cloth. Dw (worn). *(Washton)* **$100 [≈£67]**
- Medieval French Miniatures. New York: Abrams, (1959). 1st edn. Mtd plates. Dw (sl worn). *(Hermitage)* **$125 [≈£83]**

Porny, Marc Antoine (Antoine Pyron du Martre)

- The Elements of Heraldry ... The Fifth Edition, with considerable Alterations and Additions. London: Robinson ..., 1795. 24 plates. Later half calf, rubbed. *(Jarndyce)* **£30 [≈$45]**

Portfolio ...

- Portfolio. A Quarterly of New Ideas made Visible. New York: 1959-1964. Vols 1-8, all published. Lge 4to. Bds. *(Ars Libri)* **$300 [≈£200]**

Portoghesi, Paolo

- Rome of the Renaissance. London: 1972. Sq 4to. 450 pp. 446 ills. Orig cloth. Dw. *(Washton)* **$100 [≈£67]**

Posner, Donald

- Annibale Carracci. A Study in the Reform of Italian Painting around 1590. London: Phaidon, 1971. 2 vols. 10 cold plates, 472 ills. Orig cloth. Dws. *(Leicester Art Books)* **£550 [≈$825]**

Postan, Alexander

- The Complete Graphic Work of Paul Nash. London: 1973. 87 pp. 79 ills. B'plate. Orig cloth. Dw. *(Fine Art)* **£55 [≈$83]**
- The Complete Graphic Work of Paul Nash. London: 1973. 87 pp. 82 ills. Orig cloth. Dw. *(Leicester Art Books)* **£40 [≈$60]**

Postenkno, O.

- The Cathedral of St. Sophia in Kiev. New York: Ukrainian Academy of Arts & Sciences, 1954. 4to. 469 pp. 336 ills. Backstrip sl worn. *(Washton)* **$150 [≈£100]**

Potter, Margaret & Alexander

- Houses. Being a Record of the Changes in Construction Style and Plan of the Smaller English Home from Mediaeval Times ... London: Murray, 1948. 1st edn. 4to. 48 pp. Ills. Orig cloth gilt. Dw. *(Hollett)* **£25 [≈$38]**

Potterton, Homan

- National Gallery of Ireland Illustrated Summary Catalogue of Paintings. Dublin: Gill & MacMillan, 1981. 363 pp. Num ills. Orig cloth. Dw. *(Fine Art)* **£30 [≈$45]**

Poulik, Josef

- Prehistoric Art. London: Spring Books, n.d. 1st edn. 4to. 47,[5] pp. Frontis, 189 ills. Orig cloth. Dw (worn). *(Bookpress)* **$85 [≈£57]**

Pouncey, Philip & Gere, J.A.

- Italian Drawings in the Department of Prints & Drawings in the British Museum: Raphael and his Circle ... London: BM, 1962. 2 vols (text & plates). 278 plates. Orig cloth. Dws. *(Clarice Davis)* **$150 [≈£100]**

Pound, Ezra

- Gaudier-Brzeska: A Memoir. London: Marvell Press, 1960. New edn. 147 pp. 30 plates. Orig cloth. Dw. *(Fine Art)* **£22.50 [≈$35]**

Powell, Nicholas

- From Baroque to Rococo. An Introduction to Austrian and German Architecture 1580-1790. London: 1959. 1st edn. 4to. Plates, ills. Dw (v sl nicked). *(Adam Blakeney)* **£35 [≈$53]**

Powys, John Cowper

- Lucifer. A Poem. With Wood Engravings by Agnes Miller Parker. London: Macdonald, [1956]. One of 560 signed by the author. 8vo. Orig leather & cloth gilt. Acetate dw. *(Dermont)* **$175 [≈£117]**

Powys, Llewelyn

- The Twelve Months. London: Bodley Head, 1936. 1st edn. 88 pp. 28 w'engvs by Robert Gibbings. Endpapers v sl browned. Orig 2-tone cloth. Dw (sl marked). *(Waddington)* **£58 [≈$87]**

- The Twelve Months. London: Bodley Head, 1936 [1937]. 1st trade edn. 108 pp. W'engvs by Robert Gibbings. Orig cloth gilt, touch of soiling at tail edge. Dw (chipped, sl soiled). *(Bookworks)* **£48 [≈$72]**
- The Twelve Months. Wood-Engravings by Robert Gibbings. London: 1936. 1st edn. Orig cloth gilt. Dw (sl worn). *(Margaret Nangle)* **£85 [≈$128]**

Powys, Marian

- Lace and Lake-Making. Boston: Charles T. Branford, 1953. 1st edn. 4to. Num ills. Orig cloth. Dw (sl frayed). *(David Slade)* **£65 [≈$98]**

Powys, T.F.

- Goat Green, or the Better Gift. Golden Cockerel Press: 1937. One of 150 signed by the author. W'engvs by Gwenda Morgan. Orig qtr mor, spine sl sunned. *(Waddington)* **£120 [≈$180]**

Poynter, Sir Edward J.

- Lectures on Art. London: Chapman & Hall, 1885. 3rd edn. 283 pp. Prize calf gilt, sl worn & faded. *(Willow House)* **£30 [≈$45]**
- The National Gallery. London: Cassell, 1899. One of 1000. 2 vols. 4to. Num photo plates. Contemp mor gilt extra, t.e.g., by Zaehnsdorf, v sl scratched. *(Wilkinson)* **£120 [≈$180]**

Pozzo, Andrea

- Rules and Examples of Perspective Proper for Painters and Architects ... London: Benjamin Motte, 1707. 1st edn in English. Folio. [xx],130 pp. 103 plates inc 2 engvd titles. Contemp calf, spine darkened, hinges beginning to crack. *(Bookpress)* **$3,500 [≈£2,333]**

The Practice of Perspective ...

- See Dubreuil, Jean

Prasse, Leona E.

- Lyonel Feininger. A Definitive Catalogue of the Graphic Work. Etchings. Lithographs. Woodcuts. Cleveland: 1972. 304 pp. 571 ills. Orig cloth. *(Leicester Art Books)* **£160 [≈$240]**
- Lyonel Feininger. Das Graphische Werk ... A Definitive Catalogue of his Graphic Work ... Berlin & Cleveland: 1972. Lge 4to. 304 pp. Num ills. Orig cloth. *(Ars Libri)* **$650 [≈£433]**

Praz, Mario

- Conversation Pieces: A Survey of the Informal Group Portrait in Europe and America. London: 1971. 287 pp. 380 ills. Orig cloth. Dw. *(Fine Art)* **£36 [≈$54]**
- An Illustrated History of Interior Decoration, from Pompeii to Art Nouveau. New York: Thames & Hudson, (1981). 4to. 396 pp. Num ills. Orig cloth. Dw. *(Karmiole)* **$50 [≈£33]**

Prescott, William Hickling

- History of the Reign of Ferdinand and Isabella. New York: The Limited Editions Club, 1967. One of 1500 signed by the illustrator. Tall 8vo. Orig calf. Slipcase. *(Oak Knoll)* **$55 [≈£37]**

Pressly, William L.

- The Life and Art of James Barry. New Haven: Yale UP, 1981. xiv,320 pp. 157 ills. Orig cloth. Dw. *(Leicester Art Books)* **£50 [≈$75]**

Preston, Rupert

- The Seventeenth-Century Marine Painters of the Netherlands. Leigh-on-Sea: 1974. 4to. viii, 102 pp. 91 ills on plates. Orig cloth. Dw. *(Washton)* **$60 [≈£40]**

Price, F.G. Hilton

- Old Base Metal Spoons: with Illustrations and Marks. London: Batsford, 1908. 99 pp. 16 plates, ills. Orig dec cloth, t.e.g., hd of spine damaged. *(Castle Bookshop)* **£85 [≈$128]**

Price, Francis

- A Series of Particular and Useful Observations ... upon ... the Cathedral-Church of Salisbury ... London: Ackers for Baldwin, 1753. 1st edn. 4to. Subscribers. Frontis, 13 plates. Contemp calf, backstrip relaid, crnrs reprd. *(Spelman)* **£320 [≈$480]**

Price, Frederic Newlin

- The Etchings and Lithographs of Arthur B. Davies. With an Introduction. New York & London: 1929. One of 200 with an orig etching. 23,[210] pp. 205 plates. Orig qtr mor gilt, t.e.g. Slipcase. *(Ars Libri)* **$850 [≈£567]**

Prideaux, E.K., & others

- Bosses & Corbels of Exeter Cathedral. An Illustrated Study in Decorative & Symbolic Design. London: Chatto & Windus; & Exeter: Commin, 1910. [iv],228 pp. Pocket plan, ills. Orig cloth gilt, sl damaged patch upper bd. *(Hollett)* **£30 [≈$45]**

Priestley, Mary (editor)

- A Book of Birds. Illustrated by C.F. Tunnicliffe. London: Gollancz, 1937. 1st edn. 384 pp. 82 w'engvs. Silk marker. Orig cloth, leather label, edges spotted. Dw (spine ends chipped, few faint spots). *(Bookworks)* **£75 [≈$113]**
- A Book of Birds. Illustrated by C.F. Tunnicliffe. London: Gollancz, 1937. 1st edn. 384 pp. 82 w'engvs. Silk marker. Orig cloth, leather label, v sl marked, crnrs v sl bruised. *(Bookworks)* **£45 [≈$68]**

Principles ...

- Principles and Power of Harmony ... see Stillingfleet, Benjamin

Print ...

- Print, A Quarterly Journal of the Graphic Arts. Vol 1 No 1 - Vol 8, No 6. New Haven & New York: W.E. Rudge, 1940-54. Complete run for these dates. 4to. Num ills. Inserts. Orig pict wraps. *(The Veatchs)* **$200 [≈£133]**

Printing and the Mind of Man ...

- Printing and the Mind of Man. Compiled and Edited by John Carter and Percy H. Muir, assisted by Nicolas Barker. London: 1967. Lge 4to. Ills. Orig cloth. Dw. *(Traylen)* **£105 [≈$158]**

Printing Historical Society

- Journal. Edited by James Mosley. Numbers 1 to 18. London: St. Bride Institute, 1965-84. 19 parts, inc index vols 1-10. Ills. Orig wraps. *(Cooper Hay)* **£100 [≈$150]**
- Journal. Nos 1-21 with the index to nos 1-10. London: 1965-92. 1st edn. 21 issues in 20. Orig wraps. *(Claude Cox)* **£120 [≈$180]**

Prior, Edward S.

- A History of Gothic Art in England. With Illustrations by Gerald C. Horsley. London: George Bell & Sons, 1900. 4to. xiv,465 pp. 340 ills. Orig clothgilt, extrs sl worn, hd of spine snagged. *(Hollett)* **£35 [≈$53]**
- A History of Gothic Art in England. London: 1900. Roy 8vo. 340 ills, plans, diags. Orig cloth. *(Traylen)* **£30 [≈$45]**

Proctor, Robert

- An Index of German Books 1501-1520 in the British Museum. London: Holland Press, 1954. 4to. 273 pp. Orig cloth. Dw. *(Lamb)* **£25 [≈$38]**
- An Index of German Books 1501-1520 in the British Museum. London: 1954. Sm 4to. Num ills. Orig cloth. *(Traylen)* **£24 [≈$36]**
- Jan Van Doesborgh, Printer at Antwerp. An Essay in Bibliography. London: Chiswick Press for the Bibl Soc., 1894. 4to. Plates. Orig canvas backed bds, uncut. *(Traylen)* **£75 [≈$113]**

Progressive Drawing Book ...

- Progressive Drawing Book; containing a Series of Easy and Comprehensive Lessons for Drawing Landscape, Architecture, the Human Figure ... London: Bohn, 1853. Oblong 4to. [4],56 pp. Frontis, 87 plates. Occas foxing. Orig cloth, ft of spine & crnrs reprd. *(Spelman)* **£90 [≈$135]**

Proteaux, A.

- Practical Guide for the Manufacture of Paper and Boards. Translated from the French ... [with] a Chapter on the Manufacture of Paper from Wood in the United States by Henry T. Brown. Phila: 1866. 8vo. 292,[23 ctlg] pp. 6 plates. Orig cloth, worn. *(The Veatchs)* **$150 [≈£100]**

Proust, Marcel

- Swann's Way. Illustrations by Bernard LaMotte. New York: The Limited Editions Club, 1954. One of 1500 signed by the illustrator. 4to. Orig cloth. Slipcase (rubbed). *(Oak Knoll)* **$45 [≈£30]**

Prout, Samuel

- A New Drawing Book, in the Manner of Chalk, containing Twelve Views in the West of England. London: Ackermann, 1819. 1st edn. Oblong 4to. 12 uncold soft ground etchings. Some page edges dusty. Orig ptd wraps, uncut, sl soiled, spine reprd. *(Spelman)* **£220 [≈$330]**
- Picturesque Studies of Cottages, Old Houses, Castles, Bridges, Ruins, Etc. in the Manner of Chalk. London: Ackermann's Repository, 1816 [but ca 1840]. Folio. 16 views. Sm repr to final plate. Orig front wrapper preserved, new rear wrapper. *(Spelman)* **£65 [≈$98]**
- Progressive Fragments, Drawn and Etched in a Broad and Simple Manner . .. for the Use of Young Students in Landscape-Drawing. London: for R. Ackermann, 1818. Oblong 4to. 2 pp. 24 uncold soft-ground etchings. Sl crnr marks. Orig cloth backed wraps, ptd label. *(Spelman)* **£95 [≈$143]**
- Prout's Microcosm. The Artist's Sketch-Book of Groups of Figures, Shipping, and other Picturesque Objects. London: Tilt & Bogue, 1841. 1st edn. Folio. 4 pp. Advt leaf.

24 tinted litho plates. Occas foxing. Orig cloth, recased, sm reprs.
(Spelman) **£140 [≈$210]**

- Rudiments of Landscape: in Progressive Studies, in Imitation of Chalk, and Colours. London: for R. Ackermann, 1814. 1st edn, 2nd issue. Oblong folio. iv,5-26 pp. 64 plates (16 hand cold). Rec crushed mor, gilt spine , t.e.g. *(Spelman)* **£1,400 [≈$2,100]**

Prown, Jules David

- John Singleton Copley in America 1738-1774. Cambridge: Harvard UP, 1966. 2 vols. Cold frontis, 678 ills. Orig buckram. Slipcase. *(Leicester Art Books)* **£100 [≈$150]**

Pudney, John

- Bristol Fashion. London: 1960. 1st edn. Ills by David Gentleman. Orig cloth. Dw. *(Margaret Nangle)* **£18.50 [≈$29]**

Pugin, Augustus Charles

- Specimens of the Architecture of Normandy, from the XIth to the XVIth Century ... New Edition, Edited by Richard Phene Spiers. London: 1874. 4to. xvi,88 pp. 79 plates. Foxing & dust marks. Contemp half calf, gilt spine, crnrs rubbed. *(Bow Windows)* **£125 [≈$188]**

Pugin, Augustus Welby

- Details of Ancient Timber Houses of the 15th & 16th Centuries ... London: Ackermann, 1836. 1st edn. 4to. Advt leaf at end. Engvd title, 21 plates (sl foxed). Orig cloth, worn. *(Bookpress)* **$185 [≈£123]**
- Glossary of Ecclesiastical Ornaments and Costume ... Second Edition Enlarged and Revised by the Reverend Bernard Smith. London: Bohn, 1846. 4to. xvi,245,[1] pp. Chromolitho title, 1 uncold & 72 cold plates. Some foxing. Sm lib stamps. Contemp qtr mor, t.e.g. *(Bow Windows)* **£250 [≈$375]**
- A Treatise on Chancel Screens and Rood Lofts. London: Charles Dolman, 1851. 1st edn. v,124 pp. 14 plates. Orig cloth. *(Bookpress)* **$185 [≈£123]**
- The True Principles of Pointed or Christian Architecture [with] An Apology for the Revival of Christian Architecture in England. London: 1853, 1843. 2 vols in one. 4to. vi,56; viii,51,[1] pp. Frontis, 20 plates, text ills; 10 plates. Occas sl marks. Orig cloth, sl worn. *(Bow Windows)* **£95 [≈$143]**
- The True Principles of Pointed or Christian Architecture: set forth in Two Lectures delivered at St. Mary's Oscott ... Edinburgh: John Grant, 1895. 4to. [iv],51,[1] pp. Cold frontis, 9 plates, 11 plates of vignettes, text engvs. Orig cloth, sm nick in spine. *(Young's)* **£40 [≈$60]**

Puleston, J.H. & Price, J.E.

- Roman Antiquities recently discovered on the site of the National Safe Deposit Company's Premises, Mansion House, London. London: 1873. 4to. 80 pp. Map, 12 plates, text ills. Prelims foxed. Orig cloth, worn. *(Castle Bookshop)* **£38 [≈$57]**

Puppi, Lionello

- Andrea Palladio. London: 1975. Lge 4to. 467 pp. 629 ills & plans. Orig cloth. Dw. *(Washton)* **$165 [≈£110]**

Pushkin, A.S.

- Pushkin's Fairy Tales. Translated by Janet Dalley. Illustrated by Arthur Boyd. London: Barrie & Jenkins, 1978. One of 250. 4to. 93,[3] pp. 20 ills. Orig qtr cloth. Slipcase (rubbed & damp stained). Signed by the artist. *(Cooper Hay)* **£28 [≈$42]**

Putnam, Samuel

- The World of Jean de Bosschere. A Monograph. London: Fortune Press, [1942]. One of 900. 8vo. 21 plates, num text ills. Orig buckram, t.e.g. Dw (sl creased and dusty, ft of spine torn, spine darkened). *(Ulysses Bookshop)* **£75 [≈$113]**

Pye, John

- Patronage of British Art, an Historical Sketch ... London: Longman, Brown ..., 1845. 1st edn. 8vo. viii,422,[32] pp. Fldg table, text ills. Orig cloth, sl worn & reprd. *(Bookpress)* **$225 [≈£150]**

Pyke, E.J.

- A Biographical Dictionary of Wax Modellers. OUP: 1973. lxvi,216 pp. 314 ills. Orig cloth. Dw. *(Fine Art)* **£30 [≈$45]**
- A Biographical Dictionary of Wax-Modellers. Oxford: Clarendon Press 1973. 1st edn. 8vo. lxvi,216 pp. 312 ills. Orig cloth. Dw (chipped). *(Bookpress)* **$125 [≈£83]**

Pyne, George

- A Rudimentary and Practical Treatise on Perspective for Beginners ... Twelfth Edition. London: John Weale, 1879. Sm 8vo. iv,[2],168,[32 advt] pp. 86 text ills. Orig cloth. *(Spelman)* **£20 [≈$30]**

Quaritch, Bernard

- Contributions towards a Dictionary of English Book Collectors. London: Quaritch,

1892-1921. 1st edn. 14 parts in one vol. Lge 8vo. Orig cloth, orig wraps bound in.
(Bookpress) **$250 [≈£167]**

- Facsimiles of Some Examples of the Art of Book-Ornamentation during the Middle Ages. London: 1900. 1st edn. Folio. 10 chromolithos. Orig wraps, tear at ft of spine.
(Bookpress) **$110 [≈£73]**

The Queen's Story Book ...

- see Gomme, Laurence (editor)

Quennell, Nancy

- The Epicure's Anthology. Golden Cockerel Press: 1936. One of 150 signed by the illustrator, Osbert Lancaster. Orig leather, t.e.g., rubbed, dusty, sl bowed.
(Ulysses Bookshop) **£95 [≈$143]**

Quiller-Couch, Sir Arthur

- In Powder and Crinoline. Illustrated by Kay Nielsen. London: Hodder & Stoughton, n.d. 1st edn (?). 24 mtd cold plates, b/w decs. Occas foxing of text. Orig pict cloth, extrs worn, hd of spine chipped.
(Stella Books) **£285 [≈$428]**

Quinn, Edward

- Max Ernst. London: Thames & Hudson, 1972. One of 750 with orig lithograph by Ernst. 444 pp. 683 ills. Orig cloth. Dw. Slipcase. *(Leicester Art Books)* **£160 [≈$240]**

Quinn, Edward & Penrose, Roland

- Picasso at Work. New York: Doubleday, n.d. 4to. 282 ills. Orig pict bds. Wraparound band. Glassine dw. *(Abacus)* **$75 [≈£50]**

Quiz (pseudonym)

- Flunkeyism or Our Domestics. London: Read & Co., 1859. 1st edn. 24mo. 20 b/w ills by Quiz. Fold-out. Orig cloth, pict onlay, somewhat worn. *(Davidson)* **$325 [≈£217]**

Rabelais, Francois

- The Complete Works ... Illustrations by Frank C. Pape. London: John Lane, 1927. One of 4300. 2 vols. 24 plates, ills. Orig cloth gilt, uncut, minor fading sides.
(Claude Cox) **£35 [≈$53]**
- The Works ... Illustrated by W. Heath Robinson. London: Privately Printed for the Navarre Society, 1921. 2 vols. 8vo. Frontis, ills. Orig buckram gilt, t.e.g., sl soiled, spines darkened. *(Claude Cox)* **£18 [≈$27]**
- The Works ... Illustrated by W. Heath Robinson. London: Navarre Society, [ca 1921]. 1st edn thus. 2 vols. Num ills. Orig dec cloth, t.e.g. *(Argonaut)* **$250 [≈£167]**

Rackham, Arthur

- The Allies' Fairy Book. Introduction by Edmund Gosse. London: Heinemann, (1918). 1st edn. Sm 4to. 12 cold plates. Occas foxing. Orig pict gilt cloth.
(Barbara Stone) **£85 [≈$128]**
- The Allies' Fairy Book. With an Introduction by Edmund Gosse. London: [1916]. One of 525 signed by the artist. 4to. 12 mtd cold plates, 24 ills. Sl foxing. Crushed red mor gilt, by The Harcourt Bindery.
(Heritage) **$1,500 [≈£1,000]**
- The Land of Enchantment. London: Cassell, 1907. 1st edn. 36 ills. Rec calf.
(Old Cathay) **£150 [≈$225]**

Rackham, Bernard

- The Ancient Glass of Canterbury Cathedral. London: Humphries & Co. ..., 1949. 1st edn. 194 pp. 25 cold & 80 b/w plates. Orig cloth, t.e.g. *(Hermitage)* **$200 [≈£133]**
- Early Staffordshire Pottery. London: Faber, 1951. xvi,46 pp. 100 plates. Ex-lib. Orig cloth. Dw (torn).
(Castle Bookshop) **£25 [≈$38]**
- Italian Maiolica. London: Faber, 1952. xvi, 35 pp. 100 plates. Orig cloth. Dw.
(Castle Bookshop) **£20 [≈$30]**

Racz, Istvan

- Art Treasures of Medieval Finland. Helsinki: 1961. Lge 4to. 252 pp. 244 plates. Orig cloth. Dw. *(Washton)* **$75 [≈£50]**
- Treasures of Finnish Renaissance and Baroque Art. New York: 1967. Lge 4to. 239 pp. 209 plates. Orig cloth. Dw.
(Washton) **$75 [≈£50]**

Rahlves, Friedrich

- Cathedrals and Monasteries of Spain. London: Nicholas Kaye, 1966. Lge 8vo. 310 pp. Fldg map, 167 ills. Orig cloth gilt. Dw.
(Hollett) **£30 [≈$45]**

Raine, Kathleen

- Blake and Tradition. London: Routledge ..., 1969. 2 vols. 4to. Num ills. Orig bndg, sl bump top crnr vol 1.
(Mermaid Books) **£48 [≈$72]**

Ramsay, Sir W.M. & Bell, Gertrude L.

- The Thousand and One Churches. London: Hodder & Stoughton, 1909. 8vo. xv,580 pp. 4 maps, 390 ills. Lib stamps on ills. Cloth.
(Quest Books) **£70 [≈$105]**

Ramsden, E.H.

- The Letters of Michelangelo. Translated from the Original Tuscan. London: Peter Owen, 1963. 2 vols. 60 plates. Orig buckram gilt, t.e.g. Slipcase. *(Leicester Art Books)* **£70 [≈$105]**
- Sculpture: Theme and Variations. Towards a Contemporary Aesthetic. London: Lund Humphries, 1953. 56 pp. 103 plates. Prelims & endpapers foxed. Orig cloth & bds. *(Fine Art)* **£20 [≈$30]**

Ramsey, S.C.

- Small Houses of the Late Georgian Period 1750-1820. Volume I. Exteriors. London: (1919) 1924. Sm folio. vi,16 pp. Frontis, 100 plates. Orig cloth, back faded & stained. *(Whitehart)* **£35 [≈$53]**

Randall, Lilian M.C.

- Images in the Margins of Gothic Manuscripts. Berkeley: 1966. 4to. viii,235 pp. 739 ills on 158 plates. Orig cloth. Dw. *(Washton)* **$150 [≈£100]**

Randhawa, M.S.

- Basohli Painting. Calcutta: (1959). 1st edn. Sm folio. 125 pp. Frontis, 38 mtd cold ills. Orig cloth. Dw, sl worn. *(Bookpress)* **$85 [≈£57]**

Raphael, Max

- The Demands of Art. Princeton: UP, (1968). 1st edn. Folio. xxiii,258 pp. 32 plates. Orig cloth. Dw. *(Bookpress)* **$65 [≈£43]**

Rasmo, Nicolo

- Michael Pacher. London: Phaidon, 1971. 264 pp. 96 ills. Orig cloth. *(Leicester Art Books)* **£38 [≈$57]**

Raspe, Rudolph Erich

- The Singular Adventures of Baron Munchausen. Illustrated by Fritz Kredel. New York: The Limited Editions Club, 1952. One of 1500 signed by the illustrator. 8vo. Orig qtr leather (spine sl rubbed). Slipcase. *(Oak Knoll)* **$95 [≈£63]**

Rastell, John

- The Four Elements. Edited by Roger Coleman. Cambridge: 1971. One of 500. 4to. Ills. Orig cloth bds. *(Traylen)* **£52 [≈$78]**
- The Four Elements. Edited by Roger Coleman. Cambridge: [Privately Printed, Christmas] 1971. One of 500. vi,73 pp. Ills. Orig buckram backed bds. *(Claude Cox)* **£28 [≈$42]**

Ratcliff, Carter

- Botero. New York: Abbeville Press, 1980. Sq folio. 272 pp. 228 ills. Orig cloth. Dw. *(Ars Libri)* **$350 [≈£233]**

Rattray, R.S.

- Religion & Art in Ashanti. Oxford: Clarendon Press, 1927. 1st edn. 8vo. xviii, 414 pp. Frontis, 278 ills (some cold). Few faint pencil marks. Orig cloth gilt, sl faded & rubbed. *(Oriental and African)* **£145 [≈$218]**

Raverat, Gwen

- The Wood Engravings of Gwen Raverat. Selected, with an Introduction by Reynolds Stone. London: Faber, 1959. 1st edn. 4to. 136 pp. Ills. Orig cloth gilt. *(Hollett)* **£85 [≈$128]**

Ravilious, Eric

- The Wood Engravings of Eric Ravilious. Introduced by J.M. Richards. Lion and Unicorn Press: 1972. One of 500. 232 pp. Num ills inc 3 fldg plates & 3 fldg indexes. Orig (remainder issue) dec grey cloth, spine v sl faded. *(Bookworks)* **£550 [≈$825]**

Ravilious, Tirzah

- The Wood Engravings of Tirzah Ravilious. London: Gordon Fraser Gallery, 1987. One of 1000. Orig card wrappers. *(Mermaid Books)* **£18 [≈$27]**

Rawlins, Thomas

- Familiar Architecture; or, Original Designs for Houses, for Gentlemen and Tradesmen ... With Plans, Sections ... London: I. & J. Taylor, 1795. New edn. Sm folio. 26,[4 advt] pp. 51 plates. New qtr calf. *(Young's)* **£480 [≈$720]**

Rawlinson, W.G. & Finberg, A.J.

- The Water-Colours of J.M.W. Turner. London: Studio Special Number, Spring 1909. 42 pp. 30 mtd cold plates. Orig wraps, spine chipped. *(Willow House)* **£30 [≈$45]**

Ray, Cyril

- Merry England. Illustrated by Edward Ardizzone. London: Vista Books, 1960. 1st edn. 8vo. 208 pp. Num tinted plates. Orig cloth. Dw. *(Sotheran's)* **£38 [≈$57]**

Ray, Gordon N.

- The Illustrator and the Book in England from 1790 to 1914. New York: Pierpont Morgan Library, 1976. 4to. xxxiii,336 pp. Num ills. Orig cloth. *(The Veatchs)* **$150 [≈£100]**

Ray, Paul C.

- The Surrealist Movement in England. Cornell: UP, 1971. xi,331 pp. Orig cloth. Dw (worn). *(Fine Art)* **£20 [≈$30]**

Ray, Peter

- Designers in Britain. London: Allan Wingate, Society of Industrial Artists, 1947. 4to. 291 pp. Over 100 ills. Orig cloth. Dw (reprd). *(Cooper Hay)* **£35 [≈$53]**

Read, Herbert

- Art and Industry. The Principles of Industrial Design. London: Faber, 1934. 1st edn. Lge 8vo. 143 pp. Ills. Orig dec cloth. *(Spelman)* **£25 [≈$38]**
- The Art of Jean Arp. New York: Abrams, (1968). 8vo. 216 pp. 169 ills. Orig cloth. Dw. *(Karmiole)* **$30 [≈£20]**
- Paul Nash. Ten Coloured Plates with a Critical Appreciation. London: Soho Gallery, Contemporary British Painters, 1937. 1st edn. [30] pp. Port frontis, 10 mtd cold plates (one on upper cvr), 2 ills. V few spots. Orig card cvrs, yapp edges sl chipped. *(Bookworks)* **£85 [≈$128]**

Reade, Brian

- Beardsley. With an Introduction by John Rothenstein. London: Studio Vista, 1974. Reprint. 372 pp. 502 ills. Orig cloth. Dw. *(Leicester Art Books)* **£30 [≈$45]**
- Regency Antiques. London: Batsford, 1953. 1st edn. Sm 4to. 270 pp. Cold frontis, 181 plates. Orig cloth gilt. Price-clipped dw. *(Hollett)* **£45 [≈$68]**

Real, Daniel

- The Batiks of Java ... London: Ernest Benn, 1924. 4to. 15 pp. 46 plates. Orig qtr cloth, crnrs sl bumped & rubbed, lib mark ft of spine. *(Rankin)* **£110 [≈$165]**

Rearick, Janet Cox

- The Drawings of Pontormo. Cambridge: Harvard UP, 1964. 2 vols. 393 ills. Orig cloth. *(Leicester Art Books)* **£200 [≈$300]**

Redesdale, Lord

- Second Address of Lord Redesdale ... at the Campden School of Arts & Crafts ... Campden: Essex House Press, 1905. 1st edn. 8vo. 14,[2] pp. Orig cloth, sl soiled. *(Oak Knoll)* **$65 [≈£43]**

Redgrave, F.M.

- Richard Redgrave. A Memoir. Compiled from his Diary. London: Cassell, 1891. viii,399 pp. 4 plates. Orig cloth. *(Leicester Art Books)* **£35 [≈$53]**

Redoute, Pierre-Joseph

- Roses. With an Introduction and Notes by Eva Mannering. New York: The Ariel Press, (1954). 1st edn thus. Folio. xv,[i] pp. 24 plates. Orig cloth, minor wear. *(Bookpress)* **$75 [≈£50]**
- Roses. Selected and Introduced by Eva Mannering. London: 1954. 3rd imp. Folio. xv pp. 24 cold plates. Limp bds. *(Wheldon & Wesley)* **£45 [≈$68]**

Reeves, James

- Arcadian Ballads. Illustrated by Edward Ardizzone. Andoversford: The Whittington Press, 1977. One of 50 (of 250) signed by the author and illustrator. Mor, spine faded. Slipcase (sl worn and bumped). *(Ulysses Bookshop)* **£195 [≈$293]**
- The Lion that Flew. Illustrated by Edward Ardizzone. London: 1974. 1st edn. Ills. Orig pict bds, hd of spine sl bumped. *(Ulysses Bookshop)* **£28 [≈$42]**

Reff, Theodore

- The Notebooks of Edgar Degas. A Catalogue of the Thirty-Eight Notebooks in the Bibliotheque Nationale and other Countries. Oxford: Clarendon Press 1976. 2 vols. Over 1300 ills. Orig buckram. Dw. *(Leicester Art Books)* **£120 [≈$180]**

Reich, Sheldon

- John Marin. A Stylistic Analysis and Catalogue Raisonne. Tucson: Arizona UP, 1970. 1st edn. 2 vols. 4to. Num ills. Orig cloth gilt. Dws (sl chipped). Slipcase. *(Karmiole)* **$250 [≈£167]**

Reid, Anthony

- A Checklist of the Book Illustrations of John Buckland Wright together with a Personal Memoir. Pinner: PLA, 1968. Num ills. Orig cloth bds. Glassine dw. *(Michael Taylor)* **£28 [≈$42]**

Reid, John

- The Young Surveyor's Preceptor; a clear and comprehensive Analysis of the Art of Architectural Mensuration, Dimensions, Quantities and Value of Builder's work. London: J. Basevi, 1848. 1st edn. 4to. Errata slip. 16 plates. Orig cloth. *(Traylen)* **£35 [≈$53]**

Reilly, Bernard

- Currier & Ives. A Catalogue Raisonne. Detroit: Gale Research, 1984. 2 vols. Num ills. Orig cloth. Slipcase. *(Leicester Art Books)* **£140 [≈$210]**

Reilly, Robin & Savage, George

- The Dictionary of Wedgwood. Antique Collectors' Club: 1980. 4to. 414 pp. 23 cold plates. Orig cloth gilt. Dw. *(Hollett)* **£30 [≈$45]**

Reiner, Imre

- Modern and Historical Typography. An Illustrated Guide. New York: Paul A. Struck, 1946. 1st edn in English. Sm 4to. 128 pp. Orig cloth. Dw (sl soiled). *(Oak Knoll)* **$65 [≈£43]**
- Modern and Historical Typography. An Illustrated Guide. Second Volume. New York: Paul A. Struck, 1946. 1st edn in English. Sm 4to. 128 pp. Orig bds. Dw (worn). *(Oak Knoll)* **$45 [≈£30]**
- Woodcut / Wood Engraving. A Contribution to the History of the Art. Publix: 1947. 1st edn. 4to. 111 pp. Num ills. Spine darkened. Dw (defective). *(Waddington)* **£55 [≈$83]**

Reiner, Imre & Reiner, Hedwig

- Lettering in Book Art. St. Gall: Zollikofer & Co., 1948. Sm 4to. 95 pp . Ills. Orig bds. Dw (sl chipped). *(Oak Knoll)* **$65 [≈£43]**

Reinz, Gerhard F.

- Bernard Buffet. Gravures, Engravings, Radierungen, 1948-1967. New York: Tudor, (1968). 1st edn. Tall 4to. 88,[2] pp. 296 ills. Orig cloth. *(Karmiole)* **$125 [≈£83]**

Reiss, Stephen

- Albert Cuyp. Boston: 1975. Sm 4to. 223 pp. 12 cold plates, 160 ills. Orig cloth. Dw. *(Washton)* **$85 [≈£57]**
- Albert Cuyp. London: Zwemmer, 1975. 223 pp. 172 ills. Orig cloth. Dw. *(Leicester Art Books)* **£65 [≈$98]**

Remarque, Erich Maria

- All Quiet on the Western Front. With Illustrations by John Groth. New York: The Limited Editions Club, 1969. One of 1500 signed by the illustrator. Sm 4to. Orig cloth (spine sl faded). Slipcase. *(Oak Knoll)* **$85 [≈£57]**

Remey, Charles Mason

- Architectural Compositions in the Indian Style. N.p.: the author, 1923. 1st edn. 4to. Ills. Cloth, sl worn. *(Bookpress)* **$185 [≈£123]**

Remington, Frederic

- Done in the Open. New York: P.F. Collier, 1902. Folio. 8 pp. Frontis, 39 plates. Sl marg marks. Cloth backed bds, worn. *(Bookpress)* **$150 [≈£100]**
- Done in the Open. Drawings. New York: Collier, 1903. 80 b/w plates. Orig cloth backed pict bds, worn. *(Clarice Davis)* **$225 [≈£150]**

Renn, D.F.

- Norman Castles in Britain. London: John Baker, 1968. 8vo. Cold frontis, 6 maps, 76 plans, 48 plates. Dw. *(David Slade)* **£35 [≈$53]**

Restany, Pierre

- Cesar. New York: Abrams, 1976. Lge oblong 4to. 231 pp. 201 ills. Orig cloth. Dw. *(Ars Libri)* **$125 [≈£83]**
- G.H. Rothe: Master of the Mezzotint. New York: Hammer Publishing, (1983). Sq 4to. 271 pp. 171 cold plates, ills. Orig cloth. Dw. *(Abacus)* **$60 [≈£40]**

The Revelation of St. John the Divine ...

- The Revelation of St. John the Divine. Gregynog Press: 1932. One of 250. Folio. Engvs by Blair Hughes-Stanton. B'plate removed. Orig rust brown calf, spine sl rubbed. *(Spelman)* **£300 [≈$450]**

Revi, Albert Christian

- American Pressed Glass & Figure Bottles. US: Nelson, 1964. 4to. 446 pp. Num plates & ills. Sl foredge stain. Cvrs rubbed. *(Paul Brown)* **£35 [≈$53]**
- Nineteenth Century Glass. Its Genesis and Development. London: Galahad, 1967. Rvsd edn. 4to. 310 pp. 8 cold plates, num b/w ills. Price-clipped dw. *(Paul Brown)* **£32 [≈$48]**

Rewald, John

- Degas Sculpture. Complete Works. London: Thames & Hudson, 1957. 165 pp. 115 ills. Orig cloth. Dw (chipped & reprd). *(Leicester Art Books)* **£45 [≈$68]**
- Degas Sculpture. New York: Abrams, (1956). 4to. 165 pp. 114 ills. Orig cloth. Dw. *(Abacus)* **$225 [≈£150]**
- Paul Cezanne, The Watercolors, a Catalogue Raisonne. Boston: Little, Brown, for the New York Graphic Society, 1983. 1st edn. 4to. 488 pp. Orig cloth. Slipcase. *(First Folio)* **$165 [≈£110]**
- Paul Cezanne. The Watercolours. A

Catalogue Raisonne. London: Thames & Hudson, 1983. 487 pp. 759 ills. Orig cloth. Slipcase. *(Leicester Art Books)* **£180 [≈$270]**

Rey, Jose Lopez

- Velazquez. A Catalogue Raisonne of his Oeuvre with an Introductory Study. London: 1963. 4to. 367 pp. 231 plates. Orig cloth. *(Washton)* **$145 [≈£97]**

Reynolds, Graham

- The Later Paintings and Drawings of John Constable. New Haven: Yale UP, 1984. 2 vols. 1087 ills. Orig cloth. Dw. *(Leicester Art Books)* **£170 [≈$255]**

Reynolds, Jan

- Birket Foster. London: Batsford, 1984. 224 pp. 4 cold & 109 b/w plates. Orig cloth. Slipcase. *(Fine Art)* **£45 [≈$68]**
- Birket Foster. London: Batsford, 1984. Sm folio. 4 cold plates, num ills. Orig cloth. Slipcase. *(Traylen)* **£20 [≈$30]**
- William Callow R.W.S. London: Batsford, 1980. 260 pp. 114 ills. Orig cloth. Dw. *(Leicester Art Books)* **£45 [≈$68]**
- William Callow R.W.S. London: Batsford, 1980. 1st edn. 4to. xii,257 pp. 114 ills. Orig cloth gilt. Dw. *(Hollett)* **£40 [≈$60]**
- The Williams Family of Painters. Antique Collectors' Club: 1975. 178 pp. Num ills. Orig cloth. Dw. *(Fine Art)* **£48 [≈$72]**

Reynolds, John Hamilton

- The Fancy. Illustrated by Jack Butler Yeats. Preface by John Masefield. London: Elkin Mathews, The Satchel Series, [1906]. 1st edn. 90 pp. 13 ills. Orig wraps, fine. *(Bookworks)* **£40 [≈$60]**

Reynolds, Sir Joshua

- Seven Discourses delivered in the Royal Academy by the President. London: for T. Cadell, 1778. 1st edn. Half-title. 2 advt pp. Contemp calf, spine rubbed, hinges sl weakening. The dedication is by Samuel Johnson. *(Jarndyce)* **£85 [≈$128]**

Rhead, G.W. & F.A.

- Staffordshire Pots & Potters. London: Hutchinson, 1906. 1st edn. Sm 4to. xvi,384 pp. 4 cold plates, 116 b/w plates, 90 text ills. Few sm lib stamps. Mod half mor gilt. *(Hollett)* **£95 [≈$143]**

Rheims, Maurice

- The Flowering of Art Nouveau. New York: Abrams, n.d. Lge thick 4to. Ills. Orig dec cloth, spine lightened. Glassine (chipped). *(First Folio)* **$130 [≈£87]**

Rhys, Ernest

- Sir Frederic Leighton Bart., P.R.A. London: George Bell, 1895. xxxi,74 pp. 15 plates, 99 ills. Some plates foxed. Mod cloth. *(Leicester Art Books)* **£100 [≈$150]**

Ricauti, T.J.

- Sketches for Rustic Work; including Bridges, Park and Garden Buildings, Seats and Furniture ... London: Bohn, 1848. 4to. [14] pp. 17 litho plates. Some spotting. Orig cloth. *(Claude Cox)* **£85 [≈$128]**

Ricci, Corrado

- Antonio Allegri Da Correggio. His Life, His Friends, and his Time. London: Heinemann, 1896. One of 100 on Japan. 2 vols. 37 plates, 190 ills. Lib label. Orig cloth & bds. *(Leicester Art Books)* **£110 [≈$165]**
- Correggio. London: Warne, (1930). 4to. 200 pp. 292 plates. Orig cloth, t.e.g., spine sl soiled. *(Karmiole)* **$50 [≈£33]**

Rice, D. Talbot

- English Art 871-1100. Oxford: 1952. Sm 4to. xix,280 pp. 96 plates. Orig cloth. *(Washton)* **$75 [≈£50]**

Richards, Anthony & Mortimer, Ian

- From a Satyric Country. Poems by Anthony Richards with Woodcuts by Ian Mortimer. I.M. Imprimit: 1971. One of 100. Folio. 10 w'cuts. Orig unsewn folded sheets as issued in buckram backed folder. *(Claude Cox)* **£150 [≈$225]**

Richards, G. Tilghman

- Handbook of the Collection illustrating Typewriters ... London: HMSO, Science Museum, 1938. 58 pp. Ills. Few marg blind stamps. Orig wraps. *(Hollett)* **£25 [≈$38]**

Richards, J.M.

- The Bombed Buildings of Britain. London: Architectural Press, (1947). 2nd edn. 4to. 202 pp. Frontis, ills. Orig cloth. Dw (used). *(Bookpress)* **$45 [≈£30]**

Richardson, A.E.

- Robert Mylne. Architect and Engineer, 1733 to 1811. London: Batsford, 1955. 8vo. 220 pp. 58 ills. Dw. *(Spelman)* **£30 [≈$45]**

Richardson, A.E. & Eberlein, H. Donaldson

- The English Inn Past and Present. London:

Batsford, 1925. 1st edn. Sm 4to. xi,308 pp. 277 photo plates, ills & maps. Orig pict cloth gilt, fine. *(Gough)* **£85 [≈$128]**

- The Smaller English House of the Later Renaissance 1660-1830 ... London: Batsford, 1925. 1st edn. 4to. 286 pp. Plates, ills. Occas sl foxing. Orig gilt dec bds, edges sl worn. *(Monmouth)* **£40 [≈$60]**

Richardson, C.J.

- The Englishman's House. London: Chatto & Windus, [ca 1874]. 3rd edn. 8vo. viii, 504, [40] pp. Frontis, ills. Name on title. Orig cloth. *(Bookpress)* **$150 [≈£100]**

Richardson, Edward

- The Monumental Effigies of the Temple Church, with an Account of their Restoration, in the year 1842. London: Longman, Brown ..., 1843. Folio. 32 pp. 11 tinted lithos (sl used & marked). Mod half mor gilt. *(Hollett)* **£160 [≈$240]**

Richardson, James Charles

- Architectural Remains of the Reigns of Elizabeth and James 1st ... London: the author, 1838 ["Address" dated 1839]. 1st edn. Vol 1, all published. Lge folio. [vi],8 pp. Frontis, 11 plates. Title & plate 4 hand cold. Cloth backed bds, edges rubbed. *(Bookpress)* **$450 [≈£300]**

Richmond, L. & Littlejohns, J.

- The Technique of Water-Colour Painting. London: Pitman, 1929. 8vo. 73 pp. 31 cold ills. Orig cloth. *(Rona Schneider)* **$45 [≈£30]**

Ricketts, Charles

- A Catalogue of Mr. Shannon's Lithographs with Prefatory Notes ... London: The Dutch Gallery, [1902]. 32 pp. Port engvd by Ricketts. Orig bds. *(Leicester Art Books)* **£68 [≈$102]**

Rickman, Thomas

- An Attempt to Discriminate the Styles of Architecture in England, from the Conquest to the Reformation. London: John Henry Parker, 1848. 5th edn, enlgd. 8vo. lvi,238,[ii], lxii, [xiii],[i blank] pp. 29 plates, 333 w'cut ills. Calf gilt, a.e.g. *(Sotheran's)* **£198 [≈$297]**

Riddell, Robert

- The Carpenter & Joiner, Stairbuilder & Handrailer. London: William Mackenzie, [ca 1860]. 125 pp. Frontis, tinted litho plate, 57 plates, 4 fldg models. Orig half mor gilt, upper jnt cracked. *(Willow House)* **£150 [≈$225]**

Ridler, Anne

- The Jesse Tree. Illustrated by John Piper. The Lyrebird Press: 1972. One of 62 signed by the author & artist. 4to. Orig buckram backed bds, spine ends v sl rubbed, one crnr v sl bumped. Slipcase (sl worn). *(Ulysses Bookshop)* **£120 [≈$180]**

Riggs, Lynn

- Green Grow the Lilacs. New York: The Limited Editions Club, 1954. One of 1500 signed by the illustrator, Thomas Hart Benton. 4to. Orig cloth (spine darkened). Slipcase (spotted). *"This play is best know by its stage production - Oklahoma." (Oak Knoll). *(Oak Knoll)* **$275 [≈£183]**

Rilke, Rainer Maria

- Duineser Elegien. London: Hogarth Press, 1931. One of 230 sgnd by the translators, Vita and Edward Sackville-West. 10 w'cut ills by Eric Gill. Orig half vellum, t.e.g., minute mark upper bd, edges v sl spotted. Dw (sl used). Slipcase (sl worn). *(Ulysses Bookshop)* **£1,675 [≈$2,513]**

Rimbaud, Arthur

- A Season in Hell. Translated by Norman Cameron. Illustrated by Keith Vaughan. London: 1949. 1st edn thus. 8vo. 8 lithos by Vaughan. Inscrptn. Spine lettering v sl oxidized. Dw (sl nicked & sunned, sl wear hd of spine panel). *(Adam Blakeney)* **£125 [≈$188]**
- A Season in Hell. Translated by Paul Schmidt with Photogravures by Robert Mapplethorpe. New York: The Limited Editions Club [1986]. One of 1000 signed by Mapplethorpe and Smith. Sm 4to. Orig mor. Prospectus. Hand-made slipcase. *(Dermont)* **$1,250 [≈£833]**

Rinder, Frank

- D.Y. Cameron. An Illustrated Catalogue of his Etched Work ... Glasgow: Maclehose, 1912. One of 700. xlix,259 pp. 444 ills. Orig cloth, t.e.g. *(Leicester Art Books)* **£75 [≈$113]**

Riordan, Roger

- Half a Score of Etchers: Examples of the

Etched Work of Appian, Le Page, Daubigny, Lancon, Martial, Buhot, Burnand, Chauvel, Beauverie & Nelig. New York: Dodd, Mead, 1885. Folio. 10 original etchings. Orig cloth, t.e.g. *(Abacus)* **$600 [≈£400]**

Ritchie, Carson L.A.

- Shell Carving. History and Techniques. New York: Yoseloff & Barnes, 1974. 1st edn. 4to. 208 pp. Ills. Orig cloth gilt. Dw. *(Hollett)* **£35 [≈$53]**

Ritchie, Ward

- Frederic Goudy, Joseph Foster and the Present Scripps College. San Francisco: Book Club of California, 1978. One of 550. Ills. Orig cloth backed bds. *(Hermitage)* **$65 [≈£43]**

Ritter, A.

- Elementary Theory and Calculation of Iron Bridges and Roofs. Translated by H.R. Sankey. London: Spon, 1879. 1st UK edn. 8vo. viii, 395, [1],[32 ctlg] pp. Errata slip. Text figs. Orig cloth gilt. *(Clevedon Books)* **£60 [≈$90]**

Rivers, John

- Greuze and his Models. London: Hutchinson, 1912. 282 pp. 44 plates. Orig dec cloth, t.e.g. *(Fine Art)* **£15 [≈$23]**

Rivers, Larry

- Drawings and Digressions. With Carol Brightman. New York: Clarkson N. Potter, Crown, 1979. Sq 4to. 263 pp. 285 ills. Orig cloth. Dw. *(Ars Libri)* **$75 [≈£50]**

Rivers, Larry & Brightman, Carol

- Drawings and Digressions. New York: Clarkson N. Potter, (1979). Sq 4to. 264 pp. Mtd cold frontis, 260 ills. Orig cloth. Dw. signed by the artist on pasted-in b'plate. *(Abacus)* **$100 [≈£67]**

Rivoira, G.T.

- Lombardic Architecture. Its Origin, Development and Derivatives. London: Heinemann, 1910. 1st edn. 2 vols. Lge 4to. Num ills. Orig cloth, sl worn & marked. *(Hollett)* **£75 [≈$113]**
- Lombardic Architecture ... Re-edited, with Additional Notes. Oxford: Clarendon Press, 1933. 2 vols. Lge 4to. 818 ills. Orig cloth gilt. Dws (sl torn). *(Hollett)* **£125 [≈$188]**
- Moslem Architecture. OUP: 1918. 1st edn. 4to. xvii,383 pp. 340 ills. Orig dec cloth gilt. *(Hollett)* **£125 [≈$188]**
- Roman Architecture and its Principles of Construction under the Empire ... Oxford: Clarendon Press 1925. 1st English edn. 4to. xxvi,[ii],312 pp. 358 ills. Orig cloth gilt, spine ends trifle worn. *(Hollett)* **£120 [≈$180]**

Rizzi, Aldo

- The Etchings of the Tiepolos. Complete Edition. London: 1971. Lge 4to. 456 pp. 317 ills. Sm repr front free endpaper. Orig cloth. Dw. *(Washton)* **$125 [≈£83]**

Robert, Maurice & Warde, Frederic

- A Code for the Collector of Beautiful Books. New York: The Limited Editions Club, 1936. 4to. Orig cloth-backed bds, paper label (wear along edges). *(Oak Knoll)* **$25 [≈£17]**

Roberts, Henry D.

- A History of the Royal Pavilion, Brighton. With an Account of its Original Furniture and Decoration. London: Country Life, 1939. 1st edn. xvi,224 pp. 96 plates, text ills. Orig cloth gilt, sl rubbed. *(Clevedon Books)* **£44 [≈$66]**
- A History of the Royal Pavilion Brighton. With an Account of its Original Furniture and Decoration. London: Country Life, 1939. 4to. Ills. Dw (sl frayed). *(David Slade)* **£45 [≈$68]**

Roberts, James

- Introductory Lessons, with Familiar Examples in Landscape ... of the pleasing Art of Painting in Water-colours ... London: W. Bulmer, 1800. 1st edn. Thin 4to. [4],36 pp. 8 plates (5 hand cold aquatints, hand cold table). Sl browning. Contemp half mor, rebacked. *(Spelman)* **£450 [≈$675]**

Roberts, William

- 8 Cubist Designs by William Roberts R.A. London: Favil Press, 1969. One of 200. 8 ills. Pages sl wrinkled. *(Fine Art)* **£20 [≈$30]**
- The Book-Hunter in London. Historical and Other Studies of Collectors and Collecting ... Chicago: McClurg, n.d. 1st US edn. Tall 8vo. xxxii, 323 pp. Ills. Orig pict gilt cloth, t.e.g. *(Oak Knoll)* **$95 [≈£63]**
- History of Letter-Writing from the Earliest Period to the Fifth Century. London: William Pickering, 1843. 1st edn. 8vo. [xxii], 700 pp. Orig cloth, paper label, cloth faded & spotted, label chipped. *(Clark)* **£28 [≈$42]**

Roberts-Jones, Philippe

- Beyond Time and Place: Non-Realist Painting in the Nineteenth Century. OUP:

1978. 4to. 228 pp. 24 cold & 186 b/w ills. Orig cloth. Dw. Slipcase.
(Abacus) **$45 [≈£30]**

Robertson, Bryan

- Jackson Pollock. New York: Abrams, 1960. Lge sq 4to. 215 pp. 169 ills. Orig cloth.
(Ars Libri) **$600 [≈£400]**

Robertson, David

- Sir Charles Eastlake and the Victorian Art World. Princeton: UP, (1978). 4to. 468 pp. 2 cold & 200 b/w ills. Orig cloth. Dw.
(Abacus) **$45 [≈£30]**

Robertson, Giles

- Giovanni Bellini. Oxford: Clarendon Press 1968. xxiii,171 pp. 120 plates. Orig cloth.
(Leicester Art Books) **£110 [≈$165]**
- Giovanni Bellini. Oxford: 1968. Sm 4to. xxiii,171 pp. 120 plates. Orig cloth. Dw.
(Washton) **$175 [≈£117]**
- Vincenzo Catena (Catalogue Raisonne). Edinburgh: UP, 1954. 96 pp. 52 plates. Orig cloth. Dw. *(Leicester Art Books)* **£120 [≈$180]**

Robertson, John W.

- Francis Drake and Other Early Explorers along the Pacific Coast. San Francisco: The Grabhorn Press, 1927. One of 1000. 290 pp. 28 cold maps. Orig vellum backed bds, unopened. New slipcase.
(Hermitage) **$350 [≈£233]**

Robertson, W. Graham

- The Blake Collection of W. Graham Robertson. Edited by Kerrison Preston. London: Faber, (1952). Sm 4to. 263 pp. 64 plates. Orig cloth. Dw. Slipcase.
(Abacus) **$80 [≈£53]**

Robertson, W.A.

- The Crypt of Canterbury Cathedral; its Architecture, its History and its Frescoes. London: Mitchell & Hughes, 1880. 1st edn. viii,122 pp. 25 ills (3 fldg). Top edges trifle stained in places. Mod half mor gilt, t.e.g.
(Hollett) **£95 [≈$143]**

Robins, Edward Cookworthy

- Technical School and College Building ... London: Whittaker, 1887. 4to. xii,244 pp. Frontis, 63 plates of plans, 16 w'cut ills. Orig cloth gilt. *(Hollett)* **£160 [≈$240]**

Robinson, Charles N.

- Old Naval Prints. Their Artists and Engravers. Edited by Geoffrey Holme. London: The Studio, 1924. One of 1500. 4to. x,36 pp. 96 plates (24 cold). Orig cloth, spine faded, sl worn.
(Argonaut) **$350 [≈£233]**

Robinson, Duncan

- William Morris, Edward Burne-Jones and the Kelmscott Chaucer. London: Gordon Fraser, 1982. 160 pp. 125 ills. Orig cloth. Tissue dw. *(Fine Art)* **£38 [≈$57]**
- William Morris, Edward Burne-Jones and the Kelmscott Chaucer. London: Gordon Fraser, 1982. 1st edn. 4to. 116 pp. 80 plates. Orig cloth backed bds. Dw.
(Oak Knoll) **$125 [≈£83]**

Robinson, J. Armitage

- The Fourteenth-Century Glass at Wells. Oxford: Society of Antiquaries, 1931. 4to. 85,118 pp. Plates. Mod cloth backed bds.
(Hollett) **£30 [≈$45]**

Robinson, John Martin

- The Latest Country Houses. London: Bodley Head, (1984). 1st edn. 4to. 240 pp. Frontis. Orig cloth. Dw.
(Bookpress) **$35 [≈£23]**
- The Wyatts: An Architectural Dynasty. OUP: 1979. 287 pp. 8 cold plates, 140 ills. Orig cloth. Dw. *(Fine Art)* **£25 [≈$38]**

Robinson, P.F.

- Designs for Farm Buildings. London: James Carpenter & Son, 1830. 1st edn. Lge 4to. 56 litho plates. Occas sl spotting. Old diced calf gilt, scraped & reprd, rebacked.
(Hollett) **£325 [≈$488]**

Robinson, Robert

- Thomas Bewick, his Life and Times. Newcastle: 1887. 1st edn. Imperial 8vo. xxxvi, [4],328 pp. Port frontis, vignette title, ills. Orig cloth, sl marked & rubbed.
(Spelman) **£60 [≈$90]**

Robinson, Stanford F.H.

- Celtic Illuminative Art in the Gospel Books of Durrow, Lindisfarne and Kells. Dublin: Hodges Figgis, 1908. Lge 4to. Cold frontis, 51 plates, ills. Orig buckram.
(Emerald Isle) **£110 [≈$165]**

Robinson, W. Heath

- Absurdities. A Book of Collected Drawings. London: Hutchinson, (1934). 1st edn. Title, 90 b/w ills. Lacks front free endpaper. Orig pict bds, spine & crnrs sl chipped.
(Barbara Stone) **£90 [≈$135]**

- Monarchs of Merrie England. London: Alf Cooke, n.d. 4 vols. 8 cold plates, b/w ills. Orig stiff card pict wraps, 2 spines sl rubbed. *(Barbara Stone)* **£150 [≈$225]**
- Railway Ribaldry. London: Great Western Railway, 1935. 4to. 96 pp. Plates. Orig pict wraps, v sl worn & loose. *(Weiner)* **£50 [≈$75]**
- Railway Ribaldry. London: Great Western railway, 1935. 1st edn. 4to. 95 pp. Ills. Orig pict stiff card wraps, extrs sl rubbed. *(Sotheran's)* **£128 [≈$192]**
- The Saintly Hun. A Book of German Virtues. London: Duckworth, (1917). Tall thin 4to. 48 pp. B/w ills. Orig wraps, pict onlay, sl creased. *(Barbara Stone)* **£95 [≈$143]**
- The Saintly Hun. A Book of German Virtues. London: Duckworth, [1917]. 1st edn. Folio. 48 pp. B/w ills. Orig dec wraps. *(Robert Frew)* **£100 [≈$150]**
- Some 'Frightful' War Pictures. London: Duckworth, 1915. 1st edn. Folio. Title & 24 plates, vignettes, pict endpapers. Orig cloth backed pict bds, sl marked, crnrs bumped. Dw (chipped & dusty). *(Barbara Stone)* **£135 [≈$203]**

Robinson, W. Heath & Hunt, Cecil

- How to Run a Communal Home. London: Hutchinson, [1943]. 1st edn. 8vo. viii,116 pp. Num ills. Orig pict cloth. Dw. *(Robert Frew)* **£30 [≈$45]**

Robson, Edward Robert

- School Architecture ... London: Murray, 1874. 8vo. xxiv,440 pp. Frontis, 306 w'cut ills. Few sl marks. Orig cloth, rec mor spine. *(Spelman)* **£65 [≈$98]**

Rochester, John Wilmot, Earl of

- Collected Works. Edited by John Hayward. London: The Nonesuch Press, 1926. One of 975. Lge 8vo. 408 pp. Orig linen backed bds, unopened. *(Hermitage)* **$100 [≈£67]**

Rodriguez, Antonio

- A History of Mexican Mural Painting. New York: Putnam, (1969). Stout 4to. 517 pp. 312 ills (56 cold plates). Orig cloth. *(Abacus)* **$100 [≈£67]**

Roe, F. Gordon

- The Life and Art of David Cox (1783-1859). Leigh-on-Sea: 1946. One of 500. 121 pp. 46 plates. Orig buckram. *(Leicester Art Books)* **£45 [≈$68]**
- Rowlandson. The Life and Art of a British Genius. Leigh-on-Sea: F. Lewis, 1947. One of 500. 71 pp. 48 plates. Orig buckram. *(Leicester Art Books)* **£40 [≈$60]**
- Victorian Furniture. London: Phoenix House, 1952. 1st edn. 160 pp. 17 plates. Orig cloth gilt. Dw (top edge sl worn). *(Hollett)* **£15 [≈$23]**
- Windsor Chairs. London: Phoenix House, 1953. 1st edn. 96 pp. 54 plates. Orig cloth gilt. Dw. *(Hollett)* **£35 [≈$53]**

Roe, Fred

- Ancient Church Chests and Chairs in the Home Counties round Greater London ... London: Batsford, 1929. 1st edn. 4to. xii, 130, 8 pp. 95 ills, map endpapers. Orig cloth gilt. Price-clipped dw. *(Hollett)* **£40 [≈$60]**

Roethlisberger, Marcel

- Claud Lorrain. The Drawings. Berkeley & Los Angeles: Calif UP, 1968. 2 vols. 1244 ills. Orig cloth. *(Leicester Art Books)* **£160 [≈$240]**
- Claude Lorrain. The Drawings. Catalog and Plates. Berkeley: California UP, 1968. 2 vols. xi,477 pp. 1244 ills. Orig cloth. Dws. *(Clarice Davis)* **$295 [≈£197]**

Rogers, Bruce

- An Account of the Making of the Oxford Lectern Bible. Phila: Lanston Monotype Co., [1936]. 1st edn. 4to. 15 pp inc facsimiles. Slip laid in. Orig wraps. *(Claude Cox)* **£25 [≈$38]**
- Paragraphs on Printing. New York: Rudge, 1943. 4to. xi,187 pp. Num ills. Orig cloth. *(The Veatchs)* **$125 [≈£83]**
- Paragraphs on Printing. New York: William E. Rudge's Sons, 1943. 1st edn. 4to. ix,187 pp. Orig cloth. *(Oak Knoll)* **$125 [≈£83]**
- Pi, A Hodge-Podge of the Letters, Papers and Addresses written during the last Sixty Years ... Cleveland: World, 1953. 1st edn. 8vo. x,185,[3] pp. 36 plates. Orig cloth. Dw (chipped). *(Oak Knoll)* **$75 [≈£50]**
- Report on the Typography of the Cambridge University Press prepared in `1917 ... now Printed in Honour of his Eightieth Birthday. Cambridge: Cambridge Christmas book, 1950. One of 500. Offsetting on endpapers. *(The Veatchs)* **$100 [≈£67]**

Rogers, John C.

- English Furniture. Revised and Enlarged by Margaret Jourdain. London: Country Life, 1950. Lge 8vo. 244 pp. 201 ills. Orig cloth gilt. Dw. *(Hollett)* **£20 [≈$30]**

The Rohan Book of Hours

- The Rohan Book of Hours. Introduction by Millard Meiss. Introduction and Commentaries by Marcel Thomas. London: Thames & Hudson, 1973. 1st edn. Folio. 247 pp. 127 cold plates. Orig silk cloth gilt. Slipcase. *(Claude Cox)* **£35 [≈$53]**
- The Rohan Book of Hours. Bibliotheque Nationale, Paris (MS. Latin 9471). Introduction by Millard Meiss. London: 1973. 4to. 127 cold ills. Orig cloth gilt. Slipcase. *(Traylen)* **£40 [≈$60]**

Rohan, Thomas

- Old Glass Beautiful English & Irish. London: Mills & Boon, 1930. 144 pp. 31 ills. Orig bndg. *(Paul Brown)* **£24 [≈$36]**

Roland, Jeremy

- Gathering the Decade. Poems. Drawings by Joseph Goldyne. San Francisco: Goad Press, 1972. One of 1000. 51 pp. 5 plates. Orig cloth. *(Clarice Davis)* **$55 [≈£37]**

Rolleston, T.W.

- Lohengrin after the Drama by Richard Wagner by T.W. Rolleston. Illustrated by Willy Pogany. London: Harrap, [1913]. 1st edn. 4to. 8 mtd cold plates. Orig suede gilt, sl crack in front hinge. Box (wear to edges). *(Jo Ann Reisler)* **$400 [≈£267]**
- Parsifal or the Legend of the Holy Grail retold from Ancient Sources by T.W. Rolleston. Illustrated by Willy Pogany. London: Harrap, [1912]. 1st edn. 4to. 16 cold plates. Orig suede gilt. Box (wear to sides). *(Jo Ann Reisler)* **$450 [≈£300]**

Romero, Luis

- Dali. Barcelona: Ediciones Poligrafa, 1975. English-language edn. Lge sq 4to. 356 pp. 439 ills. Orig imitation leather. Dw. *(Ars Libri)* **$60 [≈£40]**

Rooke, Noel

- Woodcuts and Wood Engravings. London: Print Collectors' Club, 1926. One of 500. 40 pp. 16 plates, 12 text ills. Orig cloth & bds. *(Fine Art)* **£18 [≈$27]**
- Woodcuts and Wood Engravings. London: Print Collectors' Club, 1926. One of 500. Sm 4to. 40 pp. Ills. Orig bds, crnrs rubbed. *(Waddington)* **£20 [≈$30]**

Rope, H.E.G.

- Pugin. Ditchling: St Dominic's Press, 1935. 1st edn. 8vo. [iv],42,[2 blank] pp. Orig buckram backed bds. *(Bow Windows)* **£60 [≈$90]**

Rose, Barbara

- Claes Oldenburg. New York: MoMA, (1970). Oblong 4to. 221 pp. 52 cold & 224 b/w ills. Orig wraps. *(Abacus)* **$55 [≈£37]**
- Claes Oldenburg. New York: MoMA, 1970. Oblong 4to. 221 pp. Cold & b/w ills. Dec endpapers. Minor fault free endpaper. Orig limp padded vinyl. *(First Folio)* **$250 [≈£167]**
- Frankenthaler. Book Design by Robert Motherwell. New York: Abrams, 1979. Sm sq folio. 274 pp. 205 ills. Orig cloth. Dw. *(Ars Libri)* **$450 [≈£300]**

Rose, Benjamin

- Report on the Indian Section of the Paris Universal Exhibition 1900. London: 1901. 4to. 160 pp. Num photo plates. Orig ptd bds. *(Bury Place)* **£30 [≈$45]**

Rose, Ingrid

- Werner Drewes. A Catalogue Raisonne of his Prints ... Edited by Ralph Jentsch. Munich & New York: 1984. One of 70 containing an orig w'cut, signed by the artist. Folio. 456 pp. 447 ills. Orig cloth. Dw. *(Ars Libri)* **$600 [≈£400]**

Rose, Ronald E.

- English Dial Clocks. Woodbridge: 1988. 4to. 42 cold plates, 430 ills. Orig cloth. Dw. *(Traylen)* **£24 [≈$36]**

Rose, Stuart

- An Essex Dozen. Benham, Colchester: Privately Printed, 1953. One of 500, signed by the artist. 30 pp. 12 plates. Orig bds, s[pine ends v sl bruised. Cellophane dw (chipped at hd). *(Bookworks)* **£75 [≈$113]**

Rosenbach, A.S.W.

- The Unpublishable Memoirs. London: 1924. 1st edn. 8vo. Frontis. Free endpapers sl browned. Orig cloth, spine ends & crnrs sl bumped. Dw (sl worn). *(Ulysses Bookshop)* **£75 [≈$113]**

Rosenberg, Harold

- The Anxious Object. Art Today and its Audience. New York: Horizon Press, 1964. 4to. 270,[2] pp. Num ills. Orig qtr cloth. *(Ars Libri)* **$40 [≈£27]**
- De Kooning. New York: Abrams, 1974. Oblong folio. 293,[3] pp. 226 plates. Orig cloth. Dw. *(Ars Libri)* **$1,800 [≈£1,200]**
- Saul Steinberg. New York: Knopf & Whitney Museum of Art, 1978. One of 300 signed by Steinberg. 4to. [2],256 pp. Num plates, text ills. Orig linen. Slipcase. *(Karmiole)* **$175 [≈£117]**

Rosenberg, Jacob

- Rembrandt. Cambridge: 1948. 2 vols. Sm 4to. 281 ills. Orig cloth. *(Washton)* **$50 [≈£33]**

Rosenberg, Jakob

- Rembrandt. Cambridge: Harvard UP, 1948. 1st edn. 2 vols. 4to. xi,[2],263; [9] pp. Frontis, 281 plates. Orig cloth, spines rubbed. *(Bookpress)* **$75 [≈£50]**
- Rembrandt. Cambridge: Harvard UP, 1948. 2 vols. Sm 4to. 281 plates. Orig cloth. Slipcase. *(Abacus)* **$50 [≈£33]**
- Rembrandt, Life and Work. London: Phaidon, (1968). 3rd edn. 4to. x,235 pp. 282 ills. Orig cloth. *(Bookpress)* **$50 [≈£33]**

Rosenberg, Louis Conrad

- The Davanzati Palace, Florence ... New York: The Architectural Book Publishing Co., 1922. 1st edn. Sm folio. [ii],v,[i],72 pp. Ills. B'plate removed. Orig cloth. *(Bookpress)* **$175 [≈£117]**

Rosenfeld, Sybil

- Georgian Scene Painters and Scene Painting. Cambridge: 1981. Sm 4to. xiv,206 pp. 78 ills on plates. Orig cloth. *(Washton)* **$85 [≈£57]**
- Georgian Scene Painters and Scene Painting. Cambridge: UP, 1981. xiv,206 pp. Frontis, 78 plates. Orig cloth. Dw. *(Fine Art)* **£35 [≈$53]**

Rosenstiel, Helene Von

- American Rugs and Carpets. New York: Morrow, 1978. 4to. 192 pp. Num ills. Orig cloth. *(Rona Schneider)* **$35 [≈£23]**

Rosenthal, Nan

- George Rickey. New York: Abrams, 1977. Lge oblong 4to. 220 pp. 223 ills. Orig cloth. Dw. *(Ars Libri)* **$375 [≈£250]**

Roses of Sharon ...

- Roses of Sharon: Poems chosen from the Flower of Ancient Hebrew Literature. Golden Cockerel Press: 1937. One of 10 (of 125) specially bound (this copy unnumbered). Tall 4to. 60 pp. 12 w'engvs by Mary Groom. Orig pigskin. *(Waddington)* **£160 [≈$240]**

Ross, A.M.

- William Henry Bartlett; Artist, Author and Traveller ... Toronto: UP, 1973. 1st edn. Lge 4to. ix,164 pp. Port frontis, 36 plates. Dw. *(Clevedon Books)* **£45 [≈$68]**

Ross, Frederick

- The Ruined Abbeys of Britain. London: William Mackenzie, [1880s]. 2 vols. 4to. 12 cold plates by Benjamin Fawcett after A.F. Lydon. Orig dec cloth gilt, inner hinges sl cracked but holding, some marking of bds, extrs sl bumped. *(Cooper Hay)* **£75 [≈$113]**
- The Ruined Abbeys of Britain. London: William Mackenzie, [1882]. 1st edn, in one vol. Folio. viii,288 pp. 12 cold plates by Benjamin Fawcett after A.F. Lydon, num w'engvs in text. Orig cloth gilt, crnrs v sl rubbed, hinges trifle tender. *(Hollett)* **£160 [≈$240]**

Ross, Robert

- Aubrey Beardsley ... With a Revised Iconography by Aymer Vallance. London: John Lane; the Bodley Head, 1909. 1st edn. 8vo. 112,[8] pp. 16 ills. Orig cloth gilt, t.e.g., spine sl faded. *(Robert Frew)* **£50 [≈$75]**

Rossetti, Christina

- Goblin Market ... Illustrated by Laurence Housman. London: Macmillan, 1893. 8vo. Endpapers sl spotted. Orig elab gilt cloth, a.e.g. *(Waterfield's)* **£275 [≈$413]**
- Goblin Market. Illustrated by Laurence Housman. London: Macmillan, 1893. 1st edn thus. Thin 8vo. B/w ills. Prelims sl spotted. Orig pict cloth gilt. *(Barbara Stone)* **£165 [≈$248]**
- Goblin Market. Illustrated by Laurence Housman. London: Macmillan, 1893. One of 160 Large Paper. 4to. B/w ills. Orig green linen, paper label chipped, spine ends v sl rubbed. *(Barbara Stone)* **£500 [≈$750]**
- Goblin Market. Illustrated by Arthur Rackham. London: Harrap, (1939). 1st edn thus. 8vo. 37,[3 blank] pp. Cold frontis, b/w ills. Few sl marks. Orig wraps. Orig envelope (torn & soiled). *(Bow Windows)* **£65 [≈$98]**
- Poems. Illustrated by Florence Harrison. London: Blackie, [1910]. 1st edn thus. 4to. xxiv,369 pp. 36 mtd cold plates, ills. Foredge v sl foxed. Orig elab gilt cloth, t.e.g. *(Sotheran's)* **£168 [≈$252]**
- Poems. Chosen by Walter de la Mare. Gregynog Press: 1930. One of 275. Port. Orig half pigskin & mrbld bds. *(Barbara Stone)* **£235 [≈$353]**
- Poems. Newtown: Gregynog Press, 1930. One of 300. Port. Orig calf & mrbld bds, spine v sl darkened. *(First Folio)* **$350 [≈£233]**

Rossetti, Dante Gabriel

- The Blessed Damozel. With Drawings by Kenyon Cox. New York: Dodd, Mead, 1886. 1st edn. Folio. [37] ff. 21 ills. Name. Orig pict gilt cloth, spine ends & crnrs sl rubbed, front hinge tender. *(Chapel Hill)* **$275 [≈£183]**

Rothe, Edith

- Mediaeval Book Illumination in Europe. The Collections of the German Democratic Republic. New York: Norton, (1968). 1st English edn. 4to. 308 pp. Ills. Orig cloth gilt. Dw. *(Karmiole)* **$75 [≈£50]**
- Mediaeval Book Illumination in Europe. The Collections of the German Democratic Republic. New York: 1968. 4to. 307 pp. 160 plates (96 cold). Orig cloth. Dw. *(Washton)* **$85 [≈£57]**
- Mediaeval Book Illumination in Europe. New York: Norton, (1968). 1st edn in English. 4to. 306,[1] pp. 160 ills. Orig cloth. *(Bookpress)* **$85 [≈£57]**

Rothenstein, John

- The Artists of the 1890s. London: Routledge, 1928. 1st edn. Ills. Orig cloth, sl rubbed & soiled. Front & back panels of dw laid in. *(Between the Covers)* **$75 [≈£50]**
- Augustus John. London: 1944. 1st edn. 4to. 96 plates. Orig cloth, spine ends & crnrs rubbed. Inscribed by Augustus John. *(Ulysses Bookshop)* **£165 [≈$248]**
- Augustus John. Oxford & London: Phaidon, 1946. 3rd edn. Lge 4to. 24,[4] pp. 90 plates. Orig cloth. *(Ars Libri)* **$45 [≈£30]**
- The Life and Death of Charles Conder. London: Dent, 1938. xx,300 pp. Cold frontis, 25 plates. Orig cloth. Dw (torn). *(Leicester Art Books)* **£48 [≈$72]**
- The Life and Death of Conder. London: Dent, 1938. xx,300 pp. Cold frontis, 25 plates. Orig cloth, v sl worn. *(Fine Art)* **£50 [≈$75]**
- Life and Death of Conder. London: Dent, 1938. 1st edn. 8vo. xx,300 pp. Cold frontis, 18 plates. Orig cloth gilt. Dw (sl frayed). *(Clevedon Books)* **£90 [≈$135]**
- Victor Hammer, Artist and Craftsman. Boston: David R. Godine, (1978). One of 500. Sm 4to. 57 pp. 19 plates. Orig cloth. Cardboard slipcase. *(Oak Knoll)* **$75 [≈£50]**

Rothenstein, William

- Twenty-Four Portraits. First and Second Series. New York: Harcourt Brace, 1920; London: Chatto & Windus, 1923. One of 2000 & 1500 respectively. Orig cloth & bds. Dws (worn). *(First Folio)* **$95 [≈£63]**

Roundell, James

- Thomas Shotter Boys 1803-1874. London: 1974. 224 pp. 102 plates, 21 figs. Orig cloth. Dw (sl worn). *(Fine Art)* **£38 [≈$57]**
- Thomas Shotter Boys. London: Octopus Books, 1974. 224 pp. Frontis, 102 plates, 21 text ills. Orig cloth. *(Leicester Art Books)* **£40 [≈$60]**

Rowell, Margit

- Miro. New York: Abrams, (1970). 4to. 46 pp. 184 plates (75 cold). Orig cloth. Dw. Slipcase. *(Abacus)* **$85 [≈£57]**

Rowland, Benjamin, Jr.

- The Wall-Paintings of India, Central Asia & Ceylon. Boston: Merrymount Press, 1938. One of 500. Folio. [i],xiii,[i],94 pp. 30 plates. Name. Inscrptn. Margs sl browned. Orig portfolio. *(Bookpress)* **$350 [≈£233]**

Rowland, Kurt

- A History of the Modern Movement: Art, Architecture, Design. New York: Van Nostrand Reinhold, (1973). 4to. 240 pp. 606 ills. Orig cloth gilt. Dw. *(Karmiole)* **$35 [≈£23]**

Rowlandson, Thomas

- Medical Caricatures with a Foreword by Morris H. Saffron. New York: Editions Medicina Rara, 1971. One of 2800. Folio. 4 pp. 12 cold plates loose as issued. Orig drop-back box (sl stained). *(Argosy)* **$250 [≈£167]**

Rowley, George

- Principles of Chinese Painting. With Illustrations from the DuBois Schanck Morris Collection. Princeton: UP, 1947. 1st edn. 4to. xii,112 pp. 51 plates. Orig cloth gilt. Dw (chipped). *(Karmiole)* **$45 [≈£30]**

Royal Academy of Arts

- Commemorative Catalogue of the Exhibition of French Art 1200-1900. London: 1933. 4to. xxix,268 pp. 248 plates. Orig cloth, edges sl foxed. *(Washton)* **$45 [≈£30]**

Royal Academy Pictures ...

- Royal Academy Pictures. Illustrating the Hundred and Twenty-Sixth Exhibition of the Royal Academy. Being the Royal Academy Supplement of "The Magazine of Art". London: 1894. 4to. 200 pp. Ca 200 ills. Orig cloth, a.e.g. *(Washton)* **$45 [≈£30]**

Royer-Collard, F.B.

- Skeleton Clocks. N.A.G. Press: 1969. 4to. 154 pp. Ills. Orig cloth gilt. Dw. *(Hollett)* **£65 [≈$98]**

Rubin, James Henry

- Eighteenth-Century French Life Drawing. Selections from the Collection of Mathias Polakovits. Princeton: The Art Museum, 1977. 4to. 103 pp. 39 plates, ills. Orig cloth. Dw. *(Washton)* **$45 [≈£30]**

Rublowsky, John

- Pop Art. Photography by Ken Hyman. New York: Basic Books, 1965. 4to. [8],174,[6] pp. 32 cold plates, ills. Orig cloth. Dw. *(Ars Libri)* **$100 [≈£67]**
- Pop Art. Photography by Ken Hyman. New York: Basic Books, (1965). 4to. 212 pp. 41 cold plates, ills. Orig cloth. Dw (lacks sm piece rear panel). *(Abacus)* **$60 [≈£40]**

Rudge, William Edwin

- From a Corner of the Housetop. New York: Privately Printed, 1930. One of 25. 8vo. Faint foxing. Orig leather gilt, t.e.g. *(Black Sun)* **$200 [≈£133]**

Rudiments ...

- Rudiments of Ancient Architecture ... The Second Edition, much enlarged. London: I. & J. Taylor, 1794. Roy 8vo. xvi,117,[i],[2 advt] pp. Frontis, title vignette, 11 plates (2-10, 4*). Sl marg browning. Contemp calf, hd of spine reprd. Anon. *(Spelman)* **£60 [≈$90]**
- Rudiments of Architecture ... The Third Edition, enlarged. London: for J. Taylor, 1804. 8vo. [ii],xvi,134,[2],[4 ctlg] pp. Frontis, title vignette, 10 plates. Tiny marg worm hole. Orig cloth backed bds, uncut, lower jnt sl cracked. *(Rankin)* **£65 [≈$98]**

Rudy, Charles

- The Cathedrals of Northern Spain. London: Werner Laurie, 1896. 1st edn. 8vo. xiv,398 pp. 32 ills. Orig dec cloth gilt. *(Hollett)* **£15 [≈$23]**

Ruhe, Harry

- Fluxus, the Most Radical and Experimental Art Movement of the Sixties. Amsterdam: 1979. Lge 4to. (340) pp. Num ills. Contents loose in 2-ring binder, as issued. *(Ars Libri)* **$200 [≈£133]**

Ruhemann, Helmut

- The Cleaning of Paintings. New York: Praeger, (1968). 4to. 508 pp. Frontis. half-title creased. Orig cloth. *(Bookpress)* **$100 [≈£67]**
- The Cleaning of Paintings. Problems and Potentialities. London: 1969. 4to. 508 pp. Num plates. Orig cloth. *(Washton)* **$100 [≈£67]**

Ruscha, Edward

- Every Building on the Sunset Strip. Los Angeles: Edward Ruscha, 1966. Sm sq 4to. 52-page leporello. Orig wraps, some wear. Slipcase (taped). *(Ars Libri)* **$175 [≈£117]**

Rush, James

- A Beilby Odyssey. Olney: Nelson & Saunders, 1987. 1st edn. 4to. 176 pp. 128 ills. Orig cloth gilt. Dw. *(Hollett)* **£30 [≈$45]**
- The Ingenious Beilbys. London: Barrie & Jenkins, 1973. 1st edn. 4to. 168 pp. Num cold plates, ills. Orig cloth. Dw. Slipcase. signed by the author. *(Bookpress)* **$125 [≈£83]**
- The Ingenious Beilbys. London: Barrie & Jenkins, 1973. 1st edn. Sm 4to. 168 pp. 98 plates. Orig cloth gilt. Price-clipped dw (sl worn). Slipcase. Signed by the author. *(Hollett)* **£35 [≈$53]**

Rushforth, G. McN.

- Medieval Christian Imagery as illustrated by the Painted Windows of Great Malvern Priory Church, Worcestershire ... Oxford: Clarendon Press 1936. 1st edn. 4to. xx,456 pp. Plan, 188 ills, 3 diags. Orig cloth gilt. *(Hollett)* **£120 [≈$180]**

Ruskin, John

- The King of the Golden River. Illustrated by Arthur Rackham. London: Harrap, [1932]. 1st edn. Orig pict wraps. Dw (some browning at spine, wear at edges). *(Mac Donnell)* **$125 [≈£83]**
- The King of the Golden River. Illustrated by Arthur Rackham. London: (1932). One of 570 signed by Rackham. Thin 8vo. 4 cold plates, text ills, pict endpapers. Orig limp vellum, t.e.g. *(Argonaut)* **$500 [≈£333]**
- Modern Painters. A New Edition. London: Smith, Elder, 1873. One of 1000 signed by the author. 5 vols. 84 plates. Orig bndg. *(Schoyer)* **$600 [≈£400]**
- Modern Painters. Complete Edition. London: George Allen, 1888. 6 vols. 4to. Plates, ills. Rebound in buckram, a.e.g. *(Mermaid Books)* **£135 [≈$203]**
- The Poetry of Architecture ... Orpington: George Allen, 1893. 1st edn. 4to. xii,261 pp. Cold frontis, 14 gravures, 7 figs. Occas sl

spotting. Orig cloth gilt, rubbed, spine ends chipped, lower bd sl marked. *(Hollett)* **£45 [≈$68]**

- The Seven Lamps of Architecture. Orpington: George Allen, 1886. 5th edn. 4to. xii,[iv],222 pp. 14 plates. Orig cloth gilt, sl worn & scuffed. *(Hollett)* **£30 [≈$45]**
- Stones of Venice. A New Edition. London: Smith, Elder, 1874. One of 1500, signed by the author. 3 vols. 47 plates. Sl foxing. Orig bndg. *(Schoyer)* **$400 [≈£267]**
- The Two Paths: being Lectures on Art, and its Application to Decoration and Manufacture ... London: Smith, Elder, 1859. 1st edn. 8vo. x,[ii],271,[1],[24 ctlg dated May 1859] pp. Orig cloth, rebacked, crnrs worn. *(Claude Cox)* **£45 [≈$68]**

Russell, Charles E.

- English Mezzotinto Portraits and their States: Catalogue of Corrections of and Additions to Chaloner Smith's "British Mezzotint Portraits". London: Halton & Truscott Smith, 1926. One of 625. 2 vols. 64 plates. Half mor, v sl worn. *(Fine Art)* **£300 [≈$450]**

Russell, John

- Francis Bacon. London: Thames & Hudson, 1971. 242 pp. 116 ills. Orig cloth. Dw. *(Leicester Art Books)* **£110 [≈$165]**
- Henry Moore. London: Allen Lane, 1968. 234 pp. 229 ills. Orig bds. Dw. *(Leicester Art Books)* **£28 [≈$42]**
- Henry Moore. New York: Putnam, 1968. 4to. 231,[1] pp. 228 ills. Orig cloth. *(Ars Libri)* **$60 [≈£40]**
- Max Ernst. Life and Work. New York: Abrams, [1967]. Lge 4to. 359 pp. 475 ills. Orig cloth. *(Ars Libri)* **$175 [≈£117]**

Russell, Margarita

- Jan van de Cappelle. Leigh-on-Sea: F. Lewis, 1975. One of 600. 112 pp. 124 ills. Orig buckram. *(Leicester Art Books)* **£85 [≈$128]**

Russoli, Franco (compiler)

- The Berenson Collection. Translated and Edited by Frances and Sidney Alexander. Milan: Arti Grafiche Ricordi, (1964). Folio. Plates, ills. Orig cloth. Dw (sl chipped). Slipcase. *(Karmiole)* **$150 [≈£100]**

Rutter, Joan

- Here's Flowers. An Anthology of Flower Poems. Compiled by Joan Rutter. Golden Cockerel Press: 1937. One of 200. 199 pp. W'engvs by John O'Connor. Orig qtr mor, spine sl sunned, some faint scattered brown stains. *(Waddington)* **£85 [≈$128]**

Rutter, Owen

- We Happy Few. An Anthology. With Wood Engravings by John O'Connor. Golden Cockerel Press: 1946. One of 100 specially bound. 11 w'engvs. Orig dec bndg gilt. Slipcase (edges v sl browned). *(Margaret Nangle)* **£190 [≈$285]**

Rutter, Owen (editor)

- We Happy Few. An Anthology ... With Eleven Engravings by John O'Connor. Golden Cockerel Press: 1946. One of 100 specials. 150 pp. Frontis, 10 w'engvs. Orig morocco & buckram gilt, t.e.g. *(Claude Cox)* **£85 [≈$128]**

Ryder, John

- Flowers & Flourishes including a newly annotated Edition of a Suite of Fleurons. London: Bodley Head, (1976). 1st edn. Tall 8vo. 168 pp. Orig cloth-backed bds. Dw. *(Oak Knoll)* **$55 [≈£37]**

Saarinen, Aline B. (editor)

- Eero Saarinen on his Work. A Selection of Buildings dating from 1947 to 1964 with Statements by the Architect. Yale: UP, 1962. Lge 4to. 108 pp. Num ills. Orig cloth backed bds. Slipcase (worn). *(Francis Edwards)* **£30 [≈$45]**

Sabarsky, Serge

- George Grosz. The Berlin Years. New York: Rizzoli, 1985. Lge sq 4to. 253,[3] pp. 191 plates, text ills. Orig cloth. Dw. *(Ars Libri)* **$65 [≈£43]**

Sadleir, Michael

- The Evolution of Publishers' Binding Styles 1770-1900. London: Constable, 1930. One of 500. x,96 pp. 12 plates. Orig vellum over mrbld bds, spine sl soiled. *(Karmiole)* **$150 [≈£100]**

Sadleir, Thomas U. & Dickinson, P.L.

- Georgian Mansions in Ireland, with some Account of Georgian Architecture and Decoration. Dublin: UP, 1915. One of 700. 4to. 103 pp. 80 plates. Orig bndg. *(Emerald Isle)* **£220 [≈$330]**

Saint, Andrew

- Richard Norman Shaw. New Haven: Yale UP, (1977). 2nd printing. 4to. xx,487 pp. Orig cloth. *(Bookpress)* **$85 [≈£57]**

Saint Pierre, Jacques Bernardin de

- Paul and Virginia, with an Original Memoir of the Author, and Three Hundred-and-Thirty Illustrations. London: W.S. Orr, 1839. Sm 4to. Engvs on India paper, w'engvs, decs. Margs of mtd plates sl soiled. Purple mor gilt. *(Mermaid Books)* **£55 [≈$83]**

Salaman, Malcolm C.

- British Book Illustration Yesterday and To-Day. London: Studio, 1923. 1st edn. 4to. viii,175 pp. Ills. Orig cloth. *(Spelman)* **£40 [≈$60]**
- The Etchings of James McBey. London: Halton & Truscott Smith; New York: Minton Balch, 1929. viii,32 pp. 96 plates. Orig cloth gilt, t.e.g. *(Leicester Art Books)* **£40 [≈$60]**
- F.L. Griggs. London: The Studio, Modern Masters of Etching No. 12, 1926. Oblong 4to. 8 pp. 12 plates. Mod cloth backed bds. *(Hollett)* **£48 [≈$72]**
- Modern Book Illustrators and their Work. London: The Studio, 1914. 192 pp. Ills. Some foxing. Orig wraps. *(Fine Art)* **£35 [≈$53]**
- Old English Mezzotints. Edited by Charles Holme. London: The Studio, 1910. Sm folio. 78 plates. Orig cloth gilt, t.e.g., sl marked & worn. *(First Folio)* **$50 [≈£33]**
- The Woodcut of To-Day at Home and Abroad. London: The Studio, 1927. 1st edn. 4to. Ills. Orig cloth. *(Spelman)* **£40 [≈$60]**

Salmi, Mario

- Italian Miniatures. New York: Abrams, (1954). 2nd edn. Folio. 214 pp. 75 cold plates, 90 text ills. Orig cloth. *(Bookpress)* **$150 [≈£100]**
- Italian Miniatures. New York: n.d. Rvsd & enlgd edn. 4to. 214 pp. 78 mtd cold plates, 99 b/w ills. Orig cloth. Dw. *(Washton)* **$90 [≈£60]**

Salmon, William

- Palladio Londinensis; or, The London Art of Building. London: Rivington ..., 1773. 8th edn. 4to. xii,80, 77-132,[28] pp. 54 plates. Contemp calf, rebacked, some wear to edges & tips. *(Bookpress)* **$950 [≈£633]**
- Polygraphice: or, the Arts of Drawing, Engraving, Etching ... Eighth Edition. Enlarged ... London: A. & J. Churchill, 1701. 2 vols in one. 8vo. [32],1-224, 301-939,[i] pp, complete. Port frontis, engvd half-title, 23 plates. Contemp calf, spine ends reprd. *(Spelman)* **£380 [≈$570]**
- Polygraphice: Or, The Arts of Drawing, Engraving, Etching, Limning, Painting, Varnishing, Japaning, Gilding ... The Eighth Edition, Enlarged ... London: A. & J. Churchill, 1701. 2 vols. 8vo. 2 ports, engvd title, 23 plates. Calf, rebacked. *(Dailey)* **$750 [≈£500]**

Salomons, Vera

- Charles Eisen, Eighteenth Century French Book Illustrator and Engraver: an Annotated Bibliography ... Amsterdam: Hissink, 1927. Reprint of 1914 edn. 8vo. 195,[2] pp. Frontis, 30 plates. Orig cloth. Dw (spine sunned). *(Bookpress)* **$45 [≈£30]**

Saltz, Jerry

- Beyond Boundaries. New York's New Art. New York: Alfred van der March, 1986. Folio. 128 pp. Num ills. Orig cloth. Dw. *(Ars Libri)* **$75 [≈£50]**

Salzman, L.F.

- Building in England down to 1540. A Documentary History. Oxford: Clarendon Press 1952. 1st edn. Thick 8vo. xv,629 pp. 21 plates. Orig cloth gilt. Dw (sl torn). *(Hollett)* **£65 [≈$98]**

Samaan-Hanna, A.

- Moods that Endure. Worcester: Stanbrook Abbey Press, 1978. One of 90 specially bound (of 340). French-folded. Orig parchment backed Thai batik silk, uncut. *(Claude Cox)* **£68 [≈$102]**

Sampson, Henry

- A History of Advertising from the Earliest Times ... London: Chatto & Windus, 1875. 1st edn. 8vo. Fldg cold frontis, 13 ills. 40 pp ctlg at end. Orig dec cloth gilt, sl marked, crnrs sl worn, spine ends sl frayed. *(Clark)* **£85 [≈$128]**

San Lazzaro, G. di (editor)

- Homage to Georges Rouault. Special Issue of XXe Siecle. New York: Tudor, (1971). 1st edn. Lge 4to. 128 pp. Num ills. Orig cloth. Dw. *(Karmiole)* **$75 [≈£50]**

Sandars, N.K.

- Prehistoric Art in Europe. London: Penguin Books, 1968. 1st edn. Lge 8vo. Cold frontis, 304 plates, 104 text figs. Dw. Slipcase. *(Claude Cox)* **£18 [≈$27]**

Sandars, William Bliss

- Half Timbered Houses and Carved Oak Furniture of the 16th and 17th Centuries.

London: Quaritch, 1894. x,51 pp. 30 plates. Orig cloth, sl lib marks. *(Quest Books)* **£40 [≈$60]**

Sanders, Henry

- The Old Testament Manuscripts in the Freer Collection. New York: Macmillan, 1910. 1st edn. 4to. vi,104,[2] pp. 9 plates. Orig cloth. Slipcase. *(Karmiole)* **$75 [≈£50]**

Sanderson, William

- Graphice, or, the Use of the Pen and Pencil ... London: Robert Crofts, 1658. 1st edn. Sm folio. [xii],[iv],87 pp. 1 plate. Lacks port. Minor foxing. 2 reprs to title. Later qtr mor. *(Bookpress)* **$875 [≈£583]**

Sandford, Christopher & Sandford, Lettice

- Clervis and Belamie. A Story. Heathercombe: Boar's Heads Press, 1932. One of 100 signed by the authors. 4to. W'engvs. Orig cloth gilt. *(Barbara Stone)* **£125 [≈$188]**
- The Magic Forest. A Story. London: Chiswick Press, 1931. One of 100 signed by the authors. 4to. W'engvs by Lettice Sandford. Orig cloth gilt. Inscribed by Christopher Sandford (1931). *(Barbara Stone)* **£125 [≈$188]**

Sandler, Irving

- Abstract Expression. The Triumph of American Painting. London: (1970). 1st edn. 4to. 301,[3 blank] pp. 24 cold & 200 b/w ills. Orig cloth. Dw. *(Bow Windows)* **£50 [≈$75]**
- Alex Katz. New York: Abrams, (1979). Oblong 4to. 222 pp. 220 ills (72 mtd cold). Orig cloth. Dw. Signed by the artist on a tipped-in b'plate. *(Abacus)* **$100 [≈£67]**

Sansone, Antonio

- The Printing of Cotton Fabric ... Manchester: Abel Heywood, 1901. 2nd edn, rvsd. 486 pp. Fldg plates, ills. 116 fabric samples. Orig cloth gilt, soiled, sl worn. *(Willow House)* **£65 [≈$98]**

Sarkar, H.

- Studies in Early Buddhist Architecture of India. Delhi: (1966). 1st edn. 8vo. [viii], 120 pp. 13 plates. Orig cloth. Dw (chipped). *(Bookpress)* **$45 [≈£30]**

Sartin, Stephen

- Thomas Sidney Cooper, C.V.O., R.A., 1803-1902. Leigh-on-Sea: F. Lewis, 1976. One of 500. 79 pp. 41 plates. Orig cloth. *(Leicester Art Books)* **£30 [≈$45]**

Sasowsky, Norman

- The Prints of Reginald Marsh. An Essay and Definitive Catalog of His Linoleum Cuts, Etchings, Engravings, and Lithographs. New York: Clarkson N. Potter, (1976). 4to. 288 pp. Num ills. Orig cloth. Dw. *(Karmiole)* **$50 [≈£33]**

Sassoon, Siegfried

- Memoirs of a Fox-Hunting Man. Illustrated by William Nicholson. London: Chiswick Press, 1929. 1st illust edn. B/w ills. Foredges, half-title & endpapers sl foxed. Orig dec buckram, spine ends & 2 crnrs bumped. Dw. *(Margaret Nangle)* **£28 [≈$42]**
- Memoirs of an Infantry Officer. Illustrations by Paul Hogarth. New York: The Limited Editions Club, 1981. One of 2000 signed by the illustrator. 8vo. Orig cloth. Slipcase. *(Oak Knoll)* **$50 [≈£33]**

Saunders, O. Elfrida

- English Illumination. Paris: The Pegasus Press, (1928). 1st edn. 2 vols. 4to. 129 plates. Orig half mor, sl shelf wear, mor sl discold. Dws. Slipcases. *(Bookpress)* **$350 [≈£233]**

Saunier, Claudius

- Treatise on Modern Horology in Theory and Practice. Translated from the French ... London: A. Fischer, [1882]. Sm thick 4to. xvi,844 pp. 21 dble-page cold plates. Few marg blind stamps. Orig half leather gilt, lib reback. *(Hollett)* **£180 [≈$270]**

Savage, George

- 18th-Century Porcelain. London: Rockliff, 1952. 1st edn. xx,435 pp. Cold frontis, 112 plates. Edges trifle spotted. Orig cloth gilt. Dw. *(Hollett)* **£35 [≈$53]**

Savage, William

- A Dictionary of the Art of Printing (1841). London: Gregg Press, 1966. 8vo. viii, 815 pp. Orig buckram. *(Claude Cox)* **£30 [≈$45]**

Savidge, Alan

- The Parsonage in England. Its History and Architecture. London: SPCK, 1954. 1st edn. xv,239 pp. 49 plates. Orig cloth gilt. Dw (sl creased & chipped). *(Hollett)* **£25 [≈$38]**

Savory, Jerold J.

- The Vanity Fair Gallery. A Collector's Guide to the Caricatures. South Brunswick & New York: 1979. Thin 4to. 209 pp. 16 cold plates, 222 figs. Sm lib stamp title verso. Dw (spine marked). *(Francis Edwards)* **£25 [≈$38]**

Sawyer, Charles J. & Harvey Darton, F.J.

- English Books 1475-1900 a Signpost for Collectors. London: Sawyer, 1927. One of 2000. 2 vols. Frontis, fldg plate, 98 ills. Orig cloth gilt. *(Cooper Hay)* **£95 [≈$143]**
- English Books 1475-1900 a Signpost for Collectors. Westminster: Sawyer, 1927. One of 2000. 2 vols. 8vo. Ills. Orig cloth gilt, t.e.g., unopened, v sl worn. *(First Folio)* **$155 [≈£103]**

Saxo Grammaticus

- The History of Amleth, Prince of Denmark ... Illustrations cut in Wood by Sigurd Vasegaard. New York: The Limited Editions Club, 1954. One of 1500 signed by Vasegaard. Sm 4to. Foxed. Orig leather-backed bds. Slipcase. *(Oak Knoll)* **$45 [≈£30]**
- The History of Amleth, Prince of Denmark. New York: The Limited Editions Club, 1954. One of 1500 sgnd by the artist, Sigurd Vasegaard. 4to. 107 pp. W'engvs. Orig morocco backed bds. Endpapers, prelims and foredge foxed. Slipcase (sl browned). *(Waddington)* **£42 [≈$63]**

Scamell, George

- Breweries and Maltings: their Arrangement, Construction and Machinery. London: A. Fullarton & Co., 1871. 1st edn. viii,134 pp. 20 litho plates. Occas spotting. Orig cloth gilt, faded. *(Hollett)* **£85 [≈$128]**

Schade, Werner

- Cranach: A Family of Master Painters. New York: Putnam, 1980. 478 pp. 379 ills. Orig cloth. *(Leicester Art Books)* **£70 [≈$105]**

Schaffer, R.J.

- The Weathering of Natural Building Stones. London: HMSO, 1932. 1st edn. 8vo. x,149,[ii] pp. Frontis, 55 ills, 19 tables. *(Hollett)* **£35 [≈$53]**

Schefer, Leopold

- The Artist's Married Life; being that of Albert Durer. Translated ... by Mrs. J.R. Stodart. London: John Chapman, 1848. 1st English edn. Sm 8vo. xx,226 pp. Port frontis, engvd plate. Sl browning. Orig brown cloth over wooden bds, gilt faded, extrs sl worn. *(Claude Cox)* **£38 [≈$57]**

Schiff, Gert

- The Amorous Illustrations of Thomas Rowlandson. London: The Cythera Press, 1969. xxxix pp. 50 cold plates. Orig cloth. *(Leicester Art Books)* **£25 [≈$38]**

Schiff, Mortimer L.

- French Signed Bindings in the Mortimer L. Schiff Collection ... see De Ricci, Seymour

Schiller, Gertrude

- Iconography of Christian Art. Greenwich: 1972. 2 vols. Sm 4to. 585 + 816 ills on plates. Orig cloth. *(Washton)* **$150 [≈£100]**

Schiller, Johann Christoph Friedrich von

- William Tell. Illustrated by Charles Hug. Zurich: The Limited Editions Club, 1951. One of 1500 signed by the illustrator. Sm 4to. Orig cloth-backed bds. Slipcase. *(Oak Knoll)* **$65 [≈£43]**

Schilling, Edmund

- The German Drawings in the Collection of Her Majesty the Queen at Windsor Castle ... London: [ca 1973]. 4to. 239 pp. 110 plates, 64 text ills. Orig cloth. Dw. *(Washton)* **$75 [≈£50]**

Schmalenbach, Werner

- Fernand Leger. New York: Abrams, (1976). 4to. 173 pp. 125 ills (48 mtd cold plates). Orig cloth. Dw. *(Abacus)* **$50 [≈£33]**
- Fernand Leger. New York: Abrams, 1976. 1st edn. Tall 4to. Mtd cold plates. Orig fabric cloth. Dw. *(First Folio)* **$75 [≈£50]**
- Kurt Schwitters. New York: Abrams, (1967). 1st edn. Lge 4to. 400 pp. 420 plates (54 mtd cold). Orig cloth. Dw (sl rubbed). *(Karmiole)* **$150 [≈£100]**

Schmeckebier, Laurence E.

- John Steuart Curry's Pageant of America. New York: American Artists Group, 1943. 4to. xviii,363 pp. 341 ills. Orig cloth. *(Ars Libri)* **$65 [≈£43]**

Schmutzler, Robert

- Art Nouveau. New York: Abrams, (1962). 4to. 321 pp. 451 ills. Orig cloth. Dw. *(Abacus)* **$100 [≈£67]**
- Art Nouveau. New York: Abrams, [ca 1964]. Lge sq 4to. Num mtd cold plates, ills. Orig gilt dec cloth. Dw. *(First Folio)* **$150 [≈£100]**

Schnabel, Charles

- Lobelia & Myrrh. Songs & Fragments of Lost and Unfinished Manuscripts. London: privately printed by George W. Jones at the Sign of the Dolphin, 1924. One of 250. Sm 4to. 32 pp. Frontis, title vignette. Orig holland backed bds. *(Claude Cox)* **£22 [≈$33]**

Schneider, Pierre

- Matisse. London: Thames & Hudson, 1984. 752 pp. 930 ills. Orig cloth. Dw. *(Leicester Art Books)* **£80 [≈$120]**

Schnessel, S. Michael

- Icart. London: Studio Vista, 1976. xiv,178 pp. 217 ills. Orig cloth. *(Leicester Art Books)* **£35 [≈$53]**

Schnitzler, Arthur

- Rhapsody. A Dream Novel ... With Illustrations by Donia Nachsen. London: Constable, 1928. One of 1000. 8vo. 192 pp. Illust title, 8 plates, 14 text ills. Occas foxing. Orig parchment backed dec bds, ft of spine marked. *(Bow Windows)* **£70 [≈$105]**

Schoenberger, Guido (editor)

- The Drawings of Mathias Gothart Nithart called Grunewald. New York: Bittner, 1948. 107 pp. 44 plates. Orig bds. Dw. *(Clarice Davis)* **$55 [≈£37]**

School of Arts ...

- The School of Arts Improved ... Gainsborough: John Mozley, 1776. 1st edn. 12mo. [ii],156 pp. Contemp mrbld bds, rebacked in leather. *(Bookpress)* **$875 [≈£583]**

Schulz, Anne Markham

- Niccolo Di Giovanni Fiorentino and Venetian Sculpture of the Early Renaissance. New York: 1970. 4to. xxiv,136 pp. 100 ills on plates. Orig cloth, sl bumped. *(Washton)* **$45 [≈£30]**
- The Sculpture of Bernardo Rossellino and His Workshop. Princeton: UP, 1977. xxiii,176 pp. 95 plates. Orig cloth. *(Leicester Art Books)* **£55 [≈$83]**

Schulz, H.C.

- French Illuminated Manuscripts. With an Original Leaf from a Miniature Book of Hours. The Grabhorn Press: 1958. One of 200. 30 pp. Orig dec bds. Dw. *(Black Sun)* **$750 [≈£500]**

Schulz, Juergen

- Venetian Paintings of the Renaissance. Berkeley: 1968. 4to. xxix,244 pp. 151 ills on plates, 90 figs. Orig cloth. Dw (worn). *(Washton)* **$100 [≈£67]**

Schwarz, Arturo

- The Complete Works of Marcel Duchamp. London: Thames & Hudson, 1969. xxii,750 pp. 765 ills. Orig cloth. Dw. Slipcase. *(Leicester Art Books)* **£425 [≈$638]**
- The Complete Works of Marcel Duchamp. Second Revised Edition. New York: Abrams, 1970. Sm stout folio. xxi,[1],630 pp. Over 780 ills. Orig cloth. Dw. *(Ars Libri)* **$1,750 [≈£1,167]**
- Man Ray. The Rigours of the Imagination. London: Thames & Hudson, 1977. 384 pp. 520 ills. Orig cloth. Dw. *(Leicester Art Books)* **£110 [≈$165]**

Scott, Frank J.

- The Art of Beautifying Suburban Home Grounds of Small Extent ... New York: Appleton, 1870. 1st edn. 8vo. 618 pp. Plates. Orig cloth, spotted & rubbed. *(Bookpress)* **$285 [≈£190]**

Scott, George Gilbert

- An Essay on the History of English Church Architecture prior to the Separation of England from the Roman Obedience. London: Simpkin, Marshall, 1881. Lge 4to. [6],vi,195 pp. 37 plates inc frontis. Orig cloth, edges dampstained. *(Sotheran's)* **£75 [≈$113]**
- An Essay on the History of English Church Architecture prior to the separation of England from the Roman Obedience. London: 1881. 1st edn. 4to. 37 plates. Sl marks. Contemp cloth, sl worn & reprd. *(Bow Windows)* **£105 [≈$158]**

Scott, Sir Walter

- Ivanhoe. Design and Original Cuts by Allen Lewis. New York: The Limited Editions Club, 1940. One of 1500 signed by the illustrator. 2 vols. 8vo. Orig cloth. Slipcase (spotted). *(Oak Knoll)* **$100 [≈£67]**
- Ivanhoe. Illustrated by Edward A. Wilson. New York: The Limited Editions Club, 1951. One of 1500 signed by the illustrator. 2 vols. 8vo. Orig cloth (some rubbing of spines). Slipcase. *(Oak Knoll)* **$65 [≈£43]**
- Kenilworth. Illustrations by Clarke Hutton. New York: The Limited Editions Club, 1966. One of 1500 signed by the illustrator. 8vo. Orig cloth, leather label. Slipcase. *(Oak Knoll)* **$45 [≈£30]**
- The Talisman. Illustrations by Federico Castellon. Ipswich: The Limited Editions Club, 1968. One of 1500 signed by the illustrator. Sm 4to. Orig qtr calf, t.e.g. Slipcase. *(Oak Knoll)* **$45 [≈£30]**
- Waverley. Illustrations by Robert Ball. New York: The Limited Editions Club, 1961. One of 1500 signed by the illustrator. 8vo. Orig leather. Slipcase. *(Oak Knoll)* **$55 [≈£37]**

Sculptura Historico-Technica ...

- Sculptura Historico-Technica: or, the History and Art of Engraving ... Extracted from Baldinucci, Florent le Compte ... The Fourth Edition. London: for J. Marks, 1770. 4th edn. 12mo. xi,[i],264 pp. 10 plates. Contemp calf, rebacked, crnrs reprd. *(Gaskell)* **£350 [≈$525]**

Seago, Edward

- A Canvas to Cover. London: Collins, 1947. 1st edn. Lge 8vo. 134 pp. Cold frontis, num ills. Orig cloth gilt, sl marked. *(Hollett)* **£30 [≈$45]**

Searle, Ronald

- To the Kwai - and Back. War Drawings 1939-1945. London: 1986. 1st edn. Folio. Num ills. Orig cloth. Dw. *(Margaret Nangle)* **£20 [≈$30]**

Searle, William George

- The Illuminated Manuscripts in the Library of the Fitzwilliam Museum Cambridge. Cambridge: UP, 1876. 8vo. lxxiv,195 pp. orig bndg. *(Quest Books)* **£35 [≈$53]**

Searles-Wood, H.D. & Adams, H. (editors)

- Modern Building. London: 1921-23. 6 vols. 51 plates, num figs. Orig cloth, sl dust stained. *(Whitehart)* **£60 [≈$90]**

Seccombe, T.S.

- Army and Navy Drolleries. London: Warne, [ca 1875]. [24,2 ctlg] pp. 24 chromolitho plates. Orig cloth, spine ends & crnrs worn, lib marks to spine. *(Holtom)* **£45 [≈$68]**

Sedding, Edmund H.

- Norman Architecture in Cornwall. A Handbook to Old Cornish Ecclesiastical Architecture. With Notes on Ancient Manor-Houses ... London: Ward & Co., 1909. xxiv,464 pp. Fldg map, num plates. Orig cloth backed bds, trifle soiled, 2 nicks in upper bd. *(Hollett)* **£45 [≈$68]**

Segy, Ladislas

- African Sculpture Speaks. New York: (1952). Num ills. *(Rob Warren)* **$45 [≈£30]**

Seidlitz, W. Von

- A History of Japanese Colour-Prints. London: 1910. Lge 8vo. xvi,207,[1] pp. 16 cold & 60 b/w plates. Some foxing. Orig cloth. *(Bow Windows)* **£125 [≈$188]**
- History of Japanese Color Prints. Phila: Lippincott, 1920. Lge 8vo. xvi,207 pp. Num plates. Orig pict gilt cloth. *(Terramedia)* **$200 [≈£133]**

Seike, Kiyosi & Terry, Charles S.

- Contemporary Japanese Houses. Tokyo: Kodansha International, 1964. 1st edn. 4to. 205 pp. Ills. Orig cloth. Dw. *(Bookpress)* **$85 [≈£57]**

Seldis, Henry J.

- Henry Moore in America. New York: Praeger, 1973. 4to. 283,[1] pp. Num ills. Orig cloth. Dw. *(Ars Libri)* **$45 [≈£30]**

The Selective Eye ...

- The Selective Eye. New York & Lausanne: 1955-60. Vols 1-4, all published. Lge 4to. Num ills. Bds. *(Ars Libri)* **$100 [≈£67]**

Seligman, Germain

- Roger de la Fresnaye. With a Catalogue Raisonne. Greenwich: New York Graphic Society, [1969]. One of 600. Sm folio. 284 pp. 731 ills. Orig cloth. Dw. *(Ars Libri)* **$600 [≈£400]**

Seligmann, G. Saville & Hughes, Talbot

- Domestic Needlework. Its Origins and Customs throughout the Centuries. London: Country Life, n.d. Folio. One of 500. 96 pp. Cold frontis, 31 cold & 100 b/w plates. Sev sm lib stamps. Last plate reprd. Sl marked. Rec qtr mor. *(Francis Edwards)* **£250 [≈$375]**

Selway, N.C.

- The Golden Age of Coaching and Sport as depicted by James Pollard. Leigh-on-Sea: F. Lewis, 1972. One of 500. 61,[2] pp. 81 ills. Orig buckram. *(Leicester Art Books)* **£48 [≈$72]**
- The Regency Road. The Coaching Prints of James Pollard. London: Faber, 1957. 118 pp. 67 plates. Orig cloth. Dw (torn). *(Leicester Art Books)* **£55 [≈$83]**

Senefelder, Alois

- The Invention of Lithography. Translated from the Original German by J .W. Muller. New York: Fuchs & Lang, 1911. 4to. xii,229 pp. Orig cloth (spine ends worn). *(Oak Knoll)* **$95 [≈£63]**
- The Invention of Lithography. Translated from the Original German by J.W. Muller. New York: Fuchs & Lang, 1911. Sm 4to. xii,299 pp. Orig cloth. *(The Veatchs)* **$110 [≈£73]**

Sensier, Alfred

- Jean-Francois Millet, Peasant and Painter. Boston: Osgood, 1881. Sq 8vo. 230 pp. 28 ills. Orig gilt dec cloth. *(Abacus)* **$50 [≈£33]**

The Sermon on the Mount ...

- The Sermon on the Mount. With an Introduction, Parallel Texts, and Commentaries by Rowan A. Greer. New York: The Limited Editions Club, 1977. One of 1600. 4to. Printed French-fold. Orig qtr leather. Slipcase. *(Oak Knoll)* **$75 [≈£50]**

Sert, Jose Luis

- Can Our Cities Survive? Cambridge: Harvard UP, 1942. 1st edn. Oblong 4to. xi,[i],259 pp. Num ills. Orig cloth. Dw (worn). *(Bookpress)* **$325 [≈£217]**

Service, A.

- Edwardian Interiors. London: Barrie & Jenkins, 1982. 4to. 160 pp. Ills. Dw. *(Monmouth)* **£30 [≈$45]**

Seuphor, Michel

- Piet Mondrian. Life and Work. New York: Abrams, n.d. 4to. 444 pp. 627 ills (34 mtd cold plates). Orig cloth. Dw. *(Abacus)* **$200 [≈£133]**
- Piet Mondrian. New York: Abrams, 1956. 444 pp. 650 ills. Orig cloth. Dw. *(Leicester Art Books)* **£120 [≈$180]**
- Piet Mondrian: Life and Work. New York: Abrams, [ca 1955]. 1st edn. 4to. 444 pp. 600 ills (34 mtd cold plates). Orig cloth, extrs sl rubbed. Dw (chipped). *(Karmiole)* **$125 [≈£83]**

Severin, Mark

- Your Wood Engraving. Sylvan Press: 1953. 1st edn. 110 pp. Ills. Dw (sl chipped). *(Waddington)* **£18 [≈$27]**

Seymour, Charles Jr.

- Jacopo della Quercia Sculptor. New Haven: 1973. 4to. xxviii,146 pp. 134 plates, 116 ills. Orig cloth. Dw. *(Washton)* **$100 [≈£67]**

Shahn, Ben

- The Complete Graphic Works. New York: Quadrangle, New York Times Book Co., (1973). 1st edn. Oblong 4to. Dw. *(Hermitage)* **$125 [≈£83]**
- Haggadah for Passover. Boston: Little, Brown; Paris: Trianon Press, 1965. 4to. 149 pp. Cold ills. Orig gilt dec cloth. Plastic dw. *(Abacus)* **$95 [≈£63]**

Shakespeare, William

- All the Love Poems of Shakespeare. New York: The Sylvan Press, 1947. One of 1450 for the US. Sm 4to. [viii],166 pp. Ills by Eric Gill. Orig dec leatherette. *(Oak Knoll)* **$95 [≈£63]**
- Shakespeare's Comedy As You Like It. With Illustrations by Hugh Thomson. London: Hodder & Stoughton, [ca 1910]. 4to. [6],144 pp. 16 mtd cold plates, vignettes. Orig dec cloth, sm abrasion front cvr, minor fraying spine extrs. *(Karmiole)* **$125 [≈£83]**
- As You Like It. Decorations by John Austen. London: 1930. One of 125 signed by Austen. 4to. xii,114,[2 blank] pp. 6 mtd cold plates, 15 text ills. Minor sl foxing. Orig buckram, t.e.g. Slipcase (worn). *(Bow Windows)* **£90 [≈$135]**
- The Comedy of Errors. London: Hacon & Ricketts, The Vale Press, 1901. One of 310. Orig dec cloth, largely unopened, sl marked. *(Claude Cox)* **£30 [≈$45]**
- Hamlet. Illustrated by John Austen. London: Selwyn & Blount, (1922). 4to. Num b/w ills. Orig buckram backed pict bds, spine v sl faded. *(Barbara Stone)* **£110 [≈$165]**
- Henry VI Part Second. London: Hacon & Ricketts, The Vale Press, 1903. One of 310. Orig dec cloth, largely unopened, sl faded & marked. *(Claude Cox)* **£30 [≈$45]**
- The Life of King Henry V. Illustrated with Paintings by Fritz Kredel. New York: The Limited Editions Club, 1951. One of 1500. 4to. Orig cloth. Slipcase. *(Oak Knoll)* **$85 [≈£57]**
- The Life of Timon of Athens. London: Vale Press, 1900. One of 310. Decs by Ricketts. Orig bndg, spine ends & crnrs v sl rubbed, spine v sl darkened. *(Ulysses Bookshop)* **£95 [≈$143]**
- Macbeth. Original Screen Images by Ronald King. Guildford: Circle Press, 1970. One of 150. Lge folio. 10 screen prints, signed by the artist. Orig unsewn sheets in cloth-bound folder & slipcase. *(Claude Cox)* **£250 [≈$375]**
- The Merry Wives of Windsor. Illustrated by Hugh Thomson. London: Heinemann, 1910. 1st edn thus. 4to. 170 pp. 40 mtd cold plates. Sl foxing. Orig pict gilt cloth. *(Carol Howard)* **£80 [≈$120]**
- A Midsommer Nights Dreame. Shakespeare Head Press: 1924. One of 550. Lge 4to. 5 cold plates & b/w ills by John Nash. Orig linen backed bds. *(Barbara Stone)* **£175 [≈$263]**
- Pericles, Prince of Tyre. London: Hacon &

Ricketts, The Vale Press, 1900. One of 310. lxxxiii,colophon pp. Orig dec cloth, partly unopened. *(Claude Cox)* **£35 [≈$53]**

- The Poems & Sonnets. Edited by Gwynn Jones. Golden Cockerel Press: 1960. One of 470. Thin folio. Orig gilt dec cloth, top edge only trimmed, crnrs bumped. *(Sotheran's)* **£198 [≈$297]**
- The Poems of William Shakespeare. With Wood Engravings by Agnes Miller Parker. New York: The Limited Editions Club, 1967. One of 1500 signed by the illustrator. Sm 4to. Orig qtr leather. Slipcase (cracked). *(Oak Knoll)* **$100 [≈£67]**
- The Poems. Hammersmith: Kelmscott Press, 1893. One of 500. 8vo. Dec borders & initials. Orig limp vellum, silk ties (broken). *(Heritage)* **$1,250 [≈£833]**
- Romeo and Juliet. With Designs by Oliver Messel. New York: Scribner, (1936). 1st edn. 4to. 96 pp. 40 plates. Orig cloth. Dw. *(Karmiole)* **$75 [≈£50]**
- Romeo and Juliet. With Illustrations by W. Hatherell. London: Hodder & Stoughton, [1912]. 1st edn thus. 4to. 22 mtd cold plates, decs. Orig pict gilt cloth, sl marked. *(Claude Cox)* **£35 [≈$53]**
- Shakespeare's Songs and Sonnets. London: Sampson Low, [ca 1890]. Num chromolitho ills by Sir John Gilbert, sepia ills. Orig bndg. *(Old Cathay)* **£55 [≈$83]**
- Shakespeare's Songs and Sonnets. London: Sampson Low, [ca 1890]. Num chromolitho ills by Sir John Gilbert, sepia ills. Orig bndg, sl worn & soiled. *(Old Cathay)* **£29 [≈$44]**
- The Tempest. Illustrated by William Shakespeare. London: Heinemann, 1926. 1st edn thus. 4to. 20 mtd cold plates. Orig cloth gilt. Dw (few tiny closed tears at folds). *(Sotheran's)* **£398 [≈$597]**
- The Tempest. Illustrated by Edmund Dulac. London: Hodder & Stoughton, 1982. Centennial Limited edition. 144 pp. 40 mtd cold plates. Dark blue mor gilt. *(Stella Books)* **£80 [≈$120]**
- Titus Andronicus. (Northampton, Massachusetts: Gehenna Press, 1973). One of 400 signed by the illustrator, Leonard Baskin. Folio. 12 etchings, text ills. Half mor. *(Argonaut)* **$500 [≈£333]**
- Twelfth Night, or What You Will. Illustrated by W. Heath Robinson. London: Hodder & Stoughton, [1920]. Reprint (with less plates than 1908 edn). 4to. xxiv,143 pp. 24 mtd cold plates. Orig pict cloth, spine sl faded & discold. *(Sotheran's)* **£188 [≈$282]**
- Venus and Adonis. Illustrated by Ben Kutcher. New York: Lincoln MacVeagh - The Dial Press, 1930. Lge 8vo. 112 pp. 12 plates. Orig cloth. Dw. *(Karmiole)* **$50 [≈£33]**
- Venus and Adonis. Paris: Harrison of Paris, 1930. One of 440. Lge 8vo. 73 pp. Orig qtr vellum, spine fading, sl edgewear. *(Bookpress)* **$150 [≈£100]**
- The Works. London: Nonesuch Press, 1953. 4 vols. 8vo. Orig cloth backed bds. *(Bookpress)* **$225 [≈£150]**
- The Complete Works ... Edited by Herbert Farjeon ... London: Nonesuch Press, 1953. 4 vols. 8vo. Engvd titles by Reynolds Stone. Orig buckram backed mrbld bds. Slipcase (worn). *(Claude Cox)* **£110 [≈$165]**

A Shakespearean Memento ...

- A Shakespearean Memento 1964. Worcester: Stanbrook Abbey Press, [1964]. One of 200. 4to. Gold initials by Margaret Adams. Orig vellum backed dec bds. *(Dermont)* **$125 [≈£83]**

Shall We Join the Ladies? ...

- Shall We Join the Ladies? Wood Engravings by Women Artists of the Twentieth Century. London: Studio One Gallery, 1979. One of 500. Lge 4to. 102 pp. 80 engvs. Orig cloth, pict onlay. Glassine dw. *(Waddington)* **£42 [≈$63]**

Shapiro, David

- Jasper Johns Drawings 1954-1984. New York: Abrams, 1984. 1st edn. Lge 4to. 152 ills inc 50 cold plates. Dw. *(Clearwater)* **£60 [≈$90]**

Shapley, Fern Rusk

- Paintings from the Samuel H. Kress Collection, Italian Schools XV-XVI Century. London: 1968. 4to. 459 pp. Num ills. Orig cloth. Dw. *(Washton)* **$175 [≈£117]**

Sharp, Cecil & Oppe, A.P.

- The Dance. An Historical Survey of Dancing in Europe. London: Halton & Truscott, 1924. 4to. 75 plates. Orig bndg. *(Mermaid Books)* **£65 [≈$98]**
- The Dance. An Historical Survey of Dancing in Europe. London: Halton & Truscott, 1924. 4to. 4 cold & 27 other plates, text ills. Sl foxing. Orig cloth gilt, t.e.g. *(David Slade)* **£50 [≈$75]**

Sharp, Mary

- Point and Pillow Lace: A Short Account of Various Kinds Ancient and Modern ...

London: Murray, 1913. [xvi],202 pp. 48 plates. Frontis v foxed. Orig cloth, spine discold. *(Schoyer)* **$50 [≈£33]**

Sharp, William

- Dante Gabriel Rossetti A Record and a Study. London: Macmillan, 1882. 8vo. 432, appendix pp. Orig cloth gilt, recased. *(First Folio)* **$95 [≈£63]**

Sharpe, Edmund

- The Seven Periods of English Architecture defined and illustrated. London: Spon, 1888. 3rd edn. Sm 4to. xiv,40,[ii,iv] pp. 20 litho plates, text w'cuts. Occas foxing, new endpapers. Orig dec cloth gilt, trifle soiled, recased. *(Hollett)* **£60 [≈$90]**

Shaw, George Bernard

- Flyleaves. Edited, with an Introduction by Dan H. Laurence and Daniel J. Leary. Austin: Bird and Bull Press for W. Thomas Taylor, 1977. One of 350. 4to. 62 pp. 2 fldg facs. Orig orange cloth. *(Karmiole)* **$75 [≈£50]**
- Pygmalion and Candida. Illustrations by Clarke Hutton. Avon, CT: The Limited Editions Club, 1974. One of 2000 signed by the illustrator. 4to. Orig half cloth. Slipcase. *(Oak Knoll)* **$55 [≈£37]**

Shaw, Graham

- Printing in Calcutta to 1800. London: 1981. 8vo. Orig cloth. *(Traylen)* **£10 [≈$15]**

Shaw, Henry

- Booke of Sundry Draughtes. London: William Pickering, 1848. 1st edn. 8vo. [7] pp. 107 plates. Orig cloth backed ptd bds, rebacked, edges sl worn. *(Bookpress)* **$300 [≈£200]**
- The Decorative Arts, Ecclesiastical and Civil, of the Middle Ages. London: William Pickering, 1851. 1st edn. Folio. 41 chromolitho plates, num text engvs. Sl foxing. Half mor, sl edge wear. *(Bookpress)* **$750 [≈£500]**
- Dresses and Decorations of the Middle Ages. London: William Pickering, 1843. 1st edn. 2 vols. Sm folio. 94 hand cold plates, num text decs. One sm crnr repr. Contemp half mor gilt, a.e.g., jnts & extrs rubbed & sl worn. *(Claude Cox)* **£330 [≈$495]**
- Dresses and Decorations of the Middle Ages. London: Bohn, 1858. 2 vols. 4to. 94 hand cold & chromolitho plates. Some foxing of ptd titles & 1st pp. Orig bds, rebacked in vellum. *(Mermaid Books)* **£250 [≈$375]**

Shaw, J. Byam

- The Drawings of Francesco Guardi. London: Faber, (1951). 86 pp. 80 plates. Orig cloth. Dw (sl soiled). *(Clarice Davis)* **$55 [≈£37]**
- Paintings by Old Masters at Christchurch, Oxford. A Catalogue. London: Phaidon, 1967. 308 pp. 235 ills. Orig cloth. Dw. *(Fine Art)* **£40 [≈$60]**

Shaw, Richard Norman

- Architectural Sketches from the Continent. London: Day & Son, 1858. 1st edn. Folio. [12] pp. 100 litho plates. Fly leaf & a few margs sl soiled. Rec qtr calf. *(Claude Cox)* **£165 [≈$248]**
- Architectural Sketches from the Continent. Views and Details from France, Italy and Germany. London: Day & Son, 1858. Sm folio. 100 litho plates. Some spotting. Half mor gilt, sl worn, top edges of bds darkened. *(Hollett)* **£85 [≈$128]**

Shaw-Sparrow, Walter

- A Book of Sporting Painters ... London: 1931. 4to. xv,240 pp. 136 ills. Orig dec cloth. *(Phenotype)* **£75 [≈$113]**
- A Book of Sporting Painters. London: John Lane; The Bodley Head, (1931). 1st edn. Demy 4to. [xviii],240 pp. Num plates. Orig dec cloth gilt. remains of dw inserted. *(Ash)* **£100 [≈$150]**
- British Farm Animals in Prints and Paintings. London: Walker's Galleries, 1932. 8vo. 50 pp. Ills. Foredge sl foxed. Orig wraps. *(Phenotype)* **£36 [≈$54]**
- Frank Brangwyn and his Work. London: Kegan Paul, 1910. xiv,260 pp. 36 plates. Orig dec cloth. *(Leicester Art Books)* **£45 [≈$68]**
- George Stubbs and Ben Marshall. London: Cassell, 1929. 1st edn. 4to. 4 cold & 82 other plates. Orig cloth, spotted, spine faded. *(Spelman)* **£50 [≈$75]**
- Henry Alken. London: Williams & Norgate, 1927. xxiv,55 pp. 8 cold & 64 b/w plates. Front free endpaper creased. Orig cloth, t.e.g. *(Fine Art)* **£65 [≈$98]**
- In Rustic England. London: Hodder & Stoughton, 1906. 1st edn. 25 mtd cold plates. Endpapers foxed. Orig cloth. *(Old Cathay)* **£79 [≈$119]**
- John Lavery and his Work. London: Kegan Paul, [1912]. 4to. xxxiv,209 pp. 12 cold plates, ills. Orig cloth gilt. *(Cooper Hay)* **£65 [≈$98]**
- Prints and Drawings by Frank Brangwyn with some other Phases of his Art ... London:

John Lane, 1919. x,288 pp. 50 plates. Orig cloth, one crnr sl bumped.
(Leicester Art Books) **£46 [≈$69]**

Sheale, Richard

- The Hountyng of the Chivyat quoth Richard Sheale. The Tern Press: 1981. One of 100 sgnd by the artist and printer. Folio. 10 w'engvs by Nicholas Parry. Orig patterned bds, sl shelfwear bottom edge.
(Waddington) **£30 [≈$45]**

Shearer, Cresswell

- The Renaissance of Architecture in Southern Italy. A Study of Frederick II of Hohenstaufen and The Capua Triumphator Archway and Towers. Cambridge: Heffer, 1935. 1st edn. 4to. x,184 pp. 81 ills. Orig cloth. Dw (sl worn). Pres copy.
(Hollett) **£40 [≈$60]**

Shearman, John

- Raphael's Cartoons in the Collection of Her Majesty the Queen and the Tapestries for the Sistine Chapel. London: 1972. 4to. 258 pp. 50 plates, 90 ills. Orig cloth. Dw.
(Washton) **$85 [≈£57]**
- Raphael's Cartoons in the Collection of Her Majesty the Queen and the Tapestries for the Sistine Chapel. London: Phaidon, 1972. viii,258 pp. 50 plates, 90 ills. Orig cloth. Dw.
(Fine Art) **£60 [≈$90]**
- Raphael's Cartoons in the Collection of Her Majesty the Queen and the Tapestries for the Sistine Chapel. London: Phaidon, 1972. viii,258 pp. 140 ills. Orig cloth. Dw.
(Leicester Art Books) **£45 [≈$68]**

Sheldon, G.W.

- American Painters: With Eighty-Three Examples of Their Work Engraved on Wood. New York: Appleton, 1879. 4to. 184 pp. 83 ills. Orig elab bndg, edges scuffed.
(Rona Schneider) **$175 [≈£117]**

Shelley, Percy Bysshe

- [Poems]. London: Doves Press, 1914. One of 200 (of 212). 4to. 181 pp. Orig limp vellum, uncut. *(Finch)* **£550 [≈$825]**
- The Poetical Works. Hammersmith: Kelmscott Press, 1895. One of 250. 3 vols. 8vo. Orig limp vellum, unopened. Qtr mor case. *(Heritage)* **$2,750 [≈£1,833]**
- Zastrozzi, a Romance. Golden Cockerel Press: 1955. One of 200. 8 w'engvs by Cecil Keling. B'plate. Orig qtr mor. Slipcase.
(Waddington) **£65 [≈$98]**

Shenstone, William

- Men and Manners. Selected and Edited by Havelock Ellis. Golden Cockerel Press: 1927. One of 500. Orig leather backed bds, t.e.g. Dw. *(Margaret Nangle)* **£42 [≈$63]**

Shenton, A. & R.

- The Price Guide to Collectable Clocks, 1840-1940. Woodbridge: 1985. 4to. 34 cold plates, over 700 ills. Orig cloth. Dw.
(Traylen) **£15 [≈$23]**

Shepard, Rupert

- Passing Scene. Eighteen Images of Southern Africa. The Stourton Press: 1966. One of 200 signed by the artist. Lge folio. [12] pp. 18 cold prints. Orig dec buckram, uncut.
(Claude Cox) **£45 [≈$68]**

Shepherd, E.G.

- Design and Print. London: 1963. 8vo. xii, 195 pp. Ills. Orig cloth. Dw.
(The Veatchs) **$30 [≈£20]**

Sheridan, Richard Brinsley

- The Rivals, a Comedy. Illustrations by Rene Ben Sussan. New York: The Limited Editions Club, 1953. One of 1500 signed by the illustrator. Tall 8vo. Orig cloth (spine darkened). Slipcase. *(Oak Knoll)* **$60 [≈£40]**
- The School for Scandal. Illustrated by Lucius Rossi. London: Raphael Tuck, n.d. Folio. 38 pp. Orig green cloth, pict onlays, some marks & sl wear. *(Carol Howard)* **£36 [≈$54]**
- The School for Scandal. Illustrated by Hugh Thomson. London: Hodder & Stoughton, (1911). One of 350 signed by Thomson. 4to. 25 mtd cold plates. Orig pict gilt vellum, sl marked, lacks ties.
(Barbara Stone) **£250 [≈$375]**

Sherman, M. (editor)

- Daily Mail Ideal Home Book. London: 1947-48. Lge 4to. 268 pp. Cold plates, num ills. Orig cloth, trifle marked. Silver Jubilee issue.
(Clevedon Books) **£27 [≈$41]**

Shipp, Horace

- Edward Seago. Painter in the English Tradition. London: Collins, 1952. 46 pp. 89 plates. Orig cloth. Dw (chipped).
(Leicester Art Books) **£45 [≈$68]**
- The New Art. A Study of the Principles of Non-Representational Art and their Application in the Work of Lawrence Atkinson. London: Cecil Palmer, 1922. xii,115 pp. 20 plates. Orig cloth.
(Leicester Art Books) **£45 [≈$68]**

Shirley, The Hon Andrew

- Bonington. London: Kegan Paul, 1940. ix, 166 pp. 204 plates. Orig cloth. *(Leicester Art Books)* **£100 [≈$150]**
- Bonington. London: Kegan Paul, 1941. 157 pp. 202 ills. Endpapers sl foxed. Orig cloth. *(Fine Art)* **£100 [≈$150]**

Shoolman, Regina & Slatkin, Charles E.

- Six Centuries of French Master Drawings in America. New York: OUP, 1950. xxviii,257 pp. Cold frontis, 145 b/w plates. Orig cloth. Dw (few edge tears). *(Clarice Davis)* **$45 [≈£30]**
- Treasury of American Drawings. New York: OUP, 1947. xviii,35 pp. 163 plates. Orig cloth. Dw (a few tears). *(Clarice Davis)* **$70 [≈£47]**

Shuffrey, William Arthur

- The Churches of the Deanery of North Craven. Leeds: J. Whitehead, for subscribers only, 1914. 1st edn. Lge 8vo. 251 pp. 28 plates. Orig cloth gilt, trifle rubbed. *(Hollett)* **£95 [≈$143]**

Shure, David S.

- Hester Bateman. Queen of English Silversmiths. London: W.H. Allen, 1959. 1st edn. 4to. 32 pp. 87 plates. Orig cloth gilt. Dw. *(Hollett)* **£150 [≈$225]**

Shute, John

- The First & Chief Groundes of Architecture ... First printed in 1563 ... With an Introduction by Lawrence Weaver. London: Country Life, 1912. One of 1000 (this copy out of series). Sm folio. Orig cloth backed bds, sl rubbed & marked. *(Hollett)* **£85 [≈$128]**

Sidney, Sir Philip

- Astrophel & Stella. Edited by Mona Wilson. London: Nonesuch Press, 1931. One of 725. Orig dec bds. card folder. Slipcase. *(Claude Cox)* **£40 [≈$60]**

Signature

- Signature. A Quadrimestrial of Typography and Graphic Arts. Edited by Oliver Simon. New Series Nos 1-18. London: 1946-54. Complete set of the New Series. 4to. Orig wraps, all but 3 in orig glassine dws. *(Barbara Stone)* **£225 [≈$338]**

Silber, Evelyn

- The Sculpture of Epstein. London: Phaidon, 1986. 1st edn. 240 pp. 586 ills. Orig dec cloth. Dw. *(Bookworks)* **£65 [≈$98]**

Siltzer, Frank

- The Story of British Sporting Prints. New York: 1925. 409 pp. 20 ills. Orig cloth, 2 crnrs bumped, spine sl faded, minor wear. *(John K. King)* **$125 [≈£83]**
- The Story of British Sporting Prints. London: Hutchinson, [1925]. 1st edn. Roy 8vo. (410) pp. Plates. Orig pict cloth gilt, edges v sl spotted. *(Ash)* **£75 [≈$113]**

Silver, Larry

- The Paintings of Quinten Massys with Catalogue Raisonne. Oxford: Phaidon, 1984. 361 pp. 183 ills. Orig cloth. Dw. *(Leicester Art Books)* **£90 [≈$135]**

Silver, Rollo G.

- Typefounding in America, 1787-1825. Virginia: UP, 1965. 1st edn. xiv,139,colophon pp. 36 ills. Orig cloth backed bds. *(Claude Cox)* **£22 [≈$33]**

Simon, Andre L.

- What About Wine? London: Newman Neame, 1953. 1st edn. 56 pp. Frontis & 24 w'engvs by David Gentleman. Dw (sl marked, 2 tears). *(Waddington)* **£16 [≈$24]**

Simon, Caroline

- The Art and Life of Terrick Williams: Mist and Morning Sunshine. London: Whitford & Hughes, 1984. 80 pp. 81 plates. Orig cloth. Dw. *(Fine Art)* **£24 [≈$36]**

Simon, Helena

- Eleven Poems. The Whittington Press for The Acorn Press: 1978. One of 50 signed by the author and the artist, Hellmuth Weissenborn, 1978. Wrappers. Dw. *(Ulysses Bookshop)* **£95 [≈$143]**

Simon, James

- Essay on Irish Coins and of the Currency of Foreign Monies in Ireland, with Mr. Snelling's Supplement ... Dublin: for the editors by G.A. Proctor, 1810. 4to. Plates. Antique style half calf, uncut. *(Emerald Isle)* **£2002 [≈$300]**

Simon, Oliver

- Printer and Playground. An Autobiography. London: Faber, 1956. 1st edn. 8vo. xvi,156 pp. 4 plates, 37 ills. Orig cloth. *(Claude Cox)* **£20 [≈$30]**

Simon, Oliver & Rodenberg, Julius

- Printing of To-Day. An Illustrated Survey of

Post-War Typography in Europe and the United States. With a General Introduction by Aldous Huxley. London: Peter Davies; New York: Harper, 1928. Lge 4to. Num ills. Orig cloth backed bds. Dw (chipped). *(Barbara Stone)* **£75 [≈$113]**

- Printing of Today. An Illustrated Survey of Post-War Typography ... Introduction by Aldous Huxley. London: Peter Davies, 1928. 1st edn. Folio. xix,53 pp. 122 plates. Orig cloth backed bds, spine darkened. *(Claude Cox)* **£30 [≈$45]**

Simonson, Lee

- The Art of Scenic Design. New York: Harper, (1950). 1st edn. 4to. xiv,174 pp. Frontis, ills. Orig cloth. *(Bookpress)* **$150 [≈£100]**

Simpson, John W.

- Essays and Memorials by John W. Simpson, President of the R.I.B.A. 1920-1921. London: Architectural Press, 1923. 8vo. (viii), 174 pp. Frontis, 10 plates, 90 text figs. Orig cloth backed bds. *(Hollett)* **£25 [≈$38]**

Simpson, William

- The Autobiography. Edited by George Eyre Todd. London: Fisher Unwin, 1903. 8vo. xv,351 pp. Frontis, 23 plates. Orig cloth gilt, sl dusty. *(Cooper Hay)* **£55 [≈$83]**
- Picturesque People. London: W.M. Thompson, 1876. 1st edn. Folio. 18 chromolitho plates. Orig cloth, spine sunned. *(Bookpress)* **$425 [≈£283]**

Sindbad the Sailor ...

- Sindbad the Sailor and Other Stories from the Arabian Nights. Illustrated by Edmund Dulac. London: Hodder & Stoughton, [1914]. 1st Dulac edn. 4to. 221 pp. 23 mtd cold plates, decs. Occas v sl foxing. Orig elab dec cloth gilt. *(Sotheran's)* **£398 [≈$597]**
- Sindbad the Sailor and Other Stories from the Arabian Nights. Illustrated by Edmund Dulac. London: Hodder & Stoughton, [1914]. Lge 4to. 23 cold plates, decs, dec endpapers. Orig pict cloth gilt, lower cvr sl marked. *(Barbara Stone)* **£295 [≈$443]**

Sinel, Joseph (compiler)

- A Book of American Trademarks & Devices. New York: Knopf, 1924. One of 2050. Folio. 64 pp, french-folded. Ca 200 marks. Orig cloth backed dec bds. Dw (reprd, sl soiled). *(Claude Cox)* **£95 [≈$143]**

Singer, Isaac Bashevis

- Zlateh the Goat and Other Stories. New York: Harper & Row, (1966). 1st edn. 8vo. 17 b/w ills by Maurice Sendak. worn). *(Jo Ann Reisler)* **$75 [≈£50]**

Singh, Madanjeet

- Himalayan Art. Greenwich: New York Graphic Society, (1968). 1st edn. Lge 4to. 295 pp. Num ills. Orig cloth. Dw. *(J &J House)* **$90 [≈£60]**

Sir Gawain and the Green Knight ...

- Sir Gawain and the Green Knight. Introduction by Gwyn Jones. Illustrated by Dorothea Braby. London: Golden Cockerel Press, 1952. One of 360. Tall 4to. 95 pp. Orig cloth gilt. *(Hermitage)* **$225 [≈£150]**
- Sir Gawain and the Green Knight. Introductory Essay by Gwyn Jones. Illustrated by Dorothea Braby. Golden Cockerel Press: 1952. One of 360. Folio. Page edges v sl browned. Orig vellum paper gilt, unopened. *(Waddington)* **£90 [≈$135]**

Siren, Osvald

- A History of Early Chinese Painting. London: The Medici Society, (1933). One of 525. 2 vols. Folio. 226 plates. Ex-lib. Orig cloth. Dws. *(Bookpress)* **$450 [≈£300]**

Sisson, Marjorie

- The Cave. With Engravings on Wood by Frank Martin. Hemingford Grey: The Vine Press, 1957. One of 200. Orig cloth, t.e.g. Glassine dw. *(Claude Cox)* **£35 [≈$53]**

Sitwell, Osbert

- C.R.W. Nevinson. New York: Scribner, 1925. 32 pp. 36 plates. Orig cloth & bds. *(Leicester Art Books)* **£40 [≈$60]**

Sitwell, Pauline

- Green Song. Poems and Wood Engravings. Opal Press: 1979. One of 150 signed by the author. 4to. 32 pp. 10 w'engvs. Orig bds, sm area of upper bd roughened and watermarked. *(Waddington)* **£18 [≈$27]**

Sitwell, Sacheverell

- Narrative Pictures. A Survey of English Genre and its Painters .. London: Batsford, (1937). 1st edn. Lge 8vo. 133 ills. Few sl marks. Half calf. *(Bow Windows)* **£75 [≈$113]**
- Old-Fashioned Flowers. London: 1939. 1st edn. 4to. Cold lithos by John Farleigh, 16 ills. Orig cloth. Dw (sl worn). *(Margaret Nangle)* **£62 [≈$93]**

Skeet, Francis John Angus

- Stuart Papers, Pictures, Relics, Medals and Books in the Collection of Miss Maria Widdrington. Leeds: John Whitehead, 1930. One of 375 signed by the author. Lge 8vo. xi,98 pp. 6 plates. Orig cloth gilt, t.e.g. *(Hollett)* **£60 [≈$90]**

Skeeters, Paul W.

- Maxfield Parrish. the Early Years 1893-1930. Los Angeles: Nash Publishing, 1973. 350 pp. Num ills. Orig hessian cvrd bds. *(Leicester Art Books)* **£60 [≈$90]**
- Sidney H. Sime, Master of Fantasy. Pasadena: Ward Ritchie Press, (1978). One of 26 signed by the author and Ray Bradbury. 4to. 128 pp. Num ills. Orig fabricoid gilt. *(Karmiole)* **$100 [≈£67]**

Sketches ...

- Sketches of the Lives of Correggio and Parmegiano ... see Coxe, William

Slack, Raymond

- English Pressed Glass 1830-1900. London: Barrie & Jenkins, 1987. Cr 4to. 208 pp. 33 plates, 100 b/w ills. Dw. *(Paul Brown)* **£30 [≈$45]**

Slater, J. Herbert

- Illustrated Sporting Books. London: Upcott Gill, 1899. 1st edn. 8vo. viii,203,[17] pp. Orig cloth. *(Bookpress)* **$85 [≈£57]**

Slater, J.H.

- The Romance of Book Collecting. London: 1898. Sm 8vo. Frontis. Orig cloth. *(Traylen)* **£15 [≈$23]**

Slive, Seymour

- Frans Hals. London: Phaidon, 1970-74. 3 vols. 16 cold plates, 778 ills. Orig cloth. *(Leicester Art Books)* **£380 [≈$570]**
- Rembrandt and his Critics 1630-1730. The Hague: Martinus Nijhoff, 1953. Lge 8vo. xii, 240 pp. 45 plates. Orig cloth. *(Karmiole)* **$75 [≈£50]**

Small, Tunstall & Woodbridge, Christopher

- Houses of the Wren and Early Georgian Periods. London: Architectural Press, [1928]. 139 pp. Ills. Orig cloth gilt. *(Willow House)* **£45 [≈$68]**
- Houses of the Wren and Early Georgian Periods. London: Architectural Press, 1928. Frontis, 139 plates. Orig cloth, sm reprs spine ends, crnrs sl bumped. *(Quest Books)* **£28 [≈$42]**

Smart, Alastair

- The Life and Art of Allan Ramsay. London: Routledge, (1952). 1st edn. 8vo. xii,236 pp. 39 ills. Orig cloth. Dw (chipped, sl soiled). *(Karmiole)* **$35 [≈£23]**

Smart, Alistair

- The Life and Art of Allan Ramsay. London: Routledge, 1952. xii,235 pp. 24 plates. Orig cloth. *(Leicester Art Books)* **£50 [≈$75]**

Smart, Christopher

- A Song to David. Edited by J.B. Broadbent. Cambridge: Rampant Lions Press, (1960). One of 600. 4to. xxi,40 pp. Frontis by Lynton lamb. Inscrptn. Orig bds. Dw (sl worn). prospectus inserted. *(Oak Knoll)* **$75 [≈£50]**

Smiddy, Richard

- An Essay on the Druids. The Ancient Churches and the Round Towers of Ireland. Dublin: Kelly, 1871. 266 pp. Orig bndg. *(Emerald Isle)* **£48 [≈$72]**

Smith, Mr.

- A Short and Direct Method of Painting in Water-Colour. Written by the late ingenious Mr. Smith. London: Mary Smith, 1730. 8vo. [2], 22 pp. Some soiling, sm marg reprs. Later qtr mor. *(Spelman)* **£650 [≈$975]**

Smith, Aaron

- The Atrocities of the Pirates. Golden Cockerel Press: 1929. One of 600. 156 pp. 10 w'engvs by Eric Ravilious. Orig qtr buckram, paper sides sl mottled, hd of spine sl worn with sm chip. *(Waddington)* **£120 [≈$180]**

Smith, Bernard

- Australian Painting 1788-1960. OUP: 1962. 1st edn. 372 pp. 191 ills. Orig cloth, spine enamel sl spotted. Dw. *(Bookworks)* **£34 [≈$51]**

Smith, Bradley & Weng, Wan-go

- China - A History in Art. Gemini Smith: 1979. Lge 4to. 296 pp. Cold ills. Orig cloth. Dw (sl used). *(Hollett)* **£25 [≈$38]**

Smith, C. Fox

- Here and There in England with the Painter Brangwyn. Leigh-on-Sea: F. Lewis, 1845. One of 500. 4to. 68 pp. 72 mtd cold plates. Orig buckram gilt, extrs sl faded. Dw (sl chipped). *(Hollett)* **£75 [≈$113]**

Smith, G.E. Kidder

- Sweden Builds. New York: Reinhold,

(1957). 2nd edn. 4to. 270 pp. Frontis, ills. Orig cloth. Dw. *(Bookpress)* **$65 [≈£43]**

Smith, George Barnett (editor)

- Illustrated British Ballads, Old and New. London: 1886. 2 vols in one. Roy 8vo. viii, 384; xvi,384 pp. Num ills. Occas sl spotting. Half calf, edges sl rubbed, lower hinge tender. *(Francis Edwards)* **£55 [≈$83]**

Smith, John Chaloner

- British Mezzotinto Portraits ... accompanied by Biographical Notes and an Appendix of a selection of the Prices produced at Public Sales ... London: Sotheran, 1883. Illustrated edn. 4 vols. [1780] pp. 125 ports. Half leather, t.e.g., 2 vols rebacked. *(Fine Art)* **£300 [≈$450]**

Smith, John Thomas

- Nollekens and his Times ... Second Edition. London: Colburn, 1829. 2 vols. 8vo. x,393; vi,494 pp. Port frontis. Orig cloth backed bds, paper labels. *(Spelman)* **£180 [≈$270]**

Smith, Leon Polk

- Torn Drawings. New York: 1965. One of 490 signed by the artist. Sm folio. [4] pp. 10 cold plates. Orig wraps, contents loose, as issued. *(Ars Libri)* **$125 [≈£83]**

Smith, P.

- Houses of the Welsh Countryside. London: HMSO, 1975. 1st edn. 4to. 604 pp. Plans, 108 plates, plans. Sm lib stamp title verso. Orig cloth. Dw. *(Monmouth)* **£30 [≈$45]**

Smith, Percival Gordon

- Hints and Suggestions as to the Planning of Poor Law Buildings ... London: Knight & Co., 1901. 1st edn. Tall 8vo. viii,152,[ii] pp. 12 litho plans. 1 section trifle sprung. Orig cloth gilt. *(Hollett)* **£160 [≈$240]**

Smith, Sydney Ure & Stevens, Bertram

- The Art of J.J. Hillier. Sydney: Angus & Robertson, 1918. 50 pp. 29 mtd cold plates, 20 ills. Orig bds. *(Leicester Art Books)* **£50 [≈$75]**

Smith, T. Roger

- Acoustics in relation to Architecture and Building ... New Edition. London: Virtue, [ca 1885]. 8vo. vi,165,32 pp. 19 ills. Orig limp cloth gilt, label rubbed. *(Hollett)* **£20 [≈$30]**

Smollett, Tobias

- The Adventures of Peregrine Pickle in which is included Memoirs of a Lady of Quality. With an Introduction by G.K. Chesterton and Illustrations by John Austen. New York: The Limited Editions Club, 1936. One of 1500 signed by the illustrator. 2 vols. 4to. Orig cloth. Dws. Slipcase (sl rubbed & spotted. *(Oak Knoll)* **$125 [≈£83]**

Smyth, Ethel

- Inordinate (?) Affection. A Story for Dog Lovers. London: Cresset Press, [ca 1936]. One of 50 signed by the author and the artist. 8vo. 118,[2 blank] pp. Ills. Orig vellum. Slipcase. *(Bow Windows)* **£125 [≈$188]**

'Snaffles' (pseudonym of Charles Johnson)

- My Sketch Book in the Shiny. Second Edition. London: n.d. 4to. 51 ff. Ills. Orig dec cloth. Dw, fine. *(Bow Windows)* **£195 [≈$293]**

Snowman, Kenneth

- Eighteenth Century Gold Boxes of Europe. With a Foreword by Sacheverell Sitwell. Boston: 1966. 1st edn. Lge 4to. 192 pp. 750 ills. Orig buckram, t.e.g. Dw. *(Claude Cox)* **£85 [≈$128]**

Solly, N. Neal

- Memoir of the Life of W.J. Muller. With Original Letters and an Account of his Travels and of his Principal Works. London: Chapman & Hall, 1875. xxii,370 pp. 18 plates (8 woodburytypes & photographs). Orig dec cloth gilt bds mtd on buckram, t.e.g. *(Leicester Art Books)* **£70 [≈$105]**

Solodokoff, Alexander von

- Russian Gold and Silver. London: Trefoil Books, 1981. 1st English edn. Sq 4to. 238 pp. 245 ills. Orig cloth gilt. Dw. *(Hollett)* **£40 [≈$60]**

Solomon, Alan

- New York: The New Art Scene. Photographs by Ugo Mulas. New York: Holt, Rinehart & Winston, 1967. Sm folio. 337,[9] pp. Num ills. Orig cloth. *(Ars Libri)* **$150 [≈£100]**

Solon, M.L.

- A Brief History of Old English Porcelain and its Manufactures ... London: Bemrose, 1903. One of 1250. Sm thick 4to. 20 cold plates. Orig cloth backed bds, t.e.g., sl soiled, spine faded. *(Hollett)* **£85 [≈$128]**
- A History and Description of Italian Majolica. London: 1907. Thick 4to. xvi,208 pp. 23 cold & 49 plain plates. Orig cloth gilt,

trifle used. *(Hollett)* **£55 [≈$83]**

Solvyns, Balt

- The Costume of Hindoostan ... with Descriptions in English and French, taken in the Years 1798 and 1799. London: Edward Orme, 1804. Folio. 60 hand cold plates (sl foxing, some offsetting). Contemp mor gilt, a.e.g.. *(J &J House)* **$1,500 [≈£1,000]**

Some Contemporary English Artists ...

- Some Contemporary English Artists. London: Birrell & Garnett, 1921. 1st edn. Ills. Inscrptn. Orig wraps, v sl rubbed. *(Blakeney)* **£65 [≈$98]**

Sophocles

- Antigone. Illustrated by Harry Bennett. N.p.: The Limited Editions Club, 1975. One of 2000 signed by the illustrator. 4to. Orig cloth. Slipcase. *(Oak Knoll)* **$75 [≈£50]**
- The Banquet of Plato. Translated from the Greek by Percy Bysshe Shelley. (Boston: Riverside Press) 1908. One of 440. 8vo. Orig bds, paper label, fine. Designed by Bruce Rogers. *(The Veatchs)* **$175 [≈£117]**
- Oedipus the King. Illustrated by Demetrios Galanis. New York: The Limited Editions Club, One of 1500 signed by the artist. Lge 4to. prelims v sl foxed. Slipcase. *(Waddington)* **£45 [≈$68]**

Sopotinsky, Oleg

- Art in the Soviet Union. Painting, Sculpture, Graphic Arts. Leningrad: Aurora, 1978. Folio. 497,[3] pp. 373 cold plates. Orig cloth. Dw. *(Ars Libri)* **$150 [≈£100]**

Sorlier, Charles

- Chagall's Posters. A Catalogue Raisonne. New York: Crown, 1975. 4to. Cold ills. Orig cloth. Dw. *(First Folio)* **$165 [≈£110]**
- Chagall's Posters. A Catalogue Raisonne. Preface by Jean Adhemar. New York: Crown, 1975. Lge 4to. 146,[14] pp. Num ills. Orig cloth. Dw. *(Ars Libri)* **$200 [≈£133]**
- Marc Chagall: Lithographs VI (1980-1985). Notes, Catalogue and Preface by Charles Sorlier. New York: Crown, 1986. 1st Amer edn. Folio. Orig cloth. Dw. Slipcase. *(Cooper Hay)* **£90 [≈$135]**

Soustelle, Jacques

- Arts of Ancient Mexico. New York: Viking, 1967. Thick 4to. Ills. Orig cloth. Dw. *(First Folio)* **$45 [≈£30]**

Southey, Robert

- The Chronicle of the Cid. Illustrations by Rene Ben Sussan. New York: The Limited Editions Club, 1958. One of 1500 signed by the illustrator. Sm 4to. Orig cloth. Slipcase. *(Oak Knoll)* **$55 [≈£37]**

Soyer, Raphael

- A Painter's Pilgrimage: An Account of a Journey. New York: Crown, (1962). 4to. 80 pp. 42 plates. Orig cloth. Dw. signed by the artist. *(Abacus)* **$50 [≈£33]**

Sparrow, John

- Lapidaria Quinta. Cambridge: 1965. One of 200. 8vo. (40) pp. Title & colophon engvd by Reynolds Stone. Orig wraps, unopened. *(Claude Cox)* **£22 [≈$33]**
- Lapidaria Sexta. Cambridge: 1969. One of 200. 8vo. (52) pp. Orig wraps, unopened. *(Claude Cox)* **£18 [≈$27]**
- Lapidaria Septima. Rampant Lions Press for Cambridge UP: 1975. One of 200. Orig bndg. *(Lamb)* **£18 [≈$27]**
- Lapidaria Sexta. Rampant Lions Press for Cambridge UP: 1969. One of 200. Orig bndg. *(Lamb)* **£18 [≈$27]**
- Visible Worlds. A Study of Inscriptions in and as Books and Works of Art. Cambridge: UP, 1969. Sm 4to. xvi,152 pp. 63 ills. Dw (sl soiled). *(Francis Edwards)* **£35 [≈$53]**

Sparrow, Walter Shaw

- See Shaw-Sparrow, Walter

Speed, Flora and Lancelot

- The Limbersnigs, or the Adventures of Prince Kebole. London: Lawrence & Jellicoe, [ca 1896]. 1st edn. Num plates & b/w ills, pict endpapers. Orig pict cloth, hd of spine worn. *(Old Cathay)* **£39 [≈$59]**

Speer, William

- The Oldest and the Newest Empire: China and the United States. Hartford: S.S. Scranton; San Francisco: H.H. Bancroft, 1870. 681 pp. 40 ills. Orig bndg, worn. *(Rona Schneider)* **$120 [≈£80]**

Spelman, W.W.R.

- Lowestoft China. Norwich: Jarrold, 1905. One of 500. 4to. 78 pp. Cold frontis, 97 plates. Orig cloth gilt, t.e.g. *(Hollett)* **£130 [≈$195]**

Spence, Basil

- Phoenix at Coventry. The Building of a Cathedral. London: Geoffrey Bles, 1962.

8vo. xvii,141 pp. 45 ills. Orig cloth gilt. Dw. *(Hollett)* **£17.50 [≈$27]**

- Phoenix at Coventry. The Building of a Cathedral. London: Geoffrey Bles, 1962. 8vo. xvii,141 pp. 45 ills. Orig cloth gilt. Dw. *(Hollett)* **£17.50 [≈$27]**

Spence, H.D.M.

- Dreamland in History. The Story of the Norman Dukes. London: Isbister, 1891. 4to. xii,228 pp. 60 ills by Herbert Railton. Few sl spots. Orig dec cloth gilt. *(Hollett)* **£45 [≈$68]**

Spencer, Charles

- Erte. New York: Clarkson N. Potter, 1970. Lge 4to. 198 pp. 182 ills. Orig cloth. Dw. Inscribed by the artist. *(Ars Libri)* **$85 [≈£57]**

Spencer, Isobel

- Walter Crane. New York: Macmillan, 1975. 208 pp. 150 ills. Orig cloth. Dw. *(Leicester Art Books)* **£28 [≈$42]**

Spender, Stephen

- Henry Moore. Sculptures in Landscape. New York: Clarkson N. Potter, n.d. Lge 4to. 129 pp. 80 cold plates, num text ills. Orig cloth. Dw. *(Ars Libri)* **$75 [≈£50]**

Spenser, Edmund

- The Faerie Queen ... Decorations Drawn by John Austen and Illustrations engraved in wood by Agnes Miller Parker. New York: The Limited Editions Club, 1953. One of 1500 signed by Parker. 2 vols. Thick 4to. Orig cloth. Dws (spotted). Slipcase (broken). *(Oak Knoll)* **$100 [≈£67]**
- Four Hymns on Earthly and Heavenly Love & Beauty. London: LCC Central School of Arts & Crafts, 1912. Sm folio. 51,colophon pp. Orig folded sheets, unopened & unbound. Designed by J.H. Mason. *(Claude Cox)* **£35 [≈$53]**
- The Wedding Songs. Golden Cockerel Press: 1923. One of 345 (this copy unnumbered). Sm 8vo. Cold w'engvs by Ethelbert White. Orig canvas backed bds, label crnrs chipped, top edge of bds sl darkened. *(Waddington)* **£78 [≈$117]**
- The Wedding Songs. Waltham St. Lawrence: Golden Cockerel Press, (1923). One of 320. Cr 8vo. Cold w'engvs by Ethelbert White. Orig canvas backed bds, v sl darkened, label v sl chipped. *(Ash)* **£95 [≈$143]**

Spielmann, M.H.

- The History of Punch. London: Cassell, 1895. Large Paper. Half mor gilt, t.e.g., hd of spine reprd, spine rubbed. *(Carol Howard)* **£30 [≈$45]**
- Kate Greenaway. London: A. & C. Black, Twenty Shilling Series, 1905. 1st edn. Cold plates, ills, Greenaway endpapers. Orig cloth. *(Old Cathay)* **£110 [≈$165]**
- Kate Greenaway. London: A. & C. Black, Twenty Shilling Series, 1905. 1st edn. Cold plates, ills, Greenaway endpapers. Orig cloth, some fading. *(Old Cathay)* **£69 [≈$104]**
- Kate Greenaway: Sixteen Examples in Colour. London: A. & C. Black, 1910. 1st edn. 16 ills. Orig bndg, front hinge cracked. *(Davidson)* **$125 [≈£83]**

Spielmann, M.H. & Jerrold, W.C.

- Hugh Thomson, His Art, His Letters, His Humour and His Charm. London: Black, 1931. Sm 4to. 269 pp. Ills. Orig bndg. *(Emerald Isle)* **£65 [≈$98]**

Spielmann, M.H. & Layard, G.S.

- Kate Greenaway. London: A. & C. Black, 1905. December reprint, with minor alterations. 8vo. 54 cold ills. One plate reinserted. Orig bndg, sl faded. *(Limestone Hills)* **$165 [≈£110]**

Spielmann, Percy Edwin

- Catalogue of the Library of Miniature Books ... together with some Descriptive Summaries. London: Edward Arnold, 1961. One of 500. 8vo. 4 plates. Orig qtr buckram. Dw. *(David Slade)* **£125 [≈$188]**

Spies, Werner

- The Running Fence Project: Christo. New York: Abrams, (1977). Oblong 8vo. 127 ills. Orig stiff wraps. Signed by Christo (1979). *(Abacus)* **$50 [≈£33]**
- Victor Vasarely. New York: Abrams, 1971. Lge sq 4to. 206 pp. 189 plates. Acetate overlay hinged inside rear cvr. Orig cloth. Dw. *(Ars Libri)* **$225 [≈£150]**

Spiteris, Tony

- The Art of Cyprus. New York: Reynal, (1970). Sm folio. 215 pp. Mtd cold plates, ills. Lacks front free endpaper. Dw. *(Mendelsohn)* **$60 [≈£40]**

Spoerri, Daniel

- An Anecdoted Topography of Chance (Re-Anecdoted Version) ... New York, Cologne & Paris: Something Else Press, 1966. 4to. xviii, [2],214 pp. 100 ills. Orig wraps. *(Ars Libri)* **$50 [≈£33]**
- The Mythological Travels of a Modern Sir

John Mandeville ... New York: Something Else Press, 1970. 4to. xxviii,[6],278 pp. Num ills. Orig cloth. Dw. *(Ars Libri)* **$100 [≈£67]**

Spurling, Hilary

- The Drawings of Mervyn Peake. London: Davis-Poynter, 1974. 110 ills. Orig pict cloth. *(Fine Art)* **£18.50 [≈$29]**

Stabb, John

- Some Old Devon Churches: their Rood Screens, Pulpits, Fonts etc. London: Simpkin, Marshall ..., [1908]-1916. 3 vols. 128 + 162 + 142 photo ills. Orig cloth, rubbed. *(Waterfield's)* **£100 [≈$150]**

Stainsfield, C.W.

- The Tradesmen's Tokens of the Australian Colonies, Together with an Account of the Early Silver Pieces and Gold Coinage of Australia. London: Lincoln, 1888. 8vo. 78,[vi index] pp. Orig bndg, spine faded. *(McBlain)* **$125 [≈£83]**

Standed, Edith Appleton

- European Post-Medieval Tapestries and related Hangings in the Metropolitan Museum of Art (New York). New York: Metropolitan Museum of Art, 1985. 2 vols. [848] pp. Num ills. Orig buckram. Slipcase. *(Fine Art)* **£75 [≈$113]**

Standing, Percy Cross

- Sir Lawrence Alma-Tadema O.M., R.A. London: Cassell, 1905. 128 pp. 41 plates (4 cold). Lib stamps. *(Leicester Art Books)* **£25 [≈$38]**

Stanesby, Samuel

- The Floral Gift, An Illuminated Souvenir. Illuminated by Samuel Stanesby. Printed in Colours by Thomas Bessent. London: Griffith & Farran, [1863]. Sq 8vo. 32 pp. Orig embossed dec cloth gilt, a.e.g., spine sl rubbed & sl worn at ends. *(Wilkinson)* **£59 [≈$89]**

Stannus, Mrs Graydon

- Old Irish Glass. London: The Connoisseur Series of Books for Collectors, 1921. New edn, rvsd & enlgd. Sm 4to. 16 pp. 60 plates. Orig pict cloth gilt, sl rubbed. *(Hollett)* **£75 [≈$113]**

Stanton, Theodore

- Rosa Bonheur Reminiscences. London: Andrew Melrose, 1910. xviii,414 pp. 24 plates, 15 text ills. Orig cloth, t.e.g. *(Leicester Art Books)* **£35 [≈$53]**

Starforth, John

- The Architecture of the Farm. A Series of Designs ... With Descriptions. Edinburgh: Blackwood, 1853. 4to. 60,[8 advt] pp. 4 pp subscribers. 62 lithos. Orig cloth, sl worn. *(Rankin)* **£75 [≈$113]**

Statius, Papinius

- Ode to Sleep. Translated from the Latin into English Verse by Richard Stanton Lambert. Stanton Press: 1923. [One of 90]. Oblong fcap 8vo. Orig qtr holland, untrimmed. *(Blackwell's)* **£50 [≈$75]**

Staunton, H.

- The Chess-Player's Handbook ... London: 1861. viii,518 pp. Cold frontis, 127 figs. Orig bndg, sl worn. *(Whitehart)* **£20 [≈$30]**

Stealingworth, Slim

- Tom Weselmann. New York: Abbeville, 1980. Lge sq 4to. 321,[3] pp. Num ills. Orig cloth. Dw. *(Ars Libri)* **$150 [≈£100]**
- Tom Wesselmann. New York: Abbeville, (1980). Folio. 321 pp. Cold & b/w plates, ills. Orig bds. Dws. *(Abacus)* **$85 [≈£57]**

Stebbins, Theodore E.

- American Master Drawings and Watercolors. New York: Harper, 1976. 1st edn. 4to. 464 pp. Ills. Orig cloth. Dw. *(First Folio)* **$65 [≈£43]**

Steel, Flora Annie

- Tales of the Punjab. Illustrated by David Gentleman. London: 1973. 1st edn thus. Num b/w ills. Orig cloth. Dw. *(Margaret Nangle)* **£18.50 [≈$29]**

Steel, Robert

- The Revival of Printing. A Bibliographical Catalogue of Works issued by the Chief Modern Presses. London: Macmillan, 1912. One of 350 numbered. 8 vo. xxiv,89,[3] pp. Ills. Orig cloth-backed bds. Dw (chipped). *(Oak Knoll)* **$175 [≈£117]**
- The Revival of Printing, a Bibliographical Catalogue of Works issued by the Chief Modern Presses. London: Macmillan, 1912. One of 350. 8vo. xxiv,89,[3] pp. Orig cloth backed bds. Dw (chipped). *(Oak Knoll)* **$175 [≈£117]**

Steinbeck, John

- Of Mice and Men. With Illustrations by Fletcher Martin. New York: The Limited Editions Club, 1970 . One of 1500 signed by the illustrator. Sm 4to. Orig qtr leather.

Slipcase. *(Oak Knoll)* **$135 [≈£90]**

Steinberg, Leo

- Michelangelo's Last Paintings. The Conversion of St. Paul and the Crucifixion of St. Peter in the Capella Paolina, Vatican Palace. New York: 1975. Folio. 64 pp. 64 plates, 99 text ills. Orig cloth. Dw (worn). *(Washton)* **$75 [≈£50]**

Steinberg, Paul

- The Passport. London: (1954). 1st English edn. 4to. 224 pp. Num ills. Orig cloth backed bds. Dw (reprd). *(Bow Windows)* **£40 [≈$60]**

Steinhardt, Jakob

- The Woodcuts of Jakob Steinhardt Chronologically Arranged and Fully Reproduced. Phila: Jewish Publication Society of America, 1962. 4to. Dw (chipped). *(First Folio)* **$65 [≈£43]**
- Woodcuts. Jerusalem: [ca 1955]. Lge 4to. 57 w'cuts, 16 hand cold. Orig cloth over ptd bds, plastic spiral bndg, v sl worn & soiled. Dw (worn). *(First Folio)* **$200 [≈£133]**

Steinmann, D.B. & Watson, S.R.

- Bridges and their Builders. New York: Putnam, 1941. 1st edn. 8vo. xvi,379 pp. Plates, text ills. Orig cloth. *(Clevedon Books)* **£26 [≈$39]**

Stella, Joseph G.

- The Graphic Work of Renoir. Catalogue Raisonne. London: [1975]. 112 pp. 64 ills. Orig pict wraps. *(Leicester Art Books)* **£110 [≈$165]**

Stendhal (Marie-Henri Beyle)

- The Charterhouse of Parma. Illustrations by Rafaello Busoni. New York: Limited Editions Club, 1955. One of 1500 sgnd by Busoni. Sm 4to. Orig cloth-backed bds (spine sl yellowed). Slipcase. *(Oak Knoll)* **$55 [≈£37]**

Stephens, Frederic G.

- Memoirs of Sir Edwin Landseer. A Sketch of the Life of the Artist ... London: George Bell, 1874. Roy 8vo. xv,184 pp. 24 plates (20 mtd woodburytypes). Orig cloth gilt, sl shaken. *(Fenning)* **£45 [≈$68]**

Stephens, James

- The Crock of Gold. Illustrations by Robert Lawson. New York: The Limited Editions Club, 1942. One of 1500 signed by the illustrator. 4to. Orig cloth, leather labels. Slipcase. *(Oak Knoll)* **$85 [≈£57]**

The Sterling Library ...

- The Sterling Library. A Catalogue of the Printed Books and Literary Manuscripts Collected by Sir Louis Sterling ... Compiled by Margaret Canney. Cambridge: UP: Privately Printed, 1954. 4to. Port, 7 plates. Orig cloth. *(Traylen)* **£60 [≈$90]**

Sterne, Laurence

- The Life & Opinions of Tristram Shandy, Gentleman. Illustrations by T.M. Cleland. New York: The Limited Editions Club, 1935. One of 1500 signed by the illustrator. 2 vols. 8vo. Orig cloth-backed bds, inner hinges cracked. *(Oak Knoll)* **$45 [≈£30]**
- A Sentimental Journey through France and Italy. Illustrated by Everard Hopkins. London: Williams & Norgate, 1910. 1st edn. 196 pp. 12 cold plates. Prelims & edges spotted. Orig pict gilt cloth, t.e.g., extrs sl rubbed. *(Bookworks)* **£35 [≈$53]**
- A Sentimental Journey through France & Italy. London: Williams & Norgate, 1910. 1st edn thus. 188 pp. Frontis & 11 mtd cold plates by Everard Hopkins. Minimal foxing. Orig cloth gilt, uncut, sl worn. *(Willow House)* **£25 [≈$38]**
- A Sentimental Journey. Illustrated by Valenti Angelo. New York: Dodd, Mead, 1929. 1st edn thus. 8vo. 253 pp. 12 b/w ills. Orig cloth gilt. Dw. Slipcase. *(Davidson)* **$95 [≈£63]**
- A Sentimental Journey through France and Italy. Illustrated by Polia Chentoff. Paris: Black Sun Press, 1929. One of 335. Wrappers. Glassine dw (spine sl darkened, minor paint spots, chipped). *(John K. King)* **$150 [≈£100]**

Stevens, Francis

- Domestic Architecture. A Series of Views of Cottages and Farm Houses, in England and Wales ... London: Nattali, [1815]. Lge 4to. iv, 36 pp. 54 plates. Occas marg soiling & spotting. Orig cloth, rebacked. *(Sotheran's)* **£648 [≈$972]**

Stevenson, Allen

- The Problem of the Missale Speciale. London: Bibl. Soc., 1967. 8vo. 10 plates, 5 ills. Orig cloth. *(Traylen)* **£10 [≈$15]**

Stevenson, D. Alan

- The World's Lighthouses before 1820. OUP: 1959. 7 maps, 200 ills. Dw. *(David Slade)* **£75 [≈$113]**

Stevenson, Robert Louis

- New Arabian Nights. Illustrations by Clarke

Hutton. Avon, CT: The Limited Editions Club, 1976. One of 2000 signed by the illustrator. Sm 4to. Orig cloth. Slipcase. *(Oak Knoll)* **$55 [≈£37]**

- The Strange Case of Dr. Jekyll and Mr. Hyde. Illustrated by S.G. Hulme Beaman. London: Bodley Head, (1930). 1st Beaman edn. Lge 8vo. viii,136 pp. Frontis, dec title, 7 plates. Orig cloth gilt. Dw. *(Karmiole)* **$75 [≈£50]**
- Travels with a Donkey in the Cevennes. Illustrated by Edmund Blampied. London: John Lane; The Bodley Head, 1931. 1st edn thus. 8vo. ix,189 pp. 8 ills. Orig cloth. Dw (sm nick hd of spine). *(Robert Frew)* **£50 [≈$75]**
- Travels with a Donkey. Illustrations by Roger Duvoisin. New York: The Limited Editions Club, 1957. One of 1500 signed by the illustrator. 8vo. Orig cloth (spine faded). Slipcase. *(Oak Knoll)* **$50 [≈£33]**

Stewart, Basil

- Japanese Colour-Prints and the Subjects they Illustrate. New York: Dodd, Mead, 1920. 1st Amer edn. 4to. 6 cold & 40 b/w ills. Orig buckram. *(Book Block)* **$140 [≈£93]**

Stewart, Cecil

- Topiary. An Historical Diversion. Golden Cockerel Press: 1954. One of 100 specially bound. 13 cold engvs by Peter Barker-Mill. Orig three qtr mor, dec bds. Slipcase (sl used). *(Margaret Nangle)* **£160 [≈$240]**

Stickley, Gustav

- Craftsman Homes. New York: The Craftsmen Publishing Co., 1909. 4to. 205 pp. Num ills. Orig burlap cloth. *(Rona Schneider)* **$300 [≈£200]**

Stieglitz, Alfred

- Stieglitz Memorial Portfolio, 1864-1946. New York: Twice a Year Press, (1947). 1st edn. One of 1500. Folio. (64) pp. 18 ills. Booklet laid into fldg paper portfolio (damage to one flap). *(Hermitage)* **$600 [≈£400]**

Stillingfleet, Benjamin

- Principles and Power of Harmony. London: J. & H. Hughs, sold by Baker & Leigh ..., 1771. 4to. Plate. Few marg pencil lines. Rec half calf. Anon. *(Jarndyce)* **£260 [≈$390]**

Stillman, C.G. & Cleary, R. Castle

- The Modern School. London: The Architectural Press, 1949. 1st edn. Lge 8vo. 152 pp. 151 ills. Orig cloth gilt. Dw (sl worn). *(Hollett)* **£25 [≈$38]**

Stirling, A.M.W.

- William de Morgan and His Wife. London: Butterworth, 1922. 403 pp. 33 plates, 18 text ills. Orig cloth. *(Leicester Art Books)* **£45 [≈$68]**

Stoker, Bram

- Dracula. Illustrated with Wood Engravings by Felix Hoffmann. New York: The Limited Editions Club, 1965. One of 1500 signed by the illustrator. 4to. Orig cloth. Slipcase (spine spotted). *(Oak Knoll)* **$95 [≈£63]**

Stokes, Adrian

- The Critical Writings of Adrian Stokes 1930-1967. London: Thames & Hudson, 1978. 3 vols. 209 ills. Orig cloth. Dws. *(Fine Art)* **£48 [≈$72]**

Stokes, Hugh

- Belgium ... Illustrations from Drawings by Frank Brangwyn. London: 1916. 4to. 52 ills. Orig buckram backed bds, mor label gilt. *(Traylen)* **£34 [≈$51]**

Stokes, William

- The Life and Labours in Art and Archaeology of George Petrie. London: Longmans, 1868. 445 pp. Half calf, spine gilt extra. *(Emerald Isle)* **£75 [≈$113]**

Stoll, Robert

- Architecture and Sculpture in Early Britain. Celtic Saxon Norman. London: 1967. 4to. 356 pp. 260 photo ills. Lib stamp on title verso. Dw (v sl chipped). *(Francis Edwards)* **£45 [≈$68]**

Stone, G.C.

- A Glossary of the Construction, Decoration and Use of Arms and Armour in all Countries and all times ... New York: (1961). One of 500. 4to. Frontis, over 3600 ills. Orig buckram. *(Bow Windows)* **£30 [≈$45]**

Stone, Reynolds

- Reynolds Stone Engravings with an Introduction by the Artist and An Appreciation by Kenneth Clark. London: Murray, [1977]. One of 150 signed by the author. Lge 8vo. Sgnd engraving (waterfall in

Prescelly Mountains) loosely inserted. Orig buckram. Slipcase. *(Sotheran's)* **£298 [≈$447]**

- The Wood Engravings of Gwen Raverat. Selected with an Introduction by Reynolds Stone. London: Faber, 1959. 136 pp. 267 ills. Orig cloth. Dw. *(Leicester Art Books)* **£60 [≈$90]**
- See also Raverat, Gwen; Warner, Sylvia Townsend

Stoneback, H.R.

- Cartographers of the Deus Loci: The Mill House. North Hills, PA: Bird & Bull Press, 1982. One of 240. Lge 8vo. [24] pp. 6 ills. Orig vellum over illust bds. Dw. Prospectus laid in. *(Karmiole)* **$125 [≈£83]**

Stopford, Francis

- The Romance of the Jewel. London: 1920. 1st edn. Lge 8vo. [xii],96 pp. 16 cold & 6 plain plates. Orig qtr calf, t.e.g., crnr tips rubbed. *(Bow Windows)* **£95 [≈$143]**

Storm, Colton & Peckham, H.

- Invitation to Book Collecting. Its Pleasures and Practices. New York: 1947. 1st edn. 8vo. Orig cloth. *(Traylen)* **£18 [≈$27]**

Story, Alfred Thomas

- The Life and Work of Sir Joseph Noel Paton, R.S.A. Her Majesty's Limner for Scotland. London: Art Journal Annual, 1895. 32 pp. 46 plates, ills. Orig cloth, a.e.g., sl marked. *(Fine Art)* **£16.50 [≈$26]**

Stothard, Charles Alfred

- The Monumental Effigies of Great Britain; selected from our Cathedrals and Churches ... London: McCreery for the author, 1817-32. 1st edn. Imperial 4to. 147 plates (many tinted or with hand-colouring, 12 text ills. Contemp half mor. *(Traylen)* **£180 [≈$270]**

Stower, Caleb

- The Printer's Grammar; or, Introduction to the Art of Printing ... London: Crosby, 1808. 1st edn. Thick 8vo. xviii,530,[48] pp. Later calf gilt. *(Oak Knoll)* **$1,750 [≈£1,167]**

Strachan, Walter J.

- The Artist and the Book in France: the 20th Century Livre d'Artiste. London: Peter Owen, 1969. 368 pp. 8 cold & 181 b/w plates. Orig cloth gilt. Dw. *(Fine Art)* **£55 [≈$83]**
- A Relationship with Henry Moore 1942-1976. Bishop's Stortford: 1988. Wrappers. Inscribed by the author. *(Ulysses Bookshop)* **£36 [≈$54]**

Strange, Edward Fairbrother

- The Colour-Prints of Hiroshige. London: Cassell, n.d. One of 250 deluxe. 4to. 205 pp. Frontis, ills. Ex-lib. Orig vellum, warped, some soiling. *(McBlain)* **$125 [≈£83]**

Stratton, Arthur

- The English Interior. A Review of the Decoration of English Homes from Tudor Times to the XIX Century. London: Batsford, 1920. 4to. xxviii,86 pp. Frontis, 115 plates, 82 text ills. Orig cloth gilt, t.e.g. *(Spelman)* **£60 [≈$90]**
- The English Interior. London: Batsford, [1920]. 1st edn. Folio. xxviii,86 pp. 115 plates. Orig cloth, t.e.g. *(Spelman)* **£60 [≈$90]**

Strauss, Walter L.

- Chiaroscuro. The Clair-Obscur Woodcuts by the German and Netherlandish Masters of the XVIth and XVIIIth Centuries. London: Thames & Hudson, (1973). 1st edn. 4to. xx,393 pp. 92 ills. Orig cloth. Price-clipped dw (rubbed). *(Bookpress)* **$165 [≈£110]**
- Chiaroscuro. The Clair-Obscur Woodcuts by the German and Netherlandish Masters of the XVIth and XVIIIth Centuries. A Complete Catalogue with Commentary. New York: Graphic Society, 1973. Sm 4to. xx,393 pp. 177 plates. Orig cloth. Dw (sl chipped). *(Hollett)* **£150 [≈$225]**

Strehlneek, E.A.

- Chinese Pictorial Art ... Shanghai: Commercial Press, 1914. 4to. 323,[5],73,[3] pp. Num ills. Orig silk gilt, stabbed & tied at inner marg, spine sl frayed. Inscribed by the author. *(Karmiole)* **$100 [≈£67]**

Streider, Peter

- Albrecht Durer: Paintings, Prints, Drawings. New York: Abaris Books, (1982). Folio. 400 pp. 455 ills. Orig cloth. Dw. Slipcase. *(Abacus)* **$60 [≈£40]**

Stringer, G.E.

- New Hall Porcelain. London: 1949. Sm 4to. xii,136 pp. 39 plates. Orig cloth. Dw (torn). *(Castle Bookshop)* **£42 [≈$63]**

Strong, Roy

- Art and Power. Renaissance Festivals 1450-1650. London: Boydell Press, 1984. 8vo. 115 ills. Dws. *(David Slade)* **£25 [≈$38]**
- Gloriana: The Portraits of Queen Elizabeth I. London: Thames & Hudson, 1987. 180 pp. 189 pp. Orig cloth. Dw. *(Fine Art)* **£18.50 [≈$29]**

- Holbein and Henry VIII. London: Paul Mellon Foundation for British Art, 1967. 75 pp. Cold frontis, 55 plates. Orig cloth & bds. *(Fine Art)* **£18 [≈$27]**
- Portraits of Queen Elizabeth I. OUP: 1963. xiv,143 pp. 23 plates, ills. Orig cloth. *(Fine Art)* **£20 [≈$30]**
- Portraits of Queen Elizabeth I. Oxford: Clarendon Press 1963. xiv,173 pp. Cold frontis, 22 plates, num figs. Lib b'plate. Dw (sl soiled & chipped). *(Francis Edwards)* **£25 [≈$38]**

Stroud, Dorothy

- The Architecture of Sir John Soane. London: Studio, 1961. 1st edn. 4to. 168 pp. 225 ills. Dw (reprd). *(Spelman)* **£45 [≈$68]**
- Capability Brown. With an Introduction by Christopher Hussey. London: Country Life, 1950. 1st edn. 4to. 224 pp. Cold frontis, plates. A few spots to endpapers. Orig cloth gilt. Dw. *(Hollett)* **£60 [≈$90]**
- Capability Brown. London: Country Life, 1957. 2nd edn, rvsd. 4to. 228 pp. 100 ills. Orig cloth gilt. Dw. *(Clevedon Books)* **£65 [≈$98]**
- Humphrey Repton. London: Country Life, 1962. 182 pp. 105 plates. Orig cloth. Dw. *(Fine Art)* **£35 [≈$53]**

Strutt, Edward C.

- Fra Filippo Lippi. London: Bell, 1901. 202 pp. Num plates. Orig gilt dec cloth, edges sl worn. *(Willow House)* **£28 [≈$42]**
- Fra Filippo Lippi (1902). New York: 1972. Reprint. Lge 8vo. xxiii,202 pp. Num ills. Orig cloth. *(Washton)* **$45 [≈£30]**

Strzgowski, Josef

- Early Church Art in Northern Europe with special reference to Timber Construction and Decoration. London: Batsford, 1928. 8vo. viii, 172 pp. Frontis, 52 plates, 65 text ills. Orig cloth gilt. *(Quest Books)* **£42 [≈$63]**

Stuart, James, called Athenian Stuart

- Critical Observations on the Buildings and Improvements of London. London: Dodsley, 1771. 1st edn. 4to. [ii],51 pp. Title-vignette. Lacks half-title. Sm repr last leaf. Rec half calf. Anon. *(Jarndyce)* **£450 [≈$675]**

Stubblebine, James H.

- Duccio di Buoninsegna and His School. Princeton: UP, 1979. 1st edn. 2 vols. 4to. Frontis, 599 ills. Orig cloth. One dw reprd. *(Spelman)* **£70 [≈$105]**

The Studio

- Yearbook of Decorative Art: 1907. London: The Studio, 1907. 4to. 228 pp. 19 cold plates. Orig cloth. *(Rona Schneider)* **$120 [≈£80]**

Sturgis, Russell

- A History of Architecture ... London: Batsford, 1907-10. 2 vols (only, of 4). Sm 4to. xxvi,425; xxiii,448 pp. 728 ills. Orig cloth, one spine trifle creased. 1: Antiquity; 2: Romanesque and Oriental. *(Hollett)* **£75 [≈$113]**
- Homes in City and Country. New York: Scribner, 1893. 1st edn. 8vo. x,[ii], 214,[6] pp. Frontis, 100 ills. Orig cloth. *(Bookpress)* **$385 [≈£257]**

Styan, K.E.

- A Short History of Sepulchral Cross-Slabs ... London: Bemrose, 1902. 8vo. [vi],45 pp. 71 plates. Orig cloth gilt, trifle marked. *(Hollett)* **£16 [≈$24]**

Suckling, Sir John

- A Ballad upon a Wedding. Waltham St. Lawrence: Golden Cockerel Press, 1927. One of 375. W'engvs by Eric Ravilious. Orig cloth backed bds, edges rubbed, spine sl darkened. *(Ulysses Bookshop)* **£450 [≈$675]**
- A Ballad upon a Wedding. Waltham St. Lawrence: Golden Cockerel Press, 1927. One of 375. W'engvs by Eric Ravilious. Orig canvas backed bds, uncut, sl dusty. *(Claude Cox)* **£120 [≈$180]**

Suetonius

- The Lives of the Twelve Caesars. Illustrated with Paintings by Salvatore Fiume. New York: The Limited Editions Club, 1963. One of 1500 signed by Mardersteig. Thick 8vo. Orig cloth-backed bds, front inner hinge partially cracked. Slipcase. *(Oak Knoll)* **$125 [≈£83]**

Sugden, Alan Victor & Edmondson, John Ludlam

- A History of English Wallpaper 1509-1914. New York: Scribner; London: Batsford, [1925]. 4to. 70 mtd cold plates, num ills. Orig buckram gilt, t.e.g., fine. Dw (few short tears). Orig box (sl worn). *(David Slade)* **£440 [≈$660]**

Sukarno Collection

- Paintings and Statues from the Collection of President Sukarno of the Republic of Indonesia. [Compiled by Lee Man-Fong].

Jakarta: 1964. 5 vols. Folio. 567 mtd cold plates. Orig leatheratte gilt. Dws. Slipcases. *(Karmiole)* **$450 [≈£300]**

Sullivan, Louis H.

- Kindergarten Chats of Architecture, Education and Democracy. N.p.: Scarab Fraternity Press, 1934. 1st edn. Ltd edn. 8vo. 256 pp. Ills. Orig embossed cloth. Dw (soiled, minor chips). *(First Folio)* **$445 [≈£297]**

Sullivan, Michael

- The Birth of Landscape Painting in China. London: Routledge, (1962). 1st edn. Lge 8vo. Orig cloth. Dw (v chipped). *(Bookpress)* **$100 [≈£67]**

Summerson, John

- Architecture in Britain 1530-1830. London: Pelican History of Art, 1953. 1st edn. Roy 8vo. Num ills. Orig cloth. Dw (dull). *(Fenning)* **£28.50 [≈$44]**
- John Nash, Architect to King George IV. Second Edition. London: Allen & Unwin, 1949. 8vo. 299 pp. Map, plates, ills. Dw. *(Spelman)* **£30 [≈$45]**
- The Life and Work of John Nash, Architect. London: Allen & Unwin, 1980. 217 pp. 48 plates, text ills. Orig cloth. Dw. *(Fine Art)* **£20 [≈$30]**

Sumner, Heywood

- The Ancient Earthworks of Cranborne Chase. Described, & delineated in Plans ... London: Chiswick Press, 1913. One of 200 signed by the author. 4to. xiv,82,[i] pp. Fldg hand cold map, 46 plans. Orig dec cloth gilt, sm mark lower bd. *(Hollett)* **£160 [≈$240]**

Sumner, James

- The Mysterious Marbler. With an Historical Introduction, Notes and Eleven Original Marbled Samples by Richard J. Wolfe. North Hills: Bird & Bull Press, 1976. One of 250. 8vo. Orig mor backed mrbld bds, tips v sl rubbed. *(The Veatchs)* **$425 [≈£283]**

Surtees, Robert Smith

- The Jaunts and Jollities of ... Mr. John Jorrocks ... With Illustrations in Water-Color by Gordon Ross and an Introduction by A. Edward Newton. New York: The Limited Editions Club, 1932. One of 1500 signed by the illustrator. Tall 8vo. Orig gilt dec cloth, t.e.g. Slipcase (rubbed). *(Oak Knoll)* **$85 [≈£57]**
- Mr Jorrocks Thoughts on Hunting. Illustrated by G.D. Armour. London: 1925. 12 cold & 1 half-tone plates, 11 text ills. 1 marg tear. V sl foxed. Orig pict cloth, t.e.g., spine sl faded, crnrs sl bumped. *(Stella Books)* **£30 [≈$45]**

Surtees, Virginia

- Dante Gabriel Rossetti 1824-1882. The Paintings and Drawings. A Catalogue Raisonne. Oxford: Clarendon Press 1971. 2 vols (text & plates). 504 plates. Orig cloth. Dw. *(Leicester Art Books)* **£350 [≈$525]**

Sutcliffe, John

- Drawing Book of Horses, in Progressive Lessons. London: W. Kent, [ca 1860]. Sm oblong 4to. Title & 24 litho plates (14 cold). Orig cloth gilt. *(Spelman)* **£325 [≈$488]**

Sutherland, C.H.V.

- Gold. Its Beauty, Power and Allure. London: Thames & Hudson, 1959. 1st edn. Lge 8vo. 196 pp. 69 plates, 11 ills. Orig cloth gilt. Dw. *(Hollett)* **£30 [≈$45]**

Sutro, Oscar

- Shakespeare and Some Commentators: An Address ... San Francisco: 1933. One of 125. 8vo. [ii],25,[1] pp. Orig parchment backed bds. Dw (chipped). *(Bookpress)* **$95 [≈£63]**

Sutton, Denys

- French Drawings of the Eighteenth Century. London: 1949. 4to. 62 pp. 65 plates. Orig cloth. *(Washton)* **$35 [≈£23]**

Sutton, Peter C.

- Pieter De Hooch. Complete Edition. Oxford: Phaidon, 1980. 168 pp. 16 cold plates, 194 ills. Orig cloth. *(Leicester Art Books)* **£120 [≈$180]**
- Pieter De Hooch: Complete Edition. London: Phaidon, 1980. 168 pp. 276 ills. Orig cloth. Dw. *(Fine Art)* **£60 [≈$90]**

Sutton, Thomas

- The Daniells, Artists and Travellers. London: Theodore Brun, (1954). One of 150. Sm 4to. [ii],200 pp. 7 cold plates, 24 b/w plates. Orig mor. *(Bookpress)* **$250 [≈£167]**
- The Daniells. Artists and Travellers. London: Bodley Head, 1954. Roy 8vo. 7 cold & 24 other plates. Dw. *(David Slade)* **£35 [≈$53]**

Sutzkever, Abraham

- Siberia. Illustrated by Marc Chagall. New

York: Abelard-Schumann, 1961. 1st edn. Lge 4to. 7 ills by Chagall. Orig cloth. Dw (sl dusty). *(Barbara Stone)* **£55 [≈$83]**

Swaan, Wim

- The Gothic Cathedral. With an Historical Introduction ... by Christopher Brooke. New York: 1969. Sm folio. 328 pp. 389 ills. Orig cloth. *(Washton)* **$85 [≈£57]**

Swann, Peter C.

- Chinese Monumental Art. London: Thames & Hudson, (1963). 4to. 276 pp. 157 plates. Orig cloth. Dw. *(Abacus)* **$45 [≈£30]**

Swanson, V.G.

- The Biography and Catalogue Raisonne of the Paintings of Sir Lawrence Alma Tadema. London: Garton, Scolar Press, n.d. One of 750. 448 pp. 444 ills (60 cold). Orig cloth, t.e.g. Slipcase. *(Fine Art)* **£275 [≈$413]**

Sweeney, James Johnson

- Afro. Paintings, Gouaches, Drawings. Roma: Modern Art Editions, 1961. Sq folio. 85,[3] pp. Num ills. Orig cloth. Dw. *(Ars Libri)* **$50 [≈£33]**

Swift, Jonathan

- Gulliver's Travels Illustrated by Arthur Rackham. London: Dent, 1909. One of 750 signed by Rackham. 4to. 12 mtd cold plates, 34 ills. Orig buckram gilt, t.e.g., ribbon ties, minimally soiled, spine sl browned. *(Sotheran's)* **£950 [≈$1,425]**
- Gulliver's Travels. Golden Cockerel Press: 1925. One of 450. 2 vols. 4to. 40 w'engvs by David Jones. Occas sl foxing. Orig half buckram, unopened. *(Waddington)* **£600 [≈$900]**
- Gulliver's Travels Into Several Remote Nations of the World. London: Temple Press, [1937]. Lge 8vo. 12 cold plates by Arthur Rackham. Orig cloth. *(Wilkinson)* **£35 [≈$53]**
- Gulliver's Travels and Selected Writings in Prose & Verse. Edited by John Hayward. London: Nonesuch Press, 1946. 8vo. xviii,868 pp. Orig buckram. *(Claude Cox)* **£15 [≈$23]**
- Selected Essays. Golden Cockerel Press: 1925. One 190 [issued] copies. Vol 1 [all published]. 86 pp. 14 w'engvs by John Farleigh. Orig qtr mor, uncut, spine sunned, crnrs sl worn. *(Bookworks)* **£135 [≈$203]**

Swinburne, Algernon Charles

- Hide-and-Seek. With Notes by John S. Mayfield. The Stourton Press: 1975. One of 250. Sm folio. Orig half leather, cloth sides. *(Claude Cox)* **£55 [≈$83]**
- Lucretia Borgia. The Chronicle of Tebaldeo Tebaldei. Golden Cockerel Press: 1942. One of 350. Folio. 196 pp. W'engvs by Reynolds Stone. Orig canvas gilt, ft of spine bumped. *(Waddington)* **£120 [≈$180]**
- Pasiphae a Poem. Golden Cockerel Press: 1950. 1st 'correctly printed' edn. One of 500. 40 pp. Frontis, pict title, & 4 other copper engvs by John Buckland Wright. Orig 2-tone cloth gilt, unfaded. Glassine dw. *(Claude Cox)* **£75 [≈$113]**
- Selected Poems with Illustrations and Decorations by Harry Clarke. London: John Lane, 1928. 8vo. 10 plates. Orig cloth gilt, spine faded & sl spotted. *(Claude Cox)* **£32 [≈$48]**
- Selected Poems. Illustrated by Harry Clarke. London: John Lane; The Bodley Head, (1928). 1st edn thus. 4to. Orig gilt dec cloth, side of spine sl rippled. Dw (inner reinforcement). Slipcase (cracked along one edge). *(Jo Ann Reisler)* **$350 [≈£233]**
- Selected Poems. Illustrated by Harry Clarke. New York: Dodd, Mead; London: John Lane, (1928). [xxxiv],(218) pp. Top edge sl foxed. Orig cloth gilt, largely unopened. *(Schoyer)* **$150 [≈£100]**
- The Springtide of Life. Illustrated by Arthur Rackham. London: Heinemann, 1918. 1st Rackham edn. Roy 8vo. ix,133 pp. 8 cold plates & 58 vignettes, dec endpapers. Orig cloth gilt, two tiny chips at lower edge. *(Sotheran's)* **£128 [≈$192]**
- The Springtide of Life. Illustrated by Arthur Rackham. London: Heinemann, 1918. 1st Rackham edn. 4to. 132,[2] pp. 8 cold plates, 52 head & tail pieces, pict endpapers. Free endpapers browned. Orig cloth gilt. *(Blackwell's)* **£75 [≈$113]**
- Springtide of Life. Illustrated by Arthur Rackham. Phila: Lippincott, 1918. 1st Amer edn. Cold plates, ills. Orig cloth, extrs sl rubbed. *(Davidson)* **$250 [≈£167]**

Swinburne, Charles Alfred

- Life and Work of J.M.W. Turner, R.A. London: 1902. vii,315 pp. Frontis. Title sl spotted. Few marg pencil notes. Orig cloth, t.e.g., sl faded, spine bumped. *(Francis Edwards)* **£45 [≈$68]**

Swinburne, H.L.

- The Royal Navy. London: A. & C. Black, Twenty Shilling Series, 1916. 1st edn. 61

cold plates by Norman Wilkinson and J. Jellicoe. Orig cloth, extrs sl worn, backstrip relaid. *(Old Cathay)* **£79 [≈$119]**

Swinton, George

- Sculpture of the Eskimo. Toronto: McClelland & Stewart, 1972. 4to. Ills. Orig cloth. Dw. *(First Folio)* **$85 [≈£57]**

Swope, John

- Camera Over Hollywood. With Foreword by Leland Hayward ... New York: Random House, (1939). 1st edn. 4to. 110 photo plates. Orig cloth. Dw (sl chipped). *(Karmiole)* **$150 [≈£100]**

Symonds, John

- Lottie. Illustrated by Edward Ardizzone. London: 1957. 1st edn. Ills. Free endpapers v sl browned. Orig dec bndg, spine ends & crnrs rubbed & sl bumped. Dw (nicked, sl rubbed & dusty, spine & edges browned). *(Ulysses Bookshop)* **£38 [≈$57]**

Symonds, R.W.

- English Furniture from Charles II to George II ... London: 1929. One of 1000. Lge 4to. Cold frontis, 260 ills. Orig buckram. *(Traylen)* **£150 [≈$225]**
- Masterpieces of English Furniture and Clocks. A Study of Walnut and Mahogany Furniture and of the associated Crafts of the Looking-Glass Maker and Japanner ... Thomas Tompion ... London: Batsford, 1940. One of 750. Lge 4to. ix,172 pp. 8 cold plates, 132 text ills. Orig cloth gilt. *(Hollett)* **£175 [≈$263]**
- The Ornamental Designs of Chippendale. A Selection ... London: Alec Tiranti, 1949. 1st edn. Tall 8vo. 24 pp. 80 plates. Orig cloth. Dw. *(Hollett)* **£30 [≈$45]**
- The Present State of Old English Furniture. London: 1921. 1st edn. 4to. 116 ills. Orig cloth. *(Traylen)* **£28 [≈$42]**
- The Present State of Old English Furniture. London: Duckworth, 1927. 4to. xii, 132 pp. Ills. Orig cloth gilt. Dw (worn). *(Hollett)* **£30 [≈$45]**

Synge, Patrick M.

- Plants with Personalities. Illustrated by John Nash. London: Lindsay Drummond, [1938]. 1st edn. 1st issue, in the larger format. 234 x 144 mm. 244 pp. Cold frontis, 19 plates. Orig cloth, sl cocked, crnr bumped. Dw (chipped, sl rubbed & soiled). *(Bookworks)* **£32 [≈$48]**

Szirtes, George

- An Illustrated Alphabet. Hitchin: The Mandeville Press, 1978. One of 55 signed by the author. 26 etchings on 13 plates. Orig card cvrs, mrbld wraps, paper label. *(Mermaid Books)* **£45 [≈$68]**

Szyk, Arthur

- The New Order. New York: Putnam, 1941. 4to. Title, 38 ills. Orig cloth, sm Dent front bd. Dw. *(Barbara Stone)* **£65 [≈$98]**

Taevernier, Aug.

- James Ensor. Illustrated Catalogue of his Engravings, their Critical Description and Inventory of the Plates. Ghent: Ledeberg, 1973. vi,378 pp. 171 ills. Orig cloth. Dw. *(Leicester Art Books)* **£160 [≈$240]**

Taft, Lorado

- The History of American Sculpture. New Edition. New York: 1924. Thick 4to. xiii,604 pp. 116 text figs. Orig cloth gilt. Dw (chipped). *(Hollett)* **£40 [≈$60]**

Taft, Robert

- Artists and Illustrators of the Old West, 1850-1900. New York: Scribner, (19 53). 1st edn. Thick 8vo. xxii,400 pp. Plates. Orig cloth. Dw (chipped). *(Oak Knoll)* **$65 [≈£43]**

Taki, Sei-ichi

- Japanese Fine Art. Translated by K. Takahashi. Tokyo: Fuzambo, 1931. 8vo. xi,163 pp. Photo ills. orig bndg. *(McBlain)* **$60 [≈£40]**
- Three Essays on Oriental Painting. London: Quaritch, 1910. 4to. 84 pp. 62 plates. orig bndg, spine sl faded. *(McBlain)* **$75 [≈£50]**

Talley, M.K.

- Portrait Painting in England: Studies in the Technical Literature before 1700. Paul Mellon Centre: 1981. Lge 8vo. 512 pp. 42 plates. Orig cloth. *(Spelman)* **£35 [≈$53]**

Tallis, John, publisher

- The Crystal Palace Described and Illustrated ... London: John Tallis & Co., [1851]. 3 vols. 4to. iv,268; iv,262; title, iv,110 pp. 3 frontis, cold title, 226 engvs. Few ff sl spotted. Orig half mor, gilt spines. *(Sotheran's)* **£188 [≈$282]**
- Tallis's History and Description of the Crystal Palace and the Exhibition of the World's Industry in 1851. London: J. Tallis, (1851). 3 vols. 4to. Num ills. Half mor, jnts worn. *(Traylen)* **£190 [≈$285]**

Tancock, John L.

- The Sculpture of Rodin. The Collection of the Rodin Museum, Philadelphia. Phila: Philadelphia Museum of Art, 1976. 664 pp. Num ills. Orig cloth. Dw. *(Leicester Art Books)* **£50 [≈$75]**

Tapie, Victor-L.

- The Age of Grandeur, Baroque and Classicism in Europe. London: Weidenfeld & Nicolson, 1960. 1st edn in English. Tall 8vo. 305 pp. Ills. Orig cloth. *(First Folio)* **$50 [≈£33]**

Tatham, David

- The Lure of the Striped Pig: The Illustration of Popular Music in America 1820-1870. Barre: Imprint Society, 1973. Sm folio. 157 pp. 60 ills. Orig cloth. Slipcase. *(Rona Schneider)* **$90 [≈£60]**

Taubert, Sigfred

- Bibliopola. Pictures and Texts about the Book Trade. Hamburg & London: 1966. 1st edn. 2 vols. Folio. Plates, ills. Orig linen. Slipcase. *(Claude Cox)* **£120 [≈$180]**

Taut, Bruno

- Houses and People of Japan. London: John Gifford, (1938). 1st edn. 4to. [vi], [2],xiv, 318 pp. Frontis, 553 ills. Orig cloth, minor wear spine extrs. *(Bookpress)* **$850 [≈£567]**

Tayler, Irene

- Blake's Illustrations to the Poems of Gray. Princeton: UP, 1971. 170 pp. 128 plates. Orig buckram. Dw. *(Leicester Art Books)* **£30 [≈$45]**

Taylor, Andrew T.

- The Towers & Steeples Designed by Sir Christopher Wren. London: Batsford, 1881. 1st edn. 8vo. viii,47 pp. Pict title, 13 plates. Flyleaves sl spotted. Orig cloth backed dec bds, sl soiled & rubbed, recased. *(Hollett)* **£60 [≈$90]**

Taylor, Desmond

- Edwin Cooper of Beccles 1785-1833. Leigh-on-Sea: F. Lewis, 1980. One of 500. 104 pp. Cold frontis, 65 ills. Orig cloth. Dw. *(Leicester Art Books)* **£32 [≈$48]**

Taylor, H.

- Old Halls in Lancashire and Cheshire. Including Notes on the Ancient Domestic Architecture of the Counties Palatine. Manchester: 1884. 4to. xxxii,164 pp. 33 plates. Lib cloth. *(Castle Bookshop)* **£55 [≈$83]**

Taylor, H.M. & Joan

- Anglo-Saxon Architecture. Cambridge: UP, 1965. 2 vols. 4to. Num plates. Dws. *(Peter Bell)* **£75 [≈$113]**

Taylor, John Russell

- The Art Nouveau Book in Britain. Edinburgh: Paul Harris, 1979. Rvsd edn. 8vo. 176 pp. Ills. Orig cloth. Dw. *(Cooper Hay)* **£38 [≈$57]**

Taylor, W. Thomas & Morris, Henry

- Twenty-One Years of Bird & Bull: A Bibliography 1958-1979. Taylor & Bird & Bull: 1980. One of 350 signed by Morris. 8vo. Orig leather backed bds, spine sl stained. *(Dermont)* **$250 [≈£167]**

Taylour, Mrs Basil

- Japanese Gardens. Illustrated by Walter Tyndale. London: 1928. 2nd edn. Sm 4to. xiii, 204 pp. 28 mtd cold plates. Orig cloth gilt. *(Francis Edwards)* **£65 [≈$98]**

Tellier, Jules

- Abd-Er-Rhaman in Paradise. Golden Cockerel Press: 1928. One of 400. W'engvs by Paul Nash. Orig qtr buckram, t.e.g. *(Waddington)* **£105 [≈$158]**

Temple, A.G.

- The Art of Painting in the Queen's Reign: Being a glance at the Painters and Paintings of the British School during the last Sixty Years. London: 1897. xii,398 pp. 77 plates. Lacks front free endpaper. Orig cloth, t.e.g., spine edges worn. *(Fine Art)* **£50 [≈$75]**

Temple, Nigel

- John Nash & The Village Picturesque: with special reference to the Reptons and Nash at the Blaise Castle Estate, Bristol. London: Alan Sutton, 1979. 8vo. 104 ills. Dw. *(David Slade)* **£25 [≈$38]**

Tennyson, Alfred, Lord

- The Idylls of the King. Illustrated by Gustave Dore. London: Moxon, 1868. 1st edn thus. Folio. 36 engvd plates on india paper. Sl spotting. Mor gilt extra. *(Barbara Stone)* **£325 [≈$488]**
- The Idylls of the King. Illustrated by Eleanor F. Brickdale. London: Hodder & Stoughton, n.d. 21 cold plates. Orig elab gilt blue cloth. *(Old Cathay)* **£75 [≈$113]**

- The Poems. Selected and Introduced by John D. Rosenberg. With Wood Engravings by Reynolds Stone. N.p.: The Limited Editions Club, 1974. One of 2000 signed by the illustrator. Tall 8vo. Orig qtr leather. Slipcase. *(Oak Knoll)* **$125 [≈£83]**
- Seven Poems & Two Translations. Hammersmith: The Doves Press, 1902. One of 325. 55,colophon pp. Inscrptn & sm stamp. Orig limp vellum (darkened). *(Claude Cox)* **£150 [≈$225]**
- The Story of Enid and Geraint. Illustrated by Gustave Dore. London: Moxon, (1868). Folio. 9 ills. Orig pict cloth gilt, v sl spotted. *(Barbara Stone)* **£110 [≈$165]**
- Tennyson's Guinevere and Other Poems. Illustrated by Florence Harrison. London: Blackie, 1912. 1st edn thus. 4to. 156 pp. 24 mtd cold plates, plates, ills. Orig pict cloth, sl worn. *(Marjorie James)* **£65 [≈$98]**

Terukazu, Akiyama

- Treasures of Asia: Japanese Painting. Lausanne: Skira, (1961). 4to. (219) pp. 81 mtd cold plates. Dw (edges rubbed). *(Schoyer)* **$45 [≈£30]**

Thackeray, William Makepeace

- Henry Esmond. New York: The Limited Editions Club 1956. 1st edn thus. 32 cold ills. Orig brocade, leather label. Slipcase (worn). *(Margaret Nangle)* **£110 [≈$165]**
- The History of Pendennis ... With Illustrations by Charles W. Stewart. New York: The Limited Editions Club, 1961. One of 1500 signed by the illustrator. 2 vols. Thick 8vo. Orig cloth. Slipcase. *(Oak Knoll)* **$75 [≈£50]**
- The Newcomes ... With an Introduction by Angela Thirkell and with Illustrations by Edward Ardizzone. New York: The Limited Editions Club, 1954. One of 1500 signed by the illustrator. 2 vols. Tall 8vo. Orig cloth, front hinge vol 2 split. Slipcase (shows wear). *(Oak Knoll)* **$50 [≈£33]**
- The Rose and the Ring. Illustrations drawn by Fritz Kredel ... New York: The Limited Editions Club, 1942. One of 1500. 4to. Orig cloth. Outer folder. Slipcase (worn). *(Oak Knoll)* **$65 [≈£43]**

Thelwell, Norman

- Wrestling with a Pencil. London: 1986. 1st edn. Ills. Dw. signed by the author. *(Susan Wood)* **£25 [≈$38]**

Theobald, Henry Studdy

- Crome's Etchings. A Catalogue and Appreciation with some Account of his Paintings. London: Macmillan, 1906. xii,107 pp. Orig cloth. *(Leicester Art Books)* **£50 [≈$75]**

Theocritus

- Sixe Idillia. London: Duckworth, 1922. One of 380 signed by the artist, Vivien Gribble. Lge 4to. 34 w'engvs. Endpapers v browned. Orig linen backed bds, sides faded. *(Waddington)* **£35 [≈$53]**

Thiel, Pieter Van

- All the Paintings of the Rijksmuseum in Amsterdam. Amsterdam & Maarssen: 1976. 1st edn. 4to. 911 pp. Over 5000 ills. Orig cloth. Dw (chipped). *(Bookpress)* **$150 [≈£100]**

Thiis, Jens

- Leonardo Da Vinci, the Florentine Years of Leonardo & Verrocchio. London: Herbert Jenkins, (1913). 1st edn. Sm folio. 280 pp. Frontis, 277 ills. Lib marks. Orig dec cloth, t.e.g., sl worn. *(Bookpress)* **$150 [≈£100]**

Thomas, Alan

- Great Books and Book Collectors. London: Weidenfeld & Nicolson, 1975. 1st edn. 4to. 280 pp. 40 cold plates, 250 ills. Dw (sl frayed). *(Claude Cox)* **£18 [≈$27]**

Thomas, Dylan

- Deaths and Entrances. Illustrated by John Piper. Newtown: Gwasg Gregynog, 1984. One of 268. Thin folio. Orig qtr mor. *(Mermaid Books)* **£330 [≈$495]**

Thomas, H.

- The Drawings of G.B. Piranesi. London: Faber, 1954. 1st edn. 4to. 66 pp. 80 plates. Orig cloth. Dw (sl chipped). *(Monmouth)* **£25 [≈$38]**

Thomas, Henry

- Spanish Sixteenth-Century Printing. London: Benn, 1926. 1st edn. Lge 8vo. 38 pp. 50 plates. Orig dec bds, labels chipped. *(Claude Cox)* **£30 [≈$45]**

Thomas, Hylton

- The Drawings of Giovanni Battista Piranesi. London: Faber, 1954. 66 pp. 80 plates. Orig cloth. *(Leicester Art Books)* **£25 [≈$38]**

Thomas, J.

- The Rise of the Staffordshire Potteries. London: Adams & Dart, 1971. 228 pp. 52 plates. Ex-lib. Orig cloth. Dw. *(Castle Bookshop)* **£19.50 [≈$30]**

Thomas, M.G. Lloyd (compiler)

- Travellers' Verse. Chosen by M.G. Lloyd Thomas. London: Muller, New Excursions into English Poetry Series, 1946. 1st edn. 16 lithos by Edward Bawden. Crnr cut from front free blank. Dw. *(Mermaid Books)* **£24 [≈$36]**
- Travellers' Verse. London: Muller, New Excursions into English poetry Series, 1949. 1st edn. 120 pp. 16 lithos by Edward Bawden. Orig pict cloth, tiny bruise to crnr. *(Bookworks)* **£40 [≈$60]**

Thomas, Walter G. & Fallon, John T.

- Northern Italian Details. New York: U.P.C. Book Co., 1922. 2nd edn. 4to. 24 pp. 143 plates. Orig half cloth, worn. *(Bookpress)* **$95 [≈£63]**

Thompson, A. Hamilton

- The Cathedral Churches of England. London: SPCK, 1928. 1st edn. xvi,235 pp. 31 plates. Orig cloth gilt. *(Hollett)* **£20 [≈$30]**
- Military Architecture in England during the Middle Ages. Oxford: Henry Frowde, 1912. 8vo. Num ills & plans. Orig buckram. *(David Slade)* **£30 [≈$45]**

Thompson, David Cleghorn

- The Hidden Path. Glasgow: 1943. 1st edn. 4to. Illust by Michael Ayrton. Dw (trifle dusty, one tiny chip). Two ALS by the author laid in. *(Blakeney)* **£125 [≈$188]**

Thompson, Francis

- The Hound of Heaven. Illustrated by Frideswith Huddart. London: Chatto & Windus, 1914. Roy 4to. 10 mtd b/w plates. Poems in sep booklet. Orig bndg gilt, extrs rubbed. *(Stella Books)* **£65 [≈$98]**
- The Hound of Heaven. Mount Vernon: The Peter Pauper Press, [ca 1953]. 12mo. [30] pp. Cold frontis & ills by Valenti Angelo. Orig dec bds. Dw. *(Argonaut)* **$35 [≈£23]**

Thompson, Paul

- William Butterfield. London: Routledge, 1971. xl,526 pp. 25 cold & 392 other ills. Orig cloth. Dw. *(Leicester Art Books)* **£45 [≈$68]**

Thompson, Susan Otis

- American Book Design and William Morris. New York: Bowker, 1977. 1st edn. 4to. xvii, 258 pp. 111 ills. Orig cloth. Dw. *(Oak Knoll)* **$65 [≈£43]**

Thompson, W.G.

- Tapestry Weaving in England: from the Earliest Times to the End of the XVIIIth Century. London: Batsford, 1914. 172 pp. 60 plates. Orig cloth, t.e.g., front hinge sl weak. *(Fine Art)* **£75 [≈$113]**

Thomson, David Croal

- The Brothers Maris. James, Mathew, William. London: The Studio, 1907. ix,x, xxxviii pp. 73 plates. Orig cloth. *(Leicester Art Books)* **£28 [≈$42]**
- The Water-Colour Drawings of Thomas Bewick. London: Barbizon House, 1930. One of 525 signed by the author. xxiv,84 pp. 33 mtd cold plates. Orig cloth gilt, sl stained. *(Leicester Art Books)* **£75 [≈$113]**

Thomson, Duncan

- The Life and Art of George Jamesone. Oxford: Clarendon Press 1974. xx,164 pp. 127 ills. Orig cloth. Dw. *(Leicester Art Books)* **£50 [≈$75]**

Thomson, James

- The Seasons. London: Nonesuch Press, 1927. One of 1500. Label removed from endpaper. Orig mrbld cloth, rubbed. *(John K. King)* **$100 [≈£67]**
- The Seasons. With Five Pictures by Jacquier and an Introduction by James Beresford. London: Nonesuch Press, 1927. One of 1500. Lge 8vo. 5 stencil-cold plates. Orig mrbld cloth, mor label. *(Claude Cox)* **£45 [≈$68]**

Thomson, W.G.

- A History of Tapestry from the Earliest Times until the Present Day. London: Hodder & Stoughton, 1906. 1st edn. Thick 4to. xvi,506 pp. Num plates. A few spots. Orig dec cloth gilt, trifle rubbed, upper jnt tender. *(Hollett)* **£120 [≈$180]**
- A History of Tapestry ... London: 1930. 2nd edn, rvsd. Thick 4to. viii,550 pp. Num plates. Endpapers spotted. Orig cloth, sl worn, sl soiled. *(Hollett)* **£75 [≈$113]**
- Tapestry Weaving in England. From the Earliest Times to the End of the XVIIIth Century. London: Batsford; New York: Scribner, (1914). Folio. 172 pp. 2 cold plates, b/w ills. Some soil. Orig cloth gilt, t.e.g., somewhat soiled. *(Schoyer)* **$125 [≈£83]**

Thordeman, Bengt & Andersson, Aron

- Medieval Wooden Sculpture in Sweden. Stockholm: Almqvist & Wiksell, (1964-80).

1st edn. 5 vols. Orig wraps, chipped. *(Bookpress)* **$250 [≈£167]**

Thoreau, Henry D.
- Night and Moonlight. New York: Hubert Rutherford Brown, 1921. One of 400. 16mo. W'cut by Florence Ivins. Orig bds, sl rubbed. Designed by Bruce Rogers. *(The Veatchs)* **$45 [≈£30]**

Thorn, C. Jordan
- Handbook of Old Pottery and Porcelain Marks. New York: Tudor, 1947. xiii,176 pp. 44 plates, num ills. Orig cloth gilt. Dw (sl worn). *(Hollett)* **£28 [≈$42]**

Thornbury, Walter
- Historical & Legendary Ballads & Songs. Boston: W.F. Gill, 1876. 4to. 280 pp. 81 ills, 4 w'engvs of Whistler designs. Orig dec cloth. *(Rona Schneider)* **$80 [≈£53]**
- The Life of J.M.W. Turner, R.A. London: Hurst & Blackett, 1862. 1st edn. 2 vols. 8vo. Frontis. Contemp half calf, spines faded. *(Spelman)* **£120 [≈$180]**
- The Life of J.M.W. Turner. London: Chatto & Windus, 1877. 2nd edn. xix,636 pp. 8 cold plates, 2 w'cuts. Orig cloth, front hinge sl weak. *(Fine Art)* **£25 [≈$38]**

Thorne, Edward
- Decorative Draperies & Upholstery. Grand Rapids: The Dean-Hicks Co., 1929. 4to. 277 pp. 74 cold plates. Orig cloth. *(Rona Schneider)* **$100 [≈£67]**

Thornton, Peter
- Authentic Decor: The Domestic Interior 1620-1920. London: Weidenfeld & Nicolson, 1984. 408 pp. 532 ills. Orig cloth. Dw. *(Fine Art)* **£45 [≈$68]**

Thorold, Anne
- A Catalogue of the Paintings of Lucien Pissarro. London: Athelney Books, 1983. One of 400. xx,252 pp. Num ills. Orig cloth. Slipcase. *(Leicester Art Books)* **£120 [≈$180]**

Thorp, Joseph
- Eric Gill. New York: Cape & Smith, 1929. 4to. vii,27 pp. 38 plates. Orig cloth. *(Oak Knoll)* **$75 [≈£50]**

Thorpe, Mary & Charlotte
- London Church Staves. With Some Notes on their Surroundings. London: Elliot Stock, 1895. Lge 8vo. xiii,76 pp. Ills. Orig cloth gilt, sl soiled. *(Hollett)* **£25 [≈$38]**

Thorpe, William A.
- English Glass. London: A. & C. Black, 1967. 3rd edn. 8vo. 305 pp. 104 b/w plates. Price-clipped dw. *(Paul Brown)* **£20 [≈$30]**
- English & Irish Glass, with an Introduction. London: Medici Society, 1927. 4to. xii,35 pp. 65 plates. Orig cloth gilt. Dw (sl defective). *(Fenning)* **£21.50 [≈$33]**

Thurlocke, A.R.
- The Rustic Choir and Other Poems. Cranleigh: The Samurai Press, 1908. One of 300. 8vo. [2],54 pp. Orig buckram backed bds, sl soiled, label rubbed. *(Claude Cox)* **£25 [≈$38]**

Thurston, Ada & Buehler, Curt F.
- Check List of Fifteenth Century Printing in The Pierpont Morgan Library. New York: Pierpont Morgan Library, 1939. Roy 8vo. xv,[i], 348 pp. Orig cloth gilt. *(Blackwell's)* **£65 [≈$98]**

Tidcombe, Marianne
- The Bookbindings of T.J. Cobden-Sanderson. London: The British Library, 1984. 1st edn. 4to. 407 pp. Num plates & ills. Orig cloth. Slipcase. *(Bookpress)* **$115 [≈£77]**

Tidy, Gordon
- A Little about Leech. London: Constable, 1931. 4to. 91,[1] pp. 14 mtd plates. Orig cloth. Dw. *(Cooper Hay)* **£28 [≈$42]**

Tietze, Hans
- Tintoretto. The Paintings and Drawings. London: 1948. 4to. 383 pp. 300 ills. Orig cloth, sl soiled, crnr sl bumped. *(Washton)* **$60 [≈£40]**
- Titian. The Paintings and Drawings. London: 1950. 2nd edn, rvsd. Num ills. Dw (sl rubbed & frayed). *(Adam Blakeney)* **£35 [≈$53]**

Tietze-Conrat, E.
- Mantegna. Paintings, Drawings, Engravings. London: Phaidon, 1955. 258 pp. 7 cold plates, 200 ills. Orig cloth. *(Leicester Art Books)* **£60 [≈$90]**

Tilley, F.
- Teapots and Tea. Newport: Ceramic Book Co., 1957. One of 1000. Lge 4to. xv,135 pp. 10 cold & 205 b/w plates. Orig cloth gilt, spine dulled, rear cvr stained. *(Clevedon Books)* **£105 [≈$158]**

Timm, Werner

- The Graphic Art of Edvard Munch. Greenwich: New York Graphic Society, (1969). 4to. 314 pp. 185 ills. Orig cloth. Dw (sm piece missing hd of spine). *(Abacus)* **$85 [≈£57]**
- The Graphic Work of Edvard Munch. London: Studio Vista, 1973. 2nd edn. 316 pp. 186 plates, 65 ills. Orig cloth. Dw. *(Leicester Art Books)* **£35 [≈$53]**

Timperley, Charles Henry

- A Dictionary of Printers and Printing, with the Progress of Literature ... Bibliographical Illustrations ... London: H. Johnson, 1839. 1st edn. Roy 8vo. vi,996 pp. 11 plates. Orig cloth, backstrip relaid, label sl rubbed & browned. *(Claude Cox)* **£135 [≈$203]**
- Encyclopaedia of Literary and Typographical Anecdote ... Second Edition ... Continuation ... London: Bohn, 1842. Sm folio. Plates, ills. Inner hinges strengthened. Orig cloth, spine faded. *(Jarndyce)* **£240 [≈$360]**

Tindale, Thomas Keith & Tindale, Harriet Ramsay

- The Handmade Papers of Japan. Introduction by Dard Hunter. Rutland & Tokyo: Tuttle, 1952. One of 150. 4 vols. Japanese-style dec wraps over bds with bone thongs. Fldg cloth case. Plus envelope of 5 fibre samples. Outer folder worn. *(The Veatchs)* **$7,000 [≈£4,667]**

Tinker, Chauncey B. & Pottle, Frederick A.

- A New Portrait of James Boswell. Cambridge: Harvard UP, 1927. 4to. 17 pp. 10 plates. Light offsetting on front endpapers. Orig cloth backed bds. Plain dw. Designed by Bruce Rogers. *(The Veatchs)* **$175 [≈£117]**

Tipping, H. Avray

- English Gardens. London: 1925. Folio. lxiv,375 pp. 590 ills. Orig cloth, a.e.g., spine sl faded. *(Henly)* **£145 [≈$218]**
- English Gardens. London: Country Life, 1925. 1st edn. Folio. lxiv,375 pp. 590 ills. Orig cloth, spine sunned, some dampstaining lower tips. Dw (worn). *(Bookpress)* **$295 [≈£197]**
- English Gardens. London: Country Life, 1925. 1st edn. Folio. lxiv,375 pp. Frontis, 590 ills. Orig cloth, sunned. Glassine dw. *(Bookpress)* **$395 [≈£263]**
- English Homes of the Early Renaissance. Elizabethan and Jacobean Houses and Gardens. London: Country Life, n.d. Folio. lxiv,423,16 pp. Ills. Orig cloth gilt, spine ends sl frayed. *(Hollett)* **£120 [≈$180]**
- English Homes. Period III. Vol. I. Late Tudor and Early Stuart 1558-1649. London: 1922. Folio. Num ills. Orig buckram. *(Traylen)* **£75 [≈$113]**
- English Homes. Period IV. Vol. I. Late Stuart 1649-1714. London: 1929. Folio. Num ills. Orig buckram. *(Traylen)* **£75 [≈$113]**

Toesca, Pietro

- Pietro Cavallini. London: Oldbourne Press, 1960. 22 pp. 25 cold & 18 b/w plates. Orig cloth. *(Leicester Art Books)* **£28 [≈$42]**
- San Vitale of Ravenna, the Mosaics. Preface by Marcel Brion. London: Collins, 1954. One of 250. Lge 4to. Dw. *(Mermaid Books)* **£36 [≈$54]**

Tokyo National Museum

- Pageant of Japanese Art ... Painting; Sculpture; Ceramics and Metalwork; Textiles and Lacquer; Architecture and Gardens. Edited by Staff Members of the Tokyo National Museum. Tokyo: 1952-54. 6 vols. Folio. 300 plates. Few sm marks. Orig cloth. Dws. *(Bw Windows)* **£275 [≈$413]**

Toller, Ernst

- Brockenbrow. A Tragedy ... Translated by Vera Mendel with Drawings by Georg Grosz. London: Nonesuch Press, [1926]. 1st English edn. Sm 4to. 50 pp. 6 litho plates. Orig dec bds, uncut, overlapping edge at hd of spine chipped away. *(Claude Cox)* **£65 [≈$98]**

Tolnay, Charles de

- The Drawings of Pieter Bruegel the Elder. (With a Critical Catalogue). London: Zwemmer, 1952. 95 pp. 96 plates. Orig cloth. Dw (sl torn). *(Leicester Art Books)* **£45 [≈$68]**
- Hieronymus Bosch. Second Impression. London: Eyre Methuen, 1975. 4to. 451,[2] pp. Cold plates, b/w ills. Orig cloth. Dw (sl worn). *(Spelman)* **£50 [≈$75]**
- Hieronymus Bosch. London: Methuen, 1966. 4to. 451 pp. Mtd cold plates, b/w ills. Orig cloth. Slipcase. *(Leicester Art Books)* **£75 [≈$113]**

Tolstoy, Leo

- Childhood, Boyhood, Youth. Wood Engravings by Fritz Eichenberg. New York:

The Limited Editions Club, 1972. One of 1500 signed by the illustrator. Tall 8vo. Orig cloth. Slipcase. *(Oak Knoll)* **$75 [≈£50]**
- Resurrection. Illustrated with Wood Engravings by Fritz Eichenberg. New York: The Limited Editions Club, 1963. One of 1500 signed by the illustrator. Sm 4to. Orig cloth (rubbed). Slipcase (spotted). *(Oak Knoll)* **$85 [≈£57]**

Tomkins, Calvin
- Off the Wall. Robert Rauschenberg and the Art World of our time. Garden City: Doubleday, 1980. 4to. x,[2], 324 pp. 40 plates. Orig cloth. Dw. *(Ars Libri)* **$35 [≈£23]**

Tomory, Peter
- The Life and Art of Henry Fuseli. London: Thames & Hudson, 1972. 255 pp. 13 cold plates, 254 ills. Name. Orig cloth. Dw. *(Fine Art)* **£55 [≈$83]**

Tompkins, Herbert W.
- In Constable's Country. London: Dent, 1906. 1st edn. 16 cold plates. Orig dec cloth. *(Old Cathay)* **£59 [≈$89]**

Topolski, Felix
- Topolski's Buckingham Palace Panoramas. London: Quartet Books, 1977. One of 100 specially bound for Asprey. Orig gilt dec blue mor, slipcase, fine. *(Old Cathay)* **£125 [≈$188]**

The Torch
- The Torch, Number One. A Journal produced by Students of the City of Birmingham School of Printing. Edited by Leonard Jay. Birmingham: 1933. 22 plates, text ills. Orig bds, crnrs bumped. *(Cooper Hay)* **£30 [≈$45]**

Toulouse-Lautrec, Henri de
- One Hundred and Ten Unpublished Drawings. Boston: Boston Book & Art Shop, 1955. One of 1500. 15 pp. 110 ills. Orig cloth. Slipcase. *(Clarice Davis)* **$150 [≈£100]**
- A Suite of Color Drawings. At the Circus. New York: Abrams, 1967. 7 pp text pamphlet. 21 plates. Loose in bds portfolio. *(Clarice Davis)* **$125 [≈£83]**

Towner, D.
- Creamware. London: Faber, 1978. 240 pp. 104 plates. Orig cloth. Dw. *(Castle Bookshop)* **£22.50 [≈$35]**
- English Cream Coloured Earthenware. London: Faber, 1957. xv,107 pp. 100 plates. Ex-lib. Orig cloth. Dw (sl torn). *(Castle Bookshop)* **£16 [≈$24]**

Toynbee, J.M.C.
- Art in Roman Britain. London: Phaidon, 1962. 219 pp. 261 plates. Orig cloth. Dw. *(Castle Bookshop)* **£32 [≈$48]**
- Art in Roman Britain. London: Phaidon, 1962. 4to. [vi],219 pp. 260 ills. Occas lib stamp. Dw (sl chipped). *(Francis Edwards)* **£27 [≈$41]**

Tracy, Charles
- English Gothic Choir-Stalls 1200-1400. London: Boydell Press, 1987. 1st edn. Lge 4to. xxiv,82 pp. 242 ills. Orig cloth gilt. Dw. Author's presentation copy *(Hollett)* **£45 [≈$68]**

Trade catalogues
- Hooper & Ashby Ltd.: Catalogue. Southampton: [ca 1925]. Thick 4to. 912 pp. Num ills inc cold. Orig cloth, shaken, sl stained. *(Traylen)* **£35 [≈$53]**
- Maggs Bros.: Bookbinding in Great Britain Sixteenth to the Twentieth Century. London: Maggs Bros, Cat 966, 1975. 4to. 292 pp. Num ills. Cloth backed bds, orig wraps bound in. *(Robertshaw)* **£35 [≈$53]**
- Maggs Bros.: A Selection of Books, Manuscripts, Engravings and Autograph Letters remarkable for their Interest and Beauty: Being the Five Hundredth Catalogue ... London: Maggs Bros, 1928. Folio. 375 pp. 225 plates. Orig wraps (hd of spine worn). *(Oak Knoll)* **$50 [≈£33]**
- Pearson, J., & Co.: Catalogue Descriptive of Books and Armorial Bindings of Exceptional Rarity, Beauty and Importance. London: n.d. Sm 4to. 210 pp. Orig wraps, bumped, some tears. *(Oak Knoll)* **$65 [≈£43]**
- Quaritch, Bernard: A Catalogue of Foreign and English Bookbindings ... London: 1921. 4to. 6 cold & 80 b/w plates. Orig ptd bds, ft of spine sl worn. *(Rankin)* **£85 [≈$128]**
- Quaritch, Bernard: Bernard Quaritch's Catalogue, Examples of the Art of Bookbinding and Volumes bearing Marks of Distinguished Ownership ... London: 1897. 8vo. 158,[2] pp. Orig wraps, sl worn. *(Oak Knoll)* **$55 [≈£37]**
- Quaritch, Bernard: Bookbinding. A Catalogue of Fifteen Hundred Books remarkable for the Beauty or the Age of their Bindings ... London: 1888. 8vo . 200 pp. Orig wraps (worn). *(Oak Knoll)* **$55 [≈£37]**

Trappes-Lomax, M.

- Pugin, a Medieval Victorian. London: Sheed & Ward, 1932. 1st edn. viii,358 pp. 8 plates. Orig cloth gilt. *(Clevedon Books)* **£32 [≈$48]**

Tredgold, Thomas

- Practical Essay on the Strength of Cast Iron and Other Metals ... The Fifth Edition, edited, with Notes ... by Eaton Hodgkinson ... London: John Weale, 1860-61. 8vo. ix,384, 32 pp. 6 plates. Orig cloth gilt, faded. *(Hollett)* **£140 [≈$210]**

Tree, Iris

- The Marsh Picnic. With an Introduction by John Betjeman. Cambridge: Rampant Lions Press, 1966. One of 300. Orig bds, uncut. *(Claude Cox)* **£35 [≈$53]**

Triggs, H. Inigo

- Formal Gardens in England and Scotland. London: Batsford, 1902. 1st edn. Folio. xxiv, 63,[1] pp. 122 plates. Contemp half mor. *(Spelman)* **£180 [≈$270]**

Triggs, H. Inigo & Tanner, H.

- Some Architectural Works of Inigo Jones; a Series of Measured Drawings and Other Illustrations ... London: Batsford, 1901. Lge folio. xiv,36 pp. Port frontis, 40 plates, text ills. Orig cloth, rebacked. *(Clevedon Books)* **£190 [≈$285]**

Trivick, Henry

- The Craft and Design of Monumental Brasses. London: John Baker, 1969. 1st edn. 4to. 152 pp. Num ills. Orig cloth gilt. Price-clipped dw. Slipcase. *(Hollett)* **£30 [≈$45]**

Trollope, Anthony

- Barchester Towers. With Introduction by Angela Thirkell. Illustrated by Fritz Kredel. New York: The Limited Editions Club, 1958. One of 1500 signed by the illustrator. Thick 8vo. Orig qtr leather. Slipcase. *(Oak Knoll)* **$85 [≈£57]**
- [The Barsetshire Novels]. Edited by Michael Sadleir. Oxford: Shakespeare Head Press, 1929. One of 525. 14 vols, inc Autobiography. 8vo. Orig buckram, t.e.g., sl used. *(Blackwell's)* **£775 [≈$1,163]**
- Mary Gresley and other Stories ... Wood Engravings by Joan Hassall. London: The Folio Society, 1951. 1st edn thus. Dw. *(Michael Taylor)* **£30 [≈$45]**
- The Parson's Daughter and other Stories ... Wood Engravings by Joan Hassall. London: The Folio Society, 1949. 1st edn thus. Dw (sl worn). *(Michael Taylor)* **£30 [≈$45]**
- The Warden. Introduction by Angela Thirkell. Illustrations by Fritz Kredel. New York: The Limited Editions Club, 1955. One of 1500 signed by the illustrator. 8vo. Orig cloth-backed bds (spine faded). Slipcase. *(Oak Knoll)* **$65 [≈£43]**

Tronche, Anne

- Ljuba. Translated by I. Mark Paris. New York: Alpine Fine Arts Collection, 1981. Lge sq 4to. Cold ills. Orig dec cloth. Dw. *(First Folio)* **$75 [≈£50]**

Trowell, Margaret

- Classical African Sculpture. London: Faber, 1954. 1st edn. Tall 8vo. 103 pp. 2 maps, 48 plates. Orig cloth. Dw. *(Oriental and African)* **£35 [≈$53]**

Tschichold, Jan

- Asymmetric Typography. New York: Reinhold, 1967. 8vo. Ills. Orig cloth. Dw. *(First Folio)* **$65 [≈£43]**

Tsuda, Noritake

- Handbook of Japanese Art. Tokyo: Sanseido, 1935. xiii,525 pp. Map, 10 cold plates, ills. Orig cloth, hinges reinforced with tape, spine faded. *(Schoyer)* **$45 [≈£30]**

Tuer, Andrew W.

- Bartolozzi and his Works. A Biographical & Descriptive Account of the Life and Career of Francesco Bartolozzi, R.A. Second Edition, Corrected and Revised ... London: Field & Tuer, 1885. One of 500 signed by the author. viii, 478 pp. Cvrs worn. *(Leicester Art Books)* **£50 [≈$75]**
- The Book of Delightful and Strange Designs being One Hundred Facsimile Illustrations of the Art of the Japanese Stencil-Cutter ... London: Leadenhall Press, [ca 1895]. Oblong 8vo. 24,27,26 pp. 104 ills. Orig cloth backed bds, stained & marked, jnt cracking. *(Hollett)* **£220 [≈$330]**
- Luxurious Bathing: A Sketch ... Eight Etchings by Tristram Ellis. London: Field & Tuer, 1880. 6th edn. Oblong 8vo. [4],58 pp. Etching on title, 7 plates. Orig vellum over bds, browned. *(Wilkinson)* **£68 [≈$102]**
- Old London Street Cries and the Cries of To-day ... London: Field and Tuer, 1885. 16mo. [ii],137,[7] pp. Hand cold frontis, num ills. Endpapers browned. Orig mrbld bds, rubbed, jnts reprd. *(Blackwell's)* **£45 [≈$68]**
- Old London Street Cries and the Cries of To-day ... London: Leadenhall Press, n.d. Sm sq

8vo. 146 pp. Cold frontis, ills. Orig mrbld bds, paper label, sl worn.
(Rankin) **£22 [≈$33]**

- Quads within Quads for Authors, Editors and Devils. London: Field & Tuer, The Leadenhall Press, 1884. One of 500. 92 pp. Engvd title & frontis. Endpapers sl foxed. Miniature version of same book (4 x 2 cms) laid in at end. Orig vellum gilt, extrs sl rubbed, lacks ties.
(Barbara Stone) **£450 [≈$675]**

Tunnicliffe, C.F.

- Mereside Chronicle. London: 1948. 4to. 200 pp. Ills. Cloth.
(Wheldon & Wesley) **£50 [≈$75]**
- My Country Book. London: 1942. 4to. Num ills. Cloth. Dw.
(Wheldon & Wesley) **£30 [≈$45]**
- Shorelands Summer Diary. London: 1952. 4to. 160 pp. 16 cold plates, 180 ills. Orig cloth. Dw (sl torn).
(Wheldon & Wesley) **£85 [≈$128]**
- Shorelands Summer Diary. London: 1952. 1st edn. Folio. 16 cold plates, num b/w ills. Orig cloth gilt, spine ends v sl rubbed. Dw (extrs chipped).
(Margaret Nangle) **£115 [≈$173]**

Turgenev, Ivan

- Fathers and Sons. New York: Limited Editions Club, 1951. One of 1500, signed by the artist, Fritz Eichenberg. 215 pp. 16 w'engvs. Occas v sl foxing. Orig qtr linen gilt, faint mark on spine. Slipcase.
(Waddington) **£55 [≈$83]**
- The Torrents of Spring. Illustrated by Lajos Szalay. Westport, CT: The Limited Editions Club, 1976. One of 1600 signed by the illustrator. 8vo. Orig qtr leather. Slipcase.
(Oak Knoll) **$55 [≈£37]**

Turnbull, George

- A Curious Collection of Ancient Paintings, accurately engraved from excellent Drawings, by One of the Best Hands at Rome ... London: Birt & Dod, 1744. Folio. [4],42 pp. 55 plates (6 fldg), the last unnumbered & added from the 1740 edn. Occas sl foxing. Contemp calf, rebacked.
(Spelman) **£280 [≈$420]**

Turner, Gerard L'E.

- Collecting Microscopes. Christies South Kensington Collectors Series. London: Studio Vista, 1981. 1st edn. Lge 8vo. 120 pp. Ills. Orig cloth gilt. Dw. *(Hollett)* **£30 [≈$45]**

Turner, Hilary L.

- Town Defences in England and Wales. London: John Baker, 1971. 8vo. 2 maps, 2 plans, 40 ills. Dw. *(David Slade)* **£25 [≈$38]**

Turner, Reginald

- The Spotted Dog. A Book of English Inn Signs. Illustrated by John Farleigh. London: 1948. 1st edn. 28 ills. Orig pict cloth. Dw (shabby). *(Margaret Nangle)* **£22 [≈$33]**

Turner, Silvie & Skiold, Birgit

- Handmade Paper Today. A Worldwide Survey of Mills, Papers, Techniques and Uses. London: Lund Humphries, (1983). One of 200 sgnd. 2 vols. 4to. 280 pp. 45 samples. Orig cloth. Slipcase.
(Oak Knoll) **$400 [≈£267]**

Turner, T. Hudson

- Some Account of Domestic Architecture in England ... Oxford: John Henry Parker, 1851. 2 vols. 8vo. 231 engvs. Occas sl foxing. Half mor, gilt spines, t.e.g.
(Rankin) **£75 [≈$113]**
- Some Account of Domestic Architecture in England, from the Conquest to the End of the Thirteenth Century ... Oxford: John Henry Parker, 1851. 4 vols. 8vo. Num plans, ills. Orig cloth gilt, recased, one bd damp marked. *(Hollett)* **£95 [≈$143]**
- Some Account of the Domestic Architecture in England: From Conquest ... to Richard II. Oxford: Parker, 1877-82. 2 vols. Plates, w'engvs. Ex-lib. Cloth, t.e.g., worn & rubbed. *(Castle Bookshop)* **£28 [≈$42]**

Turner, William

- The Ceramics of Swansea and Nantgarw ... London: Bemrose, 1897. Sm 4to. xii,349 pp. Frontis, 33 plates. Sm blind stamp on title. Orig cloth gilt, sl rubbed, spine darkened & worn at hd. *(Hollett)* **£125 [≈$188]**

Twain, Mark

- Roughing It. Illustrated by Noel Sickles. New York: The Limited Editions Club, 1972. One of 1500 signed by the illustrator. Thick 8vo. Orig cloth-backed bds. Slipcase.
(Oak Knoll) **$65 [≈£43]**

Twelve Parables ...

- Twelve Parables of Our Lord Illustrated and Illuminated ... London: Macmillan, 1870. 1st edn thus. 4to. Chromolitho frontis, illuminated title, 12 chromolitho plates, 12 plates in gold & colours (all mtd on thick card). Orig dec cloth gilt, a.e.g., v sl worn.
(Fenning) **£75 [≈$113]**

Twine, Laurence

- The Patterne of Painefull Adventures ... Gathered into English by Laurence Twine. New Rochelle: The Elston Press, 1903. One of 170. 8vo. 78,[2] pp. Orig cloth over bds, paper label. *(Karmiole)* **$125 [≈£83]**

Twitchett, John & Bailey, Betty

- Royal Crown Derby. London: Barrie & Jenkins, 1976. 1st edn. 4to. 224 pp. Num ills. Orig cloth gilt. Dw. *(Hollett)* **£35 [≈$53]**

Twyman, Michael

- A Directory of London Lithographic Printers 1800-1850. London: PHS, (1976). 8vo. 55,[5] pp. Orig cloth. *(The Veatchs)* **$35 [≈£23]**
- Lithography 1800-1850. The Techniques of Drawing on Stone in England and France ... London: OUP, 1970. Sm 4to. xvi,302 pp. 158 ills. Orig cloth. Dw. *(Mendelsohn)* **$75 [≈£50]**
- Printing 1770-1970, an Illustrated History of its Development and Uses in England. London: Eyre & Spottiswoode 1970. 1st edn. 4to. x,283 pp. Num ills. Orig cloth. Dw (rubbed). *(Bookpress)* **$125 [≈£83]**

Tymms, William R. & Wyatt, M. Digby

- The Art of Illuminating as Practised in Europe from the Earliest Times. London: Day & Son, [1866]. 1st 8vo edn. Roy 8vo. 96 pp. Chromo title & 96 plates in gold & colours. Orig dec cloth gilt, spine sl sunned. *(Ash)* **£75 [≈$113]**

Type specimens

- American Type Founders Co.: Specimen Book and Catalogue. Jersey City: 1923. Thick 4to. 1148 pp. Orig cloth (rubbed). *(Oak Knoll)* **$150 [≈£100]**
- Barnhart Brothers & Spindler: Specimen Book of Type. Chicago: (1900). Thick 4to. 879 pp. Orig cloth (spotted, shaken). *(Oak Knoll)* **$200 [≈£133]**
- Barnhart Brothers & Spindler: Preferred Type Faces. Book Number 10. Chicago: [ca 1913]. Sm oblong 4to. 172 pp. Stain at ft of most pp. Orig cloth (soiled, edges worn). *(Oak Knoll)* **$100 [≈£67]**
- Bauer: Bauer Types in Use. New York: Bauer Alphabets, n.d. Sm 4to. 32 broadsides in portfolio (spine ends worn). *(Oak Knoll)* **$20 [≈£13]**
- Birrell & Garnett: Catalogue of Typefounders' Specimens ... London: 1928. 4to. viii,108 pp. Num ills. Orig wraps, sl soiled. *(Claude Cox)* **£35 [≈$53]**
- Bruce Type Foundry: Our Handy Book of Types, Brass Rule and Cuts, Printing Machinery & General Supplies. New York: (1901). 8vo. xvii,592 pp. Orig cloth (minor chips spine ends). *(Oak Knoll)* **$250 [≈£167]**
- Caslon, H.W. & Co.: Caslon Old Face Roman & Italic. London: (1924). 4to. Port, 3 fldg plates, 53 pp of examples. Orig wraps. *(Traylen)* **£38 [≈$57]**
- Caslon, H.W. & Co.: Caslon Old Face, Roman & Italic ... London: (1929). Lge 4to. 63 pp. Fldg sheet, num ills. Sm lib stamp. Orig wraps. *(Fenning)* **£45 [≈$68]**
- Caslon, William: A Specimen of Printing Types. N.p.: William Caslon, [1786]. Variant A with 4 lines of small music on p 8. Folio. 8 pp. Wraps. Removed from Ephraim Chambers' Cyclopaedia, 1786. *(Oak Knoll)* **$350 [≈£233]**
- Crescent Type Foundry: Specimens of Type, Borders and Ornaments ... Chicago: 1899. 8vo. 673 pp. Frontis. Orig cloth gilt (rubbed, sl shaken). *(Oak Knoll)* **$375 [≈£250]**
- Figgins, V. & J.: Specimen of Printing Types, by V. & J. Figgins, successors to Vincent Figgins ... London: 1839. 8vo. 234 ff. Stain at top edges. Orig cloth (rubbed, spine faded). *(Oak Knoll)* **$1,350 [≈£900]**
- Hansen, H.C.: A Book of Types, Borders, Ornaments, Brass Rule, Printing Material and the Like for Printerdom. Boston: H.C. Hansen Type Foundry, 1909. 4to. 384 pp. Orig cloth. *(Oak Knoll)* **$265 [≈£177]**
- Intertype Corporation: The Book of Intertype Faces. Brooklyn: n.d. Sm 4to. viii, 507,[5] pp. Some soiling. Cloth, metal binder (rubbed). *(Oak Knoll)* **$85 [≈£57]**
- Lanston Monotype Corporation: Pastonchi, a Specimen of a New Letter for Use on the "Monotype". London: (1928). 1st trade edn. 4to. Paper samples. Orig cloth. *(Oak Knoll)* **$125 [≈£83]**
- Miller & Richard: Specimens of Wood Letter. Edinburgh & London: [ca 1900]. Title in red & green, 77,13 ff. Marg brown stain 15 ff. Orig cloth gilt. *(Claude Cox)* **£85 [≈$128]**
- Miller & Richard: Specimens of Book Newspaper Jobbing and Ornamental Types. Edinburgh & London: [ca 1870]. Title, 6-page price list, 131 ff. 2 ff with sections cut away. Sl foxing. Orig cloth gilt, extrs rubbed, sm splits in jnts. *(Claude Cox)* **£110 [≈$165]**

Tyrell-Green, E.

- Parish Church Architecture. London: SPCK,

1931. 8vo. 247 pp. Map, 64 ills. Half-title foxed, occas spotting. Orig cloth gilt. Dw. *(Hollett)* **£30 [≈$45]**

Tyrwhitt, R. St. John

- A Handbook of Pictorial Art ... With a Chapter on Perspective by A. Macdonald. Second Edition. Oxford: Clarendon Press 1875. 8vo. Mtd cold frontis, 10 plates (5 cold). Contemp prize mor. *(Waterfield's)* **£45 [≈$68]**

Uhde, W.

- The Life and Work of Vincent Van Gogh. London: Phaidon, 1936. 1st edn. Lge 4to. 18 pp. 104 plates, text ills. Orig cloth. Dw (frayed). *(Clevedon Books)* **£28 [≈$42]**

Underwood, Paul A.

- The Kariye Djami. New York: Pantheon, (1966). 3 vols. Folio. 329 pp. 553 plates. Orig cloth. Dws. Slipcase. *(Abacus)* **$150 [≈£100]**

Unwin, Raymond & Parker, Barry

- The Art of Building a Home. London: Longmans, Green, 1901. 1st edn. 8vo. [8], 133, [7] pp. 68 plates. Orig buckram, sl rubbed. *(Claude Cox)* **£25 [≈$38]**

Updike, Daniel Berkeley

- In The Day's Work. Cambridge: Harvard UP, 1924. One of 260 signed by the author. 69 pp. 1o ills. B'plate. Orig cloth, paper label, sl worn, spine sunned. Slipcase. *(The Veatchs)* **$85 [≈£57]**
- Notes on the Merrymount Press and its Work, with a Bibliographical List of Books Printed at the Press 1893-1933 by Julian Pearce Smith. Cambridge: Harvard UP, 1934. One of 500. 8vo. 279 pp. Ills. Pencil notes. Orig cloth. *(Hermitage)* **$75 [≈£50]**
- Printing Types. Their History, Forms and Use. A Study in Survivals. Cambridge: Harvard UP, 1951. 2nd edn, 2nd printing. 2 vols. 8vo. Orig cloth. Dws. *(Oak Knoll)* **$135 [≈£90]**
- Printing Types their History, Forms and Use. Cambridge: Harvard UP, 1927. 3rd printing. 2 vols. 367 ills. Orig buckram, t.e.g. *(Claude Cox)* **£85 [≈$128]**

Valentiner, W.R.

- Frans Hals Paintings in America. Westport: Frederick Fairchild Sherman, 1936. One of 200. x,16 pp. 106 plates. Orig cloth & bds. *(Leicester Art Books)* **£60 [≈$90]**
- Tino da Camaino, A Sienese Sculptor of the Fourteenth Century. Paris: 1935. One of 450. Lge 4to. x,168 pp. 83 plates, 28 ills. Front free endpaper replaced. Orig cloth. *(Washton)* **$425 [≈£283]**

Vallance, Aymer

- The Old Colleges of Oxford. Their Architectural History Illustrated and Described. London: Batsford, 1912. Folio. Frontis, engvd title, num plates, text ills. Orig buckram gilt, t.e.g. *(Traylen)* **£55 [≈$83]**
- William Morris, his Art, his Writings and his Public Life. London: Bell, Chiswick Press, 1909. 4th issue. Roy 8vo. xiv,462 pp. Port frontis, cold & other plates, text ills. Orig gilt dec cloth, spine sl faded. *(Clevedon Books)* **£95 [≈$143]**
- William Morris His Art His Writings and His Public Life (1897). London: Studio Editions, (1986). Thick 8vo. xii,462 pp. Ills. Orig cloth. Dw. *(Oak Knoll)* **$55 [≈£37]**

Vallancey, Charles

- The Art of Tanning and Currying Leather; with an Account of all the different processes made use of in Europe and Asia ... London: re-printed for J. Nourse, 1774. 12mo. xx, 244 pp. Contemp calf. Anon. *(Spelman)* **£360 [≈$540]**

Valuable Secrets ...

- Valuable Secrets concerning Arts and Trades. Or Approved Directions, from the best Artists ... London: William Hay, 1775. 1st edn. 16mo. [viii],xxxiv,312 pp. Later half calf. Anon. *(Bookpress)* **$1,100 [≈£733]**
- Valuable Secrets concerning Arts and Trades. Or Approved Directions, from the best Artists ... London: William Hay, 1775. 1st edn. 16mo. [viii],xxxiv,312 pp. Contemp calf. Anon. *(Bookpress)* **$1,350 [≈£900]**
- Valuable Secrets concerning Arts and Trades; or Approved Directions, from the best Artists ... Dublin: James Williams, 1778. 8vo. [viii],xxv ii,[i],312 pp. Contemp calf, spine ends reprd, jnts sl cracked. *(Spelman)* **£350 [≈$525]**

Van Buren, E. Douglas

- Greek Fictile Revetments in the Archaic Period. London: Murray, 1926. 4to. xx,208 pp. 39 plates, map. Hd of spine sl bumped. *(Quest Books)* **£55 [≈$83]**

Van Dyke, Henry J.

- A Prayer for Christmas Morning. London: Ernest Nister ..., [1913]. Sm 8vo. 7 plates. Orig dec padded bds, plain cloth spine.

Tissue dw, fine. *(Fenning)* **£35 [≈$53]**

Van Dyke, John C.

- The Rembrandt Drawings and Etchings. New York & London: Scribner, 1927. One of 1200. Folio. Orig bndg. *(First Folio)* **$50 [≈£33]**

Van Gogh, Vincent

- Letters to an Artist, from Vincent Van Gogh to Anton Ridder van Rappard, 1881-1885. New York: Viking Press, 1936. One of 650. 4to. xxiv,229 pp. 20 plates. Orig cloth. Slipcase (sunned). *(Bookpress)* **$225 [≈£150]**

Van Moe, Emile A.

- The Decorated Letter from the VIIIth to the XIIth Century. Paris: 1950. 4to. 120 pp. Ills. Bds. *(Washton)* **$75 [≈£50]**
- The Decorated Letter from the VIIIth to the XIIth Century. Paris: Editions du Chene, 1950. 1st edn. Folio. 120 pp. Num plates. Orig bds gilt, sl soiled. Dw. *(Karmiole)* **$60 [≈£40]**
- Illuminated Initials in Mediaeval Manuscripts. Translated by Joan Evans. London: Thames & Hudson, (1950). Tall 4to. [4],120 pp. 80 plates. Orig cloth gilt. Dw (chipped). *(Karmiole)* **$85 [≈£57]**

Van Nostrand, Jeanne

- The First Hundred Years of Painting in California 1775-1875. With Biographical Information and references relating to the Artists. San Francisco: 1980. 1st edn. 4to. 135 pp. 42 plates. Orig cloth. Dw. *(Robertshaw)* **£25 [≈$38]**

Van Os, H.W.

- Vecchietta and the Sacristy of the Siena Hospital Church. A Study in Renaissance Religious Symbolism. 's-Gravenhage: 1974. 4to. 109 pp. 59 plates. Orig cloth. Dw. *(Washton)* **$55 [≈£37]**

Varia, Radu

- Brancusi. New York: Rizzoli, 1986. Sm sq folio. 319,[1] pp. Num ills. Orig cloth. Dw. *(Ars Libri)* **$85 [≈£57]**

Vasarely, Victor

- Vasarely. Introduction by Marcel Joray; Texts and Dummy by the Artist Victor Vasarely. Neuchatel: Editions du Griffon, 1965. Lge 4to. 194 pp. Num ills. Orig cloth. *(Ars Libri)* **$100 [≈£67]**

Vasari, G.

- The Lives of the Painters, Sculptors & Architects. London: 1900. 8 vols. 12mo. Engvd titles. Orig cloth, gilt spines. *(Traylen)* **£20 [≈$30]**

Vaughan, Keith

- Journal & Drawings 1939-1965. London: Alan Ross, 1966. 1st edn. 224 pp. Num ills. Orig buckram, sm mark on edges, tiny bruises at crnrs. Dw. *(Bookworks)* **£95 [≈$143]**

Vaughan, Malcolm

- Derain. New York: Hyperion Press, (1941). 1st edn. Sm folio. 76,[2] pp. Frontis, ills. Endpapers browned, occas foxing. Orig cloth. Dw (chipped & rubbed). *(Bookpress)* **$50 [≈£33]**
- Derain. New York: Hyperion Press, 1941. Sm folio. 76,[2] pp. Num ills. Orig cloth. *(Ars Libri)* **$37.50 [≈£25]**

Vaux, Calvert

- Villas and Cottages. A Series of Designs prepared for execution in the United States. New York: Harper, 1867. 2nd edn. 8vo. 348 pp. One cold plate, num engvd ills. Orig cloth, spine ends sl bumped. *(Sotheran's)* **£125 [≈$188]**

Venables, Edmund, & others

- Episcopal Palaces of England. London: Isbister, 1895. 1st edn. 4to. 253,[ii] pp. Etched frontis, num ills by Alexander Ansted. Orig dec cloth gilt, crnrs trifle worn. *(Hollett)* **£45 [≈$68]**

Venedikov, I. & Gerassimov, T.

- Thracian Art Treasures. London: Caxton, 1975. 4to. 388 pp. Num ills. Orig cloth. *(Quest Books)* **£18 [≈$27]**

Venturi, Adolfo

- Botticelli. London: Zwemmer, 1927. 4to. 137 pp. 192 plates. Orig cloth. *(Abacus)* **$75 [≈£50]**

Venturi, Lionello

- Italian Painters of Today. New York: Universe Books, [1959]. Lge 4to. 174,[6] pp. 66 mtd cold plates. Orig cloth. Dw. *(Ars Libri)* **$85 [≈£57]**

Venturi, Lionello & Skira-Venturi, Rosabianca

- Italian Painting. The Creators of the Renaissance. Geneva: Skira, 1950. Lge 4to.

205 pp. Mtd cold plates. Orig cloth, sl spotted. Dw (worn). *(First Folio)* **$85 [≈£57]**

Verard, Antoine & MacFarlane, John
- Antoine Verard. London: Chiswick Press for the Bibl. Soc., 1900. 4to. Frontis, 79 ills. Orig linen backed bds. *(Traylen)* **£90 [≈$135]**

Verity, Frank T., & others
- Flats, Urban Houses, and Cottage Homes. London: Hodder & Stoughton, (1906). 1st edn. 4to. 160,[16] pp. Frontis, 18 cold plates. Sl foxed. Orig cloth, worn. *(Bookpress)* **$95 [≈£63]**

Verlviet, Hendrik D.L. (editor)
- The Book through Five Thousand Years ... London: Phaidon, (1972). Thick 4to. 496,[2] pp. 254 ills. Orig cloth. Dw (few tears). *(Karmiole)* **$150 [≈£100]**

Verne, Jules
- Around the World in Eighty Days. With Illustrations by Edward A. Wilson. New York: The Limited Editions Club, 1962. One of 1500 signed by the illustrator. Tall 8vo. Orig qtr parchment (spine ends yellowed). Slipcase. *(Oak Knoll)* **$85 [≈£57]**
- From the Earth to the Moon and Around the Moon. Illustrations by Robert Shore. New York: The Limited Editions Club, 1970. One of 1500 signed by the illustrator. 2 vols. Tall 8vo. Orig cloth-backed bds (sl rubbed). Slipcase. *(Oak Knoll)* **$75 [≈£50]**
- A Journey to the Center of the Earth. Introduction by Isaac Asimov. Illustrations by Edward A. Wilson. New York: The Limited Editions Club, 1966. One of 1500 signed by the illustrator. Tall 8vo. Orig qtr leather. Slipcase. *(Oak Knoll)* **$55 [≈£37]**
- The Mysterious Island. With an Introduction by Ray Bradbury and with Illustrations by Edward A. Wilson. New York: The Limited Editions Club, 1959. One of 1500 signed by the illustrator. Thick 8vo. Orig pict cloth (spine rubbed). Slipcase (spotted). *(Oak Knoll)* **$55 [≈£37]**
- Twenty Thousand Leagues under the Sea. With Hand-colored Illustrations by Edward A. Wilson. New York: The Limited Editions Club, 1956. One of 1500 signed by the illustrator. 8vo. Orig qtr leather (jnts rubbed). Slipcase. *(Oak Knoll)* **$50 [≈£33]**

Vertes, Marcel
- Variations. Greenwich: New York Graphic Society. 1961. One of 1000. Lge 4to. 115 ills. Orig pict cloth. Dw. *(Barbara Stone)* **£95 [≈$143]**

Vertue, George
- A Catalogue of Engravers, who have been born in, or resided in England ... From the MSS of Mr. George Vertue ... added, An Account of the Life and Works of the latter ... by Horace Walpole. London: Dodsley, 1782. 8vo. 304,[6] pp. Contemp calf, gilt spine, extrs sl rubbed. *(Young's)* **£55 [≈$83]**
- A Description of the Works of the Ingenious Delineator and Engraver Wenceslaus Hollar ... The Second Edition, with Additions. London: for William Bathoe, 1759. 4to. vi, engvd title, 152 pp. Title vignette, engvd table, 3 vignettes. Mod wraps. *(Rankin)* **£135 [≈$203]**

Villiers, David
- A Winter Firework. Golden Cockerel Press: 1937. One of 150. Ils by Osbert Lancaster. Orig buckram backed cloth. *(Ulysses Bookshop)* **£145 [≈$218]**

Villiers De L'Isle Adam, J.M.M.P.A., Count
- Axel. Translated by H.P.R. Finberg with Preface by W.B. Yeats. Illustrated by T. Sturge Moore. London: Jarrolds, 1925. One of 500 sgnd by Finberg. 8vo. Orig gilt dec cloth, t.e.g., spine sl darkened. *(First Folio)* **$350 [≈£233]**

Villon, Francois
- The Ballads. San Francisco: Windsor Press, 1927. One of 200. [38] pp. 2 cold ills inc title. Orig vellum gilt, somewhat soiled, sl rubbed. *(Karmiole)* **$125 [≈£83]**
- The Lyrics. With an Introduction by Leonie Adams. The Wood-blocks cut by Howard Simon. New York: The Limited Editions Club, 1933. One of 1500 signed by the illustrator. Sm 4to. Orig cloth, leather label, t.e.g. Slipcase (label reprd). *(Oak Knoll)* **$85 [≈£57]**

Vincent, J.
- Country Cottages: a Series of Designs for an Improved Class of Dwellings for Agricultural Labourers ... London: Hardwicke, 1861. 2nd edn. Folio. 21 litho plates. Some foxing & staining. Orig dec cloth, marked. *(Monmouth)* **£100 [≈$150]**

Vincent, Keith
- Nailsea Glass. Newton Abbott: David & Charles, 1975. Cr 4to. 112 pp. 118 b/w plates. Dw. *(Paul Brown)* **£25 [≈$38]**

Vinycomb, John
- Fictitious and Symbolic Creatures in Art,

with special reference to their use in British Heraldry. London: Chapman, 1906. 276 pp. Ills. Orig bndg. *(Emerald Isle)* **£25 [≈$38]**

Voet, Leon

- The Plantin Press (1555-1589). Amsterdam: Van Hoeve, 1980-83. 1st edn. 6 vols. 8vo. Orig cloth. *(Bookpress)* **$2,090 [≈£1,393]**

Voices on the Green ...

- Voices on the Green. A Miscellany of Prose and Poetry. London: 1945. 1st edn. W'engvs by Ravilious, A. Miller Parker, &c. Orig cloth. Dw. *(Margaret Nangle)* **£18 [≈$27]**

Voltaire, Francois Marie Arouet

- Candide or Optimism. Translated by Richard Aldington ... Illustrations by May Neama. New York: The Limited Editions Club, 1973. One of 1500 signed by the illustrator. Sm 4to. Orig leather-backed bds. Slipcase. *(Oak Knoll)* **$55 [≈£37]**
- Candide or Optimism. Translated by Richard Aldington ... Twenty Illustrations in Colour By Sylvain Sauvage. London: Nonesuch Press, 1939. 1st edn. 8vo. xx,148 pp. Ills. Orig buckram backed dec cloth. Card slipcase. *(Claude Cox)* **£35 [≈$53]**
- History of Zadig or Destiny, an Oriental Tale. Decorations by Sylvain Sauvage. New York: The Limited Editions Club, 1952. One of 1500 numbered. 8vo. Orig cloth (sm chip hd of spine). Slipcase. *(Oak Knoll)* **$55 [≈£37]**
- Poem upon the Lisbon Disaster. Translated into English by Anthony Hecht with Six Wood Engravings by Lynd Ward. London: Penmaen Press, 1977. One of 100 signed. Orig half cloth & mrbld bds. *(Barbara Stone)* **£195 [≈$293]**

Von Hagen, Victor Wolfgang

- The Aztec and Maya Papermakers. With an Introduction by Dard Hunter. New York: J.J. Augustin, (1944). 1st trade edn. 8vo. [x],120 pp. Mtd sample frontis, 39 plates. Orig cloth. Dw (sl chipped). *(Oak Knoll)* **$125 [≈£83]**
- The Aztec and Maya Papermakers. New York: Augustin, (1944). 1st trade edn. Frontis, 39 photo plates. Dw. *(Hermitage)* **$150 [≈£100]**

Von Neumann, Robert

- The Design and Creation of Jewelry. London: Pitman, 1968. Reprint. 228 pp. Num ills. Orig cloth. Dw (soiled). *(Willow House)* **£20 [≈$30]**

Von Simpson, Otto

- Sacred Fortress. Byzantine Art and Statecraft in Ravenna. Chicago: 1948. 4to. xv,148 pp. 48 plates. Orig cloth, sl spotted. *(Washton)* **$50 [≈£33]**

Voorn, Henk

- Old Ream Wrappers. North Hills: Bird & Bull Press, 1969. One of 375. Sm4to. 2 copperplate prints laid into separate folder. Orig leather backed bds. Parchment dw. Slipcase. Inscrbd by Henry Morris. *(Dermont)* **$450 [≈£300]**

Vriesen, Gustav & Imdahl, Max

- Robert Delaunay: Light and Color. New York: Abrams, [1969]. Lge 4to. 116 pp. 86 ills, 13 text figs. Orig cloth. Dw. *(Ars Libri)* **$125 [≈£83]**

Vuilleumier, Bernard

- The Art of Silk Weaving in China: Symbolism of Chinese Imperial Ritual Robes. London: China Institute, 1939. 4to. 34 pp. Frontis, 14 plates. Orig wraps, sl worn. *(McBlain)* **$65 [≈£43]**

Waagen, Gustav F.

- Treasures of Art in Great Britain ... London: Murray, 1854. 3 vols. 8vo. Orig cloth, sm lib labels on upper bds, inner jnts reprd. *(Fenning)* **£195 [≈$293]**

Wadsworth, Barbara

- Edward Wadsworth. A Painter's Life. Salisbury: M. Russell, 1989. 416 pp. Ills. Orig cloth. *(Fine Art)* **£28 [≈$42]**

Wagner, Richard

- The Flying Dutchman. London: Corvinus Press, 1938. One of 130. 4to. Orig vellum gilt, sl soiled. *(Karmiole)* **$175 [≈£117]**
- Lohengrin; Parsifal ... see Rolleston, T.W.
- The Rhinegold & The Valkyrie. Illustrated by Arthur Rackham. London: Heinemann, 1910. 1st edn. 4to. Dec title, 34 mtd cold plates. Some foxing. Orig gilt dec cloth. Dw (worn but complete). *(Jo Ann Reisler)* **$335 [≈£223]**
- Siegfried & The Twilight of the Gods. Illustrated by Arthur Rackham. New York: Doubleday Page, 1911. 1st Amer edn. 4to. 30 mtd cold plates, num b/w ills. Orig cloth backed bds gilt, few tiny brown spots. *(Jo Ann Reisler)* **$285 [≈£190]**
- Tannhauser. A Dramatic Poem. Illustrated by Willy Pogany. London: Harrap, 1911. One of 525 signed by Pogany. 4to. 16 mtd

cold plates, ills. Orig blind stamped grey calf, t.e.g., fine. Orig box.
(Barbara Stone) **£500 [≈$750]**

Wailes, Rex

- The English Windmill. With Drawings by Vincent Lines. London: (1954). 1st edn. 8vo. [xxiv],246 pp. Num ills. Orig cloth. Dw. *(Bow Windows)* **£45 [≈$68]**
- Windmills in England. London: 1948. 1st edn. 4to. 48 pp. Ills. Orig cloth. Dw (worn). signed by the author. *(Monmouth)* **£20 [≈$30]**
- Windmills in England. London: Architectural Press, 1948. 1st edn. 4to. viii,48 pp. Ills. Orig cloth gilt. Dw (sm repr, sl marked). *(Clevedon Books)* **£33 [≈$50]**

Wakefield, Hugh

- 19th Century British Glass. London: Faber, 1961. Roy 8vo. 64 pp. 4 cold & 171 b/w plates. Price-clipped dw. *(Paul Brown)* **£30 [≈$45]**

Wakeman, Geoffrey

- A Leaf History of British Printing, from 1610 to 1774. (Oxford): The Plough Press, 1986. One of 100. Folio. [6] pp. 10 folders. Linen fldg box, leather label. *(Karmiole)* **$250 [≈£167]**
- Printing Relief Illustrations, Kirkall to the Line Block. The Plough Press: 1977. One of 100. Sm 4to. 29 pp. Plates, 6 tipped-in specimens. Orig cloth. *(Oak Knoll)* **$225 [≈£150]**
- Victorian Book Illustration; The Technical Revolution. Newton Abbot: David & Charles, (1973). 1st edn. 8vo. 182 pp. Orig cloth. Dw. *(Bookpress)* **$95 [≈£63]**
- Victorian Colour Printing. Loughborough: The Plough Press, 1981. One of 150. 4to. 35, [5] pp. 8 plates, prints in pocket. Orig leather & mrbld bds. *(Oak Knoll)* **$425 [≈£283]**

Wakeman, Geoffrey & Bridson, Gavin D.R.

- A Guide to Nineteenth Century Colour Printers. Loughborough: The Plough Press, (1975). 1st edn. 8vo. xii,127 pp. Orig cloth. Dw. *(Oak Knoll)* **$95 [≈£63]**

Waldberg, Patrick

- Rene Magritte. Bruxelles: Andre de Rache, 1965. 357 pp. Num ills. Orig cloth. Dw (chipped). *(Leicester Art Books)* **£100 [≈$150]**

Waldman, Diane

- Anthony Caro. Oxford: Phaidon, 1982. 232 pp. 309 ills (97 cold). Orig cloth. Dw. *(Leicester Art Books)* **£55 [≈$83]**
- Ellsworth Kelly. Drawings, Collages, Prints. Greenwich: New York Graphic Society, 1971. One of 100 signed by Kelly. Sm folio. 287 pp. 240 ills. Lacks the original lithograph. Orig cloth, sl water spotting. *(Ars Libri)* **$900 [≈£600]**
- Robert Ryman. New York: Guggenheim Museum, 1972. Sm sq 4to. (48) pp. Num ills. Orig wraps. *(Ars Libri)* **$50 [≈£33]**
- Rothko: A Retrospective. New York: Abrams, 1978. 1st edn. Folio. 296 pp. Num ills. Dw. *(Between the Covers)* **$165 [≈£110]**
- Roy Lichtenstein. Drawings and Prints. London: Thames & Hudson, 1971. 256 pp. 177 ills. Orig cloth. Dw. *(Leicester Art Books)* **£120 [≈$180]**
- Roy Lichtenstein. London: Thames & Hudson, 1971. 248 pp. 183 ills. Orig cloth. Dw. *(Leicester Art Books)* **£90 [≈$135]**
- Roy Lichtenstein: Drawings and Prints. New York: Chelsea House, [1970]. Lge 4to. 256 pp. Num ills. Orig cloth. Dw. *(Ars Libri)* **$350 [≈£233]**
- Roy Lichtenstein. New York: Abrams, 1971. Lge sq 4to. 248 pp. 183 plates. Orig cloth. Dw. *(Ars Libri)* **$1,000 [≈£667]**

Waldron, Peter

- The Price Guide to Antique Silver. Antique Collectors' Club: 1982. 2nd edn. 4to. 365 pp. Ills. Orig cloth gilt. Dw. *(Hollett)* **£25 [≈$38]**

Walker, A. Katharine

- An Introduction to the Study of English Fonts, with Details of those in Sussex. London: Woodford Fawcett & Co., 1908. xii,130 pp. Map, 125 ills. Endpapers sl spotted. Orig cloth gilt, extrs v sl rubbed. Inscribed by the author. *(Hollett)* **£60 [≈$90]**

Walker, Frederick & Pinwell, G.J.

- English Rustic Pictures. Drawn by Frederick Walker and G.J. Pinwell and Engraved by the brothers Dalziel. London: Routledge, [ca 1882]. One of 300. Folio. 32 mtd india proof plates. Orig dec vellum gilt, rubbed. *(Wilkinson)* **£88 [≈$132]**

Walker, R.A.

- Some Unknown Drawings of Aubrey Beardsley Collected and Annotated by R.A. Walker. London: 1923. One of 500. Mtd cold plate, 32 plates. Sl foxing. Orig buckram gilt. *(Fine Art)* **£90 [≈$135]**

Wallace, Lew

- Ben-Hur, A Tale of the Christ. Illustrations

by Joe Mugnaini. New York: The Limited Editions Club, 1960. One of 1500 signed by the illustrator. Sm 4to. Orig qtr leather. Slipcase. *(Oak Knoll)* **$55 [≈£37]**

Wallace, Richard W.

- The Etchings of Salvator Rosa. (A Catalogue Raisonne). Princeton: UP, 1979. xxii,348 pp. 231 ills. Orig cloth. *(Leicester Art Books)* **£48 [≈$72]**

Waller, R.D.

- The Rossetti Family 1824-1854. Manchester: UP, 1932. xii,324 pp. Frontis, 18 plates. Orig cloth. *(Fine Art)* **£30 [≈$45]**

Walpole, Horace

- Anecdotes of Painting in England ... A New Edition, Revised, with Additional Notes by Ralph N. Wornum. London: Bohn, 1862. 3 vols. 8vo. 81 ports, num text w'cuts. Orig cloth. *(Spelman)* **£40 [≈$60]**
- The Castle of Otranto. New York: The Limited Editions Club, 1975. One of 2000 signed by W.S. Lewis. 4to. Orig qtr leather. Slipcase. *(Oak Knoll)* **$55 [≈£37]**

Walpole, Hugh

- The Apple Tree. Four Reminiscences. Golden Cockerel Press: 1932. One of 500 signed by the author. 88 pp. W'engvs by Lynton Lamb. Orig qtr leather, t.e.g., extrs sl worn, sm nick hd of spine. *(Bookworks)* **£58 [≈$87]**

Walpole, Robert

- Aedes Walpolianae: or, a Description of the Collections of Pictures at Houghton-Hall in Norfolk. The Second Edition, with Additions. London: [John Hughs], 1752. 4to. xxxv,[2],38-143 pp. 2 frontis plates, 2 fldg plans, 2 fldg plates. Contemp bds, rec calf spine. *(Spelman)* **£280 [≈$420]**

Walters, H.B.

- Church Bells of England. OUP: 1912. 1st edn. 8vo. xx,400,[iv] pp. 170 ills. Orig cloth. *(Hollett)* **£60 [≈$90]**

Walters, L. d'O. (compiler)

- The Year's at the Spring. An Anthology of Recent Poetry. New York: Brentano's, (1920). 1st Amer edn. Lge 4to. Orig dec cloth. 24 plates (12 cold) by Harry Clarke. Sl foxing. Dw (sm pieces missing upper edge). *(Jo Ann Reisler)* **$275 [≈£183]**

Walters, W.T.

- Notes: Critical & Biographical: Collection of W.T. Walters. [Indianopolis]: 1895. One of 975. 8vo. Contemp three qtr mor gilt, t.e.g. Partly designed by Bruce Rogers. *(The Veatchs)* **$150 [≈£100]**

Walton, Izaak

- The Compleat Angler. Illustrated by Arthur Rackham. Phila: David McKay, [1931]. 1st Amer edn. 4to. 12 cold plates, b/w ills. Orig cloth gilt, t.e.g. Dw (some edge wear). *(Jo Ann Reisler)* **$185 [≈£123]**
- Izaak Walton. His Wallet Booke. London: Field & Tuer, 1885. One of 100 Large Paper. Sm 4to. 112,[8],[48 advt] pp. Hand cold w'cuts. Linen wallets on inner front & rear bds. Prelims sl dusty. Orig vellum, stained, lacks ties, outer hinge cracked. Crawhall. *(Cooper Hay)* **£125 [≈$188]**

Wang, Shi-chieh

- A Garland of Chinese Paintings. Hong Kong: Cafa Company Ltd., 1967. 1st edn. 5 vols. Folio. 200 ills. Sl cockled. Orig cloth gilt, sl watermarked. *(Bookpress)* **$600 [≈£400]**

Ward, Humphry & Roberts, W.

- Romney. A Biographical and Critical Essay. With a Catalogue Raisonne of his Works. London: Thos. Agnew, 1904. One of 350. 2 vols. 78 plates, 2 text ills. Orig qtr mor, t.e.g. *(Leicester Art Books)* **£200 [≈$300]**

Ward-Jackson, Peter

- English Furniture Designs of the Eighteenth Century. London: HMSO, 1958. 1st edn. 4to. 69 pp. 366 ills. Orig buckram gilt. Dw. *(Hollett)* **£45 [≈$68]**

Warde, Beatrice

- The Crystal Goblet. Sixteen Essays on Typography. Cleveland: World Publishing, 1956. 1st US edn. 8vo. 221 pp. Orig cloth (spine faded). *(Oak Knoll)* **$30 [≈£20]**

Warhol, Andy

- The Philosophy of Andy Warhol. (From A to B and Back Again). New York & London: Harcourt, Brace Jovanovich, 1975. Sm 4to. [10], 240 pp. Orig cloth. Dw. *(Ars Libri)* **$50 [≈£33]**

Warhol, Andy & Hackett, Pat

- Popism. The Warhol '60s. New York & London: Harcourt, Brace Jovanovich, 1980. 4to. 310 pp. 16 plates. Orig cloth. Dw. *(Ars Libri)* **$60 [≈£40]**

Wark, Robert R.

- Drawings by Thomas Rowlandson in the

Huntington Collection. San Marino: 1975. ix,398 pp. 6 cold plates, 575 ills. Orig cloth. Dw. *(Fine Art)* **£38 [≈$57]**

Warne, E.J.

- Furniture Mouldings. Full Size Sections of Moulded Details on English Furniture from 1574 to 1820. London: 1923. 4to. xiv pp. 140 plates. Sev lib stamps. Lib cloth. *(Francis Edwards)* **£40 [≈$60]**

Warner, Sylvia Townsend

- Boxwood. Sixteen Engravings by Reynolds Stone. Illustrated in Verse by Sylvia Townsend Warner. London: The Monotype Corporation, 1957. One of 500. Orig bndg. *(Limestone Hills)* **$110 [≈£73]**

Warr, George C.

- Echoes of Hellas. The Tale of Troy & The Story of Orestes ... Presented in 82 Designs by Walter Crane. London: Marcus Ward, 1887-88. 1st edn. 2 vols. Num ills. Orig pict gilt vellum, t.e.g. *(Holtom)* **£135 [≈$203]**

Warren, Peter

- Minoan Stone Vases. Cambridge: UP, 1969. 8vo. xiv,280 pp. 119 plates, ills. Orig cloth. *(Quest Books)* **£25 [≈$38]**

Washington, Booker T.

- Up from Slavery. Illustrations by Denver Gillen. New York: The Limited Editions Club, 1970. One of 1500 signed by the illustrator. 8vo. Orig half cloth. Slipcase. *(Oak Knoll)* **$45 [≈£30]**

Waterer, J.W.

- Leather in Life, Art and Industry. London: Faber, 1966. 4to. 320 pp. 110 plates, 20 figs. Ex-lib. Orig cloth. *(Castle Bookshop)* **£32 [≈$48]**

Waterhouse, Ellis

- Gainsborough. London: 1966. 4to. 296 pp. 292 ills on plates. Orig cloth. Dw. *(Washton)* **$90 [≈£60]**
- Gainsborough. London: Spring Books, 1966. 2nd edn. 296 pp. 8 cold plates, 292 ills. Orig cloth. Dw. *(Leicester Art Books)* **£32 [≈$48]**
- Thomas Gainsborough. London: Edward Hulton, 1958. 1st edn. 4to. 296 pp. 7 cold plates, 292 b/w ills. Dw (worn). *(Spelman)* **£50 [≈$75]**

Watney, Bernard M. & Babbage, Homer D.

- Corkscrews for Collectors. London: Sotheby Parke Bernet, 1983. 2nd imp. 4to. 160 pp. Num ills. Dw. *(Gough)* **£45 [≈$68]**
- Corkscrews for Collectors. London: Sotheby, 1981. 1st edn. Lge 8vo. 150 pp. 20 cold plates, 164 ills. Orig cloth gilt. Dw. *(Hollett)* **£30 [≈$45]**

Watson, Andrew G.

- Catalogue of Dated and Datable Manuscripts c.435-1600 in Oxford Libraries. Oxford: 1984. 2 vols (text & ills). 4to. Orig cloth. *(Traylen)* **£120 [≈$180]**
- The Library of Sir Simon D'Ewes. London: 1966. 8vo. xiv,379 pp. Orig cloth. *(Lamb)* **£20 [≈$30]**

Watson, Rosamund Marriott

- The Art of the House. London: George Bell & Sons, 1897. 1st edn. 8vo. xii,185,[2] pp. Frontis, 7 plates, 32 text ills. Orig cloth, t.e.g., spine sl sunned. *(Bookpress)* **$150 [≈£100]**

Watt, Alexander

- The Art of Paper-Making. New York: Van Nostrand, 1907. 3rd edn. 8vo. xii,260,64 pp. Orig cloth. *(Bookpress)* **$150 [≈£100]**

Wayzgoose

- Wayzgoose One. The Australian Journal of Book Arts. Australia: Wayzgoose Press, 1985. One of 450. 4to. 27 cold plates. Orig wraps. *(Cooper Hay)* **£30 [≈$45]**

Weaver, Sir Lawrence

- Cottages: Their Planning, Design and Materials. London: Country Life, 1926. 8vo. xii,402 pp. Ills. Orig cloth, sl rubbed. *(Cooper Hay)* **£20 [≈$30]**
- The "Country Life" Book of Cottages ... London: Country Life, 1913. 1st edn. x,231,10 pp. 291 ills. Orig cloth gilt, sl used, stain on spine. *(Hollett)* **£35 [≈$53]**
- Lutyens Houses and Gardens. London: Country Life, 1921. 203 pp. 142 photos & plans. Orig cloth backed gilt, minor wear. *(Willow House)* **£45 [≈$68]**
- Small Country Houses of Today. London: Country Life, [1910]. 1st edn. 4to. x, 224, [viii] pp. 309 ills. Orig cloth gilt. *(Hollett)* **£48 [≈$72]**
- Tradition and Modernity in Plasterwork. London: Jackson & Sons, 1928. 1st sep edn. Lge 8vo. 63,[1] pp inc 46 pp ills. Port frontis. Orig parchment backed cloth, sides dust marked. *(Bow Windows)* **£45 [≈$68]**

Webb, M.I.
- Michael Rysbrack Sculptor. London: Country Life, 1954. 242 pp. 94 ills. Orig buckram. *(Leicester Art Books)* **£45 [≈$68]**
- Michael Rysbrack: Sculptor. London: Country Life, 1954. 244 pp. Port frontis, 94 plates. Orig cloth. Dw (torn). *(Fine Art)* **£40 [≈$60]**

Webb, Mary
- Fifty-one Poems. London: 1946. 1st edn. Decs by Joan Hassall. Orig cloth. Dw (sl soiled). *(Margaret Nangle)* **£14 [≈$21]**

Webster, Mary
- Francis Wheatley. Mellon Foundation: 1970. xii,215 pp. Frontis, 156 plates. Orig cloth. Dw (worn). *(Fine Art)* **£20 [≈$30]**

Wedgwood, Josiah
- The Selected Letters. Edited by Ann Finer and George Savage. London: Cory, Adams & Mackay, 1965. 1st edn. Lge 8vo. xii,375 pp. 15 plates. Few pencil marks. Orig cloth. Dw (trifle soiled). *(Hollett)* **£35 [≈$53]**

Wedmore, Frederick
- Etching in England. London: George Bell, 1895. 1st edn. 4to. xiv,184,[1] pp. Frontis, text ills. Occas foxing. Orig cloth backed bds. *(Bookpress)* **$110 [≈£73]**
- Etchings. New York: Putnam, 1911. 1st edn. 44 plates. Orig cloth gilt. *(Hermitage)* **$125 [≈£83]**
- Fine Prints. Edinburgh: John Grant, 1910. 8vo. 267 pp. 15 ills. Orig cloth. *(Rona Schneider)* **$30 [≈£20]**

Weems, Mason L.
- The Life of Washington, together with Curious Anecdotes ... Embellished with Historical Woodcuts by Robert Quackenbush. N.p.: The Limited Editions Club, 1974. On e of 2000 signed by the illustrator. Sm 4to. Orig cloth. Slipcase. *(Oak Knoll)* **$50 [≈£33]**

Weibel, Adele Coulin
- Two Thousand Years of Textiles. The Figured Textiles of Europe and the Near East. New York: 1952. Lge 4to. xii,169 pp. 331 plates. Orig cloth. Dw. Slipcase. *(Washton)* **$175 [≈£117]**
- Two Thousand Years of Textiles. The Figured Textiles of Europe and the Near East. New York: 1952. Lge 4to. xii,169 pp. 331 plates. Orig cloth. Dw. Slipcase. *(Washton)* **$175 [≈£117]**

Weiler, Clemens
- Heads, Faces, Meditations. London: Pall Mall Press, 1971. 140 pp. 76 ills. Orig cloth. *(Leicester Art Books)* **£90 [≈$135]**

Weinberger, Martin
- Michelangelo The Sculptor. London: Routledge; New York: Columbia UP, 1967. 2 vols (text & plates). 144 plates. Orig buckram. Slipcase. *(Leicester Art Books)* **£65 [≈$98]**

Weiner, Lawrence
- Flowed. Halifax: Nova Scotia College of Art & Design, 1971. One of 1036. [30] pp. Orig wraps. *(Ars Libri)* **$50 [≈£33]**
- Having Been Done At. Having Been Done To ... Torino: Editions Sperone, 1972. One of 1000. [112] pp. Orig wraps. *(Ars Libri)* **$50 [≈£33]**
- 10 Works. Paris: Yvon Lambert, [1971]. One of 1000. [88] pp. Orig wraps. *(Ars Libri)* **$65 [≈£43]**

Weinstein, Michael
- Precious and Semi-Precious Stones. London: Pitman, 1929. x,138 pp. Cold frontis, 16 plates. Orig cloth gilt. *(Hollett)* **£25 [≈$38]**

Weir, Julian A.
- Julian Alden Weir. An Appreciation of his Life and Works. The Phillips Publication Number One. New York: Dutton, 1922. 4to. x, 142 pp. Frontis, 24 plates. Orig cloth. *(Karmiole)* **$85 [≈£57]**

Weisberg, Gabriel P.
- The Realist Tradition: French Painting and Drawing, 1830-1900. Cleveland: Cleveland Museum of Art, 1980. 346 pp. 42 cold & 292 b/w ills. Orig cloth. *(Rona Schneider)* **$50 [≈£33]**

Weisse, Franz
- The Art of Marbling. Translated from the German with an Introduction and Fourteen Original Marbled Specimens by Richard J. Wolfe. North Hills: Bird & Bull Press, 1980. One of 300. 4to. 78 pp. 14 specimens, ills. Orig qtr mor. *(The Veatchs)* **$450 [≈£300]**

Weitenkampf, Frank
- Famous Prints. New York: Scribner, 1926. One of 1025. Folio. 70 plates. Orig cloth. *(Rona Schneider)* **$90 [≈£60]**
- How to Appreciate Prints. New York: Moffat, Yard, 1908. 1st edn. 8vo. 330 pp. 33 ills. Orig cloth. *(Rona Schneider)* **$35 [≈£23]**

- How to Appreciate Prints. New York: Moffat, Yard, 1911. 8vo. 330 pp. 33 ills. Orig cloth. *(Rona Schneider)* **$30 [≈£20]**
- How to Appreciate Prints. New York: Moffat, Yard, 1916. 2nd edn, rvsd. 8vo. 330 pp. 33 ills. Orig cloth. *(Rona Schneider)* **$30 [≈£20]**
- The Illustrated Book. Cambridge: Harvard UP, 1938. 1st edn. 314 pp. Orig cloth, crnrs sl bumped. Dw (worn). *(First Folio)* **$75 [≈£50]**
- The Illustrated Book. Cambridge: Harvard UP, 1938. One of 210. 8vo. [xiv],314 pp. 25 plates. Orig cloth, t.e.g. Slipcase. *(Bookpress)* **$200 [≈£133]**

Weitzmann, Kurt

- Age of Spirituality. Late Antique and Early Christian Art, Third to Seventh Century. New York: Metropolitan Museum, 1979. Sm 4to. xxxi,735 pp. 16 cold plates, num ills. Orig cloth. Dw. *(Mendelsohn)* **$100 [≈£67]**
- Greek Mythology in Byzantine Art. Princeton: UP, (1957) 1984. xviii,218 pp. 60 plates. Orig cloth. *(Quest Books)* **£58 [≈$87]**
- The Miniatures of the Sacra Parallela. Parisinus Graecus 923. Princeton: UP, 1979. xiii,272 pp. Cold plate, 162 plates. Orig cloth. *(Quest Books)* **£58 [≈$87]**
- The Miniatures of the Sacra Parallela. Parisinus Graecus 923. Princeton: UP, (1979). 4to. xiv,272 pp. 162 plates. Orig cloth gilt. Dw (sl chipped). *(Karmiole)* **$60 [≈£40]**

Welby, T. Earle

- The Victorian Romantics 1850-1870: The Early Work of Dante Gabriel Rossetti, William Morris, Burne-Jones, Swinburne, Simeon Solomon and their Associates. London: Gerald Howe, 1929. One of 750. x,161 pp. 21 plates. Orig cloth, t.e.g., v sl worn. *(Fine Art)* **£60 [≈$90]**

Wells, H.G.

- Tono-Bungay. Illustrated by Lynton Lamb. New York: The Limited Editions Club, 1960. One of 1500 signed by the illustrator. Tall 8vo. Orig cloth, paper label. *(Oak Knoll)* **$65 [≈£43]**

Welsh, Stuart Cary

- Room for Wonder. Indian Painting during the British Period 1760-1880. New York: Amer Federation of Arts, 1978. Sm 4to. 191 pp. Ills. Orig cloth. Dw (sl chipped). *(Cooper Hay)* **£18 [≈$27]**

Wenham, Edward

- Old Clocks for Modern Use with a Guide to their Mechanism. London: G. Bell & Sons, 1951. 1st edn. xvii,174 pp. 70 ills. Edges sl spotted. Orig cloth gilt. Dw. *(Hollett)* **£25 [≈$38]**

Wescott, Glenway

- A Calendar of Saints for Unbelievers. Paris: Harrison of Paris, 1932. One of 695. 8vo. Ills. Orig cloth. Slipcase. *(Bookpress)* **$225 [≈£150]**

West, Anthony

- John Piper. London: 1979. One of 100 with an orig sgnd litho by Piper. Orig red mor. Slipcase. *(Words Etcetera)* **£165 [≈$248]**
- John Piper. London: Secker & Warburg, 1979. 224 pp. 33 cold plates, 238 ills. Orig cloth. Dw. *(Fine Art)* **£18.50 [≈$29]**

West, Levon

- Making an Etching. London: The Studio, 1932. 1st edn. 8vo. 79 pp. Ills. Orig cloth. *(Rona Schneider)* **$55 [≈£37]**
- Making an Etching. London: The Studio, 1932. Tall 8vo. 79 pp. Ills. Orig cloth & dec bds, edges rubbed, sl worn. *(First Folio)* **$65 [≈£43]**

West, Michael

- Clair de Lune and other Troubadour Romances. Pictured by Evelyn Paul. London: Harrap, [1913]. 1st edn. Lge 8vo. [4],140 pp. 21 cold plates, ills. Orig cloth gilt, t.e.g. *(Claude Cox)* **£30 [≈$45]**

Westropp, M.S. Dudley

- Irish Glass. An Account of Glass Making in Ireland from the 16th Century to the Present Day ... London: Herbert Jenkins, [1920]. 1st edn. 4to. 40 plates. Orig cloth gilt. *(Claude Cox)* **£90 [≈$135]**

Westwood, Arthur

- Catalogue of the Books in the Library of the Assay Office Birmingham. London: Chiswick Press, 1914. 4to. [iv],307,[3] pp. Orig cloth gilt, uncut. *(Cooper Hay)* **£55 [≈$83]**

Westwood, J.O.

- Palaeographia Sacra Pictoria: Being a Series of Illustrations of the Ancient Versions of the Bible ... London: Bohn, (1845). 1st edn. Lge 4to. 50 hand cold plates. Three qtr mor, gilt spine, t.e.g., bds sl worn, crnrs & spine sl rubbed. *(Argonaut)* **$1,500 [≈£1,000]**

Wethered, Newton

- Mediaeval Craftsmanship and the Modern Amateur more particularly with reference to Metal and Enamel. London: Longmans, Green, 1923. 1st edn. xii,150 pp. 32 plates. Orig cloth gilt. *(Hollett)* **£25 [≈$38]**

Wettegren, Erik

- The Modern Decorative Arts of Sweden. Malmoe: The Malmoe Museum, [1927]. Sm 4to. 204 pp. Num ills inc mtd cold. Orig cloth backed bds, worn, front cvr spotted. *(Mendelsohn)* **$60 [≈£40]**

Whaite, H.C.

- St. Christopher in Mediaeval Wallpainting. London: Benn, 1929. 1st edn. Sm 4to. xvi,44 pp. 36 plates. Orig cloth backed bds, gilt. Dw (v soiled & torn). *(Hollett)* **£35 [≈$53]**

Whalley, Joyce Irene

- English Handwriting, 1540-1853. London: HMSO, 1969. 1st edn. Oblong folio. xxiii,[ii] pp. Frontis, 90 plates. Orig cloth. *(Bookpress)* **$65 [≈£43]**

Wharton, Edith

- Ethan Frome. With Water-Colour Drawings by Henry Varnum Poor ... New York: The Limited Editions Club, 1939. One of 1500 signed by the illustrator. Sm 4to. Orig cloth. Slipcase. *(Oak Knoll)* **$85 [≈£57]**
- The House of Mirth. Illustrations by Lily Harmon. N.p.: The Limited Editions Club, 1975. One of 2000 signed by the illustrator. Thick 8vo. Orig cloth. Slipcase. *(Oak Knoll)* **$45 [≈£30]**

Wheatley, Henry B.

- The Dedication of Books to Patron and Friend. A Chapter in Literary History. London: Elliot Stock, 1887. 1st edn, qtr cloth issue. Sm 8vo. Orig qtr buckram, bevelled edges. *(Oak Knoll)* **$65 [≈£43]**

Wheeler, Gervase

- The Choice of a Dwelling. A Practical Handbook. London: Murray, 1872. 2nd edn. 12mo. xii,305,[3],16 pp. Frontis. Orig cloth, front cvr soiled, spine & crnrs sl worn. *(Bookpress)* **$385 [≈£257]**

Whinney, M. Dickens

- The Interrelation of the Fine Arts in England in the Early Middle Ages. London: 1930. Sm 4to. xvi,30 pp. 24 ills on plates. Text sl foxed. Orig cloth & bds. *(Washton)* **$40 [≈£27]**

Whinney, Margaret & Millar, Oliver

- English Art 1625-1714. Oxford: 1957. Sm 4to. xxi,391 pp. 94 plates. Orig cloth. Dw. *(Washton)* **$75 [≈£50]**

Whistler, James McNeill

- Eden versus Whistler. The Baronet and the Butterfly. Paris: Louis-Henry May, 1899. One of 250. 8vo. Orig cloth backed bds, unopened, sl used and rubbed. Custom slipcase. *(Ulysses Bookshop)* **£450 [≈$675]**

Whistler, Laurence

- The English Festivals. London: Heinemann, 1947. 8vo. Dw. *(Lamb)* **£12 [≈$18]**
- Engraved Glass 1952-1958. London: Hart-Davis, 1959. 1st edn. Tall 8vo. 38 pp. 89 plates. Orig cloth gilt. Dw. *(Hollett)* **£60 [≈$90]**
- Rex Whistler 1905-1944: His Life and Drawings. London: Art & Technics, 1948. 1st edn. 104 pp. Plates, ills. Orig cloth gilt, sl worn. *(Willow House)* **£22 [≈$33]**
- Rex Whistler. London: Art & Technics, 1948. 1st edn. 104 pp. Num ills. Orig cloth gilt, sl bowed, extrs v sl worn. Dw (frayed). *(Bookworks)* **£28 [≈$42]**
- Scenes and Signs on Glass. London: Cupid Press, 1985. One of 1200 signed by Whistler. Tall 4to. 80 plates. Orig pict gilt cloth. Dw. *(Margaret Nangle)* **£25 [≈$38]**
- Sir John Vanbrugh: Architect and Dramatist 1664-1726. London: Macmillan, 1939. 1st edn. Lge 8vo. 327 pp. 14 plates. Orig cloth, sl worn. *(Monmouth)* **£35 [≈$53]**

Whistler, Laurence & Fuller, Ronald

- The Work of Rex Whistler. London: Batsford, 1960. 1st edn. Folio. 112 ills. Orig gilt dec cloth. Dw (sl worn & faded). *(Sotheran's)* **£475 [≈$713]**
- The Work of Rex Whistler. London: Batsford, 1960. 4to. 116 collotype ills (9 cold), text ills. Orig buckram. Dw. *(David Slade)* **£280 [≈$420]**

Whistler, Rex

- Songs of Our Grandfathers. Re-set in Guinness Time. Guinness: 1935. 23 pp. Cold ills. Orig stiff pict wraps. *(Barbara Stone)* **£75 [≈$113]**

Whitaker-Wilson, C.

- Sir Christopher Wren, his Life and Times. London: Methuen, 1932. 1st edn. 8vo. ix, 268, [8 advt] pp. 35 plates. Orig cloth gilt, edges sunned. *(Clevedon Books)* **£24 [≈$36]**

- Sir Christopher Wren. His Life and Times. London: Methuen, 1932. 1st edn. xx,268,8 pp. 35 plates. Orig cloth gilt. Dw (worn). *(Hollett)* **£25 [≈$38]**

White, Christopher

- Rembrandt as an Etcher. A Study of the Artist at Work. University Park & London: 1969. 2 vols. 4to. 263 pp. 348 ills on plates. Orig cloth. Dw. *(Washton)* **$175 [≈£117]**
- Rembrandt as an Etcher. A Study of the Artist at Work. London: 1969. 2 vols. 255 plates. Orig cloth. *(Leicester Art Books)* **£100 [≈$150]**

White, Christopher & Boon, Karel G.

- Rembrandt's Etchings. An Illustrated Critical Catalogue. Amsterdam, London & New York: 1969. 2 vols. 623 ills. Orig cloth. *(Leicester Art Books)* **£230 [≈$345]**

White, Eric Walter

- The Room and Other Poems: 1921-1926. Shaftesbury: High House Press, 1927. One of 180. Orig 2-tone mrbld bds, uncut. Dw (frayed). *(Claude Cox)* **£20 [≈$30]**

White, Gilbert

- The Writings of Gilbert White of Selborne. London: The Nonesuch Press, 1938. One of 850. 2 vols. W'engvs by Eric Ravilious. Orig buckram gilt, spines v sl faded. Slipcase (rubbed and bumped). *(Ulysses Bookshop)* **£950 [≈$1,425]**

White, Gleeson

- Children's Books and their Illustrators. London: The Studio, 1897. 1st edn. 4to. 68 pp. Text ills. Sl foxing. Cloth, paper label, sl spotted. *(Bookpress)* **$110 [≈£73]**
- English Illustration, 'The Sixties'; 1855-70 ... London: Constable, 1906. 3rd imp. Roy 8vo. 132 ills. Orig dec cloth, sl worn. *(Rankin)* **£50 [≈$75]**

White, John

- The Birth and Rebirth of Pictorial Space. New York: 1958. Sm 4to. 288 pp. 64 plates. Orig cloth. Dw (worn). *(Washton)* **$50 [≈£33]**

White, Lawrence Grant

- Sketches and Designs by Stanford White. New York: Wenzel & Krakow, 1920. 1st edn. Folio. vi,33, [1], pp. Frontis, 56 plates. Orig cloth, sl spotted, label chipped. *(Bookpress)* **$485 [≈£323]**

White, William Charles

- An Album of Chinese Bamboos: A Study of a Set of Ink-Bamboo Drawings A.D. 1785. Toronto: UP, 1939. Lge 8vo. xiv,200 pp. Photo ills. Orig bndg. *(McBlain)* **$100 [≈£67]**

Whiter, Leonard

- Spode. A History of the Family, Factory and Wares from 1733 to 1833. London: Barrie & Jenkins, 1970. 1st edn. Sm 4to. xiii,246 pp. 9 cold plates, 302 b/w plates, ills. Orig cloth gilt. Dw. *(Hollett)* **£100 [≈$150]**

Whitfield, Christopher

- Together and Alone. Golden Cockerel Press: 1945. One of 110 signed by the author and the artist, John O'Connor. Tall 8vo. 110 pp. Orig qtr mor, bottom edges of bds v sl faded. *(Waddington)* **£78 [≈$117]**

Whitlaw, Rosa M. & Wyllie, W.L.

- Lionel P. Smythe, R.A., R.W.S. His Life and Work. London: Selwyn & Blount, 1923. xvi, 241 pp. 42 plates. Orig cloth. *(Fine Art)* **£45 [≈$68]**

Whitley, William T.

- Artists and their Friends in England, 1700-1799. London: The Medici Society, 1928. 2 vols. Orig bndgs. *(Mermaid Books)* **£24 [≈$36]**
- Thomas Gainsborough. London: Smith, Elder, 1915. xviii,417 pp. 24 plates. Orig cloth. *(Leicester Art Books)* **£30 [≈$45]**

Whitman, Alfred

- British Mezzotinters. Valentine Green. London: A.H. Bullen, 1902. One of 520. 204 pp. 6 plates. Orig cloth. *(Leicester Art Books)* **£30 [≈$45]**
- Nineteenth Century Mezzotinters. Samuel Cousins. London: George Bell, 1904. One of 500. xii,144 pp. 35 plates. Orig cloth gilt, t.e.g. *(Leicester Art Books)* **£25 [≈$38]**
- Samuel William Reynolds. Nineteenth Century Mezzotinters. London: George Bell & Sons, 1903. One of 500. ix,168 pp. 29 plates. Endpapers sl foxed. Orig cloth. *(Leicester Art Books)* **£32 [≈$48]**

Whitman, Walt

- Leaves of Grass. Introduction by Mark Van Doren. New York: The Limited Editions Club, 1942. One of 1500 signed by Weston. 2 vols. Photo ills by Edward Weston. Orig pict bds, leather labels. Slipcase. *(Argonaut)* **$1,500 [≈£1,000]**

Whitney, C.S.
- Bridges: A Study in their Art, Science, and Evolution. US: Rudge, 1929. 1st edn. 4to. 363 pp. 400 plates & ills. Orig cloth. *(Monmouth)* **£80 [≈$120]**

Whitney, Geoffrey
- Whitney's "Choice of Emblems". A Facsimile Reprint. Edited by Henry Green ... London: Lovell Reeve, 1866. One of 500. 4to. Ills. Orig cloth, t.e.g., spine ends sl frayed, upper bd damp stained. *(Clark)* **£80 [≈$120]**

Whittesley, Austin
- The Renaissance Architecture of Central and North Spain. New York: Architectural Book Publ. Co., 1920. Lge 4to. 121 plates. Orig cloth. Dw. *(Karmiole)* **$100 [≈£67]**

Whittick, A.
- The Small House, Today and Tomorrow. London: Leonard Hill, 1957. 2nd edn. xiv,218 pp. 73 plates, text ills. Orig cloth. *(Clevedon Books)* **£25 [≈$38]**

Whittier, John Greenleaf
- Snow-Bound, A Winter Idyl. New York: The Limited Editions Club, 1930. One of 1500 signed by C.P. Rollins, the designer. Sm 4to. Sl foxed. Orig cloth-backed bds. Parchment jacket. Slipcase (rubbed). *(Oak Knoll)* **$75 [≈£50]**
- Snow-Bound, A Winter Idyl. New York: The Limited Editions Club, 1930. One of 1500 signed by C.P. Rollins, the designer. Sm 4to. Orig cloth-backed bds (edges rubbed). *(Oak Knoll)* **$35 [≈£23]**

Whittock, Nathaniel
- The Art of Drawing and Colouring, from Nature, Birds, Beasts, Fishes, and Insects. London: Isaac Taylor Hinton, 1830. 1st edn. 4to. [iv],100 pp. 24 litho plates (12 cold). Contemp calf, few sm spots. *(Bookpress)* **$1,500 [≈£1,000]**
- The Oxford Drawing Book, or the Art of Drawing ... A New and Improved Edition. London: E. Lacey, [ca 1830]. Oblong 4to. vi, 159,[3] pp. Frontis, 107 plates on 27 ff. Contemp roan backed bds, ptd label on upper cvr. *(Spelman)* **£220 [≈$330]**
- The Youth's New London Self-Instructing Drawing Book ... London: G. Virtue, 1834. Oblong 8vo. iv,108 pp. 104 plates. Occas foxing. Contemp half calf, gilt spine, jnts & crnrs worn. *(Spelman)* **£120 [≈$180]**

Wichmann, Siegfried
- Japonisme. New York: Harmony Books, (1981). 1st edn in English. Folio. 432 pp. Over 1100 ills. Orig cloth. Dw. *(Bookpress)* **$165 [≈£110]**

Wicksteed, Joseph H.
- Blake's Innocence and Experience. A Study of the Songs and Manuscripts. London: Dent, 1928. 1st edn. 1st issue cloth. 304 pp. 156 pp plates. Orig cloth, t.e.g., crnrs v sl bruised, spine v sl sunned. *(Bookworks)* **£60 [≈$90]**

New editions of *ARBV* are published annually on the 1st April - including numerous authors and titles previously unlisted.

Wight, Jane A.
- Brick Building in England from the Middle Ages to 1550. London: Baker, 1972. 1st edn. 439 pp. 75 plates. Lib stamp on title. Orig cloth, sl worn. Dw (worn). *(Monmouth)* **£18 [≈$27]**
- Brick Building in England from the Middle Ages to 1550. London: 1972. 4to. 439 pp. 75 plates, 20 figs. Dw. *(Francis Edwards)* **£25 [≈$38]**

Wijdeveld, H.T.
- The Life-Work of the American Architect Frank Lloyd Wright. Santpoort: C.A. Mees, 1925. 1st edn in book form. Sq folio. 164 pp. Port, 197 ills. Two-inch marg tear on title. Rear endpaper sl marked. Orig cloth, sl worn. *(Bookpress)* **$1,250 [≈£833]**

Wilbur, Richard
- A Bestiary. Compiled by Richard Wilbur. Illustrated by Alexander Calder. New York: Pantheon Books, (1955). One of 750 (of 825) signed by the author and artist. 4to. 74 pp. Ills. Orig cloth. Slipcase. *(Abacus)* **$200 [≈£133]**

Wild, Charles
- Select Examples of Architectural Grandeur in Belgium, Germany, and France: A Series of Twenty-Four Sketches drawn on the spot. London: Bohn, 1837. 1st edn. Lge 4to. 8 pp. 24 litho plates. Some spotting. Orig leather backed cloth gilt, spine sl rubbed & scraped. *(Hollett)* **£75 [≈$113]**
- Select Examples of Architectural Grandeur in Belgium, Germany, and France. London: Bohn, 1843. 2nd edn. Folio. 16 pp. 24 plates. Later cloth, rubbed. *(Bookpress)* **$175 [≈£117]**

Wilde, Johannes

- Italian Drawings in the Department of Prints and Drawings in the British Museum. Michelangelo and his Studio. London: 1975. 2nd edn. Sm 4to. xx,142 pp. 153 plates. Orig cloth. *(Washton)* **$65 [≈£43]**

Wilde, Oscar

- The Happy Prince and Other Tales ... Illustrated by Charles Robinson. London: Duckworth, (1913). 4to. 12 mtd cold plates. Orig bndg, spine sl faded. *(Waterfield's)* **£50 [≈$75]**
- A House of Pomegranates. Illustrated by Jessie M. King. New York: Brentano's, n.d. 1st Amer edn. 8vo. 162 pp. 16 mtd cold plates, illust endpapers. Some foxing & offsetting. Orig pict gilt cloth, hinges reinforced, rebacked. *(Davidson)* **$825 [≈£550]**
- Salome ... Translated from the French by Oscar Wilde. Pictured by Aubrey Beardsley. London: 1894. 1st edn. One of 500. Sm 4to. Orig cloth, extrs rubbed. *(Heritage)* **$1,000 [≈£667]**

Wildenstein, Georges

- The Paintings of Fragonard. Complete Edition. London: Phaidon, 1960. 4to. viii,339 pp. Mtd cold frontis, plates inc mtd, ills. Lib stamp title verso. B'plate. Orig cloth, spine sl faded. *(Francis Edwards)* **£125 [≈$188]**
- The Paintings of Fragonard. Complete Edition. London: 1960. Lge 4to. viii,339 pp. 142 plates, 235 ills. Orig cloth. *(Washton)* **$275 [≈£183]**
- The Paintings of Fragonard: Complete Edition. London: Phaidon, 1960. viii,339 pp. Num plates, ills. Orig cloth. Plastic dw. Slipcase (sl worn). *(Fine Art)* **£175 [≈$263]**

Wilder, Thornton

- The Bridge of San Luis Rey. Introduction by Granville Hicks. Illustrated with Lithographs in color by Jean Charlot. New York: The Limited Editions Club, 1962. One of 1500 signed by Hicks. Tall 8vo. Orig leather-backed cloth (sm hole in spine leather). Slipcase. *(Oak Knoll)* **$65 [≈£43]**
- The Bridge of San Luis Rey. New York: Albert & Charles Boni, 1929. One of 1100 signed by the author and the illustrator, Rockwell Kent. Orig pict cloth, leather label. Slipcase. *(Hermitage)* **$400 [≈£267]**
- Our Town, A Play in Three Acts. Illustrations by Robert J. Lee. Avon, CT: The Limited Editions Club, 1974. One of 200 signed by Wilder and Lee. 4to. Orig suede, leather label. Slipcase. *(Oak Knoll)* **$125 [≈£83]**

Wilenski, R.M.

- Stanley Spencer. London: Contemporary British Artists, 1924. 30 pp. Frontis, 35 plates. Orig cloth & bds. *(Fine Art)* **£20 [≈$30]**

Wiles, H.V. (compiler)

- Thomas Bewick 1753-1828. English Engraver on Wood, English Gentleman. London: privately printed, 1945. One of 350. Ills. Orig wraps (sl dusty & creased, one nick). *(Ulysses Bookshop)* **£55 [≈$83]**

Wilkinson, Gerald

- Turner Sketches 1802-20. Romantic Genius. New York: 1974. Sm 4to. 189 pp. 450 ills (110 cold). Orig cloth. Dw. *(Washton)* **$45 [≈£30]**

Wilkinson, O.N.

- Old Glass. Manufacture, Styles, Uses. London: Benn, 1968. 8vo. 200 pp. 125 plates, num ills. Dw (rubbed). *(Paul Brown)* **£18 [≈$27]**

Wilkinson, R.

- The Hallmarks of Antique Glass. London: R. Madley, 1968. 8vo. 220 pp. 279 plates. Price-clipped dw (rubbed). Signed by the author. *(Paul Brown)* **£18 [≈$27]**

Williams, D.E.

- The Life and Correspondence of Sir Thomas Lawrence Kt. President of the Royal Academy ... London: Colburn, 1831. 1st edn. 2 vols. 8vo. xxiv,473; viii,586 pp. 2 frontises. Contemp half calf. *(Young's)* **£68 [≈$102]**

Williams, Henry Smith

- The History of the Art of Writing ... Cambridge: Heffer, [ca 1900]. Lge folio. 97 plates (some cold & heightened with gold). 2 b/w plates with some surface loss. Marg lib blind stamps. Contemp three qtr mor, worn, upper jnt cracking. *(Wilkinson)* **£55 [≈$83]**

Williams, Iolo

- Early English Watercolours and Some Cognate Drawings by Artists born not later than 1785. Bath: Kingsmead Reprints, (1970). 4to. [xxiv], 266 pp. Cold frontis, ills. Dw. *(Schoyer)* **$50 [≈£33]**
- Early English Watercolours, and some

Cognate Drawings by Artists born not later than 1785. Bath: Kingsmead Reprints, 1970. 200 plates. Dw. *(Mermaid Books)* **£15 [≈$23]**

- The Elements of Book Collecting. London: 1927. Cr 8vo. Orig cloth. *(Traylen)* **£15 [≈$23]**

Williams, J. David

- America Illustrated. Boston: DeWolfe, Fiske, 1883. 4to. 121 pp. 86 ills. Num w'engvs. Orig cloth. *(Rona Schneider)* **$50 [≈£33]**

Williams, Muriel

- Charles Blomfield. His Life and Times. Auckland: Hodder & Stoughton, 1979. x,188 pp. 67 ills. Orig cloth. Dw. *(Leicester Art Books)* **£26 [≈$39]**

Williams, Sydney B.

- Antique Blue and White Spode. London: Batsford, 1945. Lge 8vo. xviii,242 pp. 123 ills. Orig cloth gilt. *(Hollett)* **£40 [≈$60]**

Williamson, Bruce

- Catalogue of Paintings and Engravings in the Possession of the Hon. Society of the Middle Temple. London: 1931. 62 pp. 12 plates. Orig cloth, front cvr sl marked. *(Fine Art)* **£18 [≈$27]**

Williamson, George C.

- Andrew and Nathaniel Plimer. Miniature Painters - Their Lives and their Works. London: George Bell, 1903. One of 365. xv,164 pp. 189 ills. Orig cloth, t.e.g. *(Leicester Art Books)* **£110 [≈$165]**
- The Book of Amber. London: 1932. xiii,15-268 pp. Cold frontis, 4 plates, 1 text ill. Lib stamps. Orig cloth, lib mark on spine. *(Whitehart)* **£20 [≈$30]**
- Daniel Gardner: Painter in Pastel and Gouache, a Brief Account of his Life and Works. London: John Lane; Bodley Head, 1911. One of 500. 190 pp. 9 cold & 6 other plates, ills. Orig cloth & bds, t.e.g., bds wrinkled. *(Fine Art)* **£80 [≈$120]**
- Daniel Gardner. Painter in Pastel and Gouache. A Brief Account of his Life and Work. London: John Lane; The Bodley Head, 1921. One of 500. xv,190 pp. 111 plates. Orig cloth & bds, t.e.g. Dw. *(Leicester Art Books)* **£110 [≈$165]**
- George Engleheart 1750-1829. Miniature Painter to George III. London: George Bell & Sons, 1902. One of 360. xv,176 pp. 87 ills. Orig cloth. *(Leicester Art Books)* **£70 [≈$105]**
- John Downman, A.R.A. His Life and Works. London: Otto Ltd., 1907. lxvii pp. 62 plates, 89 ills. Orig cloth & bds. *(Leicester Art Books)* **£25 [≈$38]**
- Life and Works of Ozias Humphry R.A. London: 1918. One of 400. xx,330 pp. 209 ills. Orig parchment backed bds, t.e.g. *(Leicester Art Books)* **£130 [≈$195]**
- Richard Cosway, R.A. and his Wife and Pupils. Miniaturist of the 18th Century. London: George Bell, 1897. One of 350. 170 pp. 56 plates. Foxed. Orig cloth, partly disbound. *(Leicester Art Books)* **£70 [≈$105]**

Williamson, Hugh Ross

- The Flowering Hawthorn. London: 1962. 1st edn. W'engvs by Clare Leighton. Orig cloth, 2 crnrs sl bumped. Dw (worn). *(Margaret Nangle)* **£28 [≈$42]**
- Letter to Julia. The Stourton Press: 1974. One of 215. 148 pp. Orig buckram, t.e.g. Dw. *(Claude Cox)* **£18 [≈$27]**

Willis, Robert

- The Architectural History of Glastonbury Abbey. Cambridge: Deighton Bell, 1866. 8vo. vii,91 pp. Frontis, 6 plans. Orig cloth, sm chip to spine. *(Quest Books)* **£28 [≈$42]**

Willitts, William

- Foundations of Chinese Art from Neolithic Pottery to Modern Architecture. New York: McGraw-Hill, (1965). 4to. 456 pp. 322 plates, figs. Dw (chipped). *(Schoyer)* **$55 [≈£37]**
- Foundations of Chinese Art from Neolithic Pottery to Modern Architecture. New York: McGraw-Hill, (1965). 4to. 456 pp. 322 plates. Dw (chipped). *(Schoyer)* **$55 [≈£37]**

Willoughby, Edwin

- Fifty Printers' Marks. Berkeley: The Book Arts Club, 1947. One of 550. xi,153 pp. Ills. Orig cloth, ft of spine faded. Dw (sl faded). *(Argonaut)* **$60 [≈£40]**
- A Printer of Shakespeare. The Books and Times of William Jaggard. New York: Dutton, (1934). 1st edn. xvi,304 pp. 17 ills. Orig cloth. Dw (defective). *(Karmiole)* **$50 [≈£33]**

Willoughby, Vera

- A Vision of Greece. London: 1925. One of 500. 4to. viii,197,[3] pp. 16 cold plates. Orig linen & dec bds. *(Bow Windows)* **£150 [≈$225]**
- A Vision of Greece. London: Philip Allan, 1925. One of 500. 4to. 16 cold plates, b/w ills. Orig cloth backed dec bds. *(Traylen)* **£35 [≈$53]**

Wilmer, Daisy
- Early English Glass. A Guide for Collectors of Table & Other Decorative Glass of the 16th, 17th & 18th Centuries. London: Bazaar, Exchange & Mart, [ca 1918]. 3rd edn, enlgd. 282 pp. B/w ills. Blank free endpaper removed. *(Paul Brown)* **£25 [≈$38]**

Wilson, Adrian
- The Design of Books. London: Studio Vista, (1967). 1st English edn. 4to. 160 pp. Orig cloth. Dw (few sm tears). *(Bookpress)* **$110 [≈£73]**
- The Design of Books. New York: (1967). 4to. 159 pp. Ills. Orig cloth. Dw. *(The Veatchs)* **$40 [≈£27]**

Wilson, David M.
- Anglo-Saxon Art. From the Seventh Century to the Norman Conquest. Woodstock: 1984. 4to. 224 pp. 285 ills (73 cold). Orig cloth. Dw. *(Washton)* **$45 [≈£30]**

Wilson, Michael
- William Kent: Architect, Designer, Painter, Gardener 1685-1748. London: Routledge, 1984. 176 pp. 100 plates. Dw. *(Fine Art)* **£28 [≈$42]**

Wilson, Mona
- The Life of William Blake. London: The Nonesuch Press, 1927. One of 480. xv,397 pp. 24 plates. Orig vellum & bds, spine sl worn. *(Leicester Art Books)* **£50 [≈$75]**

Wilson, Ralph Pinder
- Islamic Art. New York: Macmillan, 1957. 4to. 100 cold plates. Tape marks on endpapers. Orig cloth. Dw. *(First Folio)* **$45 [≈£30]**

Wilson, Thomas
- A Descriptive Catalogue of the Prints of Rembrandt. By an Amateur. London: J.F. Setchel, 1836. 8vo. [4],226,[1 errata] pp. Orig cloth, uncut, label rubbed. Anon. *(Fenning)* **£55 [≈$83]**

Wingert, Paul S.
- The Sculpture of William Zorach. New York: Pitman, 1938. Sm 4to. 74 pp. 49 plates. Orig cloth. Dw (chipped). Signed by the artist. *(Abacus)* **$85 [≈£57]**

Wingler, Hans Maria
- Oskar Kokoscha. The Work of the Painter. Salzburg: Galerie Welz; London: Faber, 1958. 401 pp. 163 ills, 393 sm ills. Orig cloth. *(Leicester Art Books)* **£300 [≈$450]**

Winkles, H. & E.
- Winkles's Architectural and Picturesque Illustrations of the Cathedral Churches of England and Wales ... Descriptions by Thomas Moule. London: 1838-42. 3 vols. Tall 8vo. Engvd titles, 178 plates. Occas spots. Orig cloth gilt, faded & spotted, crnrs bumped, rebacked. *(Hollett)* **£140 [≈$210]**

Wise, Thomas
- The Newest Young Man's Companion ... English Grammar ... Arithmetic ... Horses ... Art of Painting in Water Colours ... Berwick: R. Taylor, 1773. 9th edn. 8vo. iv,402 pp. 2 maps. Contemp calf, sl rubbed. *(Young's)* **£120 [≈$180]**

Wittkower, Rudolf
- Gian Lorenzo Bernini. The Sculptor of the Roman Baroque. Oxford: Phaidon, 1981. xii,290 pp. 264 ills. Orig cloth. Dw. *(Leicester Art Books)* **£45 [≈$68]**
- Gian Lorenzo Bernini. The Sculptor of the Roman Baroque. London: 1966. 2nd edn. 4to. xi,286 pp. 126 plates, 128 text ills. Orig cloth. Dw. *(Washton)* **$90 [≈£60]**
- Idea and Image. London: Thames & Hudson, (1978). 1st edn. Sm 4to. 255 pp. 272 ills. Orig cloth. Dw. *(Bookpress)* **$65 [≈£43]**

Wittlich, Peter
- Art Nouveau Drawings. London: Octopus Books, 1974. 4to. Ills. Orig cloth. Dw. *(First Folio)* **$45 [≈£30]**

Wittrock, Wolfgang
- Toulouse-Lautrec: The Complete Prints. London: Sotheby's, (1985). 2 vols. Folio. 831 pp. 368 ills. Orig cloth. Dws. Slipcase. *(Abacus)* **$250 [≈£167]**

Woidt, Hanna
- Chinese Handicrafts: A Picture Book. Peking: 1944. One of 50 (with rubber-stamp so stating on copyright page). Sm 4to. 53 pp. Photo ills. Orig bndg. *(McBlain)* **$100 [≈£67]**

Wolf, Edwin, II (compiler)
- A Descriptive Catalogue of the John Frederick Lewis Collection of European Manuscripts in the Free Library of Philadelphia. With an Introduction by Dr. A.S.W. Rosenbach. Phila: 1937. One of 1000. 4to. [18],219,[16] pp. 42 plates. Orig cloth. *(Karmiole)* **$100 [≈£67]**

Wolfe, Bertram D.
- The Fabulous Life of Diego Rivera. London:

Barrie & Rockliff, 1968. 1st edn. 458 pp. 164 plates, 39 decs. Orig cloth, extrs rubbed, upper jnt weakening. *(Bookworks)* **£24 [≈$36]**

Wolfe, Richard J.

- On Improvements in Marbling the Edges of Books and Paper. A Nineteenth Century Marbling Account Explained and Illustrated with Fourteen Original Marbled Samples ... Newtown: Bird & Bull Press, 1983. One of 350. 14 specimens. Orig qtr mor. *(The Veatchs)* **$225 [≈£150]**
- Three Early French Essays on Marbling, 1642-1765. With an Introduction and Thirteen Original Marbled Samples ... Newtown: Bird & Bull Press, 1987. One of 310. 13 samples, ills. Orig qtr mor. *(The Veatchs)* **$300 [≈£200]**

Wolfe, Richard J. & McKenna, Paul

- Louis Herman Kiner and Fine Bookbinding in America: A Chapter in the History of the Roycroft Shop. Newtown: Bird & Bull Press, 1985. One of 325. Tall 8vo. Ills. Orig mor & lavender bds gilt. *(Dermont)* **$275 [≈£183]**

Wood, Esther

- A Consideration of the Art of Frederick Sandys. London: Constable, Special Winter Number of "The Artist", 1896. Large Paper. 64 pp. 31 ills. sl foxed. Orig dec cloth gilt, t.e.g. *(Leicester Art Books)* **£90 [≈$135]**

Wood, John

- An Elementary Treatise on Sketching from Nature ... London: Whittaker, [1850]. 1st edn. 8vo. 52 pp. 7 plates (2 hand cold). Orig cloth, sl marked & creased. *(Spelman)* **£140 [≈$210]**

Wood, John, junior

- A Manual of Perspective being a Familiar Explanation of the Science .. . Adapted for the Use of Amateurs. Worcester: 1841. 1st edn. Lge 8vo. iv,5-28 pp. 7 plates. Orig cloth, spine & bd edges faded. *(Spelman)* **£80 [≈$120]**

Wood, Margaret

- The English Mediaeval House. London: Phoenix House, 1965. Roy 8vo. Plans, ills. Dw. *(David Slade)* **£25 [≈$38]**
- The English Mediaeval House. London: Bracken Books, 1983. Sm 4to. xxxi,448 pp. Ills. Orig cloth gilt. Dw. *(Hollett)* **£20 [≈$30]**

Wood-Jones, R.B.

- Traditional Domestic Architecture of the Banbury Region. Manchester: UP, 1963. 1st edn. 309 pp. 24 plates, plans, ills. Orig cloth. Dw. *(Monmouth)* **£40 [≈$60]**

Woodall, Mary

- The Letters of Thomas Gainsborough. London: Cupid Press, 1963. Revised edn. One of 1200. 184 pp. 27 ills. Orig cloth & mrbld bds. *(Leicester Art Books)* **£36 [≈$54]**

Woods, S. John

- John Piper, Paintings, Drawings and Theatre Designs 1932-1954. London: Faber, 1955. 1st edn. 160 pp. Orig aquatint frontis, 4 lithographs. 11 cold plates, 244 ills. Orig dec cloth. Dw. *(Fine Art)* **£350 [≈$525]**
- John Piper. Paintings, Drawings and Theatre Design. London: Faber, 1955. 1st edn. Lge 4to. Num ills. Dw. *(Clearwater)* **£250 [≈$375]**

Woodward, C.S.

- Oriental Ceramics at the Cape of Good Hope 1652-1795 ... Rotterdam: 1974. 4to. xii,228 pp. 216 plates. Orig cloth. Dw. *(Castle Bookshop)* **£48 [≈$72]**

Woodward, George & Woodward, F.W.

- Woodward's Graperies and Horticultural Buildings. New York: George E. Woodward, (1865). 1st edn. 8vo. 139 pp. Ills. Orig cloth. *(Bookpress)* **$250 [≈£167]**

Woodward, John

- Tudor and Stuart Drawings. London: Faber, 1951. 1st edn. 4to. 57,[3] pp. 64 plates. Orig cloth. *(Bookpress)* **$45 [≈£30]**

Woolnough, C.W.

- The Whole Art of Marbling as applied to Paper, Book-Edges, Etc. ... (1881). Oxford: Plough Press, 1985. One of 150. 8vo. 42,82 pp. Tipped-in specimens. Orig cloth. *(Oak Knoll)* **$400 [≈£267]**

Wortz, Melinda

- Claes Oldenburg: The Soft Screw ... Los Angeles: Gemini, 1976. Continuous horizontal scroll. 11 ills. Orig ptd wraps, cardboard cylinder. *(Ars Libri)* **$50 [≈£33]**

The Wren Society

- [Journal]. Oxford: for The Wren Society, 1924-43. 20 vols, all published. 4to. Orig qtr cloth. *(Sotheran's)* **£950 [≈$1,425]**

Wright, C.E.

- Fontes Harleianae. A Study of the Sources of the Harleian Collection of MSS. London: 1972. 8vo. xxxv,450 pp. Plates. Orig cloth. *(Lamb)* **£25 [≈$38]**

Wright, Christopher

- Poussin Paintings: A Catalogue Raisonne. London: Harlequin, 1985. 304 pp. 217 plates. Orig cloth. Dw. *(Fine Art)* **£38 [≈$57]**

Wright, Frank Lloyd

- An American Architecture. New York: Horizon Press, 1955. 1st edn. 269 pp. Ills. Dw (sl worn & faded). *(Hermitage)* **$150 [≈£100]**
- An Autobiography. London: Faber, 1945. 1st edn. 8vo. 486 pp. 76 ills. Orig cloth gilt, hd of spine faded. Dw (defective). *(Hollett)* **£45 [≈$68]**
- Buildings, Plans and Designs. New York: Horizon Press, (1963). 1st Amer edn. Folio. 32 pp. 100 plates. Portfolio. *(Bookpress)* **$1,250 [≈£833]**
- Buildings, Plans and Designs. New York: Horizon Press, 1963. One of 2600. Folio. [28] pp. Booklet & 100 plates. Plates sl dimpled. Orig cloth & bds portfolio, with ties (worn, tear to spine). *(Mendelsohn)* **$750 [≈£500]**
- Drawings for a Living Architecture. New York: Horizon Press, 1959. 1st edn. Oblong folio. 255 pp. 200 ills. Orig cloth. Dw (worn). *(Bookpress)* **$950 [≈£633]**
- The Future of Architecture. New York: Horizon Press, 1953. 1st edn. Orig cloth. Dw (minor chips, some soiling rear panel). *(First Folio)* **$150 [≈£100]**
- Genius and the Mobocracy. London: 1949. 1st edn. 8vo. 39 ills by Louis H. Sullivan. Orig cloth, spine ends v sl bumped. Dw (sl worn). Inscribed by the author (1949). *(Ulysses Bookshop)* **£395 [≈$593]**
- The Natural House. New York: Horizon Press, 1954. 1st edn. Lge 8vo. 223 pp. Ills. Orig linen over bds, edges sl spotted, sl aged. Dw (minor chips spine extrs). *(First Folio)* **$200 [≈£133]**
- Selected Drawings. Portfolio. New York: Horizon Press, (1977). 1st edn. One of 500. Folio. 50 plates. Portfolio, box. *(Bookpress)* **$3,950 [≈£2,633]**
- Studies and Executed Buildings. Palos Park: Prairie School Press, (1975). 1st edn. Oblong folio. 60 plates. Orig cloth. Dw (chipped & rubbed). *(Bookpress)* **$250 [≈£167]**

Wright, Harold J.L.

- The Etched Work of F.L. Griggs, R.A. London: Print Collector's Club, 1941. One of 300. 80 pp. 16 plates. Cvrs sl marked, hd of spine worn. *(Fine Art)* **£40 [≈$60]**
- The Etched Work of F.L. Griggs. With a Catalogue by Campbell Dodgson. London: The Print Collector's Club, 1941. One of 400. 80 pp. 16 plates. Orig cloth gilt. *(Leicester Art Books)* **£30 [≈$45]**
- The Etchings and Drypoints of Sir D.Y. Cameron. London: Print Collectors Club, 1947. One of 400. 48 pp. 18 plates. Orig cloth. *(Fine Art)* **£18 [≈$27]**

Wright, Olgivanna Lloyd

- Our House. New York: Horizon, 1959. 1st edn. 308 pp. Dw (chipped). *(Schoyer)* **$50 [≈£33]**

Wrighte, William

- Grotesque Architecture; or, Rural Amusement ... New Edition. London: J. Taylor, 1802. 8vo. 8 pp. Frontis, 28 plates. Rec qtr mor. *(Spelman)* **£480 [≈$720]**

Wu, G.D.

- Prehistoric Pottery in China. London: Kegan Paul, 1938. 1st edn. 8vo. xii,180,[4] pp. 64 plates. Orig cloth. Dw. *(Bookpress)* **$110 [≈£73]**

Wunder, Richard P.

- Extravagant Drawings of the 18th Century from the Collection of the Cooper Union Museum. New York: 1962. 107 pp. 79 plates. Orig bds. Dw (minor tears). *(Clarice Davis)* **$40 [≈£27]**

Wycherley, William

- The Complete Works. Edited by Montague Summers. Soho: The Nonesuch Press, 1924. One of 900. 4 vols. Orig cloth, paper labels. *(Hermitage)* **$400 [≈£267]**

Wyeth, Betsy James

- Wyeth at Kuerners. Boston: Houghton, Mifflin 1976. Oblong 4to. 324 pp. 370 ills. Orig cloth. Dw. *(Abacus)* **$75 [≈£50]**

Wysuph, C.L.

- Jackson Pollock: Psychoanalytic Drawings. New York: Horizon Press, 1970. Sq 4to. 123 pp. 83 plates. Orig cloth. *(Ars Libri)* **$65 [≈£43]**

Yashiro, Yukio

- Sandro Botticelli and the Florentine Renaissance. Revised Edition. Boston: Hale, Cushman & Flint, 1929. 4to. xlviii,262 pp. 106 plates. Orig cloth, spine faded. *(Karmiole)* **$65 [≈£43]**

Yates, Frances A.

- The Valois Tapestries. London: Routledge &

Kegan Paul, (1975). 2nd edn. 4to. 150 pp. 12 plates, ills. Orig cloth. Dw. *(Abacus)* **$40 [≈£27]**

The Year Book of Japanese Art ...

- The Year Book of Japanese Art, 1927. Tokyo: 1928. Sm 4to. xiv,162 pp. 120 plates. Orig illust cloth & bds, spine extrs sl frayed, crnrs sl rubbed. *(Karmiole)* **$75 [≈£50]**
- The Year Book of Japanese Art, 1928. Tokyo: 1929. Sm 4to. xiv,172 pp. 114 plates. Orig illust cloth & bds. Dw (sl soiled & chipped). *(Karmiole)* **$75 [≈£50]**

Yeats, Jack B.

- Modern Aspects of Irish Art. [Dublin]: 1922. 11 pp. Orig wraps. *(Emerald Isle)* **£200 [≈$300]**
- The Treasure of the Garden. London: Elkin Mathews, [1902]. 4to. 7 hand cold plates by the author. Book of Words. Orig wraps. Rec slipcase. *(Emerald Isle)* **£650 [≈$975]**

Yerbury, F.R.

- Modern Dutch Buildings. With Photographs Specially Taken by the Author. London: Benn, 1931. 4to. 100 plates. Orig cloth, soiled. *(Karmiole)* **$60 [≈£40]**

Yolen, Jane

- The Lady and the Merman. A Tale. With Three Wood Engravings by Barry Moser. Easthampton: Pennyroyal Press, 1977. One of 100 signed by the author and by Moser. 8vo. Orig cloth, paper label. *(Jo Ann Reisler)* **$225 [≈£150]**

Yonezawa, Yoshito & Kawakita, Michiaki

- Arts of China: Paintings in Chinese Museums: New Collections. Tokyo & Palo Alto: Kodansha International, (1970). Folio. Ills. Dw. *(Schoyer)* **$55 [≈£37]**

The Young Clerk's Assistant ...

- The Young Clerk's Assistant; or Penmanship made easy, instructive and entertaining ... London: for W. Lowndes, 1787. 8vo. Engvd frontis & title, 61engvd ff. Orig bds, rebacked, rubbed. Cloth slipcase. *(Spelman)* **£195 [≈$293]**

Young, Andrew McLaren, & others

- The Paintings of James McNeill Whistler. Yale: UP, Paul Mellon Centre, 1980. 2 vols. 4to. Num ills. Orig cloth. Dws (sl creased). *(Cooper Hay)* **£120 [≈$180]**

Young, Edward

- The Complaint, and the Consolation; or, Night Thoughts. London: 1797. 1st edn. Lge 4to. 43 engvs by William Blake. With the 2-page explanation of the engravings. Prelims sl foxed. Leather, front hinge starting. *(Heritage)* **$7,500 [≈£5,000]**

Young, Eric

- Bartolome Bermejo. The Great Hispano-Flemish Master. London: 1975. Sm 4to. 159 pp. 4 cold plates, 68 ills. Orig cloth. Dw. *(Washton)* **$50 [≈£33]**

Young, Francis Brett

- Portrait of a Village. London: Heinemann, 1937. 1st edn. 180 pp. W'engvs by Joan Hassall. Dw (torn). *(Waddington)* **£16 [≈$24]**
- Portrait of a Village. London: Heinemann, 1937. 1st edn. [vi],180 pp. 30 w'engvs by Joan Hassall, endpaper maps. Orig cloth gilt, trifle marked. *(Hollett)* **£25 [≈$38]**

Young, Jennie J.

- The Ceramic Art. New York: Harper, 1879. 1st edn. 8vo. [iv],499,[3] pp. 464 text ills. Orig cloth gilt, sl spotted. *(Bookpress)* **$275 [≈£183]**

Zaehnsdorf, Joseph W.

- The Art of Bookbinding. A Practical Treatise. London: 1890. 2nd edn, rvsd & enlgd. Sm 8vo. 8 plates & diags. Mod half mor. *(Traylen)* **£40 [≈$60]**
- The Art of Bookbinding. A Practical Treatise. London: George Bell, 1890. 2nd edn. 12mo. xix,190,[8 advt,6,24 ctlg] pp. 8 plates, text ills. Sm lib stamp on title. Orig cloth. *(The Veatchs)* **$45 [≈£30]**

Zampetti, Pietro

- Paintings from the Marches. Gentile to Raphael. London: 1971. Sq 4to. 277 pp. 40 cold & 187 b/w plates. Orig cloth. *(Washton)* **$85 [≈£57]**

Zapf, Hermann

- About Alphabets. Some Marginal Notes on Type Design. New York: The Typophiles, 1960. One of 400 (of 700). Tall 12mo. 118 pp. Orig cloth, leather label. *(Oak Knoll)* **$75 [≈£50]**

Zarnecki, G. (editor)

- English Romanesque Art 1066-1200. London: Weidenfeld & Nicolson, 1984. 4to. 416 pp. Num plates. Orig cloth. Dw. *(Castle Bookshop)* **£32 [≈$48]**

Zerner, Henri

- The School of Fontainbleu. Etchings and Engravings. London: Thames & Hudson, 1969. 1st English edn. 4to. 216 pp. 350 plates. Dw. *(Spelman)* **£60 [≈$90]**

Zervos, Christian

- Chauvin. Paris: Editions "Cahiers d'Art", [1960]. French & English texts. Sm folio. 103 pp. 121 ills. Orig cloth. *(Ars Libri)* **$150 [≈£100]**

Zhadova, Larissa

- Malevich. Suprematism and Revolution in Russian Art 1910-1930. London: Thames & Hudson, 1982. 371 pp. 445 ills. Orig cloth. *(Leicester Art Books)* **£150 [≈$225]**

Zigrosser, Carl

- Six Centuries of Fine Prints. New York: Covici Friede, 1937. 4to. 406 pp. 488 ills. Orig cloth. *(Rona Schneider)* **$35 [≈£23]**

Zola, Emile

- Nana. Illustrated by Bernard Lamotte ... New York: The Limited Editions Club, 1948. One of 1500 signed by the illustrator. Sm 4to. Orig cloth (spine faded). Slipcase (spine cracked). *(Oak Knoll)* **$55 [≈£37]**

Zweig, Stefan

- The Buried Candelabrum. Translated by Eden and Cedar Paul. Woodcuts by Margarete Hammerschlag. London: Cassell, (1937). One of 1000. Orig linen gilt. *(Karmiole)* **$40 [≈£27]**

Catalogue Booksellers Contributing to ARBV

The booksellers who have provided catalogues during 1993 specifically for the purpose of compiling the various titles in the *ARBV* series, and from whose catalogues books have been selected, are listed below in alphabetical order of the abbreviation employed for each. This listing is therefore a complete key to the booksellers contributing to the series as a whole; only a proportion of the listed names is represented in this particular subject volume.

The majority of these booksellers issue periodic catalogues free, on request, to potential customers. Sufficient indication of the type of book handled by each bookseller can be gleaned from the individual book entries set out in the main body of this work and in the companion titles in the series.

Abacus	= Abacus Bookshop, 350 East Avenue, Rochester, New York 14604, U.S.A. (716 325 7950)
Alphabet	= Alphabet Bookshop, 145 Main Street West, Port Colborne, Ontario L3K 3V3, Canada (416 834 5323)
Antic Hay	= Antic Hay Rare Books, P.O. Box 2185, Asbury Park, NJ 07712, U.S.A. (908 774 4590)
Any Amount	= Any Amount of Books, 62 Charing Cross Road, London WC2H 0BB, England (071 836 3697)
Argonaut	= Argonaut Book Shop, 786-792 Sutter Street, San Francisco, CA 94109, U.S.A. (415 474 9067)
Argosy	= Argosy Book Store, Inc., 116 East 59th Street, New York, NY 10022, U.S.A. (212 753 4455)
Ars Libri	= Ars Libri, Ltd., 560 Harrison Avenue, Boston, MA 02118, U.S.A. (617 357 5212)
Ash	= Ash Rare Books, 25 Royal Exchange, London EC3V 3LP, England (071 626 2665)
The Associates	= The Associates, Post Office Box 4747, Falls Church, Virginia 22044-0747, U.S.A. (703 578 3810)
Baker	= A.P. & R. Baker, Laigh House, Church Lane Wigtown, Newton Stewart Wigtownshire DG8 9HT, Scotland (098 84 3348)
Bates & Hindmarch	= Bates and Hindmarch, Bridge Street, Boroughbridge, North Yorkshire YO5 9LA, England (0423 324258)
Peter Bell	= Peter Bell, Bookseller & Publisher, 4 Brandon Street, Edinburgh EH3 5DX, Scotland (031 556 2198)
Between the Covers	= Between the Covers, 132 Kings Highway East, Haddonfield, NJ 08033, U.S.A. (609 354 7665)
Bibliomania	= Bibliomania, 1539 San Pablo Ave., Oakland, California 94612, U.S.A. (510 835 5733)
Black Sun	= Black Sun Books, 157 East 57 Street, New York, NY 10021, U.S.A. (212 688 6622)
Blackwell's	= Blackwell's Rare Books, 39 Holywell Street, Oxford OX1 3SW, England (0865 792792)
Adam Blakeney	= Adam Blakeney, Apartment 5, 13 Brewer Street, London W1R 3FL, England (071 437 9531)
Book Adoption Agency	= Children's Book Adoption Agency, P.O. Box 643, Kensington, MD 20895-0643, U.S.A. (301 585 3091)
Book Block	= The Book Block, 8 Loughlin Avenue, Cos Cob, CT 06807, U.S.A. (203 629 2990)
Bookmark	= Bookmark, Children's Books, Fortnight, Wick Down, Broad Hinton, Swindon, Wiltshire SN4 9NR, England (0793 731693)
Bookpress	= The Bookpress Ltd., Post Office Box KP, Williamsburg, VA 23187, U.S.A. (804 229 1260)
Bookworks	= Bookworks, 'Gernon Elms', Letchworth Lane, Letchworth, Hertfordshire SG6 3NF, England (0462 673189)
Bow Windows	= Bow Windows Book Shop, 128 High Street, Lewes, East Sussex BN7 1XL, England (0273 480780)
Box of Delights	= The Box of Delights, 25 Otley Street, Skipton, North Yorkshire BD23 1DY, England (0756 790111)

Andrew Boyle	= Andrew Boyle (Booksellers) Ltd, 21 Friar Street, Worcester WR1 2NA, England (0905 611700)
Paul Brown	= Paul Brown, 40 Elm Grove, London SE15 5DE, England (071 732 4517)
Buckley	= Brian & Margaret Buckley, 11 Convent Close, Kenilworth, Warwickshire CV8 2FQ, England (0926 55223)
Bufo Books	= Bufo Books, 32 Tadfield Road, Romsey, Hampshire SO51 8AJ, England (0794 517149)
Bury Place	= Bury Place Rare Books, Bloomsbury, London WC1, England (4046869)
Castle Bookshop	= Castle Bookshop, Castle Street, Holt, Clwyd LL13 9YW, Wales (0829 270382)
Connie Castle	= Treasures from the Castle, Connie Castle, 1720 N. Livernois, Rochester, Michigan 48306, U.S.A. (313 651 7317)
Chalmers Hallam	= E. Chalmers Hallam, "Trees", 9 Post Office Lane, St. Ives, Ringwood, Hampshire BH24 2PG, England (0425 470060)
Chapel Hill	= Chapel Hill Rare Books, P.O. Box 456, Carrboro, NC 27510, U.S.A. (919 929 8351)
Clark	= Robert Clark, 6a King Street, Jericho, Oxford OX2 6DF, England (0865 52154)
Clearwater	= Clearwater Books, 19 Matlock Road, Ferndown, Wimborne, Dorset BH22 8QT, England (0202 893263)
Clevedon Books	= Clevedon Books, 14 Woodside Road, Clevedon, Avon BS21 7JY, England (0275 872304)
Cooper Hay	= Cooper Hay Rare Books, 203 Bath Street, Glasgow G2 4HZ, Scotland (041 226 3074)
Corn Exchange	= Corn Exchange Bookshop, 55 King Street, Stirling FK8 1DR, Scotland (0786 73112)
Claude Cox	= Claude Cox, The White House, Kelsale, Saxmundham, Suffolk IP17 2PQ, England (0473 254776)
Peter Crowe	= Peter Crowe, Antiquarian Bookseller, 75 & 77 Upper St Giles' Street Norwich NR1 2AB, England (0603 624800)
D & M Books	= D & M Books, 49 Park Drive, Mirfield, West Yorkshire WF14 9NH, England (0924 495768)
Dailey	= William & Victoria Dailey, P.O. Box 69160, Los Angeles, CA 90069, U.S.A. (213 658 8515)
D & D Galleries	= D & D Galleries, Box 8413, Somerville, NJ 08876, U.S.A. (908 874 3162)
Davidson	= Ursula C. Davidson, 134 Linden Lane, San Rafael, CA 94901, U.S.A. (415 454 1087)
Clarice Davis	= L. Clarice Davis, P.O. Box 56054, Sherman Oaks, CA 91413, U.S.A. (818 787 1322)
Dermont	= Joseph A. Dermont, 13 Arthur Street, P.O. Box 654, Onset, MA 02558, U.S.A. (508 295 4760)
Carol Docheff	= Carol Docheff, Bookseller, 1390 Reliez Valley Road, Lafayette, CA 9459, U.S.A. (510 935 9595)
Edrich	= I.D. Edrich, 17 Selsdon Road, London E11 2QF, England (081 989 9541)
Francis Edwards	= Francis Edwards, The Old Cinema, Castle Street, Hay-on-Wye, via Hereford HR3 5DF, England (0497 820071)
Emerald Isle	= Emerald Isle Books, 539 Antrim Road, Belfast BT15 3BU, Northern Ireland (0232 370798)
Fenning	= James Fenning, 12 Glenview, Rochestown Avenue, Dun Laoghaire, County Dublin, Eire (353 1 285 7855)
Finch	= Simon Finch Rare Books, 10 New Bond Street, London W1Y 9PF, England (071 499 0974)
Fine Art	= Fine Art Catalogues, The Hollies, Port Carlisle, Near Carlisle, Cumbria CA5 5BU, England (06973 51398)
First Folio	= First Folio, 1206 Brentwood, Paris, TN 38242, U.S.A. (901 644 9940)
Robert Frew	= Robert Frew Ltd., 106 Great Russell Street, London WC1B 3NA, England (071 580 2311)

Fye	= W. Bruce Fye, Antiquarian Medical Books, 1607 North Wood Avenue, Marshfield, WI 54449, U.S.A. (715 384 8128)
Gach	= John Gach Books, 5620 Waterloo Road, Columbia, MD 21045, U.S.A. (410 465 9023)
Gaskell	= Roger Gaskell, 17 Ramsey Road, Warboys, Cambridgeshire PE17 2RW, England (0487 823059)
Gekoski	= R.A. Gekoski, Pied Bull Yard, 15a Bloomsbury Square, London WC1A 2LP, England (071 404 6676)
Gemmary	= The Gemmary, Inc, PO Box 816, Redondo Beach, CA 90277, U.S.A. (310 372 6149)
Goodrich	= James Tait Goodrich, Antiquarian Books and Manuscripts, 214 Everett Place, Englewood, NJ 07631, U.S.A. (201 567 0199)
Eric Goodyer	= Eric Goodyer, 20 Gladstone Street, Hathern, Leicestershire LE12 5LE, England (0509 844473)
Gough	= Simon Gough Books, 27 Cecil Court, London WC2N 4EZ, England (071 379 1993)
Gray	= T.B. & J.N. Gray, 3 Lodge Street, Haddington, East Lothian, EH41 3PX, Scotland (062 082 5851)
Great Epic Books	= Great Epic Books, 15918-20th Place West Alderwood Manor WA 98037, U.S.A. (206 745 3113)
Green Meadow	= Green Meadow Books, Kinoulton, Nottingham NG12 3EN, England (0949 81723)
Greyfriars	= Greyfriars' Books & Prints Ltd., 4 Upper Olland Street, Bungay, Suffolk NR35 1BG, England (0986 895600)
Alan Halsey	= Alan Halsey, The Poetry Bookshop, 22 Broad Street, Hay-on-Wye, Via Hereford HR3 5DB, England (0497 820 305)
Hannas	= Torgrim Hannas, 29a Canon Street, Winchester, Hampshire SO23 9JJ, England (0962 862730)
Henly	= John Henly, Bookseller, Brooklands, Walderton, Chichester, West Sussex PO18 9EE, England (0705 631426)
Heritage	= Heritage Book Shop, Inc., 8540 Melrose Avenue, Los Angeles, CA 90069, U.S.A. (310 659 3674)
Hermitage	= The Hermitage Bookshop, 290 Fillmore Street, Denver, CO 80206-5020, U.S.A. (303 388 6811)
High Latitude	= High Latitude, P.O. Box 11254, Bainbridge Island, WA 98110, U.S.A. (206 842 0202)
Hobbyhorse	= Hobbyhorse Books Inc., P.O. Box 591, Ho-Ho-Kus, NJ 07423, U.S.A. (201 327 4717)
Hollett	= R.F.G. Hollett and Son, 6 Finkle Street, Sedbergh, Cumbria LA10 5BZ, England (05396 20298)
Holtom	= Christopher Holtom, Aarons, Treburgett, St. Teath, Cornwall PL30 3LJ, England (0208 851062)
J &J House	= J & J House, Booksellers, 731 Unionville Road (Rt. 82), Box 919, Unionville, PA 19375, U.S.A. (215 444 0490)
Carol Howard	= Carol Howard Books, Jubilee Cottage, Leck, Cowan Bridge, Carnforth, Lancashire LA6 2JD, England (05242 71072)
Jacksons	= Jacksons of Ilkley, 22 Parish Ghyll Road, Ilkley LS29 9NE, England (0943 601947)
Marjorie James	= Marjorie James, The Old School, Oving, Chichester, West Sussex PO20 6DG, England (0243 781354)
Janus	= Janus Books, Post Office Box 40787, Tucson, AZ 85717, U.S.A. (602 881 8192)
Jarndyce	= Jarndyce, Antiquarian Booksellers, 46 Great Russell Street, Bloomsbury, London WC1B 3PA, England (071 631 4220)
Karmiole	= Kenneth Karmiole, Bookseller, Post Office Box 464, Santa Monica, CA 90406, U.S.A. (310 451 4342)
John K. King	= John K. King, 901 W. Lafayette, Detroit, MI 48226, U.S.A. (313 961 0622)

Kirkpatrick = Robert J. Kirkpatrick, 244 Latimer Road, London W10 6QY, England (081 968 9033)

Knollwood Books = Knollwood Books, Post Office Box 197, Oregon, WI 53575-0197, U.S.A. (608 835 8861)

Lamb = R.W. & C.R. Lamb, Talbot House, 158 Denmark Rd., Lowestoft, Suffolk NR32 2EL, England (0502 564306)

Lame Duck Books = Lame Duck Books, 90 Moraine Street, Jamaica Plain, MA 02130, U.S.A. (617 522 7827)

Leicester Art Books = Leicester Art Books, P.O. Box 4YT London W1A 4YT, England (071 485 7073)

Levin = Barry R. Levin, 726 Santa Monica Blvd., Suite 201, Santa Monica, CA 90401, U.S.A. (213 458 6111)

Lewis = John Lewis, 35 Stoneham Street, Coggeshall, Essex CO6 1UH, England (0376 561518)

Limestone Hills = Limestone Hills Book Shop, P.O. Box 1125, Glen Rose, TX 76043, U.S.A. (817 897 4991)

Lopez = Ken Lopez, Bookseller, 51 Huntington Road, Hadley, MA 01035, U.S.A. (413 584 4827)

McBlain = McBlain Books, P.O. Box 5062 Hamden, CT 06518, U.S.A. (203 281 0400)

Mac Donnell = Mac Donnell Rare Books, 9307 Glenlake Drive, Austin, TX 78730, U.S.A. (512 345 4139)

Martin = C.J. Martin, 76 Raylawn Street, Mansfield, Nottinghamshire NG18 3ND, England (0623 20691)

Mendelsohn = H.L. Mendelsohn, Fine European Books, P.O. Box 317, Belmont, MA 02178, U.S.A. (617 484 7362)

Mermaid Books = Mermaid Books, Old Hall, Norwich Road, South Burlingham, Norwich NR13 4EY, England (0493 750804)

Meyer Boswell = Meyer Boswell Books, Inc., 2141 Mission Street, San Francisco, CA 94110, U.S.A. (415 255 6400)

Monmouth = Monmouth House Books, Llanfapley, Abergavenny, Gwent NP7 8SN, Wales (060 085 236)

Moorhouse = Hartley Moorhouse Books, 142 Petersham Road, Richmond, Surrey TW10 6UX, England (081 948 7742)

Mordida = Mordida Books, P.O. Box 79322, Houston, TX 77279, U.S.A. (713 467 4280)

Margaret Nangle = Margaret Nangle, The Cottage, High Street, Bramley, Surrey GU5 OHS, England (0483 893137)

Newcastle Bookshop = Newcastle Bookshop, 1 Side, Newcastle upon Tyne NE1 3JE, England (091 261 5380)

Nouveau = Nouveau Rare Books, P.O. Box 12471 5005 Meadow Oaks Park Drive, Jackson, Mississippi 39211, U.S.A. (601 956 9950)

O'Nale = Jan L. O'Nale, Route 2, Box 1293, New Castle, Virginia 24127, Canada (3 864 6288)

Oak Knoll = Oak Knoll Books, 414 Delaware Street, New Castle, DE 19720, U.S.A. (302 328 7232)

Old Cathay = Old Cathay Fine Books, 43 Park Street, Old Hatfield, Hertfordshire AL9 5BA, England (0707 274200)

Oriental and African = Oriental and African Books, 73 Monkmoor Road, Shrewsbury, Shropshire SY2 5AT, England (0743 352575)

Page 6 Books = Page 6 Books, 18 Underwood Close, Parkside, Stafford ST16 1TB, England (0785 41153)

Parmer = Parmer Books, 7644 Forrestal Road, San Diego, CA 92120-2203, U.S.A. (619 287 0693)

Petrilla = R & A Petrilla, Antiquarian Booksellers, Roosevelt, NJ 08555-0306, U.S.A. (609 426 4999)

Phenotype = Phenotype Books, Wallridge, 39 Arthur Street, Penrith, Cumbria CA11 7TT, England (0768 63049)

Pickering & Chatto = Pickering & Chatto, 17 Pall Mall, London SW1Y 5NB, England (071 930 8627)

Piglit Books = Piglit Books, 15 Wellhouse Road, Beech, Alton, Hampshire GU34 4AH, England (0420 84884)

Larry W. Price = Larry W. Price, 353 N.W. Maywood Dr., Portland, Oregon 97210 3333, U.S.A. (503 221 1410)

Quest Books = Quest Books, Harmer Hill, Millington, York YO4 2TX, England (0759 304735)

Rankin = Alan Rankin, 72 Dundas Street, Edinburgh EH3 6QZ, Scotland, Scotland (031 556 3705)

David Rees = David Rees, 18A Prentis Road, London SW16 1QD, England (081 769 2453)

Reese = William Reese Company, 409 Temple Street, New Haven, CT 06511, U.S.A. (203 789 8081)

Jo Ann Reisler = Jo Ann Reisler, Ltd., 360 Glyndon St., NE, Vienna, VA 22180, U.S.A. (703 938 2967)

Robertshaw = John Robertshaw, 5 Fellowes Drive, Ramsey, Huntingdon, Cambridgeshire PE17 1BE, England (0487 813330)

Rona Schneider = Rona Schneider Fine Prints, 12 Monroe Place, Brooklyn, NY 11201, U.S.A. (718 875 5121)

Schoyer = Schoyer's Books, 1404 South Negley Avenue, Pittsburgh, PA 15217, U.S.A. (412 521 8464)

David Schutte = David Schutte, Myrtle Cottage, Stedham, Midhurst, West Sussex GU29 ONQ, England (0730 814654)

Sclanders = Andrew Sclanders, 11 Albany Road, Stroud Green, London N4 4RR, England (081 340 6843)

The Silver Door = The Silver Door, PO Box 3208, Redondo Beach, CA 90277, U.S.A. (310 379 6005)

David Slade = David Slade Rare Books, 85 Park Street, Bristol BS1 5PJ, England (0272 291377)

Sotheran's = Henry Sotheran Ltd., 2 Sackville Street, Piccadilly, London W1X 2DP, England (071 439 6151)

Spelman = Ken Spelman, 70 Micklegate, York YO1 1LF, England (0904 624414)

Monroe Stahr = Monroe Stahr Books, 4420 Ventura Canyon Ave., #2, Sherman Oaks, CA 91423, U.S.A. (818 784 0870)

Stella Books = Stella Books, Main Road, Tintern, Gwent, Wales (0291 689430)

Nancy Stewart = Nancy Stewart - Books, 1188 NW Weybridge Way, Beaverton, OR 97006, U.S.A. (503 645 9779)

Barbara Stone = Barbara Stone, Antiquarius, 135 Kings Road, Chelsea, London SW3 4PW, England (071 351 0963)

Sumner & Stillman = Sumner & Stillman, P.O. Box 973, Yarmouth, ME 04096, U.S.A. (207 846 6070)

Sutton = Raymond M. Sutton, Jr., P.O. Box 330, 430 Main Street, Williamsburg, Kentucky 40769, U.S.A. (606 549 3469)

Elisabeth Sykes = Elisabeth Sykes, 52 Bridge Street, Ramsbottom, Bury, Lancashire BL0 9AQ, England (0706 825322)

Talatin Books = Talatin Books, 21 Parkstone Avenue, Emerson Park, Hornchurch, Essex RM11 3LX, England (0708 447561)

Taylor & Son = Peter Taylor & Son, 1 Ganders Ash, Leavesden, Watford, Hertfordshire WD2 7HE, England (0923 663325)

Michael Taylor = Michael Taylor Rare Books, The Gables, 8 Mendham Lane, Harleston, Norfolk IP20 9DE, England (0379 853889)

Terramedia = Terramedia Books, 19 Homestead Road, Wellesley, MA 02181, U.S.A. (617 237 6485)

Tiger Books = Tiger Books, Yew Tree Cottage, Westbere, Canterbury Kent CT2 0HH, England (0227 710030)

Traylen = Charles W. Traylen, Castle House, 49-50 Quarry Street, Guildford, Surrey GU1 3UA, England (0483 572424)

Trophy Room Books	=	Trophy Room Books, Box 3041, Agoura, CA 91301, U.S.A. (818 889 2469)
Ulysses Bookshop	=	Ulysses Bookshop, 31 & 40 Museum Street, London WC1A 1LH, England (071 831 1600)
Unicorn Books	=	Unicorn Books, 56 Rowlands Avenue, Hatch End, Pinner, Middlesex HA5 4BP, England (071 431 5162)
The Veatchs	=	The Veatchs, Arts of the Book, 20 Veronica Court, Smithtown, New York 11787-1323, U.S.A. (516 265 3357)
Virgo	=	Virgo Books, Little Court, South Wraxall, Bradford-on-Avon, Wiltshire BA15 2SE, England (0225 862040)
Waddington	=	Geraldine Waddington, Brookside, High Street, Alconbury Weston, Cambridgeshire PE17 5JP, England (0480 891906)
Walcot	=	Patrick Walcot, 60 Sunnybank Road, Sutton Coldfield, West Midlands B73 5RJ, England (021 382 6381)
Rob Warren	=	Rob Warren, Skyline Books & Records, 13 W.18th Street, New York, NY 10011, U.S.A. (212 759 5463)
Washton	=	Andrew D. Washton, 411 East 83rd Street, New York, NY 10028, U.S.A. (212 481 0479)
Waterfield's	=	Waterfield's, 36 Park End Street, Oxford OX1 1HJ, England (0865 721809)
Weiner	=	Graham Weiner, 78 Rosebery Road, London N10 2LA, England (081 883 8424)
Westwood	=	Mark Westwood Books, High Town, Hay-on-Wye via Hereford HR3 5AE, England (0497 820068)
Wheldon & Wesley	=	Wheldon & Wesley Ltd., Lytton Lodge, Codicote, Hitchin, Hertfordshire SG4 8TE, England (0438 820370)
Whitehart	=	F.E. Whitehart, Rare Books, 40 Priestfield Road, Forest Hill, London SE23 2RS, England (081 699 3225)
Wilder Books	=	Wilder Books, PO Box 762 Elmhurst, Illinois 60126, U.S.A. (708 834 8529)
Wilkinson	=	Ian Wilkinson, Gothic House, Barker Gate, Nottingham NG1 1JU, England (0602 870590)
Nigel Williams	=	Nigel Williams (Books), 7 Waldeck Grove West Norwood London SE27 0BE, England (081 761 4025)
Willow House	=	Willow House Books, 58A Chapel Street, Chorley, Lancashire PR7 1BS, England (0257 269280)
J. & M. Wilson	=	J. & M. Wilson, 94 Brechin Road, Arbroath, Angus DD11 1SX, Scotland (0241 77552)
Susan Wood	=	Susan Wood, 24 Leasowe Road, Rubery, Rednal, Worcestershire B45 9TD, England (021 453 7169)
Words Etcetera	=	Words Etcetera, Spring Cottage, 3 Penny Street, Sturminster Newton, Dorset DT10 1DE, England (0258 73338)
Worldwide	=	Worldwide Antiquarian, Post Office Box 391, Cambridge, MA 02141, U.S.A. (617 876 0839)
Norman Wright	=	Norman Wright, 60 Eastbury Road, Watford, Hertfordshire WD1 4JL, England (0923 232383)
Yesterday's Books	=	Yesterday's Books, 67 Bennett Road, Bournemouth BH8 8RH, England (0202 302023)
Young's	=	Young's Antiquarian Books, Tillingham, Essex CM0 7ST, England (0621 778187)
Zeno	=	Zeno, 6 Denmark Street, London WC2H 8LP, England (071 836 2522)